In Praise of *Computer Networks: A Systems Approach* Fifth Edition

I have known and used this book for years and I always found it very valuable as a textbook for teaching computer networks as well as a reference book for networking professionals. This Fifth Edition maintains the core value of former editions and brings the clarity of explanation of network protocols in the introduction of the most up-to-date techniques, technologies and requirements of networking. Beyond describing the details of past and current networks, this book successfully motivates the curiosity, and hopefully new research, for the networks of the future.

Stefano Basagni
Northeastern University

Peterson and Davie have written an outstanding book for the computer networking world. It is a well-organized book that features a very helpful "big picture" systems approach. This book is a must have!

Yonshik Choi
Illinois Institute of Technology

The Fifth Edition of Computer Networks: A Systems Approach *is well-suited for the serious student of computer networks, though it remains accessible to the more casual reader as well. The authors' enthusiasm for their subject is evident throughout; they have a thorough and current grasp of the interesting problems of the field. They explain not only how various protocols work, but also why they work the way they do, and even why certain protocols are the important and interesting ones. The book is also filled with little touches of historical background, from the main text to the "Where Are They Now" sidebars to the papers described in each chapter's "Further Reading" section—these give the reader a perspective on how things came to be the way they are. All in all, this book provides a lucid and literate introduction to networking.*

Peter Dordal
Loyola University Chicago

I have used Computer Networks: A Systems Approach *for over five years in an introductory course on communications networks aimed at upper-level undergraduates and first-year Masters students. I have gone through several editions and over the years the book has kept what from the beginning had been its main strength, namely, that it not only describes the 'how,' but also the 'why' and equally important, the 'why not' of things. It is a book that builds engineering intuition, and in this day and age of fast-paced technology changes, this is critical to develop a student's ability to make informed decisions on how to design or select the next generation systems.*

Roch Guerin
University of Pennsylvania

This book is an outstanding introduction to computer networks that is clear, comprehensive, and chock-full of examples. Peterson and Davie have a gift for boiling networking down to simple and manageable concepts without compromising technical rigor. Computer Networks: A Systems Approach *strikes an excellent balance between the principles underlying network architecture design and the applications built on top. It should prove invaluable to students and teachers of advanced undergraduate and graduate networking courses.*

Arvind Krishnamurthy
University of Washington

Computer Networks: A Systems Approach *has always been one of the best resources available to gain an in-depth understanding of computer networks. The latest edition covers recent developments in the field. Starting with an overview in Chapter 1, the authors systematically explain the basic building blocks of networks. Both hardware and software concepts are presented. The material is capped with a final chapter on applications, which brings all the concepts together. Optional advanced topics are placed in a separate chapter. The textbook also contains a set of exercises of varying difficulty at the end of each chapter which ensure that the students have mastered the material presented.*

Karkal Prabhu
Drexel University

Peterson and Davie provide a detailed yet clear description of the Internet protocols at all layers. Students will find many study aids that will help them gain a full understanding of the technology that is transforming our society. The book gets better with each edition.

Jean Walrand
University of California at Berkeley

Fifth Edition

Computer Networks
a systems approach

Recommended Reading List

For students interested in furthering their understanding of Computer Networking, the content in the following books supplements this textbook:

Network Analysis, Architecture, and Design, 3rd Edition
By James D. McCabe
ISBN: 9780123704801

The Illustrated Network
How TCP/IP Works in a Modern Network
By Walter Goralski
ISBN: 9780123745415

Interconnecting Smart Objects with IP
The Next Internet
By Jean-Philippe Vasseur and Adam Dunkels
ISBN: 9780123751652

Network Quality of Service Know It All
Edited by Adrian Farrel
ISBN: 9780123745972

Optical Networks, 3rd Edition
A Practical Perspective
By Rajiv Ramaswami, Kumar Sivarajan and Galen Sasaki
ISBN: 9780123740922

Broadband Cable Access Networks
The HFC Plant
By David Large and James Farmer
ISBN: 9780123744012

Deploying QoS for Cisco IP and Next Generation Networks
The Definitive Guide
By Vinod Joseph and Brett Chapman
ISBN: 9780123744616

mkp.com

Fifth Edition

Computer Networks
a systems approach

Larry L. Peterson and Bruce S. Davie

ELSEVIER

AMSTERDAM • BOSTON • HEIDELBERG • LONDON
NEW YORK • OXFORD • PARIS • SAN DIEGO
SAN FRANCISCO • SINGAPORE • SYDNEY • TOKYO

Morgan Kaufmann Publishers is an imprint of Elsevier

Acquiring Editor: Rick Adams
Development Editor: Nate McFadden
Project Manager: Paul Gottehrer
Designer: Dennis Schaefer

Morgan Kaufmann is an imprint of Elsevier
30 Corporate Drive, Suite 400, Burlington, MA 01803, USA

Library of Congress Cataloging-in-Publication Data
Peterson, Larry L.
    Computer networks : a systems approach / Larry L. Peterson and Bruce S. Davie. – 5th ed.
        p. cm. – (The Morgan Kaufmann series in networking)
    Includes bibliographical references.
    ISBN 978-0-12-385059-1 (hardback)
1. Computer networks. I. Davie, Bruce S. II. Title.
    TK5105.5.P479 2011
    004.6–dc22

                                                  2011000786

British Library Cataloguing-in-Publication Data
A catalogue record for this book is available from the British Library.

ISBN: 978-0-12-385059-1

For information on all Morgan Kaufmann publications
visit our website at *www.mkp.com*

Typeset by: diacriTech, India

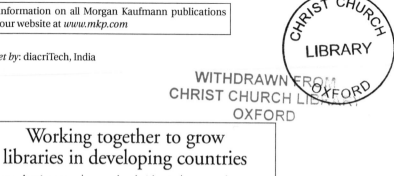

To Lee Peterson and Robert Davie

Foreword

Once again, this now-classic textbook has been revised to keep it up-to-date with our evolving field. While the Internet and its protocols now dominate networking everywhere, we see continued evolution in the technology used to support the Internet, with switching at "layer 2" providing rich functionality and powerful tools for network management. The previous edition dealt with switching and routing in two chapters, but a presentation based on layers is not always the best way to convey the essentials of the material, since what we call switching and routing actually play similar and complementary roles. This edition of the book looks at these topics in an integrated way, which brings out their functional similarities and differences. More advanced topics in routing have been moved to a second chapter that can be skipped, depending on the emphasis and level of the class.

I have never been a fan of teaching networking based on a purely layered approach, as my foreword to the first edition indicated (we've reprinted it in this edition just for fun.) Some key issues in networking, including security and performance, cannot be solved by assigning them to one layer—there cannot be a "performance" layer. These sorts of topics are both critical and cross-cutting, and the organization of this book continues to treat topics, as well as layers. The organization of this book reflects a great deal of experience using it as a classroom textbook, and as well a preference for an approach that brings out fundamentals as well as current practice.

Some moribund technologies are now missing or minimized, including token ring (one of my old favorites, but clearly it was time to go) and ATM. This edition recognizes that we need to pay more attention to application design, and not just packet forwarding. Wireless and mobility gets more attention as well.

The authors, once again, have worked hard to produce a revision that conveys the essentials of the field in a way that is pedagogically effective. I am pleased to say that I think it is better than ever.

David Clark
November, 2010

Foreword to the First Edition

The term *spaghetti code* is universally understood as an insult. All good computer scientists worship the god of modularity, since modularity brings many benefits, including the all-powerful benefit of not having to understand all parts of a problem at the same time in order to solve it. Modularity thus plays a role in presenting ideas in a book, as well as in writing code. If a book's material is organized effectively—modularly—the reader can start at the beginning and actually make it to the end.

The field of network protocols is perhaps unique in that the "proper" modularity has been handed down to us in the form of an international standard: the seven-layer reference model of network protocols from the ISO. This model, which reflects a layered approach to modularity, is almost universally used as a starting point for discussions of protocol organization, whether the design in question conforms to the model or deviates from it.

It seems obvious to organize a networking book around this layered model. However, there is a peril to doing so, because the OSI model is not really successful at organizing the core concepts of networking. Such basic requirements as reliability, flow control, or security can be addressed at most, if not all, of the OSI layers. This fact has led to great confusion in trying to understand the reference model. At times it even requires a suspension of disbelief. Indeed, a book organized strictly according to a layered model has some of the attributes of spaghetti code.

Which brings us to this book. Peterson and Davie follow the traditional layered model, but they do not pretend that this model actually helps in the understanding of the big issues in networking. Instead, the authors organize discussion of fundamental concepts in a way that is independent of layering. Thus, after reading the book, readers will understand flow control, congestion control, reliability enhancement, data representation, and synchronization, and will separately understand the implications of addressing these issues in one or another of the traditional layers.

This is a timely book. It looks at the important protocols in use today—especially the Internet protocols. Peterson and Davie have a long involvement in and much experience with the Internet. Thus their book reflects not just the theoretical issues in protocol design, but the real factors that matter in practice. The book looks at some of the protocols that are just emerging now, so the reader can be assured of an up-to-date perspective. But most importantly, the discussion of basic issues is presented in a way that derives from the fundamental nature of the problem, not the constraints of the layered reference model or the details of today's protocols. In this regard, what this book presents is both timely and timeless. The combination of real-world relevance, current examples, and careful explanation of fundamentals makes this book unique.

David D. Clark
Massachusetts Institute of Technology

Preface

When the first edition of this book was published in 1996, it was a novelty to be able to order merchandise on the Internet, and a company that advertised its domain name was considered cutting edge. The primary way for a household to connect to the Internet was via a dial-up modem. Today, Internet commerce is a fact of life, and ".com" stocks have gone through an entire boom and bust cycle. Wireless networks are everywhere and new Internet-capable devices such as smartphones and tablets appear on the market at a dizzying pace. It seems the only predictable thing about the Internet is constant change.

Despite these changes, the question we asked in the first edition is just as valid today: What are the underlying concepts and technologies that make the Internet work? The answer is that much of the TCP/IP architecture continues to function just as was envisioned by its creators more than 30 years ago. This isn't to say that the Internet architecture is uninteresting; quite the contrary. Understanding the design principles that underly an architecture that has not only survived but fostered the kind of growth and change that the Internet has seen over the past 3 decades is precisely the right place to start. Like the previous editions, the Fifth Edition makes the "why" of the Internet architecture its cornerstone.

Audience

Our intent is that the book should serve as the text for a comprehensive networking class, at either the graduate or upper-division undergraduate level. We also believe that the book's focus on core concepts should be appealing to industry professionals who are retraining for network-related assignments, as well as current network practitioners who want to understand the "whys" behind the protocols they work with every day and to see the big picture of networking.

It is our experience that both students and professionals learning about networks for the first time often have the impression that network protocols are some sort of edict handed down from on high, and that their job is to learn as many TLAs (Three-Letter Acronyms) as possible. In fact, protocols are the building blocks of a complex system developed through the application of engineering design principles. Moreover, they are constantly being refined, extended, and replaced based on real-world experience. With this in mind, our goal with this book is to do more than survey the protocols in use today. Instead, we explain the underlying principles of sound network design. We feel that this grasp of underlying principles is the best tool for handling the rate of change in the networking field.

We also recognize that there are many different ways that people approach networks. In contrast to when we wrote our first edition, most people will pick up this book having considerable experience as *users* of networks. Some will be looking to become *designers* of networking products or protocols. Others may be interested in *managing* networks, while an increasingly large number will be current or prospective *application developers* for networked devices. Our focus has traditionally been on the designers of future products and protocols, and that continues to be the case, but in this edition we have tried to address the perspectives of network managers and application developers as well.

Changes in the Fifth Edition

Even though our focus is on the underlying principles of networking, we illustrate these principles using examples from today's working Internet. Therefore, we added a significant amount of new material to track many of the important recent advances in networking. We also deleted, reorganized, and changed the focus of existing material to reflect changes that have taken place over the past decade.

Perhaps the most significant change we have noticed since writing the first edition is that almost every reader is now familiar with networked applications such as the World Wide Web and email. For this reason, we have increased the focus on applications, starting in the first chapter. We use applications as the motivation for the study of networking, and to derive a set of requirements that a useful network must meet if it is to support both current and future applications on a global scale. However, we retain the problem-solving approach of previous editions that starts with the problem of interconnecting hosts and works its way up the layers to conclude with a detailed examination of application layer issues. We believe it is important to make the topics covered in the book relevant by starting with applications and their needs. At the same time, we feel that higher layer issues, such as application layer and transport layer protocols, are best understood after the basic problems of connecting hosts and switching packets have been explained. That said, we have made it possible to approach the material in a more *top-down* manner, as described below.

As in prior editions, we have added or increased coverage of important new topics, and brought other topics up to date. Major new or substantially updated topics in this edition are:

- Updated material on wireless technology, particularly the various flavors of 802.11 (Wi-Fi) as well as cellular wireless technologies including the third generation (3G) and emerging 4G standards.
- Updated coverage of congestion control mechanisms, particularly for high bandwidth-delay product networks and wireless networks.
- Updated material on Web Services, including the SOAP and REST (Representational State Transfer) architectures.
- Expanded and updated coverage of interdomain routing and the border gateway protocol (BGP).
- Expanded coverage on protocols for multimedia applications such as voice over IP (VOIP) and video streaming.

We also reduced coverage of some topics that are less relevant today. Protocols moving into the "historic" category for this edition include asynchronous transfer mode (ATM) and token rings.

One of the most significant changes in this edition is the separation of material into "introductory" and "advanced" sections. We wanted to make the book more accessible to people new to networking technologies and protocols, without giving up the advanced material required for upper-level classes. The most apparent effect of this change is that Chapter 3 now covers the basics of switching, routing, and Internetworking, while Chapter 4 covers the more advanced routing topics such as BGP, IP version 6, and multicast. Similarly, transport protocol fundamentals are covered in Chapter 5 with the more advanced material such as TCP congestion control algorithms appearing in Chapter 6. We believe this will make it possible for readers new to the field to grasp important foundational concepts without getting overwhelmed by more complex topics.

As in the last edition, we have included a number of "where are they now?" sidebars. These short discussions, updated for this edition, focus on the success and failure of protocols in the real world. Sometimes they describe a protocol that most people have written off but which is actually enjoying unheralded success; other times they trace the fate of a protocol that failed to thrive over the long run. The goal of these sidebars is to make the material relevant by showing how technologies have fared in the competitive world of networking.

Approach

For an area that's as dynamic and changing as computer networks, the most important thing a textbook can offer is perspective—to distinguish between what's important and what's not, and between what's lasting and what's superficial. Based on our experience over the past 25-plus years doing research that has led to new networking technology, teaching undergraduate and graduate students about the latest trends in networking, and delivering advanced networking products to market, we have developed a perspective—which we call the *systems approach*—that forms the soul of this book. The systems approach has several implications:

- *First Principles*. Rather than accept existing artifacts as gospel, we start with first principles and walk you through the thought process that led to today's networks. This allows us to explain *why* networks look like they do. It is our experience that once you understand the underlying concepts, any new protocol that you are confronted with will be relatively easy to digest.

- *Non-layerist*. Although the material is loosely organized around the traditional network layers, starting at the bottom and moving up the protocol stack, we do not adopt a rigidly layerist approach. Many topics—congestion control and security are good examples—have implications up and down the hierarchy, and so we discuss them outside the traditional layered model. Similarly, routers and switches have so much in common (and are often combined as single products) that we discuss them in the same chapter. In short, we believe layering makes a good servant but a poor master; it's more often useful to take an end-to-end perspective.

- *Real-world examples*. Rather than explain how protocols work in the abstract, we use the most important protocols in use today—most of them from the TCP/IP Internet—to illustrate how networks work in practice. This allows us to include real-world experiences in the discussion.

■ *Software.* Although at the lowest levels networks are constructed from commodity hardware that can be bought from computer vendors and communication services that can be leased from the phone company, it is the software that allows networks to provide new services and adapt quickly to changing circumstances. It is for this reason that we emphasize how network software is implemented, rather than stopping with a description of the abstract algorithms involved. We also include code segments taken from a working protocol stack to illustrate how you might implement certain protocols and algorithms.

■ *End-to-end focus.* Networks are constructed from many building-block pieces, and while it is necessary to be able to abstract away uninteresting elements when solving a particular problem, it is essential to understand how all the pieces fit together to form a functioning network. We therefore spend considerable time explaining the overall end-to-end behavior of networks, not just the individual components, so that it is possible to understand how a complete network operates, all the way from the application to the hardware.

■ *Performance.* The systems approach implies doing experimental performance studies, and then using the data you gather both to quantitatively analyze various design options and to guide you in optimizing the implementation. This emphasis on empirical analysis pervades the book.

■ *Design Principles.* Networks are like other computer systems—for example, operating systems, processor architectures, distributed and parallel systems, and so on. They are all large and complex. To help manage this complexity, system builders often draw on a collection of design principles. We highlight these design principles as they are introduced throughout the book, illustrated, of course, with examples from computer networks.

Pedagogy and Features

The Fifth Edition retains the key pedagogical features from prior editions, which we encourage you to take advantage of:

■ *Problem statements.* At the start of each chapter, we describe a problem that identifies the next set of issues that must be addressed in the design of a network. This statement introduces and motivates the issues to be explored in the chapter.

■ *Shaded sidebars.* Throughout the text, shaded sidebars elaborate on the topic being discussed or introduce a related advanced topic. In many cases, these sidebars relate real-world anecdotes about networking.

■ *Where-are-they-now sidebars.* These new elements, a distinctively formatted style of sidebar, trace the success and failure of protocols in real-world deployment.

■ *Highlighted paragraphs.* These paragraphs summarize an important nugget of information that we want you to take away from the discussion, such as a widely applicable system design principle.

■ *Real protocols.* Even though the book's focus is on core concepts rather than existing protocol specifications, real protocols are used to illustrate most of the important ideas. As a result, the book can be used as a source of reference for many protocols. To help you find the descriptions of the protocols, each applicable section heading parenthetically identifies the protocols described in that section. For example, Section 5.2, which describes the principles of reliable end-to-end protocols, provides a detailed description of TCP, the canonical example of such a protocol.

■ *What's Next? discussions.* We conclude the main body of each chapter with an important issue that is currently unfolding in the research community, the commercial world, or society as a whole. We have found that discussing these forward-looking issues helps to make the subject of networking more relevant and exciting.

■ *Recommended reading.* These highly selective lists appear at the end of each chapter. Each list generally contains the seminal papers on the topics just discussed. We strongly recommend that advanced readers (e.g., graduate students) study the papers in this reading list to supplement the material covered in the chapter.

Road Map and Course Use

The book is organized as follows:

■ Chapter 1 introduces the set of core ideas that are used throughout the rest of the text. Motivated by wide-spread applications, it discusses what goes into a network architecture, provides an introduction to protocol implementation issues, and defines the quantitative performance metrics that often drive network design.

■ Chapter 2 surveys the many ways that a user can get connected to a larger network such as the Internet, thus introducing the concept of *links*. It also describes many of the issues that all link-level protocols must address, including encoding, framing, and error detection. The most important link technologies today—Ethernet and Wireless—are described here.

■ Chapter 3 introduces the basic concepts of switching and routing, starting with the virtual circuit and datagram models. Bridging and LAN switching are covered, followed by an introduction to internetworking, including the Internet Protocol (IP) and routing protocols. The chapter concludes by discussing a range of hardware- and software-based approaches to building routers and switches.

■ Chapter 4 covers advanced Internetworking topics. These include multi-area routing protocols, interdomain routing and BGP, IP version 6, multiprotocol label switching (MPLS) and multicast.

■ Chapter 5 moves up to the transport level, describing both the Internet's Transmission Control Protocol (TCP) and Remote Procedure Call (RPC) used to build client-server applications in detail. The Real-time Transport Protocol (RTP), which supports multimedia applications, is also described.

■ Chapter 6 discusses congestion control and resource allocation. The issues in this chapter cut across the link level (Chapter 2), the network level (Chapters 3 and 4) and the transport level (Chapter 5). Of particular note, this chapter describes how congestion control works in TCP, and it introduces the mechanisms used to provide quality of service in IP.

■ Chapter 7 considers the data sent through a network. This includes both the problems of presentation formatting and data compression. XML is covered here, and the compression section includes explanations of how MPEG video compression and MP3 audio compression work.

■ Chapter 8 discusses network security, beginning with an overview of cryptographic tools, the problems of key distribution, and a discussion of several authentication techniques using both public and private keys. The main focus of this chapter is the building of secure systems, using examples including Pretty Good Privacy (PGP), Secure Shell (SSH), and the IP Security architecture (IPSEC). Firewalls are also covered here.

- Chapter 9 describes a representative sample of network applications, and the protocols they use, including traditional applications like email and the Web, multimedia applications such as IP telephony and video streaming, and overlay networks like peer-to-peer file sharing and content distribution networks. Infrastructure services—the Domain Name System (DNS) and network management—are described. The Web Services architectures for developing new application protocols are also presented here.

For an undergraduate course, extra class time will most likely be needed to help students digest the introductory material in the first chapter, probably at the expense of the more advanced topics covered in Chapters 4 and 6 through 8. Chapter 9 then returns to the popular topic of network applications. An undergraduate class might reasonably skim the more advanced sections (e.g., Sections 5.3, 9.3.1, 9.3.2 and 9.2.2.)

In contrast, the instructor for a graduate course should be able to cover the first chapter in only a lecture or two—with students studying the material more carefully on their own—thereby freeing up additional class time to cover Chapter 4 and the later chapters in depth.

For those of you using the book in self-study, we believe that the topics we have selected cover the core of computer networking, and so we recommend that the book be read sequentially, from front to back. In addition, we have included a liberal supply of references to help you locate supplementary material that is relevant to your specific areas of interest, and we have included solutions to select exercises.

The book takes a unique approach to the topic of congestion control by pulling all topics related to congestion control and resource allocation together in a single place—Chapter 6. We do this because the problem of congestion control cannot be solved at any one level, and we want you to consider the various design options at the same time. (This is consistent with our view that strict layering often obscures important design trade-offs.) A more traditional treatment of congestion control is possible, however, by studying Section 6.2 in the context of Chapter 3 and Section 6.3 in the context of Chapter 5.

A Top-Down Pathway

Because most students today come to a networking class familiar with networked applications, a number of classes take the application as their starting point. While we do cover applications at a high level in Chapter 1, it is not until Chapter 9 that application layer issues are discussed in detail. Recognizing that some professors or readers may wish to follow a more top-down ordering, we suggest the following as a possible way to approach the material in this book.

- Chapter 1. This describes applications and their requirements to set the stage for the rest of the material.
- Chapter 9. The sections on traditional applications (Section 9.1) and multimedia applications (Section 9.2) will introduce readers to the concepts of network protocols using the examples of applications with which they are already familiar. Section 9.3.1 (DNS) could also be covered.
- Section 7.2 could be covered next to explain how the data that is generated by multimedia applications is encoded and compressed.
- Chapter 5. Transport protocol basics can now be covered, explaining how the data generated by the application layer protocols can be reliably carried across a network.
- Chapter 3. Switching, Internetworking, and Routing can be understood as providing the infrastructure over which transport protocols run.
- Chapter 2. Finally, the issues of how data is actually encoded and transmitted on physical media such as Ethernets and wireless links can be covered.

Clearly we have skipped quite a few sections in this ordering. For a more advanced course or comprehensive self-study, topics such as resource allocation (Chapter 6), security (Chapter 8), and the advanced topics in Chapter 4 could be added in towards the end. Security could be covered almost stand-alone, but all these advanced topics will make most sense after IP and TCP have been covered in Chapters 3 and 5 respectively.

Note that the slides made available on our companion site include a set that follows this top-down ordering in addition to the set that follows the order of the book.

Exercises

Significant effort has gone into improving the exercises with each new edition. In the Second Edition we greatly increased the number of problems and, based on class testing, dramatically improved their quality. In the Third Edition we made two other important changes, which we retained here:

- For those exercises that we felt are particularly challenging or require special knowledge not provided in the book (e.g. probability expertise) we have added an icon ☆ to indicate the extra level of difficulty

- In each chapter we added some extra representative exercises for which worked solutions are provided in the back of the book. These exercises, marked ✓ , are intended to provide some help in tackling the other exercises in the book.

In this edition we have added new exercises to reflect the updated content.

The current set of exercises are of several different styles:

- Analytical exercises that ask the student to do simple algebraic calculations that demonstrate their understanding of fundamental relationships

- Design questions that ask the student to propose and evaluate protocols for various circumstances

- Hands-on questions that ask the student to write a few lines of code to test an idea or to experiment with an existing network utility

- Library research questions that ask the student to learn more about a particular topic

Also, as described in more detail below, socket-based programming assignments, as well as simulation labs, are available online.

Supplemental Materials and Online Resources

To assist instructors, we have prepared an instructor's manual that contains solutions to selected exercises. The manual is available from the publisher.

Additional support materials, including lecture slides, figures from the text, socket-based programming assignments, and sample exams and programming assignments are available through the Morgan Kaufmann Web site at http://mkp.com/computer-networks.

And finally, as with the Fourth Edition, a set of laboratory experiments supplement the book. These labs, developed by Professor Emad Aboelela from the University of Massachusetts Dartmouth, use simulation to explore the behavior, scalability, and performance of protocols covered in the book. Sections that discuss material covered by the laboratory exercises are marked with the icon shown in the margin. The simulations use the OPNET simulation toolset, which is available for free to any one using *Computer Networks* in their course.

Acknowledgments

This book would not have been possible without the help of many people. We would like to thank them for their efforts in improving the end result. Before we do so, however, we should mention that we have done our best to correct the mistakes that the reviewers have pointed out and to accurately describe the protocols and mechanisms that our colleagues have explained to us. We alone are responsible for any remaining errors. If you should find any of these, please send an email to our publisher, Morgan Kaufmann, at netbugsPD5e@mkp.com, and we will endeavor to correct them in future printings of this book.

First, we would like to thank the many people who reviewed drafts of all or parts of the manuscript. In addition to those who reviewed prior editions, we wish to thank Peter Dordal, Stefano Basagni, Yonshik Choi, Wenbing Zhao, Sarvesh Kulkarni, James Menth, and John Doyle (and one anonymous reviewer) for their thorough reviews. Thanks also to Dina Katabi and Hari Balakrishnan for their reviews of various sections. We also wish to thank all those who provided feedback and input to help us decide what to do in this edition.

Several members of the Network Systems Group at Princeton contributed ideas, examples, corrections, data, and code to this book. In particular, we would like to thank Andy Bavier, Tammo Spalink, Mike Wawrzoniak, Stephen Soltesz, and KyoungSoo Park. Thanks also to Shankar M. Banik for developing the two comprehensive sets of slides to accompany the book.

Third, we would like to thank our series editor, David Clark, as well as all the people at Morgan Kaufmann who helped shepherd us through the book-writing process. A special thanks is due to our original sponsoring editor, Jennifer Young; our editor for this edition, Rick Adams; our developmental editor, Nate McFadden; assistant editor David Bevans; and our production editor, Paul Gottehrer. Thanks also to the publisher at MKP, Laura Colantoni, whose leadership inspired us to embark on this revision.

Contents

1

A SYSTEMS APPROACH

A SYSTEMS APPROACH

A SYSTEMS APPROACH

A SYSTEMS APPROACH

Foundation

I must Create a System, or be enslav'd by another Man's; I will not Reason and Compare: my business is to Create.

–William Blake

Suppose you want to build a computer network, one that has the potential to grow to global proportions and to support applications as diverse as teleconferencing, video on demand, electronic commerce, distributed computing, and digital libraries. What available technologies would serve as the underlying building blocks, and what kind of software architecture would you design to integrate these building blocks into an effective communication service? Answering this question is the overriding goal of this book—to describe the available building materials and

PROBLEM: BUILDING A NETWORK

then to show how they can be used to construct a network from the ground up.

Before we can understand how to design a computer network, we should first agree on exactly what a computer network is. At one time, the term *network* meant the set of serial lines used to attach dumb terminals to mainframe computers. Other important networks include the voice telephone network and the cable TV network used to disseminate video signals. The main things these networks have in common are that they are specialized to handle one particular kind of data (keystrokes, voice, or video) and they typically connect to special-purpose devices (terminals, hand receivers, and television sets).

What distinguishes a computer network from these other types of networks? Probably the most important characteristic of a computer network is its generality. Computer networks are built primarily from general-purpose programmable hardware, and they are not optimized for a particular application like making phone calls or delivering television signals. Instead, they are able to carry many different types of data, and they support a wide, and ever growing, range of applications. Today's computer networks are increasingly taking over the functions previously performed by single-use networks. This chapter looks at some typical applications of computer networks and discusses the requirements that a network designer who wishes to support such applications must be aware of.

Once we understand the requirements, how do we proceed? Fortunately, we will not be building the first network. Others, most notably the community of researchers responsible for the Internet, have gone before us. We will use the wealth of experience generated from the Internet to guide our design. This experience is embodied in a *network architecture* that identifies the available hardware and software components and shows how they can be arranged to form a complete network system.

In addition to understanding how networks are built, it is increasingly important to understand how they are operated or managed and how network applications are developed. Most of us now have computer networks in our homes, offices, and in some cases in our cars, so operating networks is no longer a matter only for a few specialists. And, with the proliferation of programmable, network-attached devices such as smartphones, many more of this generation will develop networked applications than in the past. So we need to consider networks from these multiple perspectives: builders, operators, application developers.

To start us on the road toward understanding how to build, operate, and program a network, this chapter does four things. First, it explores the requirements that different applications and different communities of people place on the network. Second, it introduces the idea of a network architecture, which lays the foundation for the rest of the book. Third, it introduces some of the key elements in the implementation of computer networks. Finally, it identifies the key metrics that are used to evaluate the performance of computer networks.

1.1 APPLICATIONS

Most people know the Internet through its applications: the World Wide Web, email, online social networking, streaming audio and video, instant messaging, file-sharing, to name just a few examples. That is to say, we interact with the Internet as *users* of the network. Internet users represent the largest class of people who interact with the Internet in some way, but there are several other important constituencies. There is the group of people who *create* the applications—a group that has greatly expanded in recent years as powerful programming platforms and new devices such as smartphones have created new opportunities to develop applications quickly and to bring them to a large market. Then there are those who *operate* or *manage* networks—mostly a behind-the-scenes job, but a critical one and often a very complex one. With the prevalence of home networks, more and more people are also becoming, if only in a small way, network operators. Finally, there are those who *design* and *build* the devices and protocols that collectively make up the Internet. That final constituency is the traditional target of networking textbooks such as this one and will continue to be our main focus. However, throughout this book we will also consider the perspectives of application developers and network operators. Considering these perspectives will enable us to better understand the diverse requirements that a network must meet. Application developers will also be able to make applications that work better if they understand how the underlying technology works and interacts with the applications. So, before we start figuring out how to build a network, let's look more closely at the types of applications that today's networks support.

1.1.1 Classes of Applications

The World Wide Web is the Internet application that catapulted the Internet from a somewhat obscure tool used mostly by scientists and engineers to the mainstream phenomenon that it is today. The Web itself has become such a powerful platform that many people confuse it with the Internet (as in "the Interwebs"), and it's a bit of a stretch to say that the Web is a single application.

In its basic form, the Web presents an intuitively simple interface. Users view pages full of textual and graphical objects and click on objects that they want to learn more about, and a corresponding new page appears. Most people are also aware that just under the covers each selectable object on a page is bound to an identifier for the next page or object to be viewed. This identifier, called a Uniform Resource Locator (URL), provides a way of identifying all the possible objects that can be viewed from your web browser. For example,

```
http://www.cs.princeton.edu/~llp/index.html
```

is the URL for a page providing information about one of this book's authors: the string http indicates that the Hypertext Transfer Protocol (HTTP) should be used to download the page, www.cs.princeton.edu is the name of the machine that serves the page, and

/~llp/index.html

uniquely identifies Larry's home page at this site.

What most web users are not aware of, however, is that by clicking on just one such URL over a dozen messages may be exchanged over the Internet, and many more than that if the web page is complicated with lots of embedded objects. This message exchange includes up to six messages to translate the server name (www.cs.princeton.edu) into its Internet Protocol (IP) address (128.112.136.35), three messages to set up a Transmission Control Protocol (TCP) connection between your browser and this server, four messages for your browser to send the HTTP "GET" request and the server to respond with the requested page (and for each side to acknowledge receipt of that message), and four messages to tear down the TCP connection. Of course, this does not include the millions of messages exchanged by Internet nodes throughout the day, just to let each other know that they exist and are ready to serve web pages, translate names to addresses, and forward messages toward their ultimate destination.

Another widespread application class of the Internet is the delivery of "streaming" audio and video. Services such as video on demand and Internet radio use this technology. While we frequently start at a website to initiate a streaming session, the delivery of audio and video has some important differences from fetching a simple web page of text and images. For example, you often don't want to download an entire video file—a process that might take minutes to hours—before watching the first scene. Streaming audio and video implies a more timely transfer of messages from sender to receiver, and the receiver displays the video or plays the audio pretty much as it arrives.

Note that the difference between streaming applications and the more traditional delivery of a page of text or still images is that humans consume audio and video streams in a continuous manner, and discontinuity—in the form of skipped sounds or stalled video—is not acceptable. By contrast, a page of text can be delivered and read in bits and pieces. This difference affects how the network supports these different classes of applications.

A subtly different application class is *real-time* audio and video. These applications have considerably tighter timing constraints than streaming applications. When using a voice-over-IP application such as Skype™ or a videoconferencing application, the interactions among the participants must be timely. When a person at one end gestures, then that action must be displayed at the other end as quickly as possible. When one person tries to interrupt another, the interrupted person needs to hear that as soon as possible[1] and decide whether to allow the interruption or to keep talking over the interrupter. Too much delay in this sort of environment makes the system unusable. Contrast this with video on demand where, if it takes several seconds from the time the user starts the video until the first image is displayed, the service is still deemed satisfactory. Also, interactive applications usually entail audio and/or video flows in both directions, while a streaming application is most likely sending video or audio in only one direction.

Videoconferencing tools that run over the Internet have been around now since the early 1990s but have achieved much more widespread use in the last couple of years, as higher network speeds and more powerful computers have become commonplace. An example of one such system is shown in Figure 1.1. Just as downloading a web page involves a bit more than meets the eye, so too with video applications. Fitting the video content into a relatively low bandwidth network, for example, or making sure that the video and audio remain in sync and arrive in time for a good user experience are all problems that network and protocol designers have to worry about. We'll look at these and many other issues related to multimedia applications later in the book.

Although they are just two examples, downloading pages from the web and participating in a videoconference demonstrate the diversity of applications that can be built on top of the Internet and hint at the complexity of the Internet's design. Later in the book we will develop a more complete taxonomy of application types to help guide our discussion of key design decisions as we seek to build, operate, and use networks that support such a wide range of applications. In Chapter 9, the book concludes by revisiting these two specific applications, as well as several others that illustrate the breadth of what is possible on today's Internet.

---

[1]Not quite "as soon as possible"—human factors research indicates 300 ms is a reasonable upper bound for how much round-trip delay can be tolerated in a telephone call before humans complain, and a 100-ms delay sounds very good.

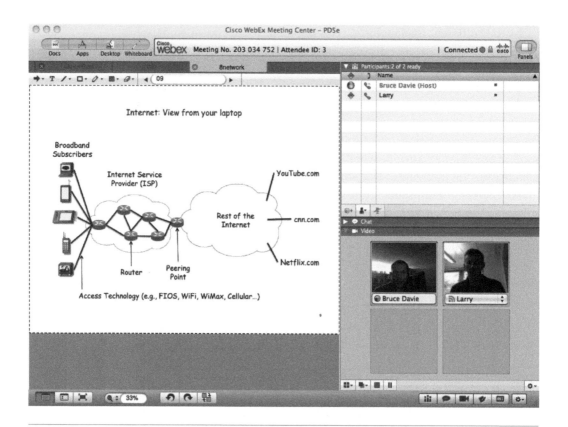

■ FIGURE 1.1 A multimedia application including videoconferencing.

LAB 00:
Introduction

For now, this quick look at a few typical applications will suffice to enable us to start looking at the problems that must be addressed if we are to build a network that supports such application diversity.

1.2 REQUIREMENTS

We have established an ambitious goal for ourselves: to understand how to build a computer network from the ground up. Our approach to accomplishing this goal will be to start from first principles and then ask the kinds of questions we would naturally ask if building an actual network. At each step, we will use today's protocols to illustrate various design choices available to us, but we will not accept these existing artifacts as gospel. Instead, we will be asking (and answering) the question of *why* networks are designed the way they are. While it is tempting to settle for just understanding the way it's done today, it is important to recognize the underlying concepts because networks are constantly changing as the technology evolves and new applications are invented. It is our experience that once you understand the fundamental ideas, any new protocol that you are confronted with will be relatively easy to digest.

1.2.1 Perspectives

As we noted above, a student of networks can take several perspectives. When we wrote the first edition of this book, the majority of the population had no Internet access at all, and those who did obtained it while at work, at a university, or by a dial-up modem at home. The set of popular applications could be counted on one's fingers. Thus, like most books at the time, ours focused on the perspective of someone who would design networking equipment and protocols. We continue to focus on this perspective, and our hope is that after reading this book you will know how to design the networking equipment and protocols of the future. However, we also want to cover the perspectives of two additional groups that are of increasing importance: those who develop networked applications and those who manage or operate networks. Let's consider how these three groups might list their requirements for a network:

- An *application programmer* would list the services that his or her application needs—for example, a guarantee that each message the application sends will be delivered without error within a certain amount of time or the ability to switch gracefully among different connections to the network as the user moves around.

- A *network operator* would list the characteristics of a system that is easy to administer and manage—for example, in which faults can be easily isolated, new devices can be added to the network and configured correctly, and it is easy to account for usage.

- A *network designer* would list the properties of a cost-effective design—for example, that network resources are efficiently utilized and fairly allocated to different users. Issues of performance are also likely to be important.

This section attempts to distill these different perspectives into a high-level introduction to the major considerations that drive network design and, in doing so, identifies the challenges addressed throughout the rest of this book.

1.2.2 Scalable Connectivity

Starting with the obvious, a network must provide connectivity among a set of computers. Sometimes it is enough to build a limited network that connects only a few select machines. In fact, for reasons of privacy and security, many private (corporate) networks have the explicit goal of limiting the set of machines that are connected. In contrast, other networks (of which the Internet is the prime example) are designed to grow in a way that allows them the potential to connect all the computers in the world. A system that is designed to support growth to an arbitrarily large size is said to *scale*. Using the Internet as a model, this book addresses the challenge of scalability.

Links, Nodes, and Clouds

To understand the requirements of connectivity more fully, we need to take a closer look at how computers are connected in a network. Connectivity occurs at many different levels. At the lowest level, a network can consist of two or more computers directly connected by some physical medium, such as a coaxial cable or an optical fiber. We call such a physical medium a *link*, and we often refer to the computers it connects as *nodes*. (Sometimes a node is a more specialized piece of hardware rather than a computer, but we overlook that distinction for the purposes of this discussion.) As illustrated in Figure 1.2, physical links are sometimes limited to a pair of nodes (such a link is said to be *point-to-point*), while in other cases more than two nodes may share a single physical link (such a link is said to be *multiple-access*). Wireless links, such as those provided by cellular networks and Wi-Fi networks, are an increasingly important class of multiple-access links. It is often the case that multiple-access links are limited in size, in terms of both the geographical distance they can cover and the number of nodes they can connect.

If computer networks were limited to situations in which all nodes are directly connected to each other over a common physical medium, then either networks would be very limited in the number of computers they could connect, or the number of wires coming out of the back of each node would quickly become both unmanageable and very expensive. Fortunately, connectivity between two nodes does not necessarily imply a direct physical connection between them—indirect connectivity may be achieved among a set of cooperating nodes. Consider the

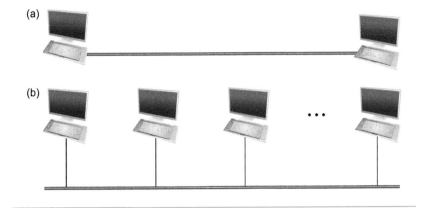

(a)

(b)

■ FIGURE 1.2 Direct links: (a) point-to-point; (b) multiple-access.

following two examples of how a collection of computers can be indirectly connected.

Figure 1.3 shows a set of nodes, each of which is attached to one or more point-to-point links. Those nodes that are attached to at least two links run software that forwards data received on one link out on another. If organized in a systematic way, these forwarding nodes form a *switched network*. There are numerous types of switched networks, of which the two most common are *circuit switched* and *packet switched*. The former is most notably employed by the telephone system, while the latter is used for the overwhelming majority of computer networks and will be the focus of this book. (Circuit switching is, however, making a bit of a comeback in the optical networking realm, which turns out to be important as demand for network capacity constantly grows.) The important feature of packet-switched networks is that the nodes in such a network send discrete blocks of data to each other. Think of these blocks of data as corresponding to some piece of application data such as a file, a piece of email, or an image. We call each block of data either a *packet* or a *message*, and for now we use these terms interchangeably; we discuss the reason they are not always the same in Section 1.2.3.

Packet-switched networks typically use a strategy called *store-and-forward*. As the name suggests, each node in a store-and-forward network first receives a complete packet over some link, stores the packet in its internal memory, and then forwards the complete packet to the next

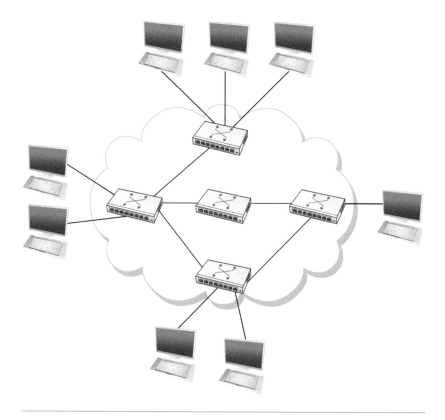

■ FIGURE 1.3 Switched network.

node. In contrast, a circuit-switched network first establishes a dedicated circuit across a sequence of links and then allows the source node to send a stream of bits across this circuit to a destination node. The major reason for using packet switching rather than circuit switching in a computer network is efficiency, discussed in the next subsection.

The cloud in Figure 1.3 distinguishes between the nodes on the inside that *implement* the network (they are commonly called *switches*, and their primary function is to store and forward packets) and the nodes on the outside of the cloud that *use* the network (they are commonly called *hosts*, and they support users and run application programs). Also note that the cloud in Figure 1.3 is one of the most important icons of computer networking. In general, we use a cloud to denote any type of network, whether it is a single point-to-point link, a multiple-access link, or a switched network. Thus, whenever you see a cloud used in a figure,

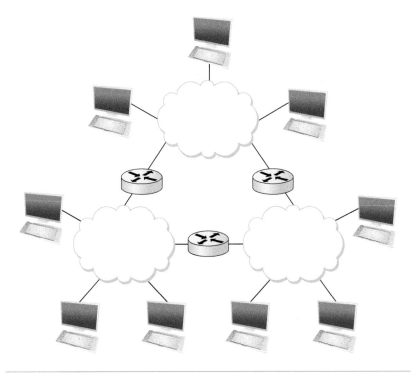

■ FIGURE 1.4 Interconnection of networks.

you can think of it as a placeholder for any of the networking technologies covered in this book.[2]

A second way in which a set of computers can be indirectly connected is shown in Figure 1.4. In this situation, a set of independent networks (clouds) are interconnected to form an *internetwork*, or internet for short. We adopt the Internet's convention of referring to a generic internetwork of networks as a lowercase *i* internet, and the currently operational TCP/IP Internet as the capital *I* Internet. A node that is connected to two or more networks is commonly called a *router* or *gateway*, and it plays much the same role as a switch—it forwards messages from one network to another. Note that an internet can itself be viewed as another kind of network, which means that an internet can be built from an interconnection of internets. Thus, we can recursively build arbitrarily large networks by interconnecting clouds to form larger clouds. It can

---

[2]Interestingly, the use of clouds in this way predates the term *cloud computing* by at least a couple of decades, but there is a connection between these two usages, which we'll discuss later.

reasonably be argued that this idea of interconnecting widely differing networks was the fundamental innovation of the Internet and that the successful growth of the Internet to global size and billions of nodes was the result of some very good design decisions by the early Internet architects, which we will discuss later.

Just because a set of hosts are directly or indirectly connected to each other does not mean that we have succeeded in providing host-to-host connectivity. The final requirement is that each node must be able to say which of the other nodes on the network it wants to communicate with. This is done by assigning an *address* to each node. An address is a byte string that identifies a node; that is, the network can use a node's address to distinguish it from the other nodes connected to the network. When a source node wants the network to deliver a message to a certain destination node, it specifies the address of the destination node. If the sending and receiving nodes are not directly connected, then the switches and routers of the network use this address to decide how to forward the message toward the destination. The process of determining systematically how to forward messages toward the destination node based on its address is called *routing*.

This brief introduction to addressing and routing has presumed that the source node wants to send a message to a single destination node (*unicast*). While this is the most common scenario, it is also possible that the source node might want to *broadcast* a message to all the nodes on the network. Or, a source node might want to send a message to some subset of the other nodes but not all of them, a situation called *multicast*. Thus, in addition to node-specific addresses, another requirement of a network is that it support multicast and broadcast addresses.

The main idea to take away from this discussion is that we can define a *network* recursively as consisting of two or more nodes connected by a physical link, or as two or more networks connected by a node. In other words, a network can be constructed from a nesting of networks, where at the bottom level, the network is implemented by some physical medium. Among the key challenges in providing network connectivity are the definition of an address for each node that is reachable on the network (including support for broadcast and multicast), and the use of such addresses to forward messages toward the appropriate destination node(s).

1.2.3 Cost-Effective Resource Sharing

As stated above, this book focuses on packet-switched networks. This section explains the key requirement of computer networks—efficiency—that leads us to packet switching as the strategy of choice.

Given a collection of nodes indirectly connected by a nesting of networks, it is possible for any pair of hosts to send messages to each other across a sequence of links and nodes. Of course, we want to do more than support just one pair of communicating hosts—we want to provide all pairs of hosts with the ability to exchange messages. The question, then, is how do all the hosts that want to communicate share the network, especially if they want to use it at the same time? And, as if that problem isn't hard enough, how do several hosts share the same *link* when they all want to use it at the same time?

To understand how hosts share a network, we need to introduce a fundamental concept, *multiplexing*, which means that a system resource is shared among multiple users. At an intuitive level, multiplexing can be explained by analogy to a timesharing computer system, where a single physical processor is shared (multiplexed) among multiple jobs, each of which believes it has its own private processor. Similarly, data being sent by multiple users can be multiplexed over the physical links that make up a network.

To see how this might work, consider the simple network illustrated in Figure 1.5, where the three hosts on the left side of the network (senders S1–S3) are sending data to the three hosts on the right (receivers R1–R3) by sharing a switched network that contains only one physical link. (For simplicity, assume that host S1 is sending data to host R1, and so on.) In this situation, three flows of data—corresponding to the three pairs of hosts—are multiplexed onto a single physical link by switch 1 and then *demultiplexed* back into separate flows by switch 2. Note that we are being intentionally vague about exactly what a "flow of data" corresponds to. For the purposes of this discussion, assume that each host on the left has a large supply of data that it wants to send to its counterpart on the right.

There are several different methods for multiplexing multiple flows onto one physical link. One common method is *synchronous time-division multiplexing* (STDM). The idea of STDM is to divide time into equal-sized quanta and, in a round-robin fashion, give each flow a chance

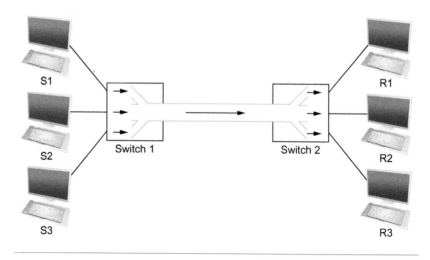

■ FIGURE 1.5 Multiplexing multiple logical flows over a single physical link.

to send its data over the physical link. In other words, during time quantum 1, data from S1 to R1 is transmitted; during time quantum 2, data from S2 to R2 is transmitted; in quantum 3, S3 sends data to R3. At this point, the first flow (S1 to R1) gets to go again, and the process repeats. Another method is *frequency-division multiplexing* (FDM). The idea of FDM is to transmit each flow over the physical link at a different frequency, much the same way that the signals for different TV stations are transmitted at a different frequency over the airwaves or on a coaxial cable TV link.

Although simple to understand, both STDM and FDM are limited in two ways. First, if one of the flows (host pairs) does not have any data to send, its share of the physical link—that is, its time quantum or its frequency—remains idle, even if one of the other flows has data to transmit. For example, S3 had to wait its turn behind S1 and S2 in the previous paragraph, even if S1 and S2 had nothing to send. For computer communication, the amount of time that a link is idle can be very large—for example, consider the amount of time you spend reading a web page (leaving the link idle) compared to the time you spend fetching the page. Second, both STDM and FDM are limited to situations in which the maximum number of flows is fixed and known ahead of time. It is not practical to resize the quantum or to add additional quanta in the case of STDM or to add new frequencies in the case of FDM.

The form of multiplexing that addresses these shortcomings, and of which we make most use in this book, is called *statistical multiplexing*. Although the name is not all that helpful for understanding the concept, statistical multiplexing is really quite simple, with two key ideas. First, it is like STDM in that the physical link is shared over time—first data from one flow is transmitted over the physical link, then data from another flow is transmitted, and so on. Unlike STDM, however, data is transmitted from each flow on demand rather than during a predetermined time slot. Thus, if only one flow has data to send, it gets to transmit that data without waiting for its quantum to come around and thus without having to watch the quanta assigned to the other flows go by unused. It is this avoidance of idle time that gives packet switching its efficiency.

As defined so far, however, statistical multiplexing has no mechanism to ensure that all the flows eventually get their turn to transmit over the physical link. That is, once a flow begins sending data, we need some way to limit the transmission, so that the other flows can have a turn. To account for this need, statistical multiplexing defines an upper bound on the size of the block of data that each flow is permitted to transmit at a given time. This limited-size block of data is typically referred to as a *packet*, to distinguish it from the arbitrarily large *message* that an application program might want to transmit. Because a packet-switched network limits the maximum size of packets, a host may not be able to send a complete message in one packet. The source may need to fragment the message into several packets, with the receiver reassembling the packets back into the original message.

In other words, each flow sends a sequence of packets over the physical link, with a decision made on a packet-by-packet basis as to which flow's packet to send next. Notice that, if only one flow has data to send, then it can send a sequence of packets back-to-back; however, should more than one of the flows have data to send, then their packets are interleaved on the link. Figure 1.6 depicts a switch multiplexing packets from multiple sources onto a single shared link.

The decision as to which packet to send next on a shared link can be made in a number of different ways. For example, in a network consisting of switches interconnected by links such as the one in Figure 1.5, the

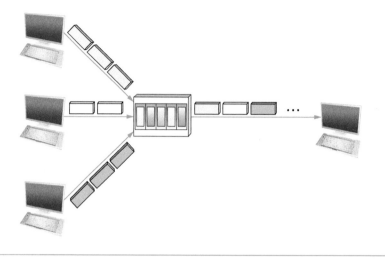

decision would be made by the switch that transmits packets onto the shared link. (As we will see later, not all packet-switched networks actually involve switches, and they may use other mechanisms to determine whose packet goes onto the link next.) Each switch in a packet-switched network makes this decision independently, on a packet-by-packet basis. One of the issues that faces a network designer is how to make this decision in a fair manner. For example, a switch could be designed to service packets on a first-in, first-out (FIFO) basis. Another approach would be to transmit the packets from each of the different flows that are currently sending data through the switch in a round-robin manner. This might be done to ensure that certain flows receive a particular share of the link's bandwidth or that they never have their packets delayed in the switch for more than a certain length of time. A network that attempts to allocate bandwidth to particular flows is sometimes said to support *quality of service* (QoS), a topic that we return to in Chapter 6.

Also, notice in Figure 1.6 that since the switch has to multiplex three incoming packet streams onto one outgoing link, it is possible that the switch will receive packets faster than the shared link can accommodate. In this case, the switch is forced to buffer these packets in its memory. Should a switch receive packets faster than it can send them for an extended period of time, then the switch will eventually run out of buffer space, and some packets will have to be dropped. When a switch is operating in this state, it is said to be *congested*.

The bottom line is that statistical multiplexing defines a cost-effective way for multiple users (e.g., host-to-host flows of data) to share network resources (links and nodes) in a fine-grained manner. It defines the packet as the granularity with which the links of the network are allocated to different flows, with each switch able to schedule the use of the physical links it is connected to on a per-packet basis. Fairly allocating link capacity to different flows and dealing with congestion when it occurs are the key challenges of statistical multiplexing.

SANs, LANs, MANs, and WANs

One way to characterize networks is according to their size. Two well-known examples are local area networks (LANs) and wide area networks (WANs); the former typically extend less than 1 km, while the latter can be worldwide. Other networks are classified as metropolitan area networks (MANs), which usually span tens of kilometers. The reason such classifications are interesting is that the size of a network often has implications for the underlying technology that can be used, with a key factor being the amount of time it takes for data to propagate from one end of the network to the other; we discuss this issue more in later chapters.

An interesting historical note is that the term *wide area network* was not applied to the first WANs because there was no other sort of network to differentiate them from. When computers were incredibly rare and expensive, there was no point in thinking about how to connect all the computers in the local area—there was only one computer in that area. Only as computers began to proliferate did LANs become necessary, and the term "WAN" was then introduced to describe the larger networks that interconnected geographically distant computers.

Another kind of network that we need to be aware of is SANs (usually now expanded as *storage area networks*, but formerly also known as *system area networks*). SANs are usually confined to a single room and connect the various components of a large computing system. For example, Fibre Channel is a common SAN technology used to connect high-performance computing systems to storage servers and data vaults. Although this book does not describe such networks in detail, they are worth knowing about because they are often at the leading edge in terms of performance, and because it is increasingly common to connect such networks into LANs and WANs.

1.2.4 Support for Common Services

The previous section outlined the challenges involved in providing cost-effective connectivity among a group of hosts, but it is overly simplistic to view a computer network as simply delivering packets among a collection of computers. It is more accurate to think of a network as providing the means for a set of application processes that are distributed over those computers to communicate. In other words, the next requirement of a computer network is that the application programs running on the hosts connected to the network must be able to communicate in a meaningful way. From the application developer's perspective, the network needs to make his or her life easier.

When two application programs need to communicate with each other, a lot of complicated things must happen beyond simply sending a message from one host to another. One option would be for application designers to build all that complicated functionality into each application program. However, since many applications need common services, it is much more logical to implement those common services once and then to let the application designer build the application using those services. The challenge for a network designer is to identify the right set of common services. The goal is to hide the complexity of the network from the application without overly constraining the application designer.

Intuitively, we view the network as providing logical *channels* over which application-level processes can communicate with each other; each channel provides the set of services required by that application. In other words, just as we use a cloud to abstractly represent connectivity among a set of computers, we now think of a channel as connecting one process to another. Figure 1.7 shows a pair of application-level processes communicating over a logical channel that is, in turn, implemented on top of a cloud that connects a set of hosts. We can think of the channel as being like a pipe connecting two applications, so that a sending application can put data in one end and expect that data to be delivered by the network to the application at the other end of the pipe.

The challenge is to recognize what functionality the channels should provide to application programs. For example, does the application require a guarantee that messages sent over the channel are delivered, or is it acceptable if some messages fail to arrive? Is it necessary that messages arrive at the recipient process in the same order in which they are sent, or does the recipient not care about the order in which messages

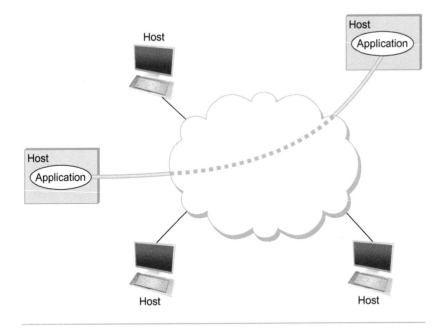

■ FIGURE 1.7 Processes communicating over an abstract channel.

arrive? Does the network need to ensure that no third parties are able to eavesdrop on the channel, or is privacy not a concern? In general, a network provides a variety of different types of channels, with each application selecting the type that best meets its needs. The rest of this section illustrates the thinking involved in defining useful channels.

Identifying Common Communication Patterns

Designing abstract channels involves first understanding the communication needs of a representative collection of applications, then extracting their common communication requirements, and finally incorporating the functionality that meets these requirements in the network.

One of the earliest applications supported on any network is a file access program like the File Transfer Protocol (FTP) or Network File System (NFS). Although many details vary—for example, whether whole files are transferred across the network or only single blocks of the file are read/written at a given time—the communication component of remote file access is characterized by a pair of processes, one that requests that a file be read or written and a second process that honors this request. The process that requests access to the file is called the *client*, and the process that supports access to the file is called the *server*.

Reading a file involves the client sending a small request message to a server and the server responding with a large message that contains the data in the file. Writing works in the opposite way—the client sends a large message containing the data to be written to the server, and the server responds with a small message confirming that the write to disk has taken place.

A digital library is a more sophisticated application than file transfer, but it requires similar communication services. For example, the *Association for Computing Machinery* (ACM) operates a large digital library of computer science literature at

http://portal.acm.org/dl.cfm

This library has a wide range of searching and browsing features to help users find the articles they want, but ultimately much of what it does is respond to user requests for files, such as electronic copies of journal articles, much like an FTP server.

Using file access, a digital library, and the two video applications described in the introduction (videoconferencing and video on demand) as a representative sample, we might decide to provide the following two types of channels: *request/reply* channels and *message stream* channels. The request/reply channel would be used by the file transfer and digital library applications. It would guarantee that every message sent by one side is received by the other side and that only one copy of each message is delivered. The request/reply channel might also protect the privacy and integrity of the data that flows over it, so that unauthorized parties cannot read or modify the data being exchanged between the client and server processes.

The message stream channel could be used by both the video on demand and videoconferencing applications, provided it is parameterized to support both one-way and two-way traffic and to support different delay properties. The message stream channel might not need to guarantee that all messages are delivered, since a video application can operate adequately even if some video frames are not received. It would, however, need to ensure that those messages that are delivered arrive in the same order in which they were sent, to avoid displaying frames out of sequence. Like the request/reply channel, the message stream channel might want to ensure the privacy and integrity of the video data. Finally, the message stream channel might need to support multicast, so that multiple parties can participate in the teleconference or view the video.

While it is common for a network designer to strive for the smallest number of abstract channel types that can serve the largest number of applications, there is a danger in trying to get away with too few channel abstractions. Simply stated, if you have a hammer, then everything looks like a nail. For example, if all you have are message stream and request/ reply channels, then it is tempting to use them for the next application that comes along, even if neither type provides exactly the semantics needed by the application. Thus, network designers will probably be inventing new types of channels—and adding options to existing channels—for as long as application programmers are inventing new applications.

Also note that independent of exactly *what* functionality a given channel provides, there is the question of *where* that functionality is implemented. In many cases, it is easiest to view the host-to-host connectivity of the underlying network as simply providing a *bit pipe*, with any high-level communication semantics provided at the end hosts. The advantage of this approach is that it keeps the switches in the middle of the network as simple as possible—they simply forward packets—but it requires the end hosts to take on much of the burden of supporting semantically rich process-to-process channels. The alternative is to push additional functionality onto the switches, thereby allowing the end hosts to be "dumb" devices (e.g., telephone handsets). We will see this question of how various network services are partitioned between the packet switches and the end hosts (devices) as a recurring issue in network design.

Reliability

As suggested by the examples just considered, reliable message delivery is one of the most important functions that a network can provide. It is difficult to determine how to provide this reliability, however, without first understanding how networks can fail. The first thing to recognize is that computer networks do not exist in a perfect world. Machines crash and later are rebooted, fibers are cut, electrical interference corrupts bits in the data being transmitted, switches run out of buffer space, and, as if these sorts of physical problems aren't enough to worry about, the software that manages the hardware may contain bugs and sometimes forwards packets into oblivion. Thus, a major requirement of a network is to recover from certain kinds of failures, so that application programs don't have to deal with them or even be aware of them.

There are three general classes of failure that network designers have to worry about. First, as a packet is transmitted over a physical link, *bit errors* may be introduced into the data; that is, a 1 is turned into a 0 or *vice versa*. Sometimes single bits are corrupted, but more often than not a *burst error* occurs—several consecutive bits are corrupted. Bit errors typically occur because outside forces, such as lightning strikes, power surges, and microwave ovens, interfere with the transmission of data. The good news is that such bit errors are fairly rare, affecting on average only one out of every 10^6 to 10^7 bits on a typical copper-based cable and one out of every 10^{12} to 10^{14} bits on a typical optical fiber. As we will see, there are techniques that detect these bit errors with high probability. Once detected, it is sometimes possible to correct for such errors—if we know which bit or bits are corrupted, we can simply flip them—while in other cases the damage is so bad that it is necessary to discard the entire packet. In such a case, the sender may be expected to retransmit the packet.

The second class of failure is at the packet, rather than the bit, level; that is, a complete packet is lost by the network. One reason this can happen is that the packet contains an uncorrectable bit error and therefore has to be discarded. A more likely reason, however, is that one of the nodes that has to handle the packet—for example, a switch that is forwarding it from one link to another—is so overloaded that it has no place to store the packet and therefore is forced to drop it. This is the problem of congestion mentioned in Section 1.2.3. Less commonly, the software running on one of the nodes that handles the packet makes a mistake. For example, it might incorrectly forward a packet out on the wrong link, so that the packet never finds its way to the ultimate destination. As we will see, one of the main difficulties in dealing with lost packets is distinguishing between a packet that is indeed lost and one that is merely late in arriving at the destination.

The third class of failure is at the node and link level; that is, a physical link is cut, or the computer it is connected to crashes. This can be caused by software that crashes, a power failure, or a reckless backhoe operator. Failures due to misconfiguration of a network device are also common. While any of these failures can eventually be corrected, they can have a dramatic effect on the network for an extended period of time. However, they need not totally disable the network. In a packet-switched network, for example, it is sometimes possible to route around a failed node or link. One of the difficulties in dealing with this third class of failure is distinguishing between a failed computer and one that is merely slow or, in the case of a link, between one that has been cut and one that is very flaky and therefore introducing a high number of bit errors.

The key idea to take away from this discussion is that defining useful channels involves both understanding the applications' requirements and recognizing the limitations of the underlying technology. The challenge is to fill in the gap between what the application expects and what the underlying technology can provide. This is sometimes called the *semantic gap*.

1.2.5 **Manageability**

A final requirement, which seems to be neglected or left till last all too often,[3] is that networks need to be managed. Managing a network includes making changes as the network grows to carry more traffic or reach more users, and troubleshooting the network when things go wrong or performance isn't as desired.

This requirement is partly related to the issue of scalability discussed above—as the Internet has scaled up to support billions of users and at least hundreds of millions of hosts, the challenges of keeping the whole thing running correctly and correctly configuring new devices as they are added have become increasingly problematic. Configuring a single router in a network is often a task for a trained expert; configuring thousands of routers and figuring out why a network of such a size is not behaving as expected can become a task beyond any single human. Furthermore, to make the operation of a network scalable and cost-effective, network operators typically require many management tasks to be automated or at least performed by relatively unskilled personnel.

An important development in networking since we wrote the first edition of this book is that networks in the home are now commonplace. This means that network management is no longer the province of experts but needs to be accomplished by consumers with little to no special training. This is sometimes stated as a requirement that networking devices should be "plug-and-play"—a goal that has proven quite elusive. We will discuss

---

[3]As we have done in this section.

some ways that this requirement has been addressed in part later on, but it is worth noting for now that improving the manageability of networks remains an important area of current research.

1.3 NETWORK ARCHITECTURE

In case you hadn't noticed, the previous section established a pretty substantial set of requirements for network design—a computer network must provide general, cost-effective, fair, and robust connectivity among a large number of computers. As if this weren't enough, networks do not remain fixed at any single point in time but must evolve to accommodate changes in both the underlying technologies upon which they are based as well as changes in the demands placed on them by application programs. Furthermore, networks must be manageable by humans of varying levels of skill. Designing a network to meet these requirements is no small task.

To help deal with this complexity, network designers have developed general blueprints—usually called *network architectures*—that guide the design and implementation of networks. This section defines more carefully what we mean by a network architecture by introducing the central ideas that are common to all network architectures. It also introduces two of the most widely referenced architectures—the OSI (or 7-layer) architecture and the Internet architecture.

1.3.1 Layering and Protocols

Abstraction—the hiding of details behind a well-defined interface—is the fundamental tool used by system designers to manage complexity. The idea of an abstraction is to define a model that can capture some important aspect of the system, encapsulate this model in an object that provides an interface that can be manipulated by other components of the system, and hide the details of how the object is implemented from the users of the object. The challenge is to identify abstractions that simultaneously provide a service that proves useful in a large number of situations and that can be efficiently implemented in the underlying system. This is exactly what we were doing when we introduced the idea of a channel in the previous section: we were providing an abstraction for applications that hides the complexity of the network from application writers.

Abstractions naturally lead to layering, especially in network systems. The general idea is that you start with the services offered by the underlying hardware and then add a sequence of layers, each providing a higher (more abstract) level of service. The services provided at the high layers are implemented in terms of the services provided by the low layers. Drawing on the discussion of requirements given in the previous section, for example, we might imagine a simple network as having two layers of abstraction sandwiched between the application program and the underlying hardware, as illustrated in Figure 1.8. The layer immediately above the hardware in this case might provide host-to-host connectivity, abstracting away the fact that there may be an arbitrarily complex network topology between any two hosts. The next layer up builds on the available host-to-host communication service and provides support for process-to-process channels, abstracting away the fact that the network occasionally loses messages, for example.

Layering provides two nice features. First, it decomposes the problem of building a network into more manageable components. Rather than implementing a monolithic piece of software that does everything you will ever want, you can implement several layers, each of which solves one part of the problem. Second, it provides a more modular design. If you decide that you want to add some new service, you may only need to modify the functionality at one layer, reusing the functions provided at all the other layers.

Thinking of a system as a linear sequence of layers is an oversimplification, however. Many times there are multiple abstractions provided at any given level of the system, each providing a different service to the higher layers but building on the same low-level abstractions. To see this, consider the two types of channels discussed in Section 1.2.4: One provides a

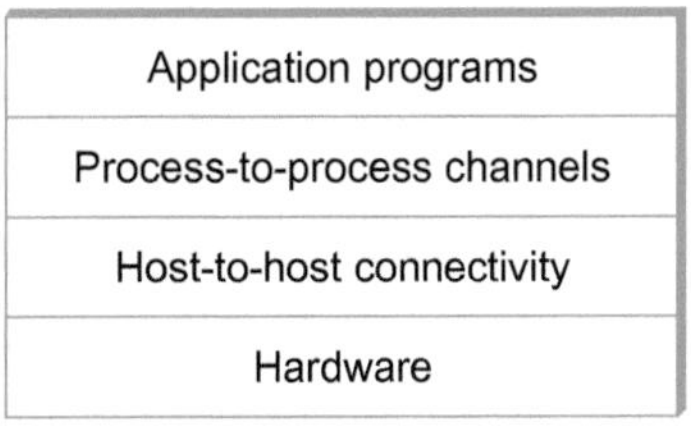

| Application programs |
| Process-to-process channels |
| Host-to-host connectivity |
| Hardware |

■ FIGURE 1.8 Example of a layered network system.

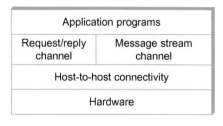

Application programs	
Request/reply channel	Message stream channel
Host-to-host connectivity	
Hardware	

request/reply service and one supports a message stream service. These two channels might be alternative offerings at some level of a multilevel networking system, as illustrated in Figure 1.9.

Using this discussion of layering as a foundation, we are now ready to discuss the architecture of a network more precisely. For starters, the abstract objects that make up the layers of a network system are called *protocols*. That is, a protocol provides a communication service that higher-level objects (such as application processes, or perhaps higher-level protocols) use to exchange messages. For example, we could imagine a network that supports a request/reply protocol and a message stream protocol, corresponding to the request/reply and message stream channels discussed above.

Each protocol defines two different interfaces. First, it defines a *service interface* to the other objects on the same computer that want to use its communication services. This service interface defines the operations that local objects can perform on the protocol. For example, a request/reply protocol would support operations by which an application can send and receive messages. An implementation of the HTTP protocol could support an operation to fetch a page of hypertext from a remote server. An application such as a web browser would invoke such an operation whenever the browser needs to obtain a new page (e.g., when the user clicks on a link in the currently displayed page).

Second, a protocol defines a *peer interface* to its counterpart (peer) on another machine. This second interface defines the form and meaning of messages exchanged between protocol peers to implement the communication service. This would determine the way in which a request/reply protocol on one machine communicates with its peer on another machine. In the case of HTTP, for example, the protocol specification

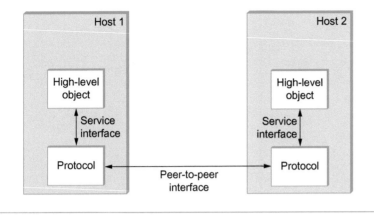

■ FIGURE 1.10 Service interfaces and peer interfaces.

defines in detail how a *GET* command is formatted, what arguments can be used with the command, and how a web server should respond when it receives such a command. (We will look more closely at this particular protocol in Section 9.1.2.)

To summarize, a protocol defines a communication service that it exports locally (the service interface), along with a set of rules governing the messages that the protocol exchanges with its peer(s) to implement this service (the peer interface). This situation is illustrated in Figure 1.10.

Except at the hardware level, where peers directly communicate with each other over a link, peer-to-peer communication is indirect—each protocol communicates with its peer by passing messages to some lower-level protocol, which in turn delivers the message to *its* peer. In addition, there are potentially multiple protocols at any given level, each providing a different communication service. We therefore represent the suite of protocols that make up a network system with a *protocol graph*. The nodes of the graph correspond to protocols, and the edges represent a *depends on* relation. For example, Figure 1.11 illustrates a protocol graph for the hypothetical layered system we have been discussing—protocols RRP (Request/Reply Protocol) and MSP (Message Stream Protocol) implement two different types of process-to-process channels, and both depend on the Host-to-Host Protocol (HHP) which provides a host-to-host connectivity service.

In this example, suppose that the file access program on host 1 wants to send a message to its peer on host 2 using the communication service

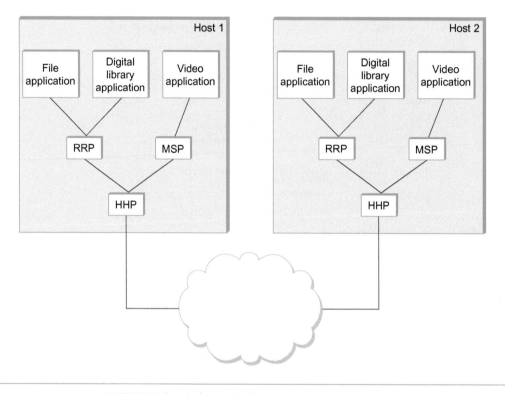

■ FIGURE 1.11 Example of a protocol graph.

offered by RRP. In this case, the file application asks RRP to send the message on its behalf. To communicate with its peer, RRP invokes the services of HHP, which in turn transmits the message to its peer on the other machine. Once the message has arrived at the instance of HHP on host 2, HHP passes the message up to RRP, which in turn delivers the message to the file application. In this particular case, the application is said to employ the services of the *protocol stack* RRP/HHP.

Note that the term *protocol* is used in two different ways. Sometimes it refers to the abstract interfaces—that is, the operations defined by the service interface and the form and meaning of messages exchanged between peers, and sometimes it refers to the module that actually implements these two interfaces. To distinguish between the interfaces and the module that implements these interfaces, we generally refer to the former as a *protocol specification*. Specifications are generally expressed using a combination of prose, pseudocode, state transition diagrams, pictures of packet formats, and other abstract notations. It should be the case that a given protocol can be implemented in different ways by different programmers, as long as each adheres to the specification. The challenge is ensuring that two different implementations of the same specification can successfully exchange messages. Two or more protocol modules that do accurately implement a protocol specification are said to *interoperate* with each other.

We can imagine many different protocols and protocol graphs that satisfy the communication requirements of a collection of applications. Fortunately, there exist standardization bodies, such as the Internet Engineering Task Force (IETF) and the International Standards Organization (ISO), that establish policies for a particular protocol graph. We call the set of rules governing the form and content of a protocol graph a *network architecture*. Although beyond the scope of this book, standardization bodies have established well-defined procedures for introducing, validating, and finally approving protocols in their respective architectures. We briefly describe the architectures defined by the IETF and ISO shortly, but first there are two additional things we need to explain about the mechanics of protocol layering.

Encapsulation

Consider what happens in Figure 1.11 when one of the application programs sends a message to its peer by passing the message to RRP. From RRP's perspective, the message it is given by the application is an uninterpreted string of bytes. RRP does not care that these bytes represent an array of integers, an email message, a digital image, or whatever; it is simply charged with sending them to its peer. However, RRP must communicate control information to its peer, instructing it how to handle the message when it is received. RRP does this by attaching a *header* to the message. Generally speaking, a header is a small data structure—from a few bytes to a few dozen bytes—that is used among peers to communicate with each other. As the name suggests, headers are usually attached to the front of a message. In some cases, however, this peer-to-peer control information is sent at the end of the message, in which case it is called a *trailer*. The exact format for the header attached by RRP is defined by its protocol specification. The rest of the message—that is, the data being transmitted on behalf of the application—is called the message's *body* or *payload*. We say that the application's data is *encapsulated* in the new message created by RRP.

This process of encapsulation is then repeated at each level of the protocol graph; for example, HHP encapsulates RRP's message by attaching a header of its own. If we now assume that HHP sends the message to its peer over some network, then when the message arrives at the destination host, it is processed in the opposite order: HHP first interprets the HHP header at the front of the message (i.e., takes whatever action is appropriate given the contents of the header) and passes the body of the message (but not the HHP header) up to RRP, which takes whatever action is indicated by the RRP header that its peer attached and passes the body of the message (but not the RRP header) up to the application program. The message passed up from RRP to the application on host 2 is exactly the same message as the application passed down to RRP on host 1; the application does not see any of the headers that have been attached to it to implement the lower-level communication services. This whole process is illustrated in Figure 1.12. Note that in this example, nodes in the

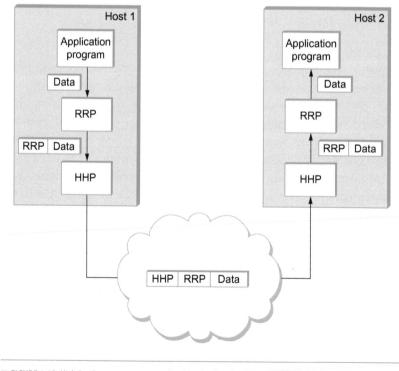

■ **FIGURE 1.12** High-level messages are encapsulated inside of low-level messages.

network (e.g., switches and routers) may inspect the HHP header at the front of the message.

Note that when we say a low-level protocol does not interpret the message it is given by some high-level protocol, we mean that it does not know how to extract any meaning from the data contained in the message. It is sometimes the case, however, that the low-level protocol applies some simple transformation to the data it is given, such as to compress or encrypt it. In this case, the protocol is transforming the entire body of the message, including both the original application's data and all the headers attached to that data by higher-level protocols.

Multiplexing and Demultiplexing

Recall from Section 1.2.3 that a fundamental idea of packet switching is to multiplex multiple flows of data over a single physical link. This same idea applies up and down the protocol graph, not just to switching nodes. In Figure 1.11, for example, we can think of RRP as implementing a logical communication channel, with messages from two different applications multiplexed over this channel at the source host and then demultiplexed back to the appropriate application at the destination host.

Practically speaking, this simply means that the header that RRP attaches to its messages contains an identifier that records the application to which the message belongs. We call this identifier RRP's *demultiplexing key*, or *demux key* for short. At the source host, RRP includes the appropriate demux key in its header. When the message is delivered to RRP on the destination host, it strips its header, examines the demux key, and demultiplexes the message to the correct application.

RRP is not unique in its support for multiplexing; nearly every protocol implements this mechanism. For example, HHP has its own demux key to determine which messages to pass up to RRP and which to pass up to MSP. However, there is no uniform agreement among protocols—even those within a single network architecture—on exactly what constitutes a demux key. Some protocols use an 8-bit field (meaning they can support only 256 high-level protocols), and others use 16- or 32-bit fields. Also, some protocols have a single demultiplexing field in their header, while others have a pair of demultiplexing fields. In the former case, the same demux key is used on both sides of the communication, while in the latter case each side uses a different key to identify the high-level protocol (or application program) to which the message is to be delivered.

The 7-Layer Model

The ISO was one of the first organizations to formally define a common way to connect computers. Their architecture, called the *Open Systems Interconnection* (OSI) architecture and illustrated in Figure 1.13, defines a partitioning of network functionality into seven layers, where one or more protocols implement the functionality assigned to a given layer. In this sense, the schematic given in Figure 1.13 is not a protocol graph, *per se*, but rather a *reference model* for a protocol graph. It is often referred to as the 7-layer model.

Starting at the bottom and working up, the *physical* layer handles the transmission of raw bits over a communications link. The *data link* layer then collects a stream of bits into a larger aggregate called a *frame*. Network adaptors, along with device drivers running in the node's operating

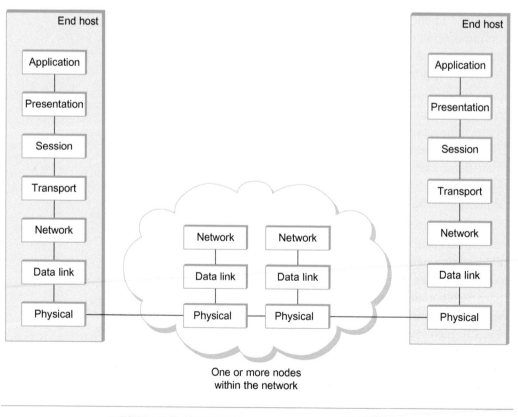

system, typically implement the data link level. This means that frames, not raw bits, are actually delivered to hosts. The *network* layer handles routing among nodes within a packet-switched network. At this layer, the unit of data exchanged among nodes is typically called a *packet* rather than a frame, although they are fundamentally the same thing. The lower three layers are implemented on all network nodes, including switches within the network and hosts connected to the exterior of the network. The *transport* layer then implements what we have up to this point been calling a *process-to-process channel*. Here, the unit of data exchanged is commonly called a *message* rather than a packet or a frame. The transport layer and higher layers typically run only on the end hosts and not on the intermediate switches or routers.

There is less agreement about the definition of the top three layers, in part because they are not always all present, as we will see below. Skipping ahead to the top (seventh) layer, we find the *application* layer. Application layer protocols include things like the Hypertext Transfer Protocol (HTTP), which is the basis of the World Wide Web and is what enables web browsers to request pages from web servers. Below that, the *presentation* layer is concerned with the format of data exchanged between peers—for example, whether an integer is 16, 32, or 64 bits long, whether the most significant byte is transmitted first or last, or how a video stream is formatted. Finally, the *session* layer provides a name space that is used to tie together the potentially different transport streams that are part of a single application. For example, it might manage an audio stream and a video stream that are being combined in a teleconferencing application.

1.3.2 Internet Architecture

The Internet architecture, which is also sometimes called the TCP/IP architecture after its two main protocols, is depicted in Figure 1.14. An alternative representation is given in Figure 1.15. The Internet architecture evolved out of experiences with an earlier packet-switched network called the ARPANET. Both the Internet and the ARPANET were funded by the Advanced Research Projects Agency (ARPA), one of the research and development funding agencies of the U.S. Department of Defense. The Internet and ARPANET were around before the OSI architecture, and the experience gained from building them was a major influence on the OSI reference model.

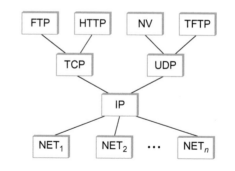

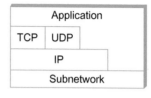

◼ FIGURE 1.15 Alternative view of the Internet architecture. The *subnetwork* layer was historically referred to as the *network* layer and is now often referred to as the layer or simply *layer 2*.

While the 7-layer OSI model can, with some imagination, be applied to the Internet, a 4-layer model is often used instead. At the lowest level is a wide variety of network protocols, denoted NET_1, NET_2, and so on. In practice, these protocols are implemented by a combination of hardware (e.g., a network adaptor) and software (e.g., a network device driver). For example, you might find Ethernet or wireless protocols (such as the 802.11 Wi-Fi standards) at this layer. (These protocols in turn may actually involve several sublayers, but the Internet architecture does not presume anything about them.) The second layer consists of a single protocol—the *Internet Protocol* (IP). This is the protocol that supports the interconnection of multiple networking technologies into a single, logical internetwork. The third layer contains two main protocols—the *Transmission Control Protocol* (TCP) and the *User Datagram Protocol* (UDP). TCP and UDP provide alternative logical channels to application programs: TCP provides a reliable byte-stream channel, and UDP provides an unreliable datagram delivery channel (*datagram* may be thought of as a synonym for message). In the language of the Internet, TCP and UDP are sometimes called *end-to-end* protocols, although it is equally correct to refer to them as *transport* protocols.

Running above the transport layer is a range of application protocols, such as HTTP, FTP, Telnet (remote login), and the Simple Mail Transfer Protocol (SMTP), that enable the interoperation of popular applications. To understand the difference between an application layer protocol and an application, think of all the different World Wide Web browsers that are or have been available (e.g., Firefox, Safari, Netscape, Mosaic, Internet Explorer). There is a similarly large number of different implementations of web servers. The reason that you can use any one of these application programs to access a particular site on the Web is that they all conform to the same application layer protocol: HTTP. Confusingly, the same term sometimes applies to both an application and the application layer protocol that it uses (e.g., FTP is often used as the name of an application that implements the FTP protocol).

Most people who work actively in the networking field are familiar with both the Internet architecture and the 7-layer OSI architecture, and there is general agreement on how the layers map between architectures. The Internet's application layer is considered to be at layer 7, its transport layer is layer 4, the IP (internetworking or just network) layer is layer 3, and the link or subnet layer below IP is layer 2.

The Internet architecture has three features that are worth highlighting. First, as best illustrated by Figure 1.15, the Internet architecture does not imply strict layering. The application is free to bypass the defined transport layers and to directly use IP or one of the underlying networks. In fact, programmers are free to define new channel abstractions or applications that run on top of any of the existing protocols.

Second, if you look closely at the protocol graph in Figure 1.14, you will notice an hourglass shape—wide at the top, narrow in the middle, and wide at the bottom. This shape actually reflects the central philosophy of the architecture. That is, IP serves as the focal point for the architecture— it defines a common method for exchanging packets among a wide collection of networks. Above IP there can be arbitrarily many transport protocols, each offering a different channel abstraction to application programs. Thus, the issue of delivering messages from host to host is completely separated from the issue of providing a useful process-to-process communication service. Below IP, the architecture allows for arbitrarily many different network technologies, ranging from Ethernet to wireless to single point-to-point links.

A final attribute of the Internet architecture (or more accurately, of the IETF culture) is that in order for a new protocol to be officially included in the architecture, there must be both a protocol specification and at least one (and preferably two) representative implementations of the specification. The existence of working implementations is required for standards to be adopted by the IETF. This cultural assumption of the design community helps to ensure that the architecture's protocols can be efficiently implemented. Perhaps the value the Internet culture places on working software is best exemplified by a quote on T-shirts commonly worn at IETF meetings:

> *We reject kings, presidents, and voting. We believe in rough consensus and running code.*
>
> **(David Clark)**

Of these three attributes of the Internet architecture, the hourglass design philosophy is important enough to bear repeating. The hourglass's narrow waist represents a minimal and carefully chosen set of global capabilities that allows both higher-level applications and lower-level communication technologies to coexist, share capabilities, and evolve rapidly. The narrow-waisted model is critical to the Internet's ability to adapt rapidly to new user demands and changing technologies.

1.4 IMPLEMENTING NETWORK SOFTWARE

Network architectures and protocol specifications are essential things, but a good blueprint is not enough to explain the phenomenal success of the Internet: The number of computers connected to the Internet has grown exponentially for almost 3 decades (although precise numbers are now hard to come by). The number of users of the Internet was estimated to be around 1.8 billion in 2009—an impressive percentage of the world's population.

What explains the success of the Internet? There are certainly many contributing factors (including a good architecture), but one thing that has made the Internet such a runaway success is the fact that so much of its functionality is provided by software running in general-purpose computers. The significance of this is that new functionality can be added readily with "just a small matter of programming." As a result, new applications and services—electronic commerce, videoconferencing, and IP telephony, to name a few—have been showing up at an incredible pace.

A related factor is the massive increase in computing power available in commodity machines. Although computer networks have always been capable in principle of transporting any kind of information, such as digital voice samples, digitized images, and so on, this potential was not particularly interesting if the computers sending and receiving that data were too slow to do anything useful with the information. Virtually all of today's computers are capable of playing back digitized voice at full speed and can display video at a speed and resolution that are useful for some (but by no means all) applications. Thus, today's networks are increasingly used to carry multimedia, and their support for it will only improve as computing hardware becomes faster.

In the years since the first edition of this book appeared, the writing of networked applications has become a much more mainstream activity and less a job just for a few specialists. Many factors have played into this, including better tools to make the job easier for nonspecialists and the opening up of new markets such as applications for smartphones.

The point to note is that knowing how to implement network software is an essential part of understanding computer networks, and while the odds are you will not be tasked to implement a low-level protocol like IP, there is a good chance you will find reason to implement an application-level protocol—the elusive "killer app" that will lead to unimaginable fame and fortune. To get you started, this section introduces some of the issues involved in implementing a network application on top of the Internet. Typically, such programs are simultaneously an application (i.e., designed to interact with users) and a protocol (i.e., communicates with peers across the network). Chapter 9 concludes the book by returning to the topic of network applications (application-level protocols) by exploring several popular examples.

1.4.1 Application Programming Interface (Sockets)

The place to start when implementing a network application is the interface exported by the network. Since most network protocols are implemented in software (especially those high in the protocol stack), and nearly all computer systems implement their network protocols as part of the operating system, when we refer to the interface "exported by the network," we are generally referring to the interface that the OS provides to its networking subsystem. This interface is often called the network *application programming interface* (API).

Although each operating system is free to define its own network API (and most have), over time certain of these APIs have become widely supported; that is, they have been ported to operating systems other than their native system. This is what has happened with the *socket interface* originally provided by the Berkeley distribution of Unix, which is now supported in virtually all popular operating systems, and is the foundation of language-specific interfaces, such as the Java socket library. The advantages of industry-wide support for a single API are that applications can be easily ported from one OS to another and developers can easily write applications for multiple operating systems.

Before describing the socket interface, it is important to keep two concerns separate in your mind. Each protocol provides a certain set of *services*, and the API provides a *syntax* by which those services can be invoked on a particular computer system. The implementation is then responsible for mapping the tangible set of operations and objects defined by the API onto the abstract set of services defined by the protocol. If you have done a good job of defining the interface, then it will be possible to use the syntax of the interface to invoke the services of many different protocols. Such generality was certainly a goal of the socket interface, although it's far from perfect.

The main abstraction of the socket interface, not surprisingly, is the *socket*. A good way to think of a socket is as the point where a local application process attaches to the network. The interface defines operations for creating a socket, attaching the socket to the network, sending/receiving messages through the socket, and closing the socket. To simplify the discussion, we will limit ourselves to showing how sockets are used with TCP.

The first step is to create a socket, which is done with the following operation:

```
int socket(int domain, int type, int protocol)
```

The reason that this operation takes three arguments is that the socket interface was designed to be general enough to support any underlying protocol suite. Specifically, the domain argument specifies the protocol *family* that is going to be used: PF_INET denotes the Internet family, PF_UNIX denotes the Unix pipe facility, and PF_PACKET denotes direct access to the network interface (i.e., it bypasses the TCP/IP protocol stack). The type argument indicates the semantics of the communication. SOCK_STREAM is used to denote a byte stream. SOCK_DGRAM is an alternative that denotes a message-oriented service, such as that provided by UDP. The protocol argument identifies the specific protocol that is going to be used. In our case, this argument is UNSPEC because the combination of PF_INET and SOCK_STREAM implies TCP. Finally, the return value from socket is a *handle* for the newly created socket—that is, an identifier by which we can refer to the socket in the future. It is given as an argument to subsequent operations on this socket.

The next step depends on whether you are a client or a server. On a server machine, the application process performs a *passive* open—the server says that it is prepared to accept connections, but it does not actually establish a connection. The server does this by invoking the following three operations:

```
int bind(int socket, struct sockaddr *address, int addr_len)
int listen(int socket, int backlog)
int accept(int socket, struct sockaddr *address, int *addr_len)
```

The bind operation, as its name suggests, binds the newly created socket to the specified address. This is the network address of the *local* participant—the server. Note that, when used with the Internet protocols, address is a data structure that includes both the IP address of the server and a TCP port number. (As we will see in Chapter 5, ports are used to indirectly identify processes. They are a form of *demux keys* as defined in Section 1.3.1.) The port number is usually some well-known number specific to the service being offered; for example, web servers commonly accept connections on port 80.

The listen operation then defines how many connections can be pending on the specified socket. Finally, the accept operation carries out the passive open. It is a blocking operation that does not return until a remote participant has established a connection, and when it does complete it returns a *new* socket that corresponds to this just-established connection, and the address argument contains the *remote* participant's address. Note that when accept returns, the original socket that was given as an argument still exists and still corresponds to the passive open; it is used in future invocations of accept.

On the client machine, the application process performs an *active open*; that is, it says who it wants to communicate with by invoking the following single operation:

```
int connect(int socket, struct sockaddr *address, int addr_len)
```

This operation does not return until TCP has successfully established a connection, at which time the application is free to begin sending data. In this case, address contains the remote participant's address. In practice, the client usually specifies only the remote participant's address and lets the system fill in the local information. Whereas a server usually listens for messages on a well-known port, a client typically does not care which port it uses for itself; the OS simply selects an unused one.

Once a connection is established, the application processes invoke the following two operations to send and receive data:

```
int send(int socket, char *message, int msg_len, int flags)
int recv(int socket, char *buffer, int buf_len, int flags)
```

The first operation sends the given message over the specified socket, while the second operation receives a message from the specified socket into the given buffer. Both operations take a set of flags that control certain details of the operation.

1.4.2 Example Application

We now show the implementation of a simple client/server program that uses the socket interface to send messages over a TCP connection. The program also uses other Unix networking utilities, which we introduce as we go. Our application allows a user on one machine to type in and send text to a user on another machine. It is a simplified version of the Unix talk program, which is similar to the program at the core of an instant messaging application.

Client

We start with the client side, which takes the name of the remote machine as an argument. It calls the Unix utility gethostbyname to translate this name into the remote host's IP address. The next step is to construct the address data structure (sin) expected by the socket interface. Notice that this data structure specifies that we'll be using the socket to connect to the Internet (AF_INET). In our example, we use TCP port 5432 as the well-known server port; this happens to be a port that has not been assigned to any other Internet service. The final step in setting up the connection is to call **socket** and **connect**. Once the **connect** operation returns, the connection is established and the client program enters its main loop, which reads text from standard input and sends it over the socket.

```c
#include <stdio.h>
#include <sys/types.h>
#include <sys/socket.h>
#include <netinet/in.h>
#include <netdb.h>

#define SERVER_PORT 5432
#define MAX_LINE 256

int
main(int argc, char * argv[])
{
    FILE *fp;
    struct hostent *hp;
    struct sockaddr_in sin;
    char *host;
    char buf[MAX_LINE];
    int s;
    int len;

    if (argc==2) {
        host = argv[1];
    }
    else {
        fprintf(stderr, "usage: simplex-talk host\n");
        exit(1);
    }

    /* translate host name into peer's IP address */
    hp = gethostbyname(host);
    if (!hp) {
        fprintf(stderr, "simplex-talk: unknown host: %s\n", host);
        exit(1);
    }
```

```
/* build address data structure */
bzero((char *)&sin, sizeof(sin));
sin.sin_family = AF_INET;
bcopy(hp->h_addr, (char *)&sin.sin_addr, hp->h_length);
sin.sin_port = htons(SERVER_PORT);

/* active open */
if ((s = socket(PF_INET, SOCK_STREAM, 0)) < 0) {
  perror("simplex-talk: socket");
  exit(1);
}
if (connect(s, (struct sockaddr *)&sin, sizeof(sin)) < 0)
{
  perror("simplex-talk: connect");
  close(s);
  exit(1);
}
/* main loop: get and send lines of text */
while (fgets(buf, sizeof(buf), stdin)) {
  buf[MAX_LINE-1] = '\0';
  len = strlen(buf) + 1;
  send(s, buf, len, 0);
}
}
```

Server

The server is equally simple. It first constructs the address data structure by filling in its own port number (**SERVER_PORT**). By not specifying an IP address, the application program is willing to accept connections on any of the local host's IP addresses. Next, the server performs the preliminary steps involved in a passive open; it creates the socket, binds it to the local address, and sets the maximum number of pending connections to be allowed. Finally, the main loop waits for a remote host to try to connect, and when one does, it receives and prints out the characters that arrive on the connection.

```
#include <stdio.h>
#include <sys/types.h>
#include <sys/socket.h>
```

```
#include <netinet/in.h>
#include <netdb.h>

#define SERVER_PORT  5432
#define MAX_PENDING  5
#define MAX_LINE     256

int
main()
{
  struct sockaddr_in sin;
  char buf[MAX_LINE];
  int len;
  int s, new_s;

  /* build address data structure */
  bzero((char *)&sin, sizeof(sin));
  sin.sin_family = AF_INET;
  sin.sin_addr.s_addr = INADDR_ANY;
  sin.sin_port = htons(SERVER_PORT);

  /* setup passive open */
  if ((s = socket(PF_INET, SOCK_STREAM, 0)) < 0) {
    perror("simplex-talk: socket");
    exit(1);
  }
  if ((bind(s, (struct sockaddr *)&sin, sizeof(sin))) < 0) {
    perror("simplex-talk: bind");
    exit(1);
  }
  listen(s, MAX_PENDING);

  /* wait for connection, then receive and print text */
  while(1) {
    if ((new_s = accept(s, (struct sockaddr *)&sin, &len)) < 0) {
      perror("simplex-talk: accept");
      exit(1);
    }
    while (len = recv(new_s, buf, sizeof(buf), 0))
```

```
        fputs(buf, stdout);
      close(new_s);
  }
}
```

1.5 PERFORMANCE

Up to this point, we have focused primarily on the functional aspects of network. Like any computer system, however, computer networks are also expected to perform well. This is because the effectiveness of computations distributed over the network often depends directly on the efficiency with which the network delivers the computation's data. While the old programming adage "first get it right and then make it fast" is valid in many settings, in networking it is usually necessary to "design for performance." It is therefore important to understand the various factors that impact network performance.

1.5.1 Bandwidth and Latency

Network performance is measured in two fundamental ways: *bandwidth* (also called *throughput*) and *latency* (also called *delay*). The bandwidth of a network is given by the number of bits that can be transmitted over the network in a certain period of time. For example, a network might have a bandwidth of 10 million bits/second (Mbps), meaning that it is able to deliver 10 million bits every second. It is sometimes useful to think of bandwidth in terms of how long it takes to transmit each bit of data. On a 10-Mbps network, for example, it takes 0.1 microsecond (μs) to transmit each bit.

While you can talk about the bandwidth of the network as a whole, sometimes you want to be more precise, focusing, for example, on the bandwidth of a single physical link or of a logical process-to-process channel. At the physical level, bandwidth is constantly improving, with no end in sight. Intuitively, if you think of a second of time as a distance you could measure with a ruler and bandwidth as how many bits fit in that distance, then you can think of each bit as a pulse of some width. For example, each bit on a 1-Mbps link is 1 μs wide, while each bit on a 2-Mbps link is 0.5 μs wide, as illustrated in Figure 1.16. The more sophisticated the transmitting and receiving technology, the narrower each bit can become and, thus, the higher the bandwidth. For logical process-to-process channels, bandwidth is also influenced by other factors, including how many times the software that implements the channel has to handle, and possibly transform, each bit of data.

Bandwidth and Throughput

Bandwidth and *throughput* are two of the most confusing terms used in networking. While we could try to give you a precise definition of each term, it is important that you know how other people might use them and for you to be aware that they are often used interchangeably. First of all, bandwidth is literally a measure of the width of a frequency band. For example, a voice-grade telephone line supports a frequency band ranging from 300 to 3300 Hz; it is said to have a bandwidth of $3300 \text{ Hz} - 300 \text{ Hz} = 3000 \text{ Hz}$. If you see the word *bandwidth* used in a situation in which it is being measured in hertz, then it probably refers to the range of signals that can be accommodated.

When we talk about the bandwidth of a communication link, we normally refer to the number of bits per second that can be transmitted on the link. This is also sometimes called the *data rate*. We might say that the bandwidth of an Ethernet link is 10 Mbps. A useful distinction can also be made, however, between the maximum data rate that is available on the link and the number of bits per second that we can actually transmit over the link in practice. We tend to use the word *throughput* to refer to the *measured performance* of a system. Thus, because of various inefficiencies of implementation, a pair of nodes connected by a link with a bandwidth of 10 Mbps might achieve a throughput of only 2 Mbps. This would mean that an application on one host could send data to the other host at 2 Mbps.

Finally, we often talk about the bandwidth *requirements* of an application. This is the number of bits per second that it needs to transmit over the network to perform acceptably. For some applications, this might be "whatever I can get"; for others, it might be some fixed number (preferably no more than the available link bandwidth); and for others, it might be a number that varies with time. We will provide more on this topic later in this section.

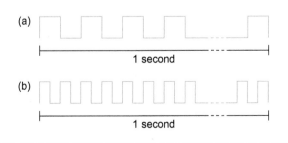

(a)   1 second

(b)   1 second

■ **FIGURE 1.16** Bits transmitted at a particular bandwidth can be regarded as having some width: (a) bits transmitted at 1 Mbps (each bit is 1 μs wide); (b) bits transmitted at 2 Mbps (each bit is 0.5 μs wide).

The second performance metric, latency, corresponds to how long it takes a message to travel from one end of a network to the other. (As with bandwidth, we could be focused on the latency of a single link or an end-to-end channel.) Latency is measured strictly in terms of time. For example, a transcontinental network might have a latency of 24 milliseconds (ms); that is, it takes a message 24 ms to travel from one coast of North America to the other. There are many situations in which it is more important to know how long it takes to send a message from one end of a network to the other and back, rather than the one-way latency. We call this the *round-trip time* (RTT) of the network.

We often think of latency as having three components. First, there is the speed-of-light propagation delay. This delay occurs because nothing, including a bit on a wire, can travel faster than the speed of light. If you know the distance between two points, you can calculate the speed-of-light latency, although you have to be careful because light travels across different media at different speeds: It travels at 3.0×10^8 m/s in a vacuum, 2.3×10^8 m/s in a copper cable, and 2.0×10^8 m/s in an optical fiber. Second, there is the amount of time it takes to transmit a unit of data. This is a function of the network bandwidth and the size of the packet in which the data is carried. Third, there may be queuing delays inside the network, since packet switches generally need to store packets for some time before forwarding them on an outbound link, as discussed in Section 1.2.3. So, we could define the total latency as

$$Latency = Propagation + Transmit + Queue$$

$$Propagation = Distance/SpeedOfLight$$

$$Transmit = Size/Bandwidth$$

where Distance is the length of the wire over which the data will travel, SpeedOfLight is the effective speed of light over that wire, Size is the size of the packet, and Bandwidth is the bandwidth at which the packet is transmitted. Note that if the message contains only one bit and we are talking about a single link (as opposed to a whole network), then the Transmit and Queue terms are not relevant, and latency corresponds to the propagation delay only.

Bandwidth and latency combine to define the performance characteristics of a given link or channel. Their relative importance, however, depends on the application. For some applications, latency dominates bandwidth. For example, a client that sends a 1-byte message to a server and receives a 1-byte message in return is latency bound. Assuming that no serious computation is involved in preparing the response, the application will perform much differently on a transcontinental channel with a 100-ms RTT than it will on an across-the-room channel with a 1-ms RTT. Whether the channel is 1 Mbps or 100 Mbps is relatively insignificant, however, since the former implies that the time to transmit a byte (Transmit) is 8 μs and the latter implies Transmit $= 0.08$ μs.

In contrast, consider a digital library program that is being asked to fetch a 25-megabyte (MB) image—the more bandwidth that is available, the faster it will be able to return the image to the user. Here, the bandwidth of the channel dominates performance. To see this, suppose that the channel has a bandwidth of 10 Mbps. It will take 20 seconds to transmit the image ($25 \times 10^6 \times 8$ bits $\div 10 \times 10^6$ Mbps $= 20$ seconds), making it relatively unimportant if the image is on the other side of a 1-ms channel or a 100-ms channel; the difference between a 20.001-second response time and a 20.1-second response time is negligible.

Figure 1.17 gives you a sense of how latency or bandwidth can dominate performance in different circumstances. The graph shows how long it takes to move objects of various sizes (1 byte, 2 KB, 1 MB) across networks with RTTs ranging from 1 to 100 ms and link speeds of either 1.5 or 10 Mbps. We use logarithmic scales to show relative performance. For a 1-byte object (say, a keystroke), latency remains almost exactly equal to the RTT, so that you cannot distinguish between a 1.5-Mbps network and a 10-Mbps network. For a 2-KB object (say, an email message), the link speed makes quite a difference on a 1-ms RTT network but a negligible difference on a 100-ms RTT network. And for a 1-MB object (say, a digital image), the RTT makes no difference—it is the link speed that dominates performance across the full range of RTT.

Note that throughout this book we use the terms *latency* and *delay* in a generic way to denote how long it takes to perform a particular function, such as delivering a message or moving an object. When we are referring to the specific amount of time it takes a signal to propagate from one end of a link to another, we use the term *propagation delay*. Also, we make it clear in the context of the discussion whether we are referring to the one-way latency or the round-trip time.

As an aside, computers are becoming so fast that when we connect them to networks, it is sometimes useful to think, at least figuratively, in

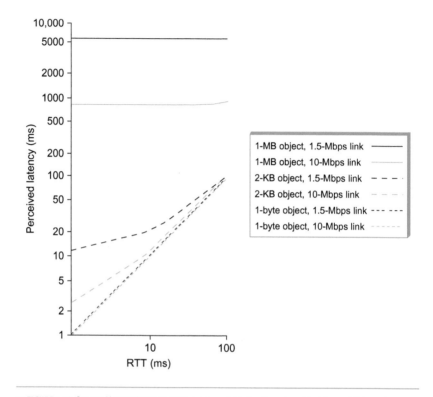

■ FIGURE 1.17 Perceived latency (response time) versus round-trip time for various object sizes and link speeds.

terms of *instructions per mile*. Consider what happens when a computer that is able to execute 1 billion instructions per second sends a message out on a channel with a 100-ms RTT. (To make the math easier, assume that the message covers a distance of 5000 miles.) If that computer sits idle the full 100 ms waiting for a reply message, then it has forfeited the ability to execute 100 million instructions, or 20,000 instructions per mile. It had better have been worth going over the network to justify this waste.

1.5.2 Delay × Bandwidth Product

It is also useful to talk about the product of these two metrics, often called the *delay × bandwidth product*. Intuitively, if we think of a channel between a pair of processes as a hollow pipe (see Figure 1.18), where the latency corresponds to the length of the pipe and the bandwidth gives the

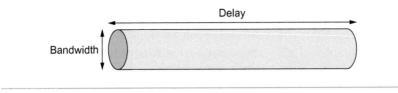

Delay

Bandwidth

■ FIGURE 1.18 Network as a pipe.

diameter of the pipe, then the delay × bandwidth product gives the volume of the pipe—the maximum number of bits that could be in transit through the pipe at any given instant. Said another way, if latency (measured in time) corresponds to the length of the pipe, then given the width of each bit (also measured in time) you can calculate how many bits fit in the pipe. For example, a transcontinental channel with a one-way latency of 50 ms and a bandwidth of 45 Mbps is able to hold

$$50 \times 10^{-3}\ \text{s} \times 45 \times 10^{6}\ \text{bits/s}$$
$$= 2.25 \times 10^{6}\ \text{bits}$$

or approximately 280 KB of data. In other words, this example channel (pipe) holds as many bytes as the memory of a personal computer from the early 1980s could hold.

The delay × bandwidth product is important to know when constructing high-performance networks because it corresponds to how many bits the sender must transmit before the first bit arrives at the receiver. If the sender is expecting the receiver to somehow signal that bits are starting to arrive, and it takes another channel latency for this signal to propagate back to the sender, then the sender can send up one RTT × bandwidth worth of data before hearing from the receiver that all is well. The bits in the pipe are said to be "in flight," which means that if the receiver tells the sender to stop transmitting it might receive up to one RTT × bandwidth's worth of data before the sender manages to respond. In our example above, that amount corresponds to 5.5×10^{6} bits (671 KB) of data. On the other hand, if the sender does not fill the pipe—send a whole RTT × bandwidth product's worth of data before it stops to wait for a signal—the sender will not fully utilize the network.

Note that most of the time we are interested in the RTT scenario, which we simply refer to as the *delay × bandwidth product*, without explicitly saying that "delay" is the RTT (i.e., the one-way delay multiplied by two). Usually, whether the "delay" in "delay × bandwidth" means one-way latency or RTT is made clear by the context. Table 1.1 shows some examples of RTT × bandwidth products for some typical network links.

How Big Is a Mega?

There are several pitfalls you need to be aware of when working with the common units of networking—MB, Mbps, KB, and kbps. The first is to distinguish carefully between bits and bytes. Throughout this book, we always use a lowercase b for bits and a capital B for bytes. The second is to be sure you are using the appropriate definition of mega (M) and kilo (K). *Mega*, for example, can mean either 2^{20} or 10^6. Similarly, *kilo* can be either 2^{10} or 10^3. What is worse, in networking we typically use both definitions. Here's why:

Network bandwidth, which is often specified in terms of Mbps, is typically governed by the speed of the clock that paces the transmission of the bits. A clock that is running at 10 MHz is used to transmit bits at 10 Mbps. Because the *mega* in MHz means 10^6 hertz, Mbps is usually also defined as 10^6 bits per second. (Similarly, kbps is 10^3 bits per second.) On the other hand, when we talk about a message that we want to transmit, we often give its size in kilobytes. Because messages are stored in the computer's memory, and memory is typically measured in powers of two, the K in KB is usually taken to mean 2^{10}. (Similarly, MB usually means 2^{20}.) When you put the two together, it is not uncommon to talk about sending a 32-KB message over a 10-Mbps channel, which should be interpreted to mean $32 \times 2^{10} \times 8$ bits are being transmitted at a rate of 10×10^6 bits per second. This is the interpretation we use throughout the book, unless explicitly stated otherwise.

The good news is that many times we are satisfied with a back-of-the-envelope calculation, in which case it is perfectly reasonable to make the approximation that 10^6 is really equal to 2^{20} (making it easy to convert between the two definitions of mega). This approximation introduces only a 5% error. We can even make the approximation in some cases that a byte has 10 bits, a 20% error but good enough for order-of-magnitude estimates.

To help you in your quick-and-dirty calculations, 100 ms is a reasonable number to use for a cross-country round-trip time—at least when the country in question is the United States—and 1 ms is a good approximation of an RTT across a local area network. In the case of the former, we increase the 48-ms round-trip time implied by the speed of light over a fiber to 100 ms because there are, as we have said, other sources of delay, such as the processing time in the switches inside the network. You can also be sure that the path taken by the fiber between two points will not be a straight line.

Table 1.1 Sample Delay × Bandwidth Products

Link type	Bandwidth (typical)	One-way distance (typical)	Round-trip delay	RTT × Bandwidth
Dial-up	56 kbps	10 km	87 μs	5 bits
Wireless LAN	54 Mbps	50 m	0.33 μs	18 bits
Satellite	45 Mbps	35,000 km	230 ms	10 Mb
Cross-country fiber	10 Gbps	4,000 km	40 ms	400 Mb

1.5.3 High-Speed Networks

The bandwidths available on today's networks are increasing at a dramatic rate, and there is eternal optimism that network bandwidth will continue to improve. This causes network designers to start thinking about what happens in the limit or, stated another way, what is the impact on network design of having infinite bandwidth available.

Although high-speed networks bring a dramatic change in the bandwidth available to applications, in many respects their impact on how we think about networking comes in what does *not* change as bandwidth increases: the speed of light. To quote Scotty from *Star Trek,* "Ye cannae change the laws of physics."[4] In other words, "high speed" does not mean that latency improves at the same rate as bandwidth; the transcontinental RTT of a 1-Gbps link is the same 100 ms as it is for a 1-Mbps link.

To appreciate the significance of ever-increasing bandwidth in the face of fixed latency, consider what is required to transmit a 1-MB file over a 1-Mbps network versus over a 1-Gbps network, both of which have an RTT of 100 ms. In the case of the 1-Mbps network, it takes 80 round-trip times to transmit the file; during each RTT, 1.25% of the file is sent. In contrast, the same 1-MB file doesn't even come close to filling 1 RTT's worth of the 1-Gbps link, which has a delay × bandwidth product of 12.5 MB.

Figure 1.19 illustrates the difference between the two networks. In effect, the 1-MB file looks like a stream of data that needs to be transmitted across a 1-Mbps network, while it looks like a single packet on a 1-Gbps network. To help drive this point home, consider that a 1-MB file is to a 1-Gbps network what a 1-KB *packet* is to a 1-Mbps network.

---

[4]Scots dialect for "You cannot change the laws of physics."

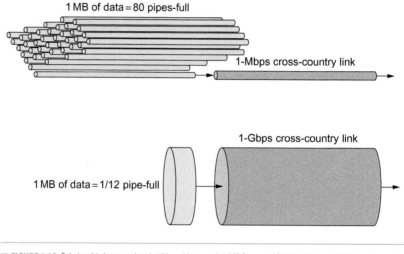

1 MB of data = 80 pipes-full

1-Mbps cross-country link

1-Gbps cross-country link

1 MB of data = 1/12 pipe-full

■ **FIGURE 1.19** Relationship between bandwidth and latency. A 1-MB file would fill the 1-Mbps link 80 times but only fill the 1-Gbps link 1/12 of one time.

Another way to think about the situation is that more data can be transmitted during each RTT on a high-speed network, so much so that a single RTT becomes a significant amount of time. Thus, while you wouldn't think twice about the difference between a file transfer taking 101 RTTs rather than 100 RTTs (a relative difference of only 1%), suddenly the difference between 1 RTT and 2 RTTs is significant—a 100% increase. In other words, latency, rather than throughput, starts to dominate our thinking about network design.

Perhaps the best way to understand the relationship between throughput and latency is to return to basics. The effective end-to-end throughput that can be achieved over a network is given by the simple relationship

$$\text{Throughput} = \text{TransferSize}/\text{TransferTime}$$

where TransferTime includes not only the elements of one-way Latency identified earlier in this section, but also any additional time spent requesting or setting up the transfer. Generally, we represent this relationship as

$$\text{TransferTime} = \text{RTT} + 1/\text{Bandwidth} \times \text{TransferSize}$$

We use RTT in this calculation to account for a request message being sent across the network and the data being sent back. For example, consider a situation where a user wants to fetch a 1-MB file across a 1-Gbps network with a round-trip time of 100 ms. The TransferTime includes both the transmit time for 1 MB (1/1 Gbps × 1 MB = 8 ms) and the 100-ms RTT, for a total transfer time of 108 ms. This means that the effective throughput will be

$$1 \text{ MB}/108 \text{ ms} = 74.1 \text{ Mbps}$$

not 1 Gbps. Clearly, transferring a larger amount of data will help improve the effective throughput, where in the limit an infinitely large transfer size will cause the effective throughput to approach the network bandwidth. On the other hand, having to endure more than 1 RTT—for example, to retransmit missing packets—will hurt the effective throughput for any transfer of finite size and will be most noticeable for small transfers.

1.5.4 Application Performance Needs

The discussion in this section has taken a network-centric view of performance; that is, we have talked in terms of what a given link or channel will support. The unstated assumption has been that application programs have simple needs—they want as much bandwidth as the network can provide. This is certainly true of the aforementioned digital library program that is retrieving a 25-MB image; the more bandwidth that is available, the faster the program will be able to return the image to the user.

However, some applications are able to state an upper limit on how much bandwidth they need. Video applications are a prime example. Suppose one wants to stream a video that is one quarter the size of a standard TV screen; that is, it has a resolution of 352 by 240 pixels. If each pixel is represented by 24 bits of information, as would be the case for 24-bit color, then the size of each frame would be

$$(352 \times 240 \times 24)/8 = 247.5 \text{ KB}$$

If the application needs to support a frame rate of 30 frames per second, then it might request a throughput rate of 75 Mbps. The ability of the network to provide more bandwidth is of no interest to such an application because it has only so much data to transmit in a given period of time.

Unfortunately, the situation is not as simple as this example suggests. Because the difference between any two adjacent frames in a video stream is often small, it is possible to compress the video by transmitting only the differences between adjacent frames. Each frame can also be compressed because not all the detail in a picture is readily perceived by a human eye. The compressed video does not flow at a constant rate, but varies with time according to factors such as the amount of action and detail in the picture and the compression algorithm being used. Therefore, it is possible to say what the average bandwidth requirement will be, but the instantaneous rate may be more or less.

The key issue is the time interval over which the average is computed. Suppose that this example video application can be compressed down to the point that it needs only 2 Mbps, on average. If it transmits 1 megabit in a 1-second interval and 3 megabits in the following 1-second interval, then over the 2-second interval it is transmitting at an average rate of 2 Mbps; however, this will be of little consolation to a channel that was engineered to support no more than 2 megabits in any one second. Clearly, just knowing the average bandwidth needs of an application will not always suffice.

Generally, however, it is possible to put an upper bound on how large a burst an application like this is likely to transmit. A burst might be described by some peak rate that is maintained for some period of time. Alternatively, it could be described as the number of bytes that can be sent at the peak rate before reverting to the average rate or some lower rate. If this peak rate is higher than the available channel capacity, then the excess data will have to be buffered somewhere, to be transmitted later. Knowing how big of a burst might be sent allows the network designer to allocate sufficient buffer capacity to hold the burst. We will return to the subject of describing bursty traffic accurately in Chapter 6.

Analogous to the way an application's bandwidth needs can be something other than "all it can get," an application's delay requirements may be more complex than simply "as little delay as possible." In the case of delay, it sometimes doesn't matter so much whether the one-way latency of the network is 100 ms or 500 ms as how much the latency varies from packet to packet. The variation in latency is called *jitter*.

Consider the situation in which the source sends a packet once every 33 ms, as would be the case for a video application transmitting frames 30 times a second. If the packets arrive at the destination spaced out exactly 33 ms apart, then we can deduce that the delay experienced by each packet in the network was exactly the same. If the spacing

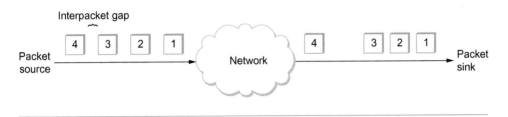

■ FIGURE 1.20 Network-induced jitter.

between when packets arrive at the destination—sometimes called the *inter-packet gap*—is variable, however, then the delay experienced by the sequence of packets must have also been variable, and the network is said to have introduced jitter into the packet stream, as shown in Figure 1.20. Such variation is generally not introduced in a single physical link, but it can happen when packets experience different queuing delays in a multihop packet-switched network. This queuing delay corresponds to the Queue component of latency defined earlier in this section, which varies with time.

To understand the relevance of jitter, suppose that the packets being transmitted over the network contain video frames, and in order to display these frames on the screen the receiver needs to receive a new one every 33 ms. If a frame arrives early, then it can simply be saved by the receiver until it is time to display it. Unfortunately, if a frame arrives late, then the receiver will not have the frame it needs in time to update the screen, and the video quality will suffer; it will not be smooth. Note that it is not necessary to eliminate jitter, only to know how bad it is. The reason for this is that if the receiver knows the upper and lower bounds on the latency that a packet can experience, it can delay the time at which it starts playing back the video (i.e., displays the first frame) long enough to ensure that in the future it will always have a frame to display when it needs it. The receiver delays the frame, effectively smoothing out the jitter, by storing it in a buffer. We return to the topic of jitter in Chapter 9.

1.6 SUMMARY

Computer networks, and in particular the Internet, have experienced enormous growth over the past 30 years and are now able to provide a wide range of services, from conducting business to providing access to entertainment to enabling social networks. Much of this growth can be attributed to the general-purpose nature of computer networks, and in particular to the ability to add new functionality to the network by writing software that runs on affordable, high-performance computers. With this in mind, the overriding goal of this book is to describe computer networks in such a way that when you finish reading it you should feel that, if you had an army of programmers at your disposal, you could actually build a fully functional computer network from the ground up. This chapter lays the foundation for realizing this goal.

The first step we have taken toward this goal is to carefully identify exactly what we expect from a network. For example, a network must first provide cost-effective and scalable connectivity among a set of computers. This is accomplished through a nested interconnection of nodes and links and by sharing this hardware base through the use of statistical multiplexing. This results in a packet-switched network, on top of which we then define a collection of process-to-process communication services.

The second step is to define a layered architecture that will serve as a blueprint for our design. The central objects of this architecture are network protocols. Protocols both provide a communication service to higher-level protocols and define the form and meaning of messages exchanged with their peers running on other machines. We have briefly surveyed two of the most widely used architectures: the 7-layer OSI architecture and the Internet architecture. This book most closely follows the Internet architecture, both in its organization and as a source of examples.

The third step is to implement the network's protocols and application programs, usually in software. Both protocols and applications need an interface by which they invoke the services of other protocols in the network subsystem. The socket interface is the most widely used interface between application programs and the network subsystem, but a slightly different interface is typically used within the network subsystem.

Finally, the network as a whole must offer high performance, where the two performance metrics we are most interested in are latency and throughput. As we will see in later chapters, it is the product of these two metrics—the so-called delay × bandwidth product—that often plays a critical role in protocol design.

It's apparent that computer networks have become an integral part of the everyday lives of vast numbers of people. What began over 40 years ago as experimental systems like the ARPANET—connecting mainframe computers over long-distance telephone lines—has turned into a pervasive part of our lives. It has also become big business, and where there is big business there are lots of players. In this case, we have the computing industry, which has become increasingly involved in integrating computation and communication; the telephone and cable operators, which recognize the market for carrying all sorts of data, not just voice and television; and, perhaps most importantly, the many entrepreneurs creating new Internet-based applications and services such as voice over IP (VOIP), online games, virtual worlds,

WHAT'S NEXT: CLOUD COMPUTING

search services, content hosting, electronic commerce, and so on. It's noteworthy that one of today's biggest names in "cloud computing," Amazon.com, achieved that position by first adopting Internet technologies to sell consumer products such as books and then making their computing infrastructure available to others as a service over the network.

A few years ago, a reasonable goal for networking might have been to provide network access to every home, but in developed countries at least that process is now far along. Ubiquitous networking now includes getting access from anywhere, including on planes and trains, and on an increasingly wide range of devices. Whereas the Internet largely evolved in an era of fixed mainframe and then personal computers, today the set of devices to be connected together includes mobile phones and even smaller devices such as sensors (which might also be mobile). Thus, it seems clear that the Internet will have to continue to scale to support several orders of magnitude more devices than today and that many of these devices will be mobile, perhaps intermittently connected over wireless links of highly variable quality. At the same time, these devices will be connected to large data centers—filled with tens of thousands of processors and many petabytes of storage—that will store and analyze the data being generated, all with the hope of enabling even more powerful applications that help us navigate our daily lives. And, the devices that we carry are often just a means of accessing "the cloud"—the amorphous set of machines that store and process our documents, photos, data, social networks, etc., which we expect to be able to access from anywhere.

Predictions about the future of networking have a tendency to look silly a few years down the road (many high-profile predictions about an imminent meltdown of the Internet, for example, have failed to come true). What we can say with confidence is that there remain plenty of technical challenges—issues of connectivity, manageability, scalability, usability, performance, reliability, security, fairness, cost-effectiveness, etc.—that stand between the current state of the art and the sort of global, ubiquitous, heterogeneous network that many believe is iminent. In other words, networking as a field is very much alive with interesting problems still to be solved, and it is these problems and the tools for solving them that are the focus of this book.

■ FURTHER READING

Computer networks are not the first communication-oriented technology to have found their way into the everyday fabric of our society. For example, the early part of this century saw the introduction of the telephone, and then during the 1950s television became widespread. When considering the future of networking—how widely it will spread and how we will use it—it is instructive to study this history. Our first reference is a good starting point for doing this (the entire issue is devoted to the first 100 years of telecommunications).

The second reference is considered one of the seminal papers on the Internet architecture. The final two papers are not specific to networking but present viewpoints that capture the "systems approach" of this book. The Saltzer et al. paper motivates and describes one of the most widely applied rules of network architecture—the *end-to-end argument*—which continues to be highly cited today. The paper by Mashey describes the thinking behind RISC (Reduced Instruction Set Computer) architectures; as we will soon discover, making good judgments about where to place functionality in a complex system is what system design is all about.

- Pierce, J. Telephony—A personal view. *IEEE Communications* 22(5):116–120, May 1984.

- Clark, D. The design philosophy of the DARPA Internet protocols. *Proceedings of the SIGCOMM '88 Symposium*, pages 106–114, August 1988.

- Saltzer, J., D. Reed, and D. Clark. End-to-end arguments in system design. *ACM Transactions on Computer Systems* 2(4):277–288, November 1984.

- Mashey, J. RISC, MIPS, and the motion of complexity. *UniForum 1986 Conference Proceedings*, pages 116–124, February 1986.

Several texts offer an introduction to computer networking: Stallings gives an encyclopedic treatment of the subject, with an emphasis on the lower levels of the OSI hierarchy [Sta07]; Comer gives a good introduction to the Internet architecture [Com05].

To put computer networking into a larger context, two books—one dealing with the past and the other looking toward the future—are must reading. The first is Holzmann and Pehrson's *The Early History of Data Networks* [HP95]. Surprisingly, many of the ideas covered in the book you are now reading were invented during the 1700s. The second is *Realizing the Information Future: The Internet and Beyond*, a book prepared by the Computer Science and Telecommunications Board of the National Research Council [NRC94].

In this book we try to bring a systems approach to the field of computer networking. We recommend Saltzer and Kaashoek's general treatment of computer systems [SK09], which teaches many important principles that apply to networking as well as other systems. Operating systems in particular are important to many aspects of networking; Tanenbaum [Tan07] provides an introduction to OS concepts.

To follow the history of the Internet from its beginning, the reader is encouraged to peruse the Internet's *Request for Comments* (RFC) series of documents. These documents, which include everything from the TCP specification to April Fools' jokes, are retrievable at http://www.ietf.org/rfc.html. For example, the protocol specifications for TCP, UDP, and IP are available in RFC 793, 768, and 791, respectively.

To gain a better appreciation for the Internet philosophy and culture, two references are recommended; both are also quite entertaining. Padlipsky gives a good description of the early days, including a pointed comparison of the Internet and OSI architectures [Pad85]. For an account of what really happens behind the scenes at the Internet Engineering Task Force, we recommend Boorsook's article [Boo95].

There is a wealth of articles discussing various aspects of protocol implementations. A good starting point is to understand two complete protocol implementation environments: the Stream mechanism from System V Unix [Rit84] and the x-kernel [HP91]. In addition, [LMKQ89] and [SW95] describe the widely used Berkeley Unix implementation of TCP/IP.

More generally, a large body of work addresses the issue of structuring and optimizing protocol implementations. Clark was one of the first to discuss the relationship between modular design and protocol performance [Cla82]. Later papers then introduce the use of upcalls in structuring protocol code [Cla85] and study the processing overheads in TCP [CJRS89]. Finally, [WM87] describes how to gain efficiency through appropriate design and implementation choices.

Several papers have introduced specific techniques and mechanisms that can be used to improve protocol performance. For example, [HMPT89] describes some of the mechanisms used in the x-kernel environment, while [MD93], [VL87], and [DP93] present a variety of techniques for improving protocol performance. Also, the performance of protocols running on parallel processors—locking is a key issue in such environments—is discussed in [BG93] and [NYKT94].

Finally, we conclude the Further Reading section of each chapter with a set of live references, URLs for locations on the World Wide Web where you can learn more about the topics discussed in that chapter. Since these references are live, it is possible that they will not remain active for an indefinite period of time. For this reason, we limit the set of live references at the end of each chapter to sites that export software, provide a service, or report on the activities of an ongoing working group or standardization body. In other words, we only give URLs for the kinds of material that cannot easily be referenced using standard citations. For this chapter, we include three live references:

- http://mkp.com/computer-networks: information about this book, including supplements, addenda, and so on

- http://www.ietf.org/: information about the IETF, its working groups, standards, etc.

- http://dblp.uni-trier.de/db/index.html: a searchable bibliography of computer science research papers

EXERCISES

1. Use anonymous FTP to connect to ftp.rfc-editor.org (directory in-notes), and retrieve the RFC index. Also, retrieve the protocol specifications for TCP, IP, and UDP.

2. The Unix utility whois can be used to find the domain name corresponding to an organization, or *vice versa*. Read the man page documentation for whois and experiment with it. Try whois princeton.edu and whois princeton, for starters. As an alternative, explore the whois interface at http://www.internic.net/whois.html.

3. Calculate the total time required to transfer a 1000-KB file in the following cases, assuming an RTT of 50 ms, a packet size of 1 KB data, and an initial $2 \times$ RTT of "handshaking" before data is sent:

   (a) The bandwidth is 1.5 Mbps, and data packets can be sent continuously.

   (b) The bandwidth is 1.5 Mbps, but after we finish sending each data packet we must wait one RTT before sending the next.

   (c) The bandwidth is "infinite," meaning that we take transmit time to be zero, and up to 20 packets can be sent per RTT.

   (d) The bandwidth is infinite, and during the first RTT we can send one packet (2^{1-1}), during the second RTT we can send two packets (2^{2-1}), during the third we can send four (2^{3-1}), and so on. (A justification for such an exponential increase will be given in Chapter 6.)

4. Calculate the total time required to transfer a 1.5-MB file in the following cases, assuming an RTT of 80 ms, a packet size of 1 KB data, and an initial $2 \times$ RTT of "handshaking" before data is sent:

   (a) The bandwidth is 10 Mbps, and data packets can be sent continuously.

   (b) The bandwidth is 10 Mbps, but after we finish sending each data packet we must wait one RTT before sending the next.

   (c) The link allows infinitely fast transmit, but limits bandwidth such that only 20 packets can be sent per RTT.

   (d) Zero transmit time as in (c), but during the first RTT we can send one packet, during the second RTT we can send two packets, during the third we can send four (2^{3-1}), etc. (A justification for such an exponential increase will be given in Chapter 6.)

5. Consider a point-to-point link 4 km in length. At what bandwidth would propagation delay (at a speed of 2×10^8 m/s) equal

transmit delay for 100-byte packets? What about 512-byte packets?

6. Consider a point-to-point link 50 km in length. At what bandwidth would propagation delay (at a speed of 2×10^8m/s) equal transmit delay for 100-byte packets? What about 512-byte packets?

7. What properties of postal addresses would be likely to be shared by a network addressing scheme? What differences might you expect to find? What properties of telephone numbering might be shared by a network addressing scheme?

8. One property of addresses is that they are unique; if two nodes had the same address, it would be impossible to distinguish between them. What other properties might be useful for network addresses to have? Can you think of any situations in which network (or postal or telephone) addresses might *not* be unique?

9. Give an example of a situation in which multicast addresses might be beneficial.

10. What differences in traffic patterns account for the fact that STDM is a cost-effective form of multiplexing for a voice telephone network and FDM is a cost-effective form of multiplexing for television and radio networks, yet we reject both as not being cost effective for a general-purpose computer network?

11. How "wide" is a bit on a 10-Gbps link? How long is a bit in copper wire, where the speed of propagation is 2.3×10^8 m/s?

12. How long does it take to transmit x KB over a y-Mbps link? Give your answer as a ratio of x and y.

13. Suppose a 1-Gbps point-to-point link is being set up between the Earth and a new lunar colony. The distance from the moon to the Earth is approximately 385,000 km, and data travels over the link at the speed of light—3×10^8 m/s.
    (a) Calculate the minimum RTT for the link.
    (b) Using the RTT as the delay, calculate the delay $\times$ bandwidth product for the link.

(c) What is the significance of the delay × bandwidth product computed in (b)?

(d) A camera on the lunar base takes pictures of the Earth and saves them in digital format to disk. Suppose Mission Control on Earth wishes to download the most current image, which is 25 MB. What is the minimum amount of time that will elapse between when the request for the data goes out and the transfer is finished?

14. Suppose a 128-kbps point-to-point link is set up between the Earth and a rover on Mars. The distance from the Earth to Mars (when they are closest together) is approximately 55 Gm, and data travels over the link at the speed of light—3×10^8 m/s.

(a) Calculate the minimum RTT for the link.

(b) Calculate the delay × bandwidth product for the link.

(c) A camera on the rover takes pictures of its surroundings and sends these to Earth. How quickly after a picture is taken can it reach Mission Control on Earth? Assume that each image is 5 Mb in size.

15. For each of the following operations on a remote file server, discuss whether they are more likely to be delay sensitive or bandwidth sensitive:

(a) Open a file.

(b) Read the contents of a file.

(c) List the contents of a directory.

(d) Display the attributes of a file.

16. Calculate the latency (from first bit sent to last bit received) for the following:

(a) 100-Mbps Ethernet with a single store-and-forward switch in the path and a packet size of 12,000 bits. Assume that each link introduces a propagation delay of 10 μs and that the switch begins retransmitting immediately after it has finished receiving the packet.

(b) Same as (a) but with three switches.

(c) Same as (a), but assume the switch implements "cut-through" switching; it is able to begin retransmitting the packet after the first 200 bits have been received.

17. Calculate the latency (from first bit sent to last bit received) for:

    (a) 1-Gbps Ethernet with a single store-and-forward switch in the path and a packet size of 5000 bits. Assume that each link introduces a propagation delay of 10 μs and that the switch begins retransmitting immediately after it has finished receiving the packet.

    (b) Same as (a) but with three switches.

    (c) Same as (b), but assume the switch implements "cut-through" switching; it is able to begin retransmitting the packet after the first 128 bits have been received.

18. Calculate the effective bandwidth for the following cases. For (a) and (b) assume there is a steady supply of data to send; for (c) simply calculate the average over 12 hours.

    (a) 100-Mbps Ethernet through three store-and-forward switches as in Exercise 16(b). Switches can send on one link while receiving on the other.

    (b) Same as (a) but with the sender having to wait for a 50-byte acknowledgment packet after sending each 12,000-bit data packet.

    (c) Overnight (12-hour) shipment of 100 DVDs that hold 4.7 GB each.

19. Calculate the delay × bandwidth product for the following links. Use one-way delay, measured from first bit sent to first bit received.

    (a) 100-Mbps Ethernet with a delay of 10 μs.

    (b) 100-Mbps Ethernet with a single store-and-forward switch like that of Exercise 16(b), packet size of 12,000 bits, and 10 μs per link propagation delay.

    (c) 1.5-Mbps T1 link, with a transcontinental one-way delay of 50 ms.

    (d) 1.5-Mbps T1 link between two groundstations communicating via a satellite in geosynchronous orbit, 35,900 km high. The only delay is speed-of-light propagation delay from Earth to the satellite *and back*.

20. Hosts A and B are each connected to a switch S via 100-Mbps links as in Figure 1.21. The propagation delay on each link is

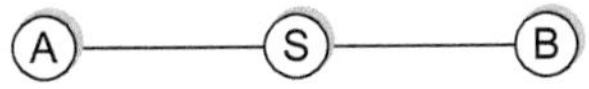

FIGURE 1.21 Diagram for Exercise 20.

20 μs. S is a store-and-forward device; it begins retransmitting a received packet 35 μs after it has finished receiving it. Calculate the total time required to transmit 10,000 bits from A to B

(a) As a single packet.

(b) As two 5000-bit packets sent one right after the other.

21. Suppose a host has a 1-MB file that is to be sent to another host. The file takes 1 second of CPU time to compress 50% or 2 seconds to compress 60%.

(a) Calculate the bandwidth at which each compression option takes the same total compression + transmission time.

(a) Explain why latency does not affect your answer.

22. Suppose that a certain communications protocol involves a per-packet overhead of 50 bytes for headers and framing. We send 1 million bytes of data using this protocol; however, one data byte is corrupted and the entire packet containing it is thus lost. Give the total number of overhead + loss bytes for packet data sizes of 1000, 10,000, and 20,000 bytes. Which size is optimal?

23. Assume you wish to transfer an n B file along a path composed of the source, destination, 7 point-to-point links, and 5 switches. Suppose each link has a propagation delay of 2 ms and a bandwidth of 4 Mbps, and that the switches support both circuit and packet switching. Thus, you can either break the file up into 1-KB packets or set up a circuit through the switches and send the file as one contiguous bitstream. Suppose that packets have 24 B of packet header information and 1000 B of payload, store-and-forward packet processing at each switch incurs a 1-ms delay after the packet had been completely received, packets may be sent continuously without waiting for acknowledgments, and circuit setup requires a 1-KB message to make one round trip on the path, incurring a 1-ms delay at each switch after the message has been completely received. Assume

switches introduce no delay to data traversing a circuit. You may also assume that filesize is a multiple of 1000 B.

(a) For what filesize n B is the total number of bytes sent across the network less for circuits than for packets?

(b) For what filesize n B is the total latency incurred before the entire file arrives at the destination less for circuits than for packets?

(c) How sensitive are these results to the number of switches along the path? To the bandwidth of the links? To the ratio of packet size to packet header size?

(d) How accurate do you think this model of the relative merits of circuits and packets is? Does it ignore important considerations that discredit one or the other approach? If so, what are they?

24. Consider a network with a ring topology, link bandwidths of 100 Mbps, and propagation speed 2×10^8 m/s. What would the circumference of the loop be to exactly contain one 1500-byte packet, assuming nodes do not introduce delay? What would the circumference be if there was a node every 100 m, and each node introduced 10 bits of delay?

25. Compare the channel requirements for voice traffic with the requirements for the real-time transmission of music, in terms of bandwidth, delay, and jitter. What would have to improve? By approximately how much? Could any channel requirements be relaxed?

26. For the following, assume that no data compression is done, although in practice this would almost never be the case. For (a) to (c), calculate the bandwidth necessary for transmitting in real time:

(a) Video at a resolution of 640×480, 3 bytes/pixel, 30 frames/second.

(b) Video at a resolution of 160×120, 1 byte/pixel, 5 frames/second.

(c) CD-ROM music, assuming one CD holds 75 minutes' worth and takes 650 MB.

(d) Assume a fax transmits an 8×10-inch black-and-white image at a resolution of 72 pixels per inch. How long would this take over a 14.4-kbps modem?

27. For the following, as in the previous problem, assume that no data compression is done. Calculate the bandwidth necessary for transmitting in real time:
    (a) High-definition video at a resolution of 1920×1080, 24 bits/pixel, 30 frames/second.
    (b) POTS (plain old telephone service) voice audio of 8-bit samples at 8 KHz.
    (c) GSM mobile voice audio of 260-bit samples at 50 Hz.
    (d) HDCD high-definition audio of 24-bit samples at 88.2 kHz.

28. Discuss the relative performance needs of the following applications in terms of average bandwidth, peak bandwidth, latency, jitter, and loss tolerance:
    (a) File server.
    (b) Print server.
    (c) Digital library.
    (d) Routine monitoring of remote weather instruments.
    (e) Voice.
    (f) Video monitoring of a waiting room.
    (g) Television broadcasting.

29. Suppose a shared medium M offers to hosts $A_1, A_2, \ldots, A_N$ in round-robin fashion an opportunity to transmit one packet; hosts that have nothing to send immediately relinquish M. How does this differ from STDM? How does network utilization of this scheme compare with STDM?

30. Consider a simple protocol for transferring files over a link. After some initial negotiation, A sends data packets of size 1 KB to B; B then replies with an acknowledgment. A always waits for each ACK before sending the next data packet; this is known as *stop-and-wait*. Packets that are overdue are presumed lost and are retransmitted.

(a) In the absence of any packet losses or duplications, explain why it is not necessary to include any "sequence number" data in the packet headers.

(b) Suppose that the link can lose occasional packets, but that packets that do arrive always arrive in the order sent. Is a 2-bit sequence number (that is, N mod 4) enough for A and B to detect and resend any lost packets? Is a 1-bit sequence number enough?

(c) Now suppose that the link can deliver out of order and that sometimes a packet can be delivered as much as 1 minute after subsequent packets. How does this change the sequence number requirements?

31. Suppose hosts A and B are connected by a link. Host A continuously transmits the current time from a high-precision clock, at a regular rate, fast enough to consume all the available bandwidth. Host B reads these time values and writes them each paired with its own time from a local clock synchronized with A's. Give qualitative examples of B's output assuming the link has

    (a) High bandwidth, high latency, low jitter.

    (b) Low bandwidth, high latency, high jitter.

    (c) High bandwidth, low latency, low jitter, occasional lost data.

    For example, a link with zero jitter, a bandwidth high enough to write on every other clock tick, and a latency of 1 tick might yield something like $(0000, 0001)$, $(0002, 0003)$, $(0004, 0005)$.

32. Obtain and build the **simplex-talk** sample socket program shown in the text. Start one server and one client, in separate windows. While the first client is running, start 10 other clients that connect to the same server; these other clients should most likely be started in the background with their input redirected from a file. What happens to these 10 clients? Do their connect()s fail, or time out, or succeed? Do any other calls block? Now let the first client exit. What happens? Try this with the server value MAX_PENDING set to 1 as well.

33. Modify the **simplex-talk** socket program so that each time the client sends a line to the server, the server sends the line back to the client. The client (and server) will now have to make alternating calls to recv() and send().

34. Modify the simplex-talk socket program so that it uses UDP as the transport protocol, rather than TCP. You will have to change SOCK_STREAM to SOCK_DGRAM in both the client and the server. Then, in the server, remove the calls to listen() and accept(), and replace the two nested loops at the end with a single loop that calls recv() with socket s. Finally, see what happens when two such UDP clients simultaneously connect to the same UDP server, and compare this to the TCP behavior.

35. Investigate the different options and parameters one can set for a TCP connection. (Do "man tcp" on Unix.) Experiment with various parameter settings to see how they affect TCP performance.

36. The Unix utility ping can be used to find the RTT to various Internet hosts. Read the man page for ping, and use it to find the RTT to www.cs.princeton.edu in New Jersey and www.cisco.com in California. Measure the RTT values at different times of day, and compare the results. What do you think accounts for the differences?

37. The Unix utility traceroute, or its Windows equivalent tracert, can be used to find the sequence of routers through which a message is routed. Use this to find the path from your site to some others. How well does the number of hops correlate with the RTT times from ping? How well does the number of hops correlate with geographical distance?

38. Use traceroute, above, to map out some of the routers within your organization (or to verify none is used).

A SYSTEMS APPROACH

A SYSTEMS APPROACH

A SYSTEMS APPROACH

A SYSTEMS APPROACH

A SYSTEMS APPROACH

2

Getting Connected

It is a mistake to look too far ahead. Only one link in the chain of destiny can be handled at a time.

–Winston Churchill

In Chapter 1 we saw that networks consist of links interconnecting nodes. One of the fundamental problems we face is how to connect two nodes together. We also introduced the "cloud" abstraction to represent a network without revealing all of its internal complexities. So we also need to address the similar problem of connecting a host to a cloud. This, in effect, is the problem every Internet Service Provider faces when it wants to connect a new customer to the network: how to connect one more nodes to the ISP's cloud?

PROBLEM: CONNECTING TO A NETWORK

Whether we want to construct a trivial two-node network with one link or connect the one-billionth host to an existing network like the Internet, we need to address a common set of issues. First, we need some physical medium over which to make the connection. The medium may be a length of wire, a piece of optical fiber, or some less tangible medium (such as air) through which electromagnetic radiation (e.g., radio waves) can be transmitted. It may cover a small area (e.g., an office building) or a wide area (e.g., transcontinental). Connecting two nodes with a suitable medium is only the first step, however. Five additional problems must be addressed before the nodes can successfully exchange packets.

The first is *encoding* bits onto the transmission medium so that they can be understood by a receiving node. Second is the matter of delineating the sequence of bits transmitted over the link into complete messages that can be delivered to the end node. This is the *framing* problem, and the messages delivered to the end hosts are often called *frames* (or sometimes *packets*). Third, because frames are sometimes corrupted during transmission, it is necessary to detect these errors and take the appropriate action; this is the *error detection* problem. The fourth issue is making a link appear reliable in spite of the fact that it corrupts frames from time to time. Finally, in those cases where the link is shared by multiple hosts—as is often the case with wireless links, for example—it is necessary to mediate access to this link. This is the *media access control* problem.

Although these five issues—encoding, framing, error detection, reliable delivery, and access mediation—can be discussed in the abstract, they are very real problems that are addressed in different ways by different networking technologies. This chapter considers these issues in the context of three specific network technologies: point-to-point links, Carrier Sense Multiple Access (CSMA) networks (of which Ethernet is the most famous example), and wireless networks (for which 802.11 is the most widespread standard[1]). The goal of this chapter is simultaneously to survey the available network technology and to explore these five fundamental issues. We will examine what it takes to make a wide variety of different physical media and link technologies useful as building blocks for the construction of robust, scalable networks.

2.1 PERSPECTIVES ON CONNECTING

As we saw in Chapter 1, networks are constructed from two classes of hardware building blocks: *nodes* and *links*. In this chapter, we focus on what it takes to make a useful link, so that large, reliable networks containing millions of links can be built.

While the operators of large networks deal with links that span hundreds or thousands of kilometers connecting refrigerator-sized routers, the typical user of a network encounters links mostly as a way to connect a computer to the global Internet. Sometimes this link will be a wireless

---

[1]Strictly speaking, 802.11 is a set of standards.

(Wi-Fi) link in a coffee shop; sometimes it is an Ethernet link in a office building or university; for an increasingly large (and fortunate) slice of the population, it is a fiber optic link provided by a telecommunications company or ISP; and many others use some sort of copper wire or cable to connect. Fortunately, there are many common strategies used on these seemingly disparate types of links so that they can all be made reliable and useful to higher layers in the protocol stack. This chapter will examine those strategies.

Figure 2.1 illustrates various types of links as seen by a typical end-user of today's Internet. On the left, we see a variety of end-user devices ranging from mobile phones to PDAs to full-fledged computers connected by various means to an Internet Service Provider. While those links might be of any type mentioned above, or some other type, they all look the same in this picture—a straight line connecting a device to a router. Also, there are some links that connect routers together inside the ISP and a link that connects the ISP to the "rest of the Internet," which consists of lots of other ISPs and the hosts to which they connect. These links all look alike not just because we're not very good artists but because part of the role of a network architecture (as discussed in Section 1.3) is to provide a common abstraction of something as complex and diverse as a link. The idea is that your laptop or smartphone doesn't have to care what sort of link it is connected to—the only thing that matters is that it has a link

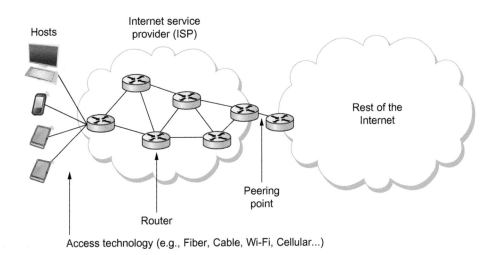

■ FIGURE 2.1 An end-user's view of the Internet.

to the Internet. Similarly, a router doesn't have to care what sort of link connects it to other routers—it can send a packet on the link with a pretty good expectation that the packet will reach the other end of the link.

How do we make all these different types of link look sufficiently alike to end users and routers? Essentially, we have to deal with all the physical limitations and shortcomings of links that exist in the real world. We sketched out some of these issues in the opening problem statement for this chapter. The first issue is that links are made of some physical material that can propagate signals (such as radio waves or other sorts of electromagnetic radiation), but what we really want to do is send *bits*. In later sections of this chapter, we'll look at how to encode bits for transmission on a physical medium, followed by the other issues mentioned above. By the end of this chapter, we'll understand how to send complete packets over just about any sort of link, no matter what physical medium is involved.

Link Capacity and the Shannon-Hartley Theorem

There has been an enormous body of work done in the related areas of signal processing and information theory, studying everything from how signals degrade over distance to how much data a given signal can effectively carry. The most notable piece of work in this area is a formula known as the *Shannon-Hartley theorem*.[2] Simply stated, this theorem gives an upper bound to the capacity of a link, in terms of bits per second (bps); as a function of the signal-to-noise ratio of the link, measured in decibels (dB); and the bandwidth of the channel, measured in Hertz (Hz). (As noted previously, *bandwidth* is a bit of an overloaded term in communications; here we use it to refer to the range of frequencies available for communication.)

As an example, we can apply the Shannon-Hartley theorem to determine the rate at which a dial-up modem can be expected to transmit binary data over a voice-grade phone line without suffering from too high an error rate. A standard voice-grade phone line typically supports a frequency range of 300 Hz to 3300 Hz, a channel bandwidth of 3 kHz.

The theorem is typically given by the following formula:

$$C = B \log_2(1 + S/N)$$

where C is the achievable channel capacity measured in bits per second, B is the bandwidth of the channel in Hz (3300 Hz   300 Hz = 3000 Hz), S is the

---

[2]Sometimes called simply *Shannon s theorem*, but Shannon actually had quite a few theorems.

average signal power, and N is the average noise power. The signal-to-noise ratio (S/N, or SNR) is usually expressed in decibels, related as follows:

$$\text{SNR} = 10 \quad \log_{10}(S/N)$$

Thus, a typical signal-to-noise ratio of 30 dB would imply that $S/N = 1000$. Thus, we have

$$C = 3000 \quad \log_{2}(1001)$$

which equals approximately 30 kbps.

When dial-up modems were the main way to connect to the Internet in the 1990s, 56 kbps was a common advertised capacity for a modem (and continues to be about the upper limit for dial-up). However, the modems often achieved lower speeds in practice, because they didn't always encounter a signal-to-noise ratio high enough to achieve 56 kbps.

The Shannon-Hartley theorem is equally applicable to all sorts of links ranging from wireless to coaxial cable to optical fiber. It should be apparent that there are really only two ways to build a high-capacity link: start with a high-bandwidth channel or achieve a high signal-to-noise ratio, or, preferably, both. Also, even those conditions won't guarantee a high-capacity link—it often takes quite a bit of ingenuity on the part of people who design channel coding schemes to achieve the theoretical limits of a channel. This ingenuity is particularly apparent today in wireless links, where there is a great incentive to get the most bits per second from a given amount of wireless spectrum (the channel bandwidth) and signal power level (and hence SNR).

2.1.1 Classes of Links

While most readers of this book have probably encountered at least a few different types of links, it will help to understand some of the broad classes of links that exist and their general properties. For a start, all practical links rely on some sort of electromagnetic radiation propagating through a medium or, in some cases, through free space. One way to characterize links, then, is by the medium they use—typically copper wire in some form, as in Digital Subscriber Line (DSL) and coaxial cable; optical fiber, as in both commercial fiber-to-the-home services and many long-distance links in the Internet's backbone; or air/free space for wireless links.

Another important link characteristic is the *frequency*, measured in hertz, with which the electromagnetic waves oscillate. The distance between a pair of adjacent maxima or minima of a wave, typically measured in meters, is called the wave's *wavelength*. Since all electromagnetic waves travel at the speed of light (which in turn depends on the medium), that speed divided by the wave's frequency is equal to its wavelength. We have already seen the example of a voice-grade telephone line, which carries continuous electromagnetic signals ranging between 300 Hz and 3300 Hz; a 300-Hz wave traveling through copper would have a wavelength of

$$\frac{\text{SpeedOfLightInCopper}}{\text{Frequency}}$$

$$= \frac{2/3 \times 3 \times 10^8}{300}$$

$$= 667 \times 10^3 \text{ meters}$$

Generally, electromagnetic waves span a much wider range of frequencies, ranging from radio waves, to infrared light, to visible light, to x-rays and gamma rays. Figure 2.2 depicts the electromagnetic spectrum and shows which media are commonly used to carry which frequency bands.

So far we understand a link to be a physical medium carrying signals in the form of electromagnetic waves. Such links provide the foundation for transmitting all sorts of information, including the kind of data we are interested in transmitting—binary data (1s and 0s). We say that the binary data is *encoded* in the signal. The problem of encoding binary data onto electromagnetic signals is a complex topic. To help make the topic more manageable, we can think of it as being divided into two layers. The lower

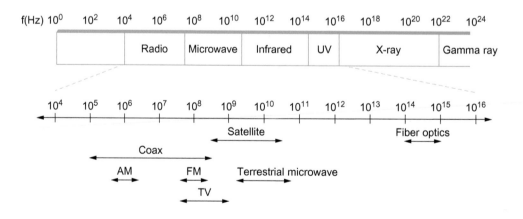

■ FIGURE 2.2 Electromagnetic spectrum.

layer is concerned with *modulation*—varying the frequency, amplitude, or phase of the signal to effect the transmission of information. A simple example of modulation is to vary the power (amplitude) of a single wavelength. Intuitively, this is equivalent to turning a light on and off. Because the issue of modulation is secondary to our discussion of links as a building block for computer networks, we simply assume that it is possible to transmit a pair of distinguishable signals—think of them as a "high" signal and a "low" signal—and we consider only the upper layer, which is concerned with the much simpler problem of encoding binary data onto these two signals. Section 2.2 discusses such encodings.

Another way to classify links is in terms of how they are used. Various economic and deployment issues tend to influence where different link types are found. Most consumers interact with the Internet either through wireless networks (which they encounter in coffee shops, airports, universities, etc.) or through so-called "last mile" links provided by Internet Service Providers, as illustrated in Figure 2.1. These link types are summarized in Table 2.1. They typically are chosen because they are cost-effective ways of reaching millions of consumers; DSL, for example, was deployed over the existing twisted pair copper wires that already existed for plain old telephone services. Most of these technologies are not sufficient for building a complete network from scratch—for example, you'll likely need some long-distance, very high-speed links to interconnect cities in a large network.

Modern long-distance links are almost exclusively fiber today, with coaxial cables having been largely replaced over the last couple of decades. These links typically use a technology called SONET (Synchronous Optical Network), which was developed to meet the demanding

Table 2.1 Common Services Available to Connect Your Home	
Service	Bandwidth (typical)
Dial-up	28–56 kbps
ISDN	64–128 kbps
DSL	128 kbps–100 Mbps
CATV (cable TV)	1–40 Mbps
FTTH (fibre to the home)	50 Mbps–1 Gbps

management requirements of telephone carriers. We'll take a closer look at SONET in Section 2.3.3.

Finally, in addition to last-mile and backbone links, there are the links that you find inside a building or a campus—generally referred to as *local area networks* (LANs). Ethernet, described in Section 2.6, has for some time been the dominant technology in this space, having displaced token ring technologies after many years. While Ethernet continues to be popular, it is now mostly seen alongside wireless technologies based around the 802.11 standards, which we will discuss in Section 2.7.

This survey of link types is by no means exhaustive but should have given you a taste of the diversity of link types that exist and some of the reasons for that diversity. In the coming sections, we will see how networking protocols can take advantage of that diversity and present a consistent view of the network to higher layers in spite of all the low-level complexity.

2.2 ENCODING (NRZ, NRZI, MANCHESTER, 4B/5B)

The first step in turning nodes and links into usable building blocks is to understand how to connect them in such a way that bits can be transmitted from one node to the other. As mentioned in the preceding section, signals propagate over physical links. The task, therefore, is to encode the binary data that the source node wants to send into the signals that the links are able to carry and then to decode the signal back into the corresponding binary data at the receiving node. We ignore the details of modulation and assume we are working with two discrete signals: high and low. In practice, these signals might correspond to two different voltages on a copper-based link or two different power levels on an optical link.

Most of the functions discussed in this chapter are performed by a *network adaptor*—a piece of hardware that connects a node to a link. The network adaptor contains a signalling component that actually encodes bits into signals at the sending node and decodes signals into bits at the receiving node. Thus, as illustrated in Figure 2.3, signals travel over a link between two signalling components, and bits flow between network adaptors.

Let's return to the problem of encoding bits onto signals. The obvious thing to do is to map the data value 1 onto the high signal and the data value 0 onto the low signal. This is exactly the mapping used by an encoding scheme called, cryptically enough, *non-return to zero* (NRZ).

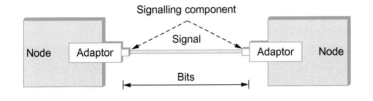

■ **FIGURE 2.3** Signals travel between signalling components; bits flow between adaptors.

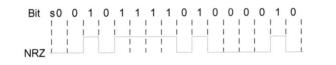

■ **FIGURE 2.4** NRZ encoding of a bit stream.

For example, Figure 2.4 schematically depicts the NRZ-encoded signal (bottom) that corresponds to the transmission of a particular sequence of bits (top).

The problem with NRZ is that a sequence of several consecutive 1s means that the signal stays high on the link for an extended period of time; similarly, several consecutive 0s means that the signal stays low for a long time. There are two fundamental problems caused by long strings of 1s or 0s. The first is that it leads to a situation known as *baseline wander*. Specifically, the receiver keeps an average of the signal it has seen so far and then uses this average to distinguish between low and high signals. Whenever the signal is significantly lower than this average, the receiver concludes that it has just seen a 0; likewise, a signal that is significantly higher than the average is interpreted to be a 1. The problem, of course, is that too many consecutive 1s or 0s cause this average to change, making it more difficult to detect a significant change in the signal.

The second problem is that frequent transitions from high to low and *vice versa* are necessary to enable *clock recovery*. Intuitively, the clock recovery problem is that both the encoding and the decoding processes are driven by a clock—every clock cycle the sender transmits a bit and the receiver recovers a bit. The sender's and the receiver's clocks have to be precisely synchronized in order for the receiver to recover the same bits the sender transmits. If the receiver's clock is even slightly faster or slower than the sender's clock, then it does not correctly decode the signal. You could imagine sending the clock to the receiver over a separate wire, but this is typically avoided because it makes the cost of cabling twice as high. So, instead, the receiver derives the clock from the received signal—the clock recovery process. Whenever the signal changes, such as on a transition from 1 to 0 or from 0 to 1, then the receiver knows it is at a clock cycle boundary, and it can resynchronize itself. However, a long period of time without such a transition leads to clock drift. Thus, clock recovery depends on having lots of transitions in the signal, no matter what data is being sent.

One approach that addresses this problem, called *non-return to zero inverted* (NRZI), has the sender make a transition from the current signal to encode a 1 and stay at the current signal to encode a 0. This solves the problem of consecutive 1s, but obviously does nothing for consecutive 0s. NRZI is illustrated in Figure 2.5. An alternative, called *Manchester encoding*, does a more explicit job of merging the clock with the signal by transmitting the exclusive OR of the NRZ-encoded data and the clock. (Think of the local clock as an internal signal that alternates from low to high; a low/high pair is considered one clock cycle.) The Manchester encoding is also illustrated in Figure 2.5. Observe that the Manchester encoding results in 0 being encoded as a low-to-high transition and 1 being encoded as a high-to-low transition. Because both 0s and 1s result in a transition to the signal, the clock can be effectively recovered at the receiver. (There is also a variant of the Manchester encoding, called *Differential Manchester*, in which a 1 is encoded with the first half of the signal equal to the last half of the previous bit's signal and a 0 is encoded with the first half of the signal opposite to the last half of the previous bit's signal.)

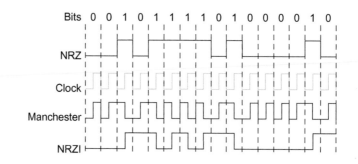

■ FIGURE 2.5 Different encoding strategies.

The problem with the Manchester encoding scheme is that it doubles the rate at which signal transitions are made on the link, which means that the receiver has half the time to detect each pulse of the signal. The rate at which the signal changes is called the link's *baud rate*. In the case of the Manchester encoding, the bit rate is half the baud rate, so the encoding is considered only 50% efficient. Keep in mind that if the receiver had been able to keep up with the faster baud rate required by the Manchester encoding in Figure 2.5, then both NRZ and NRZI could have been able to transmit twice as many bits in the same time period.

A final encoding that we consider, called *4B/5B*, attempts to address the inefficiency of the Manchester encoding without suffering from the problem of having extended durations of high or low signals. The idea of 4B/5B is to insert extra bits into the bit stream so as to break up long sequences of 0s or 1s. Specifically, every 4 bits of actual data are encoded in a 5-bit code that is then transmitted to the receiver; hence, the name 4B/5B. The 5-bit codes are selected in such a way that each one has no more than one leading 0 and no more than two trailing 0s. Thus, when sent back-to-back, no pair of 5-bit codes results in more than three consecutive 0s being transmitted. The resulting 5-bit codes are then transmitted using the NRZI encoding, which explains why the code is only concerned about consecutive 0s—NRZI already solves the problem of consecutive 1s. Note that the 4B/5B encoding results in 80% efficiency.

Table 2.2 gives the 5-bit codes that correspond to each of the 16 possible 4-bit data symbols. Notice that since 5 bits are enough to encode 32 different codes, and we are using only 16 of these for data, there are 16 codes left over that we can use for other purposes. Of these, code 11111 is used when the line is idle, code 00000 corresponds to when the line is dead, and 00100 is interpreted to mean halt. Of the remaining 13 codes, 7 of them are not valid because they violate the "one leading 0, two trailing 0s," rule, and the other 6 represent various control symbols. As we will see later in this chapter, some framing protocols make use of these control symbols.

2.3 FRAMING

Now that we have seen how to transmit a sequence of bits over a point-to-point link—from adaptor to adaptor—let's consider the scenario illustrated in Figure 2.6. Recall from Chapter 1 that we are focusing

Table 2.2 4B/5B Encoding	
4-Bit Data Symbol	**5-Bit Code**
0000	11110
0001	01001
0010	10100
0011	10101
0100	01010
0101	01011
0110	01110
0111	01111
1000	10010
1001	10011
1010	10110
1011	10111
1100	11010
1101	11011
1110	11100
1111	11101

on packet-switched networks, which means that blocks of data (called *frames* at this level), not bit streams, are exchanged between nodes. It is the network adaptor that enables the nodes to exchange frames. When node A wishes to transmit a frame to node B, it tells its adaptor to transmit a frame from the node's memory. This results in a sequence of bits being sent over the link. The adaptor on node B then collects together the sequence of bits arriving on the link and deposits the corresponding frame in B's memory. Recognizing exactly what set of bits constitutes a frame—that is, determining where the frame begins and ends—is the central challenge faced by the adaptor.

There are several ways to address the framing problem. This section uses several different protocols to illustrate the various points in the design space. Note that while we discuss framing in the context of point-to-point links, the problem is a fundamental one that must also be addressed in multiple-access networks like Ethernet and token rings.

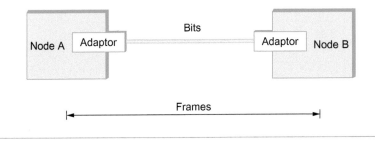

Frames

■ FIGURE 2.6 Bits flow between adaptors, frames between hosts.

2.3.1 Byte-Oriented Protocols (BISYNC, PPP, DDCMP)

One of the oldest approaches to framing—it has its roots in connecting terminals to mainframes—is to view each frame as a collection of bytes (characters) rather than a collection of bits. Such a *byte-oriented* approach is exemplified by older protocols such as the Binary Synchronous Communication (BISYNC) protocol developed by IBM in the late 1960s, and the Digital Data Communication Message Protocol (DDCMP) used in Digital Equipment Corporation's DECNET. The more recent and widely used Point-to-Point Protocol (PPP) provides another example of this approach.

Sentinel-Based Approaches

Figure 2.7 illustrates the BISYNC protocol's frame format. This figure is the first of many that you will see in this book that are used to illustrate frame or packet formats, so a few words of explanation are in order. We show a packet as a sequence of labeled fields. Above each field is a number indicating the length of that field in bits. Note that the packets are transmitted beginning with the leftmost field.

BISYNC uses special characters known as *sentinel characters* to indicate where frames start and end. The beginning of a frame is denoted by sending a special SYN (synchronization) character. The data portion of the frame is then contained between two more special characters: STX (start of text) and ETX (end of text). The SOH (start of header) field serves much the same purpose as the STX field. The problem with the sentinel approach, of course, is that the ETX character might appear in the data portion of the frame. BISYNC overcomes this problem by "escaping" the ETX character by preceding it with a DLE (data-link-escape) character whenever it appears in the body of a frame; the DLE character is also

FIGURE 2.7 BISYNC frame format.

escaped (by preceding it with an extra DLE) in the frame body. (C programmers may notice that this is analogous to the way a quotation mark is escaped by the backslash when it occurs inside a string.) This approach is often called *character stuffing* because extra characters are inserted in the data portion of the frame.

The frame format also includes a field labeled CRC (cyclic redundancy check), which is used to detect transmission errors; various algorithms for error detection are presented in Section 2.4. Finally, the frame contains additional header fields that are used for, among other things, the link-level reliable delivery algorithm. Examples of these algorithms are given in Section 2.5.

The more recent Point-to-Point Protocol (PPP), which is commonly used to carry Internet Protocol packets over various sorts of point-to-point links, is similar to BISYNC in that it also uses sentinels and character stuffing. The format for a PPP frame is given in Figure 2.8. The special start-of-text character, denoted as the Flag field in Figure 2.8, is 01111110. The Address and Control fields usually contain default values and so are uninteresting. The Protocol field is used for demultiplexing; it identifies the high-level protocol such as IP or IPX (an IP-like protocol developed by Novell). The frame payload size can be negotiated, but it is 1500 bytes by default. The Checksum field is either 2 (by default) or 4 bytes long.

The PPP frame format is unusual in that several of the field sizes are negotiated rather than fixed. This negotiation is conducted by a protocol called the Link Control Protocol (LCP). PPP and LCP work in tandem: LCP sends control messages encapsulated in PPP frames—such messages are denoted by an LCP identifier in the PPP Protocol field—and then turns around and changes PPP's frame format based on the information contained in those control messages. LCP is also involved in establishing a link between two peers when both sides detect that communication over the link is possible (e.g., when each optical receiver detects an incoming signal from the fiber to which it connects).

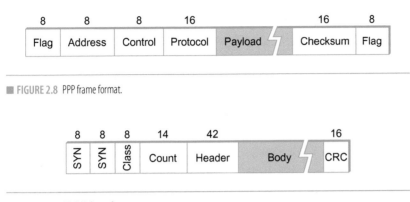

8	8	8	16		16	8
Flag	Address	Control	Protocol	Payload	Checksum	Flag

■ FIGURE 2.8 PPP frame format.

8	8	8	14	42	16	
SYN	SYN	Class	Count	Header	Body	CRC

■ FIGURE 2.9 DDCMP frame format.

Byte-Counting Approach

As every Computer Science 101 student knows, the alternative to detecting the end of a file with a sentinel value is to include the number of items in the file at the beginning of the file. The same is true in framing—the number of bytes contained in a frame can be included as a field in the frame header. The DECNET's DDCMP uses this approach, as illustrated in Figure 2.9. In this example, the COUNT field specifies how many bytes are contained in the frame's body.

One danger with this approach is that a transmission error could corrupt the count field, in which case the end of the frame would not be correctly detected. (A similar problem exists with the sentinel-based approach if the ETX field becomes corrupted.) Should this happen, the receiver will accumulate as many bytes as the bad COUNT field indicates and then use the error detection field to determine that the frame is bad. This is sometimes called a *framing error*. The receiver will then wait until it sees the next SYN character to start collecting the bytes that make up the next frame. It is therefore possible that a framing error will cause back-to-back frames to be incorrectly received.

2.3.2 Bit-Oriented Protocols (HDLC)

Unlike these byte-oriented protocols, a bit-oriented protocol is not concerned with byte boundaries—it simply views the frame as a collection of bits. These bits might come from some character set, such as ASCII; they might be pixel values in an image; or they could be instructions and operands from an executable file. The Synchronous Data Link Control

(SDLC) protocol developed by IBM is an example of a bit-oriented proto-col; SDLC was later standardized by the ISO as the High-Level Data Link Control (HDLC) protocol. In the following discussion, we use HDLC as an example; its frame format is given in Figure 2.10.

HDLC denotes both the beginning and the end of a frame with the distinguished bit sequence 01111110. This sequence is also transmitted during any times that the link is idle so that the sender and receiver can keep their clocks synchronized. In this way, both protocols essentially use the sentinel approach. Because this sequence might appear anywhere in the body of the frame—in fact, the bits 01111110 might cross byte boundaries—bit-oriented protocols use the analog of the DLE character, a technique known as *bit stuffing*.

Bit stuffing in the HDLC protocol works as follows. On the sending side, any time five consecutive 1s have been transmitted from the body of the message (i.e., excluding when the sender is trying to transmit the distin-guished 01111110 sequence), the sender inserts a 0 before transmitting the next bit. On the receiving side, should five consecutive 1s arrive, the receiver makes its decision based on the next bit it sees (i.e., the bit fol-lowing the five 1s). If the next bit is a 0, it must have been stuffed, and so the receiver removes it. If the next bit is a 1, then one of two things is true: Either this is the end-of-frame marker or an error has been introduced into the bit stream. By looking at the *next* bit, the receiver can distinguish between these two cases. If it sees a 0 (i.e., the last 8 bits it has looked at are 01111110), then it is the end-of-frame marker; if it sees a 1 (i.e., the last 8 bits it has looked at are 01111111), then there must have been an error and the whole frame is discarded. In the latter case, the receiver has to wait for the next 01111110 before it can start receiving again, and, as a consequence, there is the potential that the receiver will fail to receive two consecutive frames. Obviously, there are still ways that framing errors can go undetected, such as when an entire spurious end-of-frame pattern is generated by errors, but these failures are relatively unlikely. Robust ways of detecting errors are discussed in Section 2.4.

■ FIGURE 2.10 HDLC frame format.

An interesting characteristic of bit stuffing, as well as character stuffing, is that the size of a frame is dependent on the data that is being sent in the payload of the frame. It is in fact not possible to make all frames exactly the same size, given that the data that might be carried in any frame is arbitrary. (To convince yourself of this, consider what happens if the last byte of a frame's body is the ETX character.) A form of framing that ensures that all frames are the same size is described in the next subsection.

What's in a Layer?

One of the important contributions of the OSI reference model presented in Chapter 1 was providing some vocabulary for talking about protocols and, in particular, protocol layers. This vocabulary has provided fuel for plenty of arguments along the lines of "Your protocol does function X at layer Y, and the OSI reference model says it should be done at layer Z—that's a layer violation." In fact, figuring out the right layer at which to perform a given function can be very difficult, and the reasoning is usually a lot more subtle than "What does the OSI model say?" It is partly for this reason that this book avoids a rigidly layerist approach. Instead, it shows you a lot of functions that need to be performed by protocols and looks at some ways that they have been successfully implemented.

In spite of our nonlayerist approach, sometimes we need convenient ways to talk about classes of protocols, and the name of the layer at which they operate is often the best choice. Thus, for example, this chapter focuses primarily on link-layer protocols. (Bit encoding, described in Section 2.2, is the exception, being considered a physical-layer function.) Link-layer protocols can be identified by the fact that they run over single links—the type of network discussed in this chapter. Network-layer protocols, by contrast, run over switched networks that contain lots of links interconnected by switches or routers. Topics related to network-layer protocols are discussed in Chapters 3 and 4.

Note that protocol layers are supposed to be helpful—they provide helpful ways to talk about classes of protocols, and they help us divide the problem of building networks into manageable subtasks. However, they are not meant to be overly restrictive—the mere fact that something is a layer violation does not end the argument about whether it is a worthwhile thing to do. In other words, layering makes a good slave, but a poor master. A particularly interesting argument about the best layer in which to place a certain function comes up when we look at congestion control in Chapter 6.

2.3.3 Clock-Based Framing (SONET)

A third approach to framing is exemplified by the Synchronous Optical Network (SONET) standard. For lack of a widely accepted generic term, we refer to this approach simply as *clock-based framing*. SONET was first proposed by Bell Communications Research (Bellcore), and then developed under the American National Standards Institute (ANSI) for digital transmission over optical fiber; it has since been adopted by the ITU-T. SONET has been for many years the dominant standard for long-distance transmission of data over optical networks.

An important point to make about SONET before we go any further is that the full specification is substantially larger than this book. Thus, the following discussion will necessarily cover only the high points of the standard. Also, SONET addresses both the framing problem and the encoding problem. It also addresses a problem that is very important for phone companies—the multiplexing of several low-speed links onto one high-speed link. (In fact, much of SONET's design reflects the fact that phone companies have to be concerned with multiplexing large numbers of the 64-kbps channels that traditionally are used for telephone calls.) We begin with SONET's approach to framing and discuss the other issues following.

As with the previously discussed framing schemes, a SONET frame has some special information that tells the receiver where the frame starts and ends; however, that is about as far as the similarities go. Notably, no bit stuffing is used, so that a frame's length does not depend on the data being sent. So the question to ask is "How does the receiver know where each frame starts and ends?" We consider this question for the lowest-speed SONET link, which is known as STS-1 and runs at 51.84 Mbps. An STS-1 frame is shown in Figure 2.11. It is arranged as 9 rows of 90 bytes each, and the first 3 bytes of each row are overhead, with the rest being available for data that is being transmitted over the link. The first 2 bytes of the frame contain a special bit pattern, and it is these bytes that enable the receiver to determine where the frame starts. However, since bit stuffing is not used, there is no reason why this pattern will not occasionally turn up in the payload portion of the frame. To guard against this, the receiver looks for the special bit pattern consistently, hoping to see it appearing once every 810 bytes, since each frame is $9 \times 90 = 810$ bytes long. When

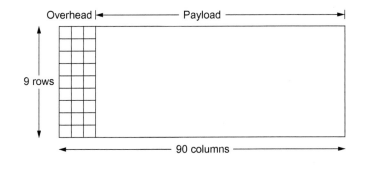

■ FIGURE 2.11 A SONET STS-1 frame.

the special pattern turns up in the right place enough times, the receiver concludes that it is in sync and can then interpret the frame correctly.

One of the things we are not describing due to the complexity of SONET is the detailed use of all the other overhead bytes. Part of this complexity can be attributed to the fact that SONET runs across the carrier's optical network, not just over a single link. (Recall that we are glossing over the fact that the carriers implement a network, and we are instead focusing on the fact that we can lease a SONET link from them and then use this link to build our own packet-switched network.) Additional complexity comes from the fact that SONET provides a considerably richer set of services than just data transfer. For example, 64 kbps of a SONET link's capacity is set aside for a voice channel that is used for maintenance.

The overhead bytes of a SONET frame are encoded using NRZ, the simple encoding described in the previous section where 1s are high and 0s are low. However, to ensure that there are plenty of transitions to allow the receiver to recover the sender's clock, the payload bytes are *scrambled*. This is done by calculating the exclusive OR (XOR) of the data to be transmitted and by the use of a well-known bit pattern. The bit pattern, which is 127 bits long, has plenty of transitions from 1 to 0, so that XORing it with the transmitted data is likely to yield a signal with enough transitions to enable clock recovery.

SONET supports the multiplexing of multiple low-speed links in the following way. A given SONET link runs at one of a finite set of possible rates, ranging from 51.84 Mbps (STS-1) to 2488.32 Mbps (STS-48), and beyond. Note that all of these rates are integer multiples of STS-1. The significance for framing is that a single SONET frame can contain sub-frames for multiple lower-rate channels. A second related feature is that each frame is 125 μs long. This means that at STS-1 rates, a SONET frame is 810 bytes long, while at STS-3 rates, each SONET frame is 2430 bytes long. Notice the synergy between these two features: $3 \times 810 = 2430$, meaning that three STS-1 frames fit exactly in a single STS-3 frame.

Intuitively, the STS-N frame can be thought of as consisting of N STS-1 frames, where the bytes from these frames are interleaved; that is, a byte from the first frame is transmitted, then a byte from the second frame is transmitted, and so on. The reason for interleaving the bytes from each STS-N frame is to ensure that the bytes in each STS-1 frame are evenly paced; that is, bytes show up at the receiver at a smooth 51 Mbps, rather than all bunched up during one particular $1/N$th of the 125-μs interval.

Although it is accurate to view an STS-N signal as being used to multiplex N STS-1 frames, the payload from these STS-1 frames can be linked together to form a larger STS-N payload; such a link is denoted STS-Nc (for *concatenated*). One of the fields in the overhead is used for this purpose. Figure 2.12 schematically depicts concatenation in the case of three STS-1 frames being concatenated into a single STS-3c frame. The significance of a SONET link being designated as STS-3c rather than STS-3 is that, in the former case, the user of the link can view it as a single 155.25-Mbps pipe, whereas an STS-3 should really be viewed as three 51.84-Mbps links that happen to share a fiber.

Finally, the preceding description of SONET is overly simplistic in that it assumes that the payload for each frame is completely contained within the frame. (Why wouldn't it be?) In fact, we should view the STS-1 frame just described as simply a placeholder for the frame, where the actual payload may *float* across frame boundaries. This situation is illustrated

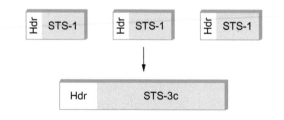

■ FIGURE 2.12 Three STS-1 frames multiplexed onto one STS-3c frame.

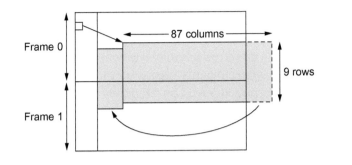

■ FIGURE 2.13 SONET frames out of phase.

in Figure 2.13. Here we see both the STS-1 payload floating across two STS-1 frames and the payload shifted some number of bytes to the right and, therefore, wrapped around. One of the fields in the frame overhead points to the beginning of the payload. The value of this capability is that it simplifies the task of synchronizing the clocks used throughout the carriers' networks, which is something that carriers spend a lot of their time worrying about.

2.4 ERROR DETECTION

As discussed in Chapter 1, bit errors are sometimes introduced into frames. This happens, for example, because of electrical interference or thermal noise. Although errors are rare, especially on optical links, some mechanism is needed to detect these errors so that corrective action can be taken. Otherwise, the end user is left wondering why the C program that successfully compiled just a moment ago now suddenly has a syntax error in it, when all that happened in the interim is that it was copied across a network file system.

There is a long history of techniques for dealing with bit errors in computer systems, dating back to at least the 1940s. Hamming and Reed-Solomon codes are two notable examples that were developed for use in punch card readers, when storing data on magnetic disks, and in early core memories. This section describes some of the error detection techniques most commonly used in networking.

Detecting errors is only one part of the problem. The other part is correcting errors once detected. Two basic approaches can be taken when the recipient of a message detects an error. One is to notify the sender that the message was corrupted so that the sender can retransmit a copy of the message. If bit errors are rare, then in all probability the retransmitted copy will be error free. Alternatively, some types of error detection algorithms allow the recipient to reconstruct the correct message even after it has been corrupted; such algorithms rely on *error-correcting codes*, discussed below.

One of the most common techniques for detecting transmission errors is a technique known as the *cyclic redundancy check* (CRC). It is used in nearly all the link-level protocols discussed in the previous section (e.g., HDLC, DDCMP), as well as in the CSMA and wireless protocols described later in this chapter. Section 2.4.3 outlines the basic CRC algorithm. Before discussing that approach, we consider two simpler schemes: *two-dimensional parity* and *checksums*. The former is used by the BISYNC protocol when it is transmitting ASCII characters (CRC is used as the error-detecting code when BISYNC is used to transmit EBCDIC[3]), and the latter is used by several Internet protocols.

The basic idea behind any error detection scheme is to add redundant information to a frame that can be used to determine if errors have been introduced. In the extreme, we could imagine transmitting two complete copies of the data. If the two copies are identical at the receiver, then it is probably the case that both are correct. If they differ, then an error was introduced into one (or both) of them, and they must be discarded. This is a rather poor error detection scheme for two reasons. First, it sends n redundant bits for an n-bit message. Second, many errors will go undetected—any error that happens to corrupt the same bit positions in the first and second copies of the message. In general, the goal of error detecting codes is to provide a high probability of detecting errors combined with a relatively low number of redundant bits.

Fortunately, we can do a lot better than this simple scheme. In general, we can provide quite strong error detection capability while sending only k redundant bits for an n-bit message, where k ≪ n. On an Ethernet, for example, a frame carrying up to 12,000 bits (1500 bytes) of data requires only a 32-bit CRC code, or as it is commonly expressed, uses CRC-32. Such a code will catch the overwhelming majority of errors, as we will see below.

---

[3]An alternative character encoding scheme used in the 1960s.

We say that the extra bits we send are redundant because they add no new information to the message. Instead, they are derived directly from the original message using some well-defined algorithm. Both the sender and the receiver know exactly what that algorithm is. The sender applies the algorithm to the message to generate the redundant bits. It then transmits both the message and those few extra bits. When the receiver applies the same algorithm to the received message, it should (in the absence of errors) come up with the same result as the sender. It compares the result with the one sent to it by the sender. If they match, it can conclude (with high likelihood) that no errors were introduced in the message during transmission. If they do not match, it can be sure that either the message or the redundant bits were corrupted, and it must take appropriate action—that is, discarding the message or correcting it if that is possible.

One note on the terminology for these extra bits. In general, they are referred to as *error-detecting codes*. In specific cases, when the algorithm to create the code is based on addition, they may be called a *checksum*. We will see that the Internet checksum is appropriately named: It is an error check that uses a summing algorithm. Unfortunately, the word *checksum* is often used imprecisely to mean any form of error-detecting code, including CRCs. This can be confusing, so we urge you to use the word *checksum* only to apply to codes that actually do use addition and to use *error-detecting code* to refer to the general class of codes described in this section.

2.4.1 Two-Dimensional Parity

Two-dimensional parity is exactly what the name suggests. It is based on "simple" (one-dimensional) parity, which usually involves adding one extra bit to a 7-bit code to balance the number of 1s in the byte. For example, odd parity sets the eighth bit to 1 if needed to give an odd number of 1s in the byte, and even parity sets the eighth bit to 1 if needed to give an even number of 1s in the byte. Two-dimensional parity does a similar calculation for each bit position across each of the bytes contained in the frame. This results in an extra parity byte for the entire frame, in addition to a parity bit for each byte. Figure 2.14 illustrates how two-dimensional even parity works for an example frame containing 6 bytes of data. Notice that the third bit of the parity byte is 1 since there is an odd number of 1s in the third bit across the 6 bytes in the frame. It can be shown that two-dimensional parity catches all 1-, 2-, and 3-bit errors, and most 4-bit

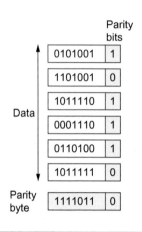

Parity
bits

0101001	1
1101001	0
1011110	1
0001110	1
0110100	1
1011111	0

Data

Parity
byte | 1111011 | 0 |

■ FIGURE 2.14 Two-dimensional parity.

errors. In this case, we have added 14 bits of redundant information to a 42-bit message, and yet we have stronger protection against common errors than the "repetition code" described above.

2.4.2 Internet Checksum Algorithm

A second approach to error detection is exemplified by the Internet checksum. Although it is not used at the link level, it nevertheless provides the same sort of functionality as CRCs and parity, so we discuss it here. We will see examples of its use in Sections 3.2, 5.1, and 5.2.

The idea behind the Internet checksum is very simple—you add up all the words that are transmitted and then transmit the result of that sum. The result is the checksum. The receiver performs the same calculation on the received data and compares the result with the received checksum. If any transmitted data, including the checksum itself, is corrupted, then the results will not match, so the receiver knows that an error occurred.

You can imagine many different variations on the basic idea of a checksum. The exact scheme used by the Internet protocols works as follows. Consider the data being checksummed as a sequence of 16-bit integers. Add them together using 16-bit ones complement arithmetic (explained below) and then take the ones complement of the result. That 16-bit number is the checksum.

In ones complement arithmetic, a negative integer $(-x)$ is represented as the complement of x; that is, each bit of x is inverted. When adding numbers in ones complement arithmetic, a carryout from the most significant bit needs to be added to the result. Consider, for example, the addition of 5 and 3 in ones complement arithmetic on 4-bit integers: +5 is 0101, so 5 is 1010; +3 is 0011, so 3 is 1100. If we add 1010 and 1100, ignoring the carry, we get 0110. In ones complement arithmetic, the fact that this operation caused a carry from the most significant bit causes us to increment the result, giving 0111, which is the ones complement representation of 8 (obtained by inverting the bits in 1000), as we would expect.

The following routine gives a straightforward implementation of the Internet's checksum algorithm. The count argument gives the length of buf measured in 16-bit units. The routine assumes that buf has already been padded with 0s to a 16-bit boundary.

```
u_short
cksum(u_short *buf, int count)
{
    register u_long sum = 0;

    while (count--)
    {
        sum += *buf++;
        if (sum & 0xFFFF0000)
        {
            /* carry occurred,
                so wrap around */
            sum &= 0xFFFF;
            sum++;
        }
    }
    return ~(sum & 0xFFFF);
}
```

This code ensures that the calculation uses ones complement arithmetic rather than the twos complement that is used in most machines. Note the if statement inside the while loop. If there is a carry into the top 16 bits of sum, then we increment sum just as in the previous example.

Compared to our repetition code, this algorithm scores well for using a small number of redundant bits—only 16 for a message of any length—but it does not score extremely well for strength of error detection. For example, a pair of single-bit errors, one of which increments a word and one of which decrements another word by the same amount, will go undetected. The reason for using an algorithm like this in spite of its relatively weak protection against errors (compared to a CRC, for example) is simple: This algorithm is much easier to implement in software. Experience in the ARPANET suggested that a checksum of this form was adequate. One reason it is adequate is that this checksum is the last line of defense in an end-to-end protocol; the majority of errors are picked up by stronger error detection algorithms, such as CRCs, at the link level.

Simple Probability Calculations

When dealing with network errors and other unlikely (we hope) events, we often have use for simple back-of-the-envelope probability estimates. A useful approximation here is that if two independent events have *small* probabilities p and q, then the probability of either event is $p + q$; the exact answer is $1 - (1 - p)(1 - q) = p + q - pq$. For $p = q = .01$, this estimate is .02, while the exact value is .0199.

For a simple application of this, suppose that the per-bit error rate on a link is 1 in 10^7. Now suppose we are interested in estimating the probability of at least one bit in a 10,000-bit packet being errored. Using the above approximation repeatedly over all the bits, we can say that we are interested in the probability of the first bit being errored, or the second bit, or the third, etc. Assuming bit errors are all independent (which they aren't), we can therefore estimate that the probability of at least one error in a 10,000-bit (10^4 bit) packet is $10^4 \times 10^{-7} = 10^{-3}$. The exact answer, computed as $1 - P(\text{no errors})$, would be $1 - (1 - 10^{-7})^{10,000} = .00099950$.

For a slightly more complex application, we compute the probability of exactly two errors in such a packet; this is the probability of an error that would sneak past a 1-parity-bit checksum. If we consider two particular bits in the packet, say bit i and bit j, the probability of those exact bits being errored is $10^{-7} \times 10^{-7}$. Now the total number of possible bit pairs in the packet is $\binom{10^4}{2} = 10^4 \times (10^4 - 1)/2 \approx 5 \times 10^7$. So again using the approximation of repeatedly adding the probabilities of many rare events (in this case, of any possible bit pair being errored), our total probability of at least two errored bits is $5 \times 10^7 \times 10^{-14} = 5 \times 10^{-7}$.

2.4.3 **Cyclic Redundancy Check**

It should be clear by now that a major goal in designing error detection algorithms is to maximize the probability of detecting errors using only a small number of redundant bits. Cyclic redundancy checks use some fairly powerful mathematics to achieve this goal. For example, a 32-bit CRC gives strong protection against common bit errors in messages that are thousands of bytes long. The theoretical foundation of the cyclic redundancy check is rooted in a branch of mathematics called *finite fields*. While this may sound daunting, the basic ideas can be easily understood.

To start, think of an $(n+1)$-bit message as being represented by an n degree polynomial, that is, a polynomial whose highest-order term is x^n. The message is represented by a polynomial by using the value of each bit in the message as the coefficient for each term in the polynomial, starting with the most significant bit to represent the highest-order term. For example, an 8-bit message consisting of the bits 10011010 corresponds to the polynomial

$$M(x) = 1 \quad x^7 + 0 \quad x^6 + 0 \quad x^5 + 1 \quad x^4$$
$$+ 1 \quad x^3 + 0 \quad x^2 + 1 \quad x^1$$
$$+ 0 \quad x^0$$
$$= x^7 + x^4 + x^3 + x^1$$

We can thus think of a sender and a receiver as exchanging polynomials with each other.

For the purposes of calculating a CRC, a sender and receiver have to agree on a *divisor* polynomial, $C(x)$. $C(x)$ is a polynomial of degree k. For example, suppose $C(x) = x^3 + x^2 + 1$. In this case, $k = 3$. The answer to the question "Where did $C(x)$ come from?" is, in most practical cases, "You look it up in a book." In fact, the choice of $C(x)$ has a significant impact on what types of errors can be reliably detected, as we discuss below. There are a handful of divisor polynomials that are very good choices for various environments, and the exact choice is normally made as part of the protocol design. For example, the Ethernet standard uses a well-known polynomial of degree 32.

When a sender wishes to transmit a message $M(x)$ that is $n+1$ bits long, what is actually sent is the $(n+1)$-bit message plus k bits. We call the complete transmitted message, including the redundant bits, $P(x)$. What we are going to do is contrive to make the polynomial representing $P(x)$ exactly divisible by $C(x)$; we explain how this is achieved below. If $P(x)$ is transmitted over a link and there are no errors introduced during transmission, then the receiver should be able to divide $P(x)$ by $C(x)$ exactly, leaving a remainder of zero. On the other hand, if some error is introduced into $P(x)$ during transmission, then in all likelihood the received polynomial will no longer be exactly divisible by $C(x)$, and thus the receiver will obtain a nonzero remainder implying that an error has occurred.

It will help to understand the following if you know a little about polynomial arithmetic; it is just slightly different from normal integer arithmetic. We are dealing with a special class of polynomial arithmetic here, where coefficients may be only one or zero, and operations on the coefficients are performed using modulo 2 arithmetic. This is referred to as "polynomial arithmetic modulo 2." Since this is a networking book, not a mathematics text, let's focus on the key properties of this type of arithmetic for our purposes (which we ask you to accept on faith):

- Any polynomial $B(x)$ can be divided by a divisor polynomial $C(x)$ if $B(x)$ is of higher degree than $C(x)$.
- Any polynomial $B(x)$ can be divided once by a divisor polynomial $C(x)$ if $B(x)$ is of the same degree as $C(x)$.
- The remainder obtained when $B(x)$ is divided by $C(x)$ is obtained by performing the exclusive OR (XOR) operation on each pair of matching coefficients.

For example, the polynomial $x^3 + 1$ can be divided by $x^3 + x^2 + 1$ (because they are both of degree 3) and the remainder would be 0 $x^3 +$ 1 $x^2 + 0$ $x^1 + 0$ $x^0 = x^2$ (obtained by XORing the coefficients of each term). In terms of messages, we could say that 1001 can be divided by 1101 and leaves a remainder of 0100. You should be able to see that the remainder is just the bitwise exclusive OR of the two messages.

Now that we know the basic rules for dividing polynomials, we are able to do long division, which is necessary to deal with longer messages. An example appears below.

Recall that we wanted to create a polynomial for transmission that is derived from the original message $M(x)$, is k bits longer than $M(x)$, and is exactly divisible by $C(x)$. We can do this in the following way:

1. Multiply $M(x)$ by x^k; that is, add k zeros at the end of the message. Call this zero-extended message $T(x)$.

2. Divide $T(x)$ by $C(x)$ and find the remainder.

3. Subtract the remainder from $T(x)$.

It should be obvious that what is left at this point is a message that is exactly divisible by $C(x)$. We may also note that the resulting message consists of $M(x)$ followed by the remainder obtained in step 2, because when we subtracted the remainder (which can be no more than k bits long), we were just XORing it with the k zeros added in step 1. This part will become clearer with an example.

Consider the message $x^7 + x^4 + x^3 + x^1$, or 10011010. We begin by multiplying by x^3, since our divisor polynomial is of degree 3. This gives 10011010000. We divide this by $C(x)$, which corresponds to 1101 in this case. Figure 2.15 shows the polynomial long-division operation. Given the rules of polynomial arithmetic described above, the long-division operation proceeds much as it would if we were dividing integers. Thus, in the first step of our example, we see that the divisor 1101 divides once into the first four bits of the message (1001), since they are of the same degree, and leaves a remainder of 100 (1101 XOR 1001). The next step is to bring down a digit from the message polynomial until we get another polynomial with the same degree as $C(x)$, in this case 1001. We calculate the remainder again (100) and continue until the calculation is complete. Note that the "result" of the long division, which appears at the top of the calculation, is not really of much interest—it is the remainder at the end that matters.

You can see from the very bottom of Figure 2.15 that the remainder of the example calculation is 101. So we know that 10011010000 minus 101 would be exactly divisible by $C(x)$, and this is what we send. The minus operation in polynomial arithmetic is the logical XOR operation, so we actually send 10011010101. As noted above, this turns out to be just the original message with the remainder from the long division calculation appended to it. The recipient divides the received polynomial by $C(x)$ and, if the result is 0, concludes that there were no errors. If the result is nonzero, it may be necessary to discard the corrupted message; with some codes, it may be possible to *correct* a small error (e.g., if the error affected only one bit). A code that enables error correction is called an *error-correcting code* (ECC).

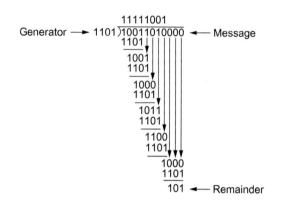

■ FIGURE 2.15 CRC calculation using polynomial long division.

Now we will consider the question of where the polynomial $C(x)$ comes from. Intuitively, the idea is to select this polynomial so that it is very unlikely to divide evenly into a message that has errors introduced into it. If the transmitted message is $P(x)$, we may think of the introduction of errors as the addition of another polynomial $E(x)$, so the recipient sees $P(x) + E(x)$. The only way that an error could slip by undetected would be if the received message could be evenly divided by $C(x)$, and since we know that $P(x)$ can be evenly divided by $C(x)$, this could only happen if $E(x)$ can be divided evenly by $C(x)$. The trick is to pick $C(x)$ so that this is very unlikely for common types of errors.

One common type of error is a single-bit error, which can be expressed as $E(x) = x^i$ when it affects bit position i. If we select $C(x)$ such that the first and the last term (that is, the x^k and x^0 terms) are nonzero, then we already have a two-term polynomial that cannot divide evenly into the one term $E(x)$. Such a $C(x)$ can, therefore, detect all single-bit errors. In general, it is possible to prove that the following types of errors can be detected by a $C(x)$ with the stated properties:

- All single-bit errors, as long as the x^k and x^0 terms have nonzero coefficients
- All double-bit errors, as long as $C(x)$ has a factor with at least three terms
- Any odd number of errors, as long as $C(x)$ contains the factor $(x + 1)$

Error Detection or Error Correction?

We have mentioned that it is possible to use codes that not only detect the presence of errors but also enable errors to be corrected. Since the details of such codes require yet more complex mathematics than that required to understand CRCs, we will not dwell on them here. However, it is worth considering the merits of correction versus detection.

At first glance, it would seem that correction is always better, since with detection we are forced to throw away the message and, in general, ask for another copy to be transmitted. This uses up bandwidth and may introduce latency while waiting for the retransmission. However, there is a downside to correction, as it generally requires a greater number of redundant bits to send an error-correcting code that is as strong (that is, able to cope with the same range of errors) as a code that only detects errors. Thus, while error detection requires more bits to be sent when errors occur, error correction requires more bits to be sent *all the time*. As a result, error correction tends to be most useful when (1) errors are quite probable, as they may be, for example, in a wireless environment, or (2) the cost of retransmission is too high, for example, because of the latency involved retransmitting a packet over a satellite link.

The use of error-correcting codes in networking is sometimes referred to as *forward error correction* (FEC) because the correction of errors is handled "in advance" by sending extra information, rather than waiting for errors to happen and dealing with them later by retransmission. FEC is commonly used in wireless networks such as 802.11.

- Any "burst" error (i.e., sequence of consecutive errored bits) for which the length of the burst is less than k bits (Most burst errors of length greater than k bits can also be detected.)

Six versions of $C(x)$ are widely used in link-level protocols (shown in Table 2.3). For example, Ethernet uses CRC-32, while HDLC uses CRC-CCITT. ATM, as described in Chapter 3, uses CRC-8, CRC-10, and CRC-32.

Finally, we note that the CRC algorithm, while seemingly complex, is easily implemented in hardware using a k-bit shift register and XOR gates. The number of bits in the shift register equals the degree of the generator polynomial (k). Figure 2.16 shows the hardware that would be used for the generator $x^3 + x^2 + 1$ from our previous example. The message is shifted

Table 2.3	Common CRC Polynomials
CRC	$C(x)$
CRC-8	$x^8 + x^2 + x^1 + 1$
CRC-10	$x^{10} + x^9 + x^5 + x^4 + x^1 + 1$
CRC-12	$x^{12} + x^{11} + x^3 + x^2 + x + 1$
CRC-16	$x^{16} + x^{15} + x^2 + 1$
CRC-CCITT	$x^{16} + x^{12} + x^5 + 1$
CRC-32	$x^{32} + x^{26} + x^{23} + x^{22} + x^{16} + x^{12} + x^{11}$
	$+x^{10} + x^8 + x^7 + x^5 + x^4 + x^2 + x + 1$

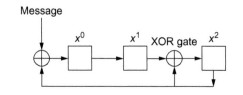

■ FIGURE 2.16 CRC calculation using shift register.

in from the left, beginning with the most significant bit and ending with the string of k zeros that is attached to the message, just as in the long division example. When all the bits have been shifted in and appropriately XORed, the register contains the remainder—that is, the CRC (most significant bit on the right). The position of the XOR gates is determined as follows: If the bits in the shift register are labeled 0 through $k - 1$, left to right, then put an XOR gate in front of bit n if there is a term x^n in the generator polynomial. Thus, we see an XOR gate in front of positions 0 and 2 for the generator $x^3 + x^2 + x^0$.

2.5 RELIABLE TRANSMISSION

As we saw in the previous section, frames are sometimes corrupted while in transit, with an error code like CRC used to detect such errors. While some error codes are strong enough also to correct errors, in practice the overhead is typically too large to handle the range of bit and burst errors that can be introduced on a network link. Even when error-correcting codes are used (e.g., on wireless links) some errors will be too severe to be corrected. As a result, some corrupt frames must be discarded. A link-level protocol that wants to deliver frames reliably must somehow recover from these discarded (lost) frames.

It's worth noting that reliability is a function that *may* be provided at the link level, but many modern link technologies omit this function. Furthermore, reliable delivery is frequently provided at higher levels, including both transport (as described in Section 5.2) and, sometimes, the application layer (Chapter 9). Exactly where it should be provided is a matter of some debate and depends on many factors. We describe the basics of reliable delivery here, since the principles are common across layers, but you should be aware that we're not just talking about a link-layer function (see the "What's in a Layer?" sidebar above for more on this).

This is usually accomplished using a combination of two fundamental mechanisms—*acknowledgments* and *timeouts*. An acknowledgment (ACK for short) is a small control frame that a protocol sends back to its peer saying that it has received an earlier frame. By control frame we mean a header without any data, although a protocol can *piggyback* an ACK on a data frame it just happens to be sending in the opposite direction. The receipt of an acknowledgment indicates to the sender of the original frame that its frame was successfully delivered. If the sender does not receive an acknowledgment after a reasonable amount of time, then it *retransmits* the original frame. This action of waiting a reasonable amount of time is called a *timeout*.

The general strategy of using acknowledgments and timeouts to implement reliable delivery is sometimes called *automatic repeat request* (normally abbreviated ARQ). This section describes three different ARQ algorithms using generic language; that is, we do not give detailed information about a particular protocol's header fields.

2.5.1 Stop-and-Wait

The simplest ARQ scheme is the *stop-and-wait* algorithm. The idea of stop-and-wait is straightforward: After transmitting one frame, the sender waits for an acknowledgment before transmitting the next frame. If the acknowledgment does not arrive after a certain period of time, the sender times out and retransmits the original frame.

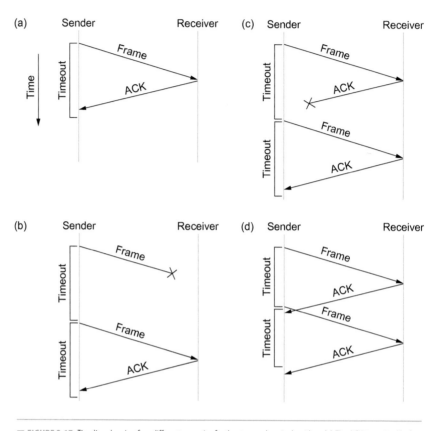

■ FIGURE 2.17 Timeline showing four different scenarios for the stop-and-wait algorithm. (a) The ACK is received before the timer expires; (b) the original frame is lost; (c) the ACK is lost; (d) the timeout fires too soon.

Figure 2.17 illustrates four different scenarios that result from this basic algorithm. This figure is a timeline, a common way to depict a protocol's behavior (see also the sidebar on this sort of diagram). The sending side is represented on the left, the receiving side is depicted on the right, and time flows from top to bottom. Figure 2.17(a) shows the situation in which the ACK is received before the timer expires; (b) and (c) show the situation in which the original frame and the ACK, respectively, are lost; and (d) shows the situation in which the timeout fires too soon. Recall that by "lost" we mean that the frame was corrupted while in transit, that this corruption was detected by an error code on the receiver, and that the frame was subsequently discarded.

Timelines and Packet Exchange Diagrams

Figures 2.17 and 2.18 are two examples of a frequently used tool in teaching, explaining, and designing protocols: the timeline or packet exchange diagram. You are going to see many more of them in this book—see Figure 9.9 for a more complex example. They are very useful because they capture visually the behavior over time of a distributed system—something that can be quite hard to analyze. When designing a protocol, you often have to be prepared for the unexpected—a system crashes, a message gets lost, or something that you expected to happen quickly turns out to take a long time. These sorts of diagrams can often help us understand what might go wrong in such cases and thus help a protocol designer be prepared for every eventuality.

There is one important subtlety in the stop-and-wait algorithm. Suppose the sender sends a frame and the receiver acknowledges it, but the acknowledgment is either lost or delayed in arriving. This situation is illustrated in timelines (c) and (d) of Figure 2.17. In both cases, the sender times out and retransmits the original frame, but the receiver will think that it is the next frame, since it correctly received and acknowledged the first frame. This has the potential to cause duplicate copies of a frame to be delivered. To address this problem, the header for a stop-and-wait protocol usually includes a 1-bit sequence number—that is, the sequence number can take on the values 0 and 1—and the sequence numbers used for each frame alternate, as illustrated in Figure 2.18. Thus, when the sender retransmits frame 0, the receiver can determine that it is seeing a second copy of frame 0 rather than the first copy of frame 1 and therefore can ignore it (the receiver still acknowledges it, in case the first ACK was lost).

The main shortcoming of the stop-and-wait algorithm is that it allows the sender to have only one outstanding frame on the link at a time, and this may be far below the link's capacity. Consider, for example, a 1.5-Mbps link with a 45-ms round-trip time. This link has a delay bandwidth product of 67.5 Kb, or approximately 8 KB. Since the sender can send only one frame per RTT, and assuming a frame size of 1 KB, this

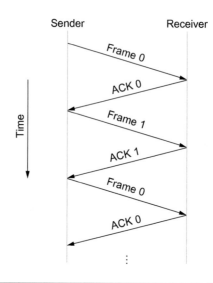

■ FIGURE 2.18 Timeline for stop-and-wait with 1-bit sequence number.

implies a maximum sending rate of

$$\frac{\text{Bits Per Frame}}{\text{Time Per Frame}}$$

$$= \frac{1024 \times 8}{0.045}$$

$$= 182 \text{ kbps}$$

or about one-eighth of the link's capacity. To use the link fully, then, we'd like the sender to be able to transmit up to eight frames before having to wait for an acknowledgment.

The significance of the delay × bandwidth product is that it represents the amount of data that could be in transit. We would like to be able to send this much data without waiting for the first acknowledgment. The principle at work here is often referred to as *keeping the pipe full*. The algorithms presented in the following two subsections do exactly this.

2.5.2 Sliding Window

Consider again the scenario in which the link has a delay × bandwidth product of 8 KB and frames are 1 KB in size. We would like the sender to be ready to transmit the ninth frame at pretty much the same moment that the ACK for the first frame arrives. The algorithm that allows us to

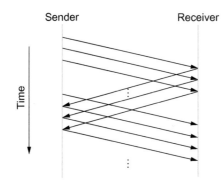

Time

Sender   Receiver

■ FIGURE 2.19 Timeline for the sliding window algorithm.

do this is called *sliding window*, and an illustrative timeline is given in Figure 2.19.

The Sliding Window Algorithm

The sliding window algorithm works as follows. First, the sender assigns a *sequence number*, denoted SeqNum, to each frame. For now, let's ignore the fact that SeqNum is implemented by a finite-size header field and instead assume that it can grow infinitely large. The sender maintains three variables: The *send window size*, denoted SWS, gives the upper bound on the number of outstanding (unacknowledged) frames that the sender can transmit; LAR denotes the sequence number of the *last acknowledgment received*; and LFS denotes the sequence number of the *last frame sent*. The sender also maintains the following invariant:

$$LFS - LAR \le SWS$$

This situation is illustrated in Figure 2.20.

When an acknowledgment arrives, the sender moves LAR to the right, thereby allowing the sender to transmit another frame. Also, the sender associates a timer with each frame it transmits, and it retransmits the frame should the timer expire before an ACK is received. Notice that the sender has to be willing to buffer up to SWS frames since it must be prepared to retransmit them until they are acknowledged.

The receiver maintains the following three variables: The *receive window size*, denoted RWS, gives the upper bound on the number of out-of-order frames that the receiver is willing to accept; LAF denotes the sequence number of the *largest acceptable frame*; and LFR denotes the

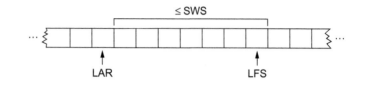

■ FIGURE 2.20 Sliding window on sender.

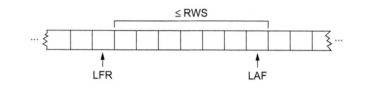

■ FIGURE 2.21 Sliding window on receiver.

sequence number of the *last frame received*. The receiver also maintains the following invariant:

$$\text{LAF} - \text{LFR} \leq \text{RWS}$$

This situation is illustrated in Figure 2.21.

When a frame with sequence number SeqNum arrives, the receiver takes the following action. If SeqNum ≤ LFR or SeqNum > LAF, then the frame is outside the receiver's window and it is discarded. If LFR < SeqNum ≤ LAF, then the frame is within the receiver's window and it is accepted. Now the receiver needs to decide whether or not to send an ACK. Let SeqNumToAck denote the largest sequence number not yet acknowledged, such that all frames with sequence numbers less than or equal to SeqNumToAck have been received. The receiver acknowledges the receipt of SeqNumToAck, even if higher numbered packets have been received. This acknowledgment is said to be cumulative. It then sets LFR = SeqNumToAck and adjusts LAF = LFR + RWS.

For example, suppose LFR = 5 (i.e., the last ACK the receiver sent was for sequence number 5), and RWS = 4. This implies that LAF = 9. Should frames 7 and 8 arrive, they will be buffered because they are within the receiver's window. However, no ACK needs to be sent since frame 6 has yet to arrive. Frames 7 and 8 are said to have arrived out of order. (Technically, the receiver could resend an ACK for frame 5 when frames 7 and 8 arrive.)

Should frame 6 then arrive—perhaps it is late because it was lost the first time and had to be retransmitted, or perhaps it was simply delayed[4]—the receiver acknowledges frame 8, bumps LFR to 8, and sets LAF to 12. If frame 6 was in fact lost, then a timeout will have occurred at the sender, causing it to retransmit frame 6.

We observe that when a timeout occurs, the amount of data in transit decreases, since the sender is unable to advance its window until frame 6 is acknowledged. This means that when packet losses occur, this scheme is no longer keeping the pipe full. The longer it takes to notice that a packet loss has occurred, the more severe this problem becomes.

Notice that, in this example, the receiver could have sent a *negative acknowledgment* (NAK) for frame 6 as soon as frame 7 arrived. However, this is unnecessary since the sender's timeout mechanism is sufficient to catch this situation, and sending NAKs adds additional complexity to the receiver. Also, as we mentioned, it would have been legitimate to send additional acknowledgments of frame 5 when frames 7 and 8 arrived; in some cases, a sender can use duplicate ACKs as a clue that a frame was lost. Both approaches help to improve performance by allowing early detection of packet losses.

Yet another variation on this scheme would be to use *selective acknowledgments*. That is, the receiver could acknowledge exactly those frames it has received rather than just the highest numbered frame received in order. So, in the above example, the receiver could acknowledge the receipt of frames 7 and 8. Giving more information to the sender makes it potentially easier for the sender to keep the pipe full but adds complexity to the implementation.

The sending window size is selected according to how many frames we want to have outstanding on the link at a given time; SWS is easy to compute for a given delay   bandwidth product.[5] On the other hand, the receiver can set RWS to whatever it wants. Two common settings are RWS = 1, which implies that the receiver will not buffer any frames that arrive out of order, and RWS = SWS, which implies that the receiver can

---

[4]It's unlikely that a packet could be delayed in this way on a point-to-point link, but later on we will see this same algorithm used on more complex networks where such delays are possible.

[5]Easy, that is, if we know the delay and the bandwidth. Sometimes we do not, and estimating them well is a challenge to protocol designers. We discuss this further in Chapter 5.

buffer any of the frames the sender transmits. It makes no sense to set RWS > SWS since it's impossible for more than SWS frames to arrive out of order.

Finite Sequence Numbers and Sliding Window

We now return to the one simplification we introduced into the algorithm—our assumption that sequence numbers can grow infinitely large. In practice, of course, a frame's sequence number is specified in a header field of some finite size. For example, a 3-bit field means that there are eight possible sequence numbers, $0 \cdots 7$. This makes it necessary to reuse sequence numbers or, stated another way, sequence numbers wrap around. This introduces the problem of being able to distinguish between different incarnations of the same sequence numbers, which implies that the number of possible sequence numbers must be larger than the number of outstanding frames allowed. For example, stop-and-wait allowed one outstanding frame at a time and had two distinct sequence numbers.

Suppose we have one more number in our space of sequence numbers than we have potentially outstanding frames; that is, SWS $\leq$ MaxSeqNum $-$ 1, where MaxSeqNum is the number of available sequence numbers. Is this sufficient? The answer depends on RWS. If RWS = 1, then MaxSeqNum $\geq$ SWS + 1 is sufficient. If RWS is equal to SWS, then having a MaxSeqNum just one greater than the sending window size is not good enough. To see this, consider the situation in which we have the eight sequence numbers 0 through 7, and SWS = RWS = 7. Suppose the sender transmits frames $0 \ldots 6$, they are successfully received, but the ACKs are lost. The receiver is now expecting frames $7, 0 \ldots 5$, but the sender times out and sends frames $0 \ldots 6$. Unfortunately, the receiver is expecting the second incarnation of frames $0 \ldots 5$ but gets the first incarnation of these frames. This is exactly the situation we wanted to avoid.

It turns out that the sending window size can be no more than half as big as the number of available sequence numbers when RWS = SWS, or stated more precisely,

$$SWS < (MaxSeqNum + 1)/2$$

Intuitively, what this is saying is that the sliding window protocol alternates between the two halves of the sequence number space, just as stop-and-wait alternates between sequence numbers 0 and 1. The only difference is that it continually slides between the two halves rather than discretely alternating between them.

Note that this rule is specific to the situation where RWS = SWS. We leave it as an exercise to determine the more general rule that works for arbitrary values of RWS and SWS. Also note that the relationship between the window size and the sequence number space depends on an assumption that is so obvious that it is easy to overlook, namely that frames are not reordered in transit. This cannot happen on a direct point-to-point link since there is no way for one frame to overtake another during transmission. However, we will see the sliding window algorithm used in a different environment in Chapter 5, and we will need to devise another rule.

Implementation of Sliding Window

The following routines illustrate how we might implement the sending and receiving sides of the sliding window algorithm. The routines are taken from a working protocol named, appropriately enough, Sliding Window Protocol (SWP). So as not to concern ourselves with the adjacent protocols in the protocol graph, we denote the protocol sitting above SWP as the high-level protocol (HLP) and the protocol sitting below SWP as the link-level protocol (LLP).

We start by defining a pair of data structures. First, the frame header is very simple: It contains a sequence number (SeqNum) and an acknowledgment number (AckNum). It also contains a Flags field that indicates whether the frame is an ACK or carries data.

```
typedef u_char SwpSeqno;

typedef struct {
    SwpSeqno   SeqNum;   /* sequence number of this frame */
    SwpSeqno   AckNum;   /* ack of received frame */
    u_char     Flags;    /* up to 8 bits worth of flags */
} SwpHdr;
```

Next, the state of the sliding window algorithm has the following structure. For the sending side of the protocol, this state includes variables LAR and LFS, as described earlier in this section, as well as a queue that holds frames that have been transmitted but not yet acknowledged (sendQ). The sending state also includes a *counting semaphore* called sendWindowNotFull. We will see how this is used below, but generally a semaphore is a synchronization primitive that supports semWait and semSignal operations. Every invocation of semSignal increments the semaphore by 1, and every invocation of semWait decrements s by 1, with the calling process blocked (suspended) should decrementing the semaphore cause its value to become less than 0. A process that is blocked during its call to semWait will be allowed to resume as soon as enough semSignal operations have been performed to raise the value of the semaphore above 0.

For the receiving side of the protocol, the state includes the variable NFE. This is the *next frame expected*, the frame with a sequence number one more that the last frame received (LFR), described earlier in this section. There is also a queue that holds frames that have been received out of order (recvQ). Finally, although not shown, the sender and receiver sliding window sizes are defined by constants SWS and RWS, respectively.

```
typedef struct {
    /* sender side state: */
    SwpSeqno    LAR;            /* seqno of last ACK
                                        received */
    SwpSeqno    LFS;            /* last frame sent */
    Semaphore   sendWindowNotFull;
    SwpHdr      hdr;            /* pre-initialized header */
    struct sendQ_slot {
        Event   timeout;       /* event associated with send
                                    -timeout */
        Msg     msg;
    }   sendQ[SWS];

    /* receiver side state: */
    SwpSeqno    NFE;           /* seqno of next frame
                                    expected */
    struct recvQ_slot {
        int     received;  /* is msg valid? */
        Msg     msg;
    }   recvQ[RWS];
} SwpState;
```

The sending side of SWP is implemented by procedure sendSWP. This routine is rather simple. First, semWait causes this process to block on a semaphore until it is OK to send another frame. Once allowed to proceed, sendSWP sets the sequence number in the frame's header, saves a copy of the frame in the transmit queue (sendQ), schedules a timeout event to handle the case in which the frame is not acknowledged, and sends the frame to the next-lower-level protocol, which we denote as LINK.

One detail worth noting is the call to store_swp_hdr just before the call to msgAddHdr. This routine translates the C structure that holds the SWP header (state-> hdr) into a byte string that can be safely attached to the front of the message (hbuf). This routine (not shown) must translate each integer field in the header into network byte order and remove any padding that the compiler has added to the C structure. The issue of byte order is discussed more fully in Section 7.1, but for now it is enough to assume that this routine places the most significant bit of a multiword integer in the byte with the highest address.

Another piece of complexity in this routine is the use of semWait and the sendWindowNotFull semaphore. sendWindowNotFull is initialized to the size of the sender's sliding window, SWS (this initialization is not shown). Each time the sender transmits a frame, the semWait operation decrements this count and blocks the sender should the count go to 0. Each time an ACK is received, the semSignal operation invoked in deliverSWP (see below) increments this count, thus unblocking any waiting sender.

```
static int
sendSWP(SwpState *state, Msg *frame)
{
    struct sendQ_slot *slot;
    hbuf[HLEN];

    /* wait for send window to open */
    semWait(&state->sendWindowNotFull);
    state->hdr.SeqNum = ++state->LFS;
    slot = &state->sendQ[state->hdr.SeqNum % SWS];
    store_swp_hdr(state->hdr, hbuf);
    msgAddHdr(frame, hbuf, HLEN);
    msgSaveCopy(&slot->msg, frame);
    slot->timeout = evSchedule(swpTimeout, slot,
        SWP_SEND_TIMEOUT);
    return send(LINK, frame);
}
```

Before continuing to the receive side of SWP, we need to reconcile a seeming inconsistency. On the one hand, we have been saying that a high-level protocol invokes the services of a low-level protocol by calling the send operation, so we would expect that a protocol that wants to send a message via SWP would call send(SWP, packet). On the other hand, the procedure that implements SWP's send operation is called sendSWP, and its first argument is a state variable (SwpState). What gives? The answer is that the operating system provides glue code that translates the generic call to send into a protocol-specific call to sendSWP. This glue code maps the first argument to send (the magic protocol variable SWP) into both a function pointer to sendSWP and a pointer to the protocol state that SWP needs to do its job. The reason we have the high-level protocol indirectly invoke the protocol-specific function through the generic function call is that we want to limit how much information the high-level protocol has coded in it about the low-level protocol. This makes it easier to change the protocol graph configuration at some time in the future.

Now we move on to SWP's protocol-specific implementation of the deliver operation, which is given in procedure deliverSWP. This routine actually handles two different kinds of incoming messages: ACKs for frames sent earlier from this node and data frames arriving at this node. In a sense, the ACK half of this routine is the counterpart to the sender side of the algorithm given in sendSWP. A decision as to whether the incoming message is an ACK or a data frame is made by checking the Flags field in the header. Note that this particular implementation does not support piggybacking ACKs on data frames.

When the incoming frame is an ACK, deliverSWP simply finds the slot in the transmit queue (sendQ) that corresponds to the ACK, cancels the timeout event, and frees the frame saved in that slot. This work is actually done in a loop since the ACK may be cumulative. The only other thing to notice about this case is the call to subroutine swpInWindow. This sub-routine, which is given below, ensures that the sequence number for the frame being acknowledged is within the range of ACKs that the sender currently expects to receive.

When the incoming frame contains data, deliverSWP first calls msgStripHdr and load_swp_hdr to extract the header from the frame. Routine load_swp_hdr is the counterpart to store_swp_hdr discussed earlier; it translates a byte string into the C data structure that holds the SWP header. deliverSWP then calls swpInWindow to make sure the sequence number of the frame is within the range of sequence numbers that it expects. If it is, the routine loops over the set of consecutive frames it has received and passes them up to the higher-level protocol by invoking the deliverHLP routine. It also sends a cumulative ACK back to the sender, but does so by looping over the receive queue (it does not use the SeqNumToAck variable used in the prose description given earlier in this section).

```c
static int
deliverSWP(SwpState state, Msg *frame)
{
    SwpHdr    hdr;
    char      *hbuf;

    hbuf = msgStripHdr(frame, HLEN);
    load_swp_hdr(&hdr, hbuf)
    if (hdr->Flags & FLAG_ACK_VALID)
    {
        /* received an acknowledgment---do SENDER side */
        if (swpInWindow(hdr.AckNum, state->LAR + 1,
            state->LFS))
        {
            do
            {
                struct sendQ_slot *slot;

                slot = &state->sendQ[++state->LAR % SWS];
                evCancel(slot->timeout);
                msgDestroy(&slot->msg);
                semSignal(&state->sendWindowNotFull);
            } while (state->LAR != hdr.AckNum);
        }
    }

    if (hdr.Flags & FLAG_HAS_DATA)
    {
        struct recvQ_slot *slot;

        /* received data packet---do RECEIVER side */
```

```
            slot = &state->recvQ[hdr.SeqNum % RWS];
            if (!swpInWindow(hdr.SeqNum, state->NFE,
                state->NFE + RWS - 1))
            {
                /* drop the message */
                return SUCCESS;
            }
            msgSaveCopy(&slot->msg, frame);
            slot->received = TRUE;
            if (hdr.SeqNum == state->NFE)
            {
                Msg m;

                while (slot->received)
                {
                    deliver(HLP, &slot->msg);
                    msgDestroy(&slot->msg);
                    slot->received = FALSE;
                    slot = &state->recvQ[++state->NFE % RWS];
                }
                /* send ACK: */
                prepare_ack(&m, state->NFE - 1);
                send(LINK, &m);
                msgDestroy(&m);
            }
        }
        return SUCCESS;
    }
```

Finally, **swpInWindow** is a simple subroutine that checks to see if a given sequence number falls between some minimum and maximum sequence number.

```
static bool
swpInWindow(SwpSeqno seqno, SwpSeqno min, SwpSeqno max)
{
    SwpSeqno pos, maxpos;
```

```
pos    = seqno - min;     /* pos *should* be in range [0..MAX) */
maxpos = max - min + 1;   /* maxpos is in range [0..MAX] */
return pos < maxpos;
}
```

Frame Order and Flow Control

The sliding window protocol is perhaps the best known algorithm in computer networking. What is easily confusing about the algorithm, however, is that it can be used to serve three different roles. The first role is the one we have been concentrating on in this section—to reliably deliver frames across an unreliable link. (In general, the algorithm can be used to reliably deliver messages across an unreliable network.) This is the core function of the algorithm.

The second role that the sliding window algorithm can serve is to preserve the order in which frames are transmitted. This is easy to do at the receiver—since each frame has a sequence number, the receiver just makes sure that it does not pass a frame up to the next-higher-level protocol until it has already passed up all frames with a smaller sequence number. That is, the receiver buffers (i.e., does not pass along) out-of-order frames. The version of the sliding window algorithm described in this section does preserve frame order, although we could imagine a variation in which the receiver passes frames to the next protocol without waiting for all earlier frames to be delivered. A question we should ask ourselves is whether we really need the sliding window protocol to keep the frames in order, or whether, instead, this is unnecessary functionality at the link level. Unfortunately, we have not yet seen enough of the network architecture to answer this question; we first need to understand how a sequence of point-to-point links is connected by switches to form an end-to-end path.

The third role that the sliding window algorithm sometimes plays is to support *flow control*—a feedback mechanism by which the receiver is able to throttle the sender. Such a mechanism is used to keep the sender from over-running the receiver—that is, from transmitting more data than the receiver is able to process. This is usually accomplished by augmenting the sliding window protocol so that the receiver not only acknowledges frames it has received but also informs the sender of how many frames it has room to receive. The number of frames that the receiver is capable of receiving corresponds to how much free buffer space it has. As in the case of ordered delivery, we need to make sure that flow control is necessary at the link level before incorporating it into the sliding window protocol.

One important concept to take away from this discussion is the system design principle we call *separation of concerns*. That is, you must be careful to distinguish between different functions that are sometimes rolled together in one mechanism, and you must make sure that each function is necessary and being supported in the most effective way. In this particular case, reliable delivery, ordered delivery, and flow control are sometimes combined in a single sliding window protocol, and we should ask ourselves if this is the right thing to do at the link level. With this question in mind, we revisit the sliding window algorithm in Chapter 3 (we show how X.25 networks use it to implement hop-by-hop flow control) and in Chapter 5 (we describe how TCP uses it to implement a reliable byte-stream channel).

2.5.3 Concurrent Logical Channels

The data link protocol used in the ARPANET provides an interesting alternative to the sliding window protocol, in that it is able to keep the pipe full while still using the simple stop-and-wait algorithm. One important consequence of this approach is that the frames sent over a given link are not kept in any particular order. The protocol also implies nothing about flow control.

The idea underlying the ARPANET protocol, which we refer to as *concurrent logical channels*, is to multiplex several logical channels onto a single point-to-point link and to run the stop-and-wait algorithm on each of these logical channels. There is no relationship maintained among the frames sent on any of the logical channels, yet because a different frame can be outstanding on each of the several logical channels the sender can keep the link full.

More precisely, the sender keeps 3 bits of state for each channel: a boolean, saying whether the channel is currently busy; the 1-bit sequence number to use the next time a frame is sent on this logical channel; and the next sequence number to expect on a frame that arrives on this channel. When the node has a frame to send, it uses the lowest idle channel, and otherwise it behaves just like stop-and-wait.

In practice, the ARPANET supported 8 logical channels over each ground link and 16 over each satellite link. In the ground-link case, the header for each frame included a 3-bit channel number and a 1-bit sequence number, for a total of 4 bits. This is exactly the number of bits the sliding window protocol requires to support up to 8 outstanding frames on the link when RWS = SWS.

2.6 ETHERNET AND MULTIPLE ACCESS NETWORKS (802.3)

LAB 01:
CSMA

Developed in the mid-1970s by researchers at the Xerox Palo Alto Research Center (PARC), the Ethernet eventually became the dominant local area networking technology, emerging from a pack of competing technologies. Today, it competes mainly with 802.11 wireless networks but remains extremely popular in campus networks and data centers. The more general name for the technology behind the Ethernet is Carrier Sense, Multiple Access with Collision Detect (CSMA/CD).

As indicated by the CSMA name, the Ethernet is a multiple-access network, meaning that a set of nodes sends and receives frames over a shared link. You can, therefore, think of an Ethernet as being like a bus that has multiple stations plugged into it. The "carrier sense" in CSMA/CD means that all the nodes can distinguish between an idle and a busy link, and "collision detect" means that a node listens as it transmits and can therefore detect when a frame it is transmitting has interfered (collided) with a frame transmitted by another node.

The Ethernet has its roots in an early packet radio network, called Aloha, developed at the University of Hawaii to support computer communication across the Hawaiian Islands. Like the Aloha network, the fundamental problem faced by the Ethernet is how to mediate access to a shared medium fairly and efficiently (in Aloha, the medium was the atmosphere, while in the Ethernet the medium is a coax cable). The core idea in both Aloha and the Ethernet is an algorithm that controls when each node can transmit.

Interestingly, modern Ethernet links are now largely point to point; that is, they connect one host to an Ethernet *switch*, or they interconnect switches. Hence, "multiple access" techniques are not used much in today's Ethernets. At the same time, wireless networks have become enormously popular, so the multiple access technologies that started in Aloha are today again mostly used in wireless networks such as 802.11 (Wi-Fi) networks. These networks will be discussed in Section 2.7.

We will discuss Ethernet switches in the next chapter. For now, we'll focus on how a single Ethernet link works. And even though multi-access Ethernet is becoming a bit of a historical curiosity, the principles of multi-access networks continue to be important enough to warrant some further discussion, which we provide below.

Digital Equipment Corporation and Intel Corporation joined Xerox to define a 10-Mbps Ethernet standard in 1978. This standard then formed the basis for IEEE standard 802.3, which additionally defines a much wider collection of physical media over which an Ethernet can operate, including 100-Mbps, 1-Gbps, and 10-Gbps versions.

2.6.1 Physical Properties

Ethernet segments were originally implemented using coaxial cable of length up to 500 m. (Modern Ethernets use twisted copper pairs, usually a particular type known as "Category 5," or optical fibers, and in some cases can be quite a lot longer than 500 m.) This cable was similar to the type used for cable TV. Hosts connected to an Ethernet segment by tapping into it. A *transceiver*, a small device directly attached to the tap, detected when the line was idle and drove the signal when the host was transmitting. It also received incoming signals. The transceiver, in turn, connected to an Ethernet adaptor, which was plugged into the host. This configuration is shown in Figure 2.22.

Multiple Ethernet segments can be joined together by *repeaters*. A repeater is a device that forwards digital signals, much like an amplifier

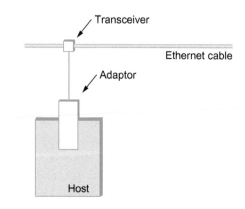

■ FIGURE 2.22 Ethernet transceiver and adaptor.

forwards analog signals. Repeaters understand only bits, not frames; however, no more than four repeaters could be positioned between any pair of hosts, meaning that a classical Ethernet had a total reach of only 2500 m. For example, using just two repeaters between any pair of hosts supports a configuration similar to the one illustrated in Figure 2.23—that is, a segment running down the spine of a building with a segment on each floor.

It's also possible to create a multiway repeater, sometimes called a *hub*, as illustrated in Figure 2.24. A hub just repeats whatever it hears on one port out all its other ports.

Any signal placed on the Ethernet by a host is broadcast over the entire network; that is, the signal is propagated in both directions, and repeaters and hubs forward the signal on all outgoing segments. Terminators attached to the end of each segment absorb the signal and keep it from bouncing back and interfering with trailing signals. The original Ethernet specifications used the Manchester encoding scheme described in Section 2.2, while 4B/5B encoding or the similar 8B/10B scheme is used today on higher speed Ethernets.

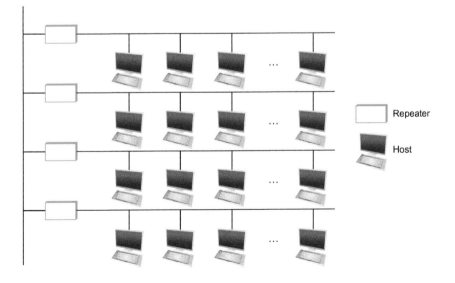

Repeater

Host

■ FIGURE 2.23 Ethernet repeater.

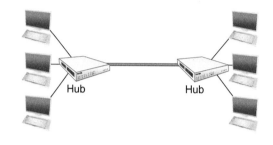

■ FIGURE 2.24 Ethernet hub.

It is important to understand that whether a given Ethernet spans a single segment, a linear sequence of segments connected by repeaters, or multiple segments connected in a star configuration by a hub, data transmitted by any one host on that Ethernet reaches all the other hosts. This is the good news. The bad news is that all these hosts are competing for access to the same link, and, as a consequence, they are said to be in the same *collision domain*. The multi-access part of the Ethernet is all about dealing with the competition for the link that arises in a collision domain.

2.6.2 Access Protocol

We now turn our attention to the algorithm that controls access to a shared Ethernet link. This algorithm is commonly called the Ethernet's *media access control* (MAC). It is typically implemented in hardware on the network adaptor. We will not describe the hardware *per se*, but instead focus on the algorithm it implements. First, however, we describe the Ethernet's frame format and addresses.

Frame Format

Each Ethernet frame is defined by the format given in Figure 2.25.[6] The 64-bit preamble allows the receiver to synchronize with the signal; it is a sequence of alternating 0s and 1s. Both the source and destination hosts are identified with a 48-bit address. The packet type field serves as the demultiplexing key; it identifies to which of possibly many higher-level protocols this frame should be delivered. Each frame contains up to 1500 bytes of data. Minimally, a frame must contain at least 46 bytes of data, even if this means the host has to pad the frame before transmitting it. The reason for this minimum frame size is that the frame must

---

[6]This frame format is from the Digital–Intel–Xerox standard; the 802.3 version differs slightly.

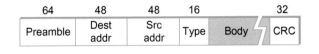

be long enough to detect a collision; we discuss this more below. Finally, each frame includes a 32-bit CRC. Like the HDLC protocol described in Section 2.3.2, the Ethernet is a bit-oriented framing protocol. Note that from the host's perspective, an Ethernet frame has a 14-byte header: two 6-byte addresses and a 2-byte type field. The sending adaptor attaches the preamble and CRC before transmitting, and the receiving adaptor removes them.

Addresses

Each host on an Ethernet—in fact, every Ethernet host in the world—has a unique Ethernet address. Technically, the address belongs to the adaptor, not the host; it is usually burned into ROM. Ethernet addresses are typically printed in a form humans can read as a sequence of six numbers separated by colons. Each number corresponds to 1 byte of the 6-byte address and is given by a pair of hexadecimal digits, one for each of the 4-bit nibbles in the byte; leading 0s are dropped. For example, 8:0:2b:e4:b1:2 is the human-readable representation of Ethernet address

00001000 00000000 00101011 11100100 10110001 00000010

To ensure that every adaptor gets a unique address, each manufacturer of Ethernet devices is allocated a different prefix that must be prepended to the address on every adaptor they build. For example, Advanced Micro Devices has been assigned the 24-bit prefix x080020 (or 8:0:20). A given manufacturer then makes sure the address suffixes it produces are unique.

Each frame transmitted on an Ethernet is received by every adaptor connected to that Ethernet. Each adaptor recognizes those frames addressed to its address and passes only those frames on to the host. (An adaptor can also be programmed to run in *promiscuous* mode, in which case it delivers all received frames to the host, but this is not the normal mode.) In addition to these *unicast* addresses, an Ethernet address consisting of all 1s is treated as a *broadcast* address; all adaptors pass frames addressed to the broadcast address up to the host. Similarly, an address that has the first bit set to 1 but is not the broadcast address is called a *multicast* address. A given host can program its adaptor to accept some set of multicast addresses. Multicast addresses are used to send messages to some subset of the hosts on an Ethernet (e.g., all file servers). To summarize, an Ethernet adaptor receives all frames and accepts

- Frames addressed to its own address
- Frames addressed to the broadcast address
- Frames addressed to a multicast address, if it has been instructed to listen to that address
- All frames, if it has been placed in promiscuous mode

It passes to the host only the frames that it accepts.

Transmitter Algorithm

As we have just seen, the receiver side of the Ethernet protocol is simple; the real smarts are implemented at the sender's side. The transmitter algorithm is defined as follows.

When the adaptor has a frame to send and the line is idle, it transmits the frame immediately; there is no negotiation with the other adaptors. The upper bound of 1500 bytes in the message means that the adaptor can occupy the line for only a fixed length of time.

When an adaptor has a frame to send and the line is busy, it waits for the line to go idle and then transmits immediately.[7] The Ethernet is said to be a *1-persistent* protocol because an adaptor with a frame to send transmits with probability 1 whenever a busy line goes idle. In general, a *p-persistent* algorithm transmits with probability $0 \leq p \leq 1$ after a line becomes idle and defers with probability $q = 1 - p$. The reasoning behind choosing a $p < 1$ is that there might be multiple adaptors waiting for the busy line to become idle, and we don't want all of them to begin transmitting at the same time. If each adaptor transmits immediately with a probability of, say, 33%, then up to three adaptors can be waiting to transmit and the odds are that only one will begin transmitting when the line becomes idle. Despite this reasoning, an Ethernet adaptor always transmits immediately after noticing that the network has become idle and has been very effective in doing so.

---

[7]To be more precise, all adaptors wait 9.6 μs after the end of one frame before beginning to transmit the next frame. This is true for both the sender of the first frame as well as those nodes listening for the line to become idle.

To complete the story about p-persistent protocols for the case when $p < 1$, you might wonder how long a sender that loses the coin flip (i.e., decides to defer) has to wait before it can transmit. The answer for the Aloha network, which originally developed this style of protocol, was to divide time into discrete slots, with each slot corresponding to the length of time it takes to transmit a full frame. Whenever a node has a frame to send and it senses an empty (idle) slot, it transmits with probability p and defers until the next slot with probability $q = 1 - p$. If that next slot is also empty, the node again decides to transmit or defer, with probabilities p and q, respectively. If that next slot is not empty—that is, some other station has decided to transmit—then the node simply waits for the next idle slot and the algorithm repeats.

Returning to our discussion of the Ethernet, because there is no centralized control it is possible for two (or more) adaptors to begin transmitting at the same time, either because both found the line to be idle or because both had been waiting for a busy line to become idle. When this happens, the two (or more) frames are said to *collide* on the network. Each sender, because the Ethernet supports collision detection, is able to determine that a collision is in progress. At the moment an adaptor detects that its frame is colliding with another, it first makes sure to transmit a 32-bit jamming sequence and then stops the transmission. Thus, a transmitter will minimally send 96 bits in the case of a collision: 64-bit preamble plus 32-bit jamming sequence.

One way that an adaptor will send only 96 bits—which is sometimes called a *runt frame*—is if the two hosts are close to each other. Had the two hosts been farther apart, they would have had to transmit longer, and thus send more bits, before detecting the collision. In fact, the worst-case scenario happens when the two hosts are at opposite ends of the Ethernet. To know for sure that the frame it just sent did not collide with another frame, the transmitter may need to send as many as 512 bits. Not coincidentally, every Ethernet frame must be at least 512 bits (64 bytes) long: 14 bytes of header plus 46 bytes of data plus 4 bytes of CRC.

Why 512 bits? The answer is related to another question you might ask about an Ethernet: Why is its length limited to only 2500 m? Why not 10 or 1000 km? The answer to both questions has to do with the fact that the farther apart two nodes are, the longer it takes for a frame sent by one to reach the other, and the network is vulnerable to a collision during this time.

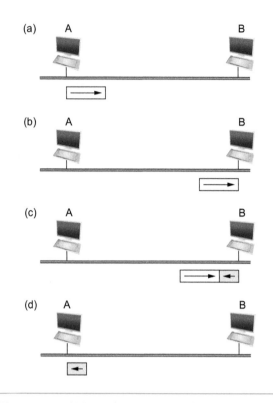

■ **FIGURE 2.26** Worst-case scenario: (a) A sends a frame at time t; (b) A's frame arrives at B at time $t + d$; (c) B begins transmitting at time $t + d$ and collides with A's frame; (d) B's runt (32-bit) frame arrives at A at time $t + 2d$.

Figure 2.26 illustrates the worst-case scenario, where hosts A and B are at opposite ends of the network. Suppose host A begins transmitting a frame at time t, as shown in (a). It takes it one link latency (let's denote the latency as d) for the frame to reach host B. Thus, the first bit of A's frame arrives at B at time $t + d$, as shown in (b). Suppose an instant before host A's frame arrives (i.e., B still sees an idle line), host B begins to transmit its own frame. B's frame will immediately collide with A's frame, and this collision will be detected by host B (c). Host B will send the 32-bit jamming sequence, as described above. (B's frame will be a runt.) Unfortunately, host A will not know that the collision occurred until B's frame reaches it, which will happen one link latency later, at time $t + 2$ d, as shown in (d). Host A must continue to transmit until this time in order to detect the collision. In other words, host A must transmit for 2 d

to be sure that it detects all possible collisions. Considering that a maximally configured Ethernet is 2500 m long, and that there may be up to four repeaters between any two hosts, the round-trip delay has been determined to be 51.2 μs, which on a 10-Mbps Ethernet corresponds to 512 bits. The other way to look at this situation is that we need to limit the Ethernet's maximum latency to a fairly small value (e.g., 51.2 μs) for the access algorithm to work; hence, an Ethernet's maximum length must be something on the order of 2500 m.

Once an adaptor has detected a collision and stopped its transmission, it waits a certain amount of time and tries again. Each time it tries to transmit but fails, the adaptor doubles the amount of time it waits before trying again. This strategy of doubling the delay interval between each retransmission attempt is a general technique known as *exponential backoff*. More precisely, the adaptor first delays either 0 or 51.2 μs, selected at random. If this effort fails, it then waits 0, 51.2, 102.4, or 153.6 μs (selected randomly) before trying again; this is $k \times 51.2$ for $k = 0\ldots3$. After the third collision, it waits $k \times 51.2$ for $k = 0\ldots2^3 - 1$, again selected at random. In general, the algorithm randomly selects a k between 0 and $2^n - 1$ and waits $k \times 51.2$ μs, where n is the number of collisions experienced so far. The adaptor gives up after a given number of tries and reports a transmit error to the host. Adaptors typically retry up to 16 times, although the backoff algorithm caps n in the above formula at 10.

2.6.3 Experience with Ethernet

Because Ethernets have been around for so many years and are so popular, we have a great deal of experience in using them. One of the most important observations people have made about multi-access Ethernets is that they work best under lightly loaded conditions. This is because under heavy loads (typically, a utilization of over 30% is considered heavy on an Ethernet) too much of the network's capacity is wasted by collisions.

To mitigate these concerns, multi-access Ethernets were typically used in a far more conservative way than the standard allows. For example, most Ethernets had fewer than 200 hosts connected to them, which is far fewer than the maximum of 1024. Similarly, most Ethernets were far shorter than 2500 m, with a round-trip delay of closer to 5 μs than 51.2 μs. Another factor that made Ethernets practical is that, even though Ethernet adaptors do not implement link-level flow control, the hosts typically provide an end-to-end flow-control mechanism, as we will see later. As a result, it is rare to find situations in which any one host is continuously pumping frames onto the network.

Finally, it is worth saying a few words about why Ethernets have been so successful, so that we can understand the properties we should emulate with any LAN technology that tries to replace it. First, an Ethernet is extremely easy to administer and maintain: There were no switches in the original Ethernets, no routing or configuration tables to be kept up-to-date, and it is easy to add a new host to the network. It is hard to imagine a simpler network to administer. Second, it is inexpensive: Cable is cheap, and the only other cost is the network adaptor on each host. Ethernet became deeply entrenched for these reasons, and any switch-based approach that aspired to displace it required additional investment in infrastructure (the switches), on top of the cost of each adaptor. As we will see in the next chapter, a switch-based technology did eventually succeed in replacing multi-access Ethernet: switched Ethernet. Retaining the simplicity of administration (and familiarity) was a key reason for this success.

**LAB 02:
WLAN**

2.7 WIRELESS

Wireless technologies differ from wired links in some important ways, while at the same time sharing many common properties. Like wired links, issues of bit errors are of great concern—typically even more so due to the unpredictable noise environment of most wireless links. Framing and reliability also have to be addressed. Unlike wired links, power is a big issue for wireless, especially because wireless links are often used by small mobile devices (like phones and sensors) that have limited access to power (e.g., a small battery). Furthermore, you can't go blasting away at arbitrarily high power with a radio transmitter—there are concerns about interference with other devices and usually regulations about how much power a device may emit at any given frequency.

Wireless media are also inherently multi-access; it's difficult to direct your radio transmission to just a single receiver or to avoid receiving radio signals from any transmitter with enough power in your neighborhood. Hence, media access control is a central issue for wireless links. And, because it's hard to control who receives your signal when you transmit over the air, issues of eavesdropping may also have to be addressed.

LAB APPENDIX A:
Token Ring

Where Are They Now?

TOKEN RINGS

For many years, there were two main ways to build a LAN: Ethernet or token ring. The most prevalent form of token ring was invented by IBM, and standardized as IEEE 802.5. Token rings have a number of things in common with Ethernet: The ring behaves like a single shared medium and employs a distributed algorithm to decide which station can transmit onto that medium at any given time, and every node on a given ring can see all the packets transmitted by other nodes.

The most obvious difference between token ring and Ethernet is the topology; whereas an Ethernet is a bus, the nodes in a token ring form a loop. That is, each node is connected to a pair of neighbors, one upstream and one downstream. The "token" is just a special sequence of bits that circulates around the ring; each node receives and then forwards the token. When a node that has a frame to transmit sees the token, it takes the token off the ring (i.e., it does not forward the special bit pattern) and instead inserts its frame into the ring. Each node along the way simply forwards the frame, with the destination node saving a copy and forwarding the message onto the next node on the ring. When the frame makes its way back around to the sender, this node strips its frame off the ring (rather than continuing to forward it) and reinserts the token. In this way, some node downstream will have the opportunity to transmit a frame. The media access algorithm is fair in the sense that as the token circulates around the ring, each node gets a chance to transmit. Nodes are serviced in a round-robin fashion.

Many different variants of token rings appeared over the decades, with the Fiber Distributed Data Interface (FDDI) being one of the last to see significant deployment. In the end, token rings lost out to the Ethernet, especially with the advent of Ethernet switching and high-speed Ethernet variants (100-Mbit and gigabit Ethernet).

There is a baffling assortment of different wireless technologies, each of which makes different tradeoffs in various dimensions. One simple way to categorize the different technologies is by the data rates they provide and how far apart communicating nodes can be. Other important differences include which part of the electromagnetic spectrum they use (including whether it requires a license) and how much power they consume. In this section, we discuss three prominent wireless technologies:

Table 2.4 Overview of Leading Wireless Technologies

	Bluetooth (802.15.1)	Wi-Fi (802.11)	3G Cellular
Typical link length	10 m	100 m	Tens of kilometers
Typical data rate	2 Mbps (shared)	54 Mbps (shared)	Hundreds of kbps (per connection)
Typical use	Link a peripheral to a computer	Link a computer to a wired base	Link a mobile phone to a wired tower
Wired technology analogy	USB	Ethernet	DSL

Wi-Fi (more formally known as 802.11), Bluetooth®, and the third-generation or "3G" family of cellular wireless standards. Table 2.4 gives an overview of these technologies and how they compare to each other.

You may recall from Section 1.5 that bandwidth sometimes means the width of a frequency band in hertz and sometimes the data rate of a link. Because both these concepts come up in discussions of wireless networks, we're going to use *bandwidth* here in its stricter sense—width of a frequency band—and use the term *data rate* to describe the number of bits per second that can be sent over the link, as in Table 2.4.

Because wireless links all share the same medium, the challenge is to share that medium efficiently, without unduly interfering with each other. Most of this sharing is accomplished by dividing it up along the dimensions of frequency and space. Exclusive use of a particular frequency in a particular geographic area may be allocated to an individual entity such as a corporation. It is feasible to limit the area covered by an electromagnetic signal because such signals weaken, or *attenuate*, with the distance from their origin. To reduce the area covered by your signal, reduce the power of your transmitter.

These allocations are typically determined by government agencies, such as the Federal Communications Commission (FCC) in the United States. Specific bands (frequency ranges) are allocated to certain uses. Some bands are reserved for government use. Other bands are reserved for uses such as AM radio, FM radio, television, satellite communication, and cellular phones. Specific frequencies within these bands are then licensed to individual organizations for use within certain geographical areas. Finally, several frequency bands are set aside for license-exempt usage—bands in which a license is not needed.

Devices that use license-exempt frequencies are still subject to certain restrictions to make that otherwise unconstrained sharing work. Most important of these is a limit on transmission power. This limits the range of a signal, making it less likely to interfere with another signal. For example, a cordless phone (a common unlicensed device) might have a range of about 100 feet.

One idea that shows up a lot when spectrum is shared among many devices and applications is *spread spectrum*. The idea behind spread spectrum is to spread the signal over a wider frequency band, so as to minimize the impact of interference from other devices. (Spread spectrum was originally designed for military use, so these "other devices" were often attempting to jam the signal.) For example, *frequency hopping* is a spread spectrum technique that involves transmitting the signal over a random sequence of frequencies; that is, first transmitting at one frequency, then a second, then a third, and so on. The sequence of frequencies is not truly random but is instead computed algorithmically by a pseudorandom number generator. The receiver uses the same algorithm as the sender and initializes it with the same seed; hence, it is able to hop frequencies in sync with the transmitter to correctly receive the frame. This scheme reduces interference by making it unlikely that two signals would be using the same frequency for more than the infrequent isolated bit.

A second spread spectrum technique, called *direct sequence*, adds redundancy for greater tolerance of interference. Each bit of data is represented by multiple bits in the transmitted signal so that, if some of the transmitted bits are damaged by interference, there is usually enough redundancy to recover the original bit. For each bit the sender wants to transmit, it actually sends the exclusive-OR of that bit and n random bits. As with frequency hopping, the sequence of random bits is generated by a pseudorandom number generator known to both the sender and the receiver. The transmitted values, known as an n-bit *chipping code*, spread the signal across a frequency band that is n times wider than the frame would have otherwise required. Figure 2.27 gives an example of a 4-bit chipping sequence.

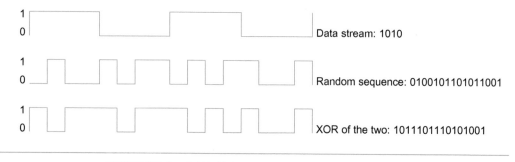

FIGURE 2.27 Example 4-bit chipping sequence.

Different parts of the electromagnetic spectrum have different properties, making some better suited to communication, and some less so. For example, some can penetrate buildings and some cannot. Governments regulate only the prime communication portion: the radio and microwave ranges. As demand for prime spectrum increases, there is great interest in the spectrum that is becoming available as analog television is phased out in favor of digital.[8]

In many wireless networks today we observe that there are two different classes of endpoints. One endpoint, sometimes described as the *base station*, usually has no mobility but has a wired (or at least high-bandwidth) connection to the Internet or other networks, as shown in Figure 2.28. The node at the other end of the link—shown here as a client node—is often mobile and relies on its link to the base station for all of its communication with other nodes.

Observe that in Figure 2.28 we have used a wavy pair of lines to represent the wireless "link" abstraction provided between two devices (e.g., between a base station and one of its client nodes). One of the interesting aspects of wireless communication is that it naturally supports point-to-multipoint communication, because radio waves sent by one device can be simultaneously received by many devices. However, it is often useful to create a point-to-point link abstraction for higher layer protocols, and we will see examples of how this works later in this section.

Note that in Figure 2.28, communication between non-base (client) nodes is routed via the base station. This is in spite of the fact that radio waves emitted by one client node may well be received by other

---

[8]Thanks to advances in video coding and modulation, digital video broadcasts require less spectrum to be allocated for each TV channel.

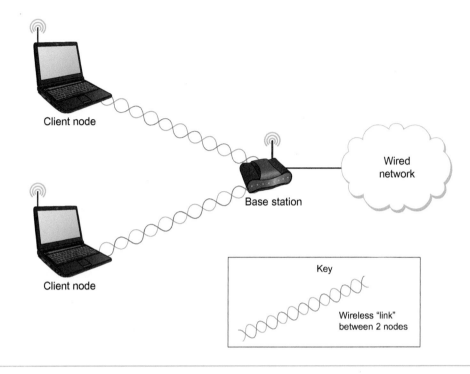

Key

Wireless "link"
between 2 nodes

■ FIGURE 2.28 A wireless network using a base station.

client nodes—the common base station model does not permit direct communication between the client nodes.

This topology implies three qualitatively different levels of mobility. The first level is no mobility, such as when a receiver must be in a fixed location to receive a directional transmission from the base station. The second level is mobility within the range of a base, as is the case with Bluetooth. The third level is mobility between bases, as is the case with cell phones and Wi-Fi.

An alternative topology that is seeing increasing interest is the *mesh* or *ad hoc* network. In a wireless mesh, nodes are peers; that is, there is no special base station node. Messages may be forwarded via a chain of peer nodes as long as each node is within range of the preceding node. This is illustrated in Figure 2.29. This allows the wireless portion of a network to extend beyond the limited range of a single radio. From the point of view of competition between technologies, this allows a shorter-range technology to extend its range and potentially compete with a longer-range technology. Meshes also offer fault tolerance by providing

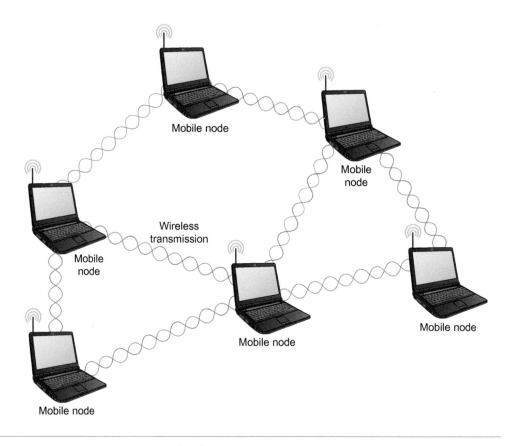

multiple routes for a message to get from point A to point B. A mesh network can be extended incrementally, with incremental costs. On the other hand, a mesh network requires non-base nodes to have a certain level of sophistication in their hardware and software, potentially increasing per-unit costs and power consumption, a critical consideration for battery-powered devices. Wireless mesh networks are of considerable research interest (see the further reading section for some references), but they are still in their relative infancy compared to networks with base stations. Wireless sensor networks, another hot emerging technology, often form wireless meshes.

Now that we have covered some of the common wireless issues, let's take a look at the details of a few common wireless technologies.

2.7.1 **802.11/Wi-Fi**

Most readers will have used a wireless network based on the IEEE 802.11 standards, often referred to as *Wi-Fi*.[9] Wi-Fi is technically a trademark, owned by a trade group called the Wi-Fi Alliance, which certifies product compliance with 802.11. Like Ethernet, 802.11 is designed for use in a limited geographical area (homes, office buildings, campuses), and its primary challenge is to mediate access to a shared communication medium—in this case, signals propagating through space.

Physical Properties

802.11 defines a number of different physical layers that operate in various frequency bands and provide a range of different data rates. At the time of writing, 802.11n provides the highest maximum data rate, topping out at 600 Mbps.

The original 802.11 standard defined two radio-based physical layers standards, one using frequency hopping (over 79 1-MHz-wide frequency bandwidths) and the other using direct sequence spread spectrum (with an 11-bit chipping sequence). Both provided data rates in the 2 Mbps range. The physical layer standard 802.11b was added subsequently. Using a variant of direct sequence, 802.11b provides up to 11 Mbps. These three standards all operated in the license-exempt 2.4-GHz frequency band of the electromagnetic spectrum. Then came 802.11a, which delivers up to 54 Mbps using a variant of FDM called *orthogonal frequency division multiplexing (OFDM)*; 802.11a runs in the license-exempt 5-GHz band. On one hand, this band is less used, so there is less interference. On the other hand, there is more absorption of the signal and it is limited to almost line of sight. 802.11g followed; 802.11g also uses OFDM, delivers up to 54 Mbps, and is backward compatible with 802.11b (and returns to the 2.4-GHz band).

Most recently 802.11n has appeared on the scene, with a standard that was approved in 2009 (although pre-standard products also existed). 802.11n achieves considerable advances in maximum possible data rate using multiple antennas and allowing greater wireless channel bandwidths. The use of multiple antennas is often called *MIMO* for multiple-input, multiple-output.

---

[9]There is some debate over whether Wi-Fi stands for "wireless fidelity," by analogy to Hi-Fi, or whether it is just a catchy name that doesn't stand for anything other than 802.11.

It is common for commercial products to support more than one flavor of 802.11; some base stations support all four variants (a,b, g, and n). This not only ensures compatibility with any device that supports any one of the standards but also makes it possible for two such products to choose the highest bandwidth option for a particular environment.

It is worth noting that while all the 802.11 standards define a *maximum* bit rate that can be supported, they mostly support lower bit rates as well; for example, 802.11a allows for bit rates of 6, 9, 12, 18, 24, 36, 48, and 54 Mbps. At lower bit rates, it is easier to decode transmitted signals in the presence of noise. Different modulation schemes are used to achieve the various bit rates; in addition, the amount of redundant information in the form of error-correcting codes is varied. (See Section 2.4 for an introduction to error-detecting codes.) More redundant information means higher resilience to bit errors at the cost of lowering the effective data rate (since more of the transmitted bits are redundant).

The systems try to pick an optimal bit rate based on the noise environment in which they find themselves; the algorithms for bit rate selection can be quite complex (see the Further Reading section for an example). Interestingly, the 802.11 standards do not specify a particular approach but leave the algorithms to the various vendors. The basic approach to picking a bit rate is to estimate the bit error rate either by directly measuring the signal-to-noise ratio (SNR) at the physical layer or by estimating the SNR by measuring how often packets are successfully transmitted and acknowledged. In some approaches, a sender will occasionally probe a higher bit rate by sending one or more packets at that rate to see if it succeeds.

Collision Avoidance

At first glance, it might seem that a wireless protocol would follow the same algorithm as the Ethernet—wait until the link becomes idle before transmitting and back off should a collision occur—and, to a first approximation, this is what 802.11 does. The additional complication for wireless is that, while a node on an Ethernet receives every other node's transmissions and can transmit and receive at the same time, neither of these conditions holds for wireless nodes. This makes detection of collisions rather more complex. The reason why wireless nodes cannot usually transmit and receive at the same time (on the same frequency) is that the power generated by the transmitter is much higher than any received

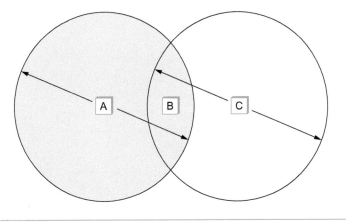

■ FIGURE 2.30 The hidden node problem. Although A and C are hidden from each other, their signals can collide at B. (B's reach is not shown.)

signal is likely to be and so swamps the receiving circuitry. The reason why a node may not receive transmissions from another node is because that node may be too far away or blocked by an obstacle. This situation is a bit more complex than it first appears, as the following discussion will illustrate.

Consider the situation depicted in Figure 2.30, where A and C are both within range of B but not each other. Suppose both A and C want to communicate with B and so they each send it a frame. A and C are unaware of each other since their signals do not carry that far. These two frames collide with each other at B, but unlike an Ethernet, neither A nor C is aware of this collision. A and C are said to be *hidden nodes* with respect to each other.

A related problem, called the *exposed node problem*, occurs under the circumstances illustrated in Figure 2.31, where each of the four nodes is able to send and receive signals that reach just the nodes to its immediate left and right. For example, B can exchange frames with A and C but it cannot reach D, while C can reach B and D but not A. Suppose B is sending to A. Node C is aware of this communication because it hears B's transmission. It would be a mistake, however, for C to conclude that it cannot transmit to anyone just because it can hear B's transmission. For example, suppose C wants to transmit to node D. This is not a problem since C's transmission to D will not interfere with A's ability to receive from B. (It would interfere with A sending to B, but B is transmitting in our example.)

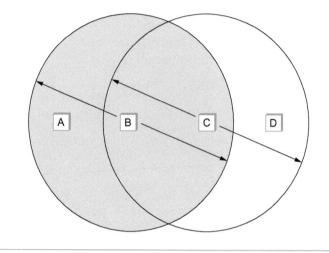

■ FIGURE 2.31 The exposed node problem. Although B and C are exposed to each other's signals, there is no interference if B transmits to A while C transmits to D. (A and D's reaches are not shown.)

802.11 addresses these problems by using CSMA/CA, where the CA stands for collision *avoidance*, in contrast to the collision *detection* of CSMA/CD used on Ethernets. There are a few pieces to make this work.

The Carrier Sense part seems simple enough: Before sending a packet, the transmitter checks if it can hear any other transmissions; if not, it sends. However, because of the hidden terminal problem, just waiting for the absence of signals from other transmitters does not guarantee that a collision will not occur from the perspective of the receiver. For this reason, one part of CSMA/CA is an explicit ACK from the receiver to the sender. If the packet was successfully decoded and passed its CRC at the receiver, the receiver sends an ACK back to the sender.

Note that if a collision does occur, it will render the entire packet useless.[10] For this reason, 802.11 adds an optional mechanism called RTS-CTS (Ready to Send-Clear to Send). This goes some way toward addressing the hidden terminal problem. The sender sends an RTS— a short packet—to the intended receiver, and if that packet is received successfully the receiver responds with another short packet, the CTS. Even though the RTS may not have been heard by a hidden terminal, the CTS probably will be. This effectively tells the nodes within range of the receiver that they should not send anything for a while—the amount of

---

[10]Current research tries to recover partial packets, but that is not yet part of 802.11.

time of the intended transmission is included in the RTS and CTS packets. After that time plus a small interval has passed, the carrier can be assumed to be available again, and another node is free to try to send.

Of course, two nodes might detect an idle link and try to transmit an RTS frame at the same time, causing their RTS frames to collide with each other. The senders realize the collision has happened when they do not receive the CTS frame after a period of time, in which case they each wait a random amount of time before trying again. The amount of time a given node delays is defined by an exponential backoff algorithm very much like that used on the Ethernet (see Section 2.6.2).

After a successful RTS-CTS exchange, the sender sends its data packet and, if all goes well, receives an ACK for that packet. In the absence of a timely ACK, the sender will try again to request usage of the channel again, using the same process described above. By this time, of course, other nodes may again be trying to get access to the channel as well.

Distribution System

As described so far, 802.11 would be suitable for a network with a mesh (*ad hoc*) topology, and development of an 802.11s standard for mesh networks is nearing completion. At the current time, however, nearly all 802.11 networks use a base-station-oriented topology.

Instead of all nodes being created equal, some nodes are allowed to roam (e.g., your laptop) and some are connected to a wired network infrastructure. 802.11 calls these base stations *access points* (APs), and they are connected to each other by a so-called *distribution system*. Figure 2.32 illustrates a distribution system that connects three access points, each of which services the nodes in some region. Each access point operates on some channel in the appropriate frequency range, and each AP will typically be on a different channel than its neighbors.

The details of the distribution system are not important to this discussion—it could be an Ethernet, for example. The only important point is that the distribution network operates at the link layer, the same protocol layer as the wireless links. In other words, it does not depend on any higher-level protocols (such as the network layer).

Although two nodes can communicate directly with each other if they are within reach of each other, the idea behind this configuration is that each node associates itself with one access point. For node A to communicate with node E, for example, A first sends a frame to its access

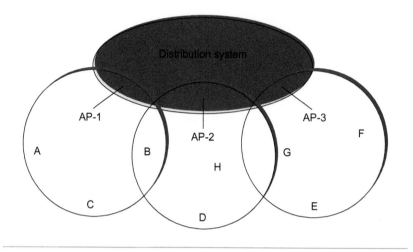

■ FIGURE 2.32 Access points connected to a distribution system.

point (AP-1), which forwards the frame across the distribution system to AP-3, which finally transmits the frame to E. How AP-1 knew to forward the message to AP-3 is beyond the scope of 802.11; it may have used the bridging protocol described in the next chapter (Section 3.1.4). What 802.11 does specify is how nodes select their access points and, more interestingly, how this algorithm works in light of nodes moving from one cell to another.

The technique for selecting an AP is called *scanning* and involves the following four steps:

1. The node sends a Probe frame.
2. All APs within reach reply with a Probe Response frame.
3. The node selects one of the access points and sends that AP an Association Request frame.
4. The AP replies with an Association Response frame.

A node engages this protocol whenever it joins the network, as well as when it becomes unhappy with its current AP. This might happen, for example, because the signal from its current AP has weakened due to the node moving away from it. Whenever a node acquires a new AP, the new AP notifies the old AP of the change (this happens in step 4) via the distribution system.

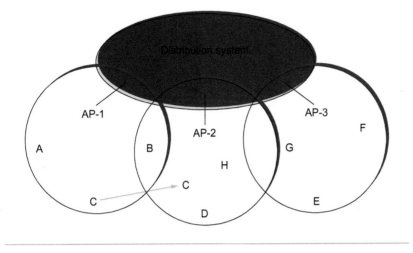

■ FIGURE 2.33 Node mobility.

Consider the situation shown in Figure 2.33, where node C moves from the cell serviced by AP-1 to the cell serviced by AP-2. As it moves, it sends Probe frames, which eventually result in Probe Response frames from AP-2. At some point, C prefers AP-2 over AP-1, and so it associates itself with that access point.

The mechanism just described is called *active scanning* since the node is actively searching for an access point. APs also periodically send a Beacon frame that advertises the capabilities of the access point; these include the transmission rates supported by the AP. This is called *passive scanning*, and a node can change to this AP based on the Beacon frame simply by sending an Association Request frame back to the access point.

Frame Format

Most of the 802.11 frame format, which is depicted in Figure 2.34, is exactly what we would expect. The frame contains the source and destination node addresses, each of which is 48 bits long; up to 2312 bytes of data; and a 32-bit CRC. The Control field contains three subfields of interest (not shown): a 6-bit Type field that indicates whether the frame carries data, is an RTS or CTS frame, or is being used by the scanning algorithm, and a pair of 1-bit fields—called ToDS and FromDS—that are described below.

The peculiar thing about the 802.11 frame format is that it contains four, rather than two, addresses. How these addresses are interpreted

16	16	48	48	48	16	48	0–18,496	32
Control	Duration	Addr1	Addr2	Addr3	SeqCtrl	Addr4	Payload	CRC

■ FIGURE 2.34 802.11 frame format.

depends on the settings of the ToDS and FromDS bits in the frame's Control field. This is to account for the possibility that the frame had to be forwarded across the distribution system, which would mean that the original sender is not necessarily the same as the most recent transmitting node. Similar reasoning applies to the destination address. In the simplest case, when one node is sending directly to another, both the DS bits are 0, Addr1 identifies the target node, and Addr2 identifies the source node. In the most complex case, both DS bits are set to 1, indicating that the message went from a wireless node onto the distribution system, and then from the distribution system to another wireless node. With both bits set, Addr1 identifies the ultimate destination, Addr2 identifies the immediate sender (the one that forwarded the frame from the distribution system to the ultimate destination), Addr3 identifies the intermediate destination (the one that accepted the frame from a wireless node and forwarded it across the distribution system), and Addr4 identifies the original source. In terms of the example given in Figure 2.32, Addr1 corresponds to E, Addr2 identifies AP-3, Addr3 corresponds to AP-1, and Addr4 identifies A.

2.7.2 Bluetooth® (802.15.1)

Bluetooth fills the niche of very short range communication between mobile phones, PDAs, notebook computers, and other personal or peripheral devices. For example, Bluetooth can be used to connect a mobile phone to a headset or a notebook computer to a keyboard. Roughly speaking, Bluetooth is a more convenient alternative to connecting two devices with a wire. In such applications, it is not necessary to provide much range or bandwidth. This means that Bluetooth radios can use quite low power transmission, since transmission power is one of the main factors affecting bandwidth and range of wireless links. This matches the target applications for Bluetooth-enabled devices—most of them are battery powered (such as the ubiquitous phone headset) and hence it is important that they not consume much power.[11]

---

[11] And who really wants a high-power radio transmitter in their ear?

Bluetooth operates in the license-exempt band at 2.45 GHz. Bluetooth links have typical bandwidths around 1 to 3 Mbps and a range of about 10 m. For this reason, and because the communicating devices typically belong to one individual or group, Bluetooth is sometimes categorized as a Personal Area Network (PAN).

Bluetooth is specified by an industry consortium called the *Bluetooth Special Interest Group*. It specifies an entire suite of protocols, going beyond the link layer to define application protocols, which it calls *profiles*, for a range of applications. For example, there is a profile for synchronizing a PDA with a personal computer. Another profile gives a mobile computer access to a wired LAN in the manner of 802.11, although this was not Bluetooth's original goal. The IEEE 802.15.1 standard is based on Bluetooth but excludes the application protocols.

The basic Bluetooth network configuration, called a *piconet*, consists of a master device and up to seven slave devices, as shown in Figure 2.35. Any communication is between the master and a slave; the slaves do not communicate directly with each other. Because slaves have a simpler role, their Bluetooth hardware and software can be simpler and cheaper.

Since Bluetooth operates in an license-exempt band, it is required to use a spread spectrum technique (as discussed at the start of this section) to deal with possible interference in the band. It uses frequency-hopping with 79 *channels* (frequencies), using each for 625 μs at a time. This provides a natural time slot for Bluetooth to use for synchronous time division multiplexing. A frame takes up 1, 3, or 5 consecutive time slots. Only the master can start to transmit in odd-numbered slots. A slave can start to transmit in an even-numbered slot—but only in response to a request from the master during the previous slot, thereby preventing any contention between the slave devices.

A slave device can be *parked*; that is, it is set to an inactive, low-power state. A parked device cannot communicate on the piconet; it can only be reactivated by the master. A piconet can have up to 255 parked devices in addition to its active slave devices.

In the realm of very low-power, short-range communication there are a few other technologies besides Bluetooth. One of these is ZigBee®, devised by the ZigBee alliance and standardized as IEEE 802.15.4. It is designed for situations where the bandwidth requirements are low and power consumption must be very low to give very long battery life. It is also intended to be simpler and cheaper than Bluetooth, making it

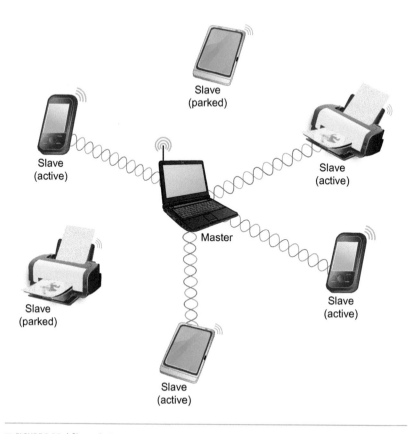

■ FIGURE 2.35 A Bluetooth piconet.

financially feasible to incorporate in cheaper devices such as *sensors*. Sensors are becoming an increasingly important class of networked device, as technology advances to the point where very cheap small devices can be deployed in large quantities to monitor things like temperature, humidity, and energy consumption in a building.

2.7.3 Cell Phone Technologies

While cellular telephone technology had its beginnings around voice communication, data services based on cellular standards have become increasingly popular (thanks in part to the increasing capabilities of mobile phones or *smartphones*). One drawback compared to the technologies just described has tended to be the cost to users, due in part to cellular's use of licensed spectrum (which has historically been sold off to cellular phone operators for astronomical sums). The frequency bands that are used for cellular telephones (and now for cellular data) vary around the world. In Europe, for example, the main bands for cellular phones are at 900 MHz and 1800 MHz. In North America, 850-MHz and 1900-MHz bands are used. This global variation in spectrum usage creates problems for users who want to travel from one part of the world to another and has created a market for phones that can operate at multiple frequencies (e.g., a tri-band phone can operate at three of the four frequency bands mentioned above). That problem, however, pales in comparison to the proliferation of incompatible standards that have plagued the cellular communication business. Only recently have some signs of convergence on a small set of standards appeared. And, finally, there is the problem that, because most cellular technology was designed for voice communication, high-bandwidth data communication has been a relatively recent addition to the standards.

Like 802.11 and WiMAX, cellular technology relies on the use of base stations that are part of a wired network. The geographic area served by a base station's antenna is called a *cell*. A base station could serve a single cell or use multiple directional antennas to serve multiple cells. Cells don't have crisp boundaries, and they overlap. Where they overlap, a mobile phone could potentially communicate with multiple base stations. This is somewhat similar to the 802.11 picture shown in Figure 2.32. At any time, however, the phone is in communication with, and under the control of, just one base station. As the phone begins to leave a cell, it moves into an area of overlap with one or more other cells. The current base station senses the weakening signal from the phone and gives control of the phone to whichever base station is receiving the strongest signal from it. If the phone is involved in a call at the time, the call must be transferred to the new base station in what is called a *handoff*.

As we noted above, there is not one unique standard for cellular, but rather a collection of competing technologies that support data traffic in different ways and deliver different speeds. These technologies are loosely categorized by *generation*. The first generation (1G) was analog, and thus of limited interest from a data communications perspective. Second-generation standards moved to digital and introduced wireless data services, while third generation (3G) allowed greater bandwidths and simultaneous voice and data transmission. Most of the widely deployed mobile phone networks today support some sort of 3G, with 4G starting to appear. Because each of the generations encompasses a family of standards and technologies, it's often a matter of some debate (and marketing interest) as to whether a particular network is 3G or some other generation.

The concept of a third generation was established before there was any implementation of 3G technologies, with the aim of shaping a single international standard that would provide much higher data bandwidth than 2G. Unfortunately, a single standard did not emerge, and this trend seems likely to continue with 4G. Interestingly, however, most of the 3G standards are based on variants of CDMA (Code Division Multiple Access).

CDMA uses a form of spread spectrum to multiplex the traffic from multiple devices into a common wireless channel. Each transmitter uses a pseudorandom chipping code at a frequency that is high relative to the data rate and sends the exclusive OR of the data with the chipping code. Each transmitter's code follows a sequence that is known to the intended receiver—for example, a base station in a cellular network assigns a unique code sequence to each mobile device with which it is currently associated. When a large number of devices broadcast their signals in the same cell and frequency band, the sum of all the transmissions looks like random noise. However, a receiver who knows the code being used by a given transmitter can extract that transmitter's data from the apparent noise.

Compared to other multiplexing techniques, CDMA has some good properties for bursty data. There is no hard limit on how many users can share a piece of spectrum—you just need to make sure they all have unique chipping codes. The bit error rate does however go up with increasing numbers of concurrent transmitters. This makes it very well suited for applications where many users exist but at any given instant many of them are not transmitting—which pretty well describes many data applications such as web surfing. And, in practical systems when it is hard to achieve very tight synchronization among all the mobile handsets, CDMA achieves better spectral efficiency (i.e., it gets closer to the theoretical limits of the Shannon–Hartley theorem) than other multiplexing schemes like TDMA.

Cross-Layer Issues in Wireless

One interesting aspect of wireless networks that has received a great deal of attention in the research community in recent years is the way they challenge the conventions of layered protocol architectures. For example, the 802.11 standards enable you to create a link abstraction that connects one node to another in what appears to be a point-to-point manner. Having done that, any higher layer protocol can just treat the link like any other point-to-point link. But is that the right approach?

Consider, for example, three nodes A, B, and C in a row such as shown in Figure 2.30. If we want to get a packet from A to C, a conventional approach would be for A to send a packet to B and B to send the packet to C. But, in reality, the range over which a given node can send packets isn't a nice crisply defined circle as shown here, but rather it drops off slowly with increasing distance. So it may well be that A can send a packet to C with, say, 30% likelihood of success while it can send a packet to B with 80% likelihood of success. So sometimes (30% of the time) there would be no need for B to forward the packet to C, as C would already have it. Hence, it might be nice for C to tell B "Don't bother to forward that packet—I've got it already." Such an approach was actually tested on a wireless testbed called Roofnet near the Massachusetts Institute of Technology and was shown to increase throughput substantially over conventional approaches. But this approach also means that A, B, and C can no longer just act like they are connected by simple links; we have passed information that is specifically related to wireless links up to a higher layer. Some people shout "layer violation" when they see such a thing, while others (like the authors of this book) admire the ingenuity of those who improved performance by thinking beyond traditional layering.

There are countless other examples where passing some information up from the wireless link layer to higher layers can provide benefits; also, it can help to pass information up from the physical layer to the link layer. There is a fine balancing act here. Layering is a great tool—without it, networks would be impossibly difficult to reason about and to construct on a large scale. But we need to be aware that whenever we hide information—which layering does—we might lose something we really would have been better not hiding. We should think of layering (or any other form of abstraction) as a tool rather than an inviolable rule.

Security of Wireless Links

One of the fairly obvious problems of wireless links compared to wires or fibers is that you can't be too sure where your data has gone. You can probably figure out if it was received by the intended receiver, but there is no telling how many other receivers might have also picked up your transmission. So, if you are concerned about the privacy of your data, wireless networks present a challenge.

Even if you are not concerned about data privacy—or perhaps have taken care of it in some other way (see Chapter 8 for discussion of this topic)—you may be concerned about an unauthorized user injecting data into your network. If nothing else, such a user might be able to consume resources that you would prefer to consume yourself, such as the finite bandwidth between your house and your ISP.

For these reasons, wireless networks typically come with some sort of mechanism to control access to both the link itself and the transmitted data. These mechanisms are often categorized as *wireless security*. Security is a large topic in its own right, to which we devote Chapter 8, and we'll look at the details of wireless security in that context in Section 8.4.5.

Satellite Communications

One other form of wireless communication that sees application in certain scenarios is based around the use of satellites. Satellite phones (satphones) use communication satellites as base stations, communicating on frequency bands that have been reserved internationally for satellite use. Consequently, service is available even where there are no cellular base stations. Satellite phones are rarely used where cellular is available, since service is typically much more expensive. (Someone has to pay for putting the satellites into orbit.) Satphones are also larger and heavier than modern cell phones, because of the need to transmit and receive over much longer distances to reach satellites rather than cell phone towers. Satellite communication is more extensively used in television and radio broadcasting, taking advantage of the fact that the signal is broadcast, not point-to-point. High-bandwidth data communication via satellite is commercially available, but its relatively high price (for both equipment and service) limits its use to regions where no alternative is available.

2.8 SUMMARY

This chapter introduced the many and varied types of links that are used to connect users to existing networks and to construct large networks from scratch. While links vary enormously in their detailed characteristics, there are many problems and techniques for solving them that are common. We looked at the five key problems that must be solved so that two or more nodes connected by some medium can exchange messages with each other.

The first problem is to encode the bits that make up a binary message into the signal at the source node and then to recover the bits from the signal at the receiving node. This is the encoding problem, and it is made challenging by the need to keep the sender's and receiver's clocks synchronized. We discussed four different encoding techniques—NRZ, NRZI, Manchester, and 4B/5B—which differ largely in how they encode clock information along with the data being transmitted. One of the key attributes of an encoding scheme is its efficiency, the ratio of signal pulses to encoded bits.

Once it is possible to transmit bits between nodes, the next step is to figure out how to package these bits into frames. This is the framing problem, and it boils down to being able to recognize the beginning and end of each frame. Again, we looked at several different techniques, including byte-oriented protocols, bit-oriented protocols, and clock-based protocols.

Assuming that each node is able to recognize the collection of bits that make up a frame, the third problem is to determine if those bits are in fact correct or if they have possibly been corrupted in transit. This is the error detection problem, and we looked at three different approaches: cyclic redundancy check, two-dimensional parity, and checksums. Of these, the CRC approach gives the strongest guarantees and is the most widely used at the link level.

Given that some frames will arrive at the destination node containing errors and thus will have to be discarded, the next problem is how to recover from such losses. The goal is to make the link appear reliable. The general approach to this problem is called *ARQ* and involves using a combination of acknowledgments and timeouts. We looked at three specific ARQ algorithms: stop-and-wait, sliding window, and concurrent channels. What makes these algorithms interesting is how effectively they use the link, with the goal being to keep the pipe full.

The final problem is not relevant to point-to-point links, but it is the central issue in multiple-access links: how to mediate access to a shared link so that all nodes eventually have a chance to transmit their data. In this case, we looked at a variety of media access protocols—Ethernet and several wireless protocols—that have been put to practical use in building local area networks. Media access in wireless networks is made more complicated by the fact that some nodes may be hidden from each other due to range limitations of radio transmission. Most of the common wireless protocols today designate some nodes as wired or base-station nodes, while the other mobile nodes communicate with a base station. Wireless standards and technologies are rapidly evolving, with mesh networks, in which all nodes communicate as peers, now beginning to emerge.

As the processing power and memory capacity of small, inexpensive, low-power devices have continued to increase, the very concept of an Internet "host" has undergone a significant shift. Whereas the Internet of the 1970s and 1980s was mostly used to connect fixed computers, and today's Internet hosts are often laptops or mobile phones, it is becoming feasible to think of much smaller objects, such as sensors and actuators, as legitimate Internet hosts. These devices are so small and potentially numerous that they have led to the concept of an "Internet of Things"—an Internet in which the majority of objects, ranging from light switches to boxes of inventory in a factory, might be addressable Internet "hosts."

WHAT'S NEXT: "THE INTERNET OF THINGS"

While the concept of networking vast numbers of tiny objects might sound like science fiction (and perhaps dystopian fiction at that), there are many concrete and practical applications of this idea. One of the most popular is the idea of controlling energy consumption through the application of networking to everyday appliances. Light switches, power outlets, and appliances could all be fitted with sensors (to measure electrical load, ambient temperature, etc.) and actuators (e.g., to control when devices are active, such as postponing the use of a washing machine until an off-peak period when electricity is cheaper). This concept often appears under the title of "smart grids" and is actively being pursued by energy companies and equipment vendors today.

Pushing networking out to trillions of small, lower-power, inexpensive, and intermittently connected devices raises a host of technical challenges. As a simple example, the design of IP version 6, which we'll discuss in Chapter 4, was somewhat influenced by the realization that the number of addresses needed may be much larger than the number of conventional computers in the world. Similarly, new routing protocols are being developed to move data efficiently among devices that may have very low energy budgets and unreliable wireless connections to the rest of the world. There are even new operating systems developed specifically to run on tiny devices with limited power, CPU, and memory resources.

Exactly how this "Internet of Things" vision will play out remains to be seen, but at this point it seems clear that the Internet is moving beyond the original vision of just interconnecting computers. The applications that are enabled by interconnecting trillions of smart objects are just beginning to be realized.

■ FURTHER READING

One of the most important contributions in computer networking over the last 20 years is the original paper by Metcalf and Boggs (1976) introducing the Ethernet. Many years later, Boggs, Mogul, and Kent (1988) reported their practical experiences with Ethernet, debunking many of the myths that had found their way into the literature over the years. Both papers are must reading. The third paper laid much of the groundwork for the development of wireless networks including 802.11.

- Metcalf, R., and D. Boggs. Ethernet: Distributed packet switching for local computer networks. *Communications of the ACM* 19(7):395–403, July 1976.
- Boggs, D., J. Mogul, and C. Kent. Measured capacity of an Ethernet. *Proceedings of the SIGCOMM 88 Symposium*, pages 222–234, August 1988.
- Bharghavan, V., A. Demers, S. Shenker, and L. Zhang. MACAW: A media access protocol for wireless LANs. *Proceedings of the SIGCOMM 94 Symposium*, pages 212–225, August 1994.

There are countless textbooks with a heavy emphasis on the lower levels of the network hierarchy, with a particular focus on *telecommunications*—networking from the phone company's perspective. Books by Spragins et al. [SHP91] and Minoli [Min93] are two good examples. Several other books concentrate on various local area network technologies. Of these, Stallings's book is the most comprehensive [Sta00], while Jain [Jai94] gives a good introduction to the low-level details of optical communication.

Wireless networking is a very active area of research, with many novel and interesting papers appearing each year. Gupta and Kumar's paper [GK00] establishes the theory behind capacity of wireless networks. Basagni et al. [BCGS04] provide a good introduction to *ad hoc* wireless networks. Bicket et al. [BABM05] describe the Roofnet wireless mesh network experiment, and Biswas and Morris [BM05] present ExOR, which ran on Roofnet. The latter paper was an early example of using cross-layer information to improve performance of a wireless network. A different use of cross-layer techniques to improve throughput in the face of bit errors is described by Jamieson et al. [JB07]. Wong et al. [WYLB06] look at the problem of how to pick the correct rate of data transmission given all the tradeoffs around error rate and bandwidth in a wireless channel. Katti et al. [KRH$^+$06] established the viability of using network coding to improve the performance of wireless networks.

A recent book by Xiao et al. [XCL10] surveys many aspects of sensor networking. Vasseur and Dunkels [VD10] provide a forward-looking view of how the "Internet of Things" might play out with the adoption of Internet protocols to interconnect sensors and other smart objects.

For an introduction to information theory, Blahut's book is a good place to start [Bla87], along with Shannon's seminal paper on link capacity [Sha48].

For a general introduction to the mathematics behind error codes, Rao and Fujiwara [RF89] is recommended. For a detailed discussion of the mathematics of CRCs in particular, along with some more information about the hardware used to calculate them, see Peterson and Brown [PB61].

Finally, we recommend the following live reference:

- http://standards.ieee.org/: status of various IEEE network-related standards, including Ethernet and 802.11

EXERCISES

1. Show the NRZ, Manchester, and NRZI encodings for the bit pattern shown in Figure 2.36. Assume that the NRZI signal starts out low.

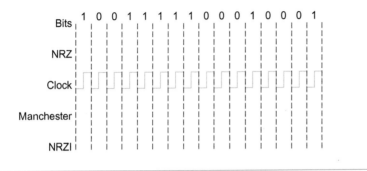

■ **FIGURE 2.36** Diagram for Exercise 1.

2. Show the 4B/5B encoding, and the resulting NRZI signal, for the following bit sequence:

    1110 0101 0000 0011

3. Show the 4B/5B encoding, and the resulting NRZI signal, for the following bit sequence:

    1101 1110 1010 1101 1011 1110 1110 1111

4. In the 4B/5B encoding (Table 2.2), only two of the 5-bit codes used end in two 0s. How many possible 5-bit sequences are there (used by the existing code or not) that meet the stronger restriction of having at most one leading and at most one trailing 0? Could all 4-bit sequences be mapped to such 5-bit sequences?

5. Assuming a framing protocol that uses bit stuffing, show the bit sequence transmitted over the link when the frame contains the following bit sequence:

    110101111101011111101011111110

    Mark the stuffed bits.

6. Suppose the following sequence of bits arrives over a link:

   11010111110101111100101111110110

   Show the resulting frame after any stuffed bits have been removed. Indicate any errors that might have been introduced into the frame.

7. Suppose the following sequence of bits arrives over a link:

   011010111110101001111111011001111110

   Show the resulting frame after any stuffed bits have been removed. Indicate any errors that might have been introduced into the frame.

8. Suppose you want to send some data using the BISYNC framing protocol and the last 2 bytes of your data are DLE and ETX. What sequence of bytes would be transmitted immediately prior to the CRC?

9. For each of the following framing protocols, give an example of a byte/bit sequence that should never appear in a transmission:
   (a) BISYNC
   (b) HDLC

10. Assume that a SONET receiver resynchronizes its clock whenever a 1 bit appears; otherwise, the receiver samples the signal in the middle of what it believes is the bit's time slot.
    (a) What relative accuracy of the sender's and receiver's clocks is required in order to receive correctly 48 zero bytes (one ATM cell's worth) in a row?
    (b) Consider a forwarding station A on a SONET STS-1 line, receiving frames from the downstream end B and retransmitting them upstream. What relative accuracy of A's and B's clocks is required to keep A from accumulating more than one extra frame per minute?

11. Show that two-dimensional parity allows detection of all 3-bit errors.

12. Give an example of a 4-bit error that would not be detected by two-dimensional parity, as illustrated in Figure 2.14. What is the general set of circumstances under which 4-bit errors will be undetected?

13. Show that two-dimensional parity provides the receiver enough information to correct any 1-bit error (assuming the receiver knows only 1 bit is bad), but not any 2-bit error.

14. Show that the Internet checksum will never be 0xFFFF (that is, the final value of sum will not be 0x0000) unless every byte in the buffer is 0. (Internet specifications in fact require that a checksum of 0x0000 be transmitted as 0xFFFF; the value 0x0000 is then reserved for an omitted checksum. Note that, in ones complement arithmetic, 0x0000 and 0xFFFF are both representations of the number 0.)

15. Prove that the Internet checksum computation shown in the text is independent of byte order (host order or network order) except that the bytes in the final checksum should be swapped later to be in the correct order. Specifically, show that the sum of 16-bit words can be computed in either byte order. For example, if the one's complement sum (denoted by $+'$) of 16-bit words is represented as follows,

$$[A,B] +' [C,D] +' \quad +' [Y,Z]$$

the following swapped sum is the same as the original sum above:

$$[B,A] +' [D,C] +' \quad +' [Z,Y]$$

16. Suppose that one byte in a buffer covered by the Internet checksum algorithm needs to be decremented (e.g., a header hop count field). Give an algorithm to compute the revised checksum without rescanning the entire buffer. Your algorithm should consider whether the byte in question is low order or high order.

17. Show that the Internet checksum can be computed by first taking the 32-bit ones complement sum of the buffer in 32-bit units, then taking the 16-bit ones complement sum of the upper and lower halfwords, and finishing as before by complementing the result. (To take a 32-bit ones complement sum on 32-bit twos complement hardware, you need access to the "overflow" bit.)

18. Suppose we want to transmit the message 11100011 and protect it from errors using the CRC polynomial $x^3 + 1$.
    (a) Use polynomial long division to determine the message that should be transmitted.

(b) Suppose the leftmost bit of the message is inverted due to noise on the transmission link. What is the result of the receiver's CRC calculation? How does the receiver know that an error has occurred?

19. Suppose we want to transmit the message 1011 0010 0100 1011 and protect it from errors using the CRC8 polynomial $x^8 + x^2 + x^1 + 1$.

    (a) Use polynomial long division to determine the message that should be transmitted.

    (b) Suppose the leftmost bit of the message is inverted due to noise on the transmission link. What is the result of the receiver's CRC calculation? How does the receiver know that an error has occurred?

20. The CRC algorithm as presented in this chapter requires lots of bit manipulations. It is, however, possible to do polynomial long division taking multiple bits at a time, via a table-driven method, that enables efficient software implementations of CRC. We outline the strategy here for long division 3 bits at a time (see Table 2.5); in practice, we would divide 8 bits at a time, and the table would have 256 entries.

    Let the divisor polynomial $C = C(x)$ be $x^3 + x^2 + 1$, or 1101. To build the table for C, we take each 3-bit sequence, p, append three trailing 0s, and then find the quotient $q = p^\frown 000 \quad C$,

Table 2.5 Table-Driven CRC Calculation

p	$q = p^\frown 000 \div C$	$C \times q$
000	000	000 000
001	001	001 101
010	011	010 ----
011	0---	011 ----
100	111	100 011
101	110	101 110
110	100	110 ----
111	----	111 ----

ignoring the remainder. The third column is the product $C \quad q$, the first 3 bits of which should equal p.

(a) Verify, for $p = 110$, that the quotients $p \frown 000 \quad C$ and $p \frown 111 \quad C$ are the same; that is, it doesn't matter what the trailing bits are.

(b) Fill in the missing entries in the table.

(c) Use the table to divide 101 001 011 001 100 by C. Hint: The first 3 bits of the dividend are $p = 101$, so from the table the corresponding first 3 bits of the quotient are $q = 110$. Write the 110 above the second 3 bits of the dividend, and subtract $C \quad q = 101\ 110$, again from the table, from the first 6 bits of the dividend. Keep going in groups of 3 bits. There should be no remainder.

21. With 1 parity bit we can detect all 1-bit errors. Show that at least one generalization fails, as follows:

(a) Show that if messages m are 8 bits long, then there is no error detection code $e = e(m)$ of size 2 bits that can detect all 2-bit errors. Hint: Consider the set M of all 8-bit messages with a single 1 bit; note that any message from M can be transmuted into any other with a 2-bit error, and show that some pair of messages m_1 and m_2 in M must have the same error code e.

(b) Find an N (not necessarily minimal) such that no 32-bit error detection code applied to N-bit blocks can detect all errors altering up to 8 bits.

22. Consider an ARQ protocol that uses only negative acknowledgments (NAKs), but no positive acknowledgments (ACKs). Describe what timeouts would have to be scheduled. Explain why an ACK-based protocol is usually preferred to a NAK-based protocol.

23. Consider an ARQ algorithm running over a 40-km point-to-point fiber link.

(a) Compute the one-way propagation delay for this link, assuming that the speed of light is $2 \quad 10^8$ m/s in the fiber.

(b) Suggest a suitable timeout value for the ARQ algorithm to use.

(c) Why might it still be possible for the ARQ algorithm to time out and retransmit a frame, given this timeout value?

24. Suppose you are designing a sliding window protocol for a 1-Mbps point-to-point link to the moon, which has a one-way latency of 1.25 seconds. Assuming that each frame carries 1 KB of data, what is the minimum number of bits you need for the sequence number?

✓ 25. Suppose you are designing a sliding window protocol for a 1-Mbps point-to-point link to the stationary satellite revolving around the Earth at an altitude of 3×10^4 km. Assuming that each frame carries 1 KB of data, what is the minimum number of bits you need for the sequence number in the following cases? Assume the speed of light is 3×10^8 m/s.

    (a) RWS=1

    (b) RWS=SWS

26. The text suggests that the sliding window protocol can be used to implement flow control. We can imagine doing this by having the receiver delay ACKs, that is, not send the ACK until there is free buffer space to hold the next frame. In doing so, each ACK would simultaneously acknowledge the receipt of the last frame and tell the source that there is now free buffer space available to hold the next frame. Explain why implementing flow control in this way is not a good idea.

27. Implicit in the stop-and-wait scenarios of Figure 2.17 is the notion that the receiver will retransmit its ACK immediately on receipt of the duplicate data frame. Suppose instead that the receiver keeps its own timer and retransmits its ACK only after the next expected frame has not arrived within the timeout interval. Draw timelines illustrating the scenarios in Figure 2.17(b) to (d); assume the receiver's timeout value is twice the sender's. Also redraw (c) assuming the receiver's timeout value is half the sender's.

28. In stop-and-wait transmission, suppose that both sender and receiver retransmit their last frame immediately on receipt of a duplicate ACK or data frame; such a strategy is superficially reasonable because receipt of such a duplicate is most likely to mean the other side has experienced a timeout.

    (a) Draw a timeline showing what will happen if the first data frame is somehow duplicated, but no frame is lost. How long will the duplications continue? This situation is known as the Sorcerer's Apprentice bug.

(b) Suppose that, like data, ACKs are retransmitted if there is no response within the timeout period. Suppose also that both sides use the same timeout interval. Identify a reasonably likely scenario for triggering the Sorcerer's Apprentice bug.

29. Give some details of how you might augment the sliding window protocol with flow control by having ACKs carry additional information that reduces the SWS as the receiver runs out of buffer space. Illustrate your protocol with a timeline for a transmission; assume the initial SWS and RWS are 4, the link speed is instantaneous, and the receiver can free buffers at the rate of one per second (i.e., the receiver is the bottleneck). Show what happens at $T = 0, T = 1, \ldots, T = 4$ seconds.

30. Describe a protocol combining the sliding window algorithm with selective ACKs. Your protocol should retransmit promptly, but not if a frame simply arrives one or two positions out of order. Your protocol should also make explicit what happens if several consecutive frames are lost.

31. Draw a timeline diagram for the sliding window algorithm with SWS = RWS = 3 frames, for the following two situations. Use a timeout interval of about 2 × RTT.

    (a) Frame 4 is lost.

    (b) Frames 4 to 6 are lost.

32. Draw a timeline diagram for the sliding window algorithm with SWS = RWS = 4 frames in the following two situations. Assume the receiver sends a duplicate acknowledgment if it does not receive the expected frame. For example, it sends DUPACK[2] when it expects to see Frame[2] but receives Frame[3] instead. Also, the receiver sends a cumulative acknowledgment after it receives all the outstanding frames. For example, it sends ACK[5] when it receives the lost frame Frame[2] after it already received Frame[3], Frame[4], and Frame[5]. Use a timeout interval of about 2 × RTT.

    (a) Frame 2 is lost. Retransmission takes place upon timeout (as usual).

(b) Frame 2 is lost. Retransmission takes place either upon receipt of the first DUPACK or upon timeout. Does this scheme reduce the transaction time? (Note that some end-to-end protocols, such as variants of TCP, use similar schemes for fast retransmission.)

33. Suppose that we attempt to run the sliding window algorithm with SWS = RWS = 3 and with MaxSeqNum = 5. The Nth packet DATA[N] thus actually contains N mod 5 in its sequence number field. Give an example in which the algorithm becomes confused; that is, a scenario in which the receiver expects DATA[5] and accepts DATA[0]—which has the same transmitted sequence number—in its stead. No packets may arrive out of order. Note that this implies MaxSeqNum 6 is necessary as well as sufficient.

34. Consider the sliding window algorithm with SWS = RWS = 3, with no out-of-order arrivals and with infinite-precision sequence numbers.
    (a) Show that if DATA[6] is in the receive window, then DATA[0] (or in general any older data) cannot arrive at the receiver (and hence that MaxSeqNum = 6 would have sufficed).
    (b) Show that if ACK[6] may be sent (or, more literally, that DATA[5] is in the sending window), then ACK[2] (or earlier) cannot be received.
       These amount to a proof of the formula given in Section 2.5.2, particularized to the case SWS = 3. Note that part (b) implies that the scenario of the previous problem cannot be reversed to involve a failure to distinguish ACK[0] and ACK[5].

35. Suppose that we run the sliding window algorithm with SWS = 5 and RWS = 3, and no out-of-order arrivals.
    (a) Find the smallest value for MaxSeqNum. You may assume that it suffices to find the smallest MaxSeqNum such that if DATA[MaxSeqNum] is in the receive window, then DATA[0] can no longer arrive.
    (b) Give an example showing that MaxSeqNum 1 is not sufficient.
    (c) State a general rule for the minimum MaxSeqNum in terms of SWS and RWS.

36. Suppose A is connected to B via an intermediate router R, as shown in Figure 2.37. The A–R and R–B links each accept and transmit only one packet per second in each direction (so two packets take 2 seconds), and the two directions transmit independently. Assume A sends to B using the sliding window protocol with SWS = 4.

    (a) For Time = 0, 1, 2, 3, 4, 5, state what packets arrive at and leave each node, or label them on a timeline.

    (b) What happens if the links have a propagation delay of 1.0 second, but accept immediately as many packets as are offered (i.e., latency = 1 second but bandwidth is infinite)?

37. Suppose A is connected to B via an intermediate router R, as in the previous problem. The A–R link is instantaneous, but the R–B link transmits only one packet each second, one at a time (so two packets take 2 seconds). Assume A sends to B using the sliding window protocol with SWS = 4. For Time = 0, 1, 2, 3, 4, state what packets arrive at and are sent from A and B. How large does the queue at R grow?

38. Consider the situation in the previous exercise, except this time assume that the router has a queue size of 1; that is, it can hold one packet in addition to the one it is sending (in each direction). Let A's timeout be 5 seconds, and let SWS again be 4. Show what happens at each second from Time = 0 until all four packets from the first window-full are successfully delivered.

39. What kind of problems can arise when two hosts on the same Ethernet share the same hardware address? Describe what happens and why that behavior is a problem.

40. The 1982 Ethernet specification allowed between any two stations up to 1500 m of coaxial cable, 1000 m of other point-to-point link cable, and two repeaters. Each station or repeater connects to the coaxial cable via up to 50 m of "drop

Table 2.6 Typical Delays Associated with Various Devices (Exercise 40)

Item	Delay
Coaxial cable	Propagation speed .77c
Link/drop cable	Propagation speed .65c
Repeaters	Approximately 0.6 μs each
Transceivers	Approximately 0.2 μs each

cable." Typical delays associated with each device are given in Table 2.6 (where $c =$ speed of light in a vacuum $= 3 \times 10^8$ m/s). What is the worst-case round-trip propagation delay, measured in bits, due to the sources listed? (This list is not complete; other sources of delay include sense time and signal rise time.)

41. Coaxial cable Ethernet was limited to a maximum of 500 m between repeaters, which regenerate the signal to 100% of its original amplitude. Along one 500-m segment, the signal could decay to no less than 14% of its original value (8.5 dB). Along 1500 m, then, the decay might be $(0.14)^3 = 0.3\%$. Such a signal, even along 2500 m, is still strong enough to be read; why then are repeaters required every 500 m?

42. Suppose the round-trip propagation delay for Ethernet is 46.4 μs. This yields a minimum packet size of 512 bits (464 bits corresponding to propagation delay + 48 bits of jam signal).
    (a) What happens to the minimum packet size if the delay time is held constant, and the signalling rate rises to 100 Mbps?
    (b) What are the drawbacks to so large a minimum packet size?
    (c) If compatibility were not an issue, how might the specifications be written so as to permit a smaller minimum packet size?

43. Let A and B be two stations attempting to transmit on an Ethernet. Each has a steady queue of frames ready to send; A's frames will be numbered A_1, A_2, and so on, and B's similarly. Let $T = 51.2$ μs be the exponential backoff base unit.
    Suppose A and B simultaneously attempt to send frame 1, collide, and happen to choose backoff times of $0 \times T$ and $1 \times T$, respectively, meaning A wins the race and transmits A_1 while B

waits. At the end of this transmission, B will attempt to retransmit B_1 while A will attempt to transmit A_2. These first attempts will collide, but now A backs off for either $0 \times T$ or $1 \times T$, while B backs off for time equal to one of $0 \times T, \dots, 3 \times T$.

(a) Give the probability that A wins this second backoff race immediately after this first collision; that is, A's first choice of backoff time $k \times 51.2$ is less than B's.

(b) Suppose A wins this second backoff race. A transmits A_3, and when it is finished, A and B collide again as A tries to transmit A_4 and B tries once more to transmit B_1. Give the probability that A wins this third backoff race immediately after the first collision.

(c) Give a reasonable lower bound for the probability that A wins all the remaining backoff races.

(d) What then happens to the frame B_1?

This scenario is known as the Ethernet *capture effect*.

44. Suppose the Ethernet transmission algorithm is modified as follows: After each successful transmission attempt, a host waits one or two slot times before attempting to transmit again, and otherwise backs off the usual way.

(a) Explain why the capture effect of the previous exercise is now much less likely.

(b) Show how the strategy above can now lead to a pair of hosts capturing the Ethernet, alternating transmissions, and locking out a third.

(c) Propose an alternative approach, for example, by modifying the exponential backoff. What aspects of a station's history might be used as parameters to the modified backoff?

45. Ethernets use Manchester encoding. Assuming that hosts sharing the Ethernet are not perfectly synchronized, why does this allow collisions to be detected soon after they occur, without waiting for the CRC at the end of the packet?

46. Suppose A, B, and C all make their first carrier sense, as part of an attempt to transmit, while a fourth station D is transmitting. Draw a timeline showing one possible sequence of transmissions, attempts, collisions, and exponential backoff choices. Your timeline should also meet the following criteria: (i) initial

transmission attempts should be in the order A, B, C but successful transmissions should be in the order C, B, A, and (ii) there should be at least four collisions.

47. Repeat the previous exercise, now with the assumption that Ethernet is p-persistent with $p = 0.33$ (that is, a waiting station transmits immediately with probability p when the line goes idle and otherwise defers one 51.2-μs slot time and repeats the process). Your timeline should meet criterion (i) of the previous problem, but in lieu of criterion (ii) you should show at least one collision and at least one run of four deferrals on an idle line. Again, note that many solutions are possible.

☆ 48. Suppose Ethernet physical addresses are chosen at random (using true random bits).
   (a) What is the probability that on a 1024-host network, two addresses will be the same?
   (b) What is the probability that the above event will occur on one or more of 2^{20} networks?
   (c) What is the probability that, of the 2^{30} hosts in all the networks of (b), some pair has the same address?
   Hint: The calculation for (a) and (c) is a variant of that used in solving the so-called Birthday Problem: Given N people, what is the probability that two of their birthdays (addresses) will be the same? The second person has probability $1 - \frac{1}{365}$ of having a different birthday from the first, the third has probability $1 - \frac{2}{365}$ of having a different birthday from the first two, and so on. The probability that all birthdays are different is thus

$$\left(1 - \frac{1}{365}\right) \left(1 - \frac{2}{365}\right) \cdots \left(1 - \frac{N-1}{365}\right)$$

which for smallish N is about

$$1 - \frac{1 + 2 + \cdots + (N-1)}{365}$$

49. Suppose five stations are waiting for another packet to finish on an Ethernet. All transmit at once when the packet is finished and collide.
   (a) Simulate this situation up until the point when one of the five waiting stations succeeds. Use coin flips or some other

genuine random source to determine backoff times. Make the following simplifications: Ignore inter-frame spacing, ignore variability in collision times (so that retransmission is always after an exact integral multiple of the 51.2-µs slot time), and assume that each collision uses up exactly one slot time.

(b) Discuss the effect of the listed simplifications in your simulation versus the behavior you might encounter on a real Ethernet.

50. Write a program to implement the simulation discussed above, this time with N stations waiting to transmit. Again, model time as an integer, T, in units of slot times, and again treat collisions as taking one slot time (so a collision at time T followed by a backoff of $k = 0$ would result in a retransmission attempt at time T + 1). Find the average delay before *one* station transmits successfully, for $N = 20$, $N = 40$, and $N = 100$. Does your data support the notion that the delay is linear in N? Hint: For each station, keep track of that station's NextTimeToSend and CollisionCount. You are done when you reach a time T for which there is only one station with NextTimeToSend == T. If there is no such station, increment T. If there are two or more, schedule the retransmissions and try again.

51. Suppose that N Ethernet stations, all trying to send at the same time, require $N/2$ slot times to sort out who transmits next. Assuming the average packet size is 5 slot times, express the available bandwidth as a function of N.

52. Consider the following Ethernet model. Transmission attempts are at random times with an average spacing of λ slot times; specifically, the interval between consecutive attempts is an exponential random variable $x = -\lambda \log u$, where u is chosen randomly in the interval $0 \le u \le 1$. An attempt at time t results in a collision if there is another attempt in the range from $t - 1$ to $t + 1$, where t is measured in units of the 51.2-µs slot time; otherwise, the attempt succeeds.

(a) Write a program to simulate, for a given value of λ, the average number of slot times needed before a successful transmission, called the *contention interval*. Find the minimum value of the contention interval. Note that you will have to find one attempt past the one that succeeds in order to determine if there was a collision. Ignore retransmissions, which probably do not fit the random model above.

(b) The Ethernet alternates between contention intervals and successful transmissions. Suppose the average successful transmission lasts 8 slot times (512 bytes). Using your minimum length of the contention interval from above, what fraction of the theoretical 10-Mbps bandwidth is available for transmissions?

53. How can a wireless node interfere with the communications of another node when the two nodes are separated by a distance greater than the transmission range of either node?

54. Why is collision detection more complex in wireless networks than in wired networks such as Ethernet?

55. How can hidden terminals be detected in 802.11 networks?

56. Why might a wireless mesh topology be superior to a base station topology for communications in a natural disaster?

57. Why isn't it practical for each node in a sensor net to learn its location by using GPS? Describe a practical alternative.

A SYSTEMS APPROACH

3

A SYSTEMS APPROACH

A SYSTEMS APPROACH

A SYSTEMS APPROACH

A SYSTEMS APPROACH

Internetworking

Nature seems ... to reach many of her ends by long circuitous routes.

–Rudolph Lotze

I n the previous chapter, we saw how to connect one node to another or to an existing network. Many technologies can be used to build "last-mile" links or to connect a modest number of nodes together, but how do we build networks of global scale? A single Ethernet can interconnect no more than 1024 hosts; a point-to-point link connects only two. Wireless networks are limited by the ranges of their radios. To build a global network, we need a way to interconnect these different types of links and networks. The concept of interconnecting different types of networks to

PROBLEM: NOT ALL NETWORKS ARE DIRECTLY CONNECTED

build a large, global network is the core idea of the Internet and is often referred to as *internetworking*.

We can divide the internetworking problem up into a few subproblems. First of all, we need a way to interconnect links. Devices that interconnect links of the same type are often called *switches*, and these devices are the first topic of this chapter. A particularly important class of switches today are those used to interconnect Ethernet segments; these switches are also sometimes called *bridges*. The core job of a switch is to take packets that arrive on an input and *forward* (or *switch*) them to the right output so that they will reach their appropriate destination. There are a variety of ways that the switch can determine the "right" output for a packet, which can be broadly categorized as connectionless and connection-oriented approaches. These two approaches have both found important application areas over the years.

Given the enormous diversity of network types, we also need a way to interconnect disparate networks and links (i.e., deal with *heterogeneity*). Devices that perform this task, once called *gateways*, are now mostly known as *routers*. The protocol that was invented to deal with interconnection of disparate network types, the Internet Protocol (IP), is the topic of our second section.

Once we interconnect a whole lot of links and networks with switches and routers, there are likely to be many different possible ways to get from one point to another. Finding a suitable path or *route* through a network is one of the fundamental problems of networking. Such paths should be efficient (e.g., no longer than necessary), loop free, and able to respond to the fact that networks are not static—nodes may fail or reboot, links may break, and new nodes or links may be added. Our third section looks at some of the algorithms and protocols that have been developed to address these issues.

Once we understand the problems of switching and routing, we need some devices to perform those functions. This chapter concludes with some discussion of the ways switches and routers are built. While many packet switches and routers are quite similar to a general-purpose computer, there are many situations where more specialized designs are used. This is particularly the case at the high end, where there seems to be a never-ending need for bigger and faster routers to handle the ever-increasing traffic load in the Internet's core.

LAB 03:
Switched LANs

3.1 SWITCHING AND BRIDGING

In the simplest terms, a switch is a mechanism that allows us to interconnect links to form a larger network. A switch is a multi-input, multi-output device that transfers packets from an input to one or more outputs. Thus, a switch adds the star topology (see Figure 3.1) to the point-to-point link, bus (Ethernet), and ring topologies established in the last chapter. A star topology has several attractive properties:

- Even though a switch has a fixed number of inputs and outputs, which limits the number of hosts that can be connected to a single switch, large networks can be built by interconnecting a number of switches.

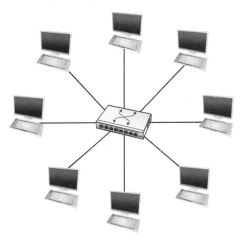

■ FIGURE 3.1 A switch provides a star topology.

- We can connect switches to each other and to hosts using point-to-point links, which typically means that we can build networks of large geographic scope.

- Adding a new host to the network by connecting it to a switch does not necessarily reduce the performance of the network for other hosts already connected.

This last claim cannot be made for the shared-media networks discussed in the last chapter. For example, it is impossible for two hosts on the same 10-Mbps Ethernet segment to transmit continuously at 10 Mbps because they share the same transmission medium. Every host on a switched network has its own link to the switch, so it may be entirely possible for many hosts to transmit at the full link speed (bandwidth), provided that the switch is designed with enough aggregate capacity. Providing high aggregate throughput is one of the design goals for a switch; we return to this topic later. In general, switched networks are considered more *scalable* (i.e., more capable of growing to large numbers of nodes) than shared-media networks because of this ability to support many hosts at full speed.

A switch is connected to a set of links and, for each of these links, runs the appropriate data link protocol to communicate with the node at the other end of the link. A switch's primary job is to receive incoming packets on one of its links and to transmit them on some other link. This function is sometimes referred to as either *switching* or *forwarding*, and in terms of the Open Systems Interconnection (OSI) architecture, it is the main function of the network layer.

The question, then, is how does the switch decide which output link to place each packet on? The general answer is that it looks at the header of the packet for an identifier that it uses to make the decision. The details of how it uses this identifier vary, but there are two common approaches. The first is the *datagram* or *connectionless* approach. The second is the *virtual circuit* or *connection-oriented* approach. A third approach, *source routing*, is less common than these other two, but it does have some useful applications.

One thing that is common to all networks is that we need to have a way to identify the end nodes. Such identifiers are usually called *addresses*. We have already seen examples of addresses in the previous chapter, such as the 48-bit address used for Ethernet. The only requirement for Ethernet addresses is that no two nodes on a network have the same address. This is accomplished by making sure that all Ethernet cards are assigned a *globally unique* identifier. For the following discussions, we assume that each host has a globally unique address. Later on, we consider other useful properties that an address might have, but global uniqueness is adequate to get us started.

Another assumption that we need to make is that there is some way to identify the input and output ports of each switch. There are at least two sensible ways to identify ports: One is to number each port, and the other is to identify the port by the name of the node (switch or host) to which it leads. For now, we use numbering of the ports.

3.1.1 Datagrams

The idea behind datagrams is incredibly simple: You just include in every packet enough information to enable any switch to decide how to get it to its destination. That is, every packet contains the complete destination address. Consider the example network illustrated in Figure 3.2, in which the hosts have addresses A, B, C, and so on. To decide how to forward a packet, a switch consults a *forwarding table* (sometimes called a *routing table*), an example of which is depicted in Table 3.1. This particular table shows the forwarding information that switch 2 needs to forward datagrams in the example network. It is pretty easy to figure out such a table when you have a complete map of a simple network like that depicted here; we could imagine a network operator configuring

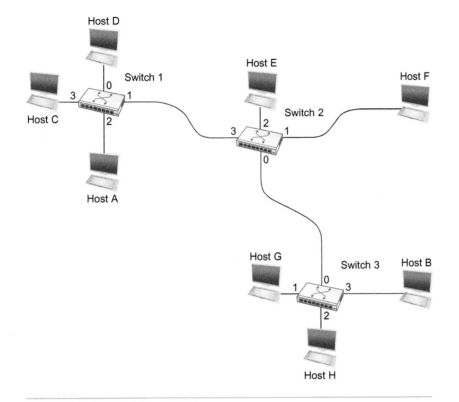

■ FIGURE 3.2 Datagram forwarding: an example network.

Table 3.1 Forwarding Table for Switch 2	
Destination	**Port**
A	3
B	0
C	3
D	3
E	2
F	1
G	0
H	0

the tables statically. It is a lot harder to create the forwarding tables in large, complex networks with dynamically changing topologies and multiple paths between destinations. That harder problem is known as *routing* and is the topic of Section 3.3. We can think of routing as a process that takes place in the background so that, when a data packet turns up, we will have the right information in the forwarding table to be able to forward, or switch, the packet.

Datagram networks have the following characteristics:

- A host can send a packet anywhere at any time, since any packet that turns up at a switch can be immediately forwarded (assuming a correctly populated forwarding table). For this reason, datagram networks are often called *connectionless*; this contrasts with the *connection-oriented* networks described below, in which some *connection state* needs to be established before the first data packet is sent.

- When a host sends a packet, it has no way of knowing if the network is capable of delivering it or if the destination host is even up and running.

- Each packet is forwarded independently of previous packets that might have been sent to the same destination. Thus, two successive packets from host A to host B may follow completely different paths (perhaps because of a change in the forwarding table at some switch in the network).

- A switch or link failure might not have any serious effect on communication if it is possible to find an alternate route around the failure and to update the forwarding table accordingly.

This last fact is particularly important to the history of datagram networks. One of the important design goals of the Internet is robustness to failures, and history has shown it to be quite effective at meeting this goal.[1]

3.1.2 Virtual Circuit Switching

A second technique for packet switching, which differs significantly from the datagram model, uses the concept of a *virtual circuit* (VC).

---

[1]The oft-repeated claim that the ARPANET was built to withstand nuclear attack does not appear to be substantiated by those who actually worked on its design, but robustness to failure of individual components was certainly a goal.

This approach, which is also referred to as a *connection-oriented model*, requires setting up a virtual connection from the source host to the destination host before any data is sent. To understand how this works, consider Figure 3.3, where host A again wants to send packets to host B. We can think of this as a two-stage process. The first stage is "connection setup." The second is data transfer. We consider each in turn.

In the connection setup phase, it is necessary to establish a "connection state" in each of the switches between the source and destination hosts. The connection state for a single connection consists of an entry in a "VC table" in each switch through which the connection passes. One entry in the VC table on a single switch contains:

- A *virtual circuit identifier* (VCI) that uniquely identifies the connection at this switch and which will be carried inside the header of the packets that belong to this connection
- An incoming interface on which packets for this VC arrive at the switch
- An outgoing interface in which packets for this VC leave the switch
- A potentially different VCI that will be used for outgoing packets

The semantics of one such entry is as follows: If a packet arrives on the designated incoming interface and that packet contains the designated VCI value in its header, then that packet should be sent out the specified outgoing interface with the specified outgoing VCI value having been first placed in its header.

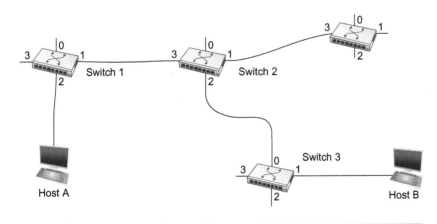

FIGURE 3.3 An example of a virtual circuit network.

Note that the combination of the VCI of packets as they are received at the switch *and* the interface on which they are received uniquely identifies the virtual connection. There may of course be many virtual connections established in the switch at one time. Also, we observe that the incoming and outgoing VCI values are generally not the same. Thus, the VCI is not a globally significant identifier for the connection; rather, it has significance only on a given link (i.e., it has *link-local scope*).

Whenever a new connection is created, we need to assign a new VCI for that connection on each link that the connection will traverse. We also need to ensure that the chosen VCI on a given link is not currently in use on that link by some existing connection.

There are two broad approaches to establishing connection state. One is to have a network administrator configure the state, in which case the virtual circuit is "permanent." Of course, it can also be deleted by the administrator, so a permanent virtual circuit (PVC) might best be thought of as a long-lived or administratively configured VC. Alternatively, a host can send messages into the network to cause the state to be established. This is referred to as *signalling*, and the resulting virtual circuits are said to be *switched*. The salient characteristic of a switched virtual circuit (SVC) is that a host may set up and delete such a VC dynamically without the involvement of a network administrator. Note that an SVC should more accurately be called a *signalled* VC, since it is the use of signalling (not switching) that distinguishes an SVC from a PVC.

Let's assume that a network administrator wants to manually create a new virtual connection from host A to host B.[2] First, the administrator needs to identify a path through the network from A to B. In the example network of Figure 3.3, there is only one such path, but in general this may not be the case. The administrator then picks a VCI value that is currently unused on each link for the connection. For the purposes of our example, let's suppose that the VCI value 5 is chosen for the link from host A to switch 1, and that 11 is chosen for the link from switch 1 to switch 2. In that case, switch 1 needs to have an entry in its VC table configured as shown in Table 3.2.

Similarly, suppose that the VCI of 7 is chosen to identify this connection on the link from switch 2 to switch 3 and that a VCI of 4 is chosen for

---

[2]In practice, the process would likely be much more automated than described here, perhaps using some sort of graphical network management tool. The following steps illustrate the state that has to be established in any case.

Table 3.2 Virtual Circuit Table Entry for Switch 1			
Incoming Interface	**Incoming VCI**	**Outgoing Interface**	**Outgoing VCI**
2	5	1	11

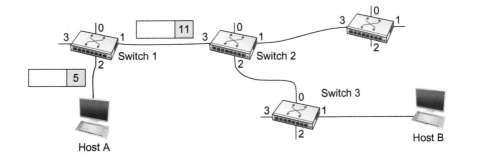

■ FIGURE 3.4 A packet is sent into a virtual circuit network.

the link from switch 3 to host B. In that case, switches 2 and 3 need to be configured with VC table entries as shown in Table 3.3. Note that the "outgoing" VCI value at one switch is the "incoming" VCI value at the next switch.

Once the VC tables have been set up, the data transfer phase can proceed, as illustrated in Figure 3.4. For any packet that it wants to send to host B, A puts the VCI value of 5 in the header of the packet and sends it to switch 1. Switch 1 receives any such packet on interface 2, and it uses the combination of the interface and the VCI in the packet header to find the appropriate VC table entry. As shown in Table 3.2, the table entry in this

Table 3.3 Virtual Circuit Table Entries for Switches 2 and 3			
VC Table Entry at Switch 2			
Incoming Interface	**Incoming VCI**	**Outgoing Interface**	**Outgoing VCI**
3	11	2	7
VC Table Entry at Switch 3			
Incoming Interface	**Incoming VCI**	**Outgoing Interface**	**Outgoing VCI**
0	7	1	4

case tells switch 1 to forward the packet out of interface 1 and to put the VCI value 11 in the header when the packet is sent. Thus, the packet will arrive at switch 2 on interface 3 bearing VCI 11. Switch 2 looks up interface 3 and VCI 11 in its VC table (as shown in Table 3.3) and sends the packet on to switch 3 after updating the VCI value in the packet header appropriately, as shown in Figure 3.5. This process continues until it arrives at host B with the VCI value of 4 in the packet. To host B, this identifies the packet as having come from host A.

In real networks of reasonable size, the burden of configuring VC tables correctly in a large number of switches would quickly become excessive using the above procedures. Thus, either a network management tool or some sort of signalling (or both) is almost always used, even when setting up "permanent" VCs. In the case of PVCs, signalling is initiated by the network administrator, while SVCs are usually set up using signalling by one of the hosts. We consider now how the same VC just described could be set up by signalling from the host.

To start the signalling process, host A sends a setup message into the network—that is, to switch 1. The setup message contains, among other things, the complete destination address of host B. The setup message needs to get all the way to B to create the necessary connection state in every switch along the way. We can see that getting the setup message to B is a lot like getting a datagram to B, in that the switches have to know which output to send the setup message to so that it eventually reaches B. For now, let's just assume that the switches know enough about the network topology to figure out how to do that, so that the setup message flows on to switches 2 and 3 before finally reaching host B.

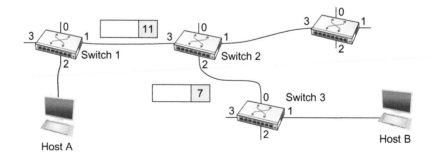

■ FIGURE 3.5 A packet makes its way through a virtual circuit network.

When switch 1 receives the connection request, in addition to sending it on to switch 2, it creates a new entry in its virtual circuit table for this new connection. This entry is exactly the same as shown previously in Table 3.2. The main difference is that now the task of assigning an unused VCI value on the interface is performed by the switch for that port. In this example, the switch picks the value 5. The virtual circuit table now has the following information: "When packets arrive on port 2 with identifier 5, send them out on port 1." Another issue is that, somehow, host A will need to learn that it should put the VCI value of 5 in packets that it wants to send to B; we will see how that happens below.

When switch 2 receives the setup message, it performs a similar process; in this example, it picks the value 11 as the incoming VCI value. Similarly, switch 3 picks 7 as the value for its incoming VCI. Each switch can pick any number it likes, as long as that number is not currently in use for some other connection on that port of that switch. As noted above, VCIs have link-local scope; that is, they have no global significance.

Finally, the setup message arrives as host B. Assuming that B is healthy and willing to accept a connection from host A, it too allocates an incoming VCI value, in this case 4. This VCI value can be used by B to identify all packets coming from host A.

Now, to complete the connection, everyone needs to be told what their downstream neighbor is using as the VCI for this connection. Host B sends an acknowledgment of the connection setup to switch 3 and includes in that message the VCI that it chose (4). Now switch 3 can complete the virtual circuit table entry for this connection, since it knows the outgoing value must be 4. Switch 3 sends the acknowledgment on to switch 2, specifying a VCI of 7. Switch 2 sends the message on to switch 1, specifying a VCI of 11. Finally, switch 1 passes the acknowledgment on to host A, telling it to use the VCI of 5 for this connection.

At this point, everyone knows all that is necessary to allow traffic to flow from host A to host B. Each switch has a complete virtual circuit table entry for the connection. Furthermore, host A has a firm acknowledgment that everything is in place all the way to host B. At this point, the connection table entries are in place in all three switches just as in the administratively configured example above, but the whole process happened automatically in response to the signalling message sent from A. The data transfer phase can now begin and is identical to that used in the PVC case.

When host A no longer wants to send data to host B, it tears down the connection by sending a teardown message to switch 1. The switch removes the relevant entry from its table and forwards the message on to the other switches in the path, which similarly delete the appropriate table entries. At this point, if host A were to send a packet with a VCI of 5 to switch 1, it would be dropped as if the connection had never existed.

There are several things to note about virtual circuit switching:

- Since host A has to wait for the connection request to reach the far side of the network and return before it can send its first data packet, there is at least one round-trip time (RTT) of delay before data is sent.[3]

- While the connection request contains the full address for host B (which might be quite large, being a global identifier on the network), each data packet contains only a small identifier, which is only unique on one link. Thus, the per-packet overhead caused by the header is reduced relative to the datagram model.

- If a switch or a link in a connection fails, the connection is broken and a new one will need to be established. Also, the old one needs to be torn down to free up table storage space in the switches.

- The issue of how a switch decides which link to forward the connection request on has been glossed over. In essence, this is the same problem as building up the forwarding table for datagram forwarding, which requires some sort of *routing algorithm*. Routing is described in Section 3.3, and the algorithms described there are generally applicable to routing setup requests as well as datagrams.

One of the nice aspects of virtual circuits is that by the time the host gets the go-ahead to send data, it knows quite a lot about the network— for example, that there really is a route to the receiver and that the receiver is willing and able to receive data. It is also possible to allocate resources to the virtual circuit at the time it is established. For example, X.25 was an early (and now largely obsolete) virtual-circuit-based

---

[3]This is not strictly true. Some people have proposed "optimistically" sending a data packet immediately after sending the connection request. However, most current implementations wait for connection setup to complete before sending data.

networking technology. X.25 networks employ the following three-part strategy:

1. Buffers are allocated to each virtual circuit when the circuit is initialized.

2. The sliding window protocol (Section 2.5) is run between each pair of nodes along the virtual circuit, and this protocol is augmented with flow control to keep the sending node from over-running the buffers allocated at the receiving node.

3. The circuit is rejected by a given node if not enough buffers are available at that node when the connection request message is processed.

In doing these three things, each node is ensured of having the buffers it needs to queue the packets that arrive on that circuit. This basic strategy is usually called *hop-by-hop flow control.*

By comparison, a datagram network has no connection establishment phase, and each switch processes each packet independently, making it less obvious how a datagram network would allocate resources in a meaningful way. Instead, each arriving packet competes with all other packets for buffer space. If there are no free buffers, the incoming packet must be discarded. We observe, however, that even in a datagram-based network a source host often sends a sequence of packets to the same destination host. It is possible for each switch to distinguish among the set of packets it currently has queued, based on the source/destination pair, and thus for the switch to ensure that the packets belonging to each source/destination pair are receiving a fair share of the switch's buffers. We discuss this idea in much greater depth in Chapter 6.

In the virtual circuit model, we could imagine providing each circuit with a different *quality of service* (QoS). In this setting, the term *quality of service* is usually taken to mean that the network gives the user some kind of performance-related guarantee, which in turn implies that switches set aside the resources they need to meet this guarantee. For example, the switches along a given virtual circuit might allocate a percentage of each outgoing link's bandwidth to that circuit. As another example, a sequence of switches might ensure that packets belonging to a particular circuit not be delayed (queued) for more than a certain amount of time. We return to the topic of quality of service in Section 6.5.

Introduction to Congestion

One important issue that switch designers face is *contention*. Contention occurs when multiple packets have to be queued at a switch because they are competing for the same output link. We'll look at how switches deal with this issue in Section 1.4. You can think of contention as something that happens at the timescale of individual packet arrivals. Congestion, by contrast, happens at a slightly longer timescale, when a switch has so many packets queued that it runs out of buffer space and has to start dropping packets. We'll return to the topic of congestion in Chapter 6, after we have seen the transport protocol component of the network architecture. At this point, however, we observe that how you deal with congestion is related to the issue of whether your network uses virtual circuits or datagrams.

On the one hand, suppose that each switch allocates enough buffers to handle the packets belonging to each virtual circuit it supports, as is done in an X.25 network. In this case, the network has defined away the problem of congestion—a switch never encounters a situation in which it has more packets to queue than it has buffer space, since it does not allow the connection to be established in the first place unless it can dedicate enough resources to it to avoid this situation. The problem with this approach, however, is that it is extremely conservative—it is unlikely that all the circuits will need to use all of their buffers at the same time, and as a consequence the switch is potentially underutilized.

On the other hand, the datagram model seemingly invites congestion—you do not know that there is enough contention at a switch to cause congestion until you run out of buffers. At that point, it is too late to prevent the congestion, and your only choice is to try to recover from it. The good news, of course, is that you may be able to get better utilization out of your switches since you are not holding buffers in reserve for a worst-case scenario that is unlikely to happen.

As is quite often the case, nothing is strictly black and white—there are design advantages for defining congestion away (as the X.25 model does) and for doing nothing about congestion until after it happens (as the simple datagram model does). There are also intermediate points between these two extremes. We describe some of these design points in Chapter 6.

There have been a number of successful examples of virtual circuit technologies over the years, notably X.25, Frame Relay, and Asynchronous Transfer Mode (ATM). With the success of the Internet's connectionless model, however, none of them enjoys great popularity today. One of the most common applications of virtual circuits for many years was the construction of *virtual private networks* (VPNs), a subject discussed in Section 3.2.9. Even that application is now mostly supported using Internet-based technologies today.

Optical Switching

To a casual observer of the networking industry around the year 2000, it might have appeared that the most interesting sort of switching was optical switching. Indeed, optical switching did become an important technology in the late 1990s, due to a confluence of several factors. One factor was the commercial availability of dense wavelength division multiplexing (DWDM) equipment, which makes it possible to send a great deal of information down a single fiber by transmitting on a large number of optical wavelengths (or colors) at once. Thus, for example, one might send data on 100 or more different wavelengths, and each wavelength might carry as much as 10 Gbps of data.

A second factor was the commercial availability of optical amplifiers. Optical signals are attenuated as they pass through fiber, and after some distance (about 40 km or so) they need to be made stronger in some way. Before optical amplifiers, it was necessary to place *repeaters* in the path to recover the optical signal, convert it to a digital electronic signal, and then convert it back to optical again. Before you could get the data into a repeater, you would have to demultiplex it using a DWDM terminal. Thus, a large number of DWDM terminals would be needed just to drive a single fiber pair for a long distance. Optical amplifiers, unlike repeaters, are *analog* devices that boost whatever signal is sent along the fiber, even if it is sent on a hundred different wavelengths. Optical amplifiers therefore made DWDM gear much more attractive, because now a pair of DWDM terminals could talk to each other when separated by a distance of hundreds of kilometers. Furthermore, you could even upgrade the DWDM gear at the ends without touching the optical amplifiers in the middle of the path, because they will amplify 100 wavelengths as easily as 50 wavelengths.

With DWDM and optical amplifiers, it became possible to build optical networks of huge capacity. But at least one more type of device is needed to make these networks useful—the *optical switch*. Most so-called optical switches today actually perform their switching function electronically, and from an architectural point of view they have more in common with the circuit switches of the telephone network than the packet switches described in this chapter. A typical optical switch has a large number of interfaces that understand SONET framing and is able to cross-connect a SONET channel from an incoming interface to an outgoing interface. Thus, with an optical switch, it becomes possible to provide SONET channels from point A to point B via point C even if there is no direct fiber path from A to B—there just needs to be a path from A to C, a switch at C, and a path from C to B. In this respect, an optical switch bears some relationship to the switches in Figure 3.3, in that it creates the illusion of a connection between two points even when there is no direct physical connection between them. However, optical switches do not provide virtual circuits, they provide "real" circuits (e.g., a SONET channel). There are even some newer types of optical switches that use microscopic, electronically controlled mirrors to deflect all the light from one switch port to another, so that there could be an uninterrupted optical channel from point A to point B. The technology behind these devices is called *MEMS (microelectromechanical systems).*

We don't cover optical networking extensively in this book, in part because of space considerations. For many practical purposes, you can think of optical networks as a piece of the infrastructure that enables telephone companies to provide SONET links or other types of circuits where and when you need them. However, it is worth noting that many of the technologies that are discussed later in this book, such as routing protocols and multiprotocol label switching, do have application to the world of optical networking.

Asynchronous Transfer Mode (ATM)

Asynchronous Transfer Mode (ATM) is probably the most well-known virtual circuit-based networking technology, although it is now somewhat past its peak in terms of deployment. ATM became an important technology in the 1980s and early 1990s for a variety of reasons, not the least of which is that it was embraced by the telephone industry, which had historically been less than active in data communications (other than as a supplier of links from which other people built networks). ATM also happened to be in the right place at the right time, as a high-speed switching technology that appeared on the scene just when shared media like Ethernet and token rings were starting to look a bit too slow for many users of computer networks. In some ways ATM was a competing technology with Ethernet switching, and it was seen by many as a competitor to IP as well.

There are a few aspects of ATM that are worth examining. The picture of the ATM packet format—more commonly called an ATM *cell*—in Figure 3.6 will illustrate the main points. We'll skip the generic flow control (GFC) bits, which never saw much use, and start with the 24 bits that are labelled VPI (virtual path identifier—8 bits) and VCI (virtual circuit identifier—16 bits). If you consider these bits together as a single 24-bit

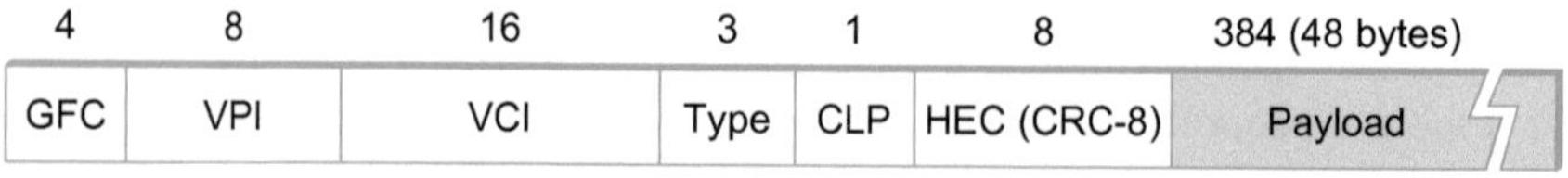

4	8	16	3	1	8	384 (48 bytes)
GFC	VPI	VCI	Type	CLP	HEC (CRC-8)	Payload

■ FIGURE 3.6 ATM cell format at the UNI.

field, they correspond to the virtual circuit identifier introduced above. The reason for breaking the field into two parts was to allow for a level of hierarchy: All the circuits with the same VPI could, in some cases, be treated as a group (a virtual path) and could all be switched together looking only at the VPI, simplifying the work of a switch that could ignore all the VCI bits and reducing the size of the VC table considerably.

Skipping to the last header byte we find an 8-bit cyclic redundancy check (CRC), known as the *header error check* (HEC). It uses the CRC-8 polynomial given in Section 2.4.3 and provides error detection and single-bit error correction capability on the cell header only. Protecting the cell header is particularly important because an error in the VCI will cause the cell to be misdelivered.

Probably the most significant thing to notice about the ATM cell, and the reason it is called a cell and not a packet, is that it comes in only one size: 53 bytes. What was the reason for this? A big reason was to facilitate the implementation of hardware switches. When ATM was being created in the mid- and late 1980s, 10-Mbps Ethernet was the cutting-edge technology in terms of speed. To go much faster, most people thought in terms of hardware. Also, in the telephone world, people think big when they think of switches—telephone switches often serve tens of thousands of customers. Fixed-length packets turn out to be a very helpful thing if you want to build fast, highly scalable switches. There are two main reasons for this:

1. It is easier to build hardware to do simple jobs, and the job of processing packets is simpler when you already know how long each one will be.

2. If all packets are the same length, then you can have lots of switching elements all doing much the same thing in parallel, each of them taking the same time to do its job.

This second reason, the enabling of parallelism, greatly improves the scalability of switch designs. It would be overstating the case to say that fast parallel hardware switches can only be built using fixed-length cells. However, it is certainly true that cells ease the task of building such hardware and that there was a lot of knowledge available about how to build cell switches in hardware at the time the ATM standards were being defined. As it turns out, this same principle is still applied in many switches and routers today, even if they deal in variable length packets—they cut those packets into some sort of cell in order to switch them, as we'll see in Section 3.4.

Having decided to use small, fixed-length packets, the next question is what is the right length to fix them at? If you make them too short, then the amount of header information that needs to be carried around relative to the amount of data that fits in one cell gets larger, so the percentage of link bandwidth that is actually used to carry data goes down. Even more seriously, if you build a device that processes cells at some maximum number of cells per second, then as cells get shorter the total data rate drops in direct proportion to cell size. An example of such a device might be a network adaptor that reassembles cells into larger units before handing them up to the host. The performance of such a device depends directly on cell size. On the other hand, if you make the cells too big, then there is a problem of wasted bandwidth caused by the need to pad transmitted data to fill a complete cell. If the cell payload size is 48 bytes and you want to send 1 byte, you'll need to send 47 bytes of padding. If this happens a lot, then the utilization of the link will be very low. The combination of relatively high header-to-payload ratio plus the frequency of sending partially filled cells did actually lead to some noticeable inefficiency in ATM networks that some detractors called the *cell tax*.

As it turns out, 48 bytes was picked for the ATM cell payload as a compromise. There were good arguments for both larger and smaller cells, but 48 made almost no one happy—a power of two would certainly have been better for computers to work with.

3.1.3 Source Routing

A third approach to switching that uses neither virtual circuits nor conventional datagrams is known as *source routing*. The name derives from the fact that all the information about network topology that is required to switch a packet across the network is provided by the source host.

There are various ways to implement source routing. One would be to assign a number to each output of each switch and to place that number in the header of the packet. The switching function is then very simple: For each packet that arrives on an input, the switch would read the port number in the header and transmit the packet on that output. However, since there will in general be more than one switch in the path between the sending and the receiving host, the header for the packet needs to contain enough information to allow every switch in the path to

---

Where Are They Now?

ATM

There was a period of time in the late 1980s and early 1990s when ATM seemed (to many people) poised to take over the world. The major telecommunication companies were supporting it, and the promise of high-speed networks that could smoothly integrate voice, video, and data onto a common network seemed compelling. Proponents of ATM referred to anything that used variable-length packets—technologies such as Ethernet and IP—as "legacy" technologies. Today, however, Ethernet and IP dominate, and ATM is viewed as yesterday's technology. You can still find pockets of ATM deployment, primarily as a way to get access to IP networks. Notably, a lot of Digital Subscriber Line (DSL) access networks were built using ATM, so some amount of broadband Internet access today is actually over ATM links, although this fact is completely hidden by the DSL modems, which take Ethernet frames and chop them into cells which are subsequently reassembled inside the access network.

There is room for debate as to why ATM didn't take over the world. One thing that seems fundamentally important in retrospect was that IP was well on its way to becoming completely entrenched by the time ATM appeared. Even though the Internet wasn't on the radar of a lot of people in the 1980s, it was already achieving global reach and the number of hosts connected was doubling every year. And, since the whole point of IP was to smoothly interconnect all sorts of different networks, when ATM appeared, rather than displace IP as its proponents imagined it might, ATM was quickly absorbed as just another network type over which IP could run. At that point, ATM was more directly in competition with Ethernet than with IP, and the arrival of inexpensive Ethernet switches and 100-Mbps Ethernet without expensive optics ensured that the Ethernet remained entrenched as a local area technology.

---

determine which output the packet needs to be placed on. One way to do this would be to put an ordered list of switch ports in the header and to rotate the list so that the next switch in the path is always at the front of the list. Figure 3.7 illustrates this idea.

In this example, the packet needs to traverse three switches to get from host A to host B. At switch 1, it needs to exit on port 1, at the next switch it needs to exit at port 0, and at the third switch it needs to exit at port 3. Thus, the original header when the packet leaves host A contains the list of ports (3, 0, 1), where we assume that each switch reads the rightmost element of the list. To make sure that the next switch gets the appropriate information, each switch rotates the list after it has read its own entry. Thus, the packet header as it leaves switch 1 en route to switch 2 is now

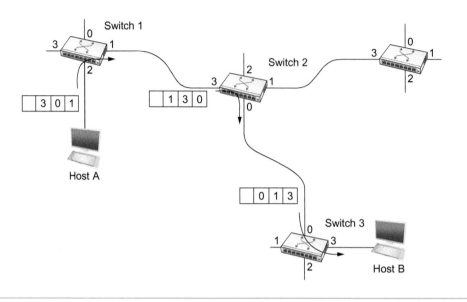

■ **FIGURE 3.7** Source routing in a switched network (where the switch reads the rightmost number).

(1, 3, 0); switch 2 performs another rotation and sends out a packet with (0, 1, 3) in the header. Although not shown, switch 3 performs yet another rotation, restoring the header to what it was when host A sent it.

There are several things to note about this approach. First, it assumes that host A knows enough about the topology of the network to form a header that has all the right directions in it for every switch in the path. This is somewhat analogous to the problem of building the forwarding tables in a datagram network or figuring out where to send a setup packet in a virtual circuit network. Second, observe that we cannot predict how big the header needs to be, since it must be able to hold one word of information for every switch on the path. This implies that headers are probably of variable length with no upper bound, unless we can predict with absolute certainty the maximum number of switches through which a packet will ever need to pass. Third, there are some variations on this approach. For example, rather than rotate the header, each switch could just strip the first element as it uses it. Rotation has an advantage over stripping, however: Host B gets a copy of the complete header, which may help it figure out how to get back to host A. Yet another alternative is to have the header carry a pointer to the current "next port" entry, so that each switch just updates the pointer rather than rotating the header; this may be more efficient to implement. We show these three approaches in

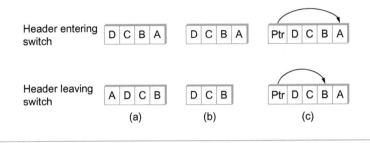

Header entering switch

| D | C | B | A |

| D | C | B | A |

| Ptr | D | C | B | A |

Header leaving switch

| A | D | C | B |

| D | C | B |

| Ptr | D | C | B | A |

(a)   (b)   (c)

■ FIGURE 3.8 Three ways to handle headers for source routing: (a) rotation; (b) stripping; (c) pointer. The labels are read right to left.

Figure 3.8. In each case, the entry that this switch needs to read is **A**, and the entry that the next switch needs to read is **B**.

Source routing can be used in both datagram networks and virtual circuit networks. For example, the Internet Protocol, which is a datagram protocol, includes a source route option that allows selected packets to be source routed, while the majority are switched as conventional datagrams. Source routing is also used in some virtual circuit networks as the means to get the initial setup request along the path from source to destination.

Source routes are sometimes categorized as "strict" or "loose." In a strict source route, every node along the path must be specified, whereas a loose source route only specifies a set of nodes to be traversed, without saying exactly how to get from one node to the next. A loose source route can be thought of as a set of waypoints rather than a completely specified route. The loose option can be helpful to limit the amount of information that a source must obtain to create a source route. In any reasonably large network, it is likely to be hard for a host to get the complete path information it needs to construct a correct strict source route to any destination. But both types of source routes do find application in certain scenarios, one of which is described in Section 4.3.

3.1.4 Bridges and LAN Switches

Having discussed some of the basic ideas behind switching, we now focus more closely on some specific switching technologies. We begin by considering a class of switch that is used to forward packets between LANs (local area networks) such as Ethernets. Such switches are sometimes known by the obvious name of LAN switches; historically, they have also

LAB 04: VLAN

been referred to as *bridges*, and they are very widely used in campus and enterprise networks.

Suppose you have a pair of Ethernets that you want to interconnect. One approach you might try is to put a repeater between them, as described in Chapter 2. This would not be a workable solution, however, if doing so exceeded the physical limitations of the Ethernet. (Recall that no more than two repeaters between any pair of hosts and no more than a total of 2500 m in length are allowed.) An alternative would be to put a node with a pair of Ethernet adaptors between the two Ethernets and have the node forward frames from one Ethernet to the other. This node would differ from a repeater, which operates on bits, not frames, and just blindly copies the bits received on one interface to another. Instead, this node would fully implement the Ethernet's collision detection and media access protocols on each interface. Hence, the length and number-of-host restrictions of the Ethernet, which are all about managing collisions, would not apply to the combined pair of Ethernets connected in this way. This device operates in promiscuous mode, accepting all frames transmitted on either of the Ethernets, and forwarding them to the other.

The node we have just described is typically called a *bridge*, and a collection of LANs connected by one or more bridges is usually said to form an *extended LAN*. In their simplest variants, bridges simply accept LAN frames on their inputs and forward them out on all other outputs. This simple strategy was used by early bridges but has some pretty serious limitations as we'll see below. A number of refinements have been added over the years to make bridges an effective mechanism for interconnecting a set of LANs. The rest of this section fills in the more interesting details.

Note that a bridge meets our definition of a switch from the previous section: a multi-input, multi-output device, which transfers packets from an input to one or more outputs. And recall that this provides a way to increase the total bandwidth of a network. For example, while a single Ethernet segment might carry only 100 Mbps of total traffic, an Ethernet bridge can carry as much as $100n$ Mbps, where n is the number of ports (inputs and outputs) on the bridge.

Learning Bridges

The first optimization we can make to a bridge is to observe that it need not forward all frames that it receives. Consider the bridge in Figure 3.9. Whenever a frame from host A that is addressed to host B arrives on port 1,

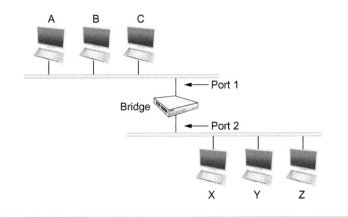

■ FIGURE 3.9 Illustration of a learning bridge.

Table 3.4 Forwarding Table Maintained by a Bridge	
Host	Port
A	1
B	1
C	1
X	2
Y	2
Z	2

there is no need for the bridge to forward the frame out over port 2. The question, then, is how does a bridge come to learn on which port the various hosts reside?

One option would be to have a human download a table into the bridge similar to the one given in Table 3.4. Then, whenever the bridge receives a frame on port 1 that is addressed to host A, it would not forward the frame out on port 2; there would be no need because host A would have already directly received the frame on the LAN connected to port 1. Anytime a frame addressed to host A was received on port 2, the bridge would forward the frame out on port 1.

No one actually builds bridges in which the table is configured by hand. Having a human maintain this table is too burdensome, and there is a simple trick by which a bridge can learn this information for itself. The idea is for each bridge to inspect the *source* address in all the frames it receives. Thus, when host A sends a frame to a host on either side of the bridge, the bridge receives this frame and records the fact that a frame from host A was just received on port 1. In this way, the bridge can build a table just like Table 3.4.

Note that a bridge using such a table implements a version of the datagram (or connectionless) model of forwarding described in Section 3.1.1. Each packet carries a global address, and the bridge decides which output to send a packet on by looking up that address in a table.

When a bridge first boots, this table is empty; entries are added over time. Also, a timeout is associated with each entry, and the bridge discards the entry after a specified period of time. This is to protect against the situation in which a host—and, as a consequence, its LAN address—is moved from one network to another. Thus, this table is not necessarily complete. Should the bridge receive a frame that is addressed to a host not currently in the table, it goes ahead and forwards the frame out on all the other ports. In other words, this table is simply an optimization that filters out some frames; it is not required for correctness.

Implementation

The code that implements the learning bridge algorithm is quite simple, and we sketch it here. Structure BridgeEntry defines a single entry in the bridge's forwarding table; these are stored in a Map structure (which supports mapCreate, mapBind, and mapResolve operations) to enable entries to be efficiently located when packets arrive from sources already in the table. The constant MAX_TTL specifies how long an entry is kept in the table before it is discarded.

```
#define BRIDGE_TAB_SIZE   1024   /* max. size of bridging
                                        table */
#define MAX_TTL            120   /* time (in seconds) before
                                     an entry is flushed */


typedef struct {
    MacAddr      destination;   /* MAC address of a node */
    int          ifnumber;      /* interface to reach it */
    u_short      TTL;           /* time to live */
    Binding      binding;       /* binding in the Map */
```

```
} BridgeEntry;

int     numEntries = 0;
Map     bridgeMap = mapCreate(BRIDGE_TAB_SIZE,
                                  sizeof(BridgeEntry));
```

The routine that updates the forwarding table when a new packet arrives is given by updateTable. The arguments passed are the source media access control (MAC) address contained in the packet and the interface number on which it was received. Another routine, not shown here, is invoked at regular intervals, scans the entries in the forwarding table, and decrements the TTL (time to live) field of each entry, discarding any entries whose TTL has reached 0. Note that the TTL is reset to MAX_TTL every time a packet arrives to refresh an existing table entry and that the interface on which the destination can be reached is updated to reflect the most recently received packet.

```
void
updateTable (MacAddr src, int inif)
{
    BridgeEntry        *b;

    if (mapResolve(bridgeMap, &src, (void **)&b) == FALSE )
    {
        /* this address is not in the table, so try to add it */
        if (numEntries < BRIDGE_TAB_SIZE)
        {
            b = NEW(BridgeEntry);
            b->binding = mapBind( bridgeMap, &src, b);
            /* use source address of packet as dest. address in table */
            b->destination = src;
            numEntries++;
        }
        else
        {
            /* can't fit this address in the table now, so give up */
            return;
        }
    }
}
```

```
/* reset TTL and use most recent input interface */
b->TTL = MAX_TTL;
b->ifnumber = inif;
}
```

Note that this implementation adopts a simple strategy in the case where the bridge table has become full to capacity—it simply fails to add the new address. Recall that completeness of the bridge table is not necessary for correct forwarding; it just optimizes performance. If there is some entry in the table that is not currently being used, it will eventually time out and be removed, creating space for a new entry. An alternative approach would be to invoke some sort of cache replacement algorithm on finding the table full; for example, we might locate and remove the entry with the smallest TTL to accommodate the new entry.

Spanning Tree Algorithm

The preceding strategy works just fine until the extended LAN has a loop in it, in which case it fails in a horrible way—frames potentially loop through the extended LAN forever. This is easy to see in the example depicted in Figure 3.10, where, for example, bridges B1, B4, and B6 form

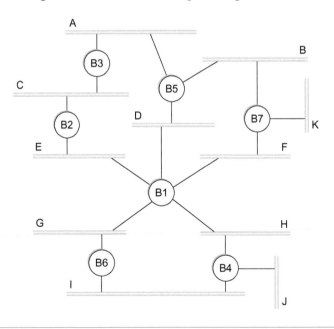

■ FIGURE 3.10 Extended LAN with loops.

a loop. Suppose that a packet enters bridge B4 from Ethernet J and that the destination address is one not yet in any bridge's forwarding table: B4 sends a copy of the packet out to Ethernets H and I. Now bridge B6 forwards the packet to Ethernet G, where B1 would see it and forward it back to Ethernet H; B4 still doesn't have this destination in its table, so it forwards the packet back to Ethernets I and J. There is nothing to stop this cycle from repeating endlessly, with packets looping in both directions among B1, B4, and B6.

Why would an extended LAN come to have a loop in it? One possibility is that the network is managed by more than one administrator, for example, because it spans multiple departments in an organization. In such a setting, it is possible that no single person knows the entire configuration of the network, meaning that a bridge that closes a loop might be added without anyone knowing. A second, more likely scenario is that loops are built into the network on purpose—to provide redundancy in case of failure. After all, a network with no loops needs only one link failure to become split into two separate partitions.

Whatever the cause, bridges must be able to correctly handle loops. This problem is addressed by having the bridges run a distributed *spanning tree* algorithm. If you think of the extended LAN as being represented by a graph that possibly has loops (cycles), then a spanning tree is a subgraph of this graph that covers (spans) all the vertices but contains no cycles. That is, a spanning tree keeps all of the vertices of the original graph but throws out some of the edges. For example, Figure 3.11 shows a cyclic graph on the left and one of possibly many spanning trees on the right.

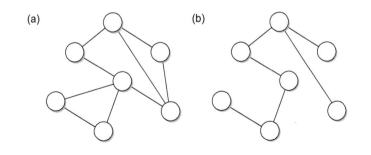

■ FIGURE 3.11 Example of (a) a cyclic graph; (b) a corresponding spanning tree.

The idea of a spanning tree is simple enough: It's a subset of the actual network topology that has no loops and that reaches all the LANs in the extended LAN. The hard part is how all of the bridges coordinate their decisions to arrive at a single view of the spanning tree. After all, one topology is typically able to be covered by multiple spanning trees. The answer lies in the spanning tree protocol, which we'll describe now.

The spanning tree algorithm, which was developed by Radia Perlman at the Digital Equipment Corporation, is a protocol used by a set of bridges to agree upon a spanning tree for a particular extended LAN. (The IEEE 802.1 specification for LAN bridges is based on this algorithm.) In practice, this means that each bridge decides the ports over which it is and is not willing to forward frames. In a sense, it is by removing ports from the topology that the extended LAN is reduced to an acyclic tree.[4] It is even possible that an entire bridge will not participate in forwarding frames, which seems kind of strange at first glance. The algorithm is dynamic, however, meaning that the bridges are always prepared to reconfigure themselves into a new spanning tree should some bridge fail, and so those unused ports and bridges provide the redundant capacity needed to recover from failures.

The main idea of the spanning tree is for the bridges to select the ports over which they will forward frames. The algorithm selects ports as follows. Each bridge has a unique identifier; for our purposes, we use the labels B1, B2, B3, and so on. The algorithm first elects the bridge with the smallest ID as the root of the spanning tree; exactly how this election takes place is described below. The root bridge always forwards frames out over all of its ports. Next, each bridge computes the shortest path to the root and notes which of its ports is on this path. This port is also selected as the bridge's preferred path to the root. Finally, all the bridges connected to a given LAN elect a single *designated* bridge that will be responsible for forwarding frames toward the root bridge. Each LAN's designated bridge is the one that is closest to the root. If two or more bridges are equally close to the root, then the bridges' identifiers are used to break ties, and

---

[4]Representing an extended LAN as an abstract graph is a bit awkward. Basically, you let both the bridges and the LANs correspond to the vertices of the graph and the ports correspond to the graph's edges. However, the spanning tree we are going to compute for this graph needs to span only those nodes that correspond to networks. It is possible that nodes corresponding to bridges will be disconnected from the rest of the graph. This corresponds to a situation in which all the ports connecting a bridge to various networks get removed by the algorithm.

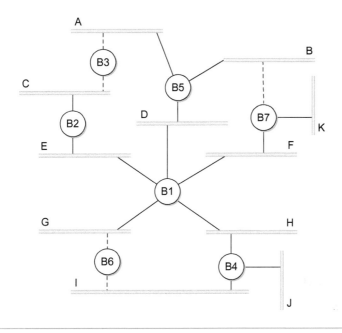

the smallest ID wins. Of course, each bridge is connected to more than one LAN, so it participates in the election of a designated bridge for each LAN it is connected to. In effect, this means that each bridge decides if it is the designated bridge relative to each of its ports. The bridge forwards frames over those ports for which it is the designated bridge.

Figure 3.12 shows the spanning tree that corresponds to the extended LAN shown in Figure 3.10. In this example, B1 is the root bridge, since it has the smallest ID. Notice that both B3 and B5 are connected to LAN A, but B5 is the designated bridge since it is closer to the root. Similarly, both B5 and B7 are connected to LAN B, but in this case B5 is the designated bridge since it has the smaller ID; both are an equal distance from B1.

While it is possible for a human to look at the extended LAN given in Figure 3.10 and to compute the spanning tree given in Figure 3.12 accord-ing to the rules given above, the bridges in an extended LAN do not have the luxury of being able to see the topology of the entire network, let alone peek inside other bridges to see their ID. Instead, the bridges have to exchange configuration messages with each other and then decide whether or not they are the root or a designated bridge based on these messages.

Specifically, the configuration messages contain three pieces of information:

1. The ID for the bridge that is sending the message
2. The ID for what the sending bridge believes to be the root bridge
3. The distance, measured in hops, from the sending bridge to the root bridge

Each bridge records the current *best* configuration message it has seen on each of its ports ("best" is defined below), including both messages it has received from other bridges and messages that it has itself transmitted.

Initially, each bridge thinks it is the root, and so it sends a configuration message out on each of its ports identifying itself as the root and giving a distance to the root of 0. Upon receiving a configuration message over a particular port, the bridge checks to see if that new message is better than the current best configuration message recorded for that port. The new configuration message is considered *better* than the currently recorded information if any of the following is true:

- It identifies a root with a smaller ID.
- It identifies a root with an equal ID but with a shorter distance.
- The root ID and distance are equal, but the sending bridge has a smaller ID

If the new message is better than the currently recorded information, the bridge discards the old information and saves the new information. However, it first adds 1 to the distance-to-root field since the bridge is one hop farther away from the root than the bridge that sent the message.

When a bridge receives a configuration message indicating that it is not the root bridge—that is, a message from a bridge with a smaller ID—the bridge stops generating configuration messages on its own and instead only forwards configuration messages from other bridges, after first adding 1 to the distance field. Likewise, when a bridge receives a configuration message that indicates it is not the designated bridge for that port—that is, a message from a bridge that is closer to the root or equally far from the root but with a smaller ID—the bridge stops sending configuration messages over that port. Thus, when the system stabilizes, only the root bridge is still generating configuration messages, and the other bridges are forwarding these messages only over ports for which they are the designated bridge. At this point, a spanning tree has been built, and all the bridges are in agreement on which ports are in use for the spanning tree. Only those ports may be used for forwarding data packets in the extended LAN.

Let's see how this works with an example. Consider what would happen in Figure 3.12 if the power had just been restored to the building housing this network, so that all the bridges boot at about the same time. All the bridges would start off by claiming to be the root. We denote a configuration message from node X in which it claims to be distance d from root node Y as (Y, d, X). Focusing on the activity at node B3, a sequence of events would unfold as follows:

1. B3 receives (B2, 0, B2).

2. Since $2 < 3$, B3 accepts B2 as root.

3. B3 adds one to the distance advertised by B2 (0) and thus sends (B2, 1, B3) toward B5.

4. Meanwhile, B2 accepts B1 as root because it has the lower ID, and it sends (B1, 1, B2) toward B3.

5. B5 accepts B1 as root and sends (B1, 1, B5) toward B3.

6. B3 accepts B1 as root, and it notes that both B2 and B5 are closer to the root than it is; thus, B3 stops forwarding messages on both its interfaces.

This leaves B3 with both ports not selected, as shown in Figure 3.12.

Even after the system has stabilized, the root bridge continues to send configuration messages periodically, and the other bridges continue to forward these messages as described in the previous paragraph. Should a particular bridge fail, the downstream bridges will not receive these configuration messages, and after waiting a specified period of time they will once again claim to be the root, and the algorithm just described will kick in again to elect a new root and new designated bridges.

One important thing to notice is that although the algorithm is able to reconfigure the spanning tree whenever a bridge fails, it is not able to forward frames over alternative paths for the sake of routing around a congested bridge.

Broadcast and Multicast

The preceding discussion has focused on how bridges forward unicast frames from one LAN to another. Since the goal of a bridge is to transparently extend a LAN across multiple networks, and since most LANs support both broadcast and multicast, then bridges must also support these two features. Broadcast is simple—each bridge forwards a frame with a destination broadcast address out on each active (selected) port other than the one on which the frame was received.

Multicast can be implemented in exactly the same way, with each host deciding for itself whether or not to accept the message. This is exactly what is done in practice. Notice, however, that since not all the LANs in an extended LAN necessarily have a host that is a member of a particular multicast group, it is possible to do better. Specifically, the spanning tree algorithm can be extended to prune networks over which multicast frames need not be forwarded. Consider a frame sent to group M by a host on LAN A in Figure 3.12. If there is no host on LAN J that belongs to group M, then there is no need for bridge B4 to forward the frames over that network. On the other hand, not having a host on LAN H that belongs to group M does not necessarily mean that bridge B1 can avoid forwarding multicast frames onto LAN H. It all depends on whether or not there are members of group M on LANs I and J.

How does a given bridge learn whether it should forward a multicast frame over a given port? It learns exactly the same way that a bridge learns whether it should forward a unicast frame over a particular port— by observing the *source* addresses that it receives over that port. Of course, groups are not typically the source of frames, so we have to cheat a little. In particular, each host that is a member of group M must periodically send a frame with the address for group M in the source field of the frame header. This frame would have as its destination address the multicast address for the bridges.

Note that, although the multicast extension just described has been proposed, it is not widely adopted. Instead, multicast is implemented in exactly the same way as broadcast on today's extended LANs.

Limitations of Bridges

The bridge-based solution just described is meant to be used in only a fairly limited setting—to connect a handful of similar LANs. The main limitations of bridges become apparent when we consider the issues of scale and heterogeneity.

On the issue of scale, it is not realistic to connect more than a few LANs by means of bridges, where in practice *few* typically means "tens of." One reason for this is that the spanning tree algorithm scales linearly; that is, there is no provision for imposing a hierarchy on the extended LAN. A second reason is that bridges forward all broadcast frames. While it is reasonable for all hosts within a limited setting (say, a department) to see each other's broadcast messages, it is unlikely that all the hosts in a larger environment (say, a large company or university) would want to have to be bothered by each other's broadcast messages. Said another way, broadcast does not scale, and as a consequence extended LANs do not scale.

One approach to increasing the scalability of extended LANs is the *virtual LAN* (VLAN). VLANs allow a single extended LAN to be partitioned into several seemingly separate LANs. Each virtual LAN is assigned an identifier (sometimes called a *color*), and packets can only travel from one segment to another if both segments have the same identifier. This has the effect of limiting the number of segments in an extended LAN that will receive any given broadcast packet.

We can see how VLANs work with an example. Figure 3.13 shows four hosts on four different LAN segments. In the absence of VLANs, any broadcast packet from any host will reach all the other hosts. Now let's suppose that we define the segments connected to hosts W and X as being in one VLAN, which we'll call VLAN 100. We also define the segments that connect to hosts Y and Z as being in VLAN 200. To do this, we need to

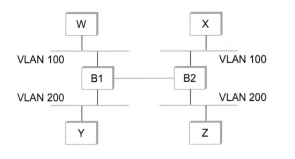

■ FIGURE 3.13 Two virtual LANs share a common backbone.

configure a VLAN ID on each port of bridges B1 and B2. The link between B1 and B2 is considered to be in both VLANs.

When a packet sent by host X arrives at bridge B2, the bridge observes that it came in a port that was configured as being in VLAN 100. It inserts a VLAN header between the Ethernet header and its payload. The interesting part of the VLAN header is the VLAN ID; in this case, that ID is set to 100. The bridge now applies its normal rules for forwarding to the packet, with the extra restriction that the packet may not be sent out an interface that is not part of VLAN 100. Thus, under no circumstances will the packet—even a broadcast packet—be sent out the interface to host Z, which is in VLAN 200. The packet is, however, forwarded on to bridge B1, which follows the same rules and thus may forward the packet to host W but not to host Y.

An attractive feature of VLANs is that it is possible to change the logical topology without moving any wires or changing any addresses. For example, if we wanted to make the segment that connects to host Z be part of VLAN 100 and thus enable X, W, and Z to be on the same virtual LAN, then we would just need to change one piece of configuration on bridge B2.

On the issue of heterogeneity, bridges are fairly limited in the kinds of networks they can interconnect. In particular, bridges make use of the network's frame header and so can support only networks that have exactly the same format for addresses. Thus, bridges can be used to connect Ethernets to Ethernets, token rings to token rings, and one 802.11 network to another. It's also possible to put a bridge between, say, an Ethernet and an 802.11 network, since both networks support the same 48-bit address format. However, bridges do not readily generalize to other kinds of networks with different addressing formats, such as ATM.[5]

Despite their limitations, bridges are a very important part of the complete networking picture. Their main advantage is that they allow multiple LANs to be transparently connected; that is, the networks can be connected without the end hosts having to run any additional protocols (or even be aware, for that matter). The one potential exception is when the hosts are expected to announce their membership in a multicast group, as described in Section 3.1.4.

---

[5]Ultimately there was quite a lot of work done to make ATM networks behave more like Ethernets, called *LAN Emulation*, to get around this limitation, but this is rarely seen today.

Notice, however, that this transparency can be dangerous. If a host or, more precisely, the application and transport protocol running on that host is programmed under the assumption that it is running on a single LAN, then inserting bridges between the source and destination hosts can have unexpected consequences. For example, if a bridge becomes congested, it may have to drop frames; in contrast, it is rare that a single Ethernet ever drops a frame. As another example, the latency between any pair of hosts on an extended LAN becomes both larger and more highly variable; in contrast, the physical limitations of a single Ethernet make the latency both small and predictable. As a final example, it is possible (although unlikely) that frames will be reordered in an extended LAN; in contrast, frame order is never shuffled on a single Ethernet. The bottom line is that it is never safe to design network software under the assumption that it will run over a single Ethernet segment. Bridges happen.

LAB 05:
Net Design

3.2 BASIC INTERNETWORKING (IP)

In the previous section, we saw that it was possible to build reasonably large LANs using bridges and LAN switches, but that such approaches were limited in their ability to scale and to handle heterogeneity. In this section, we explore some ways to go beyond the limitations of bridged networks, enabling us to build large, highly heterogeneous networks with reasonably efficient routing. We refer to such networks as *internetworks*. We'll continue the discussion of how to build a truly global internetwork in the next chapter, but for now we'll explore the basics. We start by considering more carefully what the word *internetwork* means.

3.2.1 What Is an Internetwork?

We use the term *internetwork*, or sometimes just *internet* with a lowercase *i*, to refer to an arbitrary collection of networks interconnected to provide some sort of host-to-host packet delivery service. For example, a corporation with many sites might construct a private internetwork by interconnecting the LANs at their different sites with point-to-point links leased from the phone company. When we are talking about the widely used global internetwork to which a large percentage of networks are now connected, we call it the *Internet* with a capital *I*. In keeping with the first-principles approach of this book, we mainly want you to learn about the principles of "lowercase *i*" internetworking, but we illustrate these ideas with real-world examples from the "big *I*" Internet.

Another piece of terminology that can be confusing is the difference between networks, subnetworks, and internetworks. We are going to avoid subnetworks (or subnets) altogether until Section 3.2.5. For now, we use *network* to mean either a directly connected or a switched network of the kind described in the previous section and the previous chapter. Such a network uses one technology, such as 802.11 or Ethernet. An *internetwork* is an interconnected collection of such networks. Sometimes, to avoid ambiguity, we refer to the underlying networks that we are interconnecting as *physical* networks. An internet is a *logical* network built out of a collection of physical networks. In this context, a collection of Ethernets connected by bridges or switches would still be viewed as a single network.

Figure 3.14 shows an example internetwork. An internetwork is often referred to as a "network of networks" because it is made up of lots of smaller networks. In this figure, we see Ethernets, a wireless network,

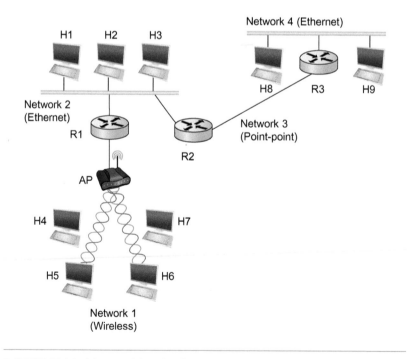

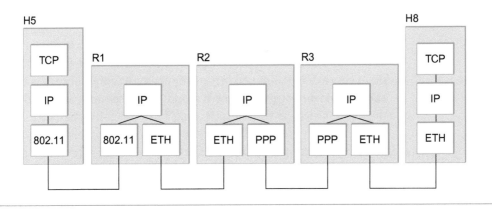

■ FIGURE 3.15   A simple internetwork, showing the protocol layers used to connect H5 to H8 in Figure 3.14. ETH is the protocol that runs over the Ethernet.

and a point-to-point link. Each of these is a single-technology network. The nodes that interconnect the networks are called *routers*. They are also sometimes called *gateways*, but since this term has several other connotations, we restrict our usage to router.

The *Internet Protocol* is the key tool used today to build scalable, heterogeneous internetworks. It was originally known as the Kahn-Cerf protocol after its inventors.[6] One way to think of IP is that it runs on all the nodes (both hosts and routers) in a collection of networks and defines the infrastructure that allows these nodes and networks to function as a single logical internetwork. For example, Figure 3.15 shows how hosts H5 and H8 are logically connected by the internet in Figure 3.14, including the protocol graph running on each node. Note that higher-level protocols, such as TCP and UDP, typically run on top of IP on the hosts.

Most of the rest of this chapter is about various aspects of IP. While it is certainly possible to build an internetwork that does not use IP—for example, Novell created an internetworking protocol called IPX, which was in turn based on the XNS internet designed by Xerox—IP is the most interesting case to study simply because of the size of the Internet. Said another way, it is only the IP Internet that has really faced the issue of scale. Thus, it provides the best case study of a scalable internetworking protocol.

---

[6]Robert Kahn and Vint Cerf received the A.M. Turing award, often referred to as the Nobel Prize of computer science, in 2005 for their design of IP.

3.2.2 Service Model

A good place to start when you build an internetwork is to define its *service model*, that is, the host-to-host services you want to provide. The main concern in defining a service model for an internetwork is that we can provide a host-to-host service only if this service can somehow be provided over each of the underlying physical networks. For example, it would be no good deciding that our internetwork service model was going to provide guaranteed delivery of every packet in 1 ms or less if there were underlying network technologies that could arbitrarily delay packets. The philosophy used in defining the IP service model, therefore, was to make it undemanding enough that just about any network technology that might turn up in an internetwork would be able to provide the necessary service.

The IP service model can be thought of as having two parts: an addressing scheme, which provides a way to identify all hosts in the internetwork, and a datagram (connectionless) model of data delivery. This service model is sometimes called *best effort* because, although IP makes every effort to deliver datagrams, it makes no guarantees. We postpone a discussion of the addressing scheme for now and look first at the data delivery model.

Datagram Delivery

The IP datagram is fundamental to the Internet Protocol. Recall from Section 3.1.1 that a datagram is a type of packet that happens to be sent in a connectionless manner over a network. Every datagram carries enough information to let the network forward the packet to its correct destination; there is no need for any advance setup mechanism to tell the network what to do when the packet arrives. You just send it, and the network makes its best effort to get it to the desired destination. The "best-effort" part means that if something goes wrong and the packet gets lost, corrupted, misdelivered, or in any way fails to reach its intended destination, the network does nothing—it made its best effort, and that is all it has to do. It does not make any attempt to recover from the failure. This is sometimes called an *unreliable* service.

Best-effort, connectionless service is about the simplest service you could ask for from an internetwork, and this is a great strength. For example, if you provide best-effort service over a network that provides a reliable service, then that's fine—you end up with a best-effort service that just happens to always deliver the packets. If, on the other hand, you had a reliable service model over an unreliable network, you would have to put lots of extra functionality into the routers to make up for the deficiencies of the underlying network. Keeping the routers as simple as possible was one of the original design goals of IP.

The ability of IP to "run over anything" is frequently cited as one of its most important characteristics. It is noteworthy that many of the technologies over which IP runs today did not exist when IP was invented. So far, no networking technology has been invented that has proven too bizarre for IP; it has even been claimed that IP can run over a network that transports messages using carrier pigeons.

Best-effort delivery does not just mean that packets can get lost. Sometimes they can get delivered out of order, and sometimes the same packet can get delivered more than once. The higher-level protocols or applications that run above IP need to be aware of all these possible failure modes.

Packet Format

Clearly, a key part of the IP service model is the type of packets that can be carried. The IP datagram, like most packets, consists of a header followed by a number of bytes of data. The format of the header is shown in Figure 3.16. Note that we have adopted a different style of representing packets than the one we used in previous chapters. This is because packet formats at the internetworking layer and above, where we will be focusing our attention

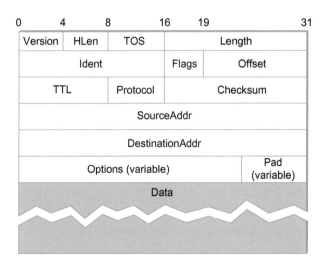

■ FIGURE 3.16 IPv4 packet header.

for the next few chapters, are almost invariably designed to align on 32-bit boundaries to simplify the task of processing them in software. Thus, the common way of representing them (used in Internet Requests for Comments, for example) is to draw them as a succession of 32-bit words. The top word is the one transmitted first, and the leftmost byte of each word is the one transmitted first. In this representation, you can easily recognize fields that are a multiple of 8 bits long. On the odd occasion when fields are not an even multiple of 8 bits, you can determine the field lengths by looking at the bit positions marked at the top of the packet.

Looking at each field in the IP header, we see that the "simple" model of best-effort datagram delivery still has some subtle features. The Version field specifies the version of IP. The current version of IP is 4, and it is sometimes called *IPv4*.[7] Observe that putting this field right at the start of the datagram makes it easy for everything else in the packet format to be redefined in subsequent versions; the header processing software starts off by looking at the version and then branches off to process the rest of the packet according to the appropriate format. The next field, HLen, specifies the length of the header in 32-bit words. When there are no options, which is most of the time, the header is 5 words (20 bytes) long. The 8-bit TOS (type of service) field has had a number of different definitions over the years, but its basic function is to allow packets to be treated differently based on application needs. For example, the TOS value might determine whether or not a packet should be placed in a special queue that receives low delay. We discuss the use of this field (which has evolved somewhat over the years) in more detail in Sections 6.4.2 and 6.5.3.

The next 16 bits of the header contain the Length of the datagram, including the header. Unlike the HLen field, the Length field counts bytes rather than words. Thus, the maximum size of an IP datagram is 65,535 bytes. The physical network over which IP is running, however, may not support such long packets. For this reason, IP supports a fragmentation and reassembly process. The second word of the header contains information about fragmentation, and the details of its use are presented in the following section entitled "Fragmentation and Reassembly."

Moving on to the third word of the header, the next byte is the TTL (time to live) field. Its name reflects its historical meaning rather than the

---

[7]The next major version of IP, which is discussed in Chapter 4, has the new version number 6 and is known as IPv6. The version number 5 was used for an experimental protocol called ST-II that was not widely used.

way it is commonly used today. The intent of the field is to catch packets that have been going around in routing loops and discard them, rather than let them consume resources indefinitely. Originally, TTL was set to a specific number of seconds that the packet would be allowed to live, and routers along the path would decrement this field until it reached 0. However, since it was rare for a packet to sit for as long as 1 second in a router, and routers did not all have access to a common clock, most routers just decremented the TTL by 1 as they forwarded the packet. Thus, it became more of a hop count than a timer, which is still a perfectly good way to catch packets that are stuck in routing loops. One subtlety is in the initial setting of this field by the sending host: Set it too high and packets could circulate rather a lot before getting dropped; set it too low and they may not reach their destination. The value 64 is the current default.

The Protocol field is simply a demultiplexing key that identifies the higher-level protocol to which this IP packet should be passed. There are values defined for the TCP (Transmission Control Protocol—6), UDP (User Datagram Protocol—17), and many other protocols that may sit above IP in the protocol graph.

The Checksum is calculated by considering the entire IP header as a sequence of 16-bit words, adding them up using ones complement arithmetic, and taking the ones complement of the result. This is the IP checksum algorithm described in Section 2.4. Thus, if any bit in the header is corrupted in transit, the checksum will not contain the correct value upon receipt of the packet. Since a corrupted header may contain an error in the destination address—and, as a result, may have been misdelivered—it makes sense to discard any packet that fails the checksum. It should be noted that this type of checksum does not have the same strong error detection properties as a CRC, but it is much easier to calculate in software.

The last two required fields in the header are the SourceAddr and the DestinationAddr for the packet. The latter is the key to datagram delivery: Every packet contains a full address for its intended destination so that forwarding decisions can be made at each router. The source address is required to allow recipients to decide if they want to accept the packet and to enable them to reply. IP addresses are discussed in Section 3.2.3—for now, the important thing to know is that IP defines its own global address space, independent of whatever physical networks it runs over. As we will see, this is one of the keys to supporting heterogeneity.

Finally, there may be a number of options at the end of the header. The presence or absence of options may be determined by examining the header length (HLen) field. While options are used fairly rarely, a complete IP implementation must handle them all.

Fragmentation and Reassembly

One of the problems of providing a uniform host-to-host service model over a heterogeneous collection of networks is that each network technology tends to have its own idea of how large a packet can be. For example, an Ethernet can accept packets up to 1500 bytes long, while FDDI (Fiber Distributed Data Interface) packets may be 4500 bytes long. This leaves two choices for the IP service model: Make sure that all IP datagrams are small enough to fit inside one packet on any network technology, or provide a means by which packets can be fragmented and reassembled when they are too big to go over a given network technology. The latter turns out to be a good choice, especially when you consider the fact that new network technologies are always turning up, and IP needs to run over all of them; this would make it hard to pick a suitably small bound on datagram size. This also means that a host will not send needlessly small packets, which wastes bandwidth and consumes processing resources by requiring more headers per byte of data sent. For example, two hosts connected to FDDI networks that are interconnected by a point-to-point link would not need to send packets small enough to fit on an Ethernet.

The central idea here is that every network type has a *maximum transmission unit* (MTU), which is the largest IP datagram that it can carry in a frame. Note that this value is smaller than the largest packet size on that network because the IP datagram needs to fit in the *payload* of the link-layer frame.[8]

When a host sends an IP datagram, therefore, it can choose any size that it wants. A reasonable choice is the MTU of the network to which the host is directly attached. Then, fragmentation will only be necessary if the path to the destination includes a network with a smaller MTU. Should the transport protocol that sits on top of IP give IP a packet larger than the local MTU, however, then the source host must fragment it.

Fragmentation typically occurs in a router when it receives a datagram that it wants to forward over a network that has an MTU that is smaller

---

[8] In ATM networks, the MTU is, fortunately, much larger than a single cell, as ATM has its own fragmentation mechanisms. The link-layer frame in ATM is called a *convergence-sublayer protocol data unit* (CS-PDU).

than the received datagram. To enable these fragments to be reassembled at the receiving host, they all carry the same identifier in the Ident field. This identifier is chosen by the sending host and is intended to be unique among all the datagrams that might arrive at the destination from this source over some reasonable time period. Since all fragments of the original datagram contain this identifier, the reassembling host will be able to recognize those fragments that go together. Should all the fragments not arrive at the receiving host, the host gives up on the reassembly process and discards the fragments that did arrive. IP does not attempt to recover from missing fragments.

To see what this all means, consider what happens when host H5 sends a datagram to host H8 in the example internet shown in Figure 3.14. Assuming that the MTU is 1500 bytes for the two Ethernets and the 802.11 network, and 532 bytes for the point-to-point network, then a 1420-byte datagram (20-byte IP header plus 1400 bytes of data) sent from H5 makes it across the 802.11 network and the first Ethernet without fragmentation but must be fragmented into three datagrams at router R2. These three fragments are then forwarded by router R3 across the second Ethernet to the destination host. This situation is illustrated in Figure 3.17. This figure also serves to reinforce two important points:

1. Each fragment is itself a self-contained IP datagram that is transmitted over a sequence of physical networks, independent of the other fragments.

2. Each IP datagram is re-encapsulated for each physical network over which it travels.

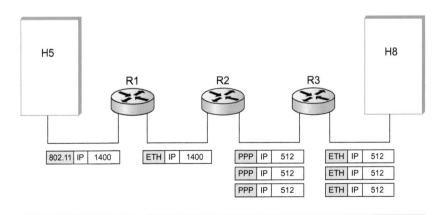

■ FIGURE 3.17 IP datagrams traversing the sequence of physical networks graphed in Figure 3.14.

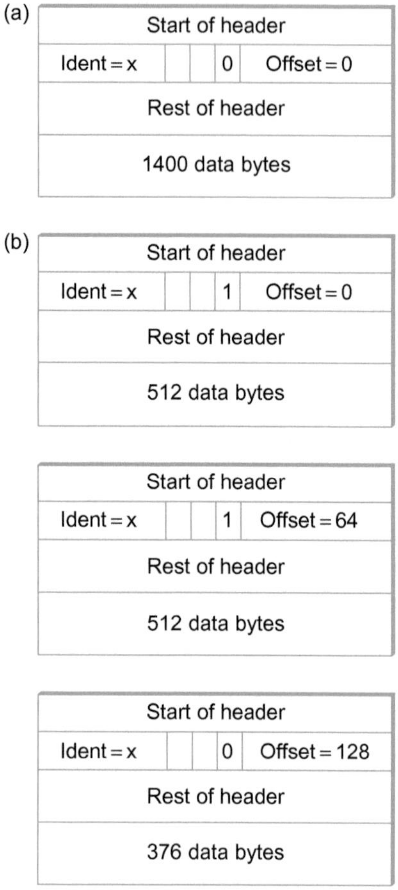

(a)

Start of header
Ident = x | | 0 | Offset = 0
Rest of header
1400 data bytes

(b)

Start of header
Ident = x | | 1 | Offset = 0
Rest of header
512 data bytes

Start of header
Ident = x | | 1 | Offset = 64
Rest of header
512 data bytes

Start of header
Ident = x | | 0 | Offset = 128
Rest of header
376 data bytes

■ FIGURE 3.18 Header fields used in IP fragmentation: (a) unfragmented packet; (b) fragmented packets.

The fragmentation process can be understood in detail by looking at the header fields of each datagram, as is done in Figure 3.18. The unfragmented packet, shown at the top, has 1400 bytes of data and a 20-byte IP header. When the packet arrives at router R2, which has an MTU of 532 bytes, it has to be fragmented. A 532-byte MTU leaves 512 bytes for data after the 20-byte IP header, so the first fragment contains 512 bytes of data. The router sets the M bit in the Flags field (see Figure 3.16), meaning that there are more fragments to follow, and it sets the Offset to 0, since this fragment contains the first part of the original datagram. The data carried in the second fragment starts with the 513th byte of the original data, so the **Offset** field in this header is set to 64, which is $512 \div 8$. Why the division by 8? Because the designers of IP decided that fragmentation should always happen on 8-byte boundaries, which means that the **Offset** field counts 8-byte chunks, not bytes. (We leave it as an exercise for you to figure out why this design decision was made.) The third fragment contains the last 376 bytes of data, and the offset is now $2 \times 512 \div 8 = 128$. Since this is the last fragment, the M bit is not set.

Observe that the fragmentation process is done in such a way that it could be repeated if a fragment arrived at another network with an even smaller MTU. Fragmentation produces smaller, valid IP datagrams that can be readily reassembled into the original datagram upon receipt, independent of the order of their arrival. Reassembly is done at the receiving host and not at each router.

IP reassembly is far from a simple process. For example, if a single fragment is lost, the receiver will still attempt to reassemble the datagram, and it will eventually give up and have to garbage-collect the resources that were used to perform the failed reassembly.[9] For this reason, among others, IP fragmentation is generally considered a good thing to avoid. Hosts are now strongly encouraged to perform "path MTU discovery," a process by which fragmentation is avoided by sending packets that are small enough to traverse the link with the smallest MTU in the path from sender to receiver.

3.2.3 Global Addresses

In the above discussion of the IP service model, we mentioned that one of the things that it provides is an addressing scheme. After all, if you want to be able to send data to any host on any network, there needs to be a way of identifying all the hosts. Thus, we need a global addressing scheme—one in which no two hosts have the same address. Global uniqueness is the first property that should be provided in an addressing scheme.[10]

Ethernet addresses are globally unique, but that alone does not suffice for an addressing scheme in a large internetwork. Ethernet addresses are also *flat*, which means that they have no structure and provide very few clues to routing protocols. (In fact, Ethernet addresses do have a

---

[9] As we will see in Chapter 8, getting a host to tie up resources needlessly can be the basis of a denial-of-service attack.

[10] For better or worse, global addressing isn't guaranteed anymore in the modern Internet, for a range of reasons, touched on in Section 4.1.

structure for the purposes of *assignment*—the first 24 bits identify the manufacturer—but this provides no useful information to routing protocols since this structure has nothing to do with network topology.) In contrast, IP addresses are *hierarchical*, by which we mean that they are made up of several parts that correspond to some sort of hierarchy in the internetwork. Specifically, IP addresses consist of two parts, usually referred to as a *network* part and a *host* part. This is a fairly logical structure for an internetwork, which is made up of many interconnected networks. The network part of an IP address identifies the network to which the host is attached; all hosts attached to the same network have the same network part in their IP address. The host part then identifies each host uniquely on that particular network. Thus, in the simple internetwork of Figure 3.14, the addresses of the hosts on network 1, for example, would all have the same network part and different host parts.

Note that the routers in Figure 3.14 are attached to two networks. They need to have an address on each network, one for each interface. For example, router R1, which sits between the wireless network and an Ethernet, has an IP address on the interface to the wireless network whose network part is the same as all the hosts on that network. It also has an IP address on the interface to the Ethernet that has the same network part as the hosts on that Ethernet. Thus, bearing in mind that a router might be implemented as a host with two network interfaces, it is more precise to think of IP addresses as belonging to interfaces than to hosts.

Now, what do these hierarchical addresses look like? Unlike some other forms of hierarchical address, the sizes of the two parts are not the same for all addresses. Originally, IP addresses were divided into three different classes, as shown in Figure 3.19, each of which defines different-sized network and host parts. (There are also class D addresses that specify a multicast group, discussed in Section 4.2, and class E addresses that are currently unused.) In all cases, the address is 32 bits long.

The class of an IP address is identified in the most significant few bits. If the first bit is 0, it is a class A address. If the first bit is 1 and the second is 0, it is a class B address. If the first two bits are 1 and the third is 0, it is a class C address. Thus, of the approximately 4 billion possible IP addresses, half are class A, one-quarter are class B, and one-eighth are class C. Each class allocates a certain number of bits for the network part of the address and the rest for the host part. Class A networks have 7 bits

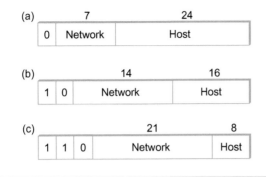

(a)

7	24

| 0 | Network | Host |

(b)

14	16

| 1 | 0 | Network | Host |

(c)

21	8

| 1 | 1 | 0 | Network | Host |

■ FIGURE 3.19 IP addresses: (a) class A; (b) class B; (c) class C.

for the network part and 24 bits for the host part, meaning that there can be only 126 class A networks (the values 0 and 127 are reserved), but each of them can accommodate up to $2^{24} - 2$ (about 16 million) hosts (again, there are two reserved values). Class B addresses allocate 14 bits for the network and 16 bits for the host, meaning that each class B network has room for 65,534 hosts. Finally, class C addresses have only 8 bits for the host and 21 for the network part. Therefore, a class C network can have only 256 unique host identifiers, which means only 254 attached hosts (one host identifier, 255, is reserved for broadcast, and 0 is not a valid host number). However, the addressing scheme supports 2^{21} class C networks.

On the face of it, this addressing scheme has a lot of flexibility, allowing networks of vastly different sizes to be accommodated fairly efficiently. The original idea was that the Internet would consist of a small number of wide area networks (these would be class A networks), a modest number of site- (campus-) sized networks (these would be class B networks), and a large number of LANs (these would be class C networks). However, it turned out not to be flexible enough, as we will see in a moment. Today, IP addresses are normally "classless"; the details of this are explained below.

Before we look at how IP addresses get used, it is helpful to look at some practical matters, such as how you write them down. By convention, IP addresses are written as four *decimal* integers separated by dots. Each integer represents the decimal value contained in 1 byte of the address, starting at the most significant. For example, the address of the computer on which this sentence was typed is 171.69.210.245.

It is important not to confuse IP addresses with Internet domain names, which are also hierarchical. Domain names tend to be ASCII strings separated by dots, such as cs.princeton.edu. We will be talking about those in Section 9.3.1. The important thing about IP addresses is that they are what is carried in the headers of IP packets, and it is those addresses that are used in IP routers to make forwarding decisions.

3.2.4 Datagram Forwarding in IP

We are now ready to look at the basic mechanism by which IP routers forward datagrams in an internetwork. Recall from Section 3.1 that *forwarding* is the process of taking a packet from an input and sending it out on the appropriate output, while *routing* is the process of building up the tables that allow the correct output for a packet to be determined. The discussion here focuses on forwarding; we take up routing in Section 3.3.

The main points to bear in mind as we discuss the forwarding of IP datagrams are the following:

- Every IP datagram contains the IP address of the destination host.
- The network part of an IP address uniquely identifies a single physical network that is part of the larger Internet.
- All hosts and routers that share the same network part of their address are connected to the same physical network and can thus communicate with each other by sending frames over that network.
- Every physical network that is part of the Internet has at least one router that, by definition, is also connected to at least one other physical network; this router can exchange packets with hosts or routers on either network.

Forwarding IP datagrams can therefore be handled in the following way. A datagram is sent from a source host to a destination host, possibly passing through several routers along the way. Any node, whether it is a host or a router, first tries to establish whether it is connected to the same physical network as the destination. To do this, it compares the network part of the destination address with the network part of the address of each of its network interfaces. (Hosts normally have only one interface, while routers normally have two or more, since they are typically connected to two or more networks.) If a match occurs, then that means that the destination lies on the same physical network as the interface, and the packet can be directly delivered over that network. Section 3.2.6 explains some of the details of this process.

If the node is not connected to the same physical network as the destination node, then it needs to send the datagram to a router. In general, each node will have a choice of several routers, and so it needs to pick the best one, or at least one that has a reasonable chance of getting the datagram closer to its destination. The router that it chooses is known as the *next hop* router. The router finds the correct next hop by consulting its forwarding table. The forwarding table is conceptually just a list of ⟨NetworkNum, NextHop⟩ pairs. (As we will see below, forwarding tables in practice often contain some additional information related to the next hop.) Normally, there is also a default router that is used if none of the entries in the table matches the destination's network number. For a host, it may be quite acceptable to have a default router and nothing else—this means that all datagrams destined for hosts not on the physical network to which the sending host is attached will be sent out through the default router.

We can describe the datagram forwarding algorithm in the following way:

```
if (NetworkNum of destination = NetworkNum of one of my interfaces) then
    deliver packet to destination over that interface
else
    if (NetworkNum of destination is in my forwarding table) then
        deliver packet to NextHop router
    else
        deliver packet to default router
```

For a host with only one interface and only a default router in its forwarding table, this simplifies to

```
if (NetworkNum of destination = my NetworkNum) then
    deliver packet to destination directly
else
    deliver packet to default router
```

Let's see how this works in the example internetwork of Figure 3.14. First, suppose that H1 wants to send a datagram to H2. Since they are on the same physical network, H1 and H2 have the same network number in their IP address. Thus, H1 deduces that it can deliver the datagram directly to H2 over the Ethernet. The one issue that needs to be resolved is how H1 finds out the correct Ethernet address for H2—this is the address resolution mechanism described in Section 3.2.6.

Bridges, Switches, and Routers

It is easy to become confused about the distinction between bridges, switches, and routers. There is good reason for such confusion, since at some level they all forward messages from one link to another. One distinction people make is based on layering: Bridges are link-level nodes (they forward frames from one link to another to implement an extended LAN), switches are network-level nodes (they forward packets from one link to another to implement a packet-switched network), and routers are internet-level nodes (they forward datagrams from one network to another to implement an internet).

The distinction between bridges and switches is now pretty much obsolete. For example, we have already seen that a multiport bridge is usually called an Ethernet switch or LAN switch. For this reason, bridges and switches are often grouped together as "layer 2 devices," where layer 2 in this context means "above the physical layer, below the internet layer."

Historically, there have been important distinctions between LAN switches (or bridges) and WAN switches (such as those based on ATM or Frame Relay). LAN switches traditionally depend on the spanning tree algorithm, while WAN switches generally run routing protocols that allow each switch to learn the topology of the whole network. This is an important distinction because knowing the whole network topology allows the switches to discriminate among different routes, while, in contrast, the spanning tree algorithm locks in a single tree over which messages are forwarded. It is also the case that the spanning tree approach does not scale as well. Again, this distinction is under threat as routing protocols from the wide area start to make their way into LAN switches.

What about switches and routers? Internally, they look quite similar (as the section on switch and router implementation will illustrate). The key distinction is the sort of packet they forward: IP datagrams in the case of routers and Layer 2 packets (Ethernet frames or ATM cells) in the case of switches.

One big difference between a network built from switches and the Internet built from routers is that the Internet is able to accommodate heterogeneity, whereas switched networks typically consists of homogeneous links. This support for heterogeneity is one of the key reasons why the Internet is so widely deployed. It is also the fact that IP runs *over* virtually every other protocol (including ATM and Ethernet) that now causes those protocols to be viewed as Layer 2 technologies.

Now suppose H5 wants to send a datagram to H8. Since these hosts are on different physical networks, they have different network numbers, so H5 deduces that it needs to send the datagram to a router. R1 is the only choice—the default router—so H1 sends the datagram over the wireless network to R1. Similarly, R1 knows that it cannot deliver a datagram directly to H8 because neither of R1's interfaces is on the same network as H8. Suppose R1's default router is R2; R1 then sends the datagram to R2 over the Ethernet. Assuming R2 has the forwarding table shown in Table 3.5, it looks up H8's network number (network 4) and forwards the datagram over the point-to-point network to R3. Finally, R3, since it is on the same network as H8, forwards the datagram directly to H8.

Table 3.5 Example Forwarding Table for Router R2 in Figure 3.14

NetworkNum	NextHop
1	R1
4	R3

Table 3.6 Complete Forwarding Table for Router R2 in Figure 3.14

NetworkNum	NextHop
1	R1
2	Interface 1
3	Interface 0
4	R3

Note that it is possible to include the information about directly connected networks in the forwarding table. For example, we could label the network interfaces of router R2 as interface 0 for the point-to-point link (network 3) and interface 1 for the Ethernet (network 2). Then R2 would have the forwarding table shown in Table 3.6.

Thus, for any network number that R2 encounters in a packet, it knows what to do. Either that network is directly connected to R2, in which case the packet can be delivered to its destination over that network, or the network is reachable via some next hop router that R2 can reach over a network to which it is connected. In either case, R2 will use ARP, described below, to find the MAC address of the node to which the packet is to be sent next.

The forwarding table used by R2 is simple enough that it could be manually configured. Usually, however, these tables are more complex and would be built up by running a routing protocol such as one of those described in Section 3.3. Also note that, in practice, the network numbers are usually longer (e.g., 128.96).

We can now see how hierarchical addressing—splitting the address into network and host parts—has improved the scalability of a large network. Routers now contain forwarding tables that list only a set of network numbers rather than all the nodes in the network. In our simple example, that meant that R2 could store the information needed to reach all the hosts in the network (of which there were eight) in a four-entry table. Even if there were 100 hosts on each physical network, R2 would still only need those same four entries. This is a good first step (although by no means the last) in achieving scalability.

This illustrates one of the most important principles of building scalable networks: To achieve scalability, you need to reduce the amount of information that is stored in each node and that is exchanged between nodes. The most common way to do that is *hierarchical aggregation*. IP introduces a two-level hierarchy, with networks at the top level and nodes at the bottom level. We have aggregated information by letting routers deal only with reaching the right network; the information that a router needs to deliver a datagram to any node on a given network is represented by a single aggregated piece of information.

3.2.5 Subnetting and Classless Addressing

The original intent of IP addresses was that the network part would uniquely identify exactly one physical network. It turns out that this approach has a couple of drawbacks. Imagine a large campus that has lots of internal networks and decides to connect to the Internet. For every network, no matter how small, the site needs at least a class C network address. Even worse, for any network with more than 255 hosts, they need a class B address. This may not seem like a big deal, and indeed it wasn't when the Internet was first envisioned, but there are only a finite number of network numbers, and there are far fewer class B addresses than class Cs. Class B addresses tend to be in particularly high demand because you never know if your network might expand beyond 255 nodes, so it is easier to use a class B address from the start than to have to renumber every host when you run out of room on a class C network. The problem we observe here is address assignment inefficiency: A network with two nodes uses an entire class C network address, thereby wasting 253 perfectly useful addresses; a class B network with slightly more than 255 hosts wastes over 64,000 addresses.

Assigning one network number per physical network, therefore, uses up the IP address space potentially much faster than we would like. While we would need to connect over 4 billion hosts to use up all the valid addresses, we only need to connect 2^{14} (about 16,000) class B networks before that part of the address space runs out. Therefore, we would like to find some way to use the network numbers more efficiently.

Assigning many network numbers has another drawback that becomes apparent when you think about routing. Recall that the amount of state that is stored in a node participating in a routing protocol is proportional to the number of other nodes, and that routing in an internet consists of building up forwarding tables that tell a router how to reach different networks. Thus, the more network numbers there are in use, the bigger the forwarding tables get. Big forwarding tables add costs to routers, and they are potentially slower to search than smaller tables for a given technology, so they degrade router performance. This provides another motivation for assigning network numbers carefully.

Subnetting provides a first step to reducing total number of network numbers that are assigned. The idea is to take a single IP network number and allocate the IP addresses with that network number to several physical networks, which are now referred to as *subnets*. Several things need to be done to make this work. First, the subnets should be close to each other. This is because at a distant point in the Internet, they will all look like a single network, having only one network number between them. This means that a router will only be able to select one route to reach any of the subnets, so they had better all be in the same general direction. A perfect situation in which to use subnetting is a large campus or corporation that has many physical networks. From outside the campus, all you need to know to reach any subnet inside the campus is where the campus connects to the rest of the Internet. This is often at a single point, so one entry in your forwarding table will suffice. Even if there are multiple points at which the campus is connected to the rest of the Internet, knowing how to get to one point in the campus network is still a good start.

The mechanism by which a single network number can be shared among multiple networks involves configuring all the nodes on each subnet with a *subnet mask*. With simple IP addresses, all hosts on the same network must have the same network number. The subnet mask enables us to introduce a *subnet number*; all hosts on the same physical network will have the same subnet number, which means that hosts may be on different physical networks but share a single network number. This concept is illustrated in Figure 3.20.

What subnetting means to a host is that it is now configured with both an IP address and a subnet mask for the subnet to which it is attached. For example, host H1 in Figure 3.21 is configured with an address of 128.96.34.15 and a subnet mask of 255.255.255.128. (All hosts on a given subnet are configured with the same mask; that is, there is exactly one subnet mask per subnet.) The bitwise AND of these two numbers defines the subnet number of the host and of all other hosts on the same subnet. In this case, 128.96.34.15 AND 255.255.255.128 equals 128.96.34.0, so this is the subnet number for the topmost subnet in the figure.

When the host wants to send a packet to a certain IP address, the first thing it does is to perform a bitwise AND between its own subnet mask and the destination IP address. If the result equals the subnet number of the sending host, then it knows that the destination host is on the same subnet and the packet can be delivered directly over the subnet.

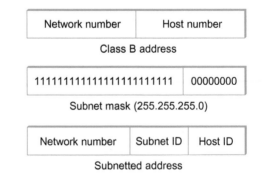

FIGURE 3.20 Subnet addressing.

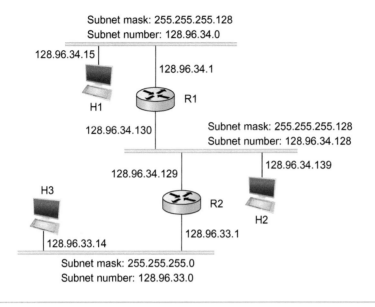

Subnet mask: 255.255.255.128
Subnet number: 128.96.34.0

128.96.34.15

128.96.34.1

H1   R1

128.96.34.130

Subnet mask: 255.255.255.128
Subnet number: 128.96.34.128

128.96.34.139

128.96.34.129

H3

R2

H2

128.96.33.1

128.96.33.14

Subnet mask: 255.255.255.0
Subnet number: 128.96.33.0

■ FIGURE 3.21 An example of subnetting.

If the results are not equal, the packet needs to be sent to a router to be forwarded to another subnet. For example, if H1 is sending to H2, then H1 ANDs its subnet mask (255.255.255.128) with the address for H2 (128.96.34.139) to obtain 128.96.34.128. This does not match the subnet number for H1 (128.96.34.0) so H1 knows that H2 is on a different subnet. Since H1 cannot deliver the packet to H2 directly over the subnet, it sends the packet to its default router R1.

The forwarding table of a router also changes slightly when we introduce subnetting. Recall that we previously had a forwarding table that consisted of entries of the form ⟨NetworkNum, NextHop⟩. To support subnetting, the table must now hold entries of the form ⟨SubnetNumber, SubnetMask, NextHop⟩. To find the right entry in the table, the router ANDs the packet's destination address with the SubnetMask for each entry in turn; if the result matches the SubnetNumber of the entry, then this is the right entry to use, and it forwards the packet to the next hop router indicated. In the example network of Figure 3.21, router R1 would have the entries shown in Table 3.7.

Continuing with the example of a datagram from H1 being sent to H2, R1 would AND H2's address (128.96.34.139) with the subnet mask of the first entry (255.255.255.128) and compare the result (128.96.34.128) with

Table 3.7 Example Forwarding Table with Subnetting for Figure 3.21

SubnetNumber	SubnetMask	NextHop
128.96.34.0	255.255.255.128	Interface 0
128.96.34.128	255.255.255.128	Interface 1
128.96.33.0	255.255.255.0	R2

the network number for that entry (128.96.34.0). Since this is not a match, it proceeds to the next entry. This time a match does occur, so R1 delivers the datagram to H2 using interface 1, which is the interface connected to the same network as H2.

We can now describe the datagram forwarding algorithm in the following way:

```
D = destination IP address
for each forwarding table entry ⟨SubnetNumber, SubnetMask, NextHop⟩
    D1 = SubnetMask & D
    if D1 = SubnetNumber
        if NextHop is an interface
            deliver datagram directly to destination
        else
            deliver datagram to NextHop (a router)
```

Although not shown in this example, a default route would usually be included in the table and would be used if no explicit matches were found. We note in passing that a naive implementation of this algorithm—one involving repeated ANDing of the destination address with a subnet mask that may not be different every time, and a linear table search—would be very inefficient.

An important consequence of subnetting is that different parts of the internet see the world differently. From outside our hypothetical campus, routers see a single network. In the example above, routers outside the campus see the collection of networks in Figure 3.21 as just the network 128.96, and they keep one entry in their forwarding tables to tell them how to reach it. Routers within the campus, however, need to be able to route packets to the right subnet. Thus, not all parts of the internet see exactly the same routing information. This is an example of *aggregation* of routing information, which is fundamental to scaling of the routing system. The next section shows how aggregation can be taken to another level.

Classless Addressing

Subnetting has a counterpart, sometimes called *supernetting*, but more often called *Classless Interdomain Routing* or CIDR, pronounced "cider." CIDR takes the subnetting idea to its logical conclusion by essentially doing away with address classes altogether. Why isn't subnetting alone sufficient? In essence, subnetting only allows us to split a classful address among multiple subnets, while CIDR allows us to coalesce several classful addresses into a single "supernet." This further tackles the address space inefficiency noted above, and does so in a way that keeps the routing system from being overloaded.

To see how the issues of address space efficiency and scalability of the routing system are coupled, consider the hypothetical case of a company whose network has 256 hosts on it. That is slightly too many for a Class C address, so you would be tempted to assign a class B. However, using up a chunk of address space that could address 65,535 to address 256 hosts has an efficiency of only $256/65{,}535 = 0.39\%$. Even though subnetting can help us to assign addresses carefully, it does not get around the fact that any organization with more than 255 hosts, or an expectation of eventually having that many, wants a class B address.

The first way you might deal with this issue would be to refuse to give a class B address to any organization that requests one unless they can show a need for something close to 64K addresses, and instead giving them an appropriate number of class C addresses to cover the expected number of hosts. Since we would now be handing out address space in chunks of 256 addresses at a time, we could more accurately match the amount of address space consumed to the size of the organization. For any organization with at least 256 hosts, we can guarantee an address utilization of at least 50%, and typically much more.

This solution, however, raises a problem that is at least as serious: excessive storage requirements at the routers. If a single site has, say, 16 class C network numbers assigned to it, that means every Internet backbone router needs 16 entries in its routing tables to direct packets to that site. This is true even if the path to every one of those networks is the same. If we had assigned a class B address to the site, the same routing information could be stored in one table entry. However, our address assignment efficiency would then be only $16 \times 255/65{,}536 = 6.2\%$.

CIDR, therefore, tries to balance the desire to minimize the number of routes that a router needs to know against the need to hand out addresses efficiently. To do this, CIDR helps us to *aggregate* routes. That is, it lets us use a single entry in a forwarding table to tell us how to reach a lot of different networks. As noted above it does this by breaking the rigid boundaries between address classes. To understand how this works, consider our hypothetical organization with 16 class C network numbers. Instead of handing out 16 addresses at random, we can hand out a block of *contiguous* class C addresses. Suppose we assign the class C network numbers from 192.4.16 through 192.4.31. Observe that the top 20 bits of all the addresses in this range are the same (11000000 00000100 0001). Thus, what we have effectively created is a 20-bit network number—something that is between a class B network number and a class C number in terms of the number of hosts that it can support. In other words, we get both the high address efficiency of handing out addresses in chunks smaller than a class B network, and a single network prefix that can be used in forwarding tables. Observe that, for this scheme to work, we need to hand out blocks of class C addresses that share a common prefix, which means that each block must contain a number of class C networks that is a power of two.

CIDR requires a new type of notation to represent network numbers, or *prefixes* as they are known, because the prefixes can be of any length. The convention is to place a /X after the prefix, where X is the prefix length in bits. So, for the example above, the 20-bit prefix for all the networks 192.4.16 through 192.4.31 is represented as 192.4.16/20. By contrast, if we wanted to represent a single class C network number, which is 24 bits long, we would write it 192.4.16/24. Today, with CIDR being the norm, it is more common to hear people talk about "slash 24" prefixes than class C networks. Note that representing a network address in this way is similar to the ⟨mask, value⟩ approach used in subnetting, as long as masks consist of contiguous bits starting from the most significant bit (which in practice is almost always the case).

The ability to aggregate routes at the edge of the network as we have just seen is only the first step. Imagine an Internet service provider network, whose primary job is to provide Internet connectivity to a large number of corporations and campuses (customers). If we assign prefixes

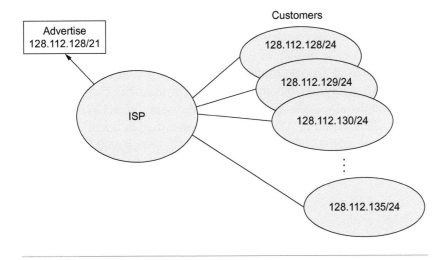

■ FIGURE 3.22 Route aggregation with CIDR.

to the customers in such a way that many different customer networks connected to the provider network share a common, shorter address prefix, then we can get even greater aggregation of routes. Consider the example in Figure 3.22. Assume that eight customers served by the provider network have each been assigned adjacent 24-bit network prefixes. Those prefixes all start with the same 21 bits. Since all of the customers are reachable through the same provider network, it can advertise a single route to all of them by just advertising the common 21-bit prefix they share. And it can do this even if not all the 24-bit prefixes have been handed out, as long as the provider ultimately *will* have the right to hand out those prefixes to a customer. One way to accomplish that is to assign a portion of address space to the provider in advance and then to let the network provider assign addresses from that space to its customers as needed. Note that, in contrast to this simple example, there is no need for all customer prefixes to be the same length.

IP Forwarding Revisited

In all our discussion of IP forwarding so far, we have assumed that we could find the network number in a packet and then look up that number in a forwarding table. However, now that we have introduced CIDR, we need to reexamine this assumption. CIDR means that prefixes may be of any length, from 2 to 32 bits. Furthermore, it is sometimes possible to have prefixes in the forwarding table that "overlap," in the sense that some addresses may match more than one prefix. For example, we might find both 171.69 (a 16-bit prefix) and 171.69.10 (a 24-bit prefix) in the forwarding table of a single router. In this case, a packet destined to, say, 171.69.10.5 clearly matches both prefixes. The rule in this case is based on the principle of "longest match"; that is, the packet matches the longest prefix, which would be 171.69.10 in this example. On the other hand, a packet destined to 171.69.20.5 would match 171.69 and *not* 171.69.10, and in the absence of any other matching entry in the routing table 171.69 would be the longest match.

The task of efficiently finding the longest match between an IP address and the variable-length prefixes in a forwarding table has been a fruitful field of research in recent years, and the Further Reading section of this chapter provides some references. The most well-known algorithm uses an approach known as a *PATRICIA tree*, which was actually developed well in advance of CIDR.

3.2.6 Address Translation (ARP)

In the previous section we talked about how to get IP datagrams to the right physical network but glossed over the issue of how to get a datagram to a particular host or router on that network. The main issue is that IP datagrams contain IP addresses, but the physical interface hardware on the host or router to which you want to send the datagram only understands the addressing scheme of that particular network. Thus, we need to translate the IP address to a link-level address that makes sense on this network (e.g., a 48-bit Ethernet address). We can then encapsulate the IP datagram inside a frame that contains that link-level address and send it either to the ultimate destination or to a router that promises to forward the datagram toward the ultimate destination.

One simple way to map an IP address into a physical network address is to encode a host's physical address in the host part of its IP address. For example, a host with physical address 00100001 01001001 (which has the decimal value 33 in the upper byte and 81 in the lower byte) might be given the IP address 128.96.33.81. While this solution has been used on some networks, it is limited in that the network's physical addresses can be no more than 16 bits long in this example; they can be only 8 bits long on a class C network. This clearly will not work for 48-bit Ethernet addresses.

A more general solution would be for each host to maintain a table of address pairs; that is, the table would map IP addresses into physical addresses. While this table could be centrally managed by a system administrator and then copied to each host on the network, a better approach would be for each host to dynamically learn the contents of the table using the network. This can be accomplished using the Address Resolution Protocol (ARP). The goal of ARP is to enable each host on a network to build up a table of mappings between IP addresses and link-level addresses. Since these mappings may change over time (e.g., because an Ethernet card in a host breaks and is replaced by a new one with a new address), the entries are timed out periodically and removed. This happens on the order of every 15 minutes. The set of mappings currently stored in a host is known as the ARP cache or ARP table.

ARP takes advantage of the fact that many link-level network technologies, such as Ethernet, support broadcast. If a host wants to send an IP datagram to a host (or router) that it knows to be on the same network (i.e., the sending and receiving node have the same IP network number), it first checks for a mapping in the cache. If no mapping is found, it needs to invoke the Address Resolution Protocol over the network. It does this by broadcasting an ARP query onto the network. This query contains the IP address in question (the target IP address). Each host receives the query and checks to see if it matches its IP address. If it does match, the host sends a response message that contains its link-layer address back to the originator of the query. The originator adds the information contained in this response to its ARP table.

The query message also includes the IP address and link-layer address of the sending host. Thus, when a host broadcasts a query message, each host on the network can learn the sender's link-level and IP addresses and place that information in its ARP table. However, not every host adds this information to its ARP table. If the host already has an entry for that host in its table, it "refreshes" this entry; that is, it resets the length of time until it discards the entry. If that host is the target of the query, then it adds the information about the sender to its table, even if it did not already have an entry for that host. This is because there is a good chance that the source host is about to send it an application-level message, and it may eventually have to send a response or ACK back to the source; it will need the source's physical address to do this. If a host is not the target and does not already have an entry for the source in its ARP table, then it does not

0	8	16	31
Hardware type = 1		ProtocolType = 0x0800	
HLen = 48	PLen = 32	Operation	
SourceHardwareAddr (bytes 0–3)			
SourceHardwareAddr (bytes 4–5)		SourceProtocolAddr (bytes 0–1)	
SourceProtocolAddr (bytes 2–3)		TargetHardwareAddr (bytes 0–1)	
TargetHardwareAddr (bytes 2–5)			
TargetProtocolAddr (bytes 0–3)			

■ FIGURE 3.23 ARP packet format for mapping IP addresses into Ethernet addresses.

add an entry for the source. This is because there is no reason to believe that this host will ever need the source's link-level address; there is no need to clutter its ARP table with this information.

Figure 3.23 shows the ARP packet format for IP-to-Ethernet address mappings. In fact, ARP can be used for lots of other kinds of mappings—the major differences are in the address sizes. In addition to the IP and link-layer addresses of both sender and target, the packet contains

- A HardwareType field, which specifies the type of physical network (e.g., Ethernet)
- A ProtocolType field, which specifies the higher-layer protocol (e.g., IP)
- HLen ("hardware" address length) and PLen ("protocol" address length) fields, which specify the length of the link-layer address and higher-layer protocol address, respectively
- An Operation field, which specifies whether this is a request or a response
- The source and target hardware (Ethernet) and protocol (IP) addresses

Note that the results of the ARP process can be added as an extra column in a forwarding table like the one in Table 4.1. Thus, for example, when R2 needs to forward a packet to network 2, it not only finds that the next hop is R1, but also finds the MAC address to place on the packet to send it to R1.

We have now seen the basic mechanisms that IP provides for dealing with both heterogeneity and scale. On the issue of heterogeneity, IP begins by defining a best-effort service model that makes minimal assumptions about the underlying networks; most notably, this service model is based on unreliable datagrams. IP then makes two important additions to this starting point: (1) a common packet format (fragmentation/reassembly is the mechanism that makes this format work over networks with different MTUs) and (2) a global address space for identifying all hosts (ARP is the mechanism that makes this global address space work over networks with different physical addressing schemes). On the issue of scale, IP uses hierarchical aggregation to reduce the amount of information needed to forward packets. Specifically, IP addresses are partitioned into network and host components, with packets first routed toward the destination network and then delivered to the correct host on that network.

3.2.7 **Host Configuration (DHCP)**

In Section 2.6, we observed that Ethernet addresses are configured into the network adaptor by the manufacturer, and this process is managed in such a way to ensure that these addresses are globally unique. This is clearly a sufficient condition to ensure that any collection of hosts connected to a single Ethernet (including an extended LAN) will have unique addresses. Furthermore, uniqueness is all we ask of Ethernet addresses.

IP addresses, by contrast, not only must be unique on a given internetwork but also must reflect the structure of the internetwork. As noted above, they contain a network part and a host part, and the network part must be the same for all hosts on the same network. Thus, it is not possible for the IP address to be configured once into a host when it is manufactured, since that would imply that the manufacturer knew which hosts were going to end up on which networks, and it would mean that a host, once connected to one network, could never move to another. For this reason, IP addresses need to be reconfigurable.

In addition to an IP address, there are some other pieces of information a host needs to have before it can start sending packets. The most notable of these is the address of a default router—the place to which it can send packets whose destination address is not on the same network as the sending host.

Most host operating systems provide a way for a system administrator, or even a user, to manually configure the IP information needed by a host; however, there are some obvious drawbacks to such manual configuration. One is that it is simply a lot of work to configure all the hosts in a large network directly, especially when you consider that such hosts are not reachable over a network until they are configured. Even more importantly, the configuration process is very error prone, since it is necessary to ensure that every host gets the correct network number and that no two hosts receive the same IP address. For these reasons, automated configuration methods are required. The primary method uses a protocol known as the *Dynamic Host Configuration Protocol* (DHCP).

DHCP relies on the existence of a DHCP server that is responsible for providing configuration information to hosts. There is at least one DHCP server for an administrative domain. At the simplest level, the DHCP server can function just as a centralized repository for host configuration information. Consider, for example, the problem of administering addresses in the internetwork of a large company. DHCP saves the network administrators from having to walk around to every host in the company with a list of addresses and network map in hand and configuring each host manually. Instead, the configuration information for each host could be stored in the DHCP server and automatically retrieved by each host when it is booted or connected to the network. However, the administrator would still pick the address that each host is to receive; he would just store that in the server. In this model, the configuration information for each host is stored in a table that is indexed by some form of unique client identifier, typically the hardware address (e.g., the Ethernet address of its network adaptor).

A more sophisticated use of DHCP saves the network administrator from even having to assign addresses to individual hosts. In this model, the DHCP server maintains a pool of available addresses that it hands out to hosts on demand. This considerably reduces the amount of configuration an administrator must do, since now it is only necessary to allocate a range of IP addresses (all with the same network number) to each network.

Since the goal of DHCP is to minimize the amount of manual configuration required for a host to function, it would rather defeat the purpose if each host had to be configured with the address of a DHCP server. Thus, the first problem faced by DHCP is that of server discovery.

To contact a DHCP server, a newly booted or attached host sends a **DHCPDISCOVER** message to a special IP address (255.255.255.255) that is an IP broadcast address. This means it will be received by all hosts and routers on that network. (Routers do not forward such packets onto other networks, preventing broadcast to the entire Internet.) In the simplest case, one of these nodes is the DHCP server for the network. The server would then reply to the host that generated the discovery message (all the other nodes would ignore it). However, it is not really desirable to require one DHCP server on every network, because this still creates a potentially large number of servers that need to be correctly and consistently configured. Thus, DHCP uses the concept of a *relay agent*. There is at least one relay agent on each network, and it is configured with just one piece of information: the IP address of the DHCP server. When a relay agent receives a **DHCPDISCOVER** message, it unicasts it to the DHCP server and awaits the response, which it will then send back to the requesting client. The process of relaying a message from a host to a remote DHCP server is shown in Figure 3.24.

Figure 3.25 shows the format of a DHCP message. The message is actually sent using a protocol called the *User Datagram Protocol* (UDP) that runs over IP. UDP is discussed in detail in the next chapter, but the only interesting thing it does in this context is to provide a demultiplexing key that says, "This is a DHCP packet."

DHCP is derived from an earlier protocol called BOOTP, and some of the packet fields are thus not strictly relevant to host configuration. When

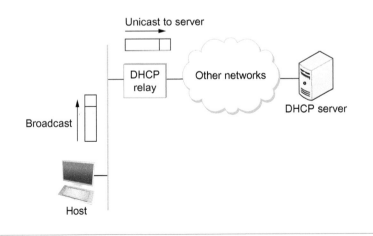

■ FIGURE 3.24 A DHCP relay agent receives a broadcast **DHCPDISCOVER** message from a host and sends a unicast **DHCPDISCOVER** to the DHCP server.

Operation	HType	HLen	Hops
Xid			
Secs		Flags	
ciaddr			
yiaddr			
siaddr			
giaddr			
chaddr (16 bytes)			
sname (64 bytes)			
file (128 bytes)			
options			

■ FIGURE 3.25 DHCP packet format.

trying to obtain configuration information, the client puts its hardware address (e.g., its Ethernet address) in the chaddr field. The DHCP server replies by filling in the yiaddr ("your" IP address) field and sending it to the client. Other information such as the default router to be used by this client can be included in the options field.

In the case where DHCP dynamically assigns IP addresses to hosts, it is clear that hosts cannot keep addresses indefinitely, as this would eventually cause the server to exhaust its address pool. At the same time, a host cannot be depended upon to give back its address, since it might have crashed, been unplugged from the network, or been turned off. Thus, DHCP allows addresses to be leased for some period of time. Once the lease expires, the server is free to return that address to its pool. A host with a leased address clearly needs to renew the lease periodically if in fact it is still connected to the network and functioning correctly.

DHCP illustrates an important aspect of scaling: the scaling of network management. While discussions of scaling often focus on keeping the state in network devices from growing too fast, it is important to pay attention to growth of network management complexity. By allowing network managers to configure a range of IP addresses per network rather than one IP address per host, DHCP improves the manageability of a network.

Note that DHCP may also introduce some more complexity into network management, since it makes the binding between physical hosts and IP addresses much more dynamic. This may make the network manager's job more difficult if, for example, it becomes necessary to locate a malfunctioning host.

3.2.8 Error Reporting (ICMP)

The next issue is how the Internet treats errors. While IP is perfectly willing to drop datagrams when the going gets tough—for example, when a router does not know how to forward the datagram or when one fragment of a datagram fails to arrive at the destination—it does not necessarily fail silently. IP is always configured with a companion protocol, known as the *Internet Control Message Protocol* (ICMP), that defines a collection of error messages that are sent back to the source host whenever a router or host is unable to process an IP datagram successfully. For example, ICMP defines error messages indicating that the destination host is unreachable (perhaps due to a link failure), that the reassembly process failed, that the TTL had reached 0, that the IP header checksum failed, and so on.

ICMP also defines a handful of control messages that a router can send back to a source host. One of the most useful control messages, called an *ICMP-Redirect*, tells the source host that there is a better route to the destination. ICMP-Redirects are used in the following situation. Suppose a host is connected to a network that has two routers attached to it, called *R1* and *R2*, where the host uses R1 as its default router. Should R1 ever receive a datagram from the host, where based on its forwarding table it knows that R2 would have been a better choice for a particular destination address, it sends an ICMP-Redirect back to the host, instructing it to use R2 for all future datagrams addressed to that destination. The host then adds this new route to its forwarding table.

ICMP also provides the basis for two widely used debugging tools, ping and traceroute. ping uses ICMP echo messages to determine if a node is reachable and alive. traceroute uses a slightly non-intuitive technique to determine the set of routers along the path to a destination, which is the topic for one of the exercises at the end of this chapter.

3.2.9 Virtual Networks and Tunnels

We conclude our introduction to IP by considering an issue you might not have anticipated, but one that is becoming increasingly important.

Our discussion up to this point has focused on making it possible for nodes on different networks to communicate with each other in an unrestricted way. This is the usually the goal in the Internet—everybody wants to be able to send email to everybody, and the creator of a new website wants to reach the widest possible audience. However, there are many situations where more controlled connectivity is required. An important example of such a situation is the *virtual private network* (VPN).

The term *VPN* is heavily overused and definitions vary, but intuitively we can define a VPN by considering first the idea of a private network. Corporations with many sites often build private networks by leasing transmission lines from the phone companies and using those lines to interconnect sites. In such a network, communication is restricted to take place only among the sites of that corporation, which is often desirable for security reasons. To make a private network *virtual*, the leased transmission lines—which are not shared with any other corporations—would be replaced by some sort of shared network. A virtual circuit (VC) is a very reasonable replacement for a leased line because it still provides a logical point-to-point connection between the corporation's sites. For example, if corporation X has a VC from site A to site B, then clearly it can send packets between sites A and B. But there is no way that corporation Y can get its packets delivered to site B without first establishing its own virtual circuit to site B, and the establishment of such a VC can be administratively prevented, thus preventing unwanted connectivity between corporation X and corporation Y.

Figure 3.26(a) shows two private networks for two separate corporations. In Figure 3.26(b) they are both migrated to a virtual circuit network. The limited connectivity of a real private network is maintained, but since the private networks now share the same transmission facilities and switches we say that two virtual private networks have been created.

In Figure 3.26, a virtual circuit network (using Frame Relay or ATM, for example) is used to provide the controlled connectivity among sites. It is also possible to provide a similar function using an IP network—an internetwork—to provide the connectivity. However, we cannot just connect the various corporations' sites to a single internetwork because that would provide connectivity between corporation X and corporation Y, which we wish to avoid. To solve this problem, we need to introduce a new concept, the *IP tunnel*.

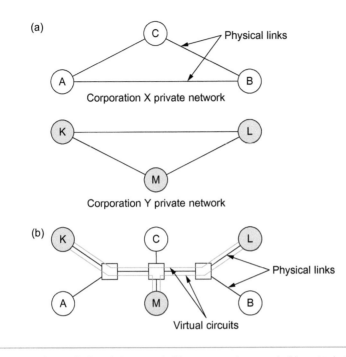

■ FIGURE 3.26 An example of virtual private networks: (a) two separate private networks; (b) two virtual private networks sharing common switches.

We can think of an IP tunnel as a virtual point-to-point link between a pair of nodes that are actually separated by an arbitrary number of networks. The virtual link is created within the router at the entrance to the tunnel by providing it with the IP address of the router at the far end of the tunnel. Whenever the router at the entrance of the tunnel wants to send a packet over this virtual link, it encapsulates the packet inside an IP datagram. The destination address in the IP header is the address of the router at the far end of the tunnel, while the source address is that of the encapsulating router.

In the forwarding table of the router at the entrance to the tunnel, this virtual link looks much like a normal link. Consider, for example, the network in Figure 3.27. A tunnel has been configured from R1 to R2 and assigned a virtual interface number of 0. The forwarding table in R1 might therefore look like Table 3.8.

R1 has two physical interfaces. Interface 0 connects to network 1; interface 1 connects to a large internetwork and is thus the default for all traffic

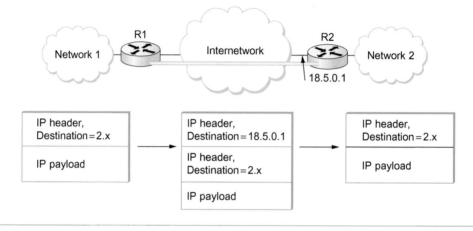

Table 3.8 Forwarding Table for Router R1 in Figure 3.27

NetworkNum	NextHop
1	Interface 0
2	Virtual interface 0
Default	Interface 1

that does not match something more specific in the forwarding table. In addition, R1 has a virtual interface, which is the interface to the tunnel. Suppose R1 receives a packet from network 1 that contains an address in network 2. The forwarding table says this packet should be sent out virtual interface 0. In order to send a packet out this interface, the router takes the packet, adds an IP header addressed to R2, and then proceeds to forward the packet as if it had just been received. R2's address is 18.5.0.1; since the network number of this address is 18, not 1 or 2, a packet destined for R2 will be forwarded out the default interface into the internetwork.

Once the packet leaves R1, it looks to the rest of the world like a normal IP packet destined to R2, and it is forwarded accordingly. All the routers in the internetwork forward it using normal means, until it arrives at R2. When R2 receives the packet, it finds that it carries its own address, so it removes the IP header and looks at the payload of the packet. What it finds is an inner IP packet whose destination address is in network 2. R2 now processes this packet like any other IP packet it receives. Since R2 is directly connected to network 2, it forwards the packet on to that network. Figure 3.27 shows the change in encapsulation of the packet as it moves across the network.

While R2 is acting as the endpoint of the tunnel, there is nothing to prevent it from performing the normal functions of a router. For example, it might receive some packets that are not tunneled, but that are addressed to networks that it knows how to reach, and it would forward them in the normal way.

You might wonder why anyone would want to go to all the trouble of creating a tunnel and changing the encapsulation of a packet as it goes across an internetwork. One reason is security, which we will discuss in more detail in Chapter 8. Supplemented with encryption, a tunnel can become a very private sort of link across a public network. Another reason may be that R1 and R2 have some capabilities that are not widely available in the intervening networks, such as multicast routing. By connecting these routers with a tunnel, we can build a virtual network in which all the routers with this capability appear to be directly connected. This in fact is how the MBone (multicast backbone) is built, as we will see in Section 4.2. A third reason to build tunnels is to carry packets from protocols other than IP across an IP network. As long as the routers at either end of the tunnel know how to handle these other protocols, the IP tunnel looks to them like a point-to-point link over which they can send non-IP packets. Tunnels also provide a mechanism by which we can force a packet to be delivered to a particular place even if its original header—the one that gets encapsulated inside the tunnel header—might suggest that it should go somewhere else. We will see an application of this when we consider mobile hosts in Section 4.4.2. Thus, we see that tunneling is a powerful and quite general technique for building virtual links across internetworks.

Tunneling does have its downsides. One is that it increases the length of packets; this might represent a significant waste of bandwidth for short packets. Longer packets might be subject to fragmentation, which has its own set of drawbacks. There may also be performance implications for the routers at either end of the tunnel, since they need to do more work than normal forwarding as they add and remove the tunnel header.

Finally, there is a management cost for the administrative entity that is responsible for setting up the tunnels and making sure they are correctly handled by the routing protocols.

3.3 **ROUTING**

So far in this chapter we have assumed that the switches and routers have enough knowledge of the network topology so they can choose the right port onto which each packet should be output. In the case of virtual circuits, routing is an issue only for the connection request packet; all subsequent packets follow the same path as the request. In datagram networks, including IP networks, routing is an issue for every packet. In either case, a switch or router needs to be able to look at a destination address and then to determine which of the output ports is the best choice to get a packet to that address. As we saw in Section 3.1.1, the switch makes this decision by consulting a forwarding table. The fundamental problem of routing is how switches and routers acquire the information in their forwarding tables.

We restate an important distinction, which is often neglected, between *forwarding* and *routing*. Forwarding consists of taking a packet, looking at its destination address, consulting a table, and sending the packet in a direction determined by that table. We saw several examples of forwarding in the preceding section. Routing is the process by which forwarding tables are built. We also note that forwarding is a relatively simple and well-defined process performed locally at a node, whereas routing depends on complex distributed algorithms that have continued to evolve throughout the history of networking.

While the terms *forwarding table* and *routing table* are sometimes used interchangeably, we will make a distinction between them here. The forwarding table is used when a packet is being forwarded and so must contain enough information to accomplish the forwarding function. This means that a row in the forwarding table contains the mapping from a network prefix to an outgoing interface and some MAC information, such as the Ethernet address of the next hop. The routing table, on the other hand, is the table that is built up by the routing algorithms as a precursor to building the forwarding table. It generally contains mappings from network prefixes to next hops. It may also contain information about how this

Table 3.9 Example Rows from (a) Routing and (b) Forwarding Tables

(a)

Prefix/Length	Next Hop
18/8	171.69.245.10

(b)

Prefix/Length	Interface	MAC Address
18/8	if0	8:0:2b:e4:b:1:2

information was learned, so that the router will be able to decide when it should discard some information.

Whether the routing table and forwarding table are actually separate data structures is something of an implementation choice, but there are numerous reasons to keep them separate. For example, the forwarding table needs to be structured to optimize the process of looking up an address when forwarding a packet, while the routing table needs to be optimized for the purpose of calculating changes in topology. In many cases, the forwarding table may even be implemented in specialized hardware, whereas this is rarely if ever done for the routing table. Table 3.9 provides an example of a row from each sort of table. In this case, the routing table tells us that network prefix 18/8 is to be reached by a next hop router with the IP address 171.69.245.10, while the forwarding table contains the information about exactly how to forward a packet to that next hop: Send it out interface number 0 with a MAC address of 8:0:2b:e4:b:1:2. Note that the last piece of information is provided by the Address Resolution Protocol.

Before getting into the details of routing, we need to remind ourselves of the key question we should be asking anytime we try to build a mechanism for the Internet: "Does this solution scale?" The answer for the algorithms and protocols described in this section is "not so much." They are designed for networks of fairly modest size—up to a few hundred nodes, in practice. However, the solutions we describe do serve as a building block for a hierarchical routing infrastructure that is used in the Internet today. Specifically, the protocols described in this section are collectively known as *intradomain* routing protocols, or *interior gateway protocols* (IGPs). To understand these terms, we need to define a routing *domain*. A good working definition is an internetwork in which all the routers are under the same administrative control (e.g., a single university campus, or the network of a single Internet Service Provider). The relevance of this definition will become apparent in the next chapter when we look at *interdomain* routing protocols. For now, the important thing to keep in mind is that we are considering the problem of routing in the context of small to midsized networks, not for a network the size of the Internet.

3.3.1 Network as a Graph

Routing is, in essence, a problem of graph theory. Figure 3.28 shows a graph representing a network. The nodes of the graph, labeled A through F, may be hosts, switches, routers, or networks. For our initial discussion, we will focus on the case where the nodes are routers. The edges of the graph correspond to the network links. Each edge has an associated *cost*, which gives some indication of the desirability of sending traffic over that link. A discussion of how edge costs are assigned is given in Section 3.3.4.[11]

The basic problem of routing is to find the lowest-cost path between any two nodes, where the cost of a path equals the sum of the costs of all the edges that make up the path. For a simple network like the one in Figure 3.28, you could imagine just calculating all the shortest paths and

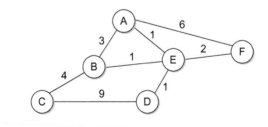

■ FIGURE 3.28 Network represented as a graph.

[11]In the example networks (graphs) used throughout this chapter, we use undirected edges and assign each edge a single cost. This is actually a slight simplification. It is more accurate to make the edges directed, which typically means that there would be a pair of edges between each node—one flowing in each direction, and each with its own edge cost.

loading them into some nonvolatile storage on each node. Such a static approach has several shortcomings:

- It does not deal with node or link failures.
- It does not consider the addition of new nodes or links.
- It implies that edge costs cannot change, even though we might reasonably wish to have link costs change over time (e.g., assigning high cost to a link that is heavily loaded).

For these reasons, routing is achieved in most practical networks by running routing protocols among the nodes. These protocols provide a distributed, dynamic way to solve the problem of finding the lowest-cost path in the presence of link and node failures and changing edge costs. Note the word *distributed* in the previous sentence; it is difficult to make centralized solutions scalable, so all the widely used routing protocols use distributed algorithms.[12]

The distributed nature of routing algorithms is one of the main reasons why this has been such a rich field of research and development—there are a lot of challenges in making distributed algorithms work well. For example, distributed algorithms raise the possibility that two routers will at one instant have different ideas about the shortest path to some destination. In fact, each one may think that the other one is closer to the destination and decide to send packets to the other one. Clearly, such packets will be stuck in a loop until the discrepancy between the two routers is resolved, and it would be good to resolve it as soon as possible. This is just one example of the type of problem routing protocols must address.

To begin our analysis, we assume that the edge costs in the network are known. We will examine the two main classes of routing protocols: *distance vector* and *link state*. In Section 3.3.4, we return to the problem of calculating edge costs in a meaningful way.

3.3.2 Distance-Vector (RIP)

The idea behind the distance-vector algorithm is suggested by its name.[13] Each node constructs a one-dimensional array (a vector) containing the "distances" (costs) to all other nodes and distributes that vector to its

LAB 06:
RIP

---

[12]This widely held assumption, however, has been re-examined in recent years—see the Further Reading section.
[13]The other common name for this class of algorithm is Bellman-Ford, after its inventors.

immediate neighbors. The starting assumption for distance-vector routing is that each node knows the cost of the link to each of its directly
connected neighbors. These costs may be provided when the router is
configured by a network manager. A link that is down is assigned an
infinite cost.

To see how a distance-vector routing algorithm works, it is easiest to
consider an example like the one depicted in Figure 3.29. In this example,
the cost of each link is set to 1, so that a least-cost path is simply the one
with the fewest hops. (Since all edges have the same cost, we do not show
the costs in the graph.) We can represent each node's knowledge about
the distances to all other nodes as a table like Table 3.10. Note that each

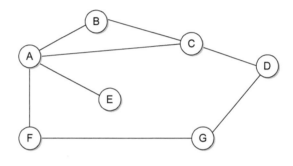

■ FIGURE 3.29 Distance-vector routing: an example network.

Table 3.10 Initial Distances Stored at Each Node (Global View)

Information Stored at Node	Distance to Reach Node						
	A	B	C	D	E	F	G
A	0	1	1	∞	1	1	∞
B	1	0	1	∞	∞	∞	∞
C	1	1	0	1	∞	∞	∞
D	∞	∞	1	0	∞	∞	1
E	1	∞	∞	∞	0	∞	∞
F	1	∞	∞	∞	∞	0	1
G	∞	∞	∞	1	∞	1	0

node knows only the information in one row of the table (the one that bears its name in the left column). The global view that is presented here is not available at any single point in the network.

We may consider each row in Table 3.10 as a list of distances from one node to all other nodes, representing the current beliefs of that node. Initially, each node sets a cost of 1 to its directly connected neighbors and ∞ to all other nodes. Thus, A initially believes that it can reach B in one hop and that D is unreachable. The routing table stored at A reflects this set of beliefs and includes the name of the next hop that A would use to reach any reachable node. Initially, then, A's routing table would look like Table 3.11.

The next step in distance-vector routing is that every node sends a message to its directly connected neighbors containing its personal list of distances. For example, node F tells node A that it can reach node G at a cost of 1; A also knows it can reach F at a cost of 1, so it adds these costs to get the cost of reaching G by means of F. This total cost of 2 is less than the current cost of infinity, so A records that it can reach G at a cost of 2 by going through F. Similarly, A learns from C that D can be reached from C at a cost of 1; it adds this to the cost of reaching C (1) and decides that D can be reached via C at a cost of 2, which is better than the old cost of infinity. At the same time, A learns from C that B can be reached from C at a cost of 1, so it concludes that the cost of reaching B via C is 2. Since this is worse than the current cost of reaching B (1), this new information is ignored.

Table 3.11 Initial Routing Table at Node A

Destination	Cost	NextHop
B	1	B
C	1	C
D	∞	—
E	1	E
F	1	F
G	∞	—

At this point, A can update its routing table with costs and next hops for all nodes in the network. The result is shown in Table 3.12.

In the absence of any topology changes, it takes only a few exchanges of information between neighbors before each node has a complete routing table. The process of getting consistent routing information to all the nodes is called *convergence*. Table 3.13 shows the final set of costs from each node to all other nodes when routing has converged. We must stress that there is no one node in the network that has all the information in this table—each node only knows about the contents of its own routing table. The beauty of a distributed algorithm like this is that it enables all

Table 3.12 Final Routing Table at Node A

Destination	Cost	NextHop
B	1	B
C	1	C
D	2	C
E	1	E
F	1	F
G	2	F

Table 3.13 Final Distances Stored at Each Node (Global View)

Information Stored at Node	Distance to Reach Node						
	A	B	C	D	E	F	G
A	0	1	1	2	1	1	2
B	1	0	1	2	2	2	3
C	1	1	0	1	2	2	2
D	2	2	1	0	3	2	1
E	1	2	2	3	0	2	3
F	1	2	2	2	2	0	1
G	2	3	2	1	3	1	0

nodes to achieve a consistent view of the network in the absence of any centralized authority.

There are a few details to fill in before our discussion of distance-vector routing is complete. First we note that there are two different circumstances under which a given node decides to send a routing update to its neighbors. One of these circumstances is the *periodic* update. In this case, each node automatically sends an update message every so often, even if nothing has changed. This serves to let the other nodes know that this node is still running. It also makes sure that they keep getting information that they may need if their current routes become unviable. The frequency of these periodic updates varies from protocol to protocol, but it is typically on the order of several seconds to several minutes. The second mechanism, sometimes called a *triggered* update, happens whenever a node notices a link failure or receives an update from one of its neighbors that causes it to change one of the routes in its routing table. Whenever a node's routing table changes, it sends an update to its neighbors, which may lead to a change in their tables, causing them to send an update to their neighbors.

Now consider what happens when a link or node fails. The nodes that notice first send new lists of distances to their neighbors, and normally the system settles down fairly quickly to a new state. As to the question of how a node detects a failure, there are a couple of different answers. In one approach, a node continually tests the link to another node by sending a control packet and seeing if it receives an acknowledgment. In another approach, a node determines that the link (or the node at the other end of the link) is down if it does not receive the expected periodic routing update for the last few update cycles.

To understand what happens when a node detects a link failure, consider what happens when F detects that its link to G has failed. First, F sets its new distance to G to infinity and passes that information along to A. Since A knows that its 2-hop path to G is through F, A would also set its distance to G to infinity. However, with the next update from C, A would learn that C has a 2-hop path to G. Thus, A would know that it could reach G in 3 hops through C, which is less than infinity, and so A would update its table accordingly. When it advertises this to F, node F would learn that it can reach G at a cost of 4 through A, which is less than infinity, and the system would again become stable.

Unfortunately, slightly different circumstances can prevent the network from stabilizing. Suppose, for example, that the link from A to E goes down. In the next round of updates, A advertises a distance of infinity to E, but B and C advertise a distance of 2 to E. Depending on the exact timing of events, the following might happen: Node B, upon hearing that E can be reached in 2 hops from C, concludes that it can reach E in 3 hops and advertises this to A; node A concludes that it can reach E in 4 hops and advertises this to C; node C concludes that it can reach E in 5 hops; and so on. This cycle stops only when the distances reach some number that is large enough to be considered infinite. In the meantime, none of the nodes actually knows that E is unreachable, and the routing tables for the network do not stabilize. This situation is known as the *count to infinity* problem.

There are several partial solutions to this problem. The first one is to use some relatively small number as an approximation of infinity. For example, we might decide that the maximum number of hops to get across a certain network is never going to be more than 16, and so we could pick 16 as the value that represents infinity. This at least bounds the amount of time that it takes to count to infinity. Of course, it could also present a problem if our network grew to a point where some nodes were separated by more than 16 hops.

One technique to improve the time to stabilize routing is called *split horizon*. The idea is that when a node sends a routing update to its neighbors, it does not send those routes it learned from each neighbor back to that neighbor. For example, if B has the route (E, 2, A) in its table, then it knows it must have learned this route from A, and so whenever B sends a routing update to A, it does not include the route (E, 2) in that update. In a stronger variation of split horizon, called *split horizon with poison reverse*, B actually sends that route back to A, but it puts negative information in the route to ensure that A will not eventually use B to get to E. For example, B sends the route (E, ∞) to A. The problem with both of these techniques is that they only work for routing loops that involve two nodes. For larger routing loops, more drastic measures are called for. Continuing the above example, if B and C had waited for a while after hearing of the link failure from A before advertising routes to E, they would have found that neither of them really had a route to E. Unfortunately, this approach delays the convergence of the protocol; speed of convergence is one of the key advantages of its competitor, link-state routing, the subject of Section 3.3.3.

Implementation

The code that implements this algorithm is very straightforward; we give only some of the basics here. Structure **Route** defines each entry in the routing table, and constant **MAX_TTL** specifies how long an entry is kept in the table before it is discarded.

```
#define MAX_ROUTES      128      /* maximum size of routing table */
#define MAX_TTL         120      /* time (in seconds) until route expires */


typedef struct {
    NodeAddr    Destination;    /* address of destination */
    NodeAddr    NextHop;        /* address of next hop */
    int         Cost;           /* distance metric */
    u_short     TTL;            /* time to live */
} Route;


int     numRoutes = 0;
Route   routingTable[MAX_ROUTES];
```

The routine that updates the local node's routing table based on a new route is given by **mergeRoute**. Although not shown, a timer function periodically scans the list of routes in the node's routing table, decrements the TTL (time to live) field of each route, and discards any routes that have a time to live of 0. Notice, however, that the TTL field is reset to MAX_TTL any time the route is reconfirmed by an update message from a neighboring node.

```
void
mergeRoute (Route *new)
{
    int i;

    for (i = 0; i < numRoutes; ++i)
    {
        if (new->Destination == routingTable[i].Destination)
        {
            if (new->Cost + 1 < routingTable[i].Cost)
            {
                /* found a better route: */
                break;
            } else if (new->NextHop == routingTable[i].NextHop) {
```

```
                                /* metric for current next-hop may have
                                      changed: */
                                break;
                        } else {
                            /* route is uninteresting---just ignore
                                it */
                            return;
                        }
                    }
                }
                if (i == numRoutes)
                {
                    /* this is a completely new route; is there room
                        for it? */
                    if (numRoutes < MAXROUTES)
                    {
                        ++numRoutes;
                    } else {
                        /* can't fit this route in table so give up */
                        return;
                    }
                }
                routingTable[i] = *new;
                /* reset TTL */
                routingTable[i].TTL = MAX_TTL;
                /* account for hop to get to next node */
                ++routingTable[i].Cost;

    }
```

Finally, the procedure updateRoutingTable is the main routine that calls mergeRoute to incorporate all the routes contained in a routing update that is received from a neighboring node.

```
void
updateRoutingTable (Route *newRoute, int numNewRoutes)
{
    int i;

    for (i=0; i < numNewRoutes; ++i)
    {
```

```
        mergeRoute(&newRoute[i]);
    }
}
```

Routing Information Protocol (RIP)

One of the more widely used routing protocols in IP networks is the Routing Information Protocol (RIP). Its widespread use in the early days of IP was due in no small part to the fact that it was distributed along with the popular Berkeley Software Distribution (BSD) version of Unix, from which many commercial versions of Unix were derived. It is also extremely simple. RIP is the canonical example of a routing protocol built on the distance-vector algorithm just described.

Routing protocols in internetworks differ very slightly from the idealized graph model described above. In an internetwork, the goal of the routers is to learn how to forward packets to various *networks*. Thus, rather than advertising the cost of reaching other routers, the routers advertise the cost of reaching networks. For example, in Figure 3.30, router C would advertise to router A the fact that it can reach networks 2 and 3 (to which it is directly connected) at a cost of 0, networks 5 and 6 at cost 1, and network 4 at cost 2.

We can see evidence of this in the RIP (version 2) packet format in Figure 3.31. The majority of the packet is taken up with ⟨address, mask, distance⟩ triples. However, the principles of the routing algorithm are just the same. For example, if router A learns from router B that network X can be reached at a lower cost via B than via the existing next hop in the routing table, A updates the cost and next hop information for the network number accordingly.

RIP is in fact a fairly straightforward implementation of distance-vector routing. Routers running RIP send their advertisements every 30 seconds;

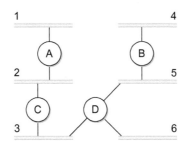

■ FIGURE 3.30 Example network running RIP.

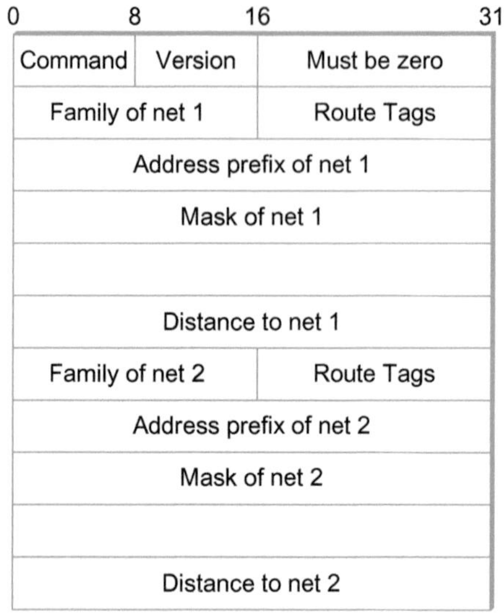

0	8	16	31
Command	Version	Must be zero	
Family of net 1		Route Tags	
Address prefix of net 1			
Mask of net 1			
Distance to net 1			
Family of net 2		Route Tags	
Address prefix of net 2			
Mask of net 2			
Distance to net 2			

■ FIGURE 3.31 RIPv2 packet format.

a router also sends an update message whenever an update from another router causes it to change its routing table. One point of interest is that it supports multiple address families, not just IP—that is the reason for the Family part of the advertisements. RIP version 2 (RIPv2) also introduced the subnet masks described in Section 3.2.5, whereas RIP version 1 worked with the old classful addresses of IP.

As we will see below, it is possible to use a range of different metrics or costs for the links in a routing protocol. RIP takes the simplest approach, with all link costs being equal to 1, just as in our example above. Thus, it always tries to find the minimum hop route. Valid distances are 1 through 15, with 16 representing infinity. This also limits RIP to running on fairly small networks—those with no paths longer than 15 hops.

3.3.3 Link State (OSPF)

LAB 07:
OSPF

Link-state routing is the second major class of intradomain routing protocol. The starting assumptions for link-state routing are rather similar to those for distance-vector routing. Each node is assumed to be capable of finding out the state of the link to its neighbors (up or down) and the cost of each link. Again, we want to provide each node with enough information to enable it to find the least-cost path to any destination. The basic idea behind link-state protocols is very simple: Every node knows how to reach its directly connected neighbors, and if we make sure that the totality of this knowledge is disseminated to every node, then every node will have enough knowledge of the network to build a complete map of the network. This is clearly a sufficient condition (although not a necessary one) for finding the shortest path to any point in the network. Thus, link-state routing protocols rely on two mechanisms: reliable dissemination of link-state information, and the calculation of routes from the sum of all the accumulated link-state knowledge.

Reliable Flooding

Reliable flooding is the process of making sure that all the nodes participating in the routing protocol get a copy of the link-state information from all the other nodes. As the term *flooding* suggests, the basic idea is for a node to send its link-state information out on all of its directly connected links; each node that receives this information then forwards it out on all of *its* links. This process continues until the information has reached all the nodes in the network.

More precisely, each node creates an update packet, also called a *link-state packet* (LSP), which contains the following information:

- The ID of the node that created the LSP
- A list of directly connected neighbors of that node, with the cost of the link to each one
- A sequence number
- A time to live for this packet

The first two items are needed to enable route calculation; the last two are used to make the process of flooding the packet to all nodes reliable. Reliability includes making sure that you have the most recent copy of the information, since there may be multiple, contradictory LSPs from one node traversing the network. Making the flooding reliable has proven to be quite difficult. (For example, an early version of link-state routing used in the ARPANET caused that network to fail in 1981.)

Flooding works in the following way. First, the transmission of LSPs between adjacent routers is made reliable using acknowledgments and retransmissions just as in the reliable link-layer protocol described in Section 2.5. However, several more steps are necessary to reliably flood an LSP to all nodes in a network.

Consider a node X that receives a copy of an LSP that originated at some other node Y. Note that Y may be any other router in the same routing domain as X. X checks to see if it has already stored a copy of an LSP from Y. If not, it stores the LSP. If it already has a copy, it compares the sequence numbers; if the new LSP has a larger sequence number, it is assumed to be the more recent, and that LSP is stored, replacing the old one. A smaller (or equal) sequence number would imply an LSP older (or not newer) than the one stored, so it would be discarded and no further action would be needed. If the received LSP was the newer one, X then sends a copy of that LSP to all of its neighbors except the neighbor from which the LSP was just received. The fact that the LSP is not sent back to the node from which it was received helps to bring an end to the flooding of an LSP. Since X passes the LSP on to all its neighbors, who then turn around and do the same thing, the most recent copy of the LSP eventually reaches all nodes.

Figure 3.32 shows an LSP being flooded in a small network. Each node becomes shaded as it stores the new LSP. In Figure 3.32(a) the LSP arrives at node X, which sends it to neighbors A and C in Figure 3.32(b). A and C do not send it back to X, but send it on to B. Since B receives two identical copies of the LSP, it will accept whichever arrived first and ignore the second as a duplicate. It then passes the LSP onto D, which has no neighbors to flood it to, and the process is complete.

Just as in RIP, each node generates LSPs under two circumstances. Either the expiry of a periodic timer or a change in topology can cause a node to generate a new LSP. However, the only topology-based reason for a node to generate an LSP is if one of its directly connected links or

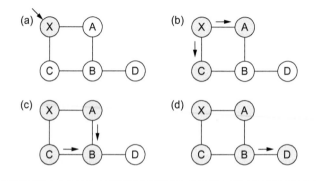

■ **FIGURE 3.32** Flooding of link-state packets: (a) LSP arrives at node X; (b) X floods LSP to A and C; (c) A and C flood LSP to B (but not X); (d) flooding is complete.

immediate neighbors has gone down. The failure of a link can be detected in some cases by the link-layer protocol. The demise of a neighbor or loss of connectivity to that neighbor can be detected using periodic "hello" packets. Each node sends these to its immediate neighbors at defined intervals. If a sufficiently long time passes without receipt of a "hello" from a neighbor, the link to that neighbor will be declared down, and a new LSP will be generated to reflect this fact.

One of the important design goals of a link-state protocol's flooding mechanism is that the newest information must be flooded to all nodes as quickly as possible, while old information must be removed from the network and not allowed to circulate. In addition, it is clearly desirable to minimize the total amount of routing traffic that is sent around the network; after all, this is just overhead from the perspective of those who actually use the network for their applications. The next few paragraphs describe some of the ways that these goals are accomplished.

One easy way to reduce overhead is to avoid generating LSPs unless absolutely necessary. This can be done by using very long timers—often on the order of hours—for the periodic generation of LSPs. Given that the flooding protocol is truly reliable when topology changes, it is safe to assume that messages saying "nothing has changed" do not need to be sent very often.

To make sure that old information is replaced by newer information, LSPs carry sequence numbers. Each time a node generates a new LSP, it increments the sequence number by 1. Unlike most sequence numbers used in protocols, these sequence numbers are not expected to wrap, so the field needs to be quite large (say, 64 bits). If a node goes down and then comes back up, it starts with a sequence number of 0. If the node was down for a long time, all the old LSPs for that node will have timed out (as described below); otherwise, this node will eventually receive a copy of its own LSP with a higher sequence number, which it can then increment and use as its own sequence number. This will ensure that its new LSP replaces any of its old LSPs left over from before the node went down.

LSPs also carry a time to live. This is used to ensure that old link-state information is eventually removed from the network. A node always decrements the TTL of a newly received LSP before flooding it to its neighbors. It also "ages" the LSP while it is stored in the node. When the TTL reaches 0, the node refloods the LSP with a TTL of 0, which is interpreted by all the nodes in the network as a signal to delete that LSP.

Route Calculation

Once a given node has a copy of the LSP from every other node, it is able to compute a complete map for the topology of the network, and from this map it is able to decide the best route to each destination. The question, then, is exactly how it calculates routes from this information. The solution is based on a well-known algorithm from graph theory—Dijkstra's shortest-path algorithm.

We first define Dijkstra's algorithm in graph-theoretic terms. Imagine that a node takes all the LSPs it has received and constructs a graphical representation of the network, in which N denotes the set of nodes in the graph, $l(i,j)$ denotes the nonnegative cost (weight) associated with the edge between nodes $i, j \in N$ and $l(i,j) = \infty$ if no edge connects i and j. In the following description, we let $s \in N$ denote this node, that is, the node executing the algorithm to find the shortest path to all the other nodes in N. Also, the algorithm maintains the following two variables: M denotes the set of nodes incorporated so far by the algorithm, and $C(n)$ denotes the cost of the path from s to each node n. Given these definitions, the algorithm is defined as follows:

$M = \{s\}$
for each n in $N - \{s\}$
   $C(n) = l(s,n)$
while $(N \neq M)$
   $M = M \cup \{w\}$ such that $C(w)$ is the minimum for all w in $(N - M)$
   for each n in $(N - M)$
      $C(n) = \mathrm{MIN}(C(n), C(w) + l(w,n))$

Basically, the algorithm works as follows. We start with M containing this node s and then initialize the table of costs (the $C(n)$s) to other nodes using the known costs to directly connected nodes. We then look for the node that is reachable at the lowest cost (w) and add it to M. Finally, we update the table of costs by considering the cost of reaching nodes through w. In the last line of the algorithm, we choose a new route to node n that goes through node w if the total cost of going from the source to w and then following the link from w to n is less than the old route we had to n. This procedure is repeated until all nodes are incorporated in M.

In practice, each switch computes its routing table directly from the LSPs it has collected using a realization of Dijkstra's algorithm called the *forward search* algorithm. Specifically, each switch maintains two lists, known as Tentative and Confirmed. Each of these lists contains a set of entries of the form (Destination, Cost, NextHop). The algorithm works as follows:

1. Initialize the Confirmed list with an entry for myself; this entry has a cost of 0.

2. For the node just added to the Confirmed list in the previous step, call it node Next and select its LSP.

3. For each neighbor (Neighbor) of Next, calculate the cost (Cost) to reach this Neighbor as the sum of the cost from myself to Next and from Next to Neighbor.

   (a) If Neighbor is currently on neither the Confirmed nor the Tentative list, then add (Neighbor, Cost, NextHop) to the Tentative list, where NextHop is the direction I go to reach Next.

   (b) If Neighbor is currently on the Tentative list, and the Cost is less than the currently listed cost for Neighbor, then replace the current entry with (Neighbor, Cost, NextHop), where NextHop is the direction I go to reach Next.

4. If the Tentative list is empty, stop. Otherwise, pick the entry from the Tentative list with the lowest cost, move it to the Confirmed list, and return to step 2.

This will become a lot easier to understand when we look at an example. Consider the network depicted in Figure 3.33. Note that, unlike our previous example, this network has a range of different edge costs. Table 3.14 traces the steps for building the routing table for node D. We denote the two outputs of D by using the names of the nodes to which they connect, B and C. Note the way the algorithm seems to head off on

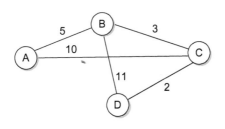

■ FIGURE 3.33 Link-state routing: an example network.

Table 3.14 Steps for Building Routing Table for Node D (Figure 3.33)

Step	Confirmed	Tentative	Comments
1	(D,0,–)		Since D is the only new member of the confirmed list, look at its LSP.
2	(D,0,–)	(B,11,B) (C,2,C)	D's LSP says we can reach B through B at cost 11, which is better than anything else on either list, so put it on Tentative list; same for C.
3	(D,0,–) (C,2,C)	(B,11,B)	Put lowest-cost member of Tentative (C) onto Confirmed list. Next, examine LSP of newly confirmed member (C).
4	(D,0,–) (C,2,C)	(B,5,C) (A,12,C)	Cost to reach B through C is 5, so replace (B,11,B). C's LSP tells us that we can reach A at cost 12.
5	(D,0,–) (C,2,C) (B,5,C)	(A,12,C)	Move lowest-cost member of Tentative (B) to Confirmed, then look at its LSP.
6	(D,0,–) (C,2,C) (B,5,C)	(A,10,C)	Since we can reach A at cost 5 through B, replace the Tentative entry.
7	(D,0,–) (C,2,C) (B,5,C) (A,10,C)		Move lowest-cost member of Tentative (A) to Confirmed, and we are all done.

false leads (like the 11-unit cost path to B that was the first addition to the Tentative list) but ends up with the least-cost paths to all nodes.

The link-state routing algorithm has many nice properties: It has been proven to stabilize quickly, it does not generate much traffic, and it responds rapidly to topology changes or node failures. On the downside, the amount of information stored at each node (one LSP for every other node in the network) can be quite large. This is one of the fundamental problems of routing and is an instance of the more general problem of scalability. Some solutions to both the specific problem (the amount of storage potentially required at each node) and the general problem (scalability) will be discussed in the next section.

The difference between the distance-vector and link-state algorithms can be summarized as follows. In distance-vector, each node talks only to its directly connected neighbors, but it tells them everything it has learned (i.e., distance to all nodes). In link-state, each node talks to all other nodes, but it tells them only what it knows for sure (i.e., only the state of its directly connected links).

The Open Shortest Path First Protocol (OSPF)

One of the most widely used link-state routing protocols is OSPF. The first word, "Open," refers to the fact that it is an open, nonproprietary standard, created under the auspices of the Internet Engineering Task Force (IETF). The "SPF" part comes from an alternative name for link-state routing. OSPF adds quite a number of features to the basic link-state algorithm described above, including the following:

- *Authentication of routing messages*—One feature of distributed routing algorithms is that they disperse information from one node to many other nodes, and the entire network can thus be impacted by bad information from one node. For this reason, it's a good idea to be sure that all the nodes taking part in the protocol can be trusted. Authenticating routing messages helps achieve this. Early versions of OSPF used a simple 8-byte password for authentication. This is not a strong enough form of authentication to prevent dedicated malicious users, but it alleviates some problems caused by misconfiguration or casual attacks. (A similar form of authentication was added to RIP in version 2.) Strong cryptographic authentication of the sort discussed in Section 8.3 was later added.

- *Additional hierarchy*—Hierarchy is one of the fundamental tools used to make systems more scalable. OSPF introduces another layer of hierarchy into routing by allowing a domain to be partitioned into *areas*. This means that a router within a domain does not necessarily need to know how to reach every network within that domain—it may be able to get by knowing only how to get to the right area. Thus, there is a reduction in the amount of information that must be transmitted to and stored in each node. We examine areas in detail in Section 4.1.1.

- *Load balancing*—OSPF allows multiple routes to the same place to be assigned the same cost and will cause traffic to be distributed evenly over those routes, thus making better use of available network capacity.

There are several different types of OSPF messages, but all begin with the same header, as shown in Figure 3.34. The Version field is currently set to 2, and the Type field may take the values 1 through 5. The SourceAddr identifies the sender of the message, and the AreaId is a 32-bit identifier

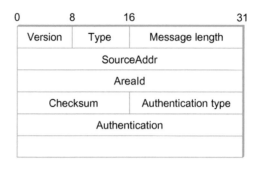

■ **FIGURE 3.34** OSPF header format.

of the area in which the node is located. The entire packet, except the authentication data, is protected by a 16-bit checksum using the same algorithm as the IP header (see Section 2.4). The Authentication type is 0 if no authentication is used; otherwise, it may be 1, implying that a simple password is used, or 2, which indicates that a cryptographic authentication checksum, of the sort described in Section 8.3, is used. In the latter cases, the Authentication field carries the password or cryptographic checksum.

Of the five OSPF message types, type 1 is the "hello" message, which a router sends to its peers to notify them that it is still alive and connected as described above. The remaining types are used to request, send, and acknowledge the receipt of link-state messages. The basic building block of link-state messages in OSPF is the link-state advertisement (LSA). One message may contain many LSAs. We provide a few details of the LSA here.

Like any internetwork routing protocol, OSPF must provide information about how to reach networks. Thus, OSPF must provide a little more information than the simple graph-based protocol described above. Specifically, a router running OSPF may generate link-state packets that advertise one or more of the networks that are directly connected to that router. In addition, a router that is connected to another router by some link must advertise the cost of reaching that router over the link. These two types of advertisements are necessary to enable all the routers in a domain to determine the cost of reaching all networks in that domain and the appropriate next hop for each network.

Figure 3.35 shows the packet format for a type 1 link-state advertisement. Type 1 LSAs advertise the cost of links between routers. Type 2

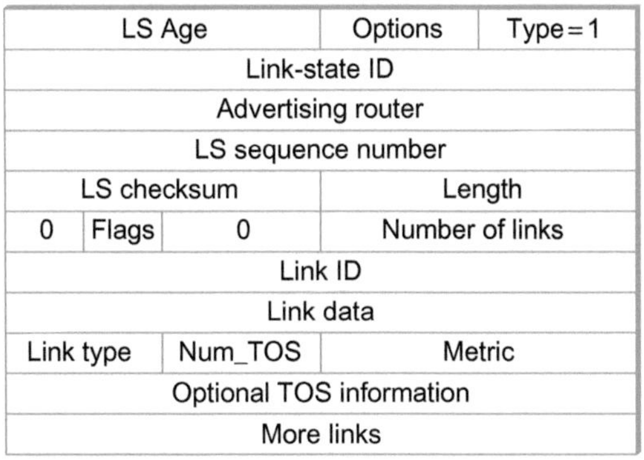

LS Age		Options	Type = 1
Link-state ID			
Advertising router			
LS sequence number			
LS checksum		Length	
0	Flags	0	Number of links
Link ID			
Link data			
Link type	Num_TOS	Metric	
Optional TOS information			
More links			

■ FIGURE 3.35 OSPF link-state advertisement.

LSAs are used to advertise networks to which the advertising router is connected, while other types are used to support additional hierarchy as described in the next section. Many fields in the LSA should be familiar from the preceding discussion. The **LS Age** is the equivalent of a time to live, except that it counts up and the LSA expires when the age reaches a defined maximum value. The **Type** field tells us that this is a type 1 LSA.

In a type 1 LSA, the **Link state ID** and the **Advertising router** field are identical. Each carries a 32-bit identifier for the router that created this LSA. While a number of assignment strategies may be used to assign this ID, it is essential that it be unique in the routing domain and that a given router consistently uses the same router ID. One way to pick a router ID that meets these requirements would be to pick the lowest IP address among all the IP addresses assigned to that router. (Recall that a router may have a different IP address on each of its interfaces.)

The **LS sequence number** is used exactly as described above to detect old or duplicate LSAs. The **LS checksum** is similar to others we have seen in Section 2.4 and in other protocols; it is, of course, used to verify that data has not been corrupted. It covers all fields in the packet except **LS Age**, so it is not necessary to recompute a checksum every time **LS Age** is incremented. **Length** is the length in bytes of the complete LSA.

Now we get to the actual link-state information. This is made a little complicated by the presence of TOS (type of service) information. Ignoring that for a moment, each link in the LSA is represented by a **Link ID**, some **Link Data**, and a metric. The first two of these fields identify the link;

a common way to do this would be to use the router ID of the router at the far end of the link as the Link ID and then use the Link Data to disambiguate among multiple parallel links if necessary. The metric is of course the cost of the link. Type tells us something about the link—for example, if it is a point-to-point link.

The TOS information is present to allow OSPF to choose different routes for IP packets based on the value in their TOS field. Instead of assigning a single metric to a link, it is possible to assign different metrics depending on the TOS value of the data. For example, if we had a link in our network that was very good for delay-sensitive traffic, we could give it a low metric for the TOS value representing low delay and a high metric for everything else. OSPF would then pick a different shortest path for those packets that had their TOS field set to that value. It is worth noting that, at the time of writing, this capability has not been widely deployed.[14]

3.3.4 Metrics

The preceding discussion assumes that link costs, or metrics, are known when we execute the routing algorithm. In this section, we look at some ways to calculate link costs that have proven effective in practice. One example that we have seen already, which is quite reasonable and very simple, is to assign a cost of 1 to all links—the least-cost route will then be the one with the fewest hops. Such an approach has several drawbacks, however. First, it does not distinguish between links on a latency basis. Thus, a satellite link with 250-ms latency looks just as attractive to the routing protocol as a terrestrial link with 1-ms latency. Second, it does not distinguish between routes on a capacity basis, making a 9.6-kbps link look just as good as a 45-Mbps link. Finally, it does not distinguish between links based on their current load, making it impossible to route around overloaded links. It turns out that this last problem is the hardest because you are trying to capture the complex and dynamic characteristics of a link in a single scalar cost.

The ARPANET was the testing ground for a number of different approaches to link-cost calculation. (It was also the place where the superior stability of link-state over distance-vector routing was demonstrated;

---

[14]Note also that the meaning of the TOS field has changed since the OSPF specification was written. This topic is discussed in Section 6.5.3.

the original mechanism used distance vector while the later version used link state.) The following discussion traces the evolution of the ARPANET routing metric and, in so doing, explores the subtle aspects of the problem.

The original ARPANET routing metric measured the number of packets that were queued waiting to be transmitted on each link, meaning that a link with 10 packets queued waiting to be transmitted was assigned a larger cost weight than a link with 5 packets queued for transmission. Using queue length as a routing metric did not work well, however, since queue length is an artificial measure of load—it moves packets toward the shortest queue rather than toward the destination, a situation all too familiar to those of us who hop from line to line at the grocery store. Stated more precisely, the original ARPANET routing mechanism suffered from the fact that it did not take either the bandwidth or the latency of the link into consideration.

A second version of the ARPANET routing algorithm, sometimes called the *new routing mechanism*, took both link bandwidth and latency into consideration and used delay, rather than just queue length, as a measure of load. This was done as follows. First, each incoming packet was timestamped with its time of arrival at the router (ArrivalTime); its departure time from the router (DepartTime) was also recorded. Second, when the link-level ACK was received from the other side, the node computed the delay for that packet as

$$\text{Delay} = (\text{DepartTime} - \text{ArrivalTime}) + \text{TransmissionTime} + \text{Latency}$$

where TransmissionTime and Latency were statically defined for the link and captured the link's bandwidth and latency, respectively. Notice that in this case, DepartTime − ArrivalTime represents the amount of time the packet was delayed (queued) in the node due to load. If the ACK did not arrive, but instead the packet timed out, then DepartTime was reset to the time the packet was *retransmitted*. In this case, DepartTime − ArrivalTime captures the reliability of the link—the more frequent the retransmission of packets, the less reliable the link, and the more we want to avoid it. Finally, the weight assigned to each link was derived from the average delay experienced by the packets recently sent over that link.

Although an improvement over the original mechanism, this approach also had a lot of problems. Under light load, it worked reasonably well, since the two static factors of delay dominated the cost. Under heavy load, however, a congested link would start to advertise a very high cost. This caused all the traffic to move off that link, leaving it idle, so then it would advertise a low cost, thereby attracting back all the traffic, and so on. The effect of this instability was that, under heavy load, many links would in fact spend a great deal of time being idle, which is the last thing you want under heavy load.

Another problem was that the range of link values was much too large. For example, a heavily loaded 9.6-kbps link could look 127 times more costly than a lightly loaded 56-kbps link. This means that the routing algorithm would choose a path with 126 hops of lightly loaded 56-kbps links in preference to a 1-hop 9.6-kbps path. While shedding some traffic from an overloaded line is a good idea, making it look so unattractive that it loses all its traffic is excessive. Using 126 hops when 1 hop will do is in general a bad use of network resources. Also, satellite links were unduly penalized, so that an idle 56-kbps satellite link looked considerably more costly than an idle 9.6-kbps terrestrial link, even though the former would give better performance for high-bandwidth applications.

A third approach, called the "revised ARPANET routing metric," addressed these problems. The major changes were to compress the dynamic range of the metric considerably, to account for the link type, and to smooth the variation of the metric with time.

The smoothing was achieved by several mechanisms. First, the delay measurement was transformed to a link utilization, and this number was averaged with the last reported utilization to suppress sudden changes. Second, there was a hard limit on how much the metric could change from one measurement cycle to the next. By smoothing the changes in the cost, the likelihood that all nodes would abandon a route at once is greatly reduced.

The compression of the dynamic range was achieved by feeding the measured utilization, the link type, and the link speed into a function that is shown graphically in Figure 3.36. Observe the following:

- A highly loaded link never shows a cost of more than three times its cost when idle.
- The most expensive link is only seven times the cost of the least expensive.

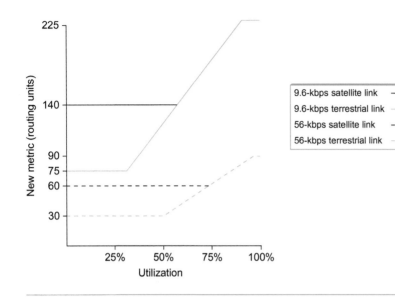

■ FIGURE 3.36 Revised ARPANET routing metric versus link utilization.

- A high-speed satellite link is more attractive than a low-speed terrestrial link.
- Cost is a function of link utilization only at moderate to high loads.

All of these factors mean that a link is much less likely to be universally abandoned, since a threefold increase in cost is likely to make the link unattractive for some paths while letting it remain the best choice for others. The slopes, offsets, and breakpoints for the curves in Figure 3.36 were arrived at by a great deal of trial and error, and they were carefully tuned to provide good performance.

We end our discussion of routing metrics with a dose of reality. In the majority of real-world network deployments at the time of writing, metrics change rarely if at all and only under the control of a network administrator, not automatically as was described above. The reason for this is partly that conventional wisdom now holds that dynamically changing metrics are too unstable, even though this probably need not be true. Perhaps more significantly, many networks today lack the great disparity of link speeds and latencies that prevailed in the ARPANET. Thus, static metrics are the norm. One common approach to setting metrics is to use a constant multiplied by (1/link_bandwidth).

Monitoring Routing Behavior

Given the complexity of routing packets through a network of the scale of the Internet, we might wonder how well the system works. We know it works some of the time because we are able to connect to sites all over the world. We suspect it doesn't work all the time, though, because sometimes we are unable to connect to certain sites. The real problem is determining what part of the system is at fault when our connections fail: Has some routing machinery failed to work properly, is the remote server too busy, or has some link or machine simply gone down?

This is really an issue of network management, and while there are tools that system administrators use to keep tabs on their own networks—for example, see the Simple Network Management Protocol (SNMP) described in Section 9.3.2—it is a largely unresolved problem for the Internet as a whole. In fact, the Internet has grown so large and complex that, even though it is constructed from a collection of man-made, largely deterministic parts, we have come to view it almost as a living organism or natural phenomenon that is to be studied. That is, we try to understand the Internet's dynamic behavior by performing experiments on it and proposing models that explain our observations.

An excellent example of this kind of study has been conducted by Vern Paxson. Paxson used the Unix traceroute tool to study 40,000 end-to-end routes between 37 Internet sites in 1995. He was attempting to answer questions about how routes fail, how stable routes are over time, and whether or not they are symmetric. Among other things, Paxson found that the likelihood of a user encountering a serious end-to-end routing problem was 1 in 30, and that such problems usually lasted about 30 seconds. He also found that two-thirds of the Internet's routes persisted for days or weeks, and that about one-third of the time the route used to get from host A to host B included at least one different routing domain than the route used to get from host B to host A. Paxson's overall conclusion was that Internet routing was becoming less and less predictable over time.

3.4 IMPLEMENTATION AND PERFORMANCE

So far, we have talked about what switches and routers must do without discussing how to do it. There is a very simple way to build a switch or router: Buy a general-purpose processor and equip it with a number of network interfaces. Such a device, running suitable software, can receive packets on one of its interfaces, perform any of the switching or forwarding functions described above, and send packets out another of its interfaces. This is, in fact, a popular way to build experimental routers and switches when you want to be able to do things like develop new routing protocols because it offers extreme flexibility and a familiar programming environment. It is also not too far removed from the architecture of many commercial mid- to low-end routers.

3.4.1 Switch Basics

Switches and routers use similar implementation techniques, so we'll start this section by looking at those common techniques, then move on to look at the specific issues affecting router implementation in Section 3.4.4. For most of this section, we'll use the word *switch* to cover both types of devices, since their internal designs are so similar (and it's tedious to say "switch or router" all the time).

Figure 3.37 shows a processor with three network interfaces used as a switch. The figure shows a path that a packet might take from the time it arrives on interface 1 until it is output on interface 2. We have assumed here that the processor has a mechanism to move data directly from an interface to its main memory without having to be directly copied by the CPU, a technique called *direct memory access* (DMA). Once the packet is in memory, the CPU examines its header to determine which interface the packet should be sent out on. It then uses DMA to move the packet out to the appropriate interface. Note that Figure 3.37 does not show the packet

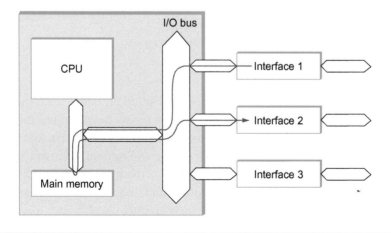

■ FIGURE 3.37 A general-purpose processor used as a packet switch.

going to the CPU because the CPU inspects only the header of the packet; it does not have to read every byte of data in the packet.

The main problem with using a general-purpose processor as a switch is that its performance is limited by the fact that all packets must pass through a single point of contention: In the example shown, each packet crosses the I/O bus twice and is written to and read from main memory once. The upper bound on aggregate throughput of such a device (the total sustainable data rate summed over all inputs) is, thus, either half the main memory bandwidth or half the I/O bus bandwidth, whichever is less. (Usually, it's the I/O bus bandwidth.) For example, a machine with a 133-MHz, 64-bit-wide I/O bus can transmit data at a peak rate of a little over 8 Gbps. Since forwarding a packet involves crossing the bus twice, the actual limit is 4 Gbps—enough to build a switch with a fair number of 100-Mbps Ethernet ports, for example, but hardly enough for a high-end router in the core of the Internet.

Moreover, this upper bound also assumes that moving data is the only problem—a fair approximation for long packets but a bad one when packets are short. In the latter case, the cost of processing each packet—parsing its header and deciding which output link to transmit it on—is likely to dominate. Suppose, for example, that a processor can perform all the necessary processing to switch 2 million packets each second. This is sometimes called the packet per second (pps) rate. (This number is representative of what is achievable on an inexpensive PC.) If the average packet is short, say, 64 bytes, this would imply

$$\text{Throughput} = \text{pps} \times (\text{BitsPerPacket})$$
$$= 2 \times 10^6 \times 64 \times 8$$
$$= 1024 \times 10^6$$

that is, a throughput of about 1 Gbps—substantially below the range that users are demanding from their networks today. Bear in mind that this 1 Gbps would be shared by all users connected to the switch, just as the bandwidth of a single (unswitched) Ethernet segment is shared among all users connected to the shared medium. Thus, for example, a 20-port switch with this aggregate throughput would only be able to cope with an average data rate of about 50 Mbps on each port.

To address this problem, hardware designers have come up with a large array of switch designs that reduce the amount of contention and provide high aggregate throughput. Note that some contention is unavoidable: If every input has data to send to a single output, then they cannot all send it at once. However, if data destined for different outputs is arriving at different inputs, then a well-designed switch will be able to move data from inputs to outputs in parallel, thus increasing the aggregate throughput.

Defining Throughput

It turns out to be difficult to define precisely the throughput of a switch. Intuitively, we might think that if a switch has n inputs that each support a link speed of s_i, then the throughput would just be the sum of all the s_i. This is actually the best possible throughput that such a switch could provide, but in practice almost no real switch can guarantee that level of performance. One reason for this is simple to understand. Suppose that, for some period of time, all the traffic arriving at the switch needed to be sent to the same output. As long as the bandwidth of that output is less than the sum of the input bandwidths, then some of the traffic will need to be either buffered or dropped. With this particular traffic pattern, the switch could not provide a sustained throughput higher than the link speed of that one output. However, a switch might be able to handle traffic arriving at the full link speed on all inputs if it is distributed across all the outputs evenly; this would be considered optimal.

Another factor that affects the performance of switches is the size of packets arriving on the inputs. For an ATM switch, this is normally not an issue because all "packets" (cells) are the same length. But, for Ethernet switches or IP routers, packets of widely varying sizes are possible. Some of the operations that a switch must perform have a constant overhead per packet, so a switch is likely to perform differently depending on whether all arriving packets are very short, very long, or mixed. For this reason, routers or switches that forward variable-length packets are often characterized by a *packet per second* rate as well as a throughput in bits per second. The pps rate is usually measured with minimum-sized packets.

The first thing to notice about this discussion is that the throughput of the switch is a function of the traffic to which it is subjected. One of the things that switch designers spend a lot of their time doing is trying to come up with traffic models that approximate the behavior of real data traffic. It turns out that it is extremely difficult to achieve accurate models. There are several elements to a traffic model. The main ones are (1) when the packets arrive, (2) what outputs they are destined for, and (3) how big they are.

Traffic modeling is a well-established science that has been extremely successful in the world of telephony, enabling telephone companies to engineer their networks to carry expected loads quite efficiently. This is partly because the way people use the phone network does not change that much over time: The frequency with which calls are placed, the amount of time taken for a call, and the tendency of everyone to make calls on Mother's Day have stayed fairly constant for many years. By contrast, the rapid evolution of computer communications, where a new application like BitTorrent can change the traffic patterns almost overnight, has made effective modeling of computer networks much more difficult. Nevertheless, there are some excellent books and articles on the subject that we list at the end of the chapter.

To give you a sense of the range of throughputs that designers need to be concerned about, a single rack router used in the core of the Internet at the time of writing might support 16 OC-768 links for a throughput of approximately 640 Gbps. A 640-Gbps switch, if called upon to handle a steady stream of 64-byte packets, would need a packet per second rate of

$$640 \times 10^9 \div (64 \times 8) = 1.25 \times 10^9 \text{ pps}$$

3.4.2 Ports

Most switches look conceptually similar to the one shown in Figure 3.38. They consist of a number of *input* and *output ports* and a *fabric*. There is usually at least one control processor in charge of the whole switch that communicates with the ports either directly or, as shown here, via the switch fabric. The ports communicate with the outside world. They may contain fiber optic receivers and lasers, buffers to hold packets that are waiting to be switched or transmitted, and often a significant amount of other circuitry that enables the switch to function. The fabric has a very

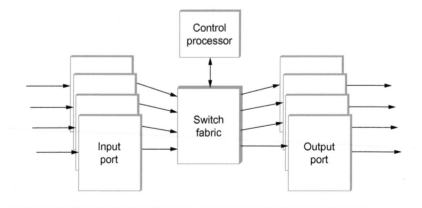

■ FIGURE 3.38 A 4 × 4 switch.

simple and well-defined job: When presented with a packet, deliver it to the right output port.

One of the jobs of the ports, then, is to deal with the complexity of the real world in such a way that the fabric can do its relatively simple job. For example, suppose that this switch is supporting a virtual circuit model of communication. In general, the virtual circuit mapping tables described in Section 3.1.2 are located in the ports. The ports maintain lists of virtual circuit identifiers that are currently in use, with information about what output a packet should be sent out on for each VCI and how the VCI needs to be remapped to ensure uniqueness on the outgoing link. Similarly, the ports of an Ethernet switch store tables that map between Ethernet addresses and output ports (bridge forwarding tables as described in Section 3.1.4). In general, when a packet is handed from an input port to the fabric, the port has figured out where the packet needs to go, and either the port sets up the fabric accordingly by communicating some control information to it, or it attaches enough information to the packet itself (e.g., an output port number) to allow the fabric to do its job automatically. Fabrics that switch packets by looking only at the information in the packet are referred to as *self-routing*, since they require no external control to route packets. An example of a self-routing fabric is discussed below.

The input port is the first place to look for performance bottlenecks. The input port has to receive a steady stream of packets, analyze information in the header of each one to determine which output port (or ports) the packet must be sent to, and pass the packet on to the fabric. The type of header analysis that it performs can range from a simple table lookup on a VCI to complex matching algorithms that examine many fields in the header. This is the type of operation that sometimes becomes a problem when the average packet size is very small. Consider, for example, 64-byte packets arriving on a port connected to an OC-48 (2.48 Gbps) link. Such a port needs to process packets at a rate of

$$2.48 \times 10^9 \div (64 \times 8) = 4.83 \times 10^6 \text{ pps}$$

In other words, when small packets are arriving as fast as possible on this link (the worst-case scenario that most ports are engineered to handle), the input port has approximately 200 nanoseconds to process each packet.

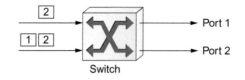

■ **FIGURE 3.39** Simple illustration of head-of-line blocking.

Another key function of ports is buffering. Observe that buffering can happen in either the input or the output port; it can also happen within the fabric (sometimes called *internal buffering*). Simple input buffering has some serious limitations. Consider an input buffer implemented as a FIFO. As packets arrive at the switch, they are placed in the input buffer. The switch then tries to forward the packets at the front of each FIFO to their appropriate output port. However, if the packets at the front of several different input ports are destined for the same output port at the same time, then only one of them can be forwarded;[15] the rest must stay in their input buffers.

The drawback of this feature is that those packets left at the front of the input buffer prevent other packets further back in the buffer from getting a chance to go to their chosen outputs, even though there may be no contention for those outputs. This phenomenon is called *head-of-line blocking*. A simple example of head-of-line blocking is given in Figure 3.39, where we see a packet destined for port 1 blocked behind a packet contending for port 2. It can be shown that when traffic is uniformly distributed among outputs, head-of-line blocking limits the throughput of an input-buffered switch to 59% of the theoretical maximum (which is the sum of the link bandwidths for the switch). Thus, the majority of switches use either pure output buffering or a mixture of internal and output buffering. Those that do rely on input buffers use more advanced buffer management schemes to avoid head-of-line blocking.

Buffers actually perform a more complex task than just holding onto packets that are waiting to be transmitted. Buffers are the main source of delay in a switch, and also the place where packets are most likely to

---

[15]For a simple input-buffered switch, exactly one packet at a time can be sent to a given output port. It is possible to design switches that can forward more than one packet to the same output at once, at a cost of higher switch complexity, but there is always some upper limit on the number.

get dropped due to lack of space to store them. The buffers therefore are the main place where the quality of service characteristics of a switch are determined. For example, if a certain packet has been sent along a VC that has a guaranteed delay, it cannot afford to sit in a buffer for very long. This means that the buffers, in general, must be managed using packet scheduling and discard algorithms that meet a wide range of QoS requirements. We talk more about these issues in Chapter 6.

3.4.3 Fabrics

While there has been an abundance of impressive research conducted on the design of efficient and scalable fabrics, it is sufficient for our purposes here to understand only the high-level properties of a switch fabric. A switch fabric should be able to move packets from input ports to output ports with minimal delay and in a way that meets the throughput goals of the switch. That usually means that fabrics display some degree of parallelism. A high-performance fabric with n ports can often move one packet from each of its n ports to one of the output ports at the same time. A sample of fabric types includes the following:

- *Shared Bus*—This is the type of "fabric" found in a conventional processor used as a switch, as described above. Because the bus bandwidth determines the throughput of the switch, high-performance switches usually have specially designed busses rather than the standard busses found in PCs.

- *Shared Memory*—In a shared memory switch, packets are written into a memory location by an input port and then read from memory by the output ports. Here it is the memory bandwidth that determines switch throughput, so wide and fast memory is typically used in this sort of design. A shared memory switch is similar in principle to the shared bus switch, except it usually uses a specially designed, high-speed memory bus rather than an I/O bus.

- *Crossbar*—A crossbar switch is a matrix of pathways that can be configured to connect any input port to any output port. Figure 3.40 shows a 4×4 crossbar switch. The main problem with crossbars is that, in their simplest form, they require each output port to be able to accept packets from all inputs at once, implying that each port would have a memory bandwidth equal to the total switch throughput. In reality, more complex designs are typically

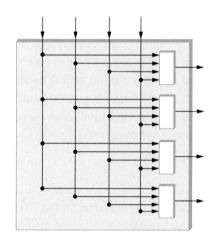

■ FIGURE 3.40 A 4×4 crossbar switch.

used to address this issue (see, for example, the Knockout switch and McKeown's virtual output-buffered approach in the Further Reading section.)

■ *Self-routing*—As noted above, self-routing fabrics rely on some information in the packet header to direct each packet to its correct output. Usually a special "self-routing header" is appended to the packet by the input port after it has determined which output the packet needs to go to, as illustrated in Figure 3.41; this extra header is removed before the packet leaves the switch. Self-routing fabrics are often built from large numbers of very simple 2×2 switching elements interconnected in regular patterns, such as the *banyan* switching fabric shown in Figure 3.42. For some examples of self-routing fabric designs, see the Further Reading section at the end of this chapter.

Self-routing fabrics are among the most scalable approaches to fabric design, and there has been a wealth of research on the topic, some of which is listed in the Further Reading section. Many self-routing fabrics resemble the one shown in Figure 3.42, consisting of regularly interconnected 2×2 switching elements. For example, the 2×2 switches in the banyan network perform a simple task: They look at 1 bit in each self-routing header and route packets toward the upper output if it is zero or toward the lower output if it is one. Obviously, if two packets arrive at a

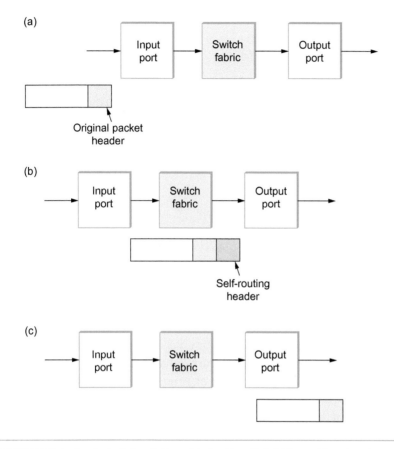

(a)

Original packet
header

(b)

Self-routing
header

(c)

■ **FIGURE 3.41** A self-routing header is applied to a packet at input to enable the fabric to send the packet to the correct output, where it is removed: (a) Packet arrives at input port; (b) input port attaches self-routing header to direct packet to correct output; (c) self-routing header is removed at output port before packet leaves switch.

banyan element at the same time and both have the bit set to the same value, then they want to be routed to the same output and a collision will occur. Either preventing or dealing with these collisions is a main challenge for self-routing switch design. The banyan network is a clever arrangement of 2×2 switching elements that routes all packets to the correct output without collisions if the packets are presented in ascending order.

We can see how this works in an example, as shown in Figure 3.42, where the self-routing header contains the output port number encoded in binary. The switch elements in the first column look at the most significant bit of the output port number and route packets to the top if that bit

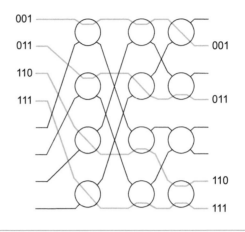

■ FIGURE 3.42 Routing packets through a banyan network. The 3-bit numbers represent values in the self-routing headers of four arriving packets.

is a 0 or the bottom if it is a 1. Switch elements in the second column look at the second bit in the header, and those in the last column look at the least significant bit. You can see from this example that the packets are routed to the correct destination port without collisions. Notice how the top outputs from the first column of switches all lead to the top half of the network, thus getting packets with port numbers 0 to 3 into the right half of the network. The next column gets packets to the right quarter of the network, and the final column gets them to the right output port. The clever part is the way switches are arranged to avoid collisions. Part of the arrangement includes the "perfect shuffle" wiring pattern at the start of the network. To build a complete switch fabric around a banyan network would require additional components to sort packets before they are presented to the banyan. The Batcher-banyan switch design is a notable example of such an approach. The Batcher network, which is also built from a regular interconnection of 2×2 switching elements, sorts packets into descending order. On leaving the Batcher network, the packets are then ready to be directed to the correct output, with no risk of collisions, by the banyan network.

One of the interesting things about switch design is the wide range of different types of switches that can be built using the same basic technology. For example, Ethernet switches, ATM switches, and Internet routers, discussed below, have all been built using designs such as those outlined in this section.

3.4.4 **Router Implementation**

We have now seen a variety of ways to build a switch, ranging from a general-purpose processor with a suitable number of network interfaces to some sophisticated hardware designs. In general, the same range of options is available for building routers, many of which look something like Figure 3.43. The control processor is responsible for running the routing protocols discussed above, among other things, and generally acts as the central point of control of the router. The switching fabric transfers packets from one port to another, just as in a switch; and the ports provide a range of functionality to allow the router to interface to links of various types (e.g., Ethernet, SONET).

A few points are worth noting about router design and how it differs from switch design. First, routers must be designed to handle variable-length packets, a constraint that does not apply to ATM switches but is certainly applicable to Ethernet or Frame Relay switches. It turns out that many high-performance routers are designed using a switching fabric that is cell based. In such cases, the ports must be able to convert variable-length packets into cells and back again. This is known as *segmentation and re-assembly* (SAR), a problem also faced by network adaptors for ATM networks.

Another consequence of the variable length of IP datagrams is that it can be harder to characterize the performance of a router than a switch that forwards only cells. Routers can usually forward a certain number of packets per second, and this implies that the total throughput in *bits*

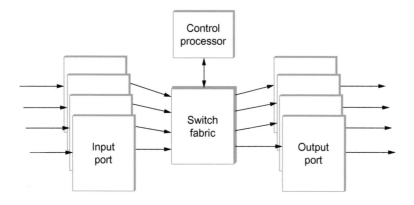

■ FIGURE 3.43 Block diagram of a router.

per second depends on packet size. Router designers generally have to make a choice as to what packet length they will support at *line rate*. That is, if pps (packets per second) is the rate at which packets arriving on a particular port can be forwarded, and linerate is the physical speed of the port in bits per second, then there will be some packetsize in bits such that:

$$packetsize \times pps = linerate$$

This is the packet size at which the router can forward at line rate; it is likely to be able to sustain line rate for longer packets but not for shorter packets. Sometimes a designer might decide that the right packet size to support is 40 bytes, since that is the minimum size of an IP packet that has a TCP header attached. Another choice might be the expected *average* packet size, which can be determined by studying traces of network traffic. For example, measurements of the Internet backbone suggest that the average IP packet is around 300 bytes long. However, such a router would fall behind and perhaps start dropping packets when faced with a long sequence of short packets, which is statistically likely from time to time and also very possible if the router is subject to an active attack (see Chapter 8). Design decisions of this type depend heavily on cost considerations and the intended application of the router.

When it comes to the task of forwarding IP packets, routers can be broadly characterized as having either a *centralized* or *distributed* forwarding model. In the centralized model, the IP forwarding algorithm, outlined earlier in this chapter, is done in a single processing engine that handles the traffic from all ports. In the distributed model, there are several processing engines, perhaps one per port, or more often one per line card, where a line card may serve one or more physical ports. Each model has advantages and disadvantages. All things being equal, a distributed forwarding model should be able to forward more packets per second through the router as a whole, because there is more processing power in total. But a distributed model also complicates the software architecture, because each forwarding engine typically needs its own copy of the forwarding table, and thus it is necessary for the control processor to ensure that the forwarding tables are updated consistently and in a timely manner.

Another aspect of router implementation that is significantly different from that of switches is the IP forwarding algorithm itself. In bridges and most ATM switches, the forwarding algorithm simply involves looking up a fixed-length identifier (MAC address or VCI) in a table, finding the correct output port in the table, and sending the packet to that port. We have already seen in Section 3.2.4 that the IP forwarding algorithm is a little more complicated than that, in part because the relevant number of bits that need to be examined when forwarding a packet is not fixed but variable, typically ranging from 8 bits to 32 bits.

Because of the relatively high complexity of the IP forwarding algorithm, there have been periods of time when it seemed IP routers might be running up against fundamental upper limits of performance. However, as we discuss in the Further Reading section of this chapter, there have been many innovative approaches to IP forwarding developed over the years, and at the time of writing there are commercial routers that can forward 40 Gbps of IP traffic *per interface*. By combining many such high-performance IP forwarding engines with the sort of very scalable switch fabrics discussed in Section 3.4, it has now become possible to build routers with many terabits of total throughput. That is more than enough to see us through the next few years of growth in Internet traffic.

Another technology of interest in the field of router implementation is the *network processor*. A network processor is intended to be a device that is just about as programmable as a standard PC processor, but that is more highly optimized for networking tasks. For example, a network processor might have instructions that are particularly well suited to performing lookups on IP addresses, or calculating checksums on IP datagrams. Such devices could be used in routers and other networking devices (e.g., firewalls).

One of the interesting and ongoing debates about network processors is whether they can do a better job than the alternatives. For example, given the continuous and remarkable improvements in performance of conventional processors, and the huge industry that drives those improvements, can network processors keep up? And can a device that strives for generality do as good a job as a custom-designed application-specific integrated circuit (ASIC) that does nothing except, say, IP forwarding? Part of the answer to questions like these depends on what you mean by "do a better job." For example, there will always be trade-offs to be made between cost of hardware, time to market, performance, power consumption, and flexibility—the ability to change the features supported by a router after it is built. We will see in later chapters just how diverse the requirements for router functionality can be. It is safe to assume that a wide range of router designs will exist for the foreseeable future and that network processors will have some role to play.

3.5 SUMMARY

This chapter has begun to look at some of the issues involved in building scalable and heterogeneous networks by using switches and routers to interconnect links and networks. The most common use of switching is the interconnection of LANs, especially Ethernet segments. LAN switches, or bridges, use techniques such as source address learning to improve forwarding efficiency and spanning tree algorithms to avoid looping. These switches are extensively used in data centers, campuses, and corporate networks.

To deal with heterogeneous networks, the Internetworking Protocol (IP) was invented and forms the basis of today's routers. IP tackles heterogeneity by defining a simple, common service model for an internetwork, which is based on the best-effort delivery of IP datagrams. An important part of the service model is the global addressing scheme, which enables any two nodes in an internetwork to uniquely identify each other for the purposes of exchanging data. The IP service model is simple enough to be supported by any known networking technology, and the ARP mechanism is used to translate global IP addresses into local link-layer addresses.

A crucial aspect of the operation of an internetwork is the determination of efficient routes to any destination in the internet. Internet routing algorithms solve this problem in a distributed fashion; this chapter introduced the two major classes of algorithms—link-state and distance-vector—along with examples of their application (RIP and OSPF).

Both switches and routers need to forward packets from inputs to outputs at a high rate and, in some circumstances, grow to a large size to accommodate hundreds or thousands of ports. Building switches that both scale and offer high performance at acceptable cost is complicated by the problem of contention; as a consequence, switches and routers often employ special-purpose hardware rather than being built from general-purpose workstations.

The Internet has without doubt been an enormous success, and it can be easy to forget that there was ever a time when it didn't exist. However, the inventors of the Internet developed it in part because the networks available at the time, such as the circuit-switched telephone network, were not well suited to the things they wanted to do. Now that the Internet is an established artifact, just as the telephone network was in the 1960s, it is reasonable to ask: What comes after the Internet?

No one knows the answer to that question at the moment, but some significant research efforts are underway to try to enable some sort of "Future Internet." While it is difficult to imagine that today's Internet will be replaced by something new any time soon (after all, the telephone network is still around, although increasingly its traffic is moving onto the

WHAT'S NEXT: THE FUTURE INTERNET

Internet), thinking beyond the constraints of incrementally deployable tweaks to today's Internet could enable some new innovations that we would otherwise miss. It is popular to talk about "clean slate" research in this context—such research looks at what might be possible if we *could* start from scratch, postponing deployment considerations for later.

For example, what if we assumed that every node in the Internet was mobile? We would probably start with a different way of identifying nodes—rather than an IP address, which includes information about what network the node is currently attached to, we might use some other form of identifier. Or, as another example, we might consider a different trust model than the one built into the current Internet. When the Internet was originally developed, it seemed reasonable to assume that every host should be able to send to every other host by default, but today in the world of spammers, phishers, and denial-of-service attacks, a different trust model—with more limited initial capabilities for newly connected or unknown nodes perhaps—might be considered. These two examples illustrate cases where, knowing today some things that were not apparent in the '70s (like the importance of mobility and security to networking), we might want to come up with a very different design for an internetwork.

A couple of points can be made here. First, you should not assume that the Internet is "done." Its architecture is inherently flexible and it will continue to evolve. We will see some examples of its evolution in the next chapter. The other point is that there's more than one way to do networking research: Developing incrementally deployable ideas is great, but in the words of Internet pioneer David Clark, "To conceive the future, it helps to let go of the present."

■ FURTHER READING

The seminal paper on bridges, in particular the spanning tree algorithm, is the article by Perlman below. Not surprisingly, countless papers have been written on various aspects of the Internet; the paper by Cerf and Kahn is the one that originally introduced the TCP/IP architecture and is worth reading for its historical perspective. Finally, McKeown's paper, one of many on switch design, describes an approach to switch design that uses cells internally but has been used commercially as the basis for high-performance routers forwarding variable-length IP packets.

- Perlman, R. An algorithm for distributed computation of spanning trees in an extended LAN. *Proceedings of the Ninth Data Communications Symposium*, pages 44–53, September 1985.
- Cerf, V., and R. Kahn. A protocol for packet network intercommunication. *IEEE Transactions on Communications* COM-22(5):637–648, May 1974.
- McKeown, N. The *i*SLIP scheduling algorithm for input-queued switches. *IEEE Transactions on Networking* 7(2):188–201, April 1999.

A good general overview of bridges and routers can be found in another work by Perlman [Per00]. There is a wealth of papers on ATM; Turner [Tur85], an ATM pioneer, was one of the first to propose the use of a cell-based network for integrated services.

Many of the techniques and protocols that are central to today's Internet are described in requests for comments (RFCs): Subnetting is described in Mogul and Postel [MP85], CIDR is described in Fuller and Li [FL06], RIPv2 is defined in Malkin [Mal98], and OSPF is defined in Moy [Moy98]. The OSPF specification, at over 200 pages, is one of the longer RFCs around, but it contains an unusual wealth of detail about how to implement a protocol. The reasons to avoid IP fragmentation are examined in Kent and Mogul [KM87] and the Path MTU discovery technique is described in Mogul and Deering [MD90].

A forward-looking paper about research on the future Internet was written by Clark et al. [CPB+05]. This paper is related to the ongoing research efforts around a future Internet for which we provide live references below.

Literally thousands of papers have been published on switch architectures. One early paper that explains Batcher networks well is, not surprisingly, one by Batcher himself [Bat68]. Sorting networks are explained by Drysdale and Young [DY75], and an interesting form of cross-bar switch is described by Yeh et al. [YHA87]. Giacopelli et al. [GHMS91] describe the "Sunshine" switch, which provides insights into the important role of traffic analysis in switch design. In particular, the Sunshine designers were among the first to realize that cells were likely to arrive at a switch in bursts and thus were able to factor correlated arrivals into their design. A good overview of the performance of different switching fabrics can be found in Robertazzi [Rob93]. An example of the design of a switch based on variable-length packets can be found in Gopal and Guerin [GG94].

There has been a lot of work aimed at developing algorithms that can be used by routers to do fast lookup of IP addresses. (Recall that the problem is that the router needs to match the longest prefix in the forwarding table.) PATRICIA trees are one of the first algorithms applied to this problem [Mor68]. More recent work is reported in [DBCP97], [WVTP97], [LS98], [SVSM98], and [EVD04]. For an overview of how algorithms like these can be used to build a high-speed router, see Partridge et al. [Par98].

Optical networking is a rich field in its own right, with its own journals, conferences, etc. We recommend Ramaswami et al. [RS01] as a good introductory text in that field.

An excellent text to read if you want to learn about the mathematical analysis of network performance is by Kleinrock [Kle75], one of the pioneers of the ARPANET. Many papers have been published on the applications of queuing theory to packet switching. We recommend the article by Paxson and Floyd [PF94] as a significant contribution focused on the Internet, and one by Leland et al. [LTWW94], a paper that introduces the important concept of "long-range dependence" and shows the inadequacy of many traditional approaches to traffic modeling.

Finally, we recommend the following live references:

- http://www.nets-find.net/: A website of the U.S. National Science Foundation that covers the "Future Internet Design" research program.
- http://www.geni.net/: A site describing the GENI networking testbed, which has been created to enable some of the "clean slate" research described above.

EXERCISES

1. Using the example network given in Figure 3.44, give the virtual circuit tables for all the switches after each of the following connections is established. Assume that the sequence of connections is cumulative; that is, the first connection is still up when the second connection is established, and so on. Also assume that the VCI assignment always picks the lowest unused

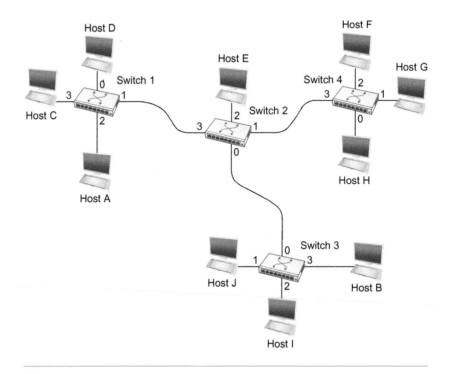

■ FIGURE 3.44 Example network for Exercises 1 and 2.

VCI on each link, starting with 0, and that a VCI is consumed for both directions of a virtual circuit.

(a) Host A connects to host C.

(b) Host D connects to host B.

(c) Host D connects to host I.

(d) Host A connects to host B.

(e) Host F connects to host J.

(f) Host H connects to host A.

2. Using the example network given in Figure 3.44, give the virtual circuit tables for all the switches after each of the following connections is established. Assume that the sequence of connections is cumulative; that is, the first connection is still up when the second connection is established, and so on. Also assume that the VCI assignment always picks the lowest unused VCI on each link, starting with 0, and that a VCI is consumed for both directions of a virtual circuit.

(a) Host D connects to host H.

(b) Host B connects to host G.

(c) Host F connects to host A.

(d) Host H connects to host C.

(e) Host I connects to host E.

(f) Host H connects to host J.

3. For the network given in Figure 3.45, give the datagram forwarding table for each node. The links are labeled with relative costs; your tables should forward each packet via the lowest-cost path to its destination.

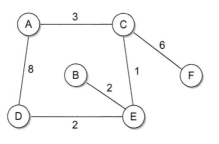

■ FIGURE 3.45 Network for Exercise 3.

4. Give forwarding tables for switches S1 to S4 in Figure 3.46. Each switch should have a default routing entry, chosen to forward packets with unrecognized destination addresses toward OUT. Any specific-destination table entries duplicated by the default entry should then be eliminated.

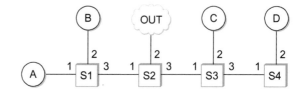

■ FIGURE 3.46 Diagram for Exercise 4.

5. Consider the virtual circuit switches in Figure 3.47. Table 3.15 lists, for each switch, what ⟨port, VCI⟩ (or ⟨VCI, interface⟩) pairs are connected to what other. Connections are bidirectional. List all endpoint-to-endpoint connections.

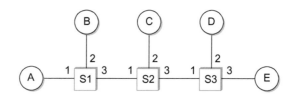

■ FIGURE 3.47 Diagram for Exercise 5.

6. In the source routing example of Section 3.1.3, the address received by B is not reversible and doesn't help B know how to reach A. Propose a modification to the delivery mechanism that does allow for reversibility. Your mechanism should *not* require giving all switches globally unique names.

7. Propose a mechanism that virtual circuit switches might use so that if one switch loses all its state regarding connections then a sender of packets along a path through that switch is informed of the failure.

8. Propose a mechanism that might be used by datagram switches so that if one switch loses all or part of its forwarding table affected senders are informed of the failure.

Table 3.15 VCI Tables for Switches in Figure 3.47

Switch S1

Port	VCI	Port	VCI
1	2	3	1
1	1	2	3
2	1	3	2

Switch S2

Port	VCI	Port	VCI
1	1	3	3
1	2	3	2

Switch S3

Port	VCI	Port	VCI
1	3	2	1
1	2	2	2

9. The virtual circuit mechanism described in Section 3.1.2 assumes that each link is point-to-point. Extend the forwarding algorithm to work in the case that links are shared-media connections (e.g., Ethernet).

10. Suppose, in Figure 3.2, that a new link has been added, connecting switch 3 port 1 (where G is now) and switch 1 port 0 (where D is now); neither switch is informed of this link. Furthermore, switch 3 mistakenly thinks that host B is reached via port 1.
    (a) What happens if host A attempts to send to host B, using datagram forwarding?
    (b) What happens if host A attempts to connect to host B, using the virtual circuit setup mechanism discussed in the text?

11. Give an example of a working virtual circuit whose path traverses some link twice. Packets sent along this path should *not*, however, circulate indefinitely.

12. In Section 3.1.2, each switch chose the VCI value for the incoming link. Show that it is also possible for each switch to choose the VCI value for the outbound link and that the same VCI values will be

chosen by each approach. If each switch chooses the outbound VCI, is it still necessary to wait one RTT before data is sent?

13. Given the extended LAN shown in Figure 3.48, indicate which ports are not selected by the spanning tree algorithm.

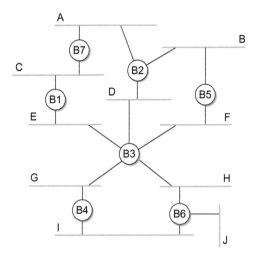

■ FIGURE 3.48 Network for Exercises 13 and 14.

14. Given the extended LAN shown in Figure 3.48, assume that bridge B1 suffers catastrophic failure. Indicate which ports are not selected by the spanning tree algorithm after the recovery process and a new tree has been formed.

15. Consider the arrangement of learning bridges shown in Figure 3.49. Assuming all are initially empty, give the forwarding tables for each of the bridges B1 to B4 after the following transmissions:

  ■ A sends to C.

  ■ C sends to A.

  ■ D sends to C.

Identify ports with the unique neighbor reached directly from that port; that is, the ports for B1 are to be labeled "A" and "B2."

16. As in the previous problem, consider the arrangement of learning bridges shown in Figure 3.49. Assuming all are initially empty, give

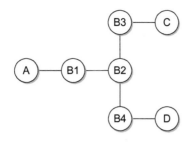

FIGURE 3.49 Network for Exercises 15 and 16.

the forwarding tables for each of the bridges B1 to B4 after the following transmissions:

- D sends to C.
- C sends to D.
- A sends to C.

17. Consider hosts X, Y, Z, W and learning bridges B1, B2, B3, with initially empty forwarding tables, as in Figure 3.50.
    (a) Suppose X sends to W. Which bridges learn where X is? Does Y's network interface see this packet?
    (b) Suppose Z now sends to X. Which bridges learn where Z is? Does Y's network interface see this packet?
    (c) Suppose Y now sends to X. Which bridges learn where Y is? Does Z's network interface see this packet?
    (d) Finally, suppose W sends to Y. Which bridges learn where W is? Does Z's network interface see this packet?

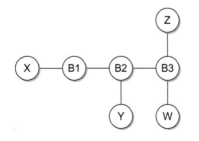

■ FIGURE 3.50 Diagram for Exercise 17.

18. Give the spanning tree generated for the extended LAN shown in Figure 3.51, and discuss how any ties are resolved.

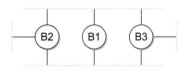

■ FIGURE 3.51 Extended LAN for Exercise 18.

19. Suppose learning bridges B1 and B2 form a loop as shown in Figure 3.52, and do *not* implement the spanning tree algorithm. Each bridge maintains a single table of ⟨*address, interface*⟩ pairs.
    (a) What will happen if M sends to L?
    (b) Suppose a short while later L replies to M. Give a sequence of events that leads to one packet from M and one packet from L circling the loop in opposite directions.

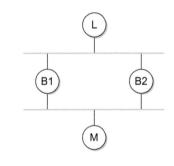

■ FIGURE 3.52 Loop for Exercises 19 and 20.

20. Suppose that M in Figure 3.52 sends to itself (this normally would never happen). State what would happen, assuming:
    (a) The bridges' learning algorithm is to install (or update) the new ⟨*sourceaddress, interface*⟩ entry *before* searching the table for the destination address.
    (b) The new source address was installed *after* destination address lookup.

21. Consider the extended LAN of Figure 3.10. What happens in the spanning tree algorithm if bridge B1 does not participate and
    (a) Simply forwards all spanning tree algorithm messages?
    (b) Drops all spanning tree messages?

22. Suppose some repeaters (hubs), rather than bridges, are connected into a loop.
    (a) What will happen when somebody transmits?
    (b) Why would the spanning tree mechanism be difficult or impossible to implement for repeaters?
    (c) Propose a mechanism by which repeaters might detect loops and shut down some ports to break the loop. Your solution is not required to work 100% of the time.

23. Suppose a bridge has two of its ports on the same network. How might the bridge detect and correct this?

24. What percentage of an ATM link's total bandwidth is consumed by the ATM cell headers? Ignore padding to fill cells or ATM adaptation layer headers.

25. Cell switching methods (like ATM) essentially always use virtual circuit switching rather than datagram forwarding. Give a specific argument why this is so (consider the preceding question).

26. Suppose a workstation has an I/O bus speed of 800 Mbps and memory bandwidth of 2 Gbps. Assuming direct memory access (DMA) is used to move data in and out of main memory, how many interfaces to 100-Mbps Ethernet links could a switch based on this workstation handle?

✓ 27. Suppose a workstation has an I/O bus speed of 1 Gbps and memory bandwidth of 2 Gbps. Assuming DMA is used to move data in and out of main memory, how many interfaces to 100-Mbps Ethernet links could a switch based on this workstation handle?

28. Suppose a switch is built using a computer workstation and that it can forward packets at a rate of 500,000 packets per second, regardless (within limits) of size. Assume the workstation uses direct memory access (DMA) to move data in and out of its main memory, which has a bandwidth of 2 Gbps, and that the I/O bus has a bandwidth of 1 Gbps. At what packet size would the bus bandwidth become the limiting factor?

29. Suppose that a switch is designed to have both input and output FIFO buffering. As packets arrive on an input port they are inserted

at the tail of the FIFO. The switch then tries to forward the packets at the head of each FIFO to the tail of the appropriate output FIFO.

(a) Explain under what circumstances such a switch can lose a packet destined for an output port whose FIFO is empty.

(b) What is this behavior called?

(c) Assume that the FIFO buffering memory can be redistributed freely. Suggest a reshuffling of the buffers that avoids the above problem, and explain why it does so.

30. A stage of an $n \times n$ banyan network consists of $(n/2)$ 2×2 switching elements. The first stage directs packets to the correct half of the network, the next stage to the correct quarter, and so on, until the packet is routed to the correct output. Derive an expression for the number of 2×2 switching elements needed to make an $n \times n$ banyan network. Verify your answer for $n = 8$.

31. Describe how a Batcher network works. (See the Further Reading section.) Explain how a Batcher network can be used in combination with a banyan network to build a switching fabric.

32. Suppose a 10-Mbps Ethernet hub (repeater) is replaced by a 10-Mbps switch, in an environment where all traffic is between a single server and N "clients." Because all traffic must still traverse the server–switch link, nominally there is no improvement in bandwidth.

(a) Would you expect *any* improvement in bandwidth? If so, why?

(b) What other advantages and drawbacks might a switch offer versus a hub?

33. What aspect of IP addresses makes it necessary to have one address per network interface, rather than just one per host? In light of your answer, why does IP tolerate point-to-point interfaces that have nonunique addresses or no addresses?

34. Why does the Offset field in the IP header measure the offset in 8-byte units? (Hint: Recall that the Offset field is 13 bits long.)

35. Some signalling errors can cause entire ranges of bits in a packet to be overwritten by all 0s or all 1s. Suppose all the bits in the packet, including the Internet checksum, are overwritten. Could a packet with all 0s or all 1s be a legal IPv4 packet? Will the Internet checksum catch that error? Why or why not?

36. Suppose a TCP message that contains 1024 bytes of data and 20 bytes of TCP header is passed to IP for delivery across two networks interconnected by a router (i.e., it travels from the source host to a router to the destination host). The first network has an MTU of 1024 bytes; the second has an MTU of 576 bytes. Each network's MTU gives the size of the largest IP datagram that can be carried in a link-layer frame. Give the sizes and offsets of the sequence of fragments delivered to the network layer at the destination host. Assume all IP headers are 20 bytes.

37. Path MTU is the smallest MTU of any link on the current path (route) between two hosts. Assume we could discover the path MTU of the path used in the previous exercise, and that we use this value as the MTU for all the path segments. Give the sizes and offsets of the sequence of fragments delivered to the network layer at the destination host.

38. Suppose an IP packet is fragmented into 10 fragments, each with a 1% (independent) probability of loss. To a reasonable approximation, this means there is a 10% chance of losing the whole packet due to loss of a fragment. What is the probability of net loss of the whole packet if the packet is transmitted twice,
    (a) Assuming all fragments received must have been part of the same transmission?
    (b) Assuming any given fragment may have been part of either transmission?
    (c) Explain how use of the Ident field might be applicable here.

39. Suppose the fragments of Figure 3.18(b) all pass through another router onto a link with an MTU of 380 bytes, not counting the link header. Show the fragments produced. If the packet were originally fragmented for this MTU, how many fragments would be produced?

40. What is the maximum bandwidth at which an IP host can send 576-byte packets without having the Ident field wrap around within 60 seconds? Suppose that IP's maximum segment lifetime (MSL) is 60 seconds; that is, delayed packets can arrive up to 60 seconds late but no later. What might happen if this bandwidth were exceeded?

41. Why do you think IPv4 has fragment reassembly done at the endpoint, rather than at the next router? Why do you think IPv6 abandoned fragmentation entirely? (Hint: Think about the differences between IP-layer fragmentation and link-layer fragmentation).

42. Having ARP table entries time out after 10 to 15 minutes is an attempt at a reasonable compromise. Describe the problems that can occur if the timeout value is too small or too large.

43. IP currently uses 32-bit addresses. If we could redesign IP to use the 6-byte MAC address instead of the 32-bit address, would we be able to eliminate the need for ARP? Explain why or why not.

44. Suppose hosts A and B have been assigned the same IP address on the same Ethernet, on which ARP is used. B starts up after A. What will happen to A's existing connections? Explain how "self-ARP" (querying the network on start-up for one's own IP address) might help with this problem.

45. Suppose an IP implementation adheres literally to the following algorithm on receipt of a packet, P, destined for IP address D:

    ```
    if (⟨Ethernet address for D is in ARP cache⟩)
        ⟨send P⟩
    else
        ⟨send out an ARP query for D⟩
        ⟨put P into a queue until the response comes back⟩
    ```

    (a) If the IP layer receives a burst of packets destined for D, how might this algorithm waste resources unnecessarily?
    (b) Sketch an improved version.
    (c) Suppose we simply drop P, after sending out a query, when cache lookup fails. How would this behave? (Some early ARP implementations allegedly did this.)

46. For the network shown in Figure 3.53, give global distance–vector tables like those of Tables 3.10 and 3.13 when
    (a) Each node knows only the distances to its immediate neighbors.
    (b) Each node has reported the information it had in the preceding step to its immediate neighbors.
    (c) Step (b) happens a second time.

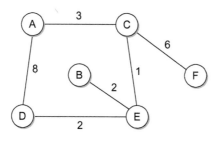

47. For the network given in Figure 3.54, give global distance–vector tables like those of Tables 3.10 and 3.13 when
   (a) Each node knows only the distances to its immediate neighbors.
   (b) Each node has reported the information it had in the preceding step to its immediate neighbors.
   (c) Step (b) happens a second time.

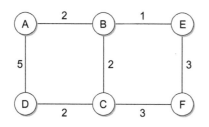

■ FIGURE 3.54 Network for Exercise 47.

48. For the network given in Figure 3.53, show how the *link-state* algorithm builds the routing table for node D.

49. Use the Unix utility traceroute (Windows tracert) to determine how many hops it is from your host to other hosts in the Internet (e.g., cs.princeton.edu or www.cisco.com). How many routers do you traverse just to get out of your local site? Read the man page or other documentation for traceroute and explain how it is implemented.

50. What will happen if traceroute is used to find the path to an unassigned address? Does it matter if the network portion or only the host portion is unassigned?

51. A site is shown in Figure 3.55. R1 and R2 are routers; R2 connects to the outside world. Individual LANs are Ethernets. RB is a *bridge-router*; it routes traffic addressed to it and acts as a bridge for other traffic. Subnetting is used inside the site; ARP is used on each subnet. Unfortunately, host A has been misconfigured and doesn't use subnets. Which of B, C, and D can A reach?

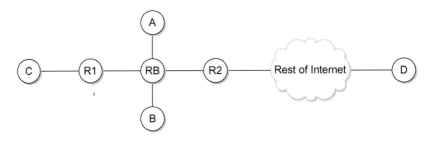

■ FIGURE 3.55 Site for Exercise 51.

52. Suppose we have the forwarding tables shown in Table 3.16 for nodes A and F, in a network where all links have cost 1. Give a diagram of the smallest network consistent with these tables.

Table 3.16 Forwarding Tables for Exercise 52

A

Node	Cost	Nexthop
B	1	B
C	2	B
D	1	D
E	2	B
F	3	D

F

Node	Cost	Nexthop
A	3	E
B	2	C
C	1	C
D	2	E
E	1	E

53. Suppose we have the forwarding tables shown in Table 3.17 for nodes A and F, in a network where all links have cost 1. Give a diagram of the smallest network consistent with these tables.

Table 3.17 Forwarding Tables for Exercise 53

A

Node	Cost	Nexthop
B	1	B
C	1	C
D	2	B
E	3	C
F	2	C

F

Node	Cost	Nexthop
A	2	C
B	3	C
C	1	C
D	2	C
E	1	E

54. For the network in Figure 3.53, suppose the forwarding tables are all established as in Exercise 46 and then the C–E link fails. Give:
    (a) The tables of A, B, D, and F after C and E have reported the news.
    (b) The tables of A and D after their next mutual exchange.
    (c) The table of C after A exchanges with it.

55. Suppose a router has built up the routing table shown in Table 3.18. The router can deliver packets directly over interfaces 0 and 1, or it can forward packets to routers R2, R3, or R4. Describe what the router does with a packet addressed to each of the following destinations:
    (a) 128.96.39.10
    (b) 128.96.40.12
    (c) 128.96.40.151
    (d) 192.4.153.17
    (e) 192.4.153.90

Table 3.18 Routing Table for Exercise 55

SubnetNumber	SubnetMask	NextHop
128.96.39.0	255.255.255.128	Interface 0
128.96.39.128	255.255.255.128	Interface 1
128.96.40.0	255.255.255.128	R2
192.4.153.0	255.255.255.192	R3
⟨default⟩		R4

56. Suppose a router has built up the routing table shown in Table 3.19. The router can deliver packets directly over interfaces 0 and 1, or it can forward packets to routers R2, R3, or R4. Assume the router does the longest prefix match. Describe what the router does with a packet addressed to each of the following destinations:
    (a) 128.96.171.92
    (b) 128.96.167.151
    (c) 128.96.163.151
    (d) 128.96.169.192
    (e) 128.96.165.121

Table 3.19 Routing Table for Exercise 56

SubnetNumber	SubnetMask	NextHop
128.96.170.0	255.255.254.0	Interface 0
128.96.168.0	255.255.254.0	Interface 1
128.96.166.0	255.255.254.0	R2
128.96.164.0	255.255.252.0	R3
⟨default⟩		R4

57. Consider the simple network in Figure 3.56, in which A and B exchange distance-vector routing information. All links have cost 1. Suppose the A–E link fails.

■ FIGURE 3.56 Simple network for Exercise 57.

(a) Give a sequence of routing table updates that leads to a routing loop between A and B.

(b) Estimate the probability of the scenario in (a), assuming A and B send out routing updates at random times, each at the same average rate.

(c) Estimate the probability of a loop forming if A broadcasts an updated report within 1 second of discovering the A–E failure, and B broadcasts every 60 seconds uniformly.

58. Consider the situation involving the creation of a routing loop in the network of Figure 3.29 when the A–E link goes down. List *all* sequences of table updates among A, B, and C, pertaining to destination E, that lead to the loop. Assume that table updates are done one at a time, that the split-horizon technique is observed by all participants, and that A sends its initial report of E's unreachability to B before C. You may ignore updates that don't result in changes.

59. Suppose a set of routers all use the split-horizon technique; we consider here under what circumstances it makes a difference if they use poison reverse in addition.

(a) Show that poison reverse makes no difference in the evolution of the routing loop in the two examples described in Section 3.3.2, given that the hosts involved use split horizon.

(b) Suppose split-horizon routers A and B somehow reach a state in which they forward traffic for a given destination X toward each other. Describe how this situation will evolve with and without the use of poison reverse.

(c) Give a sequence of events that leads A and B to a looped state as in (b), even if poison reverse is used. (Hint: Suppose B and A connect through a very slow link. They each reach X through a third node, C, and simultaneously advertise their routes to each other.)

60. *Hold down* is another distance–vector loop-avoidance technique, whereby hosts ignore updates for a period of time until link failure news has had a chance to propagate. Consider the networks in Figure 3.57, where all links have cost 1 except E–D, with cost 10. Suppose that the E–A link breaks and B reports its loop-forming E route to A immediately afterwards (this is the false route, via A).

Specify the details of a hold-down interpretation, and use this to describe the evolution of the routing loop in both networks. To what extent can hold down prevent the loop in the EAB network without delaying the discovery of the alternative route in the EABD network?

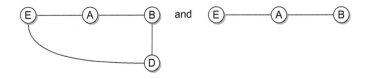

61. Consider the network in Figure 3.58, using link-state routing. Suppose the B–F link fails, and the following then occur in sequence:
    (a) Node H is added to the right side with a connection to G.
    (b) Node D is added to the left side with a connection to C.
    (c) A new link, D–A, is added.
    The failed B–F link is now restored. Describe what link-state packets will flood back and forth. Assume that the initial sequence number at all nodes is 1, that no packets time out, and that both ends of a link use the same sequence number in their LSP for that link, greater than any sequence number used before.

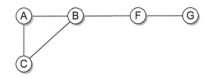

62. Give the steps as in Table 3.14 in the forward search algorithm as it builds the routing database for node A in the network shown in Figure 3.59.

63. Give the steps as in Table 3.14 in the forward search algorithm as it builds the routing database for node A in the network shown in Figure 3.60.

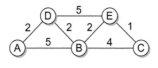

■ FIGURE 3.59 Network for Exercise 62.

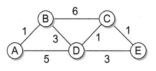

■ FIGURE 3.60 Network for Exercise 63.

64. Suppose that nodes in the network shown in Figure 3.61 participate in link-state routing, and C receives contradictory LSPs: One from A arrives claiming the A–B link is down, but one from B arrives claiming the A–B link is up.
    (a) How could this happen?
    (b) What should C do? What can C expect?
    Do not assume that the LSPs contain any synchronized timestamp.

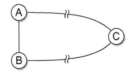

■ FIGURE 3.61 Network for Exercise 64.

65. Suppose IP routers learned about IP networks and subnets the way Ethernet learning bridges learn about hosts: by noting the appearance of new ones and the interface by which they arrive. Compare this with existing distance–vector router learning
    (a) For a leaf site with a single attachment to the Internet.
    (b) For internal use at an organization that did not connect to the Internet.
    Assume that routers only receive new-network notices from other routers and that the originating routers receive their IP network information via configuration.

66. IP hosts that are not designated routers are *required* to drop packets misaddressed to them, even if they would otherwise be able to forward them correctly. In the absence of this requirement, what would happen if a packet addressed to IP address A were inadvertently broadcast at the link layer? What other justifications for this requirement can you think of?

67. Read the man page or other documentation for the Unix/Windows utility netstat. Use netstat to display the current IP routing table on your host. Explain the purpose of each entry. What is the practical minimum number of entries?

68. An organization has been assigned the prefix 212.1.1/24 (class C) and wants to form subnets for four departments, with hosts as follows:

A	75 hosts
B	35 hosts
C	20 hosts
D	18 hosts

There are 148 hosts in all.
   (a) Give a possible arrangement of subnet masks to make this possible.
   (b) Suggest what the organization might do if department D grows to 32 hosts.

69. Suppose hosts A and B are on an Ethernet LAN with IP network address 200.0.0/24. It is desired to attach a host C to the network via a direct connection to B (see Figure 3.62). Explain how to do this with subnets; give sample subnet assignments. Assume that

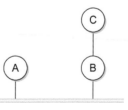

■ FIGURE 3.62 Network for Exercise 69.

an additional network prefix is not available. What does this do to the size of the Ethernet LAN?

70. An alternative method for connecting host C in Exercise 69 is to use *proxy ARP* and routing: B agrees to route traffic to and from C and also answers ARP queries for C received over the Ethernet.
    (a) Give all packets sent, with physical addresses, as A uses ARP to locate and then send one packet to C.
    (b) Give B's routing table. What peculiarity must it contain?

71. Suppose two subnets share the same physical LAN; hosts on each subnet will see the other subnet's broadcast packets.
    (a) How will DHCP fare if two servers, one for each subnet, coexist on the shared LAN? What problems might [*do!*] arise?
    (b) Will ARP be affected by such sharing?

72. Table 3.20 is a routing table using CIDR. Address bytes are in hexadecimal. The notation "/12" in C4.50.0.0/12 denotes a netmask with 12 leading 1 bits: FF.F0.0.0. Note that the last three entries cover every address and thus serve in lieu of a default route. State to what next hop the following will be delivered:
    (a) C4.5E.13.87
    (b) C4.5E.22.09
    (c) C3.41.80.02
    (d) 5E.43.91.12
    (e) C4.6D.31.2E
    (f) C4.6B.31.2E

Table 3.20 Routing Table for Exercise 72

Net/MaskLength	Nexthop
C4.50.0.0/12	A
C4.5E.10.0/20	B
C4.60.0.0/12	C
C4.68.0.0/14	D
80.0.0.0/1	E
40.0.0.0/2	F
00.0.0.0/2	G

73. Table 3.21 is a routing table using CIDR. Address bytes are in hexadecimal. The notation "/12" in C4.50.0.0/12 denotes a netmask with 12 leading 1 bits: FF.F0.0.0. State to what next hop the following will be delivered:

    (a) C4.4B.31.2E

    (b) C4.5E.05.09

    (c) C4.4D.31.2E

    (d) C4.5E.03.87

    (e) C4.5E.7F.12

    (f) C4.5E.D1.02

Table 3.21 Routing Table for Exercise 73

Net/MaskLength	Nexthop
C4.5E.2.0/23	A
C4.5E.4.0/22	B
C4.5E.C0.0/19	C
C4.5E.40.0/18	D
C4.4C.0.0/14	E
C0.0.0.0/2	F
80.0.0.0/1	G

74. An ISP that has authority to assign addresses from a /16 prefix (an old class B address) is working with a new company to allocate it a portion of address space based on CIDR. The new company needs IP addresses for machines in three divisions of its corporate network: Engineering, Marketing, and Sales. These divisions plan to grow as follows: Engineering has 5 machines as of the start of year 1 and intends to add 1 machine every week, Marketing will never need more than 16 machines, and Sales needs 1 machine for every 2 clients. As of the start of year 1, the company has no clients, but the sales model indicates that, by the start of year 2, the company will have 6 clients and each week thereafter will get one new client with probability 60%, will lose one client with probability 20%, or will maintain the same number with probability 20%.

(a) What address range would be required to support the company's growth plans for at least 7 years if Marketing uses all 16 of its addresses and the Sales and Engineering plans behave as expected?

(b) How long would this address assignment last? At the time when the company runs out of address space, how would the addresses be assigned to the three groups?

(c) If, instead of using CIDR addressing, it was necessary to use old-style classful addresses, what options would the new company have in terms of getting address space?

75. Propose a lookup algorithm for an IP forwarding table containing prefixes of varying lengths that does not require a linear search of the entire table to find the longest match.

4

A SYSTEMS APPROACH

A SYSTEMS APPROACH

A SYSTEMS APPROACH

A SYSTEMS APPROACH

A SYSTEMS APPROACH

Advanced Internetworking

Every seeming equality conceals a hierarchy.

–Mason Cooley

We have now seen how to build an internetwork that consists of a number of networks of different types. That is, we have dealt with the problem of *heterogeneity*. The second critical problem in internetworking—arguably the fundamental problem for all networking—is *scale*. To understand the problem of scaling, it is worth considering the growth of the Internet, which has roughly doubled in size each year for 30 years. This sort of growth forces us to face a number of challenges.

Chief among these is how do you build a routing system that can handle hundreds of thousands of networks and billions

PROBLEM: SCALING TO BILLIONS

of end nodes? As we will see in this chapter, most approaches to tackling the scalability of routing depend on the introduction of hierarchy. We can introduce hierarchy in the form of areas within a domain; we also use hierarchy to scale the routing system among domains. The interdomain routing protocol that has enabled the Internet to scale to its current size is BGP. We will take a look at how BGP operates, and consider the challenges faced by BGP as the Internet continues to grow.

Closely related to the scalability of routing is the problem of addressing. Even two decades ago it had become apparent that the 32-bit addressing scheme of IP version 4 would not last forever. That led to the definition of a new version of IP—version 6, since version 5 had been used in an earlier experiment. IPv6 primarily expands the address space but also adds a number of new features, some of which have been retrofitted to IPv4.

While the Internet continues to grow in size, it also needs to evolve its functionality. The final sections of this chapter cover some significant enhancements to the Internet's capabilities. The first, multicast, is an enhancement of the basic service model. We show how multicast—the ability to deliver the same packets to a group of receivers efficiently—can be incorporated into an internet, and we describe several of the routing protocols that have been developed to support multicast. The second enhancement, Multiprotocol Label Switching (MPLS), modifies the forwarding mechanism of IP networks. This modification has enabled some changes in the way IP routing is performed and in the services offered by IP networks. Finally, we look at the effects of mobility on routing and describe some enhancements to IP to support mobile hosts and routers. For each of these enhancements, issues of scalability continue to be important.

4.1 THE GLOBAL INTERNET

At this point, we have seen how to connect a heterogeneous collection of networks to create an internetwork and how to use the simple hierarchy of the IP address to make routing in an internet somewhat scalable. We say "somewhat" scalable because, even though each router does not need to know about all the hosts connected to the internet, it does, in the model described so far, need to know about all the networks connected to the internet. Today's Internet has hundreds of thousands of networks connected to it (or more, depending on how you count). Routing protocols such as those we have just discussed do not scale to those kinds of numbers. This section looks at a variety of techniques that greatly improve scalability and that have enabled the Internet to grow as far as it has.

Before getting to these techniques, we need to have a general picture in our heads of what the global Internet looks like. It is not just a random interconnection of Ethernets, but instead it takes on a shape that reflects the fact that it interconnects many different organizations. Figure 4.1 gives a simple depiction of the state of the Internet in 1990. Since that

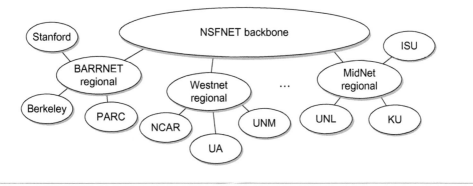

■ **FIGURE 4.1** The tree structure of the Internet in 1990.

time, the Internet's topology has grown much more complex than this figure suggests—we present a slightly more accurate picture of the current Internet in Section 4.1.2 and Figure 4.4—but this picture will do for now.

One of the salient features of this topology is that it consists of end-user sites (e.g., Stanford University) that connect to service provider networks (e.g., BARRNET was a provider network that served sites in the San Francisco Bay Area). In 1990, many providers served a limited geographic region and were thus known as *regional networks*. The regional networks were, in turn, connected by a nationwide backbone. In 1990, this backbone was funded by the National Science Foundation (NSF) and was therefore called the *NSFNET backbone*. Although the detail is not shown in this figure, the provider networks are typically built from a large number of point-to-point links (e.g., T1 and DS3 links in the past, OC-48 and OC-192 SONET links today) that connect to routers; similarly, each end-user site is typically not a single network but instead consists of multiple physical networks connected by routers and bridges.

Notice in Figure 4.1 that each provider and end-user is likely to be an administratively independent entity. This has some significant consequences on routing. For example, it is quite likely that different providers will have different ideas about the best routing protocol to use within their networks and on how metrics should be assigned to links in their network. Because of this independence, each provider's network is usually a single *autonomous system* (AS). We will define this term more precisely in Section 4.1.2, but for now it is adequate to think of an AS as a network that is administered independently of other ASs.

The fact that the Internet has a discernible structure can be used to our advantage as we tackle the problem of scalability. In fact, we need to deal with two related scaling issues. The first is the scalability of routing. We need to find ways to minimize the number of network numbers that get carried around in routing protocols and stored in the routing tables of routers. The second is address utilization—that is, making sure that the IP address space does not get consumed too quickly.

Throughout this book, we see the principle of hierarchy used again and again to improve scalability. We saw in the previous chapter how the hierarchical structure of IP addresses, especially with the flexibility provided by Classless Interdomain Routing (CIDR) and subnetting, can improve the scalability of routing. In the next two sections, we'll see further uses of hierarchy (and its partner, aggregation) to provide greater scalability, first in a single domain and then between domains. Our final subsection looks at the emerging standards for IP version 6, the invention of which was largely the result of scalability concerns.

4.1.1 Routing Areas

As a first example of using hierarchy to scale up the routing system, we'll examine how link-state routing protocols (such as OSPF and IS-IS) can be used to partition a routing domain into subdomains called *areas*. (The terminology varies somewhat among protocols—we use the OSPF terminology here.) By adding this extra level of hierarchy, we enable single domains to grow larger without overburdening the routing protocols or resorting to the more complex interdomain routing protocols described below.

An area is a set of routers that are administratively configured to exchange link-state information with each other. There is one special area—the backbone area, also known as area 0. An example of a routing domain divided into areas is shown in Figure 4.2. Routers R1, R2, and R3 are members of the backbone area. They are also members of at least one nonbackbone area; R1 is actually a member of both area 1 and area 2. A router that is a member of both the backbone area and a nonbackbone area is an area border router (ABR). Note that these are distinct from the routers that are at the edge of an AS, which are referred to as AS border routers for clarity.

Routing within a single area is exactly as described in Section 3.3.3. All the routers in the area send link-state advertisements to each other

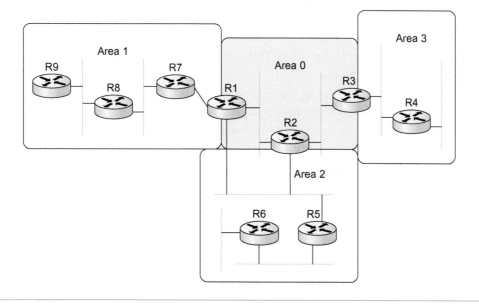

■ FIGURE 4.2 A domain divided into areas.

and thus develop a complete, consistent map of the area. However, the link-state advertisements of routers that are not area border routers do not leave the area in which they originated. This has the effect of making the flooding and route calculation processes considerably more scalable. For example, router R4 in area 3 will never see a link-state advertisement from router R8 in area 1. As a consequence, it will know nothing about the detailed topology of areas other than its own.

How, then, does a router in one area determine the right next hop for a packet destined to a network in another area? The answer to this becomes clear if we imagine the path of a packet that has to travel from one nonbackbone area to another as being split into three parts. First, it travels from its source network to the backbone area, then it crosses the backbone, then it travels from the backbone to the destination network. To make this work, the area border routers summarize routing information that they have learned from one area and make it available in their advertisements to other areas. For example, R1 receives link-state advertisements from all the routers in area 1 and can thus determine the cost of reaching any network in area 1. When R1 sends link-state advertisements into area 0, it advertises the costs of reaching the networks in area 1 much as if all those networks were directly connected to R1. This enables all the area 0 routers to learn the cost to reach all networks in area 1. The area border routers then summarize this information and advertise it into the nonbackbone areas. Thus, all routers learn how to reach all networks in the domain.

Note that, in the case of area 2, there are two ABRs and that routers in area 2 will thus have to make a choice as to which one they use to reach the backbone. This is easy enough, since both R1 and R2 will be advertising costs to various networks, so it will become clear which is the better choice as the routers in area 2 run their shortest-path algorithm. For example, it is pretty clear that R1 is going to be a better choice than R2 for destinations in area 1.

When dividing a domain into areas, the network administrator makes a tradeoff between scalability and optimality of routing. The use of areas forces all packets traveling from one area to another to go via the backbone area, even if a shorter path might have been available. For example, even if R4 and R5 were directly connected, packets would not flow between them because they are in different nonbackbone areas. It turns out that the need for scalability is often more important than the need to use the absolute shortest path.

This illustrates an important principle in network design. There is frequently a trade-off between some sort of optimality and scalability. When hierarchy is introduced, information is hidden from some nodes in the network, hindering their ability to make perfectly optimal decisions. However, information hiding is essential to scalability, since it saves all nodes from having global knowledge. It is invariably true in large networks that scalability is a more pressing design goal than perfect optimality.

Finally, we note that there is a trick by which network administrators can more flexibly decide which routers go in area 0. This trick uses the idea of a *virtual link* between routers. Such a virtual link is obtained by configuring a router that is not directly connected to area 0 to exchange backbone routing information with a router that is. For example, a virtual link could be configured from R8 to R1, thus making R8 part of the backbone. R8 would now participate in link-state advertisement flooding with the other routers in area 0. The cost of the virtual link from R8 to R1 is determined by the exchange of routing information that takes place in area 1. This technique can help to improve the optimality of routing.

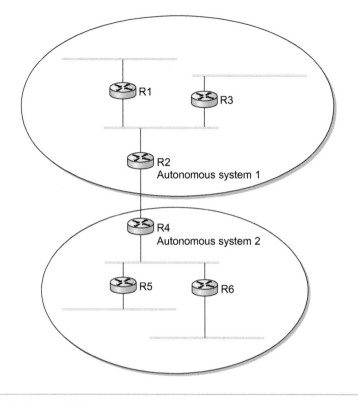

■ FIGURE 4.3 A network with two autonomous systems.

4.1.2 Interdomain Routing (BGP)

LAB 08: BGP

At the beginning of this chapter, we introduced the notion that the Internet is organized as autonomous systems, each of which is under the control of a single administrative entity. A corporation's complex internal network might be a single AS, as may the network of a single Internet Service Provider (ISP). Figure 4.3 shows a simple network with two autonomous systems.

The basic idea behind autonomous systems is to provide an additional way to hierarchically aggregate routing information in a large internet, thus improving scalability. We now divide the routing problem into two parts: routing within a single autonomous system and routing between autonomous systems. Since another name for autonomous systems in the Internet is routing *domains*, we refer to the two parts of the routing problem as interdomain routing and intradomain routing. In addition to improving scalability, the AS model decouples the intradomain routing that takes place in one AS from that taking place in another. Thus, each AS can run whatever intradomain routing protocols it chooses. It can even use static routes or multiple protocols, if desired. The interdomain routing problem is then one of having different ASs share reachability information—descriptions of the set of IP addresses that can be reached via a given AS—with each other.

Challenges in Interdomain Routing

Perhaps the most important challenge of interdomain routing today is the need for each AS to determine its own routing *policies*. A simple example routing policy implemented at a particular AS might look like this: "Whenever possible, I prefer to send traffic via AS X than via AS Y, but I'll use AS Y if it is the only path, and I never want to carry traffic from AS X to AS Y or *vice versa*." Such a policy would be typical when I have paid money to both AS X and AS Y to connect my AS to the rest of the Internet, and AS X is my preferred provider of connectivity, with AS Y being the fallback. Because I view both AS X and AS Y as providers (and presumably I paid them to play this role), I don't expect to help them out by carrying traffic between them across my network (this is called *transit* traffic). The more autonomous systems I connect to, the more complex policies I might have, especially when you consider backbone providers, who may interconnect with dozens of other providers and hundreds of customers and have different economic arrangements (which affect routing policies) with each one.

A key design goal of interdomain routing is that policies like the example above, and much more complex ones, should be supported by the interdomain routing system. To make the problem harder, I need to be able to implement such a policy without any help from other autonomous systems, and in the face of possible misconfiguration or malicious behavior by other autonomous systems. Furthermore, there is often a desire to keep the policies *private*, because the entities that run the autonomous systems—mostly ISPs—are often in competition with each other and don't want their economic arrangements made public.

There have been two major interdomain routing protocols in the history of the Internet. The first was the Exterior Gateway Protocol (EGP), which had a number of limitations, perhaps the most severe of which was that it constrained the topology of the Internet rather significantly. EGP was designed when the Internet had a treelike topology, such as that illustrated in Figure 4.1, and did not allow for the topology to become more general. Note that in this simple treelike structure there is a single backbone, and autonomous systems are connected only as parents and children and not as peers.

The replacement for EGP is the Border Gateway Protocol (BGP), which is in its fourth version at the time of this writing (BGP-4). BGP is often regarded as one of the more complex parts of the Internet. We'll cover some of its high points here.

Unlike its predecessor EGP, BGP makes virtually no assumptions about how autonomous systems are interconnected—they form an arbitrary graph. This model is clearly general enough to accommodate non-tree-structured internetworks, like the simplified picture of a multi-provider Internet shown in Figure 4.4. (It turns out there is still some sort of structure to the Internet, as we'll see below, but it's nothing like as simple as a tree, and BGP makes no assumptions about such structure.)

Unlike the simple tree-structured Internet shown in Figure 4.1, or even the fairly simple picture in Figure 4.4, today's Internet consists of a richly interconnected set of networks, mostly operated by private companies (ISPs) rather than governments. Many Internet Service Providers (ISPs)

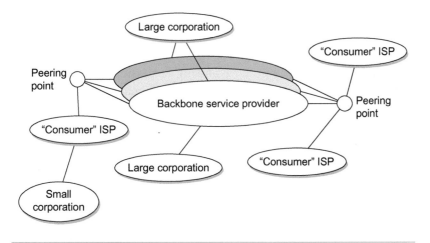

■ FIGURE 4.4 A simple multi-provider Internet.

exist mainly to provide service to "consumers" (i.e., individuals with computers in their homes), while others offer something more like the old backbone service, interconnecting other providers and sometimes larger corporations. Often, many providers arrange to interconnect with each other at a single *peering point*.

To get a better sense of how we might manage routing among this complex interconnection of autonomous systems, we can start by defining a few terms. We define *local traffic* as traffic that originates at or terminates on nodes within an AS, and *transit traffic* as traffic that passes through an AS. We can classify autonomous systems into three broad types:

- Stub AS—an AS that has only a single connection to one other AS; such an AS will only carry local traffic. The small corporation in Figure 4.4 is an example of a stub AS.

- Multihomed AS—an AS that has connections to more than one other AS but that refuses to carry transit traffic, such as the large corporation at the top of Figure 4.4.

- Transit AS—an AS that has connections to more than one other AS and that is designed to carry both transit and local traffic, such as the backbone providers in Figure 4.4.

Whereas the discussion of routing in Section 3.3 focused on finding optimal paths based on minimizing some sort of link metric, the goals of interdomain routing are rather more complex. First, it is necessary to find *some* path to the intended destination that is loop free. Second, paths must be compliant with the policies of the various autonomous systems along the path—and, as we have already seen, those policies might be almost arbitrarily complex. Thus, while intradomain focuses on a well-defined problem of optimizing the scalar cost of the path, interdomain focuses on finding a non-looping, *policy-compliant* path—a much more complex optimization problem.

There are additional factors that make interdomain routing hard. The first is simply a matter of scale. An Internet backbone router must be able to forward any packet destined anywhere in the Internet. That means having a routing table that will provide a match for any valid IP address. While CIDR has helped to control the number of distinct prefixes that are carried in the Internet's backbone routing, there is inevitably a lot of routing information to pass around—on the order of 300,000 prefixes at the time of writing.[1]

A further challenge in interdomain routing arises from the autonomous nature of the domains. Note that each domain may run its own interior routing protocols and use any scheme it chooses to assign metrics to paths. This means that it is impossible to calculate meaningful path costs for a path that crosses multiple autonomous systems. A cost of 1000 across one provider might imply a great path, but it might mean an unacceptably bad one from another provider. As a result, interdomain routing advertises only *reachability*. The concept of reachability is basically a statement that "you can reach this network through this AS." This means that for interdomain routing to pick an optimal path is essentially impossible.

The autonomous nature of interdomain raises issue of trust. Provider A might be unwilling to believe certain advertisements from provider B for fear that provider B will advertise erroneous routing information. For example, trusting provider B when he advertises a great route to anywhere in the Internet can be a disastrous choice if provider B turns out to have made a mistake configuring his routers or to have insufficient capacity to carry the traffic.

The issue of trust is also related to the need to support complex policies as noted above. For example, I might be willing to trust a particular provider only when he advertises reachability to certain prefixes, and thus I would have a policy that says, "Use AS X to reach only prefixes p and q, if and only if AS X advertises reachability to those prefixes."

Basics of BGP

Each AS has one or more *border routers* through which packets enter and leave the AS. In our simple example in Figure 4.3, routers R2 and R4 would be border routers. (Over the years, routers have sometimes also been known as *gateways*, hence the names of the protocols BGP and EGP). A border router is simply an IP router that is charged with the task of forwarding packets between autonomous systems.

Each AS that participates in BGP must also have at least one *BGP speaker*, a router that "speaks" BGP to other BGP speakers in other

---

[1]Check the live references at the end of this chapter for a current estimate of this number.

autonomous systems. It is common to find that border routers are also BGP speakers, but that does not have to be the case.

BGP does not belong to either of the two main classes of routing protocols (distance-vector and link-state protocols) described in Section 3.3. Unlike these protocols, BGP advertises *complete paths* as an enumerated list of autonomous systems to reach a particular network. It is sometimes called a *path-vector* protocol for this reason. The advertisement of complete paths is necessary to enable the sorts of policy decisions described above to be made in accordance with the wishes of a particular AS. It also enables routing loops to be readily detected.

To see how this works, consider the very simple example network in Figure 4.5. Assume that the providers are transit networks, while the customer networks are stubs. A BGP speaker for the AS of provider A (AS 2) would be able to advertise reachability information for each of the network numbers assigned to customers P and Q. Thus, it would say, in effect, "The networks 128.96, 192.4.153, 192.4.32, and 192.4.3 can be reached directly from AS 2." The backbone network, on receiving this advertisement, can advertise, "The networks 128.96, 192.4.153, 192.4.32, and 192.4.3 can be reached along the path ⟨AS 1, AS 2⟩." Similarly, it could advertise, "The networks 192.12.69, 192.4.54, and 192.4.23 can be reached along the path ⟨AS 1, AS 3⟩."

An important job of BGP is to prevent the establishment of looping paths. For example, consider the network illustrated in Figure 4.6. It differs from Figure 4.5 only in the addition of an extra link between AS 2

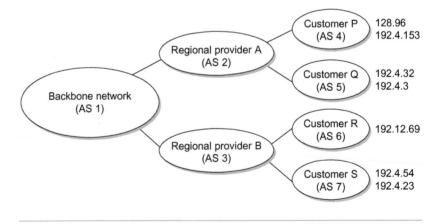

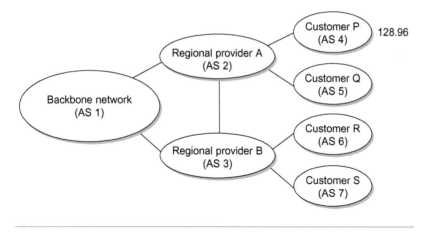

■ FIGURE 4.6 Example of loop among autonomous systems.

and AS 3, but the effect now is that the graph of autonomous systems has a loop in it. Suppose AS 1 learns that it can reach network 128.96 through AS 2, so it advertises this fact to AS 3, who in turn advertises it back to AS 2. In the absence of any loop prevention mechanism, AS 2 could now decide that AS 3 was the preferred route for packets destined for 128.96. If AS 2 starts sending packets addressed to 128.96 to AS 3, AS 3 would send them to AS 1; AS 1 would send them back to AS 2; and they would loop forever. This is prevented by carrying the complete AS path in the routing messages. In this case, the advertisement for a path to 128.96 received by AS 2 from AS 3 would contain an AS path of ⟨AS 3, AS 1, AS 2, AS 4⟩. AS 2 sees itself in this path, and thus concludes that this is not a useful path for it to use.

In order for this loop prevention technique to work, the AS numbers carried in BGP clearly need to be unique. For example, AS 2 can only recognize itself in the AS path in the above example if no other AS identifies itself in the same way. AS numbers have until recently been 16-bit numbers, and they are assigned by a central authority to assure uniqueness. While 16 bits only allows about 65,000 autonomous systems, which might not seem like a lot, we note that a stub AS does not need a unique AS number, and this covers the overwhelming majority of nonprovider networks.[2]

---

[2] 32-bit AS numbers have also been defined and came into use around 2009, thus ensuring that AS number space will not become a scarce resource.

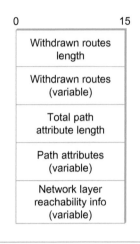

■ FIGURE 4.7 BGP-4 update packet format.

A given AS will only advertise routes that it considers good enough for itself. That is, if a BGP speaker has a choice of several different routes to a destination, it will choose the best one according to its own local policies, and then that will be the route it advertises. Furthermore, a BGP speaker is under no obligation to advertise any route to a destination, even if it has one. This is how an AS can implement a policy of not providing transit— by refusing to advertise routes to prefixes that are not contained within that AS, even if it knows how to reach them.

Given that links fail and policies change, BGP speakers need to be able to cancel previously advertised paths. This is done with a form of negative advertisement known as a *withdrawn route*. Both positive and negative reachability information are carried in a BGP update message, the format of which is shown in Figure 4.7. (Note that the fields in this figure are multiples of 16 bits, unlike other packet formats in this chapter.)

Unlike the routing protocols described in the previous chapter, BGP is defined to run on top of TCP, the reliable transport protocol described in Section 5.2. Because BGP speakers can count on TCP to be reliable, this means that any information that has been sent from one speaker to another does not need to be sent again. Thus, as long as nothing has changed, a BGP speaker can simply send an occasional *keepalive* message that says, in effect, "I'm still here and nothing has changed." If that router were to crash or become disconnected from its peer, it would stop sending the keepalives, and the other routers that had learned routes from it would assume that those routes were no longer valid.

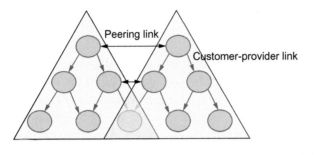

Peering link

Customer-provider link

Common AS Relationships and Policies

Having said that policies may be arbitrarily complex, there turn out to be a few common ones, reflecting common relationships between autonomous systems. The most common relationships are illustrated in Figure 4.8. The three common relationships and the policies that go with them are as follows:

- *Provider-Customer*—Providers are in the business of connecting their customers to the rest of the Internet. A customer might be a corporation, or it might be a smaller ISP (which may have customers of its own). So the common policy is to advertise all the routes I know about to my customer, and advertise routes I learn from my customer to everyone.

- *Customer-Provider*—In the other direction, the customer wants to get traffic directed to him (and his customers, if he has them) by his provider, and he wants to be able to send traffic to the rest of the Internet through his provider. So the common policy in this case is to advertise my own prefixes and routes learned from my customers to my provider, advertise routes learned from my provider to my customers, but don't advertise routes learned from one provider to another provider. That last part is to make sure the customer doesn't find himself in the business of carrying traffic from one provider to another, which isn't in his interests if he is paying the providers to carry traffic for him.

- *Peer*—The third option is a symmetrical peering between autonomous systems. Two providers who view themselves as equals usually peer so that they can get access to each other's customers without having to pay another provider. The typical policy here is to advertise routes learned from my customers to my peer, advertise routes learned from my peer to my customers, but don't advertise routes from my peer to any provider or *vice versa*.

One thing to note about this figure is the way it has brought back some structure to the apparently unstructured Internet. At the bottom of the hierarchy we have the stub networks that are customers of one or more providers, and as we move up the hierarchy we see providers who have other providers as their customers. At the top, we have providers who have customers and peers but are not customers of anyone. These providers are known as the *Tier-1* providers.

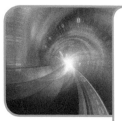

Let's return to the real question: How does all this help us to build scalable networks? First, the number of nodes participating in BGP is on the order of the number of autonomous systems, which is much smaller than the number of networks. Second, finding a good interdomain route is only a matter of finding a path to the right border router, of which there are only a few per AS. Thus, we have neatly subdivided the routing problem into manageable parts, once again using a new level of hierarchy to increase scalability. The complexity of interdomain routing is now on the order of the number of autonomous systems, and the complexity of intradomain routing is on the order of the number of networks in a single AS.

Integrating Interdomain and Intradomain Routing

While the preceding discussion illustrates how a BGP speaker learns interdomain routing information, the question still remains as to how all the other routers in a domain get this information. There are several ways this problem can be addressed.

Let's start with a very simple situation, which is also very common. In the case of a stub AS that only connects to other autonomous systems at a single point, the border router is clearly the only choice for all routes that are outside the AS. Such a router can inject a *default route* into the intradomain routing protocol. In effect, this is a statement that any network that has not been explicitly advertised in the intradomain protocol is reachable through the border router. Recall from the discussion of IP forwarding in Section 3.2 that the default entry in the forwarding table comes after all the more specific entries, and it matches anything that failed to match a specific entry.

The next step up in complexity is to have the border routers inject specific routes they have learned from outside the AS. Consider, for example, the border router of a provider AS that connects to a customer AS. That router could learn that the network prefix 192.4.54/24 is located inside the customer AS, either through BGP or because the information is configured into the border router. It could inject a route to that prefix into the routing protocol running inside the provider AS. This would be an advertisement of the sort, "I have a link to 192.4.54/24 of cost X." This would cause other routers in the provider AS to learn that this border router is the place to send packets destined for that prefix.

The final level of complexity comes in backbone networks, which learn so much routing information from BGP that it becomes too costly to inject it into the intradomain protocol. For example, if a border router wants to inject 10,000 prefixes that it learned about from another AS, it will have to send very big link-state packets to the other routers in that AS, and their shortest-path calculations are going to become very complex. For this reason, the routers in a backbone network use a variant of BGP called *interior BGP* (iBGP) to effectively redistribute the information that is learned by the BGP speakers at the edges of the AS to all the other routers in the AS. (The other variant of BGP, discussed above, runs between autonomous systems and is called *exterior BGP*, or eBGP). iBGP enables any router in the AS to learn the best border router to use when sending a packet to any address. At the same time, each router in the AS keeps track of how to get to each border router using a conventional intradomain protocol with no injected information. By combining these two sets of information, each router in the AS is able to determine the appropriate next hop for all prefixes.

To see how this all works, consider the simple example network, representing a single AS, in Figure 4.9. The three border routers, A, D, and E, speak eBGP to other autonomous systems and learn how to reach various prefixes. These three border routers communicate with other and with the interior routers B and C by building a mesh of iBGP sessions among all the routers in the AS. Let's now focus in on how router B builds up its complete view of how to forward packets to any prefix. Look at the table at the top left of Figure 4.10 which shows the information that router B learns from its iBGP sessions. It learns that some prefixes are best reached via router A, some via D, and some via E. At the same time, all the routers in the AS are also running some intradomain routing protocol such as Routing Information Protocol (RIP) or Open Shortest Path First (OSPF). (A generic term for intradomain protocols is an interior gateway protocol, or IGP.) From this completely separate protocol, B learns how

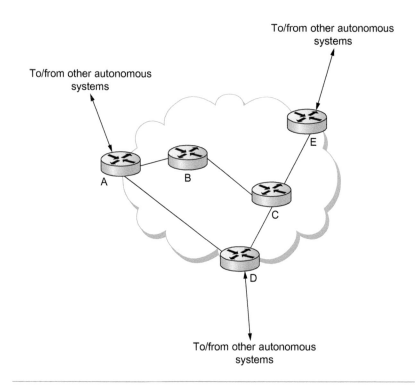

To/from other autonomous systems

To/from other autonomous systems

To/from other autonomous systems

■ **FIGURE 4.9** Example of interdomain and intradomain routing. All routers run iBGP and an intradomain routing protocol. Border routers A, D, and E also run eBGP to other autonomous systems.

to reach other nodes *inside* the domain, as shown in the top right table. For example, to reach router E, B needs to send packets toward router C. Finally, in the bottom table, B puts the whole picture together, combining the information about external prefixes learned from iBGP with the information about interior routes to the border routers learned from the IGP. Thus, if a prefix like 18.0/16 is reachable via border router E, and the best interior path to E is via C, then it follows that any packet destined for 18.0/16 should be forwarded toward C. In this way, any router in the AS can build up a complete routing table for any prefix that is reachable via some border router of the AS.

4.1.3 IP Version 6 (IPv6)

In many respects, the motivation for a new version of IP is simple: to deal with exhaustion of the IP address space. CIDR helped considerably to contain the rate at which the Internet address space is being consumed and also helped to control the growth of routing table information needed in the Internet's routers. However, there will come a point at which these

Prefix	BGP Next Hop
18.0/16	E
12.5.5/24	A
128.34/16	D
128.69./16	A

BGP table for the AS

Router	IGP Path
A	A
C	C
D	C
E	C

IGP table for router B

Prefix	IGP Path
18.0/16	C
12.5.5/24	A
128.34/16	C
128.69./16	A

Combined table for router B

■ FIGURE 4.10 BGP routing table, IGP routing table, and combined table at router B.

techniques are no longer adequate. In particular, it is virtually impossible to achieve 100% address utilization efficiency, so the address space will be exhausted well before the 4 billionth host is connected to the Internet. Even if we were able to use all 4 billion addresses, it's not too hard to imagine ways that that number could be exhausted, now that IP addresses are assigned not just to full-blown computers but also to mobile phones, televisions, and other household appliances. All of these possibilities argue that a bigger address space than that provided by 32 bits will eventually be needed.

Historical Perspective

The IETF began looking at the problem of expanding the IP address space in 1991, and several alternatives were proposed. Since the IP address is carried in the header of every IP packet, increasing the size of the address dictates a change in the packet header. This means a new version of the Internet Protocol and, as a consequence, a need for new software for every host and router in the Internet. This is clearly not a trivial matter—it is a major change that needs to be thought about very carefully.

The effort to define a new version of IP was known as IP Next Generation, or IPng. As the work progressed, an official IP version number was assigned, so IPng is now known as IPv6. Note that the version of IP discussed so far in this chapter is version 4 (IPv4). The apparent discontinuity in numbering is the result of version number 5 being used for an experimental protocol some years ago.

The significance of changing to a new version of IP caused a snowball effect. The general feeling among network designers was that if you are going to make a change of this magnitude you might as well fix as many other things in IP as possible at the same time. Consequently, the IETF solicited white papers from anyone who cared to write one, asking for input on the features that might be desired in a new version of IP. In addition to the need to accommodate scalable routing and addressing, some of the other wish list items for IPng included:

- Support for real-time services
- Security support
- Autoconfiguration (i.e., the ability of hosts to automatically configure themselves with such information as their own IP address and domain name)
- Enhanced routing functionality, including support for mobile hosts

It is interesting to note that, while many of these features were absent from IPv4 at the time IPv6 was being designed, support for all of them has made its way into IPv4 in recent years, often using similar techniques in both protocols. It can be argued that the freedom to think of IPv6 as a clean slate facilitated the design of new capabilities for IP that were then retrofitted into IPv4.

In addition to the wish list, one absolutely non-negotiable feature for IPng was that there must be a transition plan to move from the current version of IP (version 4) to the new version. With the Internet being so large and having no centralized control, it would be completely impossible to have a "flag day" on which everyone shut down their hosts and routers and installed a new version of IP. Thus, there will probably be a long transition period in which some hosts and routers will run IPv4 only, some will run IPv4 and IPv6, and some will run IPv6 only.

The IETF appointed a committee called the IPng Directorate to collect all the inputs on IPng requirements and to evaluate proposals for a protocol to become IPng. Over the life of this committee there were numerous proposals, some of which merged with other proposals, and eventually one was chosen by the Directorate to be the basis for IPng. That proposal was called *Simple Internet Protocol Plus* (SIPP). SIPP originally called for a doubling of the IP address size to 64 bits. When the Directorate selected SIPP, they stipulated several changes, one of which was another doubling of the address to 128 bits (16 bytes). It was around this time that version number 6 was assigned. The rest of this section describes some of the main features of IPv6. At the time of this writing, most of the key specifications for IPv6 are Proposed or Draft Standards in the IETF.

Addresses and Routing

First and foremost, IPv6 provides a 128-bit address space, as opposed to the 32 bits of version 4. Thus, while version 4 can potentially address 4 billion nodes if address assignment efficiency reaches 100%, IPv6 can address 3.4×10^{38} nodes, again assuming 100% efficiency. As we have seen, though, 100% efficiency in address assignment is not likely. Some analysis of other addressing schemes, such as those of the French and U.S. telephone networks, as well as that of IPv4, have turned up some empirical numbers for address assignment efficiency. Based on the most pessimistic estimates of efficiency drawn from this study, the IPv6 address space is predicted to provide over 1500 addresses per square foot of the Earth's surface, which certainly seems like it should serve us well even when toasters on Venus have IP addresses.

Address Space Allocation

Drawing on the effectiveness of CIDR in IPv4, IPv6 addresses are also classless, but the address space is still subdivided in various ways based on the leading bits. Rather than specifying different address classes, the leading bits specify different uses of the IPv6 address. The current assignment of prefixes is listed in Table 4.1.

This allocation of the address space warrants a little discussion. First, the entire functionality of IPv4's three main address classes (A, B, and C) is contained inside the "everything else" range. Global Unicast Addresses, as we will see shortly, are a lot like classless IPv4 addresses, only much longer. These are the main ones of interest at this point, with over 99% of the total IPv6 address space available to this important form of address. (At the time of writing, IPv6 unicast addresses are being allocated from

Table 4.1 Address Prefix Assignments for IPv6

Prefix	Use
00...0 (128 bits)	Unspecified
00...1 (128 bits)	Loopback
1111 1111	Multicast addresses
1111 1110 10	Link-local unicast
Everything else	Global Unicast Addresses

the block that begins 001, with the remaining address space—about 87%—being reserved for future use.)

The multicast address space is (obviously) for multicast, thereby serving the same role as class D addresses in IPv4. Note that multicast addresses are easy to distinguish—they start with a byte of all 1s. We will see how these addresses are used in Section 4.2.

The idea behind link-local use addresses is to enable a host to construct an address that will work on the network to which it is connected without being concerned about the global uniqueness of the address. This may be useful for autoconfiguration, as we will see below. Similarly, the site-local use addresses are intended to allow valid addresses to be constructed on a site (e.g., a private corporate network) that is not connected to the larger Internet; again, global uniqueness need not be an issue.

Within the global unicast address space are some important special types of addresses. A node may be assigned an IPv4-compatible IPv6 address by zero-extending a 32-bit IPv4 address to 128 bits. A node that is only capable of understanding IPv4 can be assigned an IPv4-mapped IPv6 address by prefixing the 32-bit IPv4 address with 2 bytes of all 1s and then zero-extending the result to 128 bits. These two special address types have uses in the IPv4-to-IPv6 transition (see the sidebar on this topic).

Address Notation

Just as with IPv4, there is some special notation for writing down IPv6 addresses. The standard representation is x:x:x:x:x:x:x:x, where each "x" is a hexadecimal representation of a 16-bit piece of the address. An example would be

```
47CD:1234:4422:AC02:0022:1234:A456:0124
```

Transition from IPv4 to IPv6

The most important idea behind the transition from IPv4 to IPv6 is that the Internet is far too big and decentralized to have a "flag day"—one specified day on which every host and router is upgraded from IPv4 to IPv6. Thus, IPv6 needs to be deployed incrementally in such a way that hosts and routers that only understand IPv4 can continue to function for as long as possible. Ideally, IPv4 nodes should be able to talk to other IPv4 nodes and some set of other IPv6-capable nodes indefinitely. Also, IPv6 hosts should be capable of talking to other IPv6 nodes even when some of the infrastructure between them may only support IPv4. Two major mechanisms have been defined to help this transition: *dual-stack operation* and *tunneling*.

The idea of dual stacks is fairly straightforward: IPv6 nodes run both IPv6 and IPv4 and use the Version field to decide which stack should process an arriving packet. In this case, the IPv6 address could be unrelated to the IPv4 address, or it could be the IPv4-mapped IPv6 address described earlier in this section.

The basic tunneling technique, in which an IP packet is sent as the *payload* of another IP packet, was described in Section 3.2. For IPv6 transition, tunneling is used to send an IPv6 packet over a piece of the network that only understands IPv4. This means that the IPv6 packet is encapsulated within an IPv4 header that has the address of the tunnel endpoint in its header, is transmitted across the IPv4-only piece of network, and then is decapsulated at the endpoint. The endpoint could be either a router or a host; in either case, it must be IPv6 capable to be able to process the IPv6 packet after decapsulation. If the endpoint is a host with an IPv4-mapped IPv6 address, then tunneling can be done automatically by extracting the IPv4 address from the IPv6 address and using it to form the IPv4 header. Otherwise, the tunnel must be configured manually. In this case, the encapsulating node needs to know the IPv4 address of the other end of the tunnel, since it cannot be extracted from the IPv6 header. From the perspective of IPv6, the other end of the tunnel looks like a regular IPv6 node that is just one hop away, even though there may be many hops of IPv4 infrastructure between the tunnel endpoints.

Any IPv6 address can be written using this notation. Since there are a few special types of IPv6 addresses, there are some special notations that may be helpful in certain circumstances. For example, an address with a large number of contiguous 0s can be written more compactly by omitting all the 0 fields. Thus,

```
47CD:0000:0000:0000:0000:0000:A456:0124
```

could be written

```
47CD::A456:0124
```

Clearly, this form of shorthand can only be used for one set of contiguous 0s in an address to avoid ambiguity.

The two types of IPv6 addresses that contain an embedded IPv4 address have their own special notation that makes extraction of the IPv4 address easier. For example, the IPv4-mapped IPv6 address of a host whose IPv4 address was 128.96.33.81 could be written as

```
::FFFF:128.96.33.81
```

That is, the last 32 bits are written in IPv4 notation, rather than as a pair of hexadecimal numbers separated by a colon. Note that the double colon at the front indicates the leading 0s.

Global Unicast Addresses

By far the most important sort of addressing that IPv6 must provide is plain old unicast addressing. It must do this in a way that supports the rapid rate of addition of new hosts to the Internet and that allows routing to be done in a scalable way as the number of physical networks in the Internet grows. Thus, at the heart of IPv6 is the unicast address allocation plan that determines how unicast addresses will be assigned to service providers, autonomous systems, networks, hosts, and routers.

In fact, the address allocation plan that is proposed for IPv6 unicast addresses is extremely similar to that being deployed with CIDR in IPv4. To understand how it works and how it provides scalability, it is helpful to define some new terms. We may think of a nontransit AS (i.e., a stub or multihomed AS) as a *subscriber*, and we may think of a transit AS as a *provider*. Furthermore, we may subdivide providers into *direct* and *indirect*. The former are directly connected to subscribers. The latter primarily connect other providers, are not connected directly to subscribers, and are often known as *backbone networks*.

With this set of definitions, we can see that the Internet is not just an arbitrarily interconnected set of autonomous systems; it has some intrinsic hierarchy. The difficulty lies in making use of this hierarchy without inventing mechanisms that fail when the hierarchy is not strictly observed, as happened with EGP. For example, the distinction between direct and indirect providers becomes blurred when a subscriber connects to a backbone or when a direct provider starts connecting to many other providers.

As with CIDR, the goal of the IPv6 address allocation plan is to provide aggregation of routing information to reduce the burden on intradomain routers. Again, the key idea is to use an address prefix—a set of contiguous bits at the most significant end of the address—to aggregate reachability information to a large number of networks and even to a large number of autonomous systems. The main way to achieve this is to assign an address prefix to a direct provider and then for that direct provider to assign longer prefixes that begin with that prefix to its subscribers. This is exactly what we observed in Figure 3.22. Thus, a provider can advertise a single prefix for all of its subscribers.

Of course, the drawback is that if a site decides to change providers, it will need to obtain a new address prefix and renumber all the nodes in the site. This could be a colossal undertaking, enough to dissuade most people from ever changing providers. For this reason, there is ongoing research on other addressing schemes, such as geographic addressing, in which a site's address is a function of its location rather than the provider to which it attaches. At present, however, provider-based addressing is necessary to make routing work efficiently.

Note that while IPv6 address assignment is essentially equivalent to the way address assignment has happened in IPv4 since the introduction of CIDR, IPv6 has the significant advantage of not having a large installed base of assigned addresses to fit into its plans.

One question is whether it makes sense for hierarchical aggregation to take place at other levels in the hierarchy. For example, should all providers obtain their address prefixes from within a prefix allocated to the backbone to which they connect? Given that most providers connect to multiple backbones, this probably doesn't make sense. Also, since the number of providers is much smaller than the number of sites, the benefits of aggregating at this level are much fewer.

One place where aggregation may make sense is at the national or continental level. Continental boundaries form natural divisions in the Internet topology. If all addresses in Europe, for example, had a common prefix, then a great deal of aggregation could be done, and most routers in other continents would only need one routing table entry for all networks with the Europe prefix. Providers in Europe would all select their prefixes such that they began with the European prefix. Using this scheme, an IPv6 address might look like Figure 4.11. The **RegistryID** might be an identifier

3	m	n	o	p	125–m–n–o–p
010	RegistryID	ProviderID	SubscriberID	SubnetID	InterfaceID

■ **FIGURE 4.11** An IPv6 provider-based unicast address.

assigned to a European address registry, with different IDs assigned to other continents or countries. Note that prefixes would be of different lengths under this scenario. For example, a provider with few customers could have a longer prefix (and thus less total address space available) than one with many customers.

One tricky situation could occur when a subscriber is connected to more than one provider. Which prefix should the subscriber use for his or her site? There is no perfect solution to the problem. For example, suppose a subscriber is connected to two providers, X and Y. If the subscriber takes his prefix from X, then Y has to advertise a prefix that has no relationship to its other subscribers and that as a consequence cannot be aggregated. If the subscriber numbers part of his AS with the prefix of X and part with the prefix of Y, he runs the risk of having half his site become unreachable if the connection to one provider goes down. One solution that works fairly well if X and Y have a lot of subscribers in common is for them to have three prefixes between them: one for subscribers of X only, one for subscribers of Y only, and one for the sites that are subscribers of both X and Y.

Packet Format

Despite the fact that IPv6 extends IPv4 in several ways, its header format is actually simpler. This simplicity is due to a concerted effort to remove unnecessary functionality from the protocol. Figure 4.12 shows the result. (For comparison with IPv4, see the header format shown in Figure 3.16.)

As with many headers, this one starts with a Version field, which is set to 6 for IPv6. The Version field is in the same place relative to the start of the header as IPv4's Version field so that header-processing software can immediately decide which header format to look for. The Traf cClass and FlowLabel fields both relate to quality of service issues, as discussed in Section 6.5.

The PayloadLen field gives the length of the packet, excluding the IPv6 header, measured in bytes. The NextHeader field cleverly replaces both the IP options and the Protocol field of IPv4. If options are required, then

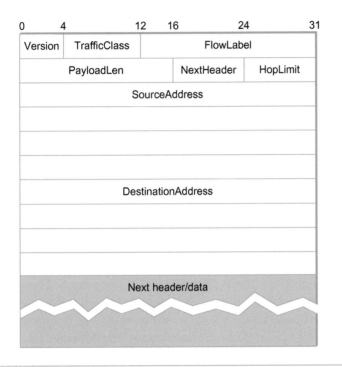

■ FIGURE 4.12 IPv6 packet header.

they are carried in one or more special headers following the IP header, and this is indicated by the value of the NextHeader field. If there are no special headers, the NextHeader field is the demux key identifying the higher-level protocol running over IP (e.g., TCP or UDP); that is, it serves the same purpose as the IPv4 Protocol field. Also, fragmentation is now handled as an optional header, which means that the fragmentation-related fields of IPv4 are not included in the IPv6 header. The HopLimit field is simply the TTL of IPv4, renamed to reflect the way it is actually used.

Finally, the bulk of the header is taken up with the source and destination addresses, each of which is 16 bytes (128 bits) long. Thus, the IPv6 header is always 40 bytes long. Considering that IPv6 addresses are four times longer than those of IPv4, this compares quite well with the IPv4 header, which is 20 bytes long in the absence of options.

The way that IPv6 handles options is quite an improvement over IPv4. In IPv4, if any options were present, every router had to parse the entire options field to see if any of the options were relevant. This is because the options were all buried at the end of the IP header, as an unordered collection of ⟨type, length, value⟩ tuples. In contrast, IPv6 treats options as *extension headers* that must, if present, appear in a specific order. This means that each router can quickly determine if any of the options are relevant to it; in most cases, they will not be. Usually this can be determined by just looking at the NextHeader field. The end result is that option processing is much more efficient in IPv6, which is an important factor in router performance. In addition, the new formatting of options as extension headers means that they can be of arbitrary length, whereas in IPv4 they were limited to 44 bytes at most. We will see how some of the options are used below.

Each option has its own type of extension header. The type of each extension header is identified by the value of the NextHeader field in the header that precedes it, and each extension header contains a NextHeader field to identify the header following it. The last extension header will be followed by a transport-layer header (e.g., TCP) and in this case the value of the NextHeader field is the same as the value of the Protocol field would be in an IPv4 header. Thus, the NextHeader field does double duty; it may either identify the type of extension header to follow, or, in the last extension header, it serves as a demux key to identify the higher-layer protocol running over IPv6.

Consider the example of the fragmentation header, shown in Figure 4.13. This header provides functionality similar to the fragmentation fields in the IPv4 header described in Section 3.2.2, but it is only present if fragmentation is necessary. Assuming it is the only extension header present, then the NextHeader field of the IPv6 header would contain the value 44, which is the value assigned to indicate the fragmentation header. The NextHeader field of the fragmentation header itself contains a value describing the header that follows it. Again, assuming no other extension headers are present, then the next header might be the TCP header, which results in NextHeader containing the value 6, just as the Protocol field would in IPv4. If the fragmentation header

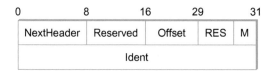

■ FIGURE 4.13 IPv6 fragmentation extension header.

were followed by, say, an authentication header, then the fragmentation header's NextHeader field would contain the value 51.

Autoconfiguration

While the Internet's growth has been impressive, one factor that has inhibited faster acceptance of the technology is the fact that getting connected to the Internet has typically required a fair amount of system administration expertise. In particular, every host that is connected to the Internet needs to be configured with a certain minimum amount of information, such as a valid IP address, a subnet mask for the link to which it attaches, and the address of a name server. Thus, it has not been possible to unpack a new computer and connect it to the Internet without some preconfiguration. One goal of IPv6, therefore, is to provide support for autoconfiguration, sometimes referred to as *plug-and-play* operation.

As we saw in Section 3.2.7, autoconfiguration is possible for IPv4, but it depends on the existence of a server that is configured to hand out addresses and other configuration information to Dynamic Host Configuration Protocol (DHCP) clients. The longer address format in IPv6 helps provide a useful, new form of autoconfiguration called *stateless* autoconfiguration, which does not require a server.

Recall that IPv6 unicast addresses are hierarchical, and that the least significant portion is the interface ID. Thus, we can subdivide the autoconfiguration problem into two parts:

1. Obtain an interface ID that is unique on the link to which the host is attached.

2. Obtain the correct address prefix for this subnet.

Network Address Translation

While IPv6 was motivated by a concern that increased usage of IP would lead to exhaustion of the address space, another technology has become popular as a way to conserve IP address space. That technology is network address translation (NAT), and its widespread use is one main reason why IPv6 deployment remains in its early stages. NAT is viewed by some as "architecturally impure," but it is also a fact of networking life that cannot be ignored.

The basic idea behind NAT is that all the hosts that might communicate with each other over the Internet do not need to have globally unique addresses. Instead, a host could be assigned a "private address" that is not necessarily globally unique, but is unique within some more limited scope—for example, within the corporate network where the host resides. The class A network number 10 is often used for this purpose, since that network number was assigned to the ARPANET and is no longer in use as a globally unique address. As long as the host communicates only with other hosts in the corporate network, a locally unique address is sufficient. If it should want to communicate with a host outside the corporate network, it does so via a *NAT box*, a device that is able to translate from the private address used by the host to some globally unique address that is assigned to the NAT box. Since it's likely that a small subset of the hosts in the corporation requires the services of the NAT box at any one time, the NAT box might be able to get by with a small pool of globally unique addresses, much smaller than the number of addresses that would be needed if every host in the corporation had a globally unique address.

So, we can imagine a NAT box receiving IP packets from a host inside the corporation and translating the IP source address from some private address (say, 10.0.1.5) to a globally unique address (say, 171.69.210.246). When packets come back from the remote host addressed to 171.69.210.246, the NAT box translates the destination address to 10.0.1.5 and forwards the packet on toward the host.

The chief drawback of NAT is that it breaks a key assumption of the IP service model—that all nodes have globally unique addresses. It turns out that lots of applications and protocols rely on this assumption. Some protocols that run over IP (e.g., application protocols such as FTP) carry IP addresses in their messages. These addresses also need to be translated by a NAT box if the higher-layer protocol is to work properly, and thus NAT boxes become much more complex than simple IP header translators. They potentially need to understand an ever-growing number of higher-layer protocols. This in turn presents an obstacle to deployment of new applications.

Even more serious is the fact that NATs make it difficult for an outside device to initiate a connection to a device on the private side of the NAT, since, in the absence of an established mapping in the NAT device, there is no public address to which to send the connection request. This situation has complicated the deployment of many applications such as Voice over IP.

It is probably safe to say that networks would be better off without NAT, but its disappearance seems unlikely. While widespread deployment of IPv6 would probably help, NAT is now popular for a range of other reasons beyond its original purpose. For example, it becomes easier to switch providers if your entire internal network has (private) IP addresses that bear no relation to the provider's address space. And, while NAT boxes cannot be considered a true solution to security threats, the fact that the addresses behind a NAT box are not globally meaningful provides a level of protection against simple attacks. It will be interesting to see how NAT fares in the future as IPv6 deployment gathers momentum.

The first part turns out to be rather easy, since every host on a link must have a unique link-level address. For example, all hosts on an Ethernet have a unique 48-bit Ethernet address. This can be turned into a valid link-local use address by adding the appropriate prefix from Table 4.1 (1111 1110 10) followed by enough 0s to make up 128 bits. For some devices—for example, printers or hosts on a small routerless network that do not connect to any other networks—this address may be perfectly adequate. Those devices that need a globally valid address depend on a router on the same link to periodically advertise the appropriate prefix for the link. Clearly, this requires that the router be configured with the correct address prefix, and that this prefix be chosen in such a way that there is enough space at the end (e.g., 48 bits) to attach an appropriate link-level address.

The ability to embed link-level addresses as long as 48 bits into IPv6 addresses was one of the reasons for choosing such a large address size. Not only does 128 bits allow the embedding, but it leaves plenty of space for the multilevel hierarchy of addressing that we discussed above.

Advanced Routing Capabilities

Another of IPv6's extension headers is the routing header. In the absence of this header, routing for IPv6 differs very little from that of IPv4 under CIDR. The routing header contains a list of IPv6 addresses that represent nodes or topological areas that the packet should visit en route to its destination. A topological area may be, for example, a backbone provider's network. Specifying that packets must visit this network would be a way of implementing provider selection on a packet-by-packet basis. Thus, a host could say that it wants some packets to go through a provider that is cheap, others through a provider that provides high reliability, and still others through a provider that the host trusts to provide security.

To provide the ability to specify topological entities rather than individual nodes, IPv6 defines an *anycast* address. An anycast address is assigned to a set of interfaces, and packets sent to that address will go to the "nearest" of those interfaces, with nearest being determined by the routing protocols. For example, all the routers of a backbone provider could be assigned a single anycast address, which would be used in the routing header.

The anycast address and the routing header are also expected to be used to provide enhanced routing support to mobile hosts. The detailed mechanisms for providing this support are still being defined.

Other Features

As mentioned at the beginning of this section, the primary motivation behind the development of IPv6 was to support the continued growth of the Internet. Once the IP header had to be changed for the sake of the addresses, however, the door was open for a wide variety of other changes, two of which we have just described—autoconfiguration and source-directed routing. IPv6 includes several additional features, most of which are covered elsewhere in this book—mobility is discussed in Section 4.4.2, network security is the topic of Chapter 8, and a new service model proposed for the Internet is described in Section 6.5. It is interesting to note that, in most of these areas, the IPv4 and IPv6 capabilities have become virtually indistinguishable, so that the main driver for IPv6 remains the need for larger addresses.

4.2 MULTICAST

As we saw in Chapter 2, multi-access networks like Ethernet implement multicast in hardware. There are, however, applications that need a broader multicasting capability that is effective at the scale of internetworks. For example, when a radio station is broadcast over the Internet, the same data must be sent to all the hosts where a user has tuned in to that station. In that example, the communication is one-to-many. Other examples of one-to-many applications include transmitting the same news, current stock prices, or software updates to multiple hosts. There are also applications whose communication is many-to-many, such as multimedia teleconferencing, online multiplayer gaming, or distributed simulations. In such cases, members of a group receive data from multiple senders, typically each other. From any particular sender, they all receive the same data.

Normal IP communication, in which each packet must be addressed and sent to a single host, is not well suited to such applications. If an application has data to send to a group, it would have to send a separate packet with the identical data to each member of the group. This redundancy consumes more bandwidth than necessary. Furthermore, the redundant traffic is not distributed evenly but rather is focused around the sending host, and may easily exceed the capacity of the sending host and the nearby networks and routers.

To better support many-to-many and one-to-many communication, IP provides an IP-level multicast analogous to the link-level multicast provided by multi-access networks like Ethernet as we saw in Chapter 2. Now that we are introducing the concept of multicast for IP, we also need a term for the traditional one-to-one service of IP that has been described so far: That service is referred to as *unicast*.

The basic IP multicast model is a many-to-many model based on multicast *groups*, where each group has its own IP *multicast address*. The hosts that are members of a group receive copies of any packets sent to that group's multicast address. A host can be in multiple groups, and it can join and leave groups freely by telling its local router using a protocol that we will discuss shortly. Thus, while we think of unicast addresses as being associated with a node or an interface, multicast addresses are associated with an abstract group, the membership of which changes dynamically over time. Further, the original IP multicast service model allows *any* host to send multicast traffic to a group; it doesn't have to be a member of the group, and there may be any number of such senders to a given group.

Using IP multicast to send the identical packet to each member of the group, a host sends a single copy of the packet addressed to the group's multicast address. The sending host doesn't need to know the individual unicast IP address of each member of the group because, as we will see, that knowledge is distributed among the routers in the internetwork. Similarly, the sending host doesn't need to send multiple copies of the packet because the routers will make copies whenever they have to forward the packet over more than one link. Compared to using unicast IP to deliver the same packets to many receivers, IP multicast is more scalable because it eliminates the redundant traffic (packets) that would have been sent many times over the same links, especially those near to the sending host.

IP's original many-to-many multicast has been supplemented with support for a form of one-to-many multicast. In this model of one-to-many multicast, called *Source-Specific Multicast* (SSM), a receiving host specifies both a multicast group and a specific sending host. The receiving host would then receive multicasts addressed to the specified group, but only if they are from the specified sender. Many Internet multicast applications (e.g., radio broadcasts) fit the SSM model. To contrast it with SSM, IP's original many-to-many model is sometimes referred to as *Any Source Multicast* (ASM).

A host signals its desire to join or leave a multicast group by communicating with its local router using a special protocol for just that purpose. In IPv4, that protocol is the *Internet Group Management Protocol* (IGMP); in IPv6, it is *Multicast Listener Discovery* (MLD). The router then has the responsibility for making multicast behave correctly with regard to that host. Because a host may fail to leave a multicast group when it should (after a crash or other failure, for example), the router periodically polls the LAN to determine which groups are still of interest to the attached hosts.

4.2.1 Multicast Addresses

IP has a subrange of its address space reserved for multicast addresses. In IPv4, these addresses are assigned in the class D address space, and IPv6 also has a portion of its address space (see Table 4.1) reserved for multicast group addresses. Some subranges of the multicast ranges are reserved for intradomain multicast, so they can be reused independently by different domains.

There are thus 28 bits of possible multicast address in IPv4 when we ignore the prefix shared by all multicast addresses. This presents a problem when attempting to take advantage of hardware multicasting on a local area network (LAN). Let's take the case of Ethernet. Ethernet multicast addresses have only 23 bits when we ignore their shared prefix. In other words, to take advantage of Ethernet multicasting, IP has to map 28-bit IP multicast addresses into 23-bit Ethernet multicast addresses. This is implemented by taking the low-order 23 bits of any IP multicast address to use as its Ethernet multicast address and ignoring the high-order 5 bits. Thus, 32 (2^5) IP addresses map into each one of the Ethernet addresses.

When a host on an Ethernet joins an IP multicast group, it configures its Ethernet interface to receive any packets with the corresponding Ethernet multicast address. Unfortunately, this causes the receiving host to receive not only the multicast traffic it desired but also traffic sent to any of the other 31 IP multicast groups that map to the same Ethernet address, if they are routed to that Ethernet. Therefore, IP at the receiving host must examine the IP header of any multicast packet to determine whether the packet really belongs to the desired group. In summary, the mismatch of multicast address sizes means that multicast traffic may place a burden on hosts that are not even interested in the group to which the traffic was sent. Fortunately, in some switched networks (such as switched Ethernet) this problem can be mitigated by schemes wherein the switches recognize unwanted packets and discard them.

One perplexing question is how senders and receivers learn which multicast addresses to use in the first place. This is normally handled by out-of-band means, and there are some quite sophisticated tools to enable group addresses to be advertised on the Internet. One example is sdr, discussed in Section 9.2.1.

4.2.2 Multicast Routing (DVMRP, PIM, MSDP)

A router's unicast forwarding tables indicate, for any IP address, which link to use to forward the unicast packet. To support multicast, a router must additionally have multicast forwarding tables that indicate, based on multicast address, which links—possibly more than one—to use to forward the multicast packet (the router duplicates the packet if it is to be forwarded over multiple links). Thus, where unicast forwarding tables collectively specify a set of paths, multicast forwarding tables collectively specify a set of trees: *multicast distribution trees.* Furthermore, to support Source-Specific Multicast (and, it turns out, for some types of Any Source Multicast), the multicast forwarding tables must indicate which links to use based on the combination of multicast address and the (unicast) IP address of the source, again specifying a set of trees.

Multicast routing is the process by which the multicast distribution trees are determined or, more concretely, the process by which the multi-cast forwarding tables are built. As with unicast routing, it is not enough that a multicast routing protocol "work"; it must also scale reasonably well as the network grows, and it must accommodate the autonomy of different routing domains.

DVMRP

Distance-vector routing, which we discussed in Section 3.3.2 for unicast, can be extended to support multicast. The resulting protocol is called

Distance Vector Multicast Routing Protocol, or DVMRP. DVMRP was the first multicast routing protocol to see widespread use.

Recall that, in the distance-vector algorithm, each router maintains a table of ⟨Destination, Cost, NextHop⟩ tuples, and exchanges a list of ⟨Destination, Cost⟩ pairs with its directly connected neighbors. Extending this algorithm to support multicast is a two-stage process. First, we create a broadcast mechanism that allows a packet to be forwarded to all the networks on the internet. Second, we need to refine this mechanism so that it prunes back networks that do not have hosts that belong to the multicast group. Consequently, DVMRP is one of several multicast routing protocols described as *ood-and-prune* protocols.

Given a unicast routing table, each router knows that the current shortest path to a given destination goes through NextHop. Thus, whenever it receives a multicast packet from source S, the router forwards the packet on all outgoing links (except the one on which the packet arrived) if and only if the packet arrived over the link that is on the shortest path to S (i.e., the packet came *from* the NextHop associated with S in the routing table). This strategy effectively floods packets outward from S but does not loop packets back toward S.

There are two major shortcomings to this approach. The first is that it truly floods the network; it has no provision for avoiding LANs that have no members in the multicast group. We address this problem below. The second limitation is that a given packet will be forwarded over a LAN by each of the routers connected to that LAN. This is due to the forwarding strategy of flooding packets on all links other than the one on which the packet arrived, without regard to whether or not those links are part of the shortest-path tree rooted at the source.

The solution to this second limitation is to eliminate the duplicate broadcast packets that are generated when more than one router is connected to a given LAN. One way to do this is to designate one router as the *parent* router for each link, relative to the source, where only the parent router is allowed to forward multicast packets from that source over the LAN. The router that has the shortest path to source S is selected as the parent; a tie between two routers would be broken according to which router has the smallest address. A given router can learn if it is the parent for the LAN (again relative to each possible source) based upon the distance-vector messages it exchanges with its neighbors.

Notice that this refinement requires that each router keep, for each source, a bit for each of its incident links indicating whether or not it is the parent for that source/link pair. Keep in mind that in an internet setting, a source is a network, not a host, since an internet router is only interested in forwarding packets between networks. The resulting mechanism is sometimes called *Reverse Path Broadcast* (RPB) or *Reverse Path Forwarding* (RPF). The path is reverse because we are considering the shortest path toward the *source* when making our forwarding decisions, as compared to unicast routing, which looks for the shortest path to a given *destination*.

The RPB mechanism just described implements shortest-path broadcast. We now want to prune the set of networks that receives each packet addressed to group G to exclude those that have no hosts that are members of G. This can be accomplished in two stages. First, we need to recognize when a *leaf* network has no group members. Determining that a network is a leaf is easy—if the parent router as described above is the only router on the network, then the network is a leaf. Determining if any group members reside on the network is accomplished by having each host that is a member of group G periodically announce this fact over the network, as described in our earlier description of link-state multicast. The router then uses this information to decide whether or not to forward a multicast packet addressed to G over this LAN.

The second stage is to propagate this "no members of G here" information up the shortest-path tree. This is done by having the router augment the ⟨Destination, Cost⟩ pairs it sends to its neighbors with the set of groups for which the leaf network is interested in receiving multicast packets. This information can then be propagated from router to router, so that for each of its links a given router knows for what groups it should forward multicast packets.

Note that including all of this information in the routing update is a fairly expensive thing to do. In practice, therefore, this information is exchanged only when some source starts sending packets to that group. In other words, the strategy is to use RPB, which adds a small amount of overhead to the basic distance-vector algorithm, until a particular multicast address becomes active. At that time, routers that are not interested in receiving packets addressed to that group speak up, and that information is propagated to the other routers.

PIM-SM

Protocol Independent Multicast, or PIM, was developed in response to the scaling problems of earlier multicast routing protocols. In particular, it was recognized that the existing protocols did not scale well in environments where a relatively small proportion of routers want to receive traffic for a certain group. For example, broadcasting traffic to all routers until they explicitly ask to be removed from the distribution is not a good design choice if most routers don't want to receive the traffic in the first place. This situation is sufficiently common that PIM divides the problem space into *sparse mode* and *dense mode,* where sparse and dense refer to the proportion of routers that will want the multicast. PIM dense mode (PIM-DM) uses a flood-and-prune algorithm like DVMRP and suffers from the same scalability problem. PIM sparse mode (PIM-SM) has become the dominant multicast routing protocol and is the focus of our discussion here. The "protocol independent" aspect of PIM, by the way, refers to the fact that, unlike earlier protocols such as DVMRP, PIM does not depend on any particular sort of unicast routing—it can be used with any unicast routing protocol, as we will see below.

In PIM-SM, routers explicitly join the multicast distribution tree using PIM protocol messages known as Join messages. Note the contrast to DVMRP's approach of creating a broadcast tree first and then pruning the uninterested routers. The question that arises is where to send those Join messages because, after all, any host (and any number of hosts) could send to the multicast group. To address this, PIM-SM assigns to each group a special router known as the *rendezvous point* (RP). In general, a number of routers in a domain are configured to be candidate RPs, and PIM-SM defines a set of procedures by which all the routers in a domain can agree on the router to use as the RP for a given group. These procedures are rather complex, as they must deal with a wide variety of scenarios, such as the failure of a candidate RP and the partitioning of a domain into two separate networks due to a number of link or node failures. For the rest of this discussion, we assume that all routers in a domain know the unicast IP address of the RP for a given group.

A multicast forwarding tree is built as a result of routers sending Join messages to the RP. PIM-SM allows two types of trees to be constructed: a *shared* tree, which may be used by all senders, and a *source-specific* tree, which may be used only by a specific sending host. The normal mode of operation creates the shared tree first, followed by one or more source-specific trees if there is enough traffic to warrant it. Because

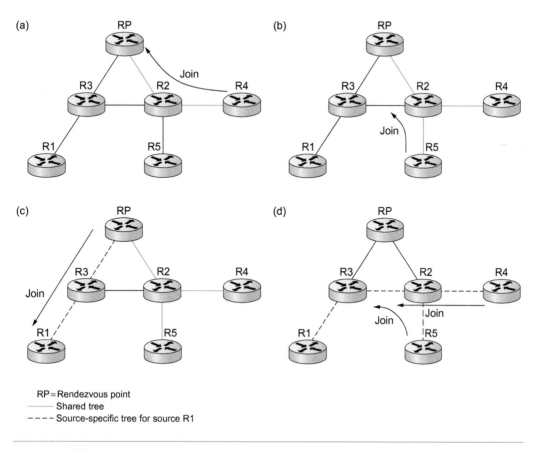

RP = Rendezvous point
——— Shared tree
– – – Source-specific tree for source R1

■ FIGURE 4.14 PIM operation: (a) R4 sends **Join** to RP and joins shared tree; (b) R5 joins shared tree; (c) RP builds source-specific tree to R1 by sending **Join** to R1; (d) R4 and R5 build source-specific tree to R1 by sending **Joins** to R1.

building trees installs state in the routers along the tree, it is important that the default is to have only one tree for a group, not one for every sender to a group.

When a router sends a Join message toward the RP for a group G, it is sent using normal IP unicast transmission. This is illustrated in Figure 4.14(a), in which router R4 is sending a Join to the rendezvous point for some group. The initial Join message is "wildcarded"; that is, it applies to all senders. A Join message clearly must pass through some sequence of routers before reaching the RP (e.g., R2). Each router along the path looks at the Join and creates a forwarding table entry for the shared tree, called a (*, G) entry (where * means "all senders"). To create the forwarding table entry, it looks at the interface on which the Join arrived and marks that interface as one on which it should forward data packets for this group. It then determines which interface it will use to forward the Join toward the RP. This will be the only acceptable interface for incoming packets sent to this group. It then forwards the Join toward the RP. Eventually, the message arrives at the RP, completing the construction of the tree branch. The shared tree thus constructed is shown as a solid line from the RP to R4 in Figure 4.14(a).

As more routers send Joins toward the RP, they cause new branches to be added to the tree, as illustrated in Figure 4.14(b). Note that, in this case, the Join only needs to travel to R2, which can add the new branch to the tree simply by adding a new outgoing interface to the forwarding table entry created for this group. R2 need not forward the Join on to the RP. Note also that the end result of this process is to build a tree whose root is the RP.

At this point, suppose a host wishes to send a message to the group. To do so, it constructs a packet with the appropriate multicast group address as its destination and sends it to a router on its local network known as the *designated router* (DR). Suppose the DR is R1 in Figure 4.14. There is no state for this multicast group between R1 and the RP at this point, so instead of simply forwarding the multicast packet, R1 *tunnels* it to the RP. That is, R1 encapsulates the multicast packet inside a PIM Register message that it sends to the unicast IP address of the RP. Just like a tunnel endpoint of the sort described in Section 3.2.9, the RP receives the packet addressed to it, looks at the payload of the Register message, and finds inside an IP packet addressed to the multicast address of this group. The RP, of course, does know what to do with such a packet—it sends it out onto the shared tree of which the RP is the root. In the example of Figure 4.14, this means that the RP sends the packet on to R2, which is able to forward it on to R4 and R5. The complete delivery of a packet from R1 to R4 and R5 is shown in Figure 4.15. We see the tunneled packet travel from R1 to the RP with an extra IP header containing the unicast address of RP, and then the multicast packet addressed to G making its way along the shared tree to R4 and R5.

At this point, we might be tempted to declare success, since all hosts can send to all receivers this way. However, there is some bandwidth inefficiency and processing cost in the encapsulation and decapsulation of packets on the way to the RP, so the RP forces knowledge about this

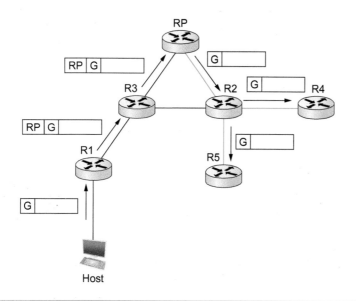

■ **FIGURE 4.15** Delivery of a packet along a shared tree. R1 tunnels the packet to the RP, which forwards it along the shared tree to R4 and R5.

group into the intervening routers so tunneling can be avoided. It sends a Join message toward the sending host (Figure 4.14(c)). As this Join travels toward the host, it causes the routers along the path (R3) to learn about the group, so that it will be possible for the DR to send the packet to the group as *native* (i.e., not tunneled) multicast packets.

An important detail to note at this stage is that the Join message sent by the RP to the sending host is specific to that sender, whereas the previous ones sent by R4 and R5 applied to all senders. Thus, the effect of the new Join is to create *sender-specific* state in the routers between the identified source and the RP. This is referred to as (S, G) state, since it applies to one sender to one group, and contrasts with the (*, G) state that was installed between the receivers and the RP that applies to all senders. Thus, in Figure 4.14(c), we see a source-specific route from R1 to the RP (indicated by the dashed line) and a tree that is valid for all senders from the RP to the receivers (indicated by the solid line).

The next possible optimization is to replace the entire shared tree with a source-specific tree. This is desirable because the path from sender to receiver via the RP might be significantly longer than the shortest possible path. This again is likely to be triggered by a high data rate being observed from some sender. In this case, the router at the downstream end of the tree—say, R4 in our example—sends a source-specific Join toward the source. As it follows the shortest path toward the source, the routers along the way create (S, G) state for this tree, and the result is a tree that has its root at the source, rather than the RP. Assuming both R4 and R5 made the switch to the source-specific tree, we would end up with the tree shown in Figure 4.14(d). Note that this tree no longer involves the RP at all. We have removed the shared tree from this picture to simplify the diagram, but in reality all routers with receivers for a group must stay on the shared tree in case new senders show up.

We can now see why PIM is protocol independent. All of its mechanisms for building and maintaining trees take advantage of unicast routing without depending on any particular unicast routing protocol. The formation of trees is entirely determined by the paths that Join messages follow, which is determined by the choice of shortest paths made by unicast routing. Thus, to be precise, PIM is "unicast routing protocol independent," as compared to DVMRP. Note that PIM is very much bound up with the Internet Protocol—it is not protocol independent in terms of network-layer protocols.

The design of PIM-SM again illustrates the challenges in building scalable networks and how scalability is sometimes pitted against some sort of optimality. The shared tree is certainly more scalable than a source-specific tree, in the sense that it reduces the total state in routers to be on the order of the number of groups rather than the number of senders times the number of groups. However, the source-specific tree is likely to be necessary to achieve efficient routing and effective use of link bandwidth.

Interdomain Multicast (MSDP)

PIM-SM has some significant shortcomings when it comes to interdomain multicast. In particular, the existence of a single RP for a group goes against the principle that domains are autonomous. For a given multicast group, all the participating domains would be dependent on the domain where the RP is located. Furthermore, if there is a particular multicast group for which a sender and some receivers shared a single domain, the multicast traffic would still have to be routed initially from the sender to those receivers via whatever domain has the RP for that multicast group. Consequently, the PIM-SM protocol is typically not used across domains, only within a domain.

To extend multicast across domains using PIM-SM, the Multicast Source Discovery Protocol (MSDP) was devised. MSDP is used to connect different domains—each running PIM-SM internally, with its own RPs—by connecting the RPs of the different domains. Each RP has one or more MSDP peer RPs in other domains. Each pair of MSDP peers is connected by a TCP connection (Section 5.2) over which the MSDP protocol runs. Together, all the MSDP peers for a given multicast group form a loose mesh that is used as a broadcast network. MSDP messages are broadcast through the mesh of peer RPs using the Reverse Path Broadcast algorithm that we discussed in the context of DVMRP.

What information does MSDP broadcast through the mesh of RPs? Not group membership information; when a host joins a group, the furthest that information will flow is its own domain's RP. Instead, it is source—multicast sender—information. Each RP knows the sources in its own domain because it receives a **Register** message whenever a new source arises. Each RP periodically uses MSDP to broadcast **Source Active** messages to its peers, giving the IP address of the source, the multicast group address, and the IP address of the originating RP.

If an MSDP peer RP that receives one of these broadcasts has active receivers for that multicast group, it sends a source-specific **Join**, on that RP's own behalf, to the source host, as shown in Figure 4.16(a). The **Join** message builds a branch of the source-specific tree to this RP, as shown in Figure 4.16(b). The result is that every RP that is part of the MSDP network and has active receivers for a particular multicast group is added to the source-specific tree of the new source. When an RP receives a multicast from the source, the RP uses its shared tree to forward the multicast to the receivers in its domain.

Source-Specific Multicast (PIM-SSM)

The original service model of PIM was, like earlier multicast protocols, a many-to-many model. Receivers joined a group, and any host could send to the group. However, it was recognized in the late 1990s that it might be useful to add a one-to-many model. Lots of multicast applications, after all, have only one legitimate sender, such as the speaker at a conference being sent over the Internet. We already saw that PIM-SM can create source-specific shortest path trees as an optimization after using the shared tree initially. In the original PIM design, this optimization was invisible to hosts—only routers joined source-specific trees. However, once the need for a one-to-many service model was recognized, it was

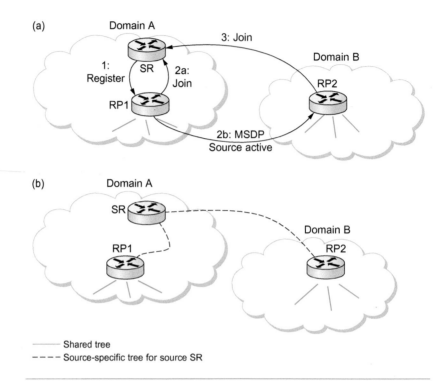

decided to make the source-specific routing capability of PIM-SM explicitly available to hosts. It turns out that this mainly required changes to IGMP and its IPv6 analog, MLD, rather than PIM itself. The newly exposed capability is now known as PIM-SSM (PIM Source-Specific Multicast).

PIM-SSM introduces a new concept, the *channel*, which is the combination of a source address S and a group address G. The group address G looks just like a normal IP multicast address, and both IPv4 and IPv6 have allocated subranges of the multicast address space for SSM. To use PIM-SSM, a host specifies both the group and the source in an IGMP Membership Report message to its local router. That router then sends a PIM-SM source-specific Join message toward the source, thereby adding a branch to itself in the source-specific tree, just as was described above for "normal" PIM-SM, but bypassing the whole shared-tree stage. Since the tree that results is source specific, only the designated source can send packets on that tree.

The introduction of PIM-SSM has provided some significant benefits, particularly since there is relatively high demand for one-to-many multicasting:

- Multicasts travel more directly to receivers.
- The address of a channel is effectively a multicast group address plus a source address. Therefore, given that a certain range of multicast group addresses will be used for SSM exclusively, multiple domains can use the same multicast group address independently and without conflict, as long as they use it only with sources in their own domains.
- Because only the specified source can send to an SSM group, there is less risk of attacks based on malicious hosts overwhelming the routers or receivers with bogus multicast traffic.
- PIM-SSM can be used across domains exactly as it is used within a domain, without reliance on anything like MSDP.

SSM, therefore, is quite a useful addition to the multicast service model.

Bidirectional Trees (BIDIR-PIM)

We round off our discussion of multicast with another enhancement to PIM known as *Bidirectional PIM*. BIDIR-PIM is a recent variant of PIM-SM that is well suited to many-to-many multicasting within a domain, especially when senders and receivers to a group may be the same, as in a multiparty videoconference, for example. As in PIM-SM, would-be receivers join groups by sending IGMP Membership Report messages (which must not be source specific), and a shared tree rooted at an RP is used to forward multicast packets to receivers. Unlike PIM-SM, however, the shared tree also has branches to the *sources*. That wouldn't make any sense with PIM-SM's unidirectional tree, but BIDIR-PIM's trees are bidirectional—a router that receives a multicast packet from a downstream branch can forward it both up the tree and down other branches. The route followed to deliver a packet to any particular receiver goes only as far up the tree as necessary before going down the branch to that receiver. See the multicast route from R1 to R2 in Figure 4.17(b) for an example. R4 forwards a multicast packet downstream to R2 at the same time that it forwards a copy of the same packet upstream to R5.

A surprising aspect of BIDIR-PIM is that there need not actually be an RP. All that is needed is a routable address, which is known as an RP

Where Are They Now?

THE FATE OF MULTICAST PROTOCOLS

A number of IP multicast protocols have fallen by the wayside since the 1991 publication of Steve Deering's doctoral thesis, "Multicast Routing in a Datagram Network." In most cases, their downfall had something to do with scaling. The most successful early multicast protocol was DVMRP, which we discussed at the start of the section. The *Multicast Open Shortest Path First* (MOSPF) protocol was based on the Open Shortest Path First (OSPF) unicast routing protocol. PIM dense mode (PIM-DM) has some similarity to DVMRP, in that it also uses a flood-and-prune approach; at the same time, it is like PIM-SM in being independent of the unicast routing protocol used. All of these protocols are more appropriate to a dense domain (i.e., one with a high proportion of routers interested in the multicast). These protocols all appeared relatively early in the history of multicast, before some of the scaling challenges were fully apparent. Although they would still make sense within a domain for multicast groups expected to be of dense interest, they are rarely used today, in part because the routers usually must support PIM-SM anyway.

Core-Based Trees (CBT) was another approach to multicast that was proposed at about the same time as PIM. The IETF was initially unable to choose between the two approaches, and both PIM and CBT were advanced as "experimental" protocols. However, PIM was more widely adopted by industry, and the main technical contributions of CBT—shared trees and bidirectional trees—were ultimately incorporated into PIM-SM and BIDIR-PIM, respectively.

Border Gateway Multicast Protocol (BGMP) also uses the concept of a bidirectional shared tree. In BGMP's case, however, the nodes of the tree are domains, with one of the domains as the root. In other words, BGMP is like MSDP in tying together domains to support interdomain multicasts. Unlike MSDP, the domains are free to choose their own intradomain protocols. BGMP was proposed at the IETF, and just a few years ago BGMP was expected to replace MSDP as the dominant interdomain routing protocol. BGMP is quite complex, however, and it requires the existence of a protocol that assigns ranges of multicast addresses to domains, in order for BGMP to know which domain is the root for a given address. Consequently, there have been, it appears, no implementations of BGMP, let alone deployments, at the time of writing.

address even though it need not be the address of an RP or anything at all. How can this be? A Join from a receiver is forwarded toward the RP address until it reaches a router with an interface on the link where the RP address would reside, where the Join terminates. Figure 4.17(a) shows a

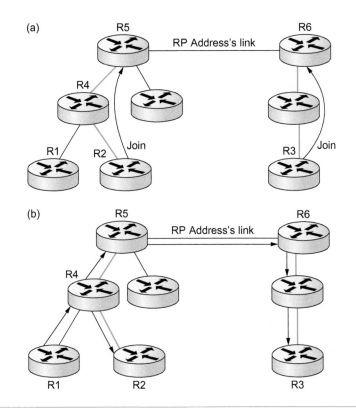

■ FIGURE 4.17 BIDIR-PIM operation: (a) R2 and R3 send **Join**s toward the RP address that terminate when they reach a router on the RP address's link. (b) A multicast packet from R1 is forwarded upstream to the RP address's link and downstream wherever it intersects a group member branch.

Join from R2 terminating at R5, and a Join from R3 terminating at R6. The upstream forwarding of a multicast packet similarly flows toward the RP address until it reaches a router with an interface on the link where the RP address would reside, but then the router forwards the multicast packet onto that link as the final step of upstream forwarding, ensuring that all other routers on that link receive the packet. Figure 4.17(b) illustrates the flow of multicast traffic originating at R1.

BIDIR-PIM cannot thus far be used across domains. On the other hand, it has several advantages over PIM-SM for many-to-many multicast within a domain:

■ There is no source registration process because the routers already know how to route a multicast packet toward the RP address.

- The routes are more direct than those that use PIM-SM's shared tree because they go only as far up the tree as necessary, not all the way to the RP.

- Bidirectional trees use much less state than the source-specific trees of PIM-SM because there is never any source-specific state. (On the other hand, the routes will be longer than those of source-specific trees.)

- The RP cannot be a bottleneck, and indeed no actual RP is needed.

One conclusion to draw from the fact that there are so many different approaches to multicast just within PIM is that multicast is a difficult problem space in which to find optimal solutions. You need to decide which criteria you want to optimize (bandwidth usage, router state, path length, etc.) and what sort of application you are trying to support (one-to-many, many-to-many, etc.) before you can make a choice of the "best" multicast mode for the task.

4.3 MULTIPROTOCOL LABEL SWITCHING (MPLS)

We continue our discussion of enhancements to IP by describing an addition to the Internet architecture that is very widely used but largely hidden from end users. The enhancement, called *Multiprotocol Label Switching* (MPLS), combines some of the properties of virtual circuits with the flexibility and robustness of datagrams. On the one hand, MPLS is very much associated with the Internet Protocol's datagram-based architecture—it relies on IP addresses and IP routing protocols to do its job. On the other hand, MPLS-enabled routers also forward packets by examining relatively short, fixed-length labels, and these labels have local scope, just like in a virtual circuit network. It is perhaps this marriage of two seemingly opposed technologies that has caused MPLS to have a somewhat mixed reception in the Internet engineering community.

Before looking at how MPLS works, it is reasonable to ask "what is it good for?" Many claims have been made for MPLS, but there are three main things that it is used for today:

- To enable IP capabilities on devices that do not have the capability to forward IP datagrams in the normal manner

- To forward IP packets along explicit routes—precalculated routes that don't necessarily match those that normal IP routing protocols would select

- To support certain types of virtual private network services

It is worth noting that one of the original goals—improving performance—is not on the list. This has a lot to do with the advances that have been made in forwarding algorithms for IP routers in recent years and with the complex set of factors beyond header processing that determine performance.

The best way to understand how MPLS works is to look at some examples of its use. In the next three sections, we will look at examples to illustrate the three applications of MPLS mentioned above.

4.3.1 Destination-Based Forwarding

One of the earliest publications to introduce the idea of attaching labels to IP packets was a paper by Chandranmenon and Vargese that described an idea called *threaded indices*. A very similar idea is now implemented in MPLS-enabled routers. The following example shows how this idea works.

Consider the network in Figure 4.18. Each of the two routers on the far right (R3 and R4) has one connected network, with prefixes 18.1.1/24 and 18.3.3/24. The remaining routers (R1 and R2) have routing tables that indicate which outgoing interface each router would use when forwarding packets to one of those two networks.

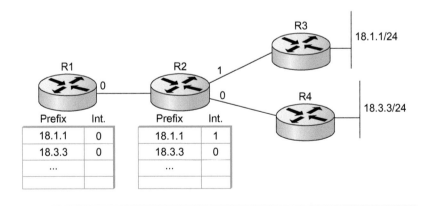

Prefix	Int.
18.1.1	0
18.3.3	0
...	

Prefix	Int.
18.1.1	1
18.3.3	0
...	

■ FIGURE 4.18 Routing tables in example network.

When MPLS is enabled on a router, the router allocates a label for each prefix in its routing table and advertises both the label and the prefix that it represents to its neighboring routers. This advertisement is carried in the Label Distribution Protocol. This is illustrated in Figure 4.19. Router R2 has allocated the label value 15 for the prefix 18.1.1 and the label value 16 for the prefix 18.3.3. These labels can be chosen at the convenience of the allocating router and can be thought of as indices into the routing table. After allocating the labels, R2 advertises the label bindings to its neighbors; in this case, we see R2 advertising a binding between the label 15 and the prefix 18.1.1 to R1. The meaning of such an advertisement is that R2 has said, in effect, "Please attach the label 15 to all packets sent to me that are destined to prefix 18.1.1." R1 stores the label in a table alongside the prefix that it represents as the remote or outgoing label for any packets that it sends to that prefix.

In Figure 4.19(c), we see another label advertisement from router R3 to R2 for the prefix 18.1.1, and R2 places the remote label that it learned from R3 in the appropriate place in its table.

At this point, we can look at what happens when a packet is forwarded in this network. Suppose a packet destined to the IP address 18.1.1.5 arrives from the left to router R1. R1 in this case is referred to as a *Label Edge Router* (LER); an LER performs a complete IP lookup on arriving IP packets and then applies labels to them as a result of the lookup. In this case, R1 would see that 18.1.1.5 matches the prefix 18.1.1 in its forwarding table and that this entry contains both an outgoing interface and a remote label value. R1 therefore attaches the remote label 15 to the packet before sending it.

When the packet arrives at R2, R2 looks only at the label in the packet, not the IP address. The forwarding table at R2 indicates that packets arriving with a label value of 15 should be sent out interface 1 and that they should carry the label value 24, as advertised by router R3. R2 therefore rewrites, or swaps, the label and forwards it on to R3.

What has been accomplished by all this application and swapping of labels? Observe that when R2 forwarded the packet in this example it never actually needed to examine the IP address. Instead, R2 looked only at the incoming label. Thus, we have replaced the normal IP destination address lookup with a label lookup. To understand why this is significant, it helps to recall that, although IP addresses are always the same length, IP prefixes are of variable length, and the IP destination address

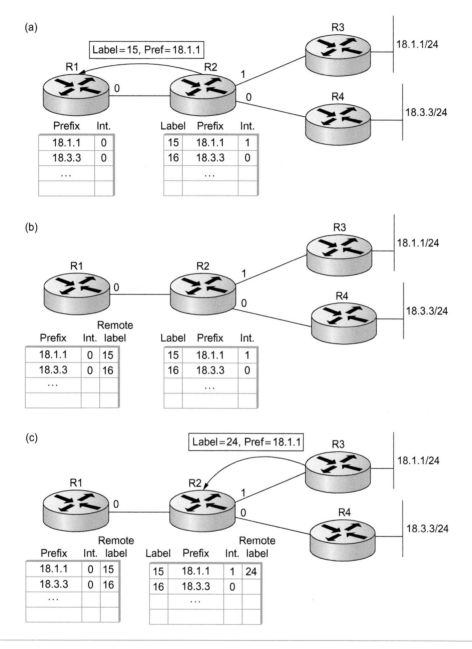

■ FIGURE 4.19 (a) R2 allocates labels and advertises bindings to R1. (b) R1 stores the received labels in a table. (c) R3 advertises another binding, and R2 stores the received label in a table.

lookup algorithm needs to find the *longest match*—the longest prefix that matches the high order bits in the IP address of the packet being forwarded. By contrast, the label forwarding mechanism just described is an *exact match* algorithm. It is possible to implement a very simple exact match algorithm, for example, by using the label as an index into an array, where each element in the array is one line in the forwarding table.

Note that, while the forwarding algorithm has been changed from longest match to exact match, the routing algorithm can be any standard IP routing algorithm (e.g., OSPF). The path that a packet will follow in this environment is the exact same path that it would have followed if MPLS were not involved—the path chosen by the IP routing algorithms. All that has changed is the forwarding algorithm.

An important fundamental concept of MPLS is illustrated by this example. Every MPLS label is associated with a *forwarding equivalence class* (FEC)—a set of packets that are to receive the same forwarding treatment in a particular router. In this example, each prefix in the routing table is an FEC; that is, all packets that match the prefix 18.1.1—no matter what the low order bits of the IP address are—get forwarded along the same path. Thus, each router can allocate one label that maps to 18.1.1, and any packet that contains an IP address whose high order bits match that prefix can be forwarded using that label.

As we will see in the subsequent examples, FECs are a very powerful and flexible concept. FECs can be formed using almost any criteria; for example, all the packets corresponding to a particular customer could be considered to be in the same FEC.

Returning to the example at hand, we observe that changing the forwarding algorithm from normal IP forwarding to label swapping has an important consequence: Devices that previously didn't know how to forward IP packets can be used to forward IP traffic in an MPLS network. The most notable early application of this result was to ATM switches, which can support MPLS without any changes to their forwarding hardware. ATM switches support the label-swapping forwarding algorithm just described, and by providing these switches with IP routing protocols and a method to distribute label bindings they could be turned into *Label Switching Routers* (LSRs)—devices that run IP control protocols but use the label switching forwarding algorithm. More recently, the same idea has been applied to optical switches of the sort described in Section 3.1.2.

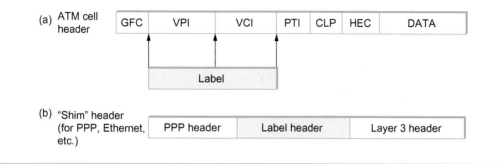

■ FIGURE 4.20   (a) Label on an ATM-encapsulated packet; (b) label on a frame-encapsulated packet.

Before we consider the purported benefits of turning an ATM switch into an LSR, we should tie up some loose ends. We have said that labels are "attached" to packets, but where exactly are they attached? The answer depends on the type of link on which packets are carried. Two common methods for carrying labels on packets are shown in Figure 4.20. When IP packets are carried as complete frames, as they are on most link types including Ethernet and PPP, the label is inserted as a "shim" between the layer 2 header and the IP (or other layer 3) header, as shown in the lower part of the figure. However, if an ATM switch is to function as an MPLS LSR, then the label needs to be in a place where the switch can use it, and that means it needs to be in the ATM cell header, exactly where one would normally find the virtual circuit identifier (VCI) and virtual path identifier (VPI) fields.

What Layer is MPLS?

There have been many debates about where MPLS belongs in the layered protocol architectures presented in Section 1.3. Since the MPLS header is normally found between the layer 3 and layer 2 headers in a packet, it is sometimes referred to as a layer 2.5 protocol. Some people argue that, since IP packets are encapsulated inside MPLS headers, MPLS must be "below" IP, making it a layer 2 protocol. Others argue that, since the control protocols for MPLS are, in large part, the same protocols as IP—MPLS uses IP routing protocols and IP addressing—then MPLS must be at the same layer as IP (i.e., layer 3). As we noted in Section 1.3, layered architectures are useful tools but they may not always exactly describe the real world, and MPLS is a good example of where strictly layerist views may be difficult to reconcile with reality.

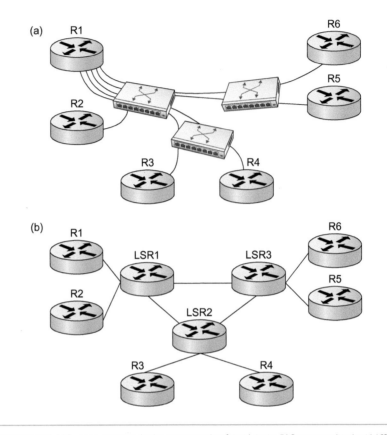

■ **FIGURE 4.21** (a) Routers connect to each other using an overlay of virtual circuits. (b) Routers peer directly with LSRs.

Having now devised a scheme by which an ATM switch can function as an LSR, what have we gained? One thing to note is that we could now build a network that uses a mixture of conventional IP routers, label edge routers, and ATM switches functioning as LSRs, and they would all use the same routing protocols. To understand the benefits of using the same protocols, consider the alternative. In Figure 4.21(a), we see a set of routers interconnected by virtual circuits over an ATM network, a configuration called an *overlay* network. At one point in time, networks of this type were often built because commercially available ATM switches supported higher total throughput than routers. Today, networks like this are less common because routers have caught up with and even surpassed ATM switches. However, these networks still exist because of the significant installed base of ATM switches in network backbones, which in turn is partly a result of ATM's ability to support a range of capabilities such as circuit emulation and virtual circuit services.

In an overlay network, each router would potentially be connected to each of the other routers by a virtual circuit, but in this case for clarity we have just shown the circuits from R1 to all of its peer routers. R1 has five routing neighbors and needs to exchange routing protocol messages with all of them—we say that R1 has five routing adjacencies. By contrast, in Figure 4.21(b), the ATM switches have been replaced with LSRs. There are no longer virtual circuits interconnecting the routers. Thus, R1 has only one adjacency, with LSR1. In large networks, running MPLS on the switches leads to a significant reduction in the number of adjacencies that each router must maintain and can greatly reduce the amount of work that the routers have to do to keep each other informed of topology changes.

A second benefit of running the same routing protocols on edge routers and on the LSRs is that the edge routers now have a full view of the topology of the network. This means that if some link or node fails inside the network, the edge routers will have a better chance of picking a good new path than if the ATM switches rerouted the affected VCs without the knowledge of the edge routers.

Note that the step of "replacing" ATM switches with LSRs is actually achieved by changing the protocols running on the switches, but typically no change to the forwarding hardware is needed; that is, an ATM switch can often be converted to an MPLS LSR by upgrading only its software. Furthermore, an MPLS LSR might continue to support standard ATM capabilities at the same time as it runs the MPLS control protocols, in what is referred to as "ships in the night" mode.

More recently, the idea of running IP control protocols on devices that are unable to forward IP packets natively has been extended to optical switches and STDM devices such as SONET multiplexors. This is known as *Generalized MPLS* (GMPLS). Part of the motivation for GMPLS was to provide routers with topological knowledge of an optical network, just as in the ATM case. Even more important was the fact that there were no standard protocols for controlling optical devices, so MPLS seemed like a natural fit for that job.

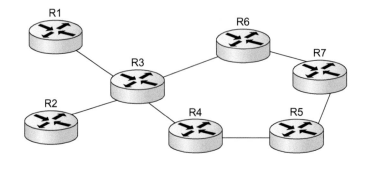

4.3.2 Explicit Routing

In Section 3.1.3, we introduced the concept of source routing. IP has a source routing option, but it is not widely used for several reasons, including the fact that only a limited number of hops can be specified and because it is usual processed outside the "fast path" on most routers.

MPLS provides a convenient way to add capabilities similar to source-routing to IP networks, although the capability is more often referred to as *explicit routing* rather than *source routing*. One reason for the distinction is that it usually isn't the real source of the packet that picks the route. More often it is one of the routers inside a service provider's network. Figure 4.22 shows an example of how the explicit routing capability of MPLS might be applied. This sort of network is often called a *fish* network because of its shape (the routers R1 and R2 form the tail; R7 is at the head).

Suppose that the operator of the network in Figure 4.22 has determined that any traffic flowing from R1 to R7 should follow the path R1-R3-R6-R7 and that any traffic going from R2 to R7 should follow the path R2-R3-R4-R5-R7. One reason for such a choice would be to make good use of the capacity available along the two distinct paths from R3 to R7. We can think of the R1-to-R7 traffic as constituting one forwarding equivalence class, and the R2-to-R7 traffic constitutes a second FEC. Forwarding traffic in these two classes along different paths is difficult with normal IP routing, because R3 doesn't normally look at where traffic came from in making its forwarding decisions.

Because MPLS uses label swapping to forward packets, it is easy enough to achieve the desired routing if the routers are MPLS enabled.

If R1 and R2 attach distinct labels to packets before sending them to R3—thus identifying them as being in different FECs—then R3 can forward packets from R1 and R2 along different paths. The question that then arises is how do all the routers in the network agree on what labels to use and how to forward packets with particular labels? Clearly, we can't use the same procedures as described in the preceding section to distribute labels, because those procedures establish labels that cause packets to follow the normal paths picked by IP routing, which is exactly what we are trying to avoid. Instead, a new mechanism is needed. It turns out that the protocol used for this task is the Resource Reservation Protocol (RSVP). We'll talk more about this protocol in Section 6.5.2, but for now it suffices to say that it is possible to send an RSVP message along an explicitly specified path (e.g., R1-R3-R6-R7) and use it to set up label forwarding table entries all along that path. This is very similar to the process of establishing a virtual circuit described in Section 3.3.

One of the applications of explicit routing is *traffic engineering*, which refers to the task of ensuring that sufficient resources are available in a network to meet the demands placed on it. Controlling exactly which paths the traffic flows on is an important part of traffic engineering. Explicit routing can also help to make networks more resilient in the face of failure, using a capability called *fast reroute*. For example, it is possible to precalculate a path from router A to router B that explicitly avoids a certain link L. In the event that link L fails, router A could send all traffic destined to B down the precalculated path. The combination of precalculation of the backup path and the explicit routing of packets along the path means that A doesn't need to wait for routing protocol packets to make their way across the network or for routing algorithms to be executed by various other nodes in the network. In certain circumstances, this can significantly reduce the time taken to reroute packets around a point of failure.

One final point to note about explicit routing is that explicit routes need not be calculated by a network operator as in the above example. Routers can use various algorithms to calculate explicit routes automatically. The most common of these is *constrained shortest path first* (CSPF), which is like the link-state algorithms described in Section 3.3.3, but which also takes various *constraints* into account. For example, if it was required to find a path from R1 to R7 that could carry an offered load of 100 Mbps, we could say that the constraint is that each link must have at least 100 Mbps of available capacity. CSPF addresses this sort of problem. More details on CSPF, and the applications of explicit routing, are provided in the Further Reading section.

4.3.3 Virtual Private Networks and Tunnels

We first talked about virtual private networks (VPNs) in Section 3.2.9, and we noted that one way to build them was using tunnels. It turns out that MPLS can be thought of as a way to build tunnels, and this makes it suitable for building VPNs of various types.

The simplest form of MPLS VPN to understand is a layer 2 VPN. In this type of VPN, MPLS is used to tunnel layer 2 data (such as Ethernet frames or ATM cells) across a network of MPLS-enabled routers. Recall from Section 3.2.9 that one reason for tunnels is to provide some sort of network service (such as multicast) that is not supported by some routers in the network. The same logic applies here: IP routers are not ATM switches, so you cannot provide an ATM virtual circuit service across a network of conventional routers. However, if you had a pair of routers interconnected by a tunnel, they could send ATM cells across the tunnel and emulate an ATM circuit. The term for this technique within the IETF is *pseudowire emulation*. Figure 4.23 illustrates the idea.

We have already seen how IP tunnels are built: The router at the entrance of the tunnel wraps the data to be tunneled in an IP header (the *tunnel header*), which represents the address of the router at the far end of the tunnel and sends the data like any other IP packet. The receiving router receives the packet with its own address in the header, strips the tunnel header, and finds the data that was tunneled, which it then processes. Exactly what it does with that data depends on what it is. For example, if it were another IP packet, it would then be forwarded on like a normal IP packet. However, it need not be an IP packet, as long as the

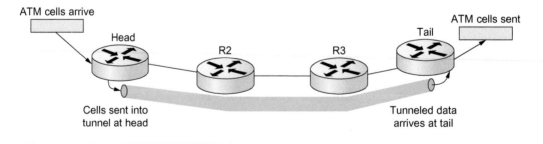

ATM cells arrive

ATM cells sent

Head

Tail

R2

R3

Cells sent into
tunnel at head

Tunneled data
arrives at tail

■ FIGURE 4.23 An ATM circuit is emulated by a tunnel.

receiving router knows what to do with non-IP packets. We'll return to the issue of how to handle non-IP data in a moment.

An MPLS tunnel is not too different from an IP tunnel, except that the tunnel header consists of an MPLS header rather than an IP header. Looking back to our first example, in Figure 4.19, we saw that router R1 attached a label (15) to every packet that it sent towards prefix 18.1.1. Such a packet would then follow the path R1-R2-R3, with each router in the path examining only the MPLS label. Thus, we observe that there was no requirement that R1 only send IP packets along this path—any data could be wrapped up in the MPLS header and it would follow the same path, because the intervening routers never look beyond the MPLS header. In this regard, an MPLS header is just like an IP tunnel header.[3] The only issue with sending non-IP traffic along a tunnel, MPLS or otherwise, is what to do with non-IP traffic when it reaches the end of the tunnel. The general solution is to carry some sort of demultiplexing identifier in the tunnel payload that tells the router at the end of the tunnel what to do. It turns out that an MPLS label is a perfect fit for such an identifier. An example will make this clear.

Let's assume we want to tunnel ATM cells from one router to another across a network of MPLS-enabled routers, as in Figure 4.23. Further, we assume that the goal is to emulate an ATM virtual circuit; that is, cells arrive at the entrance, or head, of the tunnel on a certain input port with a certain VCI and should leave the tail end of the tunnel on a certain output port and potentially different VCI. This can be accomplished by configuring the head and tail routers as follows:

- The head router needs to be configured with the incoming port, the incoming VCI, the demultiplexing label for this emulated circuit, and the address of the tunnel end router.
- The tail router needs to be configured with the outgoing port, the outgoing VCI, and the demultiplexing label.

Once the routers are provided with this information, we can see how an ATM cell would be forwarded. Figure 4.24 illustrates the steps.

1. An ATM cell arrives on the designated input port with the appropriate VCI value (101 in this example).

---

[3]Note, however, that an MPLS header is only 4 bytes long, compared to 20 for an IP header, which implies a bandwidth saving when MPLS is used.

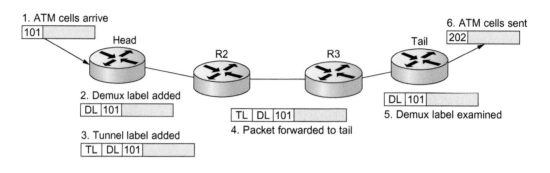

1. ATM cells arrive
101

Head

R2

R3

Tail

6. ATM cells sent
202

2. Demux label added
DL 101

3. Tunnel label added
TL DL 101

TL DL 101
4. Packet forwarded to tail

DL 101
5. Demux label examined

■ FIGURE 4.24 Forward ATM cells along a tunnel.

2. The head router attaches the demultiplexing label that identifies the emulated circuit.

3. The head router then attaches a second label, which is the tunnel label that will get the packet to the tail router. This label is learned by mechanisms just like those described in Section 4.3.1.

4. Routers between the head and tail forward the packet using only the tunnel label.

5. The tail router removes the tunnel label, finds the demultiplexing label, and recognizes the emulated circuit.

6. The tail router modifies the ATM VCI to the correct value (202 in this case) and sends it out the correct port.

One item in this example that might be surprising is that the packet has two labels attached to it. This is one of the interesting features of MPLS—labels may be stacked on a packet to any depth. This provides some useful scaling capabilities. In this example, it allows a single tunnel to carry a potentially large number of emulated circuits.

The same techniques described here can be applied to emulate many other layer 2 services, including Frame Relay and Ethernet. It is worth noting that virtually identical capabilities can be provided using IP tunnels; the main advantage of MPLS here is the shorter tunnel header.

Before MPLS was used to tunnel layer 2 services, it was also being used to support layer 3 VPNs. We won't go into the details of layer 3 VPNs, which are quite complex (see the Further Reading section for some good sources of more information), but we will note that they represent one of the most popular uses of MPLS today. Layer 3 VPNs also use stacks of MPLS labels to tunnel packets across an IP network. However, the packets that are tunneled are themselves IP packets—hence, the name *layer 3 VPNs*. In a layer 3 VPN, a single service provider operates a network of MPLS-enabled routers and provides a "virtually private" IP network service to any number of distinct customers. That is, each customer of the provider has some number of sites, and the service provider creates the illusion for each customer that there are no other customers on the network. The customer sees an IP network interconnecting his own sites and no other sites. This means that each customer is isolated from all other customers in terms of both routing and addressing. Customer A can't sent packets directly to customer B, and *vice versa.*[4] Customer A can even use IP addresses that have also been used by customer B. The basic idea is illustrated in Figure 4.25. As in layer 2 VPNs, MPLS is used to

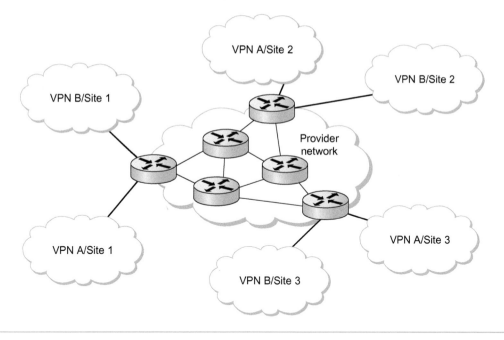

■ FIGURE 4.25 Example of a layer 3 VPN. Customers A and B each obtain a virtually private IP service from a single provider.

[4]Customer A in fact usually *can* send data to customer B in some restricted way. Most likely, both customer A and customer B have some connection to the global Internet, and thus it is probably possible for customer A to send email messages, for example, to the mail server inside customer B's network. The "privacy" offered by a VPN prevents customer A from having unrestricted access to all the machines and subnets inside customer B's network.

tunnel packets from one site to another; however, the configuration of the tunnels is performed automatically by some fairly elaborate use of BGP, which is beyond the scope of this book.

In summary, MPLS is a rather versatile tool that has been applied to a wide range of different networking problems. It combines the label-swapping forwarding mechanism that is normally associated with virtual circuit networks with the routing and control protocols of IP datagram networks to produce a class of network that is somewhere between the two conventional extremes. This extends the capabilities of IP networks to enable, among other things, more precise control of routing and the support of a range of VPN services.

Where Are They Now?

DEPLOYMENT OF MPLS

Originally conceived as a technology that would operate within the network of individual service providers, MPLS remains hidden from most consumer and academic users of the Internet today. However, it is now sufficiently popular among service providers that it has become almost mandatory for high-end router manufacturers to include MPLS capabilities in their products. The widespread success of MPLS is a relatively well-kept secret, at least to students and researchers focused on the public Internet.

Two main applications of MPLS account for most of its deployment. The layer 3 VPN application described in this section is the killer application for MPLS. Almost every service provider in the world now offers an MPLS-based layer 3 VPN service. This is often run on routers that are essentially separate from the Internet, since the main use of layer 3 VPNs is to provide private IP service to corporations, not to provide global Internet connectivity. Some providers do run their Internet service and VPN service over a common backbone, however.

The second popular usage of MPLS is explicit routing, either for traffic engineering or fast reroute, or both. Unlike the layer 3 VPN service, which is explicitly marketed to end customers, explicit routing is an internal capability that providers use to improve the reliability of their networks or reduce the cost. Providers do not usually publicize details of their internal network designs, making it more difficult to determine how many providers actually use this technology. It is clear that the explicit routing features of MPLS are used by fewer providers than the VPN features, but nevertheless there is evidence of significant usage, especially when bandwidth is expensive or when there is a strong desire to maintain low levels of congestion (e.g., to support real-time services).

4.4 ROUTING AMONG MOBILE DEVICES

LAB 09:
Mobile WLAN

It probably should not be a great surprise to learn that mobile devices present some challenges for the Internet architecture. The Internet was designed in an era when computers were large, immobile devices, and, while the Internet's designers probably had some notion that mobile devices might appear in the future, it's fair to assume it was not a top priority to accommodate them. Today, of course, mobile computers are everywhere, notably in the forms of laptops and IP-enabled mobile phones, and increasingly in other forms such as sensors. In this section, we will look at some of the challenges posed by the appearance of mobile devices and some of the current approaches to accommodating them.

4.4.1 Challenges for Mobile Networking

Most readers of this book have probably used a networked mobile device at some point, and for many of us mobile devices have become the norm. So one might reasonably think that mobile networking is a solved problem. Certainly, it is easy enough today to turn up in a wireless hotspot, connect to the Internet using 802.11 or some other wireless networking protocol, and obtain pretty good Internet service. One key enabling technology that made the hotspot feasible is DHCP (see Section 3.2.7 for details). You can settle in at a café, open your laptop, obtain an IP address for your laptop, and get your laptop talking to a default router and a Domain Name System (DNS) server (see Section 9.3.1), and for a broad class of applications you have everything you need.

If we look a little more closely, however, it's clear that for some application scenarios, just getting a new IP address every time you move—which is what DHCP does for you—isn't always enough. Suppose you are using your laptop or smartphone for a Voice over IP telephone call, and while talking on the phone you move from one hotspot to another, or even switch from 802.11 to 3G wireless for your Internet connection.

Clearly, when you move from one access network to another, you need to get a new IP address—one that corresponds to the new network. But, the computer or telephone at the other end of your conversation doesn't immediately know where you have moved or what your new IP address is. Consequently, in the absence of some other mechanism, packets would continue to be sent to the address where you *used* to be, not where you are now. This problem is illustrated in Figure 4.26; as the mobile node moves from the 802.11 network in Figure 4.26(a) to the cellular

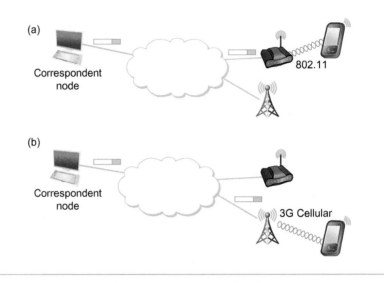

(a)

Correspondent node

802.11

(b)

Correspondent node

3G Cellular

■ FIGURE 4.26 Forwarding packets from a correspondent node to a mobile node.

network in Figure 4.26(b), somehow packets from the *correspondent node* need to find their way to the new network and then on to the mobile node.

There are many different ways to tackle the problem just described, and we will look at some of them below. Assuming that there is some way to redirect packets so that they come to your new address rather than your old address, the next immediately apparent problems relate to security. For example, if there is a mechanism by which I can say, "My new IP address is X," how do I prevent some attacker from making such a statement without my permission, thus enabling him to either receive my packets, or to redirect my packets to some unwitting third party? Thus, we see that security and mobility are quite closely related.

One issue that the above discussion highlights is the fact that IP addresses actually serve two tasks. They are used as an *identifier* of an endpoint, and they are also used to *locate* the endpoint. Think of the identifier as a long-lived name for the endpoint, and the locator as some possibly more temporary information about how to route packets to the endpoint. As long as devices do not move, or do not move often, using a single address for both jobs seem pretty reasonable. But once devices start to move, you would rather like to have an identifier that does not change as you move—this is sometimes called an *Endpoint Identifier* or *Host Identifier*—and a separate *locator*. This idea of separating locators from identifiers has been around for a long time, and most of the approaches to handling mobility described below provide such a separation in some form.

The assumption that IP addresses don't change shows up in many different places. For example, as we'll see in the next chapter, transport protocols like TCP have historically made assumptions about the IP address staying constant for the life of a connection, so transport protocols operating in a mobile world require some re-evaluation of that assumption.

While we are all familiar with endpoints that move, it is worth noting that routers can also move. This is certainly less common today than endpoint mobility, but there are plenty of environments where a mobile router might make sense. One example might be an emergency response team trying to deploy a network after some natural disaster has knocked out all the fixed infrastructure. There are additional considerations when *all* the nodes in a network, not just the endpoints, are mobile, a topic we will discuss in Section 4.4.2.

As with many technologies, support for mobility raises issues of incremental deployment. Given that, for its first couple of decades, the Internet consisted entirely of nodes that didn't move, it's fair to assume that there will be a lot of routers and hosts around for the foreseeable future that make that assumption. Hence, mobility solutions need to deal with incremental deployment. Conversely, IP version 6 had the ability to make mobility part of its design from the outset, which provides it with some advantages.

Before we start to look at some of the approaches to supporting mobile devices, a couple of points of clarification. It is common to find that people confuse wireless networks with mobility. After all, mobility and wireless often are found together for obvious reasons. But wireless communication is really about getting data from A to B without a wire, as discussed in some detail in Chapter 2, while mobility is about dealing with what happens when a node moves around as it communicates. Certainly many nodes that use wireless communication channels are not mobile, and sometimes mobile nodes will use wired communication (although this is less common).

Finally, in this chapter we are mostly interested in what we might call *network-layer mobility*. That is, we are interested in how to deal with nodes that move from one network to another. As we saw in Section 2.7, moving from one access point to another in the same 802.11 network can be handled by mechanisms specific to 802.11, and cellular telephone networks also have ways to handle mobility, of course, but in large heterogeneous systems like the Internet we need to support mobility more broadly across networks.

4.4.2 Routing to Mobile Hosts (Mobile IP)

Mobile IP is the primary mechanism in today's Internet architecture to tackle the problem of routing packets to mobile hosts. It introduces a few new capabilities but does not require any change from non-mobile hosts or most routers—thus tackling the incremental deployment issue raised above.

The mobile host is assumed to have a permanent IP address, called its *home address*, which has a network prefix equal to that of its *home network*. This is the address that will be used by other hosts when they initially send packets to the mobile host; because it does not change, it can be used by long-lived applications as the host roams. We can think of this as the long-lived identifier of the host.

When the host moves to a new foreign network away from its home network, it typically acquires a new address on that network using some means such as DHCP.[5] This address is going to change every time the host roams to a new network, so we can think of this as being more like the locator for the host, but it is important to note that the host does not lose its permanent home address when it acquires a new address on the foreign network. This home address is critical to its ability to sustain communications as it moves, as we'll see below.

While the majority of routers remain unchanged, mobility support does require some new functionality in at least one router, known as the

---

[5]Because DHCP was developed around the same time as Mobile IP, the original Mobile IP standards did not require DHCP, but DHCP is ubiquitous today.

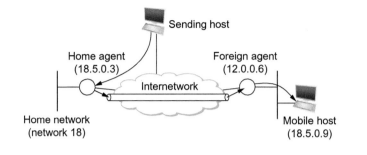

■ FIGURE 4.27 Mobile host and mobility agents.

home agent of the mobile node. This router is located on the home network of the mobile host. In some cases, a second router with enhanced functionality, the *foreign agent,* is also required. This router is located on a network to which the mobile node attaches itself when it is away from its home network. We will consider first the operation of Mobile IP when a foreign agent is used. An example network with both home and foreign agents is shown in Figure 4.27.

Both home and foreign agents periodically announce their presence on the networks to which they are attached using agent advertisement messages. A mobile host may also solicit an advertisement when it attaches to a new network. The advertisement by the home agent enables a mobile host to learn the address of its home agent before it leaves its home network. When the mobile host attaches to a foreign network, it hears an advertisement from a foreign agent and registers with the agent, providing the address of its home agent. The foreign agent then contacts the home agent, providing a *care-of address*. This is usually the IP address of the foreign agent.

At this point, we can see that any host that tries to send a packet to the mobile host will send it with a destination address equal to the home address of that node. Normal IP forwarding will cause that packet to arrive on the home network of the mobile node on which the home agent is sitting. Thus, we can divide the problem of delivering the packet to the mobile node into three parts:

1. How does the home agent intercept a packet that is destined for the mobile node?

2. How does the home agent then deliver the packet to the foreign agent?

3. How does the foreign agent deliver the packet to the mobile node?

The first problem might look easy if you just look at Figure 4.27, in which the home agent is clearly the only path between the sending host and the home network and thus must receive packets that are destined to the mobile node. But what if the sending (correspondent) node were on network 18, or what if there were another router connected to network 18 that tried to deliver the packet without its passing through the home agent? To address this problem, the home agent actually impersonates the mobile node, using a technique called *proxy ARP*. This works just like Address Resolution Protocol (ARP) as described in Section 3.2.6, except that the home agent inserts the IP address of the mobile node, rather than its own, in the ARP messages. It uses its own hardware address, so that all the nodes on the same network learn to associate the hardware address of the home agent with the IP address of the mobile node. One subtle aspect of this process is the fact that ARP information may be cached in other nodes on the network. To make sure that these caches are invalidated in a timely way, the home agent issues an ARP message as soon as the mobile node registers with a foreign agent. Because the ARP message is not a response to a normal ARP request, it is termed a *gratuitous ARP*.

The second problem is the delivery of the intercepted packet to the foreign agent. Here we use the tunneling technique described in Section 3.2.9. The home agent simply wraps the packet inside an IP header that is destined for the foreign agent and transmits it into the internetwork. All the intervening routers just see an IP packet destined for the IP address of the foreign agent. Another way of looking at this is that an IP tunnel is established between the home agent and the foreign agent, and the home agent just drops packets destined for the mobile node into that tunnel.

When a packet finally arrives at the foreign agent, it strips the extra IP header and finds inside an IP packet destined for the home address of the mobile node. Clearly the foreign agent cannot treat this like any old IP packet because this would cause it to send it back to the home network.

Instead, it has to recognize the address as that of a registered mobile node. It then delivers the packet to the *hardware* address of the mobile node (e.g., its Ethernet address), which was learned as part of the registration process.

One observation that can be made about these procedures is that it is possible for the foreign agent and the mobile node to be in the same box; that is, a mobile node can perform the foreign agent function itself. To make this work, however, the mobile node must be able to dynamically acquire an IP address that is located in the address space of the foreign network (e.g., using DHCP). This address will then be used as the care-of address. In our example, this address would have a network number of 12. This approach has the desirable feature of allowing mobile nodes to attach to networks that don't have foreign agents; thus, mobility can be achieved with only the addition of a home agent and some new software on the mobile node (assuming DHCP is used on the foreign network).

What about traffic in the other direction (i.e., from mobile node to fixed node)? This turns out to be much easier. The mobile node just puts the IP address of the fixed node in the destination field of its IP packets while putting its permanent address in the source field, and the packets are forwarded to the fixed node using normal means. Of course, if both nodes in a conversation are mobile, then the procedures described above are used in each direction.

Route Optimization in Mobile IP

There is one significant drawback to the above approach: The route from the correspondent node to the mobile node can be significantly suboptimal. One of the most extreme examples is when a mobile node and the correspondent node are on the same network, but the home network for the mobile node is on the far side of the Internet. The sending correspondent node addresses all packets to the home network; they traverse the Internet to reach the home agent, which then tunnels them back across the Internet to reach the foreign agent. Clearly, it would be nice if the correspondent node could find out that the mobile node is actually on the same network and deliver the packet directly. In the more general case, the goal is to deliver packets as directly as possible from correspondent node to mobile node without passing through a home agent. This is sometimes referred to as the *triangle routing problem* since the path from correspondent to mobile node via home agent takes two sides of a triangle, rather than the third side that is the direct path.

The basic idea behind the solution to triangle routing is to let the correspondent node know the care-of address of the mobile node. The correspondent node can then create its own tunnel to the foreign agent. This is treated as an optimization of the process just described. If the sender has been equipped with the necessary software to learn the care-of address and create its own tunnel, then the route can be optimized; if not, packets just follow the suboptimal route.

When a home agent sees a packet destined for one of the mobile nodes that it supports, it can deduce that the sender is not using the optimal route. Therefore, it sends a "binding update" message back to the source, in addition to forwarding the data packet to the foreign agent. The source, if capable, uses this binding update to create an entry in a *binding cache*, which consists of a list of mappings from mobile node addresses to care-of addresses. The next time this source has a data packet to send to that mobile node, it will find the binding in the cache and can tunnel the packet directly to the foreign agent.

There is an obvious problem with this scheme, which is that the binding cache may become out-of-date if the mobile host moves to a new network. If an out-of-date cache entry is used, the foreign agent will receive tunneled packets for a mobile node that is no longer registered on its network. In this case, it sends a *binding warning* message back to the sender to tell it to stop using this cache entry. This scheme works only in the case where the foreign agent is not the mobile node itself, however. For this reason, cache entries need to be deleted after some period of time; the exact amount is specified in the binding update message.

As noted above, mobile routing provides some interesting security challenges, which are clearer now that we have seen how Mobile IP works. For example, an attacker wishing to intercept the packets destined to some other node in an internetwork could contact the home agent for that node and announce itself as the new foreign agent for the node. Thus, it is clear that some authentication mechanisms are required. We discuss such mechanisms in Chapter 8.

Mobility in IPv6

There are a handful of significant differences between mobility support in IPv4 and IPv6. Most importantly, it was possible to build mobility support into the standards for IPv6 pretty much from the beginning, thus alleviating a number of incremental deployment problems. (It may be more correct to say that IPv6 is one big incremental deployment problem, which, if solved, will deliver mobility support as part of the package.)

Since all IPv6-capable hosts can acquire an address whenever they are attached to a foreign network (using several mechanisms defined as part of the core v6 specifications), Mobile IPv6 does away with the foreign agent and includes the necessary capabilities to act as a foreign agent in every host.

One other interesting aspect of IPv6 that comes into play with Mobile IP is its inclusion of a flexible set of extension headers, as described in Section 4.1.3. This is used in the optimized routing scenario described above. Rather than *tunneling* a packet to the mobile node at its care-of address, an IPv6 node can send an IP packet to the care-of address with the home address contained in a *routing header*. This header is ignored by all the intermediate nodes, but it enables the mobile node to treat the packet as if it were sent to the home address, thus enabling it to continue presenting higher layer protocols with the illusion that its IP address is fixed. Using an extension header rather than a tunnel is more efficient from the perspective of both bandwidth consumption and processing.

Finally, we note that many open issues remain in mobile networking. Managing the power consumption of mobile devices is increasingly important, so that smaller devices with limited battery power can by built. There is also the problem of *ad hoc* mobile networks—enabling a group of mobile nodes to form a network in the absence of any fixed nodes—which has some special challenges (see the sidebar). A particularly challenging class of mobile networks, *sensor networks*, was mentioned previously. Sensors typically are small, inexpensive, and often battery powered, meaning that issues of very low power consumption and limited processing capability must also be considered. Furthermore, since wireless communications and mobility typically go hand in hand, the continual advances in wireless technologies keep on producing new challenges and opportunities for mobile networking.

Mobile *Ad Hoc* Networks

For most of this section, we've been assuming that only the end nodes (hosts) are mobile. This is certainly a good description of the way most of us deal with networks today. Our laptops and phones move around, and connect to fixed infrastructure, such as cell towers and 802.11 access points, which connect over fixed links to the Internet's backbone. However, many modern routers are also quite small enough to be mobile, and there are environments where mobile routers would be useful, such as building networks among moving vehicles. Because routing protocols are dynamic, you might imagine that the occasional mobile router would not be a problem, and that is roughly correct. However, what if all or most of the nodes in a network where mobile? Taken to the logical extreme, you could have a network with no fixed infrastructure at all—just a collection of mobile nodes, some or all of which function as routers. Would standard routing protocols work in such an environment?

The environment where everything is mobile and there is no fixed infrastructure is often called a Mobile *Ad Hoc* Network (MANET, which is the name of an IETF working group tackling the problem space). To understand why special solutions might be needed for the mobile *ad hoc* environment, consider the fact that, unlike a fixed network, the neighbors of any given *ad hoc* router are likely to change very frequently as the nodes move. Since any change in neighbor relationships typically requires a routing protocol message to be sent and a new routing table to be calculated, it's easy to see that there may be concerns about using a protocol not optimized for this environment. Compounding this issue is the fact that communication is likely to be wireless, which consumes power, and many mobile nodes are likely to run off power-constrained batteries. Link bandwidths are also likely to be constrained. Hence, reducing the overhead caused by sending routing protocol messages, and reflooding them to all of one's neighbors, is a key concern for *ad hoc* routing.

At the time of writing, several approaches to optimizing routing for mobile *ad hoc* environments have been developed. These are broadly characterized as reactive and proactive approaches. Optimized Link State Routing (OLSR) is the dominant proactive approach, and its name gives a good sense of what it is; it resembles a conventional link-state protocol (like OSPF, Section 3.3.3), with a number of optimizations to reduce the amount of flooding of routing messages. Reactive protocols include *Ad Hoc* On-Demand Distance Vector (AODV) and Dynamic MANET On Demand (DYMO), both of which are based on distance vector protocols as described in Section 3.3.2. These approaches seek to reduce the amount of routing protocol overhead by only building routes as needed, such as when a given node has traffic for a particular destination. There is a rich solution space in which tradeoffs can be made, and this space continues to be explored.

4.5 SUMMARY

The main theme of this chapter was dealing with the continued growth of the Internet. The Internet keeps on attaching more users, and each user sends more traffic as applications such as video streaming become more bandwidth intensive. Thus, while the Internet has proved to be a hugely scalable system, new scaling issues continue to demand solutions. In addition to scaling, the Internet also needs to evolve to support new capabilities and services.

The major scaling issues today are the efficient use of address space and the growth of routing tables as the Internet grows. The hierarchical IP address format, with its network and host parts, gives us one level of hierarchy to manage scale. Routing areas provide another level of hierarchy. Autonomous systems allow us to partition the routing problem into two parts, interdomain and intradomain routing, each of which is much smaller than the total routing problem would be. BGP, the interdomain routing protocol of the Internet, has been remarkably successful in dealing with the growth of the Internet.

In spite of the many steps taken to scale IPv4, it is clear that a new, longer address format will soon be needed. This requires a new IP datagram format and a new version of the protocol. Originally known as Next Generation IP (IPng), this new protocol is now known as IPv6, and it provides a 128-bit address with (mostly) CIDR-like addressing and routing. While many new capabilities have been claimed for IPv6, its main advantage remains its ability to support an extremely large number of addressable devices.

Finally, the Internet also needs to evolve in function as well as size. In that regard, we looked at three enhancements to the original IP datagram model. The first, multicast, enables efficient delivery of the same data to groups of receivers. As with unicast, many of the challenges in multicast relate to scaling, and a number of different protocols and multicast modes have been developed to optimize scaling and routing in different environments. The second enhancement, MPLS, brings some of the aspects of virtual circuit networks to IP and has been widely used to extend the capabilities of IP. Applications of MPLS range from traffic engineering to the support of virtual private networks over the Internet. And, finally, mobility support, which was far from the minds of the original designers of IP, is increasingly important as more networked devices, both hosts and routers, become mobile.

Roughly 20 years have elapsed since the shortage of IPv4 address space became serious enough to warrant proposals for a new version of IP. The original IPv6 specification is now more than 15 years old. IPv6-capable host operating systems are now widely available and the major router vendors offer varying degrees of support for IPv6 in their products. Yet, the deployment of IPv6 in the Internet can only be described as embryonic. It is worth wondering when deployment is likely to begin in earnest and what will cause it.

One reason why IPv6 has *not* been needed sooner is because of the extensive use of Network Address Translation (NAT), described earlier in this chapter. As providers viewed IPv4 addresses as a scarce resource, they handed out fewer of them to their customers,

WHAT'S NEXT: DEPLOYMENT OF IPv6

or charged for the number of addresses used; customers responded by hiding many of their devices behind a NAT box and a single IPv4 address. For example, it is generally the case that home networks with more than one IP-capable device have some sort of NAT in the network to conserve addresses. So one factor that might drive IPv6 deployment would be applications that don't work well with NAT. While client–server applications work reasonably well when the client's address is hidden behind a NAT box, peer-to-peer applications fare less well. Examples of applications that would work better without NAT and would therefore benefit from more liberal address allocation policies are multiplayer gaming and IP telephony. Yet, even these applications have found ways to deal with NAT, and NAT traversal technologies are now widely available.

Obtaining blocks of IPv4 addresses has been getting more difficult for years, and this is particularly noticeable in countries outside of the United States. As the difficulty increases, the incentive for providers to start offering IPv6 addresses to their customers also rises. At the same time, for existing providers, offering IPv6 is a substantial additional cost, because they don't get to stop supporting IPv4 when they start to offer IPv6. This means, for example, that the size of a provider's routing tables can only increase initially, because they need to carry all the existing IPv4 prefixes plus new IPv6 prefixes.

At the moment, IPv6 deployment has been led by research networks. A few service providers are starting to offer it, especially outside the United States (often with some incentive from national governments). Commercial routers and host operating systems support IPv6 to varying degrees. It seems certain that IPv6 deployment will continue to accelerate, but it also seems likely that the overwhelming majority of hosts and networks will be IPv4-only for several more years at least.

■ FURTHER READING

Our first selection, an RFC by Bradner and Mankin, gives an informative overview on how the rapidly growing Internet has stressed the scalability of the original architecture, ultimately resulting IPv6. The paper by Paxson describes a study of how routers behave in the Internet. Even though it is more than 15 years old, it continues to be highly cited and is a good example of how researchers study the dynamic behavior of the Internet. The final paper discusses multicast, presenting the approach to multicast originally used on the MBone.

- Bradner, S., and A. Mankin. The recommendation for the next generation IP protocol. *Request for Comments* 1752, January 1995.
- Paxson, V. End-to-end routing behavior in the Internet. *SIGCOMM 96*, pages 25–38, August 1996.
- Deering, S., and D. Cheriton. Multicast routing in datagram internetworks and extended LANs. *ACM Transactions on Computer Systems* 8(2):85–110, May 1990.

Some interesting experimental studies of the behavior of Internet routing are presented in Labovitz et al. [LAAJ00]. Another useful paper on the stability of BGP is by Gao and Rexford [GR01].

A collection of RFCs related to IPv6 can be found in Bradner and Mankin [BM95], and the most recent IPv6 spec is by Deering and Hinden [DH98]. There are dozens of other IPv6-related RFCs.

Protocol Independent Multicast (PIM) is described in Deering et al. [DEF⁺96] and Fenner et al. [FHHK06]; PIM-SSM is described in [Bha03]. [Wil00] and [HC99] are both very readable introductions to multicast with interesting historical details.

Multiprotocol Label Switching and the related protocols that fed its development are described in Chandranmenon et al. [CV95], Rekhter et al. [RDR$^+$97], and Davie et al. [DR00]. The latter reference describes many applications of MPLS such as traffic engineering, fast recovery from network failures, and virtual private networks. [RR06] provides the specification of MPLS/BGP VPNs, a form of layer 3 VPN that can be provided over MPLS networks.

Mobile IP is defined in Perkins [Per02] for IPv4 and in Johnson et al. [JPA04] for IPv6. Basagni et al. [BCGS04] provide a good background of the problems and research in mobile *ad hoc* networking, while one of the primary MANET routing protocols is described by Clausen et al. [CHCB01].

Finally, we recommend the following live references:

- http://www.isoc.org/internet/history/: A collection of links related to Internet history, including some articles written by the original researchers who built the Internet.

- http://bgp.potaroo.net/: Lots of data about the growth of the routing tables in the Internet, including IPv6 deployment.

EXERCISES

1. Consider the network shown in Figure 4.28, in which horizontal lines represent transit providers and numbered vertical lines are interprovider links.

    (a) How many routes to P could provider Q's BGP speakers receive?

    (b) Suppose Q and P adopt the policy that outbound traffic is routed to the closest link to the destination's provider, thus minimizing their own cost. What paths will traffic from host A to host B and from host B to host A take?

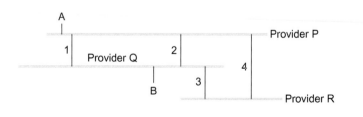

■ FIGURE 4.28 Network for Exercise 1.

(c) What could Q do to have the B $\longrightarrow$ A traffic use the closer link 1?

(d) What could Q do to have the B $\longrightarrow$ A traffic pass through R?

2. Give an example of an arrangement of routers grouped into autonomous systems so that the path with the fewest hops from a point A to another point B crosses the same AS twice. Explain what BGP would do with this situation.

3. Let A be the number of autonomous systems on the Internet, and let D (for diameter) be the maximum AS path length.

   (a) Give a connectivity model for which D is of order $\log A$ and another for which D is of order $\sqrt{A}$.

   (b) Assuming each AS number is 2 bytes and each network number is 4 bytes, give an estimate for the amount of data a BGP speaker must receive to keep track of the AS path to every network. Express your answer in terms of A, D, and the number of networks N.

4. Propose a plausible addressing plan for IPv6 that runs out of bits. Specifically, provide a diagram such as Figure 4.11, perhaps with additional ID fields, that adds up to more than 128 bits, together with plausible justifications for the size of each field. You may assume fields are divided on byte boundaries and that the InterfaceID is 64 bits. (Hint: Consider fields that would approach maximum allocation only under unusual circumstances.) Can you do this if the InterfaceID is 48 bits?

5. Suppose P, Q, and R are network service providers with respective CIDR address allocations C1.0.0.0/8, C2.0.0.0/8, and C3.0.0.0/8. Each provider's customers initially receive address allocations that are a subset of the provider's. P has the following customers:

   PA, with allocation C1.A3.0.0/16

   PB, with allocation C1.B0.0.0/12.

   Q has the following customers:

   QA, with allocation C2.0A.10.0/20

   QB, with allocation C2.0B.0.0/16.

   Assume there are no other providers or customers.

   (a) Give routing tables for P, Q, and R assuming each provider connects to both of the others.

(b) Now assume P is connected to Q and Q is connected to R, but P and R are not directly connected. Give tables for P and R.

(c) Suppose customer PA acquires a direct link to Q, and QA acquires a direct link to P, in addition to existing links. Give tables for P and Q, ignoring R.

6. In the previous problem, assume each provider connects to both others. Suppose customer PA switches to provider Q and customer QB switches to provider R. Use the CIDR longest-match rule to give routing tables for all three providers that allow PA and QB to switch without renumbering.

7. Suppose most of the Internet used some form of geographical addressing, but that a large international organization has a single IP network address and routes its internal traffic over its own links.

(a) Explain the routing inefficiency for the organization's inbound traffic inherent in this situation.

(b) Explain how the organization might solve this problem for outbound traffic.

(c) For your method above to work for inbound traffic, what would have to happen?

(d) Suppose the large organization now changes its addressing to separate geographical addresses for each office. What will its internal routing structure have to look like if internal traffic is still to be routed internally?

8. The telephone system uses geographical addressing. Why do you think this wasn't adopted as a matter of course by the Internet?

9. Suppose a small ISP X pays a larger ISP A to connect him to the rest of the Internet and also pays another ISP B to provide a fall-back connection to the Internet in the event that he loses connectivity via ISP A. If ISP X learns of a path to some prefix via ISP A, should he advertise that path to ISP B? Why or why not?

10. Suppose a site A is *multihomed*, in that it has two Internet connections from two different providers, P and Q. Provider-based addressing as in Exercise 5 is used, and A takes its address assignment from P. Q has a CIDR longest-match routing entry for A.

(a) Describe what inbound traf c might ow on the A–Q connection. Consider cases where Q does and does not advertise A to the world using BGP.

(b) What is the minimum advertising of its route to A that Q must do in order for all inbound traf c to reach A via Q if the P–A link breaks?

(c) What problems must be overcome if A is to use both links for its outbound traf c?

11. Suppose a network N within a larger organization A acquires its own direct connection to an Internet Service Provider, in addition to an existing connection via A. Let R1 be the router connecting N to its own provider, and let R2 be the router connecting N to the rest of A.

(a) Assuming N remains a subnet of A, how should R1 and R2 be con gured? What limitations would still exist with N s use of its separate connection? Would A be prevented from using N s connection? Specify your con guration in terms of what R1 and R2 should advertise, and with what paths. Assume a BGP-like mechanism is available.

(b) Now suppose N gets its own network number; how does this change your answer in (a)?

(c) Describe a router con guration that would allow A to use N s link when its own link is down.

12. How do routers determine that an incoming IP packet is to be multicast? Give answers for both IPv4 and IPv6.

13. Suppose a multicast group is intended to be private to a particular routing domain. Can an IP multicast address be assigned to the group without consulting with other domains with no risk of con icts?

14. Under what conditions could a non-router host on an Ethernet receive a IP multicast packet for a multicast group it has not joined?

15. Consider the example internet shown in Figure 4.29, in which sources D and E send packets to multicast group G. All hosts except D and E are members of G. Show the shortest-path multicast trees for each source.

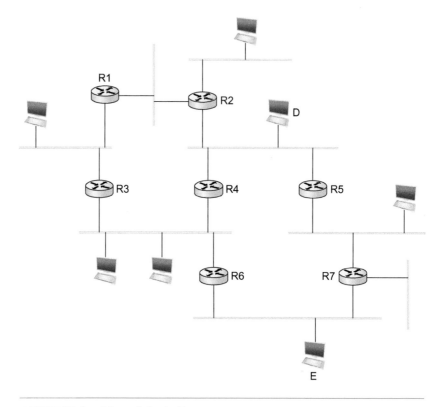

R1
R2
D
R3
R4
R5
R6
R7
E

■ FIGURE 4.29 Example internet for Exercise 15.

16. Consider the example internet shown in Figure 4.30 in which sources S1 and S2 send packets to multicast group G. All hosts except S1 and S2 are members of G. Show the shortest-path multicast trees for each source.

17. Suppose host A is sending to a multicast group; the recipients are leaf nodes of a tree rooted at A with depth N and with each nonleaf node having k children; there are thus k^N recipients.
   (a) How many individual link transmissions are involved if A sends a multicast message to all recipients?
   (b) How many individual link transmissions are involved if A sends unicast messages to each individual recipient?
   (c) Suppose A sends to all recipients, but some messages are lost and retransmission is necessary. Unicast retransmissions to what fraction of the recipients is equivalent, in terms of individual link transmissions, to a multicast retransmission to all recipients?

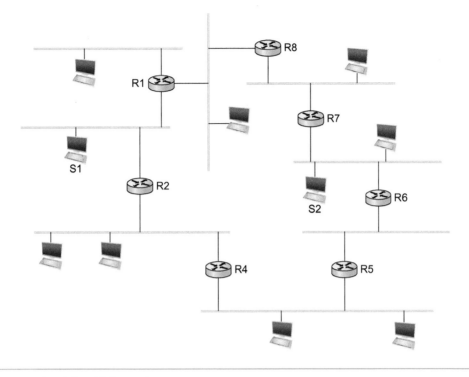

■ FIGURE 4.30 Example Network for Exercise 16.

18. The existing Internet depends in many respects on participants being good "network citizens"—cooperating above and beyond adherence to standard protocols.

   (a) In the PIM-SM scheme, who determines when to create a source-specific tree? How might this be a problem?

   (b) In the PIM-SSM scheme, who determines when to create a source-specific tree? Why is this presumably not a problem?

19. (a) Draw an example internetwork where the BIDIR-PIM route from a source's router to a group member's router is longer than the PIM-SM source-specific route.

   (b) Draw an example where they are the same.

20. Determine whether or not the following IPv6 address notations are correct:

   (a) ::0F53:6382:AB00:67DB:BB27:7332

   (b) 7803:42F2:::88EC:D4BA:B75D:11CD

   (c) ::4BA8:95CC::DB97:4EAB

(d) 74DC::02BA

(e) ::00FF:128.112.92.116

21. MPLS labels are usually 20 bits long. Explain why this provides enough labels when MPLS is used for destination-based forwarding.

22. MPLS has sometimes been claimed to improve router performance. Explain why this might be true, and suggest reasons why in practice this may not be the case.

23. Assume that it takes 32 bits to carry each MPLS label that is added to a packet when the "shim" header of Figure 4.20(b) is used.
    (a) How many additional bytes are needed to tunnel a packet using the MPLS techniques described in Section 4.3.3?
    (b) How many additional bytes are needed, at a minimum, to tunnel a packet using an additional IP header as described in Section 3.2.9?
    (c) Calculate the efficiency of bandwidth usage for each of the two tunneling approaches when the average packet size is 300 bytes. Repeat for 64-byte packets. Bandwidth efficiency is defined as (payload bytes carried) ÷ (total bytes carried).

24. RFC 791 describes the Internet Protocol and includes two options for source routing. Describe three disadvantages of using IP source route options compared to using MPLS for explicit routing. (Hint: The IP header including options may be at most 15 words long.)

25. DHCP allows a computer to acquire a new IP address whenever it moves to a new subnet. Why is this not always enough to address the communications needs of mobile hosts?

26. What is the main downside of requiring traffic destined to a mobile node to be sent first to its home agent?

27. Mobile IP allows a home agent to tell a correspondent node a new care-of address for a mobile node. How might such a mechanism be used to steal traffic? How could it be used to launch a flood of attack traffic at another node?

5

A SYSTEMS APPROACH

A SYSTEMS APPROACH

A SYSTEMS APPROACH

A SYSTEMS APPROACH

A SYSTEMS APPROACH

End-to-End Protocols

Victory is the beautiful, bright coloured flower. Transport is the stem without which it could never have blossomed.

–Winston Churchill

The previous three chapters have described various technologies that can be used to connect together a collection of computers, ranging from simple Ethernets and wireless networks to global-scale internetworks. The next problem is to turn this host-to-host packet delivery service into a process-to-process communication channel. This is the role played by the *transport* level of the network architecture, which, because it supports communication between application programs running in end nodes, is sometimes called the *end-to-end* protocol.

PROBLEM: GETTING PROCESSES TO COMMUNICATE

Two forces shape the end-to-end protocol. From above, the application-level processes that use its services have certain requirements. The following list itemizes some of the common properties that a transport protocol can be expected to provide:

- Guarantees message delivery
- Delivers messages in the same order they are sent

- Delivers at most one copy of each message
- Supports arbitrarily large messages
- Supports synchronization between the sender and the receiver
- Allows the receiver to apply flow control to the sender
- Supports multiple application processes on each host

Note that this list does not include all the functionality that application processes might want from the network. For example, it does not include security features like authentication or encryption, which are typically provided by protocols that sit above the transport level.

From below, the underlying network upon which the transport protocol operates has certain limitations in the level of service it can provide. Some of the more typical limitations of the network are that it may

- Drop messages
- Reorder messages
- Deliver duplicate copies of a given message
- Limit messages to some finite size
- Deliver messages after an arbitrarily long delay

Such a network is said to provide a *best-effort* level of service, as exemplified by the Internet.

The challenge, therefore, is to develop algorithms that turn the less-than-desirable properties of the underlying network into the high level of service required by application programs. Different transport protocols employ different combinations of these algorithms. This chapter looks at these algorithms in the context of four representative services—a simple asynchronous demultiplexing service, a reliable byte-stream service, a request/reply service, and a service for real-time applications.

In the case of the demultiplexing and byte-stream services, we use the Internet's User Datagram Protocol (UDP) and Transmission Control Protocol (TCP), respectively, to illustrate how these services are provided in practice. In the case of a request/reply service, we discuss the role it plays in a Remote Procedure Call (RPC) service and what features that entails. This discussion is capped off with a description of two widely used RPC protocols: SunRPC and DCE-RPC.

Finally, real-time applications make particular demands on the transport protocol, such as the need to carry timing information that allows audio or video samples to be played back at the appropriate point in time. We look at the requirements placed by applications on such a protocol and the most widely used example, the Real-Time Transport Protocol (RTP).

5.1 SIMPLE DEMULTIPLEXER (UDP)

The simplest possible transport protocol is one that extends the host-to-host delivery service of the underlying network into a process-to-process communication service. There are likely to be many processes running on any given host, so the protocol needs to add a level of demultiplexing, thereby allowing multiple application processes on each host to share the network. Aside from this requirement, the transport protocol adds no other functionality to the best-effort service provided by the underlying network. The Internet's User Datagram Protocol is an example of such a transport protocol.

The only interesting issue in such a protocol is the form of the address used to identify the target process. Although it is possible for processes to *directly* identify each other with an OS-assigned process id (pid), such an approach is only practical in a closed distributed system in which a single OS runs on all hosts and assigns each process a unique id. A more common approach, and the one used by UDP, is for processes to *indirectly* identify each other using an abstract locater, usually called a *port*. The basic idea is for a source process to send a message to a port and for the destination process to receive the message from a port.

The header for an end-to-end protocol that implements this demultiplexing function typically contains an identifier (port) for both the sender (source) and the receiver (destination) of the message. For example, the UDP header is given in Figure 5.1. Notice that the UDP port field is only 16 bits long. This means that there are up to 64K possible ports, clearly not enough to identify all the processes on all the hosts in the Internet. Fortunately, ports are not interpreted across the entire Internet, but only on a single host. That is, a process is really identified by a port on some particular host—a ⟨port, host⟩ pair. In fact, this pair constitutes the demultiplexing key for the UDP protocol.

The next issue is how a process learns the port for the process to which it wants to send a message. Typically, a client process initiates a message

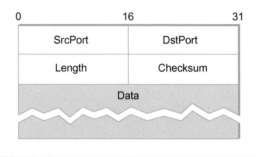

0   16   31

SrcPort	DstPort
Length	Checksum

Data

exchange with a server process. Once a client has contacted a server, the server knows the client's port (from the **SrcPrt** field contained in the message header) and can reply to it. The real problem, therefore, is how the client learns the server's port in the first place. A common approach is for the server to accept messages at a *well-known port*. That is, each server receives its messages at some fixed port that is widely published, much like the emergency telephone service available in the United States at the well-known phone number 911. In the Internet, for example, the Domain Name Server (DNS) receives messages at well-known port 53 on each host, the mail service listens for messages at port 25, and the Unix talk program accepts messages at well-known port 517, and so on. This mapping is published periodically in an RFC and is available on most Unix systems in file /etc/services. Sometimes a well-known port is just the starting point for communication: The client and server use the well-known port to agree on some other port that they will use for subsequent communication, leaving the well-known port free for other clients.

An alternative strategy is to generalize this idea, so that there is only a single well-known port—the one at which the *port mapper* service accepts messages. A client would send a message to the port mapper's well-known port asking for the port it should use to talk to the "whatever" service, and the port mapper returns the appropriate port. This strategy makes it easy to change the port associated with different services over time and for each host to use a different port for the same service.

As just mentioned, a port is purely an abstraction. Exactly how it is implemented differs from system to system, or more precisely, from OS to OS. For example, the socket API described in Chapter 1 is an example implementation of ports. Typically, a port is implemented by a message queue, as illustrated in Figure 5.2. When a message arrives, the protocol (e.g., UDP) appends the message to the end of the queue. Should the

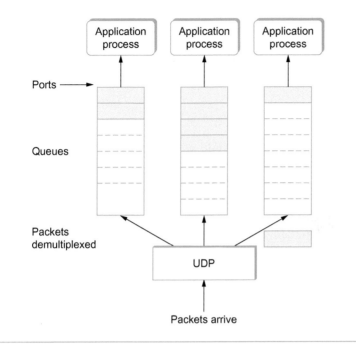

queue be full, the message is discarded. There is no flow-control mechanism in UDP to tell the sender to slow down. When an application process
wants to receive a message, one is removed from the front of the queue. If
the queue is empty, the process blocks until a message becomes available.

Finally, although UDP does not implement flow control or reliable/
ordered delivery, it does provide one more function aside from demultiplexing messages to some application process—it also ensures the correctness of the message by the use of a checksum. (The UDP checksum
is optional in IPv4 but is mandatory in IPv6.) The basic UDP checksum
algorithm is the same one used for IP, as defined in Section 2.4.2—that is,
it adds up a set of 16-bit words using ones complement arithmetic and
takes the ones complement of the result. But the input data that is used
for the checksum is a little counterintuitive.

The UDP checksum takes as input the UDP header, the contents of
the message body, and something called the *pseudoheader*. The pseudoheader consists of three fields from the IP header—protocol number,
source IP address, and destination IP address—plus the UDP length field.
(Yes, the UDP length field is included twice in the checksum calculation.)
The motivation behind having the pseudoheader is to verify that this

message has been delivered between the correct two endpoints. For example, if the destination IP address was modified while the packet was in transit, causing the packet to be misdelivered, this fact would be detected by the UDP checksum.

LAB 10: TCP

5.2 RELIABLE BYTE STREAM (TCP)

In contrast to a simple demultiplexing protocol like UDP, a more sophisticated transport protocol is one that offers a reliable, connection-oriented, byte-stream service. Such a service has proven useful to a wide assortment of applications because it frees the application from having to worry about missing or reordered data. The Internet's Transmission Control Protocol is probably the most widely used protocol of this type; it is also the most carefully tuned. It is for these two reasons that this section studies TCP in detail, although we identify and discuss alternative design choices at the end of the section.

In terms of the properties of transport protocols given in the problem statement at the start of this chapter, TCP guarantees the reliable, in-order delivery of a stream of bytes. It is a full-duplex protocol, meaning that each TCP connection supports a pair of byte streams, one flowing in each direction. It also includes a flow-control mechanism for each of these byte streams that allows the receiver to limit how much data the sender can transmit at a given time. Finally, like UDP, TCP supports a demultiplexing mechanism that allows multiple application programs on any given host to simultaneously carry on a conversation with their peers. In addition to the above features, TCP also implements a highly tuned (and still evolving) congestion-control mechanism. The idea of this mechanism is to throttle how fast TCP sends data, not for the sake of keeping the sender from over-running the receiver, but so as to keep the sender from overloading the network. A description of TCP's congestion-control mechanism is postponed until Chapter 6, where we discuss it in the larger context of how network resources are fairly allocated.

Since many people confuse congestion control and flow control, we restate the difference. *Flow control* involves preventing senders from over-running the capacity of receivers. *Congestion control* involves preventing too much data from being injected into the network, thereby causing switches or links to become overloaded. Thus, flow control is an end-to-end issue, while congestion control is concerned with how hosts and networks interact.

5.2.1 End-to-End Issues

At the heart of TCP is the sliding window algorithm. Even though this is the same basic algorithm we saw in Section 2.5.2, because TCP runs over the Internet rather than a point-to-point link, there are many important differences. This subsection identifies these differences and explains how they complicate TCP. The following subsections then describe how TCP addresses these and other complications.

First, whereas the sliding window algorithm presented in Section 2.5.2 runs over a single physical link that always connects the same two computers, TCP supports logical connections between processes that are running on any two computers in the Internet. This means that TCP needs an explicit connection establishment phase during which the two sides of the connection agree to exchange data with each other. This difference is analogous to having to dial up the other party, rather than having a dedicated phone line. TCP also has an explicit connection teardown phase. One of the things that happens during connection establishment is that the two parties establish some shared state to enable the sliding window algorithm to begin. Connection teardown is needed so each host knows it is OK to free this state.

Second, whereas a single physical link that always connects the same two computers has a fixed round-trip time (RTT), TCP connections are likely to have widely different round-trip times. For example, a TCP connection between a host in San Francisco and a host in Boston, which are separated by several thousand kilometers, might have an RTT of 100 ms, while a TCP connection between two hosts in the same room, only a few meters apart, might have an RTT of only 1 ms. The same TCP protocol must be able to support both of these connections. To make matters worse, the TCP connection between hosts in San Francisco and Boston might have an RTT of 100 ms at 3 a.m., but an RTT of 500 ms at 3 p.m. Variations in the RTT are even possible during a single TCP connection that lasts only a few minutes. What this means to the sliding window algorithm is that the timeout mechanism that triggers retransmissions must be adaptive. (Certainly, the timeout for a point-to-point link must be a settable parameter, but it is not necessary to adapt this timer for a particular pair of nodes.)

A third difference is that packets may be reordered as they cross the Internet, but this is not possible on a point-to-point link where the first packet put into one end of the link must be the first to appear at the other end. Packets that are slightly out of order do not cause a problem since the sliding window algorithm can reorder packets correctly using the sequence number. The real issue is how far out of order packets can get or, said another way, how late a packet can arrive at the destination. In the worst case, a packet can be delayed in the Internet until the IP time to live (TTL) field expires, at which time the packet is discarded (and hence there is no danger of it arriving late). Knowing that IP throws packets away after their TTL expires, TCP assumes that each packet has a maximum lifetime. The exact lifetime, known as the *maximum segment lifetime* (MSL), is an engineering choice. The current recommended setting is 120 seconds. Keep in mind that IP does not directly enforce this 120-second value; it is simply a conservative estimate that TCP makes of how long a packet might live in the Internet. The implication is significant—TCP has to be prepared for very old packets to suddenly show up at the receiver, potentially confusing the sliding window algorithm.

Fourth, the computers connected to a point-to-point link are generally engineered to support the link. For example, if a link's delay × bandwidth product is computed to be 8 KB—meaning that a window size is selected to allow up to 8 KB of data to be unacknowledged at a given time—then it is likely that the computers at either end of the link have the ability to buffer up to 8 KB of data. Designing the system otherwise would be silly. On the other hand, almost any kind of computer can be connected to the Internet, making the amount of resources dedicated to any one TCP connection highly variable, especially considering that any one host can potentially support hundreds of TCP connections at the same time. This means that TCP must include a mechanism that each side uses to "learn" what resources (e.g., how much buffer space) the other side is able to apply to the connection. This is the flow control issue.

Fifth, because the transmitting side of a directly connected link cannot send any faster than the bandwidth of the link allows, and only one host is pumping data into the link, it is not possible to unknowingly congest the link. Said another way, the load on the link is visible in the form of a queue of packets at the sender. In contrast, the sending side of a TCP connection has no idea what links will be traversed to reach the destination. For example, the sending machine might be directly connected to a relatively fast Ethernet—and capable of sending data at a rate of 100 Mbps—but somewhere out in the middle of the network, a 1.5-Mbps T1 link must be traversed. And, to make matters worse, data being generated by many different sources might be trying to traverse this same slow link. This leads to the problem of network congestion. Discussion of this topic is delayed until Chapter 6.

We conclude this discussion of end-to-end issues by comparing TCP's approach to providing a reliable/ordered delivery service with the approach used by X.25 networks. In TCP, the underlying IP network is assumed to be unreliable and to deliver messages out of order; TCP uses the sliding window algorithm on an end-to-end basis to provide reliable/ordered delivery. In contrast, X.25 networks use the sliding window protocol within the network, on a hop-by-hop basis. The assumption behind this approach is that if messages are delivered reliably and in order between each pair of nodes along the path between the source host and the destination host, then the end-to-end service also guarantees reliable/ordered delivery.

The problem with this latter approach is that a sequence of hop-by-hop guarantees does not necessarily add up to an end-to-end guarantee. First, if a heterogeneous link (say, an Ethernet) is added to one end of the path, then there is no guarantee that this hop will preserve the same service as the other hops. Second, just because the sliding window protocol guarantees that messages are delivered correctly from node A to node B, and then from node B to node C, it does not guarantee that node B behaves perfectly. For example, network nodes have been known to introduce errors into messages while transferring them from an input buffer to an output buffer. They have also been known to accidentally reorder messages. As a consequence of these small windows of vulnerability, it is still necessary to provide true end-to-end checks to guarantee reliable/ordered service, even though the lower levels of the system also implement that functionality.

This discussion serves to illustrate one of the most important principles in system design—the *end-to-end argument*. In a nutshell, the end-to-end argument says that a function (in our example, providing reliable/ordered delivery) should not be provided in the lower levels of the system unless it can be completely and correctly implemented at that level. Therefore, this rule argues in favor of the TCP/IP approach. This rule is not absolute, however. It does allow for functions to be incompletely provided at a low level as a performance optimization. This is why it is perfectly consistent with the end-to-end argument to perform error detection (e.g., CRC) on a hop-by-hop basis; detecting and retransmitting a single corrupt packet across one hop is preferable to having to retransmit an entire file end-to-end.

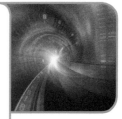

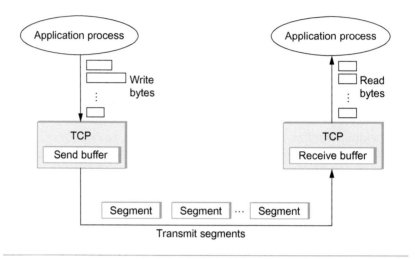

■ **FIGURE 5.3** How TCP manages a byte stream.

5.2.2 **Segment Format**

TCP is a byte-oriented protocol, which means that the sender writes bytes into a TCP connection and the receiver reads bytes out of the TCP connection. Although "byte stream" describes the service TCP offers to application processes, TCP does not, itself, transmit individual bytes over the Internet. Instead, TCP on the source host buffers enough bytes from the sending process to fill a reasonably sized packet and then sends this packet to its peer on the destination host. TCP on the destination host then empties the contents of the packet into a receive buffer, and the receiving process reads from this buffer at its leisure. This situation is illustrated in Figure 5.3, which, for simplicity, shows data flowing in only one direction. Remember that, in general, a single TCP connection supports byte streams flowing in both directions.

The packets exchanged between TCP peers in Figure 5.3 are called *segments*, since each one carries a segment of the byte stream. Each TCP segment contains the header schematically depicted in Figure 5.4. The relevance of most of these fields will become apparent throughout this section. For now, we simply introduce them.

The SrcPort and DstPort fields identify the source and destination ports, respectively, just as in UDP. These two fields, plus the source and destination IP addresses, combine to uniquely identify each TCP connection. That is, TCP's demux key is given by the 4-tuple

⟨ SrcPort, SrcIPAddr, DstPort, DstIPAddr ⟩

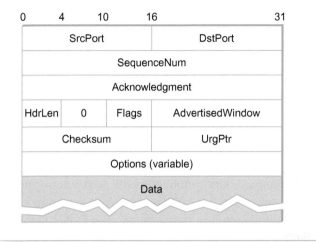

Note that because TCP connections come and go, it is possible for a connection between a particular pair of ports to be established, used to send
and receive data, and closed, and then at a later time for the same pair of
ports to be involved in a second connection. We sometimes refer to this
situation as two different *incarnations* of the same connection.

The Acknowledgment, SequenceNum, and AdvertisedWindow fields are
all involved in TCP's sliding window algorithm. Because TCP is a byte-
oriented protocol, each byte of data has a sequence number. The SequenceNum field contains the sequence number for the first byte of data
carried in that segment, and the Acknowledgment and AdvertisedWindow fields carry information about the flow of data going in the other
direction. To simplify our discussion, we ignore the fact that data can
flow in both directions, and we concentrate on data that has a particular SequenceNum flowing in one direction and Acknowledgment and
AdvertisedWindow values flowing in the opposite direction, as illustrated
in Figure 5.5. The use of these three fields is described more fully in
Section 5.2.4.

The 6-bit Flags field is used to relay control information between TCP
peers. The possible flags include SYN, FIN, RESET, PUSH, URG, and
ACK. The SYN and FIN flags are used when establishing and terminating a
TCP connection, respectively. Their use is described in Section 5.2.3. The
ACK flag is set any time the Acknowledgment field is valid, implying that
the receiver should pay attention to it. The URG flag signifies that this segment contains urgent data. When this flag is set, the UrgPtr field indicates

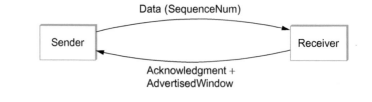

■ **FIGURE 5.5** Simplified illustration (showing only one direction) of the TCP process, with data flow in one direction and ACKs in the other.

where the nonurgent data contained in this segment begins. The urgent data is contained at the front of the segment body, up to and including a value of UrgPtr bytes into the segment. The **PUSH** flag signifies that the sender invoked the push operation, which indicates to the receiving side of TCP that it should notify the receiving process of this fact. We discuss these last two features more in Section 5.2.7. Finally, the **RESET** flag signifies that the receiver has become confused—for example, because it received a segment it did not expect to receive—and so wants to abort the connection.

Finally, the Checksum field is used in exactly the same way as for UDP—it is computed over the TCP header, the TCP data, and the pseudoheader, which is made up of the source address, destination address, and length fields from the IP header. The checksum is required for TCP in both IPv4 and IPv6. Also, since the TCP header is of variable length (options can be attached after the mandatory fields), a HdrLen field is included that gives the length of the header in 32-bit words. This field is also known as the Offset field, since it measures the offset from the start of the packet to the start of the data.

5.2.3 Connection Establishment and Termination

A TCP connection begins with a client (caller) doing an active open to a server (callee). Assuming that the server had earlier done a passive open, the two sides engage in an exchange of messages to establish the connection. (Recall from Chapter 1 that a party wanting to initiate a connection performs an active open, while a party willing to accept a connection does a passive open.) Only after this connection establishment phase is over do the two sides begin sending data. Likewise, as soon as a participant is done sending data, it closes one direction of the connection, which causes TCP to initiate a round of connection termination messages. Notice that,

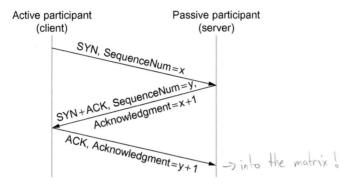

■ FIGURE 5.6 Timeline for three-way handshake algorithm.

while connection setup is an asymmetric activity (one side does a passive open and the other side does an active open), connection teardown is
symmetric (each side has to close the connection independently).[1] Therefore, it is possible for one side to have done a close, meaning that it can
no longer send data, but for the other side to keep the other half of the
bidirectional connection open and to continue sending data.

Three-Way Handshake

The algorithm used by TCP to establish and terminate a connection is
called a *three-way handshake*. We first describe the basic algorithm and
then show how it is used by TCP. The three-way handshake involves
the exchange of three messages between the client and the server, as
illustrated by the timeline given in Figure 5.6.

The idea is that two parties want to agree on a set of parameters, which,
in the case of opening a TCP connection, are the starting sequence numbers the two sides plan to use for their respective byte streams. In general,
the parameters might be any facts that each side wants the other to know
about. First, the client (the active participant) sends a segment to the
server (the passive participant) stating the initial sequence number it
plans to use (**Flags** = **SYN, SequenceNum** = x). The server then responds
with a single segment that both acknowledges the client's sequence number (**Flags** = **ACK, Ack** = $x + 1$) and states its own beginning sequence
number (**Flags** = **SYN, SequenceNum** = y). That is, both the **SYN** and

---

[1] To be more precise, connection setup can be symmetric, with both sides trying to open
the connection at the same time, but the common case is for one side to do an active
open and the other side to do a passive open.

ACK bits are set in the Flags field of this second message. Finally, the client responds with a third segment that acknowledges the server's sequence number (Flags = ACK, Ack = $y + 1$). The reason why each side acknowledges a sequence number that is one larger than the one sent is that the Acknowledgment field actually identifies the "next sequence number expected," thereby implicitly acknowledging all earlier sequence numbers. Although not shown in this timeline, a timer is scheduled for each of the first two segments, and if the expected response is not received the segment is retransmitted.

You may be asking yourself why the client and server have to exchange starting sequence numbers with each other at connection setup time. It would be simpler if each side simply started at some "well-known" sequence number, such as 0. In fact, the TCP specification requires that each side of a connection select an initial starting sequence number at random. The reason for this is to protect against two incarnations of the same connection reusing the same sequence numbers too soon—that is, while there is still a chance that a segment from an earlier incarnation of a connection might interfere with a later incarnation of the connection.

State-Transition Diagram

TCP is complex enough that its specification includes a state-transition diagram. A copy of this diagram is given in Figure 5.7. This diagram shows only the states involved in opening a connection (everything above ESTABLISHED) and in closing a connection (everything below ESTABLISHED). Everything that goes on while a connection is open—that is, the operation of the sliding window algorithm—is hidden in the ESTABLISHED state.

TCP's state-transition diagram is fairly easy to understand. Each circle denotes a state that one end of a TCP connection can find itself in. All connections start in the CLOSED state. As the connection progresses, the connection moves from state to state according to the arcs. Each arc is labeled with a tag of the form *event/action*. Thus, if a connection is in the LISTEN state and a SYN segment arrives (i.e., a segment with the SYN flag set), the connection makes a transition to the SYN_RCVD state and takes the action of replying with an ACK + SYN segment.

Notice that two kinds of events trigger a state transition: (1) a segment arrives from the peer (e.g., the event on the arc from LISTEN to

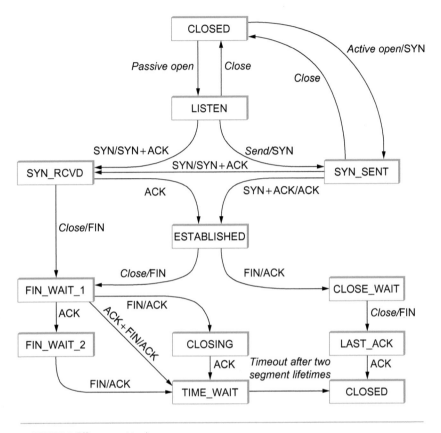

SYN_RCVD), or (2) the local application process invokes an operation on TCP (e.g., the *active open* event on the arc from CLOSED to SYN_SENT). In other words, TCP's state-transition diagram effectively defines the *semantics* of both its peer-to-peer interface and its service interface, as defined in Section 1.3.1. The *syntax* of these two interfaces is given by the segment format (as illustrated in Figure 5.4) and by some application programming interface (an example of which is given in Section 1.4.1), respectively.

Now let's trace the typical transitions taken through the diagram in Figure 5.7. Keep in mind that at each end of the connection, TCP makes different transitions from state to state. When opening a connection, the server first invokes a passive open operation on TCP, which causes TCP to move to the LISTEN state. At some later time, the client does an active open, which causes its end of the connection to send a SYN segment to the server and to move to the SYN_SENT state. When the SYN segment arrives at the server, it moves to the SYN_RCVD state and responds with a SYN + ACK segment. The arrival of this segment causes the client to move to the ESTABLISHED state and to send an ACK back to the server. When this ACK arrives, the server finally moves to the ESTABLISHED state. In other words, we have just traced the three-way handshake.

There are three things to notice about the connection establishment half of the state-transition diagram. First, if the client's ACK to the server is lost, corresponding to the third leg of the three-way handshake, then the connection still functions correctly. This is because the client side is already in the ESTABLISHED state, so the local application process can start sending data to the other end. Each of these data segments will have the ACK flag set, and the correct value in the Acknowledgment field, so the server will move to the ESTABLISHED state when the first data segment arrives. This is actually an important point about TCP—every segment reports what sequence number the sender is expecting to see next, even if this repeats the same sequence number contained in one or more previous segments.

The second thing to notice about the state-transition diagram is that there is a funny transition out of the LISTEN state whenever the local process invokes a *send* operation on TCP. That is, it is possible for a passive participant to identify both ends of the connection (i.e., itself and the remote participant that it is willing to have connect to it), and then for it to change its mind about waiting for the other side and instead actively establish the connection. To the best of our knowledge, this is a feature of TCP that no application process actually takes advantage of.

The final thing to notice about the diagram is the arcs that are not shown. Specifically, most of the states that involve sending a segment to the other side also schedule a timeout that eventually causes the segment to be present if the expected response does not happen. These retransmissions are not depicted in the state-transition diagram. If after several tries the expected response does not arrive, TCP gives up and returns to the CLOSED state.

Turning our attention now to the process of terminating a connection, the important thing to keep in mind is that the application process on both sides of the connection must independently close its half of the connection. If only one side closes the connection, then this means it has no more data to send, but it is still available to receive data from the other side. This complicates the state-transition diagram because it must account for the possibility that the two sides invoke the *close* operator at the same time, as well as the possibility that first one side invokes close and then, at some later time, the other side invokes close. Thus, on any one side there are three combinations of transitions that get a connection from the ESTABLISHED state to the CLOSED state:

- This side closes first: ESTABLISHED → FIN_WAIT_1 → FIN_WAIT_2 → TIME_WAIT → CLOSED.
- The other side closes first: ESTABLISHED → CLOSE_WAIT → LAST_ACK → CLOSED.
- Both sides close at the same time: ESTABLISHED → FIN_WAIT_1 → CLOSING → TIME_WAIT → CLOSED.

There is actually a fourth, although rare, sequence of transitions that leads to the CLOSED state; it follows the arc from FIN_WAIT_1 to TIME_WAIT. We leave it as an exercise for you to figure out what combination of circumstances leads to this fourth possibility.

The main thing to recognize about connection teardown is that a connection in the TIME_WAIT state cannot move to the CLOSED state until it has waited for two times the maximum amount of time an IP datagram might live in the Internet (i.e., 120 seconds). The reason for this is that, while the local side of the connection has sent an ACK in response to the other side's FIN segment, it does not know that the ACK was successfully delivered. As a consequence, the other side might retransmit its FIN segment, and this second FIN segment might be delayed in the network. If the connection were allowed to move directly to the CLOSED state, then another pair of application processes might come along and open the same connection (i.e., use the same pair of port numbers), and the delayed FIN segment from the earlier incarnation of the connection would immediately initiate the termination of the later incarnation of that connection.

5.2.4 Sliding Window Revisited

We are now ready to discuss TCP's variant of the sliding window algorithm, which serves several purposes: (1) it guarantees the reliable delivery of data, (2) it ensures that data is delivered in order, and (3) it enforces flow control between the sender and the receiver. TCP's use of the sliding window algorithm is the same as we saw in Section 2.5.2 in the case of the first two of these three functions. Where TCP differs from the earlier algorithm is that it folds the flow-control function in as well. In particular, rather than having a fixed-size sliding window, the receiver *advertises* a window size to the sender. This is done using the AdvertisedWindow field in the TCP header. The sender is then limited to having no more than a value of AdvertisedWindow bytes of unacknowledged data at any given time. The receiver selects a suitable value for AdvertisedWindow based on the amount of memory allocated to the connection for the purpose of buffering data. The idea is to keep the sender from over-running the receiver's buffer. We discuss this at greater length below.

Reliable and Ordered Delivery

To see how the sending and receiving sides of TCP interact with each other to implement reliable and ordered delivery, consider the situation illustrated in Figure 5.8. TCP on the sending side maintains a send buffer. This buffer is used to store data that has been sent but not yet acknowledged, as well as data that has been written by the sending application but not transmitted. On the receiving side, TCP maintains a receive buffer. This buffer holds data that arrives out of order, as well as data that is in the correct order (i.e., there are no missing bytes earlier in the stream) but that the application process has not yet had the chance to read.

To make the following discussion simpler to follow, we initially ignore the fact that both the buffers and the sequence numbers are of some finite

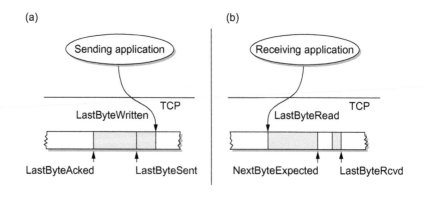

■ FIGURE 5.8 Relationship between TCP send buffer (a) and receive buffer (b).

size and hence will eventually wrap around. Also, we do not distinguish between a pointer into a buffer where a particular byte of data is stored and the sequence number for that byte.

Looking first at the sending side, three pointers are maintained into the send buffer, each with an obvious meaning: LastByteAcked, LastByteSent, and LastByteWritten. Clearly,

$$\text{LastByteAcked} \leq \text{LastByteSent}$$

since the receiver cannot have acknowledged a byte that has not yet been sent, and

$$\text{LastByteSent} \leq \text{LastByteWritten}$$

since TCP cannot send a byte that the application process has not yet written. Also note that none of the bytes to the left of LastByteAcked need to be saved in the buffer because they have already been acknowledged, and none of the bytes to the right of LastByteWritten need to be buffered because they have not yet been generated.

A similar set of pointers (sequence numbers) are maintained on the receiving side: LastByteRead, NextByteExpected, and LastByteRcvd. The inequalities are a little less intuitive, however, because of the problem of out-of-order delivery. The first relationship

$$\text{LastByteRead} < \text{NextByteExpected}$$

is true because a byte cannot be read by the application until it is received *and* all preceding bytes have also been received. NextByteExpected points to the byte immediately after the latest byte to meet this criterion. Second,

$$\text{NextByteExpected} \leq \text{LastByteRcvd} + 1$$

since, if data has arrived in order, NextByteExpected points to the byte after LastByteRcvd, whereas if data has arrived out of order, then NextByteExpected points to the start of the first gap in the data, as in Figure 5.8. Note that bytes to the left of LastByteRead need not be buffered because they have already been read by the local application process, and bytes to the right of LastByteRcvd need not be buffered because they have not yet arrived.

Flow Control

Most of the above discussion is similar to that found in Section 2.5.2; the only real difference is that this time we elaborated on the fact that the sending and receiving application processes are filling and emptying their local buffer, respectively. (The earlier discussion glossed over the fact that data arriving from an upstream node was filling the send buffer and data being transmitted to a downstream node was emptying the receive buffer.)

You should make sure you understand this much before proceeding because now comes the point where the two algorithms differ more significantly. In what follows, we reintroduce the fact that both buffers are of some finite size, denoted MaxSendBuffer and MaxRcvBuffer, although we don't worry about the details of how they are implemented. In other words, we are only interested in the number of bytes being buffered, not in where those bytes are actually stored.

Recall that in a sliding window protocol, the size of the window sets the amount of data that can be sent without waiting for acknowledgment from the receiver. Thus, the receiver throttles the sender by advertising a window that is no larger than the amount of data that it can buffer. Observe that TCP on the receive side must keep

$$\mathsf{LastByteRcvd} - \mathsf{LastByteRead} \leq \mathsf{MaxRcvBuffer}$$

to avoid overflowing its buffer. It therefore advertises a window size of

$$\mathsf{AdvertisedWindow} = \mathsf{MaxRcvBuffer} - ((\mathsf{NextByteExpected} - 1)$$
$$- \mathsf{LastByteRead})$$

which represents the amount of free space remaining in its buffer. As data arrives, the receiver acknowledges it as long as all the preceding bytes have also arrived. In addition, LastByteRcvd moves to the right (is incremented), meaning that the advertised window potentially shrinks. Whether or not it shrinks depends on how fast the local application process is consuming data. If the local process is reading data just as fast as it arrives (causing LastByteRead to be incremented at the same rate as LastByteRcvd), then the advertised window stays open (i.e., AdvertisedWindow = MaxRcvBuffer). If, however, the receiving process falls behind, perhaps because it performs a very expensive operation on each byte of data that it reads, then the advertised window grows smaller with every segment that arrives, until it eventually goes to 0.

TCP on the send side must then adhere to the advertised window it gets from the receiver. This means that at any given time, it must ensure that

$$\mathsf{LastByteSent} - \mathsf{LastByteAcked} \leq \mathsf{AdvertisedWindow}$$

Said another way, the sender computes an *effective* window that limits how much data it can send:

EffectiveWindow = AdvertisedWindow − (LastByteSent − LastByteAcked)

Clearly, EffectiveWindow must be greater than 0 before the source can send more data. It is possible, therefore, that a segment arrives acknowledging x bytes, thereby allowing the sender to increment LastByteAcked by x, but because the receiving process was not reading any data, the advertised window is now x bytes smaller than the time before. In such a situation, the sender would be able to free buffer space, but not to send any more data.

All the while this is going on, the send side must also make sure that the local application process does not overflow the send buffer—that is, that

$$\text{LastByteWritten} - \text{LastByteAcked} \leq \text{MaxSendBuffer}$$

If the sending process tries to write y bytes to TCP, but

$$(\text{LastByteWritten} - \text{LastByteAcked}) + y > \text{MaxSendBuffer}$$

then TCP blocks the sending process and does not allow it to generate more data.

It is now possible to understand how a slow receiving process ultimately stops a fast sending process. First, the receive buffer fills up, which means the advertised window shrinks to 0. An advertised window of 0 means that the sending side cannot transmit any data, even though data it has previously sent has been successfully acknowledged. Finally, not being able to transmit any data means that the send buffer fills up, which ultimately causes TCP to block the sending process. As soon as the receiving process starts to read data again, the receive-side TCP is able to open its window back up, which allows the send-side TCP to transmit data out of its buffer. When this data is eventually acknowledged, LastByteAcked is incremented, the buffer space holding this acknowledged data becomes free, and the sending process is unblocked and allowed to proceed.

There is only one remaining detail that must be resolved—how does the sending side know that the advertised window is no longer 0? As mentioned above, TCP *always* sends a segment in response to a received data segment, and this response contains the latest values for the Acknowledge and AdvertisedWindow fields, even if these values have not changed since the last time they were sent. The problem is this. Once the receive side has advertised a window size of 0, the sender is not permitted to send any more data, which means it has no way to discover that the advertised window is no longer 0 at some time in the future. TCP on the receive side does not spontaneously send nondata segments; it only sends them in response to an arriving data segment.

TCP deals with this situation as follows. Whenever the other side advertises a window size of 0, the sending side persists in sending a segment with 1 byte of data every so often. It knows that this data will probably not be accepted, but it tries anyway, because each of these 1-byte segments triggers a response that contains the current advertised window. Eventually, one of these 1-byte probes triggers a response that reports a nonzero advertised window.

Note that the reason the sending side periodically sends this probe segment is that TCP is designed to make the receive side as simple as possible—it simply responds to segments from the sender, and it never initiates any activity on its own. This is an example of a well-recognized (although not universally applied) protocol design rule, which, for lack of a better name, we call the *smart sender/dumb receiver* rule. Recall that we saw another example of this rule when we discussed the use of NAKs in Section 2.5.2.

Protecting against Wraparound

This subsection and the next consider the size of the SequenceNum and AdvertisedWindow fields and the implications of their sizes on TCP's correctness and performance. TCP's SequenceNum field is 32 bits long, and its AdvertisedWindow field is 16 bits long, meaning that TCP has easily satisfied the requirement of the sliding window algorithm that the sequence number space be twice as big as the window size: $2^{32} \gg 2 \times 2^{16}$. However, this requirement is not the interesting thing about these two fields. Consider each field in turn.

The relevance of the 32-bit sequence number space is that the sequence number used on a given connection might wrap around—a byte with sequence number x could be sent at one time, and then at a later time a second byte with the same sequence number x might be sent. Once again, we assume that packets cannot survive in the Internet for longer than the recommended MSL. Thus, we currently need to make sure that the sequence number does not wrap around within a 120-second period

Table 5.1 Time Until 32-Bit Sequence Number Space Wraps Around

Bandwidth	Time until Wraparound
T1 (1.5 Mbps)	6.4 hours
Ethernet (10 Mbps)	57 minutes
T3 (45 Mbps)	13 minutes
Fast Ethernet (100 Mbps)	6 minutes
OC-3 (155 Mbps)	4 minutes
OC-12 (622 Mbps)	55 seconds
OC-48 (2.5 Gbps)	14 seconds

of time. Whether or not this happens depends on how fast data can be transmitted over the Internet—that is, how fast the 32-bit sequence number space can be consumed. (This discussion assumes that we are trying to consume the sequence number space as fast as possible, but of course we will be if we are doing our job of keeping the pipe full.) Table 5.1 shows how long it takes for the sequence number to wrap around on networks with various bandwidths.

As you can see, the 32-bit sequence number space is adequate for most situations encountered on today's networks, but given that OC-192 links exist in the Internet backbone, and that most servers now come with gigabit Ethernet (or 10 Gbps) interfaces, it is getting close to the point where 32 bits is too small. Fortunately, the IETF has already worked out an extension to TCP that effectively extends the sequence number space to protect against the sequence number wrapping around. This and related extensions are described in Section 5.2.8.

Keeping the Pipe Full

The relevance of the 16-bit AdvertisedWindow field is that it must be big enough to allow the sender to keep the pipe full. Clearly, the receiver is free to not open the window as large as the AdvertisedWindow field allows; we are interested in the situation in which the receiver has enough buffer space to handle as much data as the largest possible AdvertisedWindow allows.

In this case, it is not just the network bandwidth but the delay × bandwidth product that dictates how big the AdvertisedWindow field needs to

Table 5.2 Required Window Size for 100-ms RTT

Bandwidth	Delay × Bandwidth Product
T1 (1.5 Mbps)	18 KB
Ethernet (10 Mbps)	122 KB
T3 (45 Mbps)	549 KB
Fast Ethernet (100 Mbps)	1.2 MB
OC-3 (155 Mbps)	1.8 MB
OC-12 (622 Mbps)	7.4 MB
OC-48 (2.5 Gbps)	29.6 MB

be—the window needs to be opened far enough to allow a full delay × bandwidth product's worth of data to be transmitted. Assuming an RTT of 100 ms (a typical number for a cross-country connection in the United States), Table 5.2 gives the delay × bandwidth product for several network technologies.

As you can see, TCP's AdvertisedWindow field is in even worse shape than its SequenceNum field—it is not big enough to handle even a T3 connection across the continental United States, since a 16-bit field allows us to advertise a window of only 64 KB. The very same TCP extension mentioned above (see Section 5.2.8) provides a mechanism for effectively increasing the size of the advertised window.

5.2.5 Triggering Transmission

We next consider a surprisingly subtle issue: how TCP decides to transmit a segment. As described earlier, TCP supports a byte-stream abstraction; that is, application programs write bytes into the stream, and it is up to TCP to decide that it has enough bytes to send a segment. What factors govern this decision?

If we ignore the possibility of flow control—that is, we assume the window is wide open, as would be the case when a connection first starts—then TCP has three mechanisms to trigger the transmission of a segment. First, TCP maintains a variable, typically called the *maximum segment size* (MSS), and it sends a segment as soon as it has collected MSS bytes from the sending process. MSS is usually set to the size of the largest segment TCP can send without causing the local IP to fragment. That is, **MSS** is set to the maximum transmission unit (MTU) of the directly connected network, minus the size of the TCP and IP headers. The second thing that triggers TCP to transmit a segment is that the sending process has explicitly asked it to do so. Specifically, TCP supports a *push* operation, and the sending process invokes this operation to effectively flush the buffer of unsent bytes. The final trigger for transmitting a segment is that a timer fires; the resulting segment contains as many bytes as are currently buffered for transmission. However, as we will soon see, this "timer" isn't exactly what you expect.

Silly Window Syndrome

Of course, we can't just ignore flow control, which plays an obvious role in throttling the sender. If the sender has **MSS** bytes of data to send and the window is open at least that much, then the sender transmits a full segment. Suppose, however, that the sender is accumulating bytes to send, but the window is currently closed. Now suppose an ACK arrives that effectively opens the window enough for the sender to transmit, say, **MSS**/2 bytes. Should the sender transmit a half-full segment or wait for the window to open to a full **MSS**? The original specification was silent on this point, and early implementations of TCP decided to go ahead and transmit a half-full segment. After all, there is no telling how long it will be before the window opens further.

It turns out that the strategy of aggressively taking advantage of any available window leads to a situation now known as the *silly window syndrome*. Figure 5.9 helps visualize what happens. If you think of a TCP stream as a conveyer belt with "full" containers (data segments) going in one direction and empty containers (ACKs) going in the reverse direction, then **MSS**-sized segments correspond to large containers and 1-byte segments correspond to very small containers. As long as the sender is sending **MSS**-sized segments and the receiver ACKs at least one **MSS** of data at a time, everything is good (Figure 5.9(a)). But, what if the receiver has to reduce the window, so that at some time the sender can't send a full **MSS** of data? If the sender aggressively fills a smaller-than-**MSS** empty container as soon as it arrives, then the receiver will ACK that smaller number of bytes, and hence the small container introduced into the system remains in the system indefinitely. That is, it is immediately filled and emptied at each end and is never coalesced with adjacent containers to

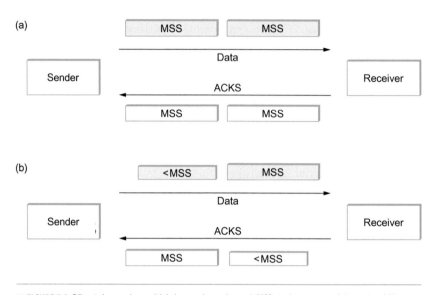

■ **FIGURE 5.9** Silly window syndrome. (a) As long as the sender sends MSS-sized segments and the receiver ACKs one MSS at a time, the system works smoothly. (b) As soon as the sender sends less than one **MSS**, or the receiver ACKs less than one **MSS**, a small "container" enters the system and continues to circulate.

create larger containers, as in Figure 5.9(b). This scenario was discovered when early implementations of TCP regularly found themselves filling the network with tiny segments.

Note that the silly window syndrome is only a problem when either the sender transmits a small segment or the receiver opens the window a small amount. If neither of these happens, then the small container is never introduced into the stream. It's not possible to outlaw sending small segments; for example, the application might do a *push* after sending a single byte. It is possible, however, to keep the receiver from introducing a small container (i.e., a small open window). The rule is that after advertising a zero window the receiver must wait for space equal to an **MSS** before it advertises an open window.

Since we can't eliminate the possibility of a small container being introduced into the stream, we also need mechanisms to coalesce them. The receiver can do this by delaying ACKs—sending one combined ACK rather than multiple smaller ones—but this is only a partial solution because the receiver has no way of knowing how long it is safe to delay waiting either for another segment to arrive or for the application to read more data (thus opening the window). The ultimate solution falls to the sender, which brings us back to our original issue: When does the TCP sender decide to transmit a segment?

Nagle's Algorithm

Returning to the TCP sender, if there is data to send but the window is open less than MSS, then we may want to wait some amount of time before sending the available data, but the question is how long? If we wait too long, then we hurt interactive applications like Telnet. If we don't wait long enough, then we risk sending a bunch of tiny packets and falling into the silly window syndrome. The answer is to introduce a timer and to transmit when the timer expires.

While we could use a clock-based timer—for example, one that fires every 100 ms—Nagle introduced an elegant *self-clocking* solution. The idea is that as long as TCP has any data in flight, the sender will eventually receive an ACK. This ACK can be treated like a timer firing, triggering the transmission of more data. Nagle's algorithm provides a simple, unified rule for deciding when to transmit:

```
When the application produces data to send
  if both the available data and the window ≥ MSS
    send a full segment
  else
    if there is unACKed data in flight
      buffer the new data until an ACK arrives
    else
      send all the new data now
```

In other words, it's always OK to send a full segment if the window allows. It's also all right to immediately send a small amount of data if there are currently no segments in transit, but if there is anything in flight the sender must wait for an ACK before transmitting the next segment. Thus, an interactive application like Telnet that continually writes one byte at a time will send data at a rate of one segment per RTT. Some segments will contain a single byte, while others will contain as many bytes as the user was able to type in one round-trip time. Because some applications cannot afford such a delay for each write it does to a TCP connection, the socket interface allows the application to turn off Nagel's algorithm by setting the TCP_NODELAY option. Setting this option means that data is transmitted as soon as possible.

5.2.6 Adaptive Retransmission

Because TCP guarantees the reliable delivery of data, it retransmits each segment if an ACK is not received in a certain period of time. TCP sets this timeout as a function of the RTT it expects between the two ends of the connection. Unfortunately, given the range of possible RTTs between any pair of hosts in the Internet, as well as the variation in RTT between the same two hosts over time, choosing an appropriate timeout value is not that easy. To address this problem, TCP uses an adaptive retransmission mechanism. We now describe this mechanism and how it has evolved over time as the Internet community has gained more experience using TCP.

Original Algorithm

We begin with a simple algorithm for computing a timeout value between a pair of hosts. This is the algorithm that was originally described in the TCP specification—and the following description presents it in those terms—but it could be used by any end-to-end protocol.

The idea is to keep a running average of the RTT and then to compute the timeout as a function of this RTT. Specifically, every time TCP sends a data segment, it records the time. When an ACK for that segment arrives, TCP reads the time again, and then takes the difference between these two times as a SampleRTT. TCP then computes an EstimatedRTT as a weighted average between the previous estimate and this new sample. That is,

$$\mathsf{EstimatedRTT} = \alpha \times \mathsf{EstimatedRTT} + (1 - \alpha) \times \mathsf{SampleRTT}$$

The parameter α is selected to *smooth* the EstimatedRTT. A small α tracks changes in the RTT but is perhaps too heavily influenced by temporary fluctuations. On the other hand, a large α is more stable but perhaps not quick enough to adapt to real changes. The original TCP specification recommended a setting of α between 0.8 and 0.9. TCP then uses EstimatedRTT to compute the timeout in a rather conservative way:

$$\mathsf{TimeOut} = 2 \times \mathsf{EstimatedRTT}$$

Karn/Partridge Algorithm

After several years of use on the Internet, a rather obvious flaw was discovered in this simple algorithm. The problem was that an ACK does not really acknowledge a transmission; it actually acknowledges the receipt of data. In other words, whenever a segment is retransmitted and then

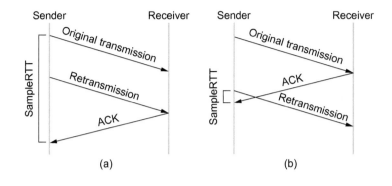

an ACK arrives at the sender, it is impossible to determine if this ACK should be associated with the first or the second transmission of the segment for the purpose of measuring the sample RTT. It is necessary to know which transmission to associate it with so as to compute an accurate SampleRTT. As illustrated in Figure 5.10, if you assume that the ACK is for the original transmission but it was really for the second, then the SampleRTT is too large (a); if you assume that the ACK is for the second transmission but it was actually for the first, then the SampleRTT is too small (b).

The solution, which was proposed in 1987, is surprisingly simple. Whenever TCP retransmits a segment, it stops taking samples of the RTT; it only measures SampleRTT for segments that have been sent only once. This solution is known as the Karn/Partridge algorithm, after its inventors. Their proposed fix also includes a second small change to TCP's timeout mechanism. Each time TCP retransmits, it sets the next timeout to be twice the last timeout, rather than basing it on the last EstimatedRTT. That is, Karn and Partridge proposed that TCP use exponential backoff, similar to what the Ethernet does. The motivation for using exponential backoff is simple: Congestion is the most likely cause of lost segments, meaning that the TCP source should not react too aggressively to a timeout. In fact, the more times the connection times out, the more cautious the source should become. We will see this idea again, embodied in a much more sophisticated mechanism, in Chapter 6.

Jacobson/Karels Algorithm
The Karn/Partridge algorithm was introduced at a time when the Internet was suffering from high levels of network congestion. Their approach

was designed to fix some of the causes of that congestion, but, although it was an improvement, the congestion was not eliminated. The following year (1988), two other researchers—Jacobson and Karels—proposed a more drastic change to TCP to battle congestion. The bulk of that proposed change is described in Chapter 6. Here, we focus on the aspect of that proposal that is related to deciding when to time out and retransmit a segment.

As an aside, it should be clear how the timeout mechanism is related to congestion—if you time out too soon, you may unnecessarily retransmit a segment, which only adds to the load on the network. As we will see in Chapter 6, the other reason for needing an accurate timeout value is that a timeout is taken to imply congestion, which triggers a congestion-control mechanism. Finally, note that there is nothing about the Jacobson/Karels timeout computation that is specific to TCP. It could be used by any end-to-end protocol.

The main problem with the original computation is that it does not take the variance of the sample RTTs into account. Intuitively, if the variation among samples is small, then the EstimatedRTT can be better trusted and there is no reason for multiplying this estimate by 2 to compute the timeout. On the other hand, a large variance in the samples suggests that the timeout value should not be too tightly coupled to the EstimatedRTT.

In the new approach, the sender measures a new SampleRTT as before. It then folds this new sample into the timeout calculation as follows:

$$\text{Difference} = \text{SampleRTT} - \text{EstimatedRTT}$$

$$\text{EstimatedRTT} = \text{EstimatedRTT} + (\delta \times \text{Difference})$$

$$\text{Deviation} = \text{Deviation} + \delta(|\text{Difference}| - \text{Deviation})$$

where δ is a fraction between 0 and 1. That is, we calculate both the mean RTT and the variation in that mean.

TCP then computes the timeout value as a function of both EstimatedRTT and Deviation as follows:

$$\text{TimeOut} = \mu \times \text{EstimatedRTT} + \phi \times \text{Deviation}$$

where based on experience, μ is typically set to 1 and ϕ is set to 4. Thus, when the variance is small, TimeOut is close to EstimatedRTT; a large variance causes the Deviation term to dominate the calculation.

Implementation

There are two items of note regarding the implementation of timeouts in TCP. The first is that it is possible to implement the calculation for Estimat-edRTT and Deviation without using floating-point arithmetic. Instead, the whole calculation is scaled by 2^n, with δ selected to be $1/2^n$. This allows us to do integer arithmetic, implementing multiplication and division using shifts, thereby achieving higher performance. The resulting calculation is given by the following code fragment, where $n = 3$ (i.e., $\delta = 1/8$). Note that EstimatedRTT and Deviation are stored in their scaled-up forms, while the value of SampleRTT at the start of the code and of TimeOut at the end are real, unscaled values. If you find the code hard to follow, you might want to try plugging some real numbers into it and verifying that it gives the same results as the equations above.

```
{
    SampleRTT -= (EstimatedRTT >> 3);
    EstimatedRTT += SampleRTT;
    if (SampleRTT < 0)
        SampleRTT = -SampleRTT;
    SampleRTT -= (Deviation >> 3);
    Deviation += SampleRTT;
    TimeOut = (EstimatedRTT >> 3) + (Deviation >> 1);
}
```

The second point of note is that the Jacobson/Karels algorithm is only as good as the clock used to read the current time. On typical Unix imple-mentations at the time, the clock granularity was as large as 500 ms, which is significantly larger than the average cross-country RTT of somewhere between 100 and 200 ms. To make matters worse, the Unix implementa-tion of TCP only checked to see if a timeout should happen every time this 500-ms clock ticked and would only take a sample of the round-trip time once per RTT. The combination of these two factors could mean that a timeout would happen 1 second after the segment was transmitted. Once again, the extensions to TCP include a mechanism that makes this RTT calculation a bit more precise.

All of the retransmission algorithms we have discussed are based on acknowledgment timeouts, which indicate that a segment has probably been lost. Note that a timeout does not, however, tell the sender whether any segments it sent after the lost segment were successfully received.

This is because TCP acknowledgments are cumulative; they identify only the last segment that was received without any preceding gaps. The reception of segments that occur after a gap grows more frequent as faster networks lead to larger windows. If ACKs also told the sender which subsequent segments, if any, had been received, then the sender could be more intelligent about which segments it retransmits, draw better conclusions about the state of congestion, and make better RTT estimates. A TCP extension supporting this is described in Section 5.2.8.

5.2.7 Record Boundaries

Since TCP is a byte-stream protocol, the number of bytes written by the sender are not necessarily the same as the number of bytes read by the receiver. For example, the application might write 8 bytes, then 2 bytes, then 20 bytes to a TCP connection, while on the receiving side the application reads 5 bytes at a time inside a loop that iterates 6 times. TCP does not interject record boundaries between the 8th and 9th bytes, nor between the 10th and 11th bytes. This is in contrast to a message-oriented protocol, such as UDP, in which the message that is sent is exactly the same length as the message that is received.

Even though TCP is a byte-stream protocol, it has two different features that can be used by the sender to insert record boundaries into this byte stream, thereby informing the receiver how to break the stream of bytes into records. (Being able to mark record boundaries is useful, for example, in many database applications.) Both of these features were originally included in TCP for completely different reasons; they have only come to be used for this purpose over time.

The first mechanism is the urgent data feature, as implemented by the URG flag and the UrgPtr field in the TCP header. Originally, the urgent data mechanism was designed to allow the sending application to send *out-of-band* data to its peer. By "out of band" we mean data that is separate from the normal flow of data (e.g., a command to interrupt an operation already under way). This out-of-band data was identified in the segment using the UrgPtr field and was to be delivered to the receiving process as soon as it arrived, even if that meant delivering it before data with an earlier sequence number. Over time, however, this feature has not been used, so instead of signifying "urgent" data, it has come to be used to signify "special" data, such as a record marker. This use has developed because, as with the push operation, TCP on the receiving side must inform the application that urgent data has arrived. That is, the urgent data in itself is not important. It is the fact that the sending process can effectively send a signal to the receiver that is important.

The second mechanism for inserting end-of-record markers into a byte is the *push* operation. Originally, this mechanism was designed to allow the sending process to tell TCP that it should send (flush) whatever bytes it had collected to its peer. The *push* operation can be used to implement record boundaries because the specification says that TCP must send whatever data it has buffered at the source when the application says push, and, optionally, TCP at the destination notifies the application whenever an incoming segment has the PUSH flag set. If the receiving side supports this option (the socket interface does not), then the push operation can be used to break the TCP stream into records.

Of course, the application program is always free to insert record boundaries without any assistance from TCP. For example, it can send a field that indicates the length of a record that is to follow, or it can insert its own record boundary markers into the data stream.

5.2.8 TCP Extensions

We have mentioned at four different points in this section that there are now extensions to TCP that help to mitigate some problem that TCP is facing as the underlying network gets faster. These extensions are designed to have as small an impact on TCP as possible. In particular, they are realized as options that can be added to the TCP header. (We glossed over this point earlier, but the reason why the TCP header has a HdrLen field is that the header can be of variable length; the variable part of the TCP header contains the options that have been added.) The significance of adding these extensions as options rather than changing the core of the TCP header is that hosts can still communicate using TCP even if they do not implement the options. Hosts that do implement the optional extensions, however, can take advantage of them. The two sides agree that they will use the options during TCP's connection establishment phase.

The first extension helps to improve TCP's timeout mechanism. Instead of measuring the RTT using a coarse-grained event, TCP can read the actual system clock when it is about to send a segment, and put this time—think of it as a 32-bit *timestamp*—in the segment's header. The receiver then echoes this timestamp back to the sender in its acknowledgment, and the sender subtracts this timestamp from the current time to measure the RTT. In essence, the timestamp option provides a convenient place for TCP to store the record of when a segment was transmitted; it stores the time in the segment itself. Note that the endpoints in the connection do not need synchronized clocks, since the timestamp is written and read at the same end of the connection.

The second extension addresses the problem of TCP's 32-bit Sequence-Num field wrapping around too soon on a high-speed network. Rather than define a new 64-bit sequence number field, TCP uses the 32-bit timestamp just described to effectively extend the sequence number space. In other words, TCP decides whether to accept or reject a segment based on a 64-bit identifier that has the SequenceNum field in the low-order 32 bits and the timestamp in the high-order 32 bits. Since the timestamp is always increasing, it serves to distinguish between two different incarnations of the same sequence number. Note that the timestamp is being used in this setting only to protect against wraparound; it is not treated as part of the sequence number for the purpose of ordering or acknowledging data.

The third extension allows TCP to advertise a larger window, thereby allowing it to fill larger delay $\times$ bandwidth pipes that are made possible by high-speed networks. This extension involves an option that defines a *scaling factor* for the advertised window. That is, rather than interpreting the number that appears in the AdvertisedWindow field as indicating how many bytes the sender is allowed to have unacknowledged, this option allows the two sides of TCP to agree that the AdvertisedWindow field counts larger chunks (e.g., how many 16-byte units of data the sender can have unacknowledged). In other words, the window scaling option specifies how many bits each side should left-shift the AdvertisedWindow field before using its contents to compute an effective window.

The fourth extension allows TCP to augment its cumulative acknowledgment with selective acknowledgments of any additional segments that have been received but aren't contiguous with all previously received segments. This is the *selective acknowledgment*, or *SACK*, option. When the SACK option is used, the receiver continues to acknowledge segments normally—the meaning of the Acknowledge field does not change—but it also uses optional fields in the header to acknowledge any additional blocks of received data. This allows the sender to retransmit just the segments that are missing according to the selective acknowledgment.

Without SACK, there are only two reasonable strategies for a sender. The pessimistic strategy responds to a timeout by retransmitting not just the segment that timed out, but any segments transmitted subsequently. In effect, the pessimistic strategy assumes the worst: that all those segments were lost. The disadvantage of the pessimistic strategy is that it may unnecessarily retransmit segments that were successfully received the first time. The other strategy is the optimistic strategy, which responds to a timeout by retransmitting only the segment that timed out. In effect, the optimistic approach assumes the rosiest scenario: that only the one segment has been lost. The disadvantage of the optimistic strategy is that it is very slow, unnecessarily, when a series of consecutive segments has been lost, as might happen when there is congestion. It is slow because each segment's loss is not discovered until the sender receives an ACK for its retransmission of the previous segment. So it consumes one RTT per segment until it has retransmitted all the segments in the lost series. With the SACK option, a better strategy is available to the sender: retransmit just the segments that fill the gaps between the segments that have been selectively acknowledged.

These extensions, by the way, are not the full story. We'll see some more extensions in the next chapter when we look at how TCP handles congestion. The Internet Assigned Numbers Authority (IANA) keeps track of all the options that are defined for TCP (and for many other Internet protocols). About 30 TCP options were defined at the time of writing (quite a few are experimental or obsolete, however). See the references at the end of the chapter for a link to IANA's protocol number registry.

5.2.9 Performance

Recall that Chapter 1 introduced the two quantitative metrics by which network performance is evaluated: latency and throughput. As mentioned in that discussion, these metrics are influenced not only by the underlying hardware (e.g., propagation delay and link bandwidth) but also by software overheads. Now that we have a complete software-based protocol graph available to us that includes alternative transport protocols, we can discuss how to meaningfully measure its performance. The importance of such measurements is that they represent the performance seen by application programs.

We begin, as any report of experimental results should, by describing our experimental method. This includes the apparatus used in the experiments; in this case, each workstation has a pair of dual CPU 2.4-GHz Xeon processors running Linux. In order to enable speeds above 1 Gbps, a pair of Ethernet adaptors (labeled NIC, for network interface card) are used on

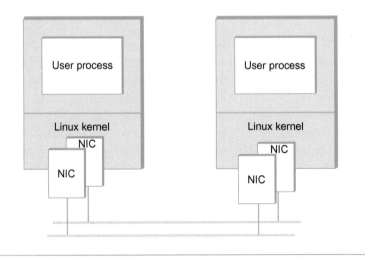

■ FIGURE 5.11 Measured system: Two Linux workstations and a pair of Gbps Ethernet links.

each machine. The Ethernet spans a single machine room so propagation is not an issue, making this a measure of processor/software overheads. A test program running on top of the socket interface simply tries to transfer data as quickly as possible from one machine to the other. Figure 5.11 illustrates the setup.

You may notice that this experimental setup is not especially bleeding edge in terms of the hardware or link speed. The point of this section is not to show how fast a particular protocol can run, but to illustrate the general methodology for measuring and reporting protocol performance.

The throughput test is performed for a variety of message sizes using a standard benchmarking tool called TTCP. The results of the throughput test are given in Figure 5.12. The key thing to notice in this graph is that throughput improves as the messages get larger. This makes sense—each message involves a certain amount of overhead, so a larger message means that this overhead is amortized over more bytes. The throughput curve flattens off above 1 KB, at which point the per-message overhead becomes insignificant when compared to the large number of bytes that the protocol stack has to process.

It's worth noting that the maximum throughput is less than 2 Gbps, the available link speed in this setup. Further testing and analysis of results would be needed to figure out where the bottleneck is (or if there is more than one). For example, looking at CPU load might give an indication

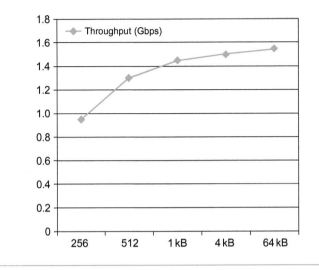

■ **FIGURE 5.12** Measured throughput using TCP, for various message sizes.

of whether the CPU is the bottleneck or whether memory bandwidth, adaptor performance, or some other issue is to blame.

We also note that the network in this test is basically "perfect." It has almost no delay or loss, so the only factors affecting performance are the TCP implementation and the workstation hardware and software. By contrast, most of the time we deal with networks that are far from perfect, notably our bandwidth-constrained, last-mile links and loss-prone wireless links. Before we can fully appreciate how these links affect TCP performance, we need to understand how TCP deals with *congestion*, which is the topic of Section 6.3.

At various times in the history of networking, the steadily increasing speed of network links has threatened to run ahead of what could be delivered to applications. For example, a large research effort was begun in the United States in 1989 to build "gigabit networks," where the goal was not only to build links and switches that could run at 1Gbps or higher but also to deliver that throughput all the way to a single application process. There were some real problems (e.g., network adaptors, workstation architectures, and operating systems all had to be designed with network-to-application throughput in mind) and also some perceived problems that turned out to be not so serious. High on the list of such problems was the concern that existing transport protocols, TCP in particular, might not be up to the challenge of gigabit operation.

As it turns out, TCP has done well keeping up with the increasing demands of high-speed networks and applications. One of the most important factors was the introduction of window scaling to deal with larger bandwidth-delay products. However, there is often a big difference between the theoretical performance of TCP and what is achieved in practice. Relatively simple problems like copying the data more times than necessary as it passes from network adaptor to application can drive down performance, as can insufficient buffer memory when the bandwidth-delay product is large. And the dynamics of TCP are complex enough (as will become even more apparent in the next chapter) that subtle interactions among network behavior, application behavior, and the TCP protocol itself can dramatically alter performance.

For our purposes, it's worth noting that TCP continues to perform very well as network speeds increase, and when it runs up against some limit (normally related to congestion, increasing bandwidth-delay products, or both), researchers rush in to find solutions. We've seen some of those in this chapter, and we'll see some more in the next.

5.2.10 Alternative Design Choices

Although TCP has proven to be a robust protocol that satisfies the needs of a wide range of applications, the design space for transport protocols is quite large. TCP is by no means the only valid point in that design space. We conclude our discussion of TCP by considering alternative design choices. While we offer an explanation for why TCP's designers made the choices they did, we observe that other protocols exist that have made other choices, and more such protocols may appear in the future.

First, we have suggested from the very first chapter of this book that there are at least two interesting classes of transport protocols: stream-oriented protocols like TCP and request/reply protocols like RPC. In other words, we have implicitly divided the design space in half and placed TCP squarely in the stream-oriented half of the world. We could further divide the stream-oriented protocols into two groups—reliable and unreliable—with the former containing TCP and the latter being more suitable for interactive video applications that would rather drop a frame than incur the delay associated with a retransmission.

This exercise in building a transport protocol taxonomy is interesting and could be continued in greater and greater detail, but the world isn't as black and white as we might like. Consider the suitability of TCP as a transport protocol for request/reply applications, for example. TCP is a full-duplex protocol, so it would be easy to open a TCP connection between the client and server, send the request message in one direction, and send the reply message in the other direction. There are two complications, however. The first is that TCP is a *byte*-oriented protocol rather than a *message*-oriented protocol, and request/reply applications always deal with messages. (We explore the issue of bytes versus messages in greater detail in a moment.) The second complication is that in those situations where both the request message and the reply message fit in a single network packet, a well-designed request/reply protocol needs only two packets to implement the exchange, whereas TCP would need at least nine: three to establish the connection, two for the message exchange, and four to tear down the connection. Of course, if the request or reply messages are large enough to require multiple network packets (e.g., it might take 100 packets to send a 100,000-byte reply message), then the overhead of setting up and tearing down the connection is inconsequential. In other words, it isn't always the case that a particular protocol cannot support a certain functionality; it's sometimes the case that one design is more efficient than another under particular circumstances.

Second, as just suggested, you might question why TCP chose to provide a reliable *byte*-stream service rather than a reliable *message*-stream service; messages would be the natural choice for a database application that wants to exchange records. There are two answers to this question. The first is that a message-oriented protocol must, by definition, establish an upper bound on message sizes. After all, an infinitely long message is a byte stream. For any message size that a protocol selects, there will be applications that want to send larger messages, rendering the transport protocol useless and forcing the application to implement its own transport-like services. The second reason is that, while message-oriented protocols are definitely more appropriate for applications that want to send records to each other, you can easily insert record boundaries into a byte stream to implement this functionality, as described in Section 5.2.7.

A third decision made in the design of TCP is that it delivers bytes *in order* to the application. This means that it may hold onto bytes that were received out of order from the network, awaiting some missing bytes to fill a hole. This is enormously helpful for many applications but turns out to be quite unhelpful if the application is capable of processing data out of order. As a simple example, a Web page containing multiple embedded images doesn't need all the images to be delivered in order before starting to display the page. In fact, there is a class of applications that would prefer to handle out-of-order data at the application layer, in return for getting data sooner when packets are dropped or misordered within the network. The desire to support such applications led to the creation of another IETF standard transport protocol known as the *Stream Control Transmission Protocol* (SCTP). SCTP provides a partially ordered delivery service, rather than the strictly ordered service of TCP. (SCTP also makes some other design decisions that differ from TCP, including message orientation and support of multiple IP addresses for a single session. See the Further Reading section for more details.)

Fourth, TCP chose to implement explicit setup/teardown phases, but this is not required. In the case of connection setup, it would certainly be possible to send all necessary connection parameters along with the first data message. TCP elected to take a more conservative approach that gives the receiver the opportunity to reject the connection before any data arrives. In the case of teardown, we could quietly close a connection that has been inactive for a long period of time, but this would complicate applications like Telnet that want to keep a connection alive for weeks at a time; such applications would be forced to send out-of-band "keep alive" messages to keep the connection state at the other end from disappearing.

Finally, TCP is a window-based protocol, but this is not the only possibility. The alternative is a *rate-based* design, in which the receiver tells the sender the rate—expressed in either bytes or packets per second—at which it is willing to accept incoming data. For example, the receiver might inform the sender that it can accommodate 100 packets a second. There is an interesting duality between windows and rate, since the number of packets (bytes) in the window, divided by the RTT, is exactly the rate. For example, a window size of 10 packets and a 100-ms RTT implies that the sender is allowed to transmit at a rate of 100 packets a second. It is by increasing or decreasing the advertised window size that the receiver is effectively raising or lowering the rate at which the sender can transmit. In TCP, this information is fed back to the sender in the AdvertisedWindow field of the ACK for every segment. One of the key issues in a rate-based protocol is how often the desired rate—which may change over time—is relayed back to the source: Is it for every packet, once per RTT, or only when the rate changes? While we have just now considered window versus rate in the context of flow control, it is an even more hotly

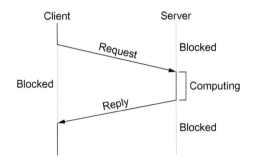

■ FIGURE 5.13 Timeline for RPC.

contested issue in the context of congestion control, which we will discuss in Chapter 6.

5.3 REMOTE PROCEDURE CALL

As discussed in Chapter 1, one common pattern of communication used by application programs is the request/reply paradigm, also called *message transaction*: A client sends a request message to a server, and the server responds with a reply message, with the client blocking (suspending execution) to wait for the reply. Figure 5.13 illustrates the basic interaction between the client and server in such a message transaction.

A transport protocol that supports the request/reply paradigm is much more than a UDP message going in one direction followed by a UDP message going in the other direction. It needs to deal with correctly identifying processes on remote hosts and correlating requests with responses. It may also need to overcome some or all of the limitations of the underlying network outlined in the problem statement at the beginning of this chapter. While TCP overcomes these limitations by providing a reliable byte-stream service, it doesn't match the request/reply paradigm very well either—going to the trouble to establish a TCP connection just to exchange a pair of messages seems like overkill. This section describes a third category of transport protocol, called *Remote Procedure Call* (RPC), that more closely matches the needs of an application involved in a request/reply message exchange.

5.3.1 RPC Fundamentals

RPC is actually more than just a protocol—it is a popular mechanism for structuring distributed systems. RPC is popular because it is based on the semantics of a local procedure call—the application program makes a call into a procedure without regard for whether it is local or remote and blocks until the call returns. An application developer can be largely unaware of whether the procedure is local or remote, simplifying his task considerably. When the procedures being called are actually methods of remote objects in an object-oriented language, RPC is known as *remote method invocation* (RMI). While the RPC concept is simple, there are two main problems that make it more complicated than local procedure calls:

- The network between the calling process and the called process has much more complex properties than the backplane of a computer. For example, it is likely to limit message sizes and has a tendency to lose and reorder messages.

- The computers on which the calling and called processes run may have significantly different architectures and data representation formats.

Thus, a complete RPC mechanism actually involves two major components:

1. A protocol that manages the messages sent between the client and the server processes and that deals with the potentially undesirable properties of the underlying network

2. Programming language and compiler support to package the arguments into a request message on the client machine and then to translate this message back into the arguments on the server machine, and likewise with the return value (this piece of the RPC mechanism is usually called a *stub compiler*)

Figure 5.14 schematically depicts what happens when a client invokes a remote procedure. First, the client calls a local stub for the procedure, passing it the arguments required by the procedure. This stub hides the fact that the procedure is remote by translating the arguments into a request message and then invoking an RPC protocol to send the request message to the server machine. At the server, the RPC protocol delivers the request message to the server stub (sometimes called a *skeleton*), which translates it into the arguments to the procedure and then calls the local procedure. After the server procedure completes, it returns the answer to the server stub, which packages this return value in a reply message that it hands off to the RPC protocol for transmission back to

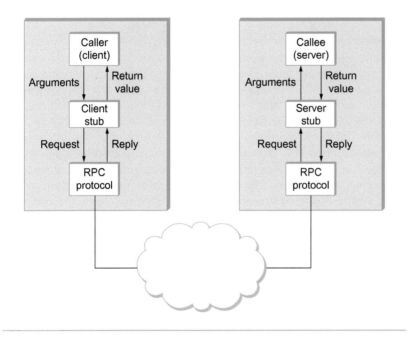

the client. The RPC protocol on the client passes this message up to the client stub, which translates it into a return value that it returns to the client program.

This section considers just the protocol-related aspects of an RPC mechanism. That is, it ignores the stubs and focuses instead on the RPC protocol, sometimes referred to as a request/reply protocol, that transmits messages between client and server. The transformation of arguments into messages and *vice versa* is covered in Chapter 7.

The term *RPC* refers to a type of protocol rather than a specific standard like TCP, so specific RPC protocols vary in the functions they perform. And, unlike TCP, which is the dominant reliable byte-stream protocol, there is no one dominant RPC protocol. Thus, in this section we will talk more about alternative design choices than previously.

Identifiers in RPC

Two functions that must be performed by any RPC protocol are:

- ■ Provide a name space for uniquely identifying the procedure to be called.
- ■ Match each reply message to the corresponding request message.

What Layer Is RPC?

Once again, the "What layer is this?" issue raises its ugly head. To many people, especially those who adhere to a strictly layerist view of protocol architecture, RPC is implemented on top of a transport protocol (usually UDP) and so cannot itself (by definition) be a transport protocol. It is certainly valid, however, to argue that the Internet should have an RPC protocol, since RPC offers a process-to-process service that is fundamentally different from that offered by TCP and UDP. The usual response to such a suggestion, however, is that the Internet architecture does not prohibit network designers from implementing their own RPC protocol on top of UDP. Whichever side of the issue of whether the Internet should have an official RPC protocol you support, the important point is that the way you implement RPC in the Internet architecture says nothing about whether RPC should be considered a transport protocol or not.

Interestingly, there are other people who believe that RPC is the most interesting protocol in the world and that TCP/IP is just what you do when you want to go "off site." This is the predominant view of the operating systems community, which has built countless OS kernels for distributed systems that contain exactly one protocol—you guessed it, RPC—running on top of a network device driver.

Our position is that any protocol that offers process-to-process service, as opposed to node-to-node or host-to-host service, qualifies as a transport protocol. Thus, RPC is a transport protocol and, in fact, can be implemented on top of other protocols that are themselves valid transport protocols.

The first problem has some similarities to the problem of identifying nodes in a network, something that we saw in previous chapters (IP addresses, for example, in Chapter 4). One of the design choices when identifying things is whether to make this name space flat or hierarchical. A flat name space would simply assign a unique, unstructured identifier (e.g., an integer) to each procedure, and this number would be carried in a single field in an RPC request message. This would require some kind of central coordination to avoid assigning the same procedure number to two different procedures. Alternatively, the protocol could implement a hierarchical name space, analogous to that used for file pathnames, which requires only that a file's "basename" be unique within its directory. This approach potentially simplifies the job of ensuring uniqueness of procedure names. A hierarchical name space for RPC could be implemented by defining a set of fields in the request message format, one for each level of naming in, say, a two- or three-level hierarchical name space.

The key to matching a reply message to the corresponding request is to uniquely identify request-replies pairs using a message ID field. A reply message had its message ID field set to the same value as the request message. When the client RPC module receives the reply, it uses the message ID to search for the corresponding outstanding request. To make the RPC transaction appear like a local procedure call to the caller, the caller is blocked (e.g., by using a semaphore) until the reply message is received. When the reply is received, the blocked caller is identified based on the request number in the reply, the remote procedure's return value is obtained from the reply, and the caller is unblocked so that it can return with that return value.

One of the recurrent challenges in RPC is dealing with unexpected responses, and we see this with message IDs. For example, consider the following pathological (but realistic) situation. A client machine sends a request message with a message ID of 0, then crashes and reboots, and then sends an unrelated request message, also with a message ID of 0. The server may not have been aware that the client crashed and rebooted and, upon seeing a request message with a message ID of 0, acknowledges it and discards it as a duplicate. The client never gets a response to the request.

One way to eliminate this problem is to use a *boot ID*. A machine's boot ID is a number that is incremented each time the machine reboots; this number is read from nonvolatile storage (e.g., a disk or flash drive), incremented, and written back to the storage device during the machine's start-up procedure. This number is then put in every message sent by that host. If a message is received with an old message ID but a new boot ID, it is recognized as a new message. In effect, the message ID and boot ID combine to form a unique ID for each transaction.

Overcoming Network Limitations
RPC protocols often perform additional functions to deal with the fact that networks are not perfect channels. Two such functions are:

- Provide reliable message delivery
- Support large message sizes through fragmentation and reassembly

An RPC protocol might implement reliability because the underlying protocols (e.g., UDP/IP) do not provide it, or perhaps to recover more quickly or efficiently from failures that otherwise would eventually be repaired by underlying protocols. An RPC protocol can implement reliability using acknowledgments and timeouts, similarly to TCP. The basic algorithm is straightforward, as illustrated by the timeline given in Figure 5.15. The client sends a request message and the server acknowledges it. Then, after executing the procedure, the server sends a reply message and the client acknowledges the reply.

Either a message carrying data (a request message or a reply message) or the ACK sent to acknowledge that message may be lost in the network. To account for this possibility, both client and server save a copy of each message they send until an ACK for it has arrived. Each side also sets a RETRANSMIT timer and resends the message should this timer expire. Both sides reset this timer and try again some agreed-upon number of times before giving up and freeing the message.

If an RPC client receives a reply message, clearly the corresponding request message must have been received by the server. Hence, the reply message itself is an *implicit acknowledgment*, and any additional acknowledgment from the server is not logically necessary. Similarly, a request message could implicitly acknowledge the preceding reply message—assuming the protocol makes request-reply transactions sequential, so that one transaction must complete before the next begins. Unfortunately, this sequentiality would severely limit RPC performance.

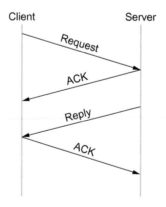

■ FIGURE 5.15 Simple timeline for a reliable RPC protocol.

A way out of this predicament is for the RPC protocol to implement a *channel* abstraction. Within a given channel, request/reply transactions are sequential—there can be only one transaction active on a given channel at any given time—but there can be multiple channels. Each message includes a channel ID field to indicate which channel the message belongs to. A request message in a given channel would implicitly acknowledge the previous reply in that channel, if it hadn't already been acknowledged. An application program can open multiple channels to a server if it wants to have more than one request/reply transaction between them at the same time (the application would need multiple threads). As illustrated in Figure 5.16, the reply message serves to acknowledge the request message, and a subsequent request acknowledges the preceding reply. Note that we saw a very similar approach— called *concurrent logical channels*—in Section 2.5.3 as a way to improve on the performance of a stop-and-wait reliability mechanism.

Another complication that RPC must address is that the server may take an arbitrarily long time to produce the result, and, worse yet, it may crash before generating the reply. Keep in mind that we are talking about the period of time after the server has acknowledged the request but before it has sent the reply. To help the client distinguish between a slow server and a dead server, the RPC's client side can periodically send an "Are you alive?" message to the server, and the server side responds with an ACK. Alternatively, the server could send "I am still alive" messages to the client without the client having first solicited them. The

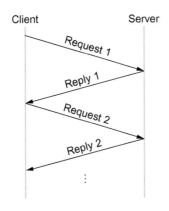

■ FIGURE 5.16 Timeline for a reliable RPC protocol using implicit acknowledgment.

client-initiated approach is more scalable because it puts more of the per-client burden (managing the timeout timer) on the clients.

RPC reliability may include the property known as *at-most-once semantics*. This means that for every request message that the client sends, at most one copy of that message is delivered to the server. Each time the client calls a remote procedure, that procedure is invoked at most one time on the server machine. We say "at most once" rather than "exactly once" because it is always possible that either the network or the server machine has failed, making it impossible to deliver even one copy of the request message.

To implement at-most-once semantics, RPC on the server side must recognize duplicate requests (and ignore them), even if it has already successfully replied to the original request. Hence, it must maintain some state information that identifies past requests. One approach is to identify requests using sequence numbers, so a server need only remember the most recent sequence number. Unfortunately, this would limit an RPC to one outstanding request (to a given server) at a time, since one request must be completed before the request with the next sequence number can be transmitted. Once again, channels provide a solution. The server could recognize duplicate requests by remembering the current sequence number for each channel, without limiting the client to one request at a time.

As obvious as at-most-once sounds, not all RPC protocols support this behavior. Some support a semantics that is facetiously called *zero-or-more* semantics; that is, each invocation on a client results in the remote procedure being invoked zero or more times. It is not difficult to understand how this would cause problems for a remote procedure that changed some local state variable (e.g., incremented a counter) or that had some externally visible side effect (e.g., launched a missile) each time it was invoked. On the other hand, if the remote procedure being invoked is *idempotent*—multiple invocations have the same effect as just one—then the RPC mechanism need not support at-most-once semantics; a simpler (possibly faster) implementation will suffice.

As was the case with reliability, the two reasons why an RPC protocol might implement message fragmentation and reassembly are that it is not provided by the underlying protocol stack or that it can be implemented more efficiently by the RPC protocol. Consider the case where RPC is implemented on top of UDP/IP and relies on IP for fragmentation and reassembly. If even one fragment of a message fails to arrive within a certain amount of time, IP discards the fragments that did arrive and the message is effectively lost. Eventually, the RPC protocol (assuming it implements reliability) would time out and retransmit the message. In contrast, consider an RPC protocol that implements its own fragmentation and reassembly and aggressively ACKs or NACKs (negatively acknowledges) individual fragments. Lost fragments would be more quickly detected and retransmitted, and only the lost fragments would be retransmitted, not the whole message.

Synchronous versus Asynchronous Protocols

One way to characterize a protocol is by whether it is *synchronous* or *asynchronous*. The precise meaning of these terms depends on where in the protocol hierarchy you use them. At the transport layer, it is most accurate to think of them as defining the extremes of a spectrum rather than as two mutually exclusive alternatives. The key attribute of any point along the spectrum is how much the sending process knows after the operation to send a message returns. In other words, if we assume that an application program invokes a send operation on a transport protocol, then exactly what does the application know about the success of the operation when the send operation returns?

At the *asynchronous* end of the spectrum, the application knows absolutely nothing when send returns. Not only does it not know if the message was received by its peer, but it doesn't even know for sure that the message has successfully left the local machine. At the *synchronous* end of the spectrum, the send operation typically returns a reply message. That is, the application not only knows that the message it sent was received by its peer, but it also knows that the peer has returned an answer. Thus, synchronous protocols implement the request/reply abstraction, while asynchronous protocols are used if the sender wants to be able to transmit many messages without having to wait for a response. Using this definition, RPC protocols are obviously synchronous protocols.

Although we have not discussed them in this chapter, there are interesting points between these two extremes. For example, the transport protocol might implement send so that it blocks (does not return) until the message has been successfully received at the remote machine, but returns before the sender's peer on that machine has actually processed and responded to it. This is sometimes called a *reliable datagram protocol*.

5.3.2 RPC Implementations (SunRPC, DCE)

We now turn our discussion to some example implementations of RPC protocols. These will serve to highlight some of the different design decisions that protocol designers have made. Our first example is SunRPC, a widely used RPC protocol also known as Open Network Computing RPC (ONC RPC). Our second example, which we will refer to as DCE-RPC, is part of the Distributed Computing Environment (DCE). DCE is a set of standards and software for building distributed systems that was defined by the Open Software Foundation (OSF), a consortium of computer companies that originally included IBM, Digital Equipment Corporation, and Hewlett-Packard; today, OSF goes by the name The Open Group. These two examples represent interesting alternative design choices in the RPC solution space.

SunRPC

SunRPC became a *de facto* standard thanks to its wide distribution with Sun workstations and the central role it plays in Sun's popular Network File System (NFS). The IETF subsequently adopted it as a standard Internet protocol under the name ONC RPC.

SunRPC can be implemented over several different transport protocols. Figure 5.17 illustrates the protocol graph when SunRPC is implemented on UDP. As we noted earlier in this section, a strict layerist might frown on the idea of running a transport protocol over a transport protocol, or argue that RPC must be something other than a transport protocol since it appears "above" the transport layer. Pragmatically, the design decision to run RPC over an existing transport layer makes quite a lot of sense, as will be apparent in the following discussion.

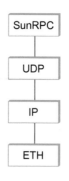

■ FIGURE 5.17 Protocol graph for SunRPC on top of UDP.

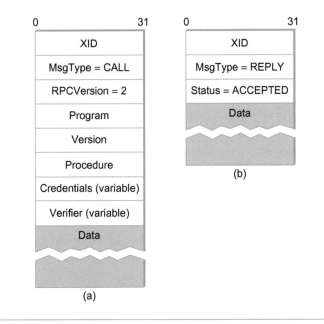

SunRPC uses two-tier identifiers to identify remote procedures: a 32-bit program number and a 32-bit procedure number. (There is also a 32-bit version number, but we ignore that in the following discussion.) For example, the NFS server has been assigned program number x00100003, and within this program getattr is procedure 1, setattr is procedure 2, read is procedure 6, write is procedure 8, and so on. The program number and procedure number are transmitted in the SunRPC request message's header, whose fields are shown in Figure 5.18. The server—which may support several program numbers—is responsible for calling the specified procedure of the specified program. A SunRPC request really represents a request to call the specified program and procedure on the particular machine to which the request was sent, even though the same program number may be implemented on other machines in the same network. Thus, the address of the server's machine (e.g., an IP address) is an implicit third tier of the RPC address.

Different program numbers may belong to different servers on the same machine. These different servers have different transport layer demux keys (e.g., UDP ports), most of which are not well-known numbers but instead are assigned dynamically. These demux keys are called *transport selectors*. How can a SunRPC client that wants to talk to a particular program determine which transport selector to use to reach the corresponding server? The solution is to assign a well-known address to *just one* program on the remote machine and let that program handle the task of telling clients which transport selector to use to reach any other program on the machine. The original version of this SunRPC program is called the *Port Mapper*, and it supports only UDP and TCP as underlying protocols. Its program number is x00100000, and its well-known port is 111. RPCBIND, which evolved from the Port Mapper, supports arbitrary underlying transport protocols. As each SunRPC server starts, it calls an RPCBIND registration procedure, on the server's own home machine, to register its transport selector and the program numbers that it supports. A remote client can then call an RPCBIND lookup procedure to look up the transport selector for a particular program number.

To make this more concrete, consider an example using the Port Mapper with UDP. To send a request message to NFS's read procedure, a client first sends a request message to the Port Mapper at well-known UDP port 111, asking that procedure 3 be invoked to map program number x00100003 to the UDP port where the NFS program currently resides.[2] The client then sends a SunRPC request message with program number x00100003 and procedure number 6 to this UDP port, and the SunRPC module listening at that port calls the NFS read procedure. The client also caches the program-to-port number mapping so that it need not go back to the Port Mapper each time it wants to talk to the NFS program.

To match up a reply message with the corresponding request, so that the result of the RPC can be returned to the correct caller, both request and reply message headers include a XID (transaction ID) field, as in Figure 5.18. A XID is a unique transaction ID used only by one request and the corresponding reply. After the server has successfully replied to a given request, it does not remember the XID. Because of this, SunRPC cannot guarantee at-most-once semantics.

The details of SunRPC's semantics depend on the underlying transport protocol. It does not implement its own reliability, so it is only reliable if the underlying transport is reliable. (Of course, any application that runs over SunRPC may also choose to implement its own reliability

---

[2]In practice, NFS is such an important program that it has been given its own well-known UDP port, but for the purposes of illustration we're pretending that's not the case.

mechanisms above the level of SunRPC.) The ability to send request and reply messages that are larger than the network MTU is also dependent on the underlying transport. In other words, SunRPC does not make any attempt to improve on the underlying transport when it comes to reliability and message size. Since SunRPC can run over many different transport protocols, this gives it considerable flexibility without complicating the design of the RPC protocol itself.

Returning to the SunRPC header format of Figure 5.18, the request message contains variable-length Credentials and Verifier fields, both of which are used by the client to authenticate itself to the server—that is, to give evidence that the client has the right to invoke the server. How a client authenticates itself to a server is a general issue that must be addressed by any protocol that wants to provide a reasonable level of security. This topic is discussed in more detail in the next chapter.

DCE-RPC

DCE-RPC is the RPC protocol at the core of the DCE system and was the basis of the RPC mechanism underlying Microsoft's DCOM and ActiveX. It can be used with the Network Data Representation (NDR) stub compiler described in Chapter 7, but it also serves as the underlying RPC protocol for the Common Object Request Broker Architecture (CORBA), which is an industry-wide standard for building distributed, object-oriented systems.

DCE-RPC, like SunRPC, can be implemented on top of several transport protocols including UDP and TCP. It is also similar to SunRPC in that it defines a two-level addressing scheme: the transport protocol demultiplexes to the correct server, DCE-RPC dispatches to a particular procedure exported by that server, and clients consult an "endpoint mapping service" (similar to SunRPC's Port Mapper) to learn how to reach a particular server. Unlike SunRPC, however, DCE-RPC implements at-most-once call semantics. (In truth, DCE-RPC supports multiple call semantics, including an idempotent semantics similar to SunRPC's, but at-most-once is the default behavior.) There are some other differences between the two approaches, which we will highlight in the following paragraphs.

Figure 5.19 gives a timeline for the typical exchange of messages, where each message is labeled by its DCE-RPC type. The client sends a Request message, the server eventually replies with a Response message, and the

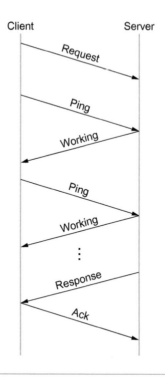

■ FIGURE 5.19 Typical DCE-RPC message exchange.

client acknowledges (Ack) the response. Instead of the server acknowledging the request messages, however, the client periodically sends a Ping message to the server, which responds with a Working message to indicate that the remote procedure is still in progress. If the server's reply is received reasonably quickly, no Pings are sent. Although not shown in the figure, other message types are also supported. For example, the client can send a Quit message to the server, asking it to abort an earlier call that is still in progress; the server responds with a Quack (quit acknowledgment) message. Also, the server can respond to a Request message with a Reject message (indicating that a call has been rejected), and it can respond to a Ping message with a Nocall message (indicating that the server has never heard of the caller).

Each request/reply transaction in DCE-RPC takes place in the context of an *activity*. An activity is a logical request/reply channel between a pair of participants. At any given time, there can be only one message transaction active on a given channel. Like the concurrent logical channel approach described above and in Section 2.5.3, the application programs have to open multiple channels if they want to have more than one request/ reply transaction between them at the same time. The activity to which a message belongs is identified by the message's ActivityId field. A Sequence-Num field then distinguishes between calls made as part of the same activity; it serves the same purpose as SunRPC's XID (transaction id) field. Unlike SunRPC, DCE-RPC keeps track of the last sequence number used as part of a particular activity, so as to ensure at-most-once semantics. To distinguish between replies sent before and after a server machine reboots, DCE-RPC uses a ServerBoot field to hold the machine's boot ID.

Another design choice made in DCE-RPC that differs from SunRPC is the support of fragmentation and reassembly in the RPC protocol. As noted above, even if an underlying protocol such as IP provides fragmentation/reassembly, a more sophisticated algorithm implemented as part of RPC can result in quicker recovery and reduced bandwidth consumption when fragments are lost. The FragmentNum field uniquely identifies each fragment that makes up a given request or reply message. Each DCE-RPC fragment is assigned a unique fragment number (0, 1, 2, 3, and so on). Both the client and server implement a selective acknowledgment mechanism, which works as follows. (We describe the mechanism in terms of a client sending a fragmented request message to the server; the same mechanism applies when a server sends a fragment response to the client.)

First, each fragment that makes up the request message contains both a unique FragmentNum and a flag indicating whether this packet is a fragment of a call (frag) or the last fragment of a call (last_frag); request messages that fit in a single packet carry a no_frag flag. The server knows it has received the complete request message when it has the last_frag packet and there are no gaps in the fragment numbers. Second, in response to each arriving fragment, the server sends a Fack (fragment acknowledgment) message to the client. This acknowledgment identifies the highest fragment number that the server has successfully received. In other words, the acknowledgment is cumulative, much like in TCP. In addition, however, the server selectively acknowledges any higher fragment numbers it has received out of order. It does so with a bit vector that identifies these out-of-order fragments relative to the highest in-order fragment it has received. Finally, the client responds by retransmitting the missing fragments.

Figure 5.20 illustrates how this all works. Suppose the server has successfully received fragments up through number 20, plus fragments 23,

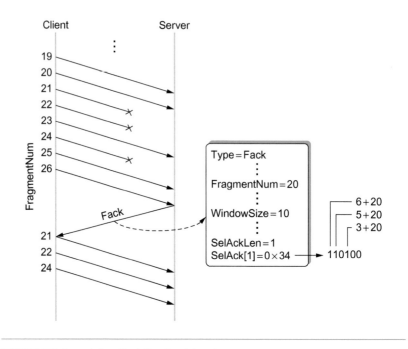

Client   Server

FragmentNum

Type = Fack

FragmentNum = 20

WindowSize = 10

SelAckLen = 1
SelAck[1] = 0 × 34

6 + 20
5 + 20
3 + 20

110100

■ FIGURE 5.20 Fragmentation with selective acknowledgments.

25, and 26. The server responds with a Fack that identifies fragment 20 as the highest in-order fragment, plus a bit-vector (SelAck) with the third $(23 = 20 + 3)$, fifth $(25 = 20 + 5)$, and sixth $(26 = 20 + 6)$ bits turned on. So as to support an (almost) arbitrarily long bit vector, the size of the vector (measured in 32-bit words) is given in the SelAckLen field.

Given DCE-RPC's support for very large messages—the FragmentNum field is 16 bits long, meaning it can support 64K fragments—it is not appropriate for the protocol to blast all the fragments that make up a message as fast as it can since doing so might overrun the receiver. Instead, DCE-RPC implements a flow-control algorithm that is very similar to TCP's. Specifically, each Fack message not only acknowledges received fragments but also informs the sender of how many fragments it may now send. This is the purpose of the WindowSize field in Figure 5.20, which serves exactly the same purpose as TCP's AdvertisedWindow field except it counts fragments rather than bytes. DCE-RPC also implements a congestion-control mechanism that is similar to TCP's, which we will see in Chapter 6. Given the complexity of congestion control, it is perhaps not surprising that some RPC protocols avoid it by avoiding fragmentation.

In summary, designers have quite a range of options open to them when designing an RPC protocol. SunRPC takes the more minimalist approach and adds relatively little to the underlying transport beyond the essentials of locating the right procedure and identifying messages. DCE-RPC adds more functionality, with the possibility of improved performance in some environments at the cost of greater complexity.

5.4 TRANSPORT FOR REAL-TIME APPLICATIONS (RTP)

In the early days of packet switching, most applications were concerned with the movement of data: accessing remote computing resources, transferring files, sending email, etc. However, at least as early as 1981, experiments were under way to carry real-time traffic, such as digitized voice samples, over packet networks. We call an application "real-time" when it has strong requirements for the timely delivery of information. Internet telephony, or Voice over IP (VoIP), is a classic example of a real-time application, because you can't easily carry on a conversation with someone if it takes more than a fraction of a second to get a response. As we will see shortly, real-time applications place some specific demands on the transport protocol that are not well met by the protocols discussed so far in this chapter.

Multimedia applications—those that involve video, audio, and data—are sometimes divided into two classes: *interactive* applications and *streaming* applications. An early and at one time popular example of the interactive class is vat, a multiparty audioconferencing tool that is often used over networks supporting IP multicast. The control panel for a typical vat conference is shown in Figure 5.21. Internet telephony is also a class of interactive application and probably the most widely used one at the time of writing. Internet-based multimedia conferencing applications, as mentioned in Chapter 1 and illustrated in Figure 1.1, provide another example. Modern instant messaging applications also use real-time audio and video. These are the sort of applications with the most stringent real-time requirements.

Streaming applications typically deliver audio or video streams from a server to a client and are typified by such commercial products as RealAudio®. Streaming video, typified by YouTube, has become one of the dominant forms of traffic on the Internet. Because streaming applications lack human-to-human interaction, they place somewhat less

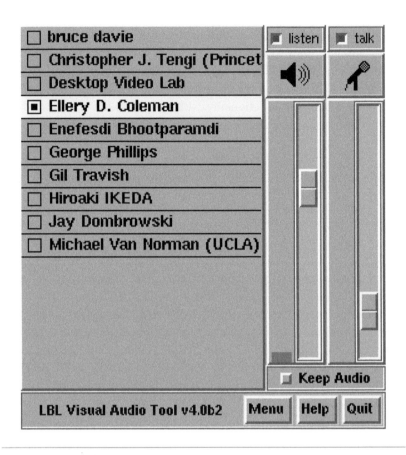

■ FIGURE 5.21 User interface of a **vat** audioconference.

stringent real-time requirements on the underlying protocols. Timeliness is still important, however—for example, you want a video to start playing soon after pushing "play," and once it starts to play, late packets will either cause it to stall or create some sort of visual degradation. So, while streaming applications are not strictly real time, they still have enough in common with interactive multimedia applications to warrant consideration of a common protocol for both types of application.

It should by now be apparent that designers of a transport protocol for real-time and multimedia applications face a real challenge in defining the requirements broadly enough to meet the needs of very different applications. They must also pay attention to the interactions among different applications, such as the synchronization of audio and video streams. We will see below how these concerns affected the design of the primary real-time transport protocol in use today, RTP.

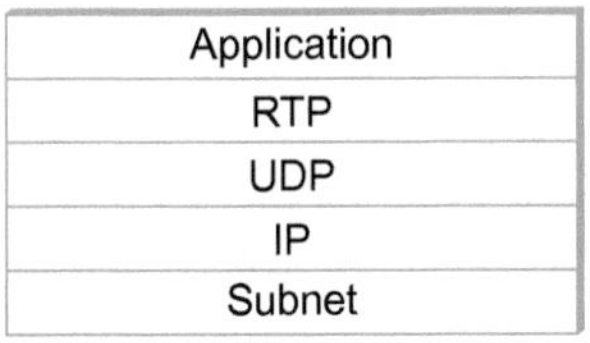

Application
RTP
UDP
IP
Subnet

■ FIGURE 5.22 Protocol stack for multimedia applications using RTP.

Much of RTP actually derives from protocol functionality that was originally embedded in the application itself. When the vat application was
first developed, it ran over UDP, and the designers figured out which
features were needed to handle the real-time nature of voice communication. Later, they realized that these features could be useful to many other
applications and defined a protocol with those features, which became
RTP. RTP can run over many lower-layer protocols, but still commonly
runs over UDP. That leads to the protocol stack shown in Figure 5.22.
Note that we are therefore running a transport protocol over a transport protocol. There is no rule against that,[3] and in fact it makes a lot
of sense, since UDP provides such a minimal level of functionality, and
the basic demultiplexing based on port numbers happens to be just what
RTP needs as a starting point. So, rather than recreate port numbers in
RTP, RTP outsources the demultiplexing function to UDP.

5.4.1 Requirements

The most basic requirement for a general-purpose multimedia protocol is that it allow similar applications to interoperate with each other.
For example, it should be possible for two independently implemented
audioconferencing applications to talk to each other. This immediately
suggests that the applications had better use the same method of encoding and compressing voice; otherwise, the data sent by one party will be
incomprehensible to the receiving party. Since there are quite a few different coding schemes for voice, each with its own trade-offs among quality,
bandwidth requirements, and computational cost, it would probably be
a bad idea to decree that only one such scheme can be used. Instead,
our protocol should provide a way that a sender can tell a receiver which
coding scheme it wants to use, and possibly negotiate until a scheme that
is available to both parties is identified.

---

[3]But it has caused some confusion as to whether RTP is really a transport protocol.

Just as with audio, there are many different video coding schemes. Thus, we see that the first common function that RTP can provide is the ability to communicate that choice of coding scheme. Note that this also serves to identify the type of application (e.g., audio or video); once we know what coding algorithm is being used, we know what type of data is being encoded as well.

Another important requirement is to enable the recipient of a data stream to determine the timing relationship among the received data. Recall from Section 6.5 that real-time applications need to place received data into a *playback buffer* to smooth out the jitter that may have been introduced into the data stream during transmission across the network. Thus, some sort of timestamping of the data will be necessary to enable the receiver to play it back at the appropriate time.

Related to the timing of a single media stream is the issue of synchronization of multiple media in a conference. The obvious example of this would be to synchronize an audio and video stream that are originating from the same sender. As we will see below, this is a slightly more complex problem than playback time determination for a single stream.

Another important function to be provided is an indication of packet loss. Note that an application with tight latency bounds generally cannot use a reliable transport like TCP because retransmission of data to correct for loss would probably cause the packet to arrive too late to be useful. Thus, the application must be able to deal with missing packets, and the first step in dealing with them is noticing that they are in fact missing. As an example, a video application using MPEG encoding may take different actions when a packet is lost, depending on whether the packet came from an I frame, a B frame, or a P frame.

Packet loss is also a potential indicator of congestion. Since multimedia applications generally do not run over TCP, they also miss out on the congestion avoidance features of TCP (described in Section 6.3). Yet, many multimedia applications are capable of responding to congestion—for example, by changing the parameters of the coding algorithm to reduce the bandwidth consumed. Clearly, to make this work, the receiver needs to notify the sender that losses are occurring so that the sender can adjust its coding parameters.

Another common function across multimedia applications is the concept of frame boundary indication. A frame in this context is application specific. For example, it may be helpful to notify a video application that a certain set of packets correspond to a single frame. In an audio application it is helpful to mark the beginning of a "talkspurt," which is a collection of sounds or words followed by silence. The receiver can then identify the silences between talkspurts and use them as opportunities to move the playback point. This follows the observation that slight shortening or lengthening of the spaces between words are not perceptible to users, whereas shortening or lengthening the words themselves is both perceptible and annoying.

A final function that we might want to put into the protocol is some way of identifying senders that is more user-friendly than an IP address. As illustrated in Figure 5.21, audio and video conferencing applications can display strings such as Joe User (user@domain.com) on their control panels, and thus the application protocol should support the association of such a string with a data stream.

In addition to the functionality that is required from our protocol, we note an additional requirement: It should make reasonably efficient use of bandwidth. Put another way, we don't want to introduce a lot of extra bits that need to be sent with every packet in the form of a long header. The reason for this is that audio packets, which are one of the most common types of multimedia data, tend to be small, so as to reduce the time it takes to fill them with samples. Long audio packets would mean high latency due to packetization, which has a negative effect on the perceived quality of conversations. (This was one of the factors in choosing the length of ATM cells.) Since the data packets themselves are short, a large header would mean that a relatively large amount of link bandwidth would be used by headers, thus reducing the available capacity for "useful" data. We will see several aspects of the design of RTP that have been influenced by the necessity of keeping the header short.

You could argue whether every single feature just described *really* needs to be in a real-time transport protocol, and you could probably find some more that could be added. The key idea here is to make life easier for application developers by giving them a useful set of abstractions and building blocks for their applications. For example, by putting a timestamping mechanism into RTP, we save every developer of a real-time application from inventing his own. We also increase the chances that two different real-time applications might interoperate.

5.4.2 **RTP Design**

Now that we have seen the rather long list of requirements for our transport protocol for multimedia, we turn to the details of the protocol that has been specified to meet those requirements. This protocol, RTP, was developed in the IETF and is in widespread use. The RTP standard actually defines a pair of protocols, RTP and the Real-time Transport Control Protocol (RTCP). The former is used for the exchange of multimedia data, while the latter is used to periodically send control information associated with a certain data flow. When running over UDP, the RTP data stream and the associated RTCP control stream use consecutive transport-layer ports. The RTP data uses an even port number and the RTCP control information uses the next higher (odd) port number.

Because RTP is designed to support a wide variety of applications, it provides a flexible mechanism by which new applications can be developed without repeatedly revising the RTP protocol itself. For each class of application (e.g., audio), RTP defines a *profile* and one or more *formats*. The profile provides a range of information that ensures a common understanding of the fields in the RTP header for that application class, as will be apparent when we examine the header in detail. The format specification explains how the data that follows the RTP header is to be interpreted. For example, the RTP header might just be followed by a sequence of bytes, each of which represents a single audio sample taken a defined interval after the previous one. Alternatively, the format of the data might be much more complex; an MPEG-encoded video stream, for example, would need to have a good deal of structure to represent all the different types of information.

The design of RTP embodies an architectural principle known as *Application Level Framing* (ALF). This principle was put forward by Clark and Tennenhouse in 1990 as a new way to design protocols for emerging multimedia applications. They recognized that these new applications were unlikely to be well served by existing protocols such as TCP, and that furthermore they might not be well served by any sort of "one-size-fits-all" protocol. At the heart of this principle is the belief that an application understands its own needs best. For example, an MPEG video application knows how best to recover from lost frames and how to react differently if an I frame or a B frame is lost. The same application also understands best how to segment the data for transmission—for example, it's better to send the data from different frames in different datagrams, so that a lost packet only corrupts a single frame, not two. It is for this reason that RTP leaves so many of the protocol details to the profile and format documents that are specific to an application.

Header Format

Figure 5.23 shows the header format used by RTP. The first 12 bytes are always present, whereas the contributing source identifiers are only used in certain circumstances. After this header there may be optional header extensions, as described below. Finally, the header is followed by the RTP payload, the format of which is determined by the application. The intention of this header is that it contain only the fields that are likely to be used by many different applications, since anything that is very specific to a single application would be more efficiently carried in the RTP payload for that application only.

The first two bits are a version identifier, which contains the value 2 in the RTP version deployed at the time of writing. You might think that the designers of the protocol were rather bold to think that 2 bits would be enough to contain all future versions of RTP, but recall that bits are at a premium in the RTP header. Furthermore, the use of profiles for different applications makes it less likely that many revisions to the base RTP protocol would be needed. In any case, if it turns out that another version of RTP is needed beyond version 2, it would be possible to consider a change to the header format so that more than one future version would be possible. For example, a new RTP header with the value 3 in the version field could have a "subversion" field somewhere else in the header.

The next bit is the *padding* (P) bit, which is set in circumstances in which the RTP payload has been padded for some reason. RTP data might be padded to fill up a block of a certain size as required by an encryption algorithm, for example. In such a case, the complete length of the RTP header, data, and padding would be conveyed by the lower-layer protocol

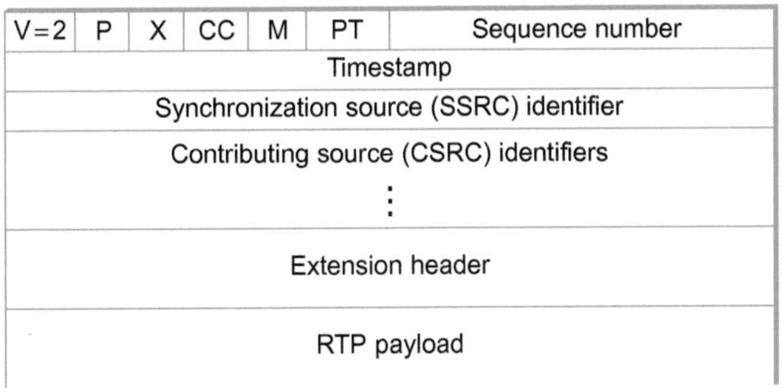

V = 2	P	X	CC	M	PT	Sequence number
Timestamp							
Synchronization source (SSRC) identifier							
Contributing source (CSRC) identifiers							
⋮							
Extension header							
RTP payload							

■ FIGURE 5.23 RTP header format.

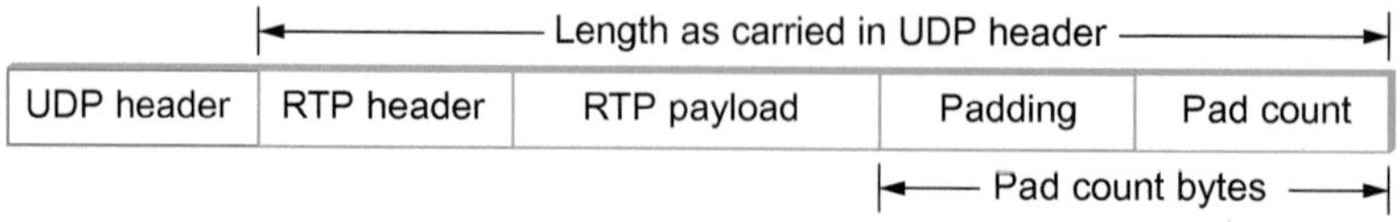

■ FIGURE 5.24 Padding of an RTP packet.

header (e.g., the UDP header), and the last byte of the padding would contain a count of how many bytes should be ignored. This is illustrated in Figure 5.24. Note that this approach to padding removes any need for a length field in the RTP header (thus serving the goal of keeping the header short); in the common case of no padding, the length is deduced from the lower-layer protocol.

The *extension* (X) bit is used to indicate the presence of an extension header, which would be defined for a specific application and follow the main header. Such headers are rarely used, since it is generally possible to define a payload-specific header as part of the payload format definition for a particular application.

The X bit is followed by a 4-bit field that counts the number of *contributing sources*, if any are included in the header. Contributing sources are discussed below.

We noted above the frequent need for some sort of frame indication; this is provided by the marker bit, which has a profile-specific use. For a voice application, it could be set at the beginning of a talkspurt, for example. The 7-bit payload type field follows; it indicates what type of multimedia data is carried in this packet. One possible use of this field would be to enable an application to switch from one coding scheme to another based on information about resource availability in the network or feedback on application quality. The exact usage of the payload type is also determined by the application profile.

Note that the payload type is generally not used as a demultiplexing key to direct data to different applications (or to different streams within a single application, such as the audio and video stream for a videoconference). This is because such demultiplexing is typically provided at a lower layer (e.g., by UDP, as described in Section 5.1). Thus, two media streams using RTP would typically use different UDP port numbers.

The sequence number is used to enable the receiver of an RTP stream to detect missing and misordered packets. The sender simply increments the value by one for each transmitted packet. Note that RTP does not do anything when it detects a lost packet, in contrast to TCP, which both corrects for the loss (by retransmission) and interprets the loss as a congestion indication (which may cause it to reduce its window size). Rather, it is left to the application to decide what to do when a packet is lost because this decision is likely to be highly application dependent. For example, a video application might decide that the best thing to do when a packet is lost is to replay the last frame that was correctly received. Some applications might also decide to modify their coding algorithms to reduce bandwidth needs in response to loss, but this is not a function of RTP. It would not be sensible for RTP to decide that the sending rate should be reduced, as this might make the application useless.

The function of the timestamp field is to enable the receiver to play back samples at the appropriate intervals and to enable different media streams to be synchronized. Because different applications may require different granularities of timing, RTP itself does not specify the units in which time is measured. Instead, the timestamp is just a counter of "ticks," where the time between ticks is dependent on the encoding in use. For example, an audio application that samples data once every $125\,\mu s$ could use that value as its clock resolution. The clock granularity is one of the details that is specified in the RTP profile or payload format for an application.

The timestamp value in the packet is a number representing the time at which the *first* sample in the packet was generated. The timestamp is not a reflection of the time of day; only the differences between timestamps are relevant. For example, if the sampling interval is $125\,\mu s$ and the first sample in packet $n+1$ was generated 10 ms after the first sample in packet n, then the number of sampling instants between these two samples is

$$\text{TimeBetweenPackets} \div \text{TimePerSample} = (10 \times 10^{-3}) \div (125 \times 10^{-6})$$

$$= 80$$

Assuming the clock granularity is the same as the sampling interval, then the timestamp in packet $n+1$ would be greater than that in packet n by 80. Note that fewer than 80 samples might have been sent due to compression techniques such as silence detection, and yet the timestamp allows the receiver to play back the samples with the correct temporal relationship.

The synchronization source (SSRC) is a 32-bit number that uniquely identifies a single source of an RTP stream. In a given multimedia conference, each sender picks a random SSRC and is expected to resolve conflicts in the unlikely event that two sources pick the same value. By making the source identifier something other than the network or transport address of the source, RTP ensures independence from the lower-layer protocol. It also enables a single node with multiple sources (e.g., several cameras) to distinguish those sources. When a single node generates different media streams (e.g., audio and video), it is not required to use the same SSRC in each stream, as there are mechanisms in RTCP (described below) to allow intermedia synchronization.

The contributing source (CSRC) is used only when a number of RTP streams pass through a mixer. A mixer can be used to reduce the bandwidth requirements for a conference by receiving data from many sources and sending it as a single stream. For example, the audio streams from several concurrent speakers could be decoded and recoded as a single audio stream. In this case, the mixer lists itself as the synchronization source but also lists the contributing sources—the SSRC values of the speakers who contributed to the packet in question.

5.4.3 Control Protocol

RTCP provides a control stream that is associated with a data stream for a multimedia application. This control stream provides three main functions:

1. Feedback on the performance of the application and the network
2. A way to correlate and synchronize different media streams that have come from the same sender
3. A way to convey the identity of a sender for display on a user interface (e.g., the vat interface shown in Figure 5.21)

The first function may be useful for detecting and responding to congestion. Some applications are able to operate at difference rates and may use performance data to decide to use a more aggressive compression scheme to reduce congestion, for example, or to send a higher-quality stream when there is little congestion. Performance feedback can also be useful in diagnosing network problems.

You might think that the second function is already provided by the synchronization source ID (SSRC) of RTP, but in fact it is not. As already noted, multiple cameras from a single node might have different SSRC values. Furthermore, there is no requirement that an audio and video stream from the same node use the same SSRC. Because collisions of SSRC values may occur, it may be necessary to change the SSRC value of a stream. To deal with this problem, RTCP uses the concept of a *canonical name* (CNAME) that is assigned to a sender, which is then associated with the various SSRC values that might be used by that sender using RTCP mechanisms.

Simply correlating two streams is only part of the problem of inter-media synchronization. Because different streams may have completely different clocks (with different granularities and even different amounts of inaccuracy, or drift), there needs to be a way to accurately synchronize streams with each other. RTCP addresses this problem by conveying timing information that correlates actual time of day with the clock-rate-dependent timestamps that are carried in RTP data packets.

RTCP defines a number of different packet types, including

- Sender reports, which enable active senders to a session to report transmission and reception statistics
- Receiver reports, which receivers who are not senders use to report reception statistics
- Source descriptions, which carry CNAMEs and other sender description information
- Application-specific control packets

These different RTCP packet types are sent over the lower-layer protocol, which, as we have noted, is typically UDP. Several RTCP packets can be packed into a single PDU of the lower-level protocol. It is required that at least two RTCP packets are sent in every lower-level PDU: One of these is a report packet; the other is a source description packet. Other packets may be included up to the size limits imposed by the lower-layer protocols.

Before looking further at the contents of an RTCP packet, we note that there is a potential problem with every member of a multicast group sending periodic control traffic. Unless we take some steps to limit it, this control traffic has the potential to be a significant consumer of bandwidth. In an audioconference, for example, no more than two or three senders are likely to send audio data at any instant, since there is no point in everyone talking at once. But there is no such social limit on everyone sending control traffic, and this could be a severe problem in a conference with thousands of participants. To deal with this problem, RTCP has a set of mechanisms by which the participants scale back their reporting frequency as the number of participants increases. These rules are somewhat complex, but the basic goal is this: Limit the total amount of RTCP traffic to a small percentage (typically 5%) of the RTP data traffic. To accomplish this goal, the participants should know how much data bandwidth is likely to be in use (e.g., the amount to send three audio streams) and the number of participants. They learn the former from means outside RTP (known as *session management*, discussed at the end of this section), and they learn the latter from the RTCP reports of other participants. Because RTCP reports might be sent at a very low rate, it might only be possible to get an approximate count of the current number of recipients, but that is typically sufficient. Also, it is recommended to allocate more RTCP bandwidth to active senders, on the assumption that most participants would like to see reports from them—for example, to find out who is speaking.

Once a participant has determined how much bandwidth it can consume with RTCP traffic, it sets about sending periodic reports at the appropriate rate. Sender reports and receiver reports differ only in that the former include some extra information about the sender. Both types of reports contain information about the data that was received from all sources in the most recent reporting period.

The extra information in a sender report consists of

- A timestamp containing the actual time of day when this report was generated
- The RTP timestamp corresponding to the time when the report was generated
- Cumulative counts of the packets and bytes sent by this sender since it began transmission

Note that the first two quantities can be used to enable synchronization of different media streams from the same source, even if those streams use different clock granularities in their RTP data streams, since it gives the key to convert time of day to the RTP timestamps.

Both sender and receiver reports contain one block of data per source that has been heard from since the last report. Each block contains the following statistics for the source in question:

- Its SSRC
- The fraction of data packets from this source that were lost since the last report was sent (calculated by comparing the number of

packets received with the number of packets expected; this last value can be determined from the RTP sequence numbers)

- Total number of packets lost from this source since the first time it was heard from
- Highest sequence number received from this source (extended to 32 bits to account for wrapping of the sequence number)
- Estimated interarrival jitter for the source (calculated by comparing the interarrival spacing of received packets with the expected spacing at transmission time)
- Last actual timestamp received via RTCP for this source
- Delay since last sender report received via RTCP for this source

As you might imagine, the recipients of this information can learn all sorts of things about the state of the session. In particular, they can see if other recipients are getting much better quality from some sender than they are, which might be an indication that a resource reservation needs to be made, or that there is a problem in the network that needs to be attended to. In addition, if a sender notices that many receivers are experiencing high loss of its packets, it might decide that it should reduce its sending rate or use a coding scheme that is more resilient to loss.

The final aspect of RTCP that we will consider is the source description packet. Such a packet contains, at a minimum, the SSRC of the sender and the sender's CNAME. The canonical name is derived in such a way that all applications that generate media streams that might need to be synchronized (e.g., separately generated audio and video streams from the same user) will choose the same CNAME even though they might choose different SSRC values. This enables a receiver to identify the media stream that came from the same sender. The most common format of the CNAME is user@host, where host is the fully qualified domain name of the sending machine. Thus, an application launched by the user whose user name is jdoe running on the machine cicada.cs.princeton.edu would use the string jdoe@cicada.cs.princeton.edu as its CNAME. The large and variable number of bytes used in this representation would make it a bad choice for the format of an SSRC, since the SSRC is sent with every data packet and must be processed in real time. Allowing CNAMEs to be bound to SSRC values in periodic RTCP messages enables a compact and efficient format for the SSRC.

Other items may be included in the source description packet, such as the real name and email address of the user. These are used in user interface displays and to contact participants, but are less essential to the operation of RTP than the CNAME.

Like TCP, RTP and RTCP are a fairly complex pair of protocols. This complexity comes in large part from the desire to make life easier for application designers. Because there is an infinite number of possible applications, the challenge in designing a transport protocol is to make it general enough to meet the widely varying needs of many different applications without making the protocol itself impossible to implement. RTP has proven very successful in this regard, forming the basis for the majority of real-time multimedia communications over the Internet today.

5.5 SUMMARY

This chapter has described four very different end-to-end protocols. The first protocol we considered is a simple demultiplexer, as typified by UDP. All such a protocol does is dispatch messages to the appropriate application process based on a port number. It does not enhance the best-effort service model of the underlying network in any way—it simply offers an unreliable, connectionless datagram service to application programs.

The second type is a reliable byte-stream protocol, and the specific example of this type that we looked at is TCP. The challenges faced with such a protocol are to recover from messages that may be lost by the network, to deliver messages in the same order in which they are sent, and to allow the receiver to do flow control on the sender. TCP uses the basic sliding window algorithm, enhanced with an advertised window, to implement this functionality. The other item of note for this protocol is the importance of an accurate timeout/retransmission mechanism. Interestingly, even though TCP is a single protocol, we saw that it employs at least five different algorithms—sliding window, Nagle, three-way handshake, Karn/Partridge, and Jacobson/Karels—all of which can be of value to any end-to-end protocol.

The third type of transport protocol we looked at is request/reply protocols that form the basis for RPC. Such protocols must dispatch requests to the correct remote procedures and match replies to the corresponding requests. They may additionally provide reliability, such as at-most-once semantics, or support large message sizes by message fragmentation and reassembly.

Finally, we looked at transport protocols for the class of applications that involve multimedia data (such as audio and video) and that have a requirement for real-time delivery. Such a transport protocol needs to provide help with recovering the timing information of a single media stream and with synchronizing multiple media streams. It also needs to provide information to upper layers (e.g., the application layer) about lost data (since there will normally not be enough time to retransmit lost packets) so that appropriate application-specific recovery and congestion avoidance methods can be employed. The protocol that has been developed to meet these needs is RTP, which includes a companion control protocol called *RTCP*.

What should be clear after reading this chapter is that transport protocol design is a tricky business. As we have seen, getting a transport protocol right in the first place is hard enough, but changing circumstances make matters more complicated. Some changes are not too hard to predict—networks keep getting faster, for example—but sometimes a new class of applications appears and changes the requirements for transport-level services. The challenge is finding ways to adapt to these changes. Sometimes existing protocols can be tweaked to deal with new circumstances—TCP options have evolved over time to achieve this—at other times it may be necessary to create a new transport protocol, as with RTP and

WHAT'S NEXT: TRANSPORT PROTOCOL DIVERSITY

SCTP. It is an open question as to when we should reuse an existing protocol versus create a new one.

In addition to making small changes to an existing protocol to accommodate changing network environments or new application needs, sometimes we might be able to tweak the application to get it to work with an existing protocol. For example, an application that needs RPC semantics would probably do best with an RPC protocol, but with a bit of work and some loss of efficiency it can use TCP. We see this happening a lot today when web-based applications need some sort of RPC. TCP is ubiquitous on the

Web and known to work in all sorts of challenging environments, such as through NAT devices and firewalls. Consequently, it turns out to be simpler sometimes to build RPC-like mechanisms that run on top of TCP (and HTTP in many cases) even if that's not strictly the most efficient approach.

Similarly, it seems that RTP should be the protocol of choice for streaming of video, and it continues to be widely used, but there is also quite a trend toward the use of TCP (and HTTP) to deliver streaming video content. This approach is increasingly popular for delivery of entertainment video such as TV shows and movies for web-browser-based viewing. It is too early to tell how this will end up, but it is not hard to imagine a future in which TCP is the dominant transport protocol for video delivery.

Looking back on the "hourglass" architecture of the Internet that we discussed in Chapter 1, it's clear that some diversity of transport protocols was expected by the Internet's designers. But, at this point in the Internet's history, it almost looks like TCP might itself become part of the waist of the hourglass, providing the ubiquitous service on which a majority of applications will depend.

■ FURTHER READING

There is no doubt that TCP is a complex protocol and that in fact it has subtleties not illuminated in this chapter; therefore, the recommended reading list for this chapter includes the original TCP specification. Our motivation for including this specification is not so much to fill in the missing details as to expose you to what an honest-to-goodness protocol specification looks like. The next paper, by Birrell and Nelson, is the seminal paper on RPC. Third, the paper by Clark and Tennenhouse on protocol architecture introduced the concept of *Application Layer Framing* which inspired the design of RTP; this paper provides considerable insight into the challenges of designing protocols as application needs change.

- USC-ISI. Transmission Control Protocol. *Request for Comments* 793, September 1981.
- Birrell, A., and B. Nelson. Implementing remote procedure calls. *ACM Transactions on Computer Systems* 2(1):39–59, February 1984.
- Clark, D., and D. Tennenhouse. Architectural considerations for a new generation of protocols. *Proceedings of the SIGCOMM '90 Symposium*, pages 200–208, September 1990.

Beyond the protocol specification, the most complete description of TCP, including its implementation in Unix, can be found in Stevens [Ste94],

[SW95]. Also, the third volume of Comer and Stevens' TCP/IP series of books describes how to write client/server applications on top of TCP and UDP, using the Posix socket interface [CS00], the Windows socket interface [CS97], and the BSD socket interface [CS96]. SCTP, a reliable transport protocol that stakes out a different point in the design space than TCP, is described in a helpful overview [OY02] and specified in [Ste07].

Several papers evaluate the performance of different transport protocols at a very detailed level. For example, the article by Clark et al. [CJRS89] measures the processing overheads of TCP, a paper by Mosberger et al. [MPBO96] explores the limitations of protocol processing overheads, and Thekkath and Levy [TL93] and Schroeder and Burrows [SB89] examine RPC's performance in great detail.

The original TCP timeout calculation was described in the TCP specification (see above), while the Karn/Partridge algorithm was described in [KP91] and the Jacobson/Karels algorithm was proposed in [Jac88]. The TCP extensions are defined by Jacobson et al. [JBB92], while O'Malley and Peterson [OP91] argue that extending TCP in this way is not the right approach to solving the problem.

Several distributed operating systems have defined their own RPC protocols. Notable examples include the V system, described by Cheriton and Zwaenepoel [CZ85]; Sprite, described by Ousterhout et al. [OCD$^+$88]; and Amoeba, described by Mullender [Mul90].

RTP is described in RFC 3550 [SCFJ03], and there are numerous other RFCs (such as RFC 3551 [SC03]) that describe the profiles of various applications that use RTP. McCanne and Jacobson [MJ95] describe vic, one of the early video applications to use RTP.

Finally, the following live reference provides lots of information related to transport and other protocols:

- http://www.iana.org/protocols/: Information about all the options, constants, port numbers, etc., that have been defined for various Internet protocols. You can find here, among other things, the lists of TCP header flags, TCP options, and well-known port numbers for protocols that run over TCP and UDP.

EXERCISES

1. If a UDP datagram is sent from host A, port P to host B, port Q, but at host B there is no process listening to port Q, then B is to

send back an ICMP Port Unreachable message to A. Like all ICMP messages, this is addressed to A as a whole, not to port P on A.

(a) Give an example of when an application might want to receive such ICMP messages.

(b) Find out what an application has to do, on the operating system of your choice, to receive such messages.

(c) Why might it not be a good idea to send such messages directly back to the originating port P on A?

2. Consider a simple UDP-based protocol for requesting files (based somewhat loosely on the Trivial File Transport Protocol, or TFTP). The client sends an initial file request, and the server answers (if the file can be sent) with the first data packet. Client and server then continue with a stop-and-wait transmission mechanism.

(a) Describe a scenario by which a client might request one file but get another; you may allow the client application to exit abruptly and be restarted with the same port.

(b) Propose a change in the protocol that will make this situation much less likely.

3. Design a simple UDP-based protocol for retrieving files from a server. No authentication is to be provided. Stop-and-wait transmission of the data may be used. Your protocol should address the following issues:

(a) Duplication of the first packet should not duplicate the "connection."

(b) Loss of the final ACK should not necessarily leave the server in doubt as to whether the transfer succeeded.

(c) A late-arriving packet from a past connection shouldn't be interpretable as part of a current connection.

4. This chapter explains three sequences of state transitions during TCP connection teardown. There is a fourth possible sequence, which traverses an additional arc (not shown in Figure 5.7) from FIN_WAIT_1 to TIME_WAIT and labelled FIN + ACK/ACK. Explain the circumstances that result in this fourth teardown sequence.

5. When closing a TCP connection, why is the two-segment-lifetime timeout not necessary on the transition from LAST_ACK to CLOSED?

6. A sender on a TCP connection that receives a 0 advertised window periodically probes the receiver to discover when the window becomes nonzero. Why would the receiver need an extra timer if it were responsible for reporting that its advertised window had become nonzero (i.e., if the sender did not probe)?

7. Read the man page (or Windows equivalent) for the Unix/ Windows utility netstat. Use netstat to see the state of the local TCP connections. Find out how long closing connections spend in TIME_WAIT.

8. The sequence number field in the TCP header is 32 bits long, which is big enough to cover over 4 billion bytes of data. Even if this many bytes were never transferred over a single connection, why might the sequence number still wrap around from $2^{32} - 1$ to 0?

9. You are hired to design a reliable byte-stream protocol that uses a sliding window (like TCP). This protocol will run over a 1-Gbps network. The RTT of the network is 100 ms, and the maximum segment lifetime is 30 seconds.
   (a) How many bits would you include in the AdvertisedWindow and SequenceNum fields of your protocol header?
   (b) How would you determine the numbers given above, and which values might be less certain?

10. You are hired to design a reliable byte-stream protocol that uses a sliding window (like TCP). This protocol will run over a 1-Gbps network. The RTT of the network is 140 ms, and the maximum segment lifetime is 60 seconds. How many bits would you include in the AdvertisedWindow and SequenceNum fields of your protocol header?

11. Suppose a host wants to establish the reliability of a link by sending packets and measuring the percentage that is received; routers, for example, do this. Explain the difficulty doing this over a TCP connection.

12. Suppose TCP operates over a 1-Gbps link.
   (a) Assuming TCP could utilize the full bandwidth continuously, how long would it take the sequence numbers to wrap around completely?

(b) Suppose an added 32-bit timestamp field increments 1000 times during the wraparound time you found above. How long would it take for the timestamp to wrap around?

13. Suppose TCP operates over a 40-Gbps STS-768 link.
    (a) Assuming TCP could utilize the full bandwidth continuously, how long would it take the sequence numbers to wrap around completely?
    (b) Suppose an added 32-bit timestamp field which increments 1000 times during the wraparound time you found above. How long would it take for the timestamp to wrap around?

14. If host A receives two SYN packets from the same port from remote host B, the second may be either a retransmission of the original or, if B has crashed and rebooted, an entirely new connection request.
    (a) Describe the difference as seen by host A between these two cases.
    (b) Give an algorithmic description of what the TCP layer needs to do upon receiving a SYN packet. Consider the duplicate/new cases above and the possibility that nothing is listening to the destination port.

15. Suppose x and y are two TCP sequence numbers. Write a function to determine whether x comes before y (in the notation of *Request for Comments* 793, "$x =< y$") or after y; your solution should work even when sequence numbers wrap around.

16. Suppose an idle TCP connection exists between sockets A and B. A third party has eavesdropped and knows the current sequence number at both ends.
    (a) Suppose the third party sends A a forged packet ostensibly from B and with 100 bytes of new data. What happens? (Hint: Look up in *Request for Comments* 793 what TCP does when it receives an ACK that is not an "acceptable ACK.")
    (b) Suppose the third party sends each end such a forged 100-byte data packet ostensibly from the other end. What happens now? What would happen if A later sent 200 bytes of data to B?

17. Suppose party A connects to the Internet via a wireless network using DHCP to assign IP addresses. A opens several Telnet

connections (using TCP) and is then disconnected from the wireless network. Party B then connects and is assigned the same IP address that A had had. Assuming B were able to guess to what host(s) A had been connected, describe a sequence of probes that could enable B to obtain sufficient state information to continue with A's connections.

18. Diagnostic programs are commonly available that record the first 100 bytes, say, of every TCP connection to a certain ⟨host, port⟩. Outline what must be done with each received TCP packet, P, in order to determine if it contains data that belongs to the first 100 bytes of a connection to host **HOST**, port **PORT**. Assume the IP header is **P.IPHEAD**, the TCP header is **P.TCPHEAD**, and header fields are as named in Figures 3.16 and 5.4. (Hint: To get initial sequence numbers (ISNs) you will have to examine every packet with the **SYN** bit set. Ignore the fact that sequence numbers will eventually be reused.)

19. If a packet arrives at host A with B's source address, it could just as easily have been forged by any third host C. If, however, A accepts a TCP connection from B, then during the three-way handshake A sent ISN_A to B's address and received an acknowledgment of it. If C is not located so as to be able to eavesdrop on ISN_A, then it might seem that C could not have forged B's response.

   However, the algorithm for choosing ISN_A does give other unrelated hosts a fair chance of guessing it. Specifically, A selects ISN_A based on a clock value at the time of connection. *Request for Comments* 793 specifies that this clock value be incremented every 4 μs; common Berkeley implementations once simplified this to incrementing by 250,000 (or 256,000) once per second.

   (a) Given this simplified increment-once-per-second implementation, explain how an arbitrary host C could masquerade as B in at least the opening of a TCP connection. You may assume that B does not respond to SYN + ACK packets A is tricked into sending to it.

   (b) Assuming real RTTs can be estimated to within 40 ms, about how many tries would you expect it to take to implement the strategy of part (a) with the unsimplified "increment every 4 μs" TCP implementation?

20. The Nagle algorithm, built into most TCP implementations, requires the sender to hold a partial segment's worth of data (even if PUSHed) until either a full segment accumulates or the most recent outstanding ACK arrives.

    (a) Suppose the letters abcdefghi are sent, one per second, over a TCP connection with an RTT of 4.1 seconds. Draw a timeline indicating when each packet is sent and what it contains.

    (b) If the above were typed over a full-duplex Telnet connection, what would the user see?

    (c) Suppose that mouse position changes are being sent over the connection. Assuming that multiple position changes are sent each RTT, how would a user perceive the mouse motion with and without the Nagle algorithm?

21. Suppose a client C repeatedly connects via TCP to a given port on a server S, and that each time it is C that initiates the close.

    (a) How many TCP connections a second can C make here before it ties up all its available ports in TIME_WAIT state? Assume client ephemeral ports are in the range of 1024 to 5119, and that TIME_WAIT lasts 60 seconds.

    (b) Berkeley-derived TCP implementations typically allow a socket in TIME_WAIT state to be reopened before TIME_WAIT expires, if the highest sequence number used by the old incarnation of the connection is less than the ISN used by the new incarnation. This solves the problem of old data being accepted as new; however, TIME_WAIT also serves the purpose of handling late final FINs. What would such an implementation have to do to address this and still achieve strict compliance with the TCP requirement that a FIN sent anytime before or during a connection's TIME_WAIT receive the same response?

22. Explain why TIME_WAIT is a somewhat more serious problem if the server initiates the close than if the client does. Describe a situation in which this might reasonably happen.

23. What is the justification for the exponential increase in timeout value proposed by Karn and Partridge? Why, specifically, might a linear (or slower) increase be less desirable?

24. The Jacobson/Karels algorithm sets TimeOut to be 4 mean deviations above the mean. Assume that individual packet round-trip times follow a statistical normal distribution, for which 4 mean deviations are π standard deviations. Using statistical tables, for example, what is the probability that a packet will take more than TimeOut time to arrive?

25. Suppose a TCP connection, with window size 1, loses every other packet. Those that do arrive have RTT $= 1$ second. What happens? What happens to TimeOut? Do this for two cases:
    (a) After a packet is eventually received, we pick up where we left off, resuming with EstimatedRTT initialized to its pre-timeout value, and TimeOut double that.
    (b) After a packet is eventually received, we resume with TimeOut initialized to the last exponentially backed-off value used for the timeout interval.
    In the following four exercises, the calculations involved are straightforward with a spreadsheet.

26. Suppose, in TCP's adaptive retransmission mechanism, that EstimatedRTT is 4.0 seconds at some point and subsequent measured RTT's all are 1.0 second. How long does it take before the TimeOut value, as calculated by the Jacobson/Karels algorithm, falls below 4.0 seconds? Assume a plausible initial value of Deviation; how sensitive is your answer to this choice? Use $\delta = 1/8$.

27. Suppose, in TCP's adaptive retransmission mechanism, that EstimatedRTT is 90 at some point and subsequent measured RTTs are all 200. How long does it take before the TimeOut value, as calculated by the Jacobson/Karels algorithm, falls below 300? Assume initial Deviation value of 25; use $\delta = 1/8$.

28. Suppose TCP's measured RTT is 1.0 second except that every Nth RTT is 4.0 seconds. What is the largest N, approximately, that doesn't result in timeouts in the steady state (i.e., for which the Jacobson/Karels TimeOut remains greater than 4.0 seconds)? Use $\delta = 1/8$.

29. Suppose that TCP is measuring RTTs of 1.0 second, with a mean deviation of 0.1 second. Suddenly the RTT jumps to 5.0 seconds,

with no deviation. Compare the behaviors of the original and Jacobson/Karels algorithms for computing TimeOut. Specifically, how many timeouts are encountered with each algorithm? What is the largest TimeOut calculated? Use $\delta = 1/8$.

30. Suppose that, when a TCP segment is sent more than once, we take SampleRTT to be the time between the original transmission and the ACK, as in Figure 5.10(a). Show that if a connection with a 1-packet window loses every other packet (i.e., each packet is transmitted twice), then EstimatedRTT increases to infinity. Assume TimeOut = EstimatedRTT; both algorithms presented in the text always set TimeOut even larger. (Hint: EstimatedRTT = EstimatedRTT + $\beta \times$ (SampleRTT $-$ EstimatedRTT).)

31. Suppose that, when a TCP segment is sent more than once, we take SampleRTT to be the time between the most recent transmission and the ACK, as in Figure 5.10(b). Assume, for definiteness, that TimeOut = $2 \times$ EstimatedRTT. Sketch a scenario in which no packets are lost but EstimatedRTT converges to a third of the true RTT, and give a diagram illustrating the final steady state. (Hint: Begin with a sudden jump in the true RTT to just over the established TimeOut.)

32. Consult *Request for Comments* 793 to find out how TCP is supposed to respond if a FIN or an RST arrives with a sequence number other than NextByteExpected. Consider both when the sequence number is within the receive window and when it is not.

33. One of the purposes of TIME_WAIT is to handle the case of a data packet from a first incarnation of a connection arriving very late and being accepted as data for the second incarnation.
    (a) Explain why, for this to happen (in the absence of TIME_WAIT), the hosts involved would have to exchange several packets in sequence *after* the delayed packet was sent but before it was delivered.
    (b) Propose a network scenario that might account for such a late delivery.

34. Propose an extension to TCP by which one end of a connection can hand off its end to a third host; that is, if A were connected to B, and A handed off its connection to C, then afterwards C would be connected to B and A would not. Specify the new states and

transitions needed in the TCP state-transition diagram and any new packet types involved. You may assume all parties will understand this new option. What state should A go into immediately after the handoff?

35. TCP's simultaneous open feature is seldom used.
    (a) Propose a change to TCP in which this is disallowed. Indicate what changes would be made in the state diagram (and if necessary in the undiagrammed event responses).
    (b) Could TCP reasonably disallow simultaneous close?
    (c) Propose a change to TCP in which simultaneous SYNs exchanged by two hosts lead to two separate connections. Indicate what state diagram changes this entails and what header changes become necessary. Note that this now means that more than one connection can exist over a given pair of ⟨host, port⟩s. (You might also look up the first "Discussion" item on page 87 of *Request for Comments* 1122.)

36. TCP is a very symmetric protocol, but the client/server model is not. Consider an asymmetric TCP-like protocol in which only the server side is assigned a port number visible to the application layers. Client-side sockets would simply be abstractions that can be connected to server ports.
    (a) Propose header data and connection semantics to support this. What will you use to replace the client port number?
    (b) What form does TIME_WAIT now take? How would this be seen through the programming interface? Assume that a client socket could now be reconnected arbitrarily many times to a given server port, resources permitting.
    (c) Look up the rsh/rlogin protocol. How would the above break this?

37. The following exercise is concerned with the TCP state FIN_WAIT_2 (see Figure 5.7).
    (a) Describe how a client might leave a suitable server in state FIN_WAIT_2 indefinitely. What feature of the server's protocol is necessary here for this scenario?
    (b) Try this with some appropriate existing server. Either write a stub client or use an existing Telnet client capable of connecting to an arbitrary port. Use the netstat utility to verify that the server is in FIN_WAIT_2 state.

38. *Request for Comments* 1122 states (of TCP):

    > A host MAY implement a "half-duplex" TCP close sequence, so that an application that has called CLOSE cannot continue to read data from the connection. If such a host issues a CLOSE call while received data is still pending in TCP, or if new data is received after CLOSE is called, its TCP SHOULD send an RST to show that data was lost.

    Sketch a scenario involving the above in which data sent by *(not to!)* the closing host is lost. You may assume that the remote host, upon receiving an RST, discards all received data still unread in buffers.

39. When TCP sends a $\langle$SYN, SequenceNum $= x\rangle$ or $\langle$FIN, SequenceNum $= x\rangle$, the consequent ACK has Acknowledgment $= x + 1$; that is, SYNs and FINs each take up one unit in sequence number space. Is this necessary? If so, give an example of an ambiguity that would arise if the corresponding Acknowledgment were x instead of $x + 1$; if not, explain why.

40. Find out the generic format for TCP header options from *Request for Comments* 793.
    (a) Outline a strategy that would expand the space available for options beyond the current limit of 44 bytes.
    (b) Suggest an extension to TCP allowing the sender of an option a way of specifying what the receiver should do if the option is not understood. List several such receiver actions that might be useful, and try to give an example application of each.

41. The TCP header does not have a boot ID field. Why isn't there a problem with one end of a TCP connection crashing and rebooting, then sending a message with an ID it had previously used?

42. Suppose we were to implement remote file system mounting using an unreliable RPC protocol that offers zero-or-more semantics. If a message reply is received, this improves to at-least-once semantics. We define read(n) to return the specified nth block, rather than the next block in sequence; this way, reading once is the same as reading twice and at-least-once semantics is thus the same as exactly once.

(a) For what other file system operations is there no difference between at-least-once and exactly once semantics? Consider open, create, write, seek, opendir, readdir, mkdir, delete (*aka* unlink), and rmdir.

(b) For the remaining operations, which can have their semantics altered to achieve equivalence of at-least-once and exactly once? What file system operations are irreconcilable with at-least-once semantics?

(c) Suppose the semantics of the rmdir system call are now that the given directory is removed if it exists, and nothing is done otherwise. How could you write a program to delete directories that distinguishes between these two cases?

43. The RPC-based NFS remote file system is sometimes considered to have slower than expected write performance. In NFS, a server's RPC reply to a client write request means that the data is physically written to the server's disk, not just placed in a queue.

(a) Explain the bottleneck we might expect, even with infinite bandwidth, if the client sends all its write requests through a single logical channel, and explain why using a pool of channels could help. Hint: You will need to know a little about disk controllers.

(b) Suppose the server's reply means only that the data has been placed in the disk queue. Explain how this could lead to data loss that wouldn't occur with a local disk. Note that a system crash immediately after data was enqueued doesn't count, because that would cause data loss on a local disk as well.

(c) An alternative would be for the server to respond immediately to acknowledge the write request and to send its own separate request later to confirm the physical write. Propose different RPC semantics to achieve the same effect, but with a single logical request and reply.

44. Consider a client and server using an RPC mechanism that includes a channel abstraction and boot IDs.

(a) Give a scenario involving server reboot in which an RPC request is sent twice by the client and is executed twice by the server, with only a single ACK.

(b) How might the client become aware this had happened? Would the client be sure it had happened?

45. Suppose an RPC request is of the form: "Increment the value of field X of disk block N by 10%." Specify a mechanism to be used by the executing server to guarantee that an arriving request is executed exactly once, even if the server crashes while in the middle of the operation. Assume that individual disk block writes are either complete or else the block is unchanged. You may also assume that some designated "undo log" blocks are available. Your mechanism should include how the RPC server is to behave at restart.

46. Consider a SunRPC client sending a request to a server.
    (a) Under what circumstances can the client be sure its request has executed exactly once?
    (b) Suppose we wished to add at-most-once semantics to SunRPC. What changes would have to be made? Explain why adding one or more fields to the existing headers would not be sufficient.

47. Suppose TCP were to be used as the underlying transport in an RPC protocol; each TCP connection is to carry a sequential stream of requests and replies. What analog, if any, would TCP have for:
    (a) Channel ID
    (b) Message ID
    (c) Boot ID
    (d) A message type for requests
    (e) A message type for replies
    (f) A message type for acknowledgments
    (g) A message type for are-you-alive? messages
    Which of these would the overlying RPC protocol have to provide? Would some analog of implicit acknowledgments exist?

48. Write a test program that uses the socket interface to send messages between a pair of Unix workstations connected by some LAN (e.g., Ethernet, 802.11). Use this test program to perform the following experiments:
    (a) Measure the round-trip latency of TCP and UDP for different message sizes (e.g., 1 byte, 100 bytes, 200 bytes,..., 1000 bytes).

(b) Measure the throughput of TCP and UDP for 1-KB, 2-KB, 3-KB, ..., 32-KB messages. Plot the measured throughput as a function of message size.

(c) Measure the throughput of TCP by sending 1 MB of data from one host to another. Do this in a loop that sends a message of some size—for example, 1024 iterations of a loop that sends 1-KB messages. Repeat the experiment with different message sizes and plot the results.

49. Try to find situations where an RTP application might reasonably do the following:

   ■ Send multiple packets at essentially the same time that need different timestamps.

   ■ Send packets at different times that need the same timestamp.

   Argue, in consequence, that RTP timestamps must, in at least some cases, be provided (at least indirectly) by the application. (Hint: Think of cases where the sending rate and playback rate might not match.)

50. Having the RTP timestamp clock count time in units of one frame time or one voice sample time would be the minimum resolution to ensure accurate playback, but the time unit is usually considerably smaller; what is the purpose of this?

51. Suppose we want returning RTCP reports from receivers to amount to no more than 5% of the outgoing primary RTP stream. If each report is 84 bytes, the RTP traffic is 320 kbps, and there are 1000 recipients, how often do individual receivers get to report? What if there are 10,000 recipients?

52. RFC 3550 specifies that the time interval between receiver RTCP reports include a randomization factor to avoid having all the receivers sending at the same time. If all the receivers sent in the same 5% subinterval of their reply time interval, the arriving upstream RTCP traffic would rival the downstream RTP traffic.

   (a) Video receivers might reasonably wait to send their reports until the higher-priority task of processing and displaying one frame is completed; this might mean their RTCP transmissions were synchronized on frame boundaries. Is this likely to be a serious concern?

(b) With 10 receivers, what is the probability of their all sending in one particular 5% subinterval?

(c) With 10 receivers, what is the probability half will send in one particular 5% subinterval? Multiply this by 20 for an estimate of the probability half will all send in the same arbitrary 5% subinterval. (Hint: How many ways can we choose 5 receivers out of 10?)

53. What might a server actually do with the packet-loss-rate data and jitter data in receiver reports?

54. Propose a mechanism for deciding when to report an RTP packet as lost. How does your mechanism compare with the TCP adaptive retransmission mechanisms of Section 5.2.6?

6

Congestion Control and Resource Allocation

The hand that hath made you fair hath made you good.

–William Shakespeare

By now we have seen enough layers of the network protocol hierarchy to understand how data can be transferred among processes across heterogeneous networks. We now turn to a problem that spans the entire protocol stack—how to effectively and fairly allocate resources among a collection of competing users. The resources being shared include the bandwidth of the links and the buffers on the routers or switches where packets are queued awaiting transmission. Packets *contend* at a router for the use of a link, with each contending packet placed in a queue waiting its turn to be transmitted over the link. When

PROBLEM: ALLOCATING RESOURCES

too many packets are contending for the same link, the queue overflows and packets have to be dropped. When such drops become common events, the network is said to be *congested*. Most networks provide a *congestion-control* mechanism to deal with just such a situation.

Congestion control and resource allocation are two sides of the same coin. On the one hand, if the network takes an active role in allocating resources—for example, scheduling which virtual circuit gets to use a given physical link during a certain period of time—then congestion may be avoided, thereby making congestion control unnecessary. Allocating network resources with any precision is difficult, however, because the resources in question are distributed throughout the network; multiple links connecting a series of routers need to be scheduled. On the other hand, you can always let packet sources send as much data as they want and then recover from congestion should it occur. This is the easier approach, but it can be disruptive because many packets may be discarded by the network before congestion can be controlled. Furthermore, it is precisely at those times when the network is congested—that is, resources have become scarce relative to demand—that the need for resource allocation among competing users is most keenly felt. There are also solutions in the middle, whereby inexact allocation decisions are made, but congestion can still occur and hence some mechanism is still needed to recover from it. Whether you call such a mixed solution congestion control or resource allocation does not really matter. In some sense, it is both.

Congestion control and resource allocation involve both hosts and network elements such as routers. In network elements, various queuing disciplines can be used to control the order in which packets get transmitted and which packets get dropped. The queuing discipline can also segregate traffic to keep one user's packets from unduly affecting another user's packets. At the end hosts, the congestion-control mechanism paces how fast sources are allowed to send packets. This is done in an effort to keep congestion from occurring in the first place and, should it occur, to help eliminate the congestion.

This chapter starts with an overview of congestion control and resource allocation. We then discuss different queuing disciplines that can be implemented on the routers inside the network, followed by a description of the congestion-control algorithm provided by TCP on the hosts. The fourth section explores various techniques involving both routers and hosts that aim to avoid congestion before it becomes a problem. Finally, we examine the broad area of *quality of service*. We consider the needs of applications to receive different levels of resource allocation in the network and describe a number of ways in which they can request these resources and the network can meet the requests.

6.1 ISSUES IN RESOURCE ALLOCATION

Resource allocation and congestion control are complex issues that have been the subject of much study ever since the first network was designed. They are still active areas of research. One factor that makes these issues complex is that they are not isolated to one single level of a protocol hierarchy. Resource allocation is partially implemented in the routers, switches, and links inside the network and partially in the transport protocol running on the end hosts. End systems may use signalling protocols to convey their resource requirements to network nodes, which respond with information about resource availability. One of the main goals of this chapter is to define a framework in which these mechanisms can be understood, as well as to give the relevant details about a representative sample of mechanisms.

We should clarify our terminology before going any further. By *resource allocation*, we mean the process by which network elements try to meet the competing demands that applications have for network resources—primarily link bandwidth and buffer space in routers or switches. Of course, it will often not be possible to meet all the demands, meaning that some users or applications may receive fewer network resources than they want. Part of the resource allocation problem is deciding when to say no and to whom.

We use the term *congestion control* to describe the efforts made by network nodes to prevent or respond to overload conditions. Since congestion is generally bad for everyone, the first order of business is making congestion subside, or preventing it in the first place. This might be achieved simply by persuading a few hosts to stop sending, thus improving the situation for everyone else. However, it is more common for congestion-control mechanisms to have some aspect of fairness—that is, they try to share the pain among all users, rather than causing great pain to a few. Thus, we see that many congestion-control mechanisms have some sort of resource allocation built into them.

It is also important to understand the difference between flow control and congestion control. Flow control, as we have seen in Section 2.5, involves keeping a fast sender from overrunning a slow receiver. Congestion control, by contrast, is intended to keep a set of senders from sending too much data *into the network* because of lack of resources at some point. These two concepts are often confused; as we will see, they also share some mechanisms.

6.1.1 Network Model

We begin by defining three salient features of the network architecture. For the most part, this is a summary of material presented in the previous chapters that is relevant to the problem of resource allocation.

Packet-Switched Network

We consider resource allocation in a packet-switched network (or internet) consisting of multiple links and switches (or routers). Since most of the mechanisms described in this chapter were designed for use on the Internet, and therefore were originally defined in terms of routers rather than switches, we use the term *router* throughout our discussion. The problem is essentially the same, whether on a network or an internetwork.

In such an environment, a given source may have more than enough capacity on the immediate outgoing link to send a packet, but somewhere in the middle of a network its packets encounter a link that is being used by many different traffic sources. Figure 6.1 illustrates this situation—two high-speed links are feeding a low-speed link. This is in contrast to shared-access networks like Ethernet and wireless networks, where the source can directly observe the traffic on the network and decide accordingly whether or not to send a packet. We have already seen the algorithms used to allocate bandwidth on shared-access networks (Chapter 2). These access-control algorithms are, in some sense, analogous to congestion-control algorithms in a switched network.

Note that congestion control is a different problem than routing. While it is true that a congested link could be assigned a large edge weight by the routing protocol, and, as a consequence, routers would route around it, "routing around" a congested link does not generally solve the congestion problem. To see this, we need look no further than the simple network depicted in Figure 6.1, where all traffic has to flow through the same router to reach the destination. Although this is an extreme example, it is common to have a certain router that it is not possible to route around.[1] This router can become congested, and there is nothing the routing mechanism can do about it. This congested router is sometimes called the *bottleneck* router.

Connectionless Flows

For much of our discussion, we assume that the network is essentially connectionless, with any connection-oriented service implemented in the transport protocol that is running on the end hosts. (We explain the qualification "essentially" in a moment.) This is precisely the model of the

---

[1]It is also worth noting that the complexity of routing in the Internet is such that simply obtaining a reasonably direct, loop-free route is about the best you can hope for. Routing around congestion would be considered icing on the cake.

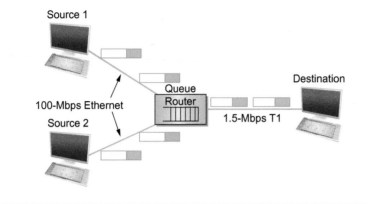

Source 1

100-Mbps Ethernet

Source 2

Queue
Router

1.5-Mbps T1

Destination

■ FIGURE 6.1 A potential bottleneck router.

Internet, where IP provides a connectionless datagram delivery service and TCP implements an end-to-end connection abstraction. Note that this assumption does not hold in virtual circuit networks such as ATM and X.25 (see Section 3.1.2). In such networks, a connection setup message traverses the network when a circuit is established. This setup message reserves a set of buffers for the connection at each router, thereby providing a form of congestion control—a connection is established only if enough buffers can be allocated to it at each router. The major shortcoming of this approach is that it leads to an underutilization of resources— buffers reserved for a particular circuit are not available for use by other traffic even if they were not currently being used by that circuit. The focus of this chapter is on resource allocation approaches that apply in an internetwork, and thus we focus mainly on connectionless networks.

We need to qualify the term *connectionless* because our classification of networks as being either connectionless or connection oriented is a bit too restrictive; there is a gray area in between. In particular, the assumption that all datagrams are completely independent in a connectionless network is too strong. The datagrams are certainly switched independently, but it is usually the case that a stream of datagrams between a particular pair of hosts flows through a particular set of routers. This idea of a *flow*—a sequence of packets sent between a source/destination pair and following the same route through the network—is an important abstraction in the context of resource allocation; it is one that we will use in this chapter.

One of the powers of the flow abstraction is that flows can be defined at different granularities. For example, a flow can be host-to-host (i.e., have the same source/destination host addresses) or process-to-process (i.e., have the same source/destination host/port pairs). In the latter case, a flow is essentially the same as a channel, as we have been using that term throughout this book. The reason we introduce a new term is that a flow is visible to the routers inside the network, whereas a channel is an end-to-end abstraction. Figure 6.2 illustrates several flows passing through a series of routers.

Because multiple related packets flow through each router, it sometimes makes sense to maintain some state information for each flow, information that can be used to make resource allocation decisions about the packets that belong to the flow. This state is sometimes called *soft state*; the main difference between soft state and hard state is that soft state need not always be explicitly created and removed by signalling. Soft state represents a middle ground between a purely connectionless network that maintains *no* state at the routers and a purely connection-oriented network that maintains hard state at the routers. In general, the correct operation of the network does not depend on soft state being present (each packet is still routed correctly without regard to this state), but when a packet happens to belong to a flow for which the router is currently maintaining soft state, then the router is better able to handle the packet.

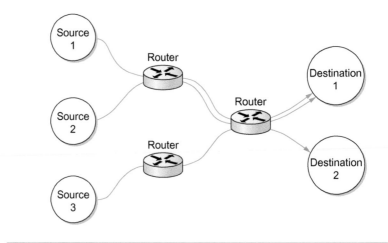

■ FIGURE 6.2 Multiple flows passing through a set of routers.

Note that a flow can be either implicitly defined or explicitly established. In the former case, each router watches for packets that happen to be traveling between the same source/destination pair—the router does this by inspecting the addresses in the header—and treats these packets as belonging to the same flow for the purpose of congestion control. In the latter case, the source sends a flow setup message across the network, declaring that a flow of packets is about to start. While explicit flows are arguably no different than a connection across a connection-oriented network, we call attention to this case because, even when explicitly established, a flow does not imply any end-to-end semantics and, in particular, does not imply the reliable and ordered delivery of a virtual circuit. It simply exists for the purpose of resource allocation. We will see examples of both implicit and explicit flows in this chapter.

Service Model

In the early part of this chapter, we will focus on mechanisms that assume the best-effort service model of the Internet. With best-effort service, all packets are given essentially equal treatment, with end hosts given no opportunity to ask the network that some packets or flows be given certain guarantees or preferential service. Defining a service model that supports some kind of preferred service or guarantee—for example, guaranteeing the bandwidth needed for a video stream—is the subject of Section 6.5. Such a service model is said to provide multiple *qualities of service* (QoS). As we will see, there is actually a spectrum of possibilities, ranging from a purely best-effort service model to one in which individual flows receive quantitative guarantees of QoS. One of the greatest challenges is to define a service model that meets the needs of a wide range of applications and even allows for the applications that will be invented in the future.

6.1.2 Taxonomy

There are countless ways in which resource allocation mechanisms differ, so creating a thorough taxonomy is a difficult proposition. For now, we describe three dimensions along which resource allocation mechanisms can be characterized; more subtle distinctions will be called out during the course of this chapter.

Router-Centric versus Host-Centric

Resource allocation mechanisms can be classified into two broad groups: those that address the problem from inside the network (i.e., at the routers or switches) and those that address it from the edges of the network (i.e., in the hosts, perhaps inside the transport protocol). Since it is the case that both the routers inside the network and the hosts at the edges of the network participate in resource allocation, the real issue is where the majority of the burden falls.

In a router-centric design, each router takes responsibility for deciding when packets are forwarded and selecting which packets are to be dropped, as well as for informing the hosts that are generating the network traffic how many packets they are allowed to send. In a host-centric design, the end hosts observe the network conditions (e.g., how many packets they are successfully getting through the network) and adjust their behavior accordingly. Note that these two groups are not mutually exclusive. For example, a network that places the primary burden for managing congestion on routers still expects the end hosts to adhere to any advisory messages the routers send, while the routers in networks that use end-to-end congestion control still have some policy, no matter how simple, for deciding which packets to drop when their queues do overflow.

Reservation-Based versus Feedback-Based

A second way that resource allocation mechanisms are sometimes classified is according to whether they use *reservations* or *feedback*. In a reservation-based system, some entity (e.g., the end host) asks the network for a certain amount of capacity to be allocated for a flow. Each router then allocates enough resources (buffers and/or percentage of the link's bandwidth) to satisfy this request. If the request cannot be satisfied at some router, because doing so would overcommit its resources, then the router rejects the reservation. This is analogous to getting a busy signal when trying to make a phone call. In a feedback-based approach, the end hosts begin sending data without first reserving any capacity and then adjust their sending rate according to the feedback they receive. This feedback can be either *explicit* (i.e., a congested router sends a "please slow down" message to the host) or *implicit* (i.e., the end host adjusts its sending rate according to the externally observable behavior of the network, such as packet losses).

Note that a reservation-based system always implies a router-centric resource allocation mechanism. This is because each router is responsible for keeping track of how much of its capacity is currently available and deciding whether new reservations can be admitted. Routers may also have to make sure each host lives within the reservation it made. If a host sends data faster than it claimed it would when it made the reservation, then that host's packets are good candidates for discarding, should the router become congested. On the other hand, a feedback-based system can imply either a router- or host-centric mechanism. Typically, if the feedback is explicit, then the router is involved, to at least some degree, in the resource allocation scheme. If the feedback is implicit, then almost all of the burden falls to the end host; the routers silently drop packets when they become congested.

Reservations do not have to be made by end hosts. It is possible for a network administrator to allocate resources to flows or to larger aggregates of traffic, as we will see in Section 6.5.3.

Window Based versus Rate Based

A third way to characterize resource allocation mechanisms is according to whether they are *window based* or *rate based*. This is one of the areas, noted above, where similar mechanisms and terminology are used for both flow control and congestion control. Both flow-control and resource allocation mechanisms need a way to express, to the sender, how much data it is allowed to transmit. There are two general ways of doing this: with a *window* or with a *rate*. We have already seen window-based transport protocols, such as TCP, in which the receiver advertises a window to the sender. This window corresponds to how much buffer space the receiver has, and it limits how much data the sender can transmit; that is, it supports flow control. A similar mechanism—window advertisement—can be used within the network to reserve buffer space (i.e., to support resource allocation). TCP's congestion-control mechanisms, described in Section 6.3, are window based.

It is also possible to control a sender's behavior using a rate—that is, how many bits per second the receiver or network is able to absorb. Rate-based control makes sense for many multimedia applications, which tend to generate data at some average rate and which need at least some minimum throughput to be useful. For example, a video codec of the sort described in Section 7.2.3 might generate video at an average rate of

1 Mbps with a peak rate of 2 Mbps. As we will see later in this chapter, rate-based characterization of flows is a logical choice in a reservation-based system that supports different qualities of service—the sender makes a reservation for so many bits per second, and each router along the path determines if it can support that rate, given the other flows it has made commitments to.

Summary of Resource Allocation Taxonomy

Classifying resource allocation approaches at two different points along each of three dimensions, as we have just done, would seem to suggest up to eight unique strategies. While eight different approaches are certainly possible, we note that in practice two general strategies seem to be most prevalent; these two strategies are tied to the underlying service model of the network.

On the one hand, a best-effort service model usually implies that feedback is being used, since such a model does not allow users to reserve network capacity. This, in turn, means that most of the responsibility for congestion control falls to the end hosts, perhaps with some assistance from the routers. In practice, such networks use window-based information. This is the general strategy adopted in the Internet and is the focus of Sections 6.3 and 6.4.

On the other hand, a QoS-based service model probably implies some form of reservation.[2] Support for these reservations is likely to require significant router involvement, such as queuing packets differently depending on the level of reserved resources they require. Moreover, it is natural to express such reservations in terms of rate, since windows are only indirectly related to how much bandwidth a user needs from the network. We discuss this topic in Section 6.5.

6.1.3 Evaluation Criteria

The final issue is one of knowing whether a resource allocation mechanism is good or not. Recall that in the problem statement at the start of this chapter we posed the question of how a network *effectively* and *fairly* allocates its resources. This suggests at least two broad measures by which a resource allocation scheme can be evaluated. We consider each in turn.

---

[2]As we will see in Section 6.5, resource reservations might be made by network managers rather than by hosts.

Effective Resource Allocation

A good starting point for evaluating the effectiveness of a resource allocation scheme is to consider the two principal metrics of networking: throughput and delay. Clearly, we want as much throughput and as little delay as possible. Unfortunately, these goals are often somewhat at odds with each other. One sure way for a resource allocation algorithm to increase throughput is to allow as many packets into the network as possible, so as to drive the utilization of all the links up to 100%. We would do this to avoid the possibility of a link becoming idle because an idle link necessarily hurts throughput. The problem with this strategy is that increasing the number of packets in the network also increases the length of the queues at each router. Longer queues, in turn, mean packets are delayed longer in the network.

To describe this relationship, some network designers have proposed using the ratio of throughput to delay as a metric for evaluating the effectiveness of a resource allocation scheme. This ratio is sometimes referred to as the *power* of the network:[3]

$$\text{Power} = \text{Throughput}/\text{Delay}$$

Note that it is not obvious that power is the right metric for judging resource allocation effectiveness. For one thing, the theory behind power is based on an M/M/1 queuing network[4] that assumes infinite queues; real networks have finite buffers and sometimes have to drop packets. For another, power is typically defined relative to a single connection (flow); it is not clear how it extends to multiple, competing connections. Despite these rather severe limitations, however, no alternatives have gained wide acceptance, and so power continues to be used.

The objective is to maximize this ratio, which is a function of how much load you place on the network. The load, in turn, is set by the resource allocation mechanism. Figure 6.3 gives a representative power curve, where, ideally, the resource allocation mechanism would operate at the peak of this curve. To the left of the peak, the mechanism is being too conservative; that is, it is not allowing enough packets to be sent to keep

---

[3]The actual definition is Power $= \text{Throughput}^{\alpha}/\text{Delay}$, where $0 < \alpha < 1$; $\alpha = 1$ results in power being maximized at the knee of the delay curve. Throughput is measured in units of data (e.g., bits) per second; delay in seconds.

[4]Since this is not a queuing theory book, we provide only this brief description of an M/M/1 queue. The 1 means it has a single server, and the Ms mean that the distribution of both packet arrival and service times is "Markovian," or exponential.

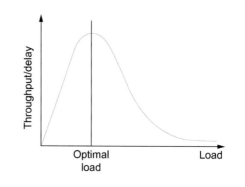

■ **FIGURE 6.3** Ratio of throughput to delay as a function of load.

the links busy. To the right of the peak, so many packets are being allowed into the network that increases in delay due to queuing are starting to dominate any small gains in throughput.

Interestingly, this power curve looks very much like the system throughput curve in a timesharing computer system. System throughput improves as more jobs are admitted into the system, until it reaches a point when there are so many jobs running that the system begins to thrash (spends all of its time swapping memory pages) and the throughput begins to drop.

As we will see in later sections of this chapter, many congestion-control schemes are able to control load in only very crude ways; that is, it is simply not possible to turn the "knob" a little and allow only a small number of additional packets into the network. As a consequence, network designers need to be concerned about what happens even when the system is operating under extremely heavy load—that is, at the rightmost end of the curve in Figure 6.3. Ideally, we would like to avoid the situation in which the system throughput goes to zero because the system is thrashing. In networking terminology, we want a system that is *stable*—where packets continue to get through the network even when the network is operating under heavy load. If a mechanism is not stable, the network may experience *congestion collapse*.

Fair Resource Allocation

The effective utilization of network resources is not the only criterion for judging a resource allocation scheme. We must also consider the issue of fairness. However, we quickly get into murky waters when we try to

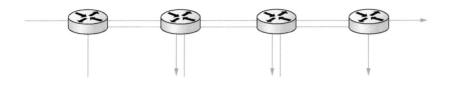

■ FIGURE 6.4 One four-hop flow competing with three one-hop flows.

define what exactly constitutes fair resource allocation. For example, a reservation-based resource allocation scheme provides an explicit way to create controlled unfairness. With such a scheme, we might use reservations to enable a video stream to receive 1 Mbps across some link while a file transfer receives only 10 kbps over the same link.

In the absence of explicit information to the contrary, when several flows share a particular link, we would like for each flow to receive an equal share of the bandwidth. This definition presumes that a *fair* share of bandwidth means an *equal* share of bandwidth. But, even in the absence of reservations, equal shares may not equate to fair shares. Should we also consider the length of the paths being compared? For example, as illustrated in Figure 6.4, what is fair when one four-hop flow is competing with three one-hop flows?

Assuming that fair implies equal and that all paths are of equal length, networking researcher Raj Jain proposed a metric that can be used to quantify the fairness of a congestion-control mechanism. Jain's fairness index is defined as follows. Given a set of flow throughputs $(x_1, x_2, \ldots, x_n)$ (measured in consistent units such as bits/second), the following function assigns a fairness index to the flows:

$$f(x_1, x_2, \ldots, x_n) = \frac{\left(\sum_{i=1}^{n} x_i\right)^2}{n \sum_{i=1}^{n} x_i^2}$$

The fairness index always results in a number between 0 and 1, with 1 representing greatest fairness. To understand the intuition behind this metric, consider the case where all n flows receive a throughput of 1 unit of data per second. We can see that the fairness index in this case is

$$\frac{n^2}{n \times n} = 1$$

Now, suppose one flow receives a throughput of $1 + \Delta$. Now the fairness index is

$$\frac{((n-1)+1+\Delta)^2}{n(n-1+(1+\Delta)^2)}$$

$$= \frac{n^2 + 2n\Delta + \Delta^2}{n^2 + 2n\Delta + n\Delta^2}$$

Note that the denominator exceeds the numerator by $(n-1)\Delta^2$. Thus, whether the odd flow out was getting more or less than all the other flows (positive or negative Δ), the fairness index has now dropped below one. Another simple case to consider is where only k of the n flows receive equal throughput, and the remaining $n - k$ users receive zero throughput, in which case the fairness index drops to k/n.

6.2 QUEUING DISCIPLINES

LAB 11:
Queues

Regardless of how simple or how sophisticated the rest of the resource allocation mechanism is, each router must implement some queuing discipline that governs how packets are buffered while waiting to be transmitted. The queuing algorithm can be thought of as allocating both bandwidth (which packets get transmitted) and buffer space (which packets get discarded). It also directly affects the latency experienced by a packet by determining how long a packet waits to be transmitted. This section introduces two common queuing algorithms—first-in, first-out (FIFO) and fair queuing (FQ)—and identifies several variations that have been proposed.

6.2.1 FIFO

The idea of FIFO queuing, also called first-come, first-served (FCFS) queuing, is simple: The first packet that arrives at a router is the first packet to be transmitted. This is illustrated in Figure 6.5(a), which shows a FIFO with "slots" to hold up to eight packets. Given that the amount of buffer space at each router is finite, if a packet arrives and the queue (buffer space) is full, then the router discards that packet, as shown in Figure 6.5(b). This is done without regard to which flow the packet belongs to or how important the packet is. This is sometimes called *tail drop*, since packets that arrive at the tail end of the FIFO are dropped.

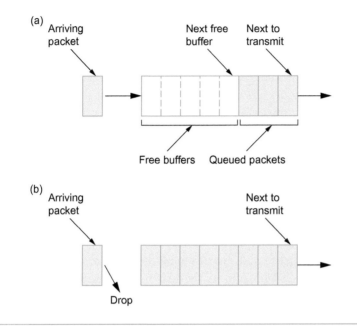

■ FIGURE 6.5 (a) FIFO queuing; (b) tail drop at a FIFO queue.

Note that tail drop and FIFO are two separable ideas. FIFO is a *scheduling discipline*—it determines the order in which packets are transmitted. Tail drop is a *drop policy*—it determines which packets get dropped. Because FIFO and tail drop are the simplest instances of scheduling discipline and drop policy, respectively, they are sometimes viewed as a bundle—the vanilla queuing implementation. Unfortunately, the bundle is often referred to simply as *FIFO queuing*, when it should more precisely be called *FIFO with tail drop*. Section 6.4 provides an example of another drop policy, which uses a more complex algorithm than "Is there a free buffer?" to decide when to drop packets. Such a drop policy may be used with FIFO, or with more complex scheduling disciplines.

FIFO with tail drop, as the simplest of all queuing algorithms, is the most widely used in Internet routers at the time of writing. This simple approach to queuing pushes all responsibility for congestion control and resource allocation out to the edges of the network. Thus, the prevalent form of congestion control in the Internet currently assumes no help from the routers: TCP takes responsibility for detecting and responding to congestion. We will see how this works in Section 6.3.

A simple variation on basic FIFO queuing is priority queuing. The idea is to mark each packet with a priority; the mark could be carried, for example, in the IP header, as we'll discuss in Section 6.5.3. The routers then implement multiple FIFO queues, one for each priority class. The router always transmits packets out of the highest-priority queue if that queue is nonempty before moving on to the next priority queue. Within each priority, packets are still managed in a FIFO manner. This idea is a small departure from the best-effort delivery model, but it does not go so far as to make guarantees to any particular priority class. It just allows high-priority packets to cut to the front of the line.

The problem with priority queuing, of course, is that the high-priority queue can starve out all the other queues; that is, as long as there is at least one high-priority packet in the high-priority queue, lower-priority queues do not get served. For this to be viable, there need to be hard limits on how much high-priority traffic is inserted in the queue. It should be immediately clear that we can't allow users to set their own packets to high priority in an uncontrolled way; we must either prevent them from doing this altogether or provide some form of "pushback" on users. One obvious way to do this is to use economics—the network could charge more to deliver high-priority packets than low-priority packets. However, there are significant challenges to implementing such a scheme in a decentralized environment such as the Internet.

One situation in which priority queuing is used in the Internet is to protect the most important packets—typically, the routing updates that are necessary to stabilize the routing tables after a topology change. Often there is a special queue for such packets, which can be identified by the Differentiated Services Code Point (formerly the TOS field) in the IP header. This is in fact a simple case of the idea of "Differentiated Services," the subject of Section 6.5.3.

6.2.2 Fair Queuing

The main problem with FIFO queuing is that it does not discriminate between different traffic sources, or, in the language introduced in the previous section, it does not separate packets according to the flow to which they belong. This is a problem at two different levels. At one level, it is not clear that any congestion-control algorithm implemented entirely at the source will be able to adequately control congestion with so little help from the routers. We will suspend judgment on this point until the next section when we discuss TCP congestion control. At another level, because the entire congestion-control mechanism is implemented at the sources and FIFO queuing does not provide a means to police how well the sources adhere to this mechanism, it is possible for an ill-behaved source (flow) to capture an arbitrarily large fraction of the network capacity. Considering the Internet again, it is certainly possible for a given application not to use TCP and, as a consequence, to bypass its end-to-end congestion-control mechanism. (Applications such as Internet telephony do this today.) Such an application is able to flood the Internet's routers with its own packets, thereby causing other applications' packets to be discarded.

Fair queuing (FQ) is an algorithm that has been proposed to address this problem. The idea of FQ is to maintain a separate queue for each flow currently being handled by the router. The router then services these queues in a sort of round-robin, as illustrated in Figure 6.6. When a flow sends packets too quickly, then its queue fills up. When a queue reaches a particular length, additional packets belonging to that flow's queue are discarded. In this way, a given source cannot arbitrarily increase its share of the network's capacity at the expense of other flows.

Note that FQ does not involve the router telling the traffic sources anything about the state of the router or in any way limiting how quickly a given source sends packets. In other words, FQ is still designed to be used in conjunction with an end-to-end congestion-control mechanism. It simply segregates traffic so that ill-behaved traffic sources do not interfere with those that are faithfully implementing the end-to-end

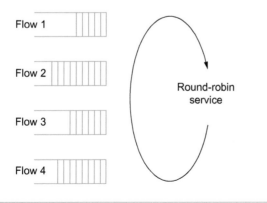

Flow 1

Flow 2

Round-robin
service

Flow 3

Flow 4

■ FIGURE 6.6 Round-robin service of four flows at a router.

algorithm. FQ also enforces fairness among a collection of flows managed by a well-behaved congestion-control algorithm.

As simple as the basic idea is, there are still a modest number of details that you have to get right. The main complication is that the packets being processed at a router are not necessarily the same length. To truly allocate the bandwidth of the outgoing link in a fair manner, it is necessary to take packet length into consideration. For example, if a router is managing two flows, one with 1000-byte packets and the other with 500-byte packets (perhaps because of fragmentation upstream from this router), then a simple round-robin servicing of packets from each flow's queue will give the first flow two-thirds of the link's bandwidth and the second flow only one-third of its bandwidth.

What we really want is bit-by-bit round-robin, where the router transmits a bit from flow 1, then a bit from flow 2, and so on. Clearly, it is not feasible to interleave the bits from different packets. The FQ mechanism therefore simulates this behavior by first determining when a given packet would finish being transmitted if it were being sent using bit-by-bit round-robin and then using this finishing time to sequence the packets for transmission.

To understand the algorithm for approximating bit-by-bit round-robin, consider the behavior of a single flow and imagine a clock that ticks once each time one bit is transmitted from all of the active flows. (A flow is active when it has data in the queue.) For this flow, let P_i denote the length of packet i, let S_i denote the time when the router starts to transmit packet i, and let F_i denote the time when the router finishes transmitting packet i. If P_i is expressed in terms of how many clock ticks it takes to transmit packet i (keeping in mind that time advances 1 tick each time this flow gets 1 bit's worth of service), then it is easy to see that $F_i = S_i + P_i$.

When do we start transmitting packet i? The answer to this question depends on whether packet i arrived before or after the router finished transmitting packet $i - 1$ from this flow. If it was before, then logically the first bit of packet i is transmitted immediately after the last bit of packet $i - 1$. On the other hand, it is possible that the router finished transmitting packet $i - 1$ long before i arrived, meaning that there was a period of time during which the queue for this flow was empty, so the round-robin mechanism could not transmit any packets from this flow. If we let A_i denote the time that packet i arrives at the router, then

$S_i = \max(F_{i-1}, A_i)$. Thus, we can compute

$$F_i = \max(F_{i-1}, A_i) + P_i$$

Now we move on to the situation in which there is more than one flow, and we find that there is a catch to determining A_i. We can't just read the wall clock when the packet arrives. As noted above, we want time to advance by one tick each time all the active flows get one bit of service under bit-by-bit round-robin, so we need a clock that advances more slowly when there are more flows. Specifically, the clock must advance by one tick when n bits are transmitted if there are n active flows. This clock will be used to calculate A_i.

Now, for every flow, we calculate F_i for each packet that arrives using the above formula. We then treat all the F_i as timestamps, and the next packet to transmit is always the packet that has the lowest timestamp—the packet that, based on the above reasoning, should finish transmission before all others.

Note that this means that a packet can arrive on a flow, and, because it is shorter than a packet from some other flow that is already in the queue waiting to be transmitted, it can be inserted into the queue in front of that longer packet. However, this does not mean that a newly arriving packet can preempt a packet that is currently being transmitted. It is this lack of preemption that keeps the implementation of FQ just described from exactly simulating the bit-by-bit round-robin scheme that we are attempting to approximate.

To better see how this implementation of fair queuing works, consider the example given in Figure 6.7. Part (a) shows the queues for two flows;

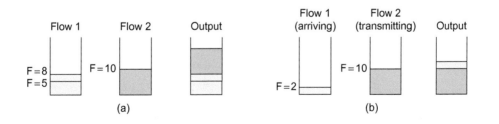

FIGURE 6.7 Example of fair queuing in action: (a) Packets with earlier finishing times are sent first; (b) sending of a packet already in progress is completed.

the algorithm selects both packets from flow 1 to be transmitted before the packet in the flow 2 queue, because of their earlier finishing times. In (b), the router has already begun to send a packet from flow 2 when the packet from flow 1 arrives. Though the packet arriving on flow 1 would have finished before flow 2 if we had been using perfect bit-by-bit fair queuing, the implementation does not preempt the flow 2 packet.

There are two things to notice about fair queuing. First, the link is never left idle as long as there is at least one packet in the queue. Any queuing scheme with this characteristic is said to be *work conserving*. One effect of being work conserving is that if I am sharing a link with a lot of flows that are not sending any data then; I can use the full link capacity for my flow. As soon as the other flows start sending, however, they will start to use their share and the capacity available to my flow will drop.

The second thing to notice is that if the link is fully loaded and there are n flows sending data, I cannot use more than $1/n$th of the link bandwidth. If I try to send more than that, my packets will be assigned increasingly large timestamps, causing them to sit in the queue longer awaiting transmission. Eventually, the queue will overflow—although whether it is my packets or someone else's that are dropped is a decision that is not determined by the fact that we are using fair queuing. This is determined by the drop policy; FQ is a scheduling algorithm, which, like FIFO, may be combined with various drop policies.

Because FQ is work conserving, any bandwidth that is not used by one flow is automatically available to other flows. For example, if we have four flows passing through a router, and all of them are sending packets, then each one will receive one-quarter of the bandwidth. But, if one of them is idle long enough that all its packets drain out of the router's queue, then the available bandwidth will be shared among the remaining three flows, which will each now receive one-third of the bandwidth. Thus, we can think of FQ as providing a guaranteed minimum share of bandwidth to each flow, with the possibility that it can get more than its guarantee if other flows are not using their shares.

It is possible to implement a variation of FQ, called *weighted fair queuing* (WFQ), that allows a weight to be assigned to each flow (queue). This weight logically specifies how many bits to transmit each time the router services that queue, which effectively controls the percentage of the link's bandwidth that that flow will get. Simple FQ gives each queue a weight of 1, which means that logically only 1 bit is transmitted from each queue each time around. This results in each flow getting $1/n$th of the bandwidth when there are n flows. With WFQ, however, one queue might have a weight of 2, a second queue might have a weight of 1, and a third queue might have a weight of 3. Assuming that each queue always contains a packet waiting to be transmitted, the first flow will get one-third of the available bandwidth, the second will get one-sixth of the available bandwidth, and the third will get one-half of the available bandwidth.

While we have described WFQ in terms of flows, note that it could be implemented on *classes* of traffic, where classes are defined in some other way than the simple flows introduced at the start of this chapter. For example, we could use some bits in the IP header to identify classes and allocate a queue and a weight to each class. This is exactly what is proposed as part of the Differentiated Services architecture described in Section 6.5.3.

Note that a router performing WFQ must learn what weights to assign to each queue from somewhere, either by manual configuration or by some sort of signalling from the sources. In the latter case, we are moving toward a reservation-based model. Just assigning a weight to a queue provides a rather weak form of reservation because these weights are only indirectly related to the bandwidth the flow receives. (The bandwidth available to a flow also depends, for example, on how many other flows are sharing the link.) We will see in Section 6.5.2 how WFQ can be used as a component of a reservation-based resource allocation mechanism.

Finally, we observe that this whole discussion of queue management illustrates an important system design principle known as *separating policy and mechanism*. The idea is to view each mechanism as a black box that provides a multifaceted service that can be controlled by a set of knobs. A policy specifies a particular setting of those knobs but does not know (or care) about how the black box is implemented. In this case, the mechanism in question is the queuing discipline, and the policy is a particular setting of which flow gets what level of service (e.g., priority or weight). We discuss some policies that can be used with the WFQ mechanism in Section 6.5.

6.3 TCP CONGESTION CONTROL

This section describes the predominant example of end-to-end congestion control in use today, that implemented by TCP. The essential strategy of TCP is to send packets into the network without a reservation and then to react to observable events that occur. TCP assumes only FIFO queuing in the network's routers, but also works with fair queuing.

TCP congestion control was introduced into the Internet in the late 1980s by Van Jacobson, roughly eight years after the TCP/IP protocol stack had become operational. Immediately preceding this time, the Internet was suffering from congestion collapse—hosts would send their packets into the Internet as fast as the advertised window would allow, congestion would occur at some router (causing packets to be dropped), and the hosts would time out and retransmit their packets, resulting in even more congestion.

Broadly speaking, the idea of TCP congestion control is for each source to determine how much capacity is available in the network, so that it knows how many packets it can safely have in transit. Once a given source has this many packets in transit, it uses the arrival of an ACK as a signal that one of its packets has left the network and that it is therefore safe to insert a new packet into the network without adding to the level of congestion. By using ACKs to pace the transmission of packets, TCP is said to be *self-clocking*. Of course, determining the available capacity in the first place is no easy task. To make matters worse, because other connections come and go, the available bandwidth changes over time, meaning that any given source must be able to adjust the number of packets it has in transit. This section describes the algorithms used by TCP to address these and other problems.

Note that, although we describe the TCP congestion-control mechanisms one at a time, thereby giving the impression that we are talking about three independent mechanisms, it is only when they are taken as a whole that we have TCP congestion control. Also, while we are going to begin here with the variant of TCP congestion control most often referred to as *standard TCP*, we will see that there are actually quite a few variants of TCP congestion control in use today, and researchers continue to explore new approaches to addressing this problem. Some of these new approaches are discussed below.

6.3.1 Additive Increase/Multiplicative Decrease

TCP maintains a new state variable for each connection, called CongestionWindow, which is used by the source to limit how much data it is allowed to have in transit at a given time. The congestion window is congestion control's counterpart to flow control's advertised window.

TCP is modified such that the maximum number of bytes of unacknowledged data allowed is now the minimum of the congestion window and the advertised window. Thus, using the variables defined in Section 5.2.4, TCP's effective window is revised as follows:

$$MaxWindow = MIN(CongestionWindow, AdvertisedWindow)$$

$$EffectiveWindow = MaxWindow - (LastByteSent - LastByteAcked).$$

That is, MaxWindow replaces AdvertisedWindow in the calculation of EffectiveWindow. Thus, a TCP source is allowed to send no faster than the slowest component—the network or the destination host—can accommodate.

The problem, of course, is how TCP comes to learn an appropriate value for CongestionWindow. Unlike the AdvertisedWindow, which is sent by the receiving side of the connection, there is no one to send a suitable CongestionWindow to the sending side of TCP. The answer is that the TCP source sets the CongestionWindow based on the level of congestion it perceives to exist in the network. This involves decreasing the congestion window when the level of congestion goes up and increasing the congestion window when the level of congestion goes down. Taken together, the mechanism is commonly called *additive increase/multiplicative decrease* (AIMD); the reason for this mouthful of a name will become apparent below.

The key question, then, is how does the source determine that the network is congested and that it should decrease the congestion window? The answer is based on the observation that the main reason packets are not delivered, and a timeout results, is that a packet was dropped due to congestion. It is rare that a packet is dropped because of an error during transmission. Therefore, TCP interprets timeouts as a sign of congestion and reduces the rate at which it is transmitting. Specifically, each time a timeout occurs, the source sets CongestionWindow to half of its previous value. This halving of the CongestionWindow for each timeout corresponds to the "multiplicative decrease" part of AIMD.

Although CongestionWindow is defined in terms of bytes, it is easiest to understand multiplicative decrease if we think in terms of whole packets. For example, suppose the CongestionWindow is currently set to 16 packets. If a loss is detected, CongestionWindow is set to 8. (Normally, a loss is detected when a timeout occurs, but as we see below, TCP has another mechanism to detect dropped packets.) Additional losses cause

CongestionWindow to be reduced to 4, then 2, and finally to 1 packet. CongestionWindow is not allowed to fall below the size of a single packet, or in TCP terminology, the *maximum segment size* (MSS).

A congestion-control strategy that only decreases the window size is obviously too conservative. We also need to be able to increase the congestion window to take advantage of newly available capacity in the network. This is the "additive increase" part of AIMD, and it works as follows. Every time the source successfully sends a CongestionWindow's worth of packets—that is, each packet sent out during the last round-trip time (RTT) has been ACKed—it adds the equivalent of 1 packet to CongestionWindow. This linear increase is illustrated in Figure 6.8. Note that, in practice, TCP does not wait for an entire window's worth of ACKs to add 1 packet's worth to the congestion window, but instead increments CongestionWindow by a little for each ACK that arrives. Specifically, the

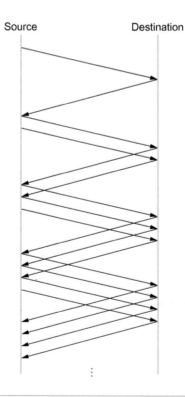

■ FIGURE 6.8 Packets in transit during additive increase, with one packet being added each RTT.

congestion window is incremented as follows each time an ACK arrives:

$$\text{Increment} = \text{MSS} \times (\text{MSS}/\text{CongestionWindow})$$

$$\text{CongestionWindow}+ = \text{Increment}$$

That is, rather than incrementing CongestionWindow by an entire MSS bytes each RTT, we increment it by a fraction of MSS every time an ACK is received. Assuming that each ACK acknowledges the receipt of MSS bytes, then that fraction is MSS/CongestionWindow.

   This pattern of continually increasing and decreasing the congestion window continues throughout the lifetime of the connection. In fact, if you plot the current value of CongestionWindow as a function of time, you get a sawtooth pattern, as illustrated in Figure 6.9. The important concept to understand about AIMD is that the source is willing to reduce its congestion window at a much faster rate than it is willing to increase its congestion window. This is in contrast to an additive increase/additive decrease strategy in which the window would be increased by 1 packet when an ACK arrives and decreased by 1 when a timeout occurs. It has been shown that AIMD is a necessary condition for a congestion-control mechanism to be stable (see the Further Reading section). One intuitive reason to decrease the window aggressively and increase it conservatively is that the consequences of having too large a window are much worse than those of it being too small. For example, when the window is too large, packets that are dropped will be retransmitted, making congestion even worse; thus, it is important to get out of this state quickly.

   Finally, since a timeout is an indication of congestion that triggers multiplicative decrease, TCP needs the most accurate timeout mechanism it

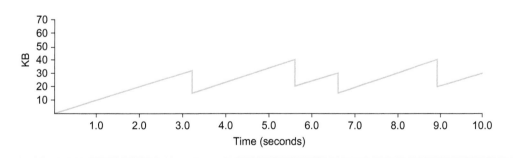

■ FIGURE 6.9 Typical TCP sawtooth pattern.

When Loss Doesn't Mean Congestion: TCP Over Wireless

There is one situation in which TCP congestion control has a tendency to fail spectacularly. When a link drops packets at a relatively high rate due to bit errors—something that is fairly common on wireless links—TCP misinterprets this as a signal of congestion. Consequently, the TCP sender reduces its rate, which typically has no effect on the rate of bit errors, so the situation can continue until the send window drops to a single packet. At this point, the throughput achieved by TCP will deteriorate to one packet per round-trip time, which may be much less than the appropriate rate for a network that is not actually experiencing congestion.

Given this situation, you may wonder how it is that TCP works at all over wireless networks. Fortunately, there are a number of ways to address the problem. Most commonly, some steps are taken at the link layer to reduce or hide packet losses due to bit errors. For example, 802.11 networks apply forward error correction (FEC) to the transmitted packets so that some number of errors can be corrected by the receiver. Another approach is to do link-layer retransmission, so that even if a packet is corrupted and dropped it eventually gets sent successfully, and the initial loss never becomes apparent to TCP. Each of these approaches has its problems: FEC wastes some bandwidth and will sometimes still fail to correct errors, while retransmission increases both the RTT of the connection and its variance, leading to worse performance.

Another approach used in some situations is to split the TCP connection into wireless and wired segments. There are many variations on this idea, but the basic approach is to treat losses on the wired segment as congestion signals but treat losses on the wireless segment as being caused by bit errors. This sort of technique has been used in satellite networks, where the RTT is so long already that you really don't want to make it any longer. Unlike the link-layer approaches, however, this one is a fundamental change to the end-to-end operation of the protocol; it also means that the forward and reverse paths of the connection have to pass through the same "middlebox" that is doing the splitting of the connection.

Another set of approaches tries to distinguish intelligently between the two difference classes of loss: congestion and bit errors. There are clues that losses are due to congestion, such as increasing RTT and correlation among successive losses. Explicit Congestion Notification (ECN) marking (see Section 6.4.2) can also provide an indication that congestion is imminent, so a subsequent loss is more likely to be congestion related. Clearly, if you can detect the difference between the two types of loss, then TCP doesn't need to reduce its window for bit-error-related losses. Unfortunately, it is hard to make this determination with 100% accuracy, and this issue continues to be an area of active research.

can afford. We already covered TCP's timeout mechanism in Section 5.2.6, so we do not repeat it here. The two main things to remember about that mechanism are that (1) timeouts are set as a function of both the average RTT and the standard deviation in that average, and (2) due to the cost of measuring each transmission with an accurate clock, TCP only samples the round-trip time once per RTT (rather than once per packet) using a coarse-grained (500-ms) clock.

6.3.2 Slow Start

The additive increase mechanism just described is the right approach to use when the source is operating close to the available capacity of the network, but it takes too long to ramp up a connection when it is starting from scratch. TCP therefore provides a second mechanism, iron-ically called *slow start,*[5] which is used to increase the congestion window rapidly from a cold start. Slow start effectively increases the congestion window exponentially, rather than linearly.

Specifically, the source starts out by setting CongestionWindow to one packet. When the ACK for this packet arrives, TCP adds 1 to Conges-tionWindow and then sends two packets. Upon receiving the correspond-ing two ACKs, TCP increments CongestionWindow by 2—one for each ACK—and next sends four packets. The end result is that TCP effectively doubles the number of packets it has in transit every RTT. Figure 6.10 shows the growth in the number of packets in transit during slow start. Compare this to the linear growth of additive increase illustrated in Figure 6.8.

Why any exponential mechanism would be called "slow" is puzzling at first, but it can be explained if put in the proper historical context. We need to compare slow start not against the linear mechanism of the pre-vious subsection, but against the original behavior of TCP. Consider what happens when a connection is established and the source first starts to send packets—that is, when it currently has no packets in transit. If the source sends as many packets as the advertised window allows—which is exactly what TCP did before slow start was developed—then even if there is a fairly large amount of bandwidth available in the network, the

---

[5] Even though the original paper describing slow start called it "slow-start," the unhy-phenated term is more commonly used today, so we omit the hyphen here.

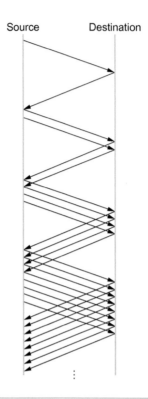

■ FIGURE 6.10 Packets in transit during slow start.

routers may not be able to consume this burst of packets. It all depends on how much buffer space is available at the routers. Slow start was therefore designed to space packets out so that this burst does not occur. In other words, even though its exponential growth is faster than linear growth, slow start is much "slower" than sending an entire advertised window's worth of data all at once.

There are actually two different situations in which slow start runs. The first is at the very beginning of a connection, at which time the source has no idea how many packets it is going to be able to have in transit at a given time. (Keep in mind that TCP runs over everything from 9600-bps links to 2.4-Gbps links, so there is no way for the source to know the network's capacity.) In this situation, slow start continues to double CongestionWindow each RTT until there is a loss, at which time a timeout causes multiplicative decrease to divide CongestionWindow by 2.

The second situation in which slow start is used is a bit more subtle; it occurs when the connection goes dead while waiting for a timeout to occur. Recall how TCP's sliding window algorithm works—when a packet is lost, the source eventually reaches a point where it has sent as much data as the advertised window allows, and so it blocks while waiting for an ACK that will not arrive. Eventually, a timeout happens, but by this time there are no packets in transit, meaning that the source will receive no ACKs to "clock" the transmission of new packets. The source will instead receive a single cumulative ACK that reopens the entire advertised window, but, as explained above, the source then uses slow start to restart the flow of data rather than dumping a whole window's worth of data on the network all at once.

Although the source is using slow start again, it now knows more information than it did at the beginning of a connection. Specifically, the source has a current (and useful) value of CongestionWindow; this is the value of CongestionWindow that existed prior to the last packet loss, divided by 2 as a result of the loss. We can think of this as the *target* congestion window. Slow start is used to rapidly increase the sending rate up to this value, and then additive increase is used beyond this point. Notice that we have a small bookkeeping problem to take care of, in that we want to remember the target congestion window resulting from multiplicative decrease as well as the *actual* congestion window being used by slow start. To address this problem, TCP introduces a temporary variable to store the target window, typically called CongestionThreshold, that is set equal to the CongestionWindow value that results from multiplicative decrease. The variable CongestionWindow is then reset to one packet, and it is incremented by one packet for every ACK that is received until it reaches CongestionThreshold, at which point it is incremented by one packet per RTT.

In other words, TCP increases the congestion window as defined by the following code fragment:

```
{
    u_int   cw = state->CongestionWindow;
    u_int   incr = state->maxseg;

    if (cw > state->CongestionThreshold)
        incr = incr * incr / cw;
```

```
    state->CongestionWindow = MIN(cw + incr, TCP_MAXWIN);
}
```

where state represents the state of a particular TCP connection and TCP_MAXWIN defines an upper bound on how large the congestion window is allowed to grow.

Figure 6.11 traces how TCP's CongestionWindow increases and decreases over time and serves to illustrate the interplay of slow start and additive increase/multiplicative decrease. This trace was taken from an actual TCP connection and shows the current value of CongestionWindow—the colored line—over time.

There are several things to notice about this trace. The first is the rapid increase in the congestion window at the beginning of the connection. This corresponds to the initial slow start phase. The slow start phase continues until several packets are lost at about 0.4 seconds into the connection, at which time CongestionWindow flattens out at about 34 KB. (Why so many packets are lost during slow start is discussed below.) The reason why the congestion window flattens is that there are no ACKs arriving, due to the fact that several packets were lost. In fact, no new packets are sent during this time, as denoted by the lack of hash marks at the top of the graph. A timeout eventually happens at approximately 2 seconds, at which time the congestion window is divided by 2 (i.e., cut from approximately 34 KB to around 17 KB) and CongestionThreshold is set to this value. Slow start then causes CongestionWindow to be reset to one packet and to start ramping up from there.

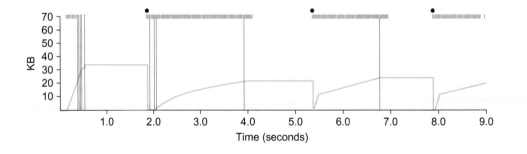

■ FIGURE 6.11 Behavior of TCP congestion control. Colored line = value of CongestionWindow over time; solid bullets at top of graph = timeouts; hash marks at top of graph = time when each packet is transmitted; vertical bars = time when a packet that was eventually retransmitted was first transmitted.

There is not enough detail in the trace to see exactly what happens when a couple of packets are lost just after 2 seconds, so we jump ahead to the linear increase in the congestion window that occurs between 2 and 4 seconds. This corresponds to additive increase. At about 4 seconds, CongestionWindow flattens out, again due to a lost packet. Now, at about 5.5 seconds:

1. A timeout happens, causing the congestion window to be divided by 2, dropping it from approximately 22 KB to 11 KB, and CongestionThreshold is set to this amount.

2. CongestionWindow is reset to one packet, as the sender enters slow start.

3. Slow start causes CongestionWindow to grow exponentially until it reaches CongestionThreshold.

4. CongestionWindow then grows linearly.

The same pattern is repeated at around 8 seconds when another timeout occurs.

We now return to the question of why so many packets are lost during the initial slow start period. At this point, TCP is attempting to learn how much bandwidth is available on the network. This is a very difficult task. If the source is not aggressive at this stage—for example, if it only increases the congestion window linearly—then it takes a long time for it to discover how much bandwidth is available. This can have a dramatic impact on the throughput achieved for this connection. On the other hand, if the source is aggressive at this stage, as TCP is during exponential growth, then the source runs the risk of having half a window's worth of packets dropped by the network.

To see what can happen during exponential growth, consider the situation in which the source was just able to successfully send 16 packets through the network, causing it to double its congestion window to 32. Suppose, however, that the network happens to have just enough capacity to support 16 packets from this source. The likely result is that 16 of the 32 packets sent under the new congestion window will be dropped by the network; actually, this is the worst-case outcome, since some of the packets will be buffered in some router. This problem will become increasingly severe as the delay $\times$ bandwidth product of networks increases. For example, a delay $\times$ bandwidth product of 500 KB means that each connection has the potential to lose up to 500 KB of data at the beginning of each connection. Of course, this assumes that both the source and the destination implement the "big windows" extension.

Some protocol designers have proposed alternatives to slow start, whereby the source tries to estimate the available bandwidth by more sophisticated means. A recent example is the *quick-start* mechanism undergoing standardization at the IETF. The basic idea is that a TCP sender can ask for an initial sending rate greater than slow start would allow by putting a requested rate in its SYN packet as an IP option. Routers along the path can examine the option, evaluate the current level of congestion on the outgoing link for this flow, and decide if that rate is acceptable, if a lower rate would be acceptable, or if standard slow start should be used. By the time the SYN reaches the receiver, it will contain either a rate that was acceptable to all routers on the path or an indication that one or more routers on the path could not support the quick-start request. In the former case, the TCP sender uses that rate to begin transmission; in the latter case, it falls back to standard slow start. If TCP is allowed to start off sending at a higher rate, a session could more quickly reach the point of filling the pipe, rather than taking many round-trip times to do so.

Clearly one of the challenges to this sort of enhancement to TCP is that it requires substantially more cooperation from the routers than standard TCP does. If a single router in the path does not support quick-start, then the system reverts to standard slow start. Thus, it could be a long time before these types of enhancements could make it into the Internet; for now, they are more likely to be used in controlled network environments (e.g., research networks).

6.3.3 Fast Retransmit and Fast Recovery

The mechanisms described so far were part of the original proposal to add congestion control to TCP. It was soon discovered, however, that the coarse-grained implementation of TCP timeouts led to long periods of time during which the connection went dead while waiting for a timer to expire. Because of this, a new mechanism called *fast retransmit* was added to TCP. Fast retransmit is a heuristic that sometimes triggers the retransmission of a dropped packet sooner than the regular timeout mechanism. The fast retransmit mechanism does not replace regular timeouts; it just enhances that facility.

The idea of fast retransmit is straightforward. Every time a data packet arrives at the receiving side, the receiver responds with an acknowledgment, even if this sequence number has already been acknowledged. Thus, when a packet arrives out of order—when TCP cannot yet acknowledge the data the packet contains because earlier data has not yet arrived—TCP resends the same acknowledgment it sent the last time. This second transmission of the same acknowledgment is called a *duplicate ACK*. When the sending side sees a duplicate ACK, it knows that the other side must have received a packet out of order, which suggests that an earlier packet might have been lost. Since it is also possible that the earlier packet has only been delayed rather than lost, the sender waits until it sees some number of duplicate ACKs and then retransmits the missing packet. In practice, TCP waits until it has seen three duplicate ACKs before retransmitting the packet.

Figure 6.12 illustrates how duplicate ACKs lead to a fast retransmit. In this example, the destination receives packets 1 and 2, but packet 3 is lost in the network. Thus, the destination will send a duplicate ACK for packet 2 when packet 4 arrives, again when packet 5 arrives, and so on. (To simplify this example, we think in terms of packets 1, 2, 3, and so on, rather

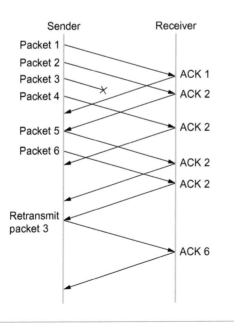

■ FIGURE 6.12   Fast retransmit based on duplicate ACKs.

than worrying about the sequence numbers for each byte.) When the sender sees the third duplicate ACK for packet 2—the one sent because the receiver had gotten packet 6—it retransmits packet 3. Note that when the retransmitted copy of packet 3 arrives at the destination, the receiver then sends a cumulative ACK for everything up to and including packet 6 back to the source.

Figure 6.13 illustrates the behavior of a version of TCP with the fast retransmit mechanism. It is interesting to compare this trace with that given in Figure 6.11, where fast retransmit was not implemented—the long periods during which the congestion window stays flat and no packets are sent has been eliminated. In general, this technique is able to eliminate about half of the coarse-grained timeouts on a typical TCP connection, resulting in roughly a 20% improvement in the throughput over what could otherwise have been achieved. Notice, however, that the fast retransmit strategy does not eliminate all coarse-grained timeouts. This is because for a small window size there will not be enough packets in transit to cause enough duplicate ACKs to be delivered. Given enough lost packets—for example, as happens during the initial slow start phase— the sliding window algorithm eventually blocks the sender until a timeout occurs. Given the current 64-KB maximum advertised window size, TCP's fast retransmit mechanism is able to detect up to three dropped packets per window in practice.

Finally, there is one last improvement we can make. When the fast retransmit mechanism signals congestion, rather than drop the congestion window all the way back to one packet and run slow start, it is

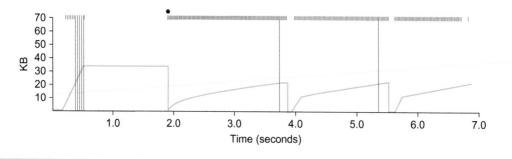

■ FIGURE 6.13 Trace of TCP with fast retransmit. Colored line = **CongestionWindow**; solid bullet = timeout; hash marks = time when each packet is transmitted; vertical bars = time when a packet that was eventually retransmitted was first transmitted.

possible to use the ACKs that are still in the pipe to clock the sending of packets. This mechanism, which is called *fast recovery*, effectively removes the slow start phase that happens between when fast retransmit detects a lost packet and additive increase begins. For example, fast recovery avoids the slow start period between 3.8 and 4 seconds in Figure 6.13 and instead simply cuts the congestion window in half (from 22 KB to 11 KB) and resumes additive increase. In other words, slow start is only used at the beginning of a connection and whenever a coarse-grained timeout occurs. At all other times, the congestion window is following a pure additive increase/multiplicative decrease pattern.

A Faster TCP?

Many times in the last two decades the argument over how fast TCP can be made to run has reared its head. First there was the claim that TCP was too complex to run fast in host software as networks headed toward the gigabit range. This claim was repeatedly disproved. More recently however, an important theoretical result has shown that there are limits to how well standard TCP can perform in very high bandwidth-delay environments. An analysis of the congestion-control behavior of TCP has shown that, in the steady state, TCP's throughput is approximately

$$Rate = \left(\frac{1.2 \times MSS}{RTT \times \sqrt{\rho}} \right)$$

In a network with an RTT of 100 ms and 10-Gbps links, it follows that a single TCP connection will only be able to achieve a throughput close to link speed if the loss rate is below one per 5 billion packets—equivalent to one congestion event every 100 minutes. Even very rare packet losses due to bit errors on the fiber will typically produce a considerably higher loss rate than this, making it impossible to fill the pipe with a single TCP connection.

A number of proposals to improve on TCP's behavior in networks with very high bandwidth delay products have been put forward, and they range from the incremental to the dramatic. Observing the dependency on MSS, one simple change that has been proposed is to increase the packet size. Unfortunately, increasing packet sizes also increases the chance that a given packet will suffer from a bit error, so at some point increasing the MSS alone may not be sufficient. Other proposals that have been advanced at the IETF and elsewhere make changes to the way TCP avoids congestion, in an attempt to make TCP better able to use bandwidth that is available. The challenges here are to be fair to standard TCP implementations and also to avoid the congestion collapse issues that led to the current behavior of TCP.

The HighSpeed TCP proposal, now an experimental RFC, makes TCP more aggressive only when it is clearly operating in a very high bandwidth-delay product environment and not competing with a lot of other traffic. In essence, when the congestion window gets very large, HighSpeed TCP starts to increase CongestionWindow by a larger amount that standard TCP. In the normal environment where CongestionWindow is relatively small (about 40 × MSS), HighSpeed TCP is indistinguishable from standard TCP. Many other proposals have been made in this vein, some of which are listed in the Further Reading section. Notably, the default TCP behavior in the Linux operating system is now based on a TCP variant called *CUBIC*, which also expands the congestion window aggressively in high bandwidth-delay product regimes, while maintaining compatibility with older TCP variants in more bandwidth-constrained environments.

The Quick-Start proposal, which changes the start-up behavior of TCP, was mentioned above. Since it can enable a TCP connection to ramp up its sending rate more quickly, its effect on TCP performance is most noticeable when connections are short, or when an application periodically stops sending data and TCP would otherwise return to slow start.

Yet another proposal, FAST TCP, takes an approach similar to TCP Vegas described in the next section. The basic idea is to anticipate the onset of congestion and avoid it, thereby not taking the performance hit associated with decreasing the congestion window.

Several proposals that involve more dramatic changes to TCP or even replace it with a new protocol have been developed. These have considerable potential to fill the pipe quickly and fairly in high bandwidth-delay environments, but they also face higher deployment challenges. We refer the reader to the end of this chapter for references to ongoing work in this area.

6.4 CONGESTION-AVOIDANCE MECHANISMS

It is important to understand that TCP's strategy is to control congestion once it happens, as opposed to trying to avoid congestion in the first place. In fact, TCP repeatedly increases the load it imposes on the network in an effort to find the point at which congestion occurs, and then it backs off from this point. Said another way, TCP *needs* to create losses to find the available bandwidth of the connection. An appealing alternative, but one that has not yet been widely adopted, is to predict when congestion is about to happen and then to reduce the rate at which hosts send data just before packets start being discarded. We call such a strategy *congestion avoidance*, to distinguish it from *congestion control*.

This section describes three different congestion-avoidance mechanisms. The first two take a similar approach: They put a small amount of additional functionality into the router to assist the end node in the anticipation of congestion. The third mechanism is very different from the first two: It attempts to avoid congestion purely from the end nodes.

6.4.1 DECbit

The first mechanism was developed for use on the Digital Network Architecture (DNA), a connectionless network with a connection-oriented transport protocol. This mechanism could, therefore, also be applied to TCP and IP. As noted above, the idea here is to more evenly split the responsibility for congestion control between the routers and the end nodes. Each router monitors the load it is experiencing and explicitly notifies the end nodes when congestion is about to occur. This notification is implemented by setting a binary congestion bit in the packets that flow through the router, hence the name *DECbit*. The destination host then copies this congestion bit into the ACK it sends back to the source. Finally, the source adjusts its sending rate so as to avoid congestion. The following discussion describes the algorithm in more detail, starting with what happens in the router.

A single congestion bit is added to the packet header. A router sets this bit in a packet if its average queue length is greater than or equal to 1 at the time the packet arrives. This average queue length is measured over a time interval that spans the last busy + idle cycle, plus the current busy cycle. (The router is *busy* when it is transmitting and *idle* when it is not.) Figure 6.14 shows the queue length at a router as a function of time. Essentially, the router calculates the area under the curve and divides this value by the time interval to compute the average queue length. Using a queue length of 1 as the trigger for setting the congestion bit is a trade-off between significant queuing (and hence higher throughput) and increased idle time (and hence lower delay). In other words, a queue length of 1 seems to optimize the power function.

Now turning our attention to the host half of the mechanism, the source records how many of its packets resulted in some router setting the congestion bit. In particular, the source maintains a congestion window, just as in TCP, and watches to see what fraction of the last window's worth of packets resulted in the bit being set. If less than 50% of the packets had the bit set, then the source increases its congestion window by

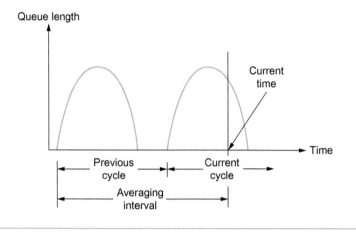

Queue length

Time

Current
time

Previous
cycle

Current
cycle

Averaging
interval

■ FIGURE 6.14 Computing average queue length at a router.

one packet. If 50% or more of the last window's worth of packets had the congestion bit set, then the source decreases its congestion window to 0.875 times the previous value. The value 50% was chosen as the threshold based on analysis that showed it to correspond to the peak of the power curve. The "increase by 1, decrease by 0.875" rule was selected because additive increase/multiplicative decrease makes the mechanism stable.

6.4.2 Random Early Detection (RED)

A second mechanism, called *random early detection* (RED), is similar to the DECbit scheme in that each router is programmed to monitor its own queue length and, when it detects that congestion is imminent, to notify the source to adjust its congestion window. RED, invented by Sally Floyd and Van Jacobson in the early 1990s, differs from the DECbit scheme in two major ways.

The first is that rather than explicitly sending a congestion notification message to the source, RED is most commonly implemented such that it *implicitly* notifies the source of congestion by dropping one of its packets. The source is, therefore, effectively notified by the subsequent timeout or duplicate ACK. In case you haven't already guessed, RED is designed to be used in conjunction with TCP, which currently detects congestion by means of timeouts (or some other means of detecting packet loss such as duplicate ACKs). As the "early" part of the RED acronym suggests, the gateway drops the packet earlier than it would have to, so as to notify the source that it should decrease its congestion window sooner than it would normally have. In other words, the router drops a few packets before it has exhausted its buffer space completely, so as to cause the source to slow down, with the hope that this will mean it does not have to drop lots of packets later on. Note that RED could easily be adapted to work with an explicit feedback scheme simply by *marking* a packet instead of *dropping* it, as discussed in the sidebar on Explicit Congestion Notification.

Explicit Congestion Notification (ECN)

While current deployments of RED almost always signal congestion by dropping packets, there has recently been much attention given to whether or not explicit notification is a better strategy. This has led to an effort to standardize ECN for the Internet.

The basic argument is that while dropping a packet certainly acts as a signal of congestion, and is probably the right thing to do for long-lived bulk transfers, doing so hurts applications that are sensitive to the delay or loss of one or more packets. Interactive traffic such as telnet and web browsing are prime examples. Learning of congestion through explicit notification is more appropriate for such applications.

Technically, ECN requires two bits; the proposed standard uses bits 6 and 7 in the IP type of service (TOS) field. One is set by the source to indicate that it is ECN capable; that is, it is able to react to a congestion notification. The other is set by routers along the end-to-end path when congestion is encountered. The latter bit is also echoed back to the source by the destination host. TCP running on the source responds to the ECN bit set in exactly the same way it responds to a dropped packet.

As with any good idea, this recent focus on ECN has caused people to stop and think about other ways in which networks can benefit from an ECN-style exchange of information between hosts at the edge of the networks and routers in the middle of the network, piggybacked on data packets. The general strategy is sometimes called *active queue management*, and recent research seems to indicate that it is particularly valuable to TCP flows that have large delay-bandwidth products. The interested reader can pursue the relevant references given at the end of the chapter.

The second difference between RED and DECbit is in the details of how RED decides when to drop a packet and what packet it decides to drop. To understand the basic idea, consider a simple FIFO queue. Rather than wait for the queue to become completely full and then be forced to drop each arriving packet (the tail drop policy of Section 6.2.1), we could decide to drop each arriving packet with some *drop probability* whenever the queue length exceeds some *drop level*. This idea is called *early random drop*. The RED algorithm defines the details of how to monitor the queue length and when to drop a packet.

In the following paragraphs, we describe the RED algorithm as originally proposed by Floyd and Jacobson. We note that several modifications have since been proposed both by the inventors and by other researchers; some of these are discussed in Further Reading. However, the key ideas are the same as those presented below, and most current implementations are close to the algorithm that follows.

First, RED computes an average queue length using a weighted running average similar to the one used in the original TCP timeout computation. That is, AvgLen is computed as

$$\mathsf{AvgLen} = (1 - \mathsf{Weight}) \times \mathsf{AvgLen} + \mathsf{Weight} \times \mathsf{SampleLen}$$

where $0 < \mathsf{Weight} < 1$ and SampleLen is the length of the queue when a sample measurement is made. In most software implementations, the queue length is measured every time a new packet arrives at the gateway. In hardware, it might be calculated at some fixed sampling interval.

The reason for using an average queue length rather than an instantaneous one is that it more accurately captures the notion of congestion. Because of the bursty nature of Internet traffic, queues can become full very quickly and then become empty again. If a queue is spending most of its time empty, then it's probably not appropriate to conclude that the router is congested and to tell the hosts to slow down. Thus, the weighted running average calculation tries to detect long-lived congestion, as indicated in the right-hand portion of Figure 6.15, by filtering out short-term changes in the queue length. You can think of the running average as a low-pass filter, where Weight determines the time constant of the filter. The question of how we pick this time constant is discussed below.

Second, RED has two queue length thresholds that trigger certain activity: MinThreshold and MaxThreshold. When a packet arrives at the gateway, RED compares the current AvgLen with these two thresholds, according to the following rules:

$$\text{if } \mathsf{AvgLen} \leq \mathsf{MinThreshold}$$
$$\longrightarrow \text{queue the packet}$$

if MinThreshold < AvgLen < MaxThreshold

⟶ calculate probability P

⟶ drop the arriving packet with probability P

if MaxThreshold ≤ AvgLen

⟶ drop the arriving packet

If the average queue length is smaller than the lower threshold, no action is taken, and if the average queue length is larger than the upper threshold, then the packet is always dropped. If the average queue length is between the two thresholds, then the newly arriving packet is dropped with some probability P. This situation is depicted in Figure 6.16. The approximate relationship between P and AvgLen is shown in Figure 6.17. Note that the probability of drop increases slowly when AvgLen is between the two thresholds, reaching MaxP at the upper threshold, at which point it jumps to unity. The rationale behind this is that, if AvgLen reaches the upper threshold, then the gentle approach (dropping a few packets) is not working and drastic measures are called for: dropping all arriving packets. Some research has suggested that a smoother transition from random dropping to complete dropping, rather than the discontinuous approach shown here, may be appropriate.

Although Figure 6.17 shows the probability of drop as a function only of AvgLen, the situation is actually a little more complicated. In fact, P is

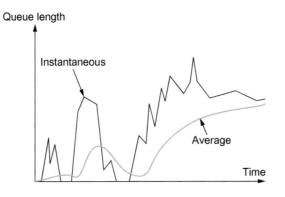

■ FIGURE 6.15 Weighted running average queue length.

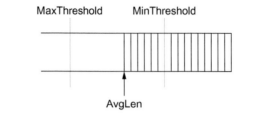

■ FIGURE 6.16 RED thresholds on a FIFO queue.

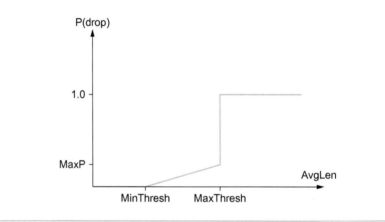

■ FIGURE 6.17 Drop probability function for RED.

a function of both AvgLen and how long it has been since the last packet was dropped. Specifically, it is computed as follows:

$$\mathsf{TempP} = \mathsf{MaxP} \times (\mathsf{AvgLen} - \mathsf{MinThreshold})/(\mathsf{MaxThreshold} - \mathsf{MinThreshold})$$
$$\mathsf{P} = \mathsf{TempP}/(1 - \mathsf{count} \times \mathsf{TempP})$$

TempP is the variable that is plotted on the y-axis in Figure 6.17, count keeps track of how many newly arriving packets have been queued (not dropped), and AvgLen has been between the two thresholds. P increases slowly as count increases, thereby making a drop increasingly likely as the time since the last drop increases. This makes closely spaced drops relatively less likely than widely spaced drops. This extra step in calculating P was introduced by the inventors of RED when they observed that, without it, the packet drops were not well distributed in time but instead tended to occur in clusters. Because packet arrivals from a certain connection are likely to arrive in bursts, this clustering of drops is likely to cause multiple drops in a single connection. This is not desirable, since only one drop per round-trip time is enough to cause a connection to reduce its window size, whereas multiple drops might send it back into slow start.

As an example, suppose that we set MaxP to 0.02 and count is initialized to zero. If the average queue length were halfway between the two thresholds, then TempP, and the initial value of P, would be half of MaxP, or 0.01. An arriving packet, of course, has a 99 in 100 chance of getting into the queue at this point. With each successive packet that is not dropped, P slowly increases, and by the time 50 packets have arrived without a drop, P would have doubled to 0.02. In the unlikely event that 99 packets arrived without loss, P reaches 1, guaranteeing that the next packet is dropped. The important thing about this part of the algorithm is that it ensures a roughly even distribution of drops over time.

The intent is that, if RED drops a small percentage of packets when AvgLen exceeds MinThreshold, this will cause a few TCP connections to reduce their window sizes, which in turn will reduce the rate at which packets arrive at the router. All going well, AvgLen will then decrease and congestion is avoided. The queue length can be kept short, while throughput remains high since few packets are dropped.

Note that, because RED is operating on a queue length averaged over time, it is possible for the instantaneous queue length to be much longer than AvgLen. In this case, if a packet arrives and there is nowhere to put it, then it will have to be dropped. When this happens, RED is operating in tail drop mode. One of the goals of RED is to prevent tail drop behavior if possible.

The random nature of RED confers an interesting property on the algorithm. Because RED drops packets randomly, the probability that RED decides to drop a particular flow's packet(s) is roughly proportional to the share of the bandwidth that that flow is currently getting at that router. This is because a flow that is sending a relatively large number of packets is providing more candidates for random dropping. Thus, there is some sense of fair resource allocation built into RED, although it is by no means precise.

Note that a fair amount of analysis has gone into setting the various RED parameters—for example, MaxThreshold, MinThreshold, MaxP, and Weight—all in the name of optimizing the power function (throughput-to-delay ratio). The performance of these parameters has also been confirmed through simulation, and the algorithm has been shown not to be overly sensitive to them. It is important to keep in mind, however, that all of this analysis and simulation hinges on a particular characterization of the network workload. The real contribution of RED is a mechanism by which the router can more accurately manage its queue length. Defining precisely what constitutes an optimal queue length depends on the traffic mix and is still a subject of research, with real information now being gathered from operational deployment of RED in the Internet.

Consider the setting of the two thresholds, MinThreshold and MaxThreshold. If the traffic is fairly bursty, then MinThreshold should be sufficiently large to allow the link utilization to be maintained at an acceptably high level. Also, the difference between the two thresholds should be larger than the typical increase in the calculated average queue length in one RTT. Setting MaxThreshold to twice MinThreshold seems to be a reasonable rule of thumb given the traffic mix on today's Internet. In addition, since we expect the average queue length to hover between the two thresholds during periods of high load, there should be enough free buffer space *above* MaxThreshold to absorb the natural bursts that occur in Internet traffic without forcing the router to enter tail drop mode.

We noted above that Weight determines the time constant for the running average low-pass filter, and this gives us a clue as to how we might pick a suitable value for it. Recall that RED is trying to send signals to TCP flows by dropping packets during times of congestion. Suppose that a router drops a packet from some TCP connection and then immediately forwards some more packets from the same connection. When those packets arrive at the receiver, it starts sending duplicate ACKs to the sender. When the sender sees enough duplicate ACKs, it will reduce its window size. So, from the time the router drops a packet until the time when the same router starts to see some relief from the affected connection in terms of a reduced window size, at least one round-trip time must elapse for that connection. There is probably not much point in having the router respond to congestion on time scales much less than the round-trip time of the connections passing through it. As noted previously, 100 ms is not a bad estimate of average round-trip times in the Internet. Thus, **Weight** should be chosen such that changes in queue length over time scales much less than 100 ms are filtered out.

Since RED works by sending signals to TCP flows to tell them to slow down, you might wonder what would happen if those signals are ignored. This is often called the *unresponsive flow* problem, and it has been a matter of some concern for several years. Unresponsive flows use more than their fair share of network resources and could cause congestive collapse if there were enough of them, just as in the days before TCP congestion control. Some of the techniques described in Section 6.5 can help with this problem by isolating certain classes of traffic from others. There is also the possibility that a variant of RED could drop more heavily from flows that are unresponsive to the initial hints that it sends; this continues to be an area of active research.

6.4.3 Source-Based Congestion Avoidance

Unlike the two previous congestion-avoidance schemes, which depended on new mechanisms in the routers, we now describe a strategy for detecting the incipient stages of congestion—before losses occur—from the end hosts. We first give a brief overview of a collection of related mechanisms that use different information to detect the early stages of congestion, and then we describe a specific mechanism in some detail.

The general idea of these techniques is to watch for some sign from the network that some router's queue is building up and that congestion will happen soon if nothing is done about it. For example, the source might notice that as packet queues build up in the network's routers, there is a measurable increase in the RTT for each successive packet it sends. One particular algorithm exploits this observation as follows: The congestion window normally increases as in TCP, but every two round-trip delays the algorithm checks to see if the current RTT is greater than the average of the minimum and maximum RTTs seen so far. If it is, then the algorithm decreases the congestion window by one-eighth.

A second algorithm does something similar. The decision as to whether or not to change the current window size is based on changes to both the RTT and the window size. The window is adjusted once every two round-trip delays based on the product

$$(\text{CurrentWindow} - \text{OldWindow}) \times (\text{CurrentRTT} - \text{OldRTT})$$

Tahoe, Reno, and Vegas

The name "TCP Vegas" is a takeoff on earlier implementations of TCP that were distributed in releases of 4.3 BSD Unix. These releases were known as Tahoe and Reno (which, like Las Vegas, are places in Nevada), and the versions of TCP became known by the names of the BSD release. TCP Tahoe, which is also known as *BSD Network Release 1.0* (BNR1), corresponds to the original implementation of Jacobson's congestion-control mechanism and includes all of the mechanisms described in Section 6.3 except fast recovery. TCP Reno, which is also known as *BSD Network Release 2.0* (BNR2), adds the fast recovery mechanism, along with an optimization known as *header prediction*—optimizing for the common case that segments arrive in order. TCP Reno also supports *delayed ACKs*—acknowledging every other segment rather than every segment—although this is a selectable option that is sometimes turned off. A version of TCP distributed in 4.4 BSD Unix added the "big windows" extensions described in Section 5.2.

With the rising popularity of the Linux operating system, and an increase in the number of researchers looking at TCP congestion control, the situation has grown considerably more complex. Linux today offers a range of settings for TCP congestion control, with Vegas being one option and a newer variant called *TCP CUBIC* being the default. The whole idea of using place names to refer to TCP variants has been taken up enthusiastically (see TCP-Illinois and TCP-Westwood, for example).

One point you should take away from this discussion of TCP's lineage is that TCP has been a rather fluid protocol over the last several years, especially in its congestion-control mechanism. In fact, you would not even find universal agreement about which technique was introduced in which release, due to the availability of intermediate versions and the fact that patch has been layered on top of patch.

All that can be said with any certainty is that any two implementations of TCP that follow the original specification, although they should interoperate, will not necessarily perform well. Recognizing the performance implications of interactions among TCP variants is a tricky business. In other words, you could argue that TCP is no longer defined by a specification but rather by an implementation. The only question is, which implementation?

If the result is positive, the source decreases the window size by one-eighth; if the result is negative or 0, the source increases the window by one maximum packet size. Note that the window changes during every adjustment; that is, it oscillates around its optimal point.

Another change seen as the network approaches congestion is the flattening of the sending rate. A third scheme takes advantage of this fact. Every RTT, it increases the window size by one packet and compares the throughput achieved to the throughput when the window was one packet smaller. If the difference is less than one-half the throughput achieved when only one packet was in transit—as was the case at the beginning of the connection—the algorithm decreases the window by one packet. This scheme calculates the throughput by dividing the number of bytes outstanding in the network by the RTT.

A fourth mechanism, the one we are going to describe in more detail, is similar to this last algorithm in that it looks at changes in the throughput rate or, more specifically, changes in the sending rate. However, it differs from the third algorithm in the way it calculates throughput, and instead of looking for a change in the slope of the throughput it compares the measured throughput rate with an expected throughput rate. The algorithm, TCP Vegas, is not widely deployed in the Internet, but the strategy it takes continues to be studied. (See the Further Reading section for additional information.)

The intuition behind the Vegas algorithm can be seen in the trace of standard TCP given in Figure 6.18. (See the preceding sidebar for an explanation of the name TCP Vegas.) The top graph shown in Figure 6.18 traces the connection's congestion window; it shows the same information as the traces given earlier in this section. The middle and bottom graphs depict new information: The middle graph shows the average sending rate as measured at the source, and the bottom graph shows the average queue length as measured at the bottleneck router. All three graphs are synchronized in time. In the period between 4.5 and 6.0 seconds (shaded region), the congestion window increases (top graph). We expect the observed throughput to also increase, but instead it stays flat (middle graph). This is because the throughput cannot increase beyond the available bandwidth. Beyond this point, any increase in the window size only results in packets taking up buffer space at the bottleneck router (bottom graph).

A useful metaphor that describes the phenomenon illustrated in Figure 6.18 is driving on ice. The speedometer (congestion window) may say that you are going 30 miles an hour, but by looking out the car window and seeing people pass you on foot (measured sending rate) you know that you are going no more than 5 miles an hour. The extra energy is being absorbed by the car's tires (router buffers).

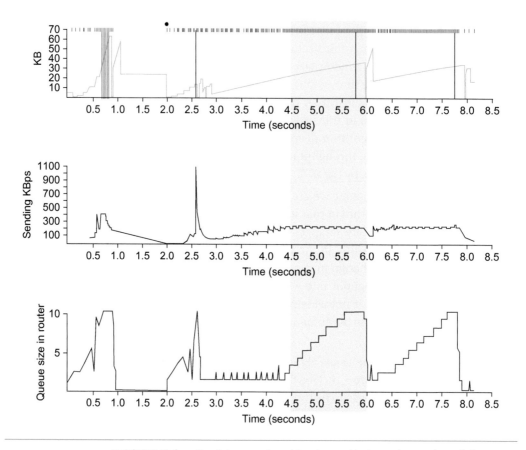

■ FIGURE 6.18 Congestion window versus observed throughput rate (the three graphs are synchronized). Top, congestion window; middle, observed throughput; bottom, buffer space taken up at the router. Colored line = CongestionWindow; solid bullet = timeout; hash marks = time when each packet is transmitted; vertical bars = time when a packet that was eventually retransmitted was first transmitted.

TCP Vegas uses this idea to measure and control the amount of extra data this connection has in transit, where by "extra data" we mean data that the source would not have transmitted had it been trying to match exactly the available bandwidth of the network. The goal of TCP Vegas is to maintain the "right" amount of extra data in the network. Obviously, if a source is sending too much extra data, it will cause long delays and possibly lead to congestion. Less obviously, if a connection is sending too little extra data, it cannot respond rapidly enough to transient increases in the available network bandwidth. TCP Vegas's congestion-avoidance actions are based on changes in the estimated amount of extra data in the network, not only on dropped packets. We now describe the algorithm in detail.

First, define a given flow's BaseRTT to be the RTT of a packet when the flow is not congested. In practice, TCP Vegas sets BaseRTT to the minimum of all measured round-trip times; it is commonly the RTT of the first packet sent by the connection, before the router queues increase due to traffic generated by this flow. If we assume that we are not overflowing the connection, then the expected throughput is given by

$$\text{ExpectedRate} = \text{CongestionWindow}/\text{BaseRTT}$$

where CongestionWindow is the TCP congestion window, which we assume (for the purpose of this discussion) to be equal to the number of bytes in transit.

Second, TCP Vegas calculates the current sending rate, ActualRate. This is done by recording the sending time for a distinguished packet, recording how many bytes are transmitted between the time that packet is sent and when its acknowledgment is received, computing the sample RTT for the distinguished packet when its acknowledgment arrives, and dividing the number of bytes transmitted by the sample RTT. This calculation is done once per round-trip time.

Third, TCP Vegas compares ActualRate to ExpectedRate and adjusts the window accordingly. We let Diff = ExpectedRate − ActualRate. Note that Diff is positive or 0 by definition, since ActualRate > ExpectedRate implies that we need to change BaseRTT to the latest sampled RTT. We also define two thresholds, $\alpha < \beta$, roughly corresponding to having too little and too much extra data in the network, respectively. When Diff $< \alpha$, TCP Vegas increases the congestion window linearly during the next RTT, and when Diff $> \beta$, TCP Vegas decreases the congestion window linearly during the next RTT. TCP Vegas leaves the congestion window unchanged when $\alpha < $ Diff $ < \beta$.

Intuitively, we can see that the farther away the actual throughput gets from the expected throughput, the more congestion there is in the network, which implies that the sending rate should be reduced. The β threshold triggers this decrease. On the other hand, when the actual throughput rate gets too close to the expected throughput, the connection is in danger of not utilizing the available bandwidth. The α threshold triggers this increase. The overall goal is to keep between α and β extra bytes in the network.

Figure 6.19 traces the TCP Vegas congestion-avoidance algorithm. The top graph traces the congestion window, showing the same information as the other traces given throughout this chapter. The bottom graph traces the expected and actual throughput rates that govern how the congestion window is set. It is this bottom graph that best illustrates how the algorithm works. The colored line tracks the ExpectedRate, while the black line tracks the ActualRate. The wide shaded strip gives the region between the α and β thresholds; the top of the shaded strip is α KBps away from ExpectedRate, and the bottom of the shaded strip is β KBps away from ExpectedRate. The goal is to keep the ActualRate between these two thresholds, within the shaded region. Whenever ActualRate falls below the shaded region (i.e., gets too far from ExpectedRate), TCP Vegas decreases the congestion window because it fears that too many packets are being buffered in the network. Likewise, whenever ActualRate goes above the shaded region (i.e., gets too close to the ExpectedRate), TCP Vegas increases the congestion window because it fears that it is underutilizing the network.

Because the algorithm, as just presented, compares the difference between the actual and expected throughput rates to the α and β thresholds, these two thresholds are defined in terms of KBps. However, it is

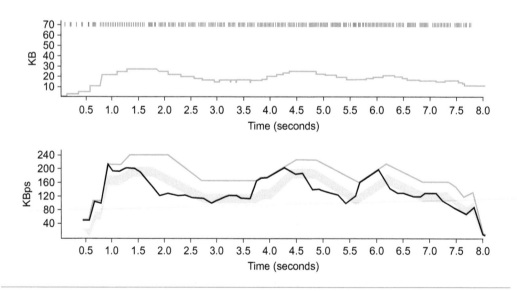

FIGURE 6.19 Trace of TCP Vegas congestion-avoidance mechanism. Top, congestion window; bottom, expected (colored line) and actual (black line) throughput. The shaded area is the region between the α and β thresholds.

perhaps more accurate to think in terms of how many extra *buffers* the connection is occupying in the network. For example, on a connection with a BaseRTT of 100 ms and a packet size of 1 KB, if $\alpha = 30$ KBps and $\beta = 60$ KBps, then we can think of α as specifying that the connection needs to be occupying at least 3 extra buffers in the network and β as specifying that the connection should occupy no more than 6 extra buffers in the network. In practice, a setting of α to 1 buffer and β to 3 buffers works well.

Finally, you will notice that TCP Vegas decreases the congestion window linearly, seemingly in conflict with the rule that multiplicative

Evaluating a New Congestion-Control Mechanism

Suppose you develop a new congestion-control mechanism and want to evaluate its performance. For example, you might want to compare it to the current mechanism running on the Internet. How do you go about measuring and evaluating your mechanism? Although at one time the Internet's primary purpose in life was to support networking research, today it is a large production network and therefore completely inappropriate for running a controlled experiment.

If your approach is purely end to end—that is, if it assumes only FIFO routers within the Internet—then it is possible to run your congestion-control mechanism on a small set of hosts and to measure the throughput your connections are able to achieve. We need to add a word of caution here, however. It is surprisingly easy to invent a congestion-control mechanism that achieves five times the throughput of TCP across the Internet. You simply blast packets into the Internet at a high rate, thereby causing congestion. All the other hosts running TCP detect this congestion and reduce the rate at which they are sending packets. Your mechanism then happily consumes all the bandwidth. This strategy is fast but hardly fair.

Experimenting directly on the Internet, even when done carefully, will not work when your congestion-control mechanism involves changes to the routers. It is simply not practical to change the software running on thousands of routers for the sake of evaluating a new congestion-control algorithm. In this case, network designers are forced to test their systems on simulated networks or private testbed networks. For example, the TCP traces presented in this chapter were generated by an implementation of TCP that was running on a network simulator. The challenge in either a simulation or a testbed is coming up with a topology and a traffic workload that are representative of the real Internet.

decrease is needed to ensure stability. The explanation is that TCP Vegas does use multiplicative decrease when a timeout occurs; the linear decrease just described is an *early* decrease in the congestion window that should happen before congestion occurs and packets start being dropped.

6.5 QUALITY OF SERVICE

For many years, packet-switched networks have offered the promise of supporting multimedia applications that combine audio, video, and data. After all, once digitized, audio and video information becomes like any other form of data—a stream of bits to be transmitted. One obstacle to the fulfillment of this promise has been the need for higher-bandwidth links. Recently, however, improvements in coding have reduced the bandwidth needs of audio and video applications, while at the same time link speeds have increased.

There is more to transmitting audio and video over a network than just providing sufficient bandwidth, however. Participants in a telephone conversation, for example, expect to be able to converse in such a way that one person can respond to something said by the other and be heard almost immediately. Thus, the timeliness of delivery can be very important. We refer to applications that are sensitive to the timeliness of data as *real-time applications*. Voice and video applications tend to be the canonical examples, but there are others such as industrial control—you would like a command sent to a robot arm to reach it before the arm crashes into something. Even file transfer applications can have timeliness constraints, such as a requirement that a database update complete overnight before the business that needs the data resumes on the next day.

The distinguishing characteristic of real-time applications is that they need some sort of assurance *from the network* that data is likely to arrive on time (for some definition of "on time"). Whereas a non-real-time application can use an end-to-end retransmission strategy to make sure that data arrives *correctly*, such a strategy cannot provide timeliness: Retransmission only adds to total latency if data arrives late. Timely arrival must be provided by the network itself (the routers), not just at the network edges (the hosts). We therefore conclude that the best-effort model, in which the network tries to deliver your data but makes no promises and leaves the cleanup operation to the edges, is not sufficient for real-time applications. What we need is a new service model, in which applications that need higher assurances can ask the network for them. The network may then respond by providing an assurance that it will do better or perhaps by saying that it cannot promise anything better at the moment. Note that such a service model is a superset of the current model: Applications that are happy with best-effort service should be able to use the new service model; their requirements are just less stringent. This implies that the network will treat some packets differently from others—something that is not done in the best-effort model. A network that can provide these different levels of service is often said to support quality of service (QoS).

At this point, you might be thinking "Hold on. Doesn't the Internet already support real-time applications?" Most of us have tried some sort of Internet telephony application such as Skype at this point, and it seems to work OK. The reason for this, in part, is because best-effort service is often quite good. (Skype in particular also does a number of clever things to try to deal with lack of QoS in the Internet.) The key word here is "often." If you want a service that is *reliably* good enough for your real-time applications, then best-effort—which by definition makes no assurances—won't be sufficient. We'll return later to the topic of just how necessary QoS really is.

6.5.1 Application Requirements

Before looking at the various protocols and mechanisms that may be used to provide quality of service to applications, we should try to understand what the needs of those applications are. To begin, we can divide applications into two types: real-time and non-real-time. The latter are sometimes called *traditional data* applications, since they have traditionally been the major applications found on data networks. They include most popular applications like telnet, FTP, email, web browsing, and so on. All of these applications can work without guarantees of timely delivery of data. Another term for this non-real-time class of applications is *elastic*, since they are able to stretch gracefully in the face of increased delay. Note that these applications can benefit from shorter-length delays, but they do not become unusable as delays increase. Also note that their delay requirements vary from the interactive applications like telnet to more asynchronous ones like email, with interactive bulk transfers like FTP in the middle.

Real-Time Audio Example

As a concrete example of a real-time application, consider an audio application similar to the one illustrated in Figure 6.20. Data is generated by collecting samples from a microphone and digitizing them using an analog-to-digital (A→D) converter. The digital samples are placed in packets, which are transmitted across the network and received at the other end. At the receiving host, the data must be *played back* at some appropriate rate. For example, if the voice samples were collected at a rate of one per 125 μs, they should be played back at the same rate. Thus, we can think of each sample as having a particular *playback time*: the point in time at which it is needed in the receiving host. In the voice example, each sample has a playback time that is 125 μs later than the preceding sample. If data arrives after its appropriate playback time, either because it was delayed in the network or because it was dropped and subsequently retransmitted, it is essentially useless. It is the complete worthlessness of late data that characterizes real-time applications. In elastic applications, it might be nice if data turns up on time, but we can still use it when it does not.

One way to make our voice application work would be to make sure that all samples take exactly the same amount of time to traverse the network. Then, since samples are injected at a rate of one per 125 μs, they will appear at the receiver at the same rate, ready to be played back. However, it is generally difficult to guarantee that all data traversing a packet-switched network will experience exactly the same delay. Packets encounter queues in switches or routers, and the lengths of these queues vary with time, meaning that the delays tend to vary with time and, as a consequence, are potentially different for each packet in the audio stream. The way to deal with this at the receiver end is to buffer up some amount of data in reserve, thereby always providing a store of packets waiting to be played back at the right time. If a packet is delayed a short

■ FIGURE 6.20 An audio application.

time, it goes in the buffer until its playback time arrives. If it gets delayed a long time, then it will not need to be stored for very long in the receiver's buffer before being played back. Thus, we have effectively added a constant offset to the playback time of all packets as a form of insurance. We call this offset the *playback point*. The only time we run into trouble is if packets get delayed in the network for such a long time that they arrive after their playback time, causing the playback buffer to be drained.

The operation of a playback buffer is illustrated in Figure 6.21. The left-hand diagonal line shows packets being generated at a steady rate. The wavy line shows when the packets arrive, some variable amount of time after they were sent, depending on what they encountered in the network. The right-hand diagonal line shows the packets being played back at a steady rate, after sitting in the playback buffer for some period of time. As long as the playback line is far enough to the right in time, the variation in network delay is never noticed by the application. However, if we move the playback line a little to the left, then some packets will begin to arrive too late to be useful.

For our audio application, there are limits to how far we can delay playing back data. It is hard to carry on a conversation if the time between when you speak and when your listener hears you is more than 300 ms. Thus, what we want from the network in this case is a guarantee that all our data will arrive within 300 ms. If data arrives early, we buffer it until

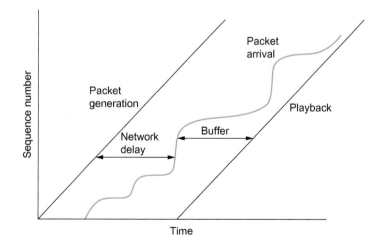

■ FIGURE 6.21 A playback buffer.

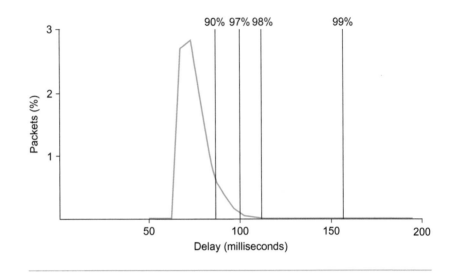

■ FIGURE 6.22 Example distribution of delays for an Internet connection.

its correct playback time. If it arrives late, we have no use for it and must discard it.

To get a better appreciation of how variable network delay can be, Figure 6.22 shows the one-way delay measured over a certain path across the Internet over the course of one particular day. While the exact numbers would vary depending on the path and the date, the key factor here is the *variability* of the delay, which is consistently found on almost any path at any time. As denoted by the cumulative percentages given across the top of the graph, 97% of the packets in this case had a latency of 100 ms or less. This means that if our example audio application were to set the playback point at 100 ms, then, on average, 3 out of every 100 packets would arrive too late to be of any use. One important thing to notice about this graph is that the tail of the curve—how far it extends to the right—is very long. We would have to set the playback point at over 200 ms to ensure that all packets arrived in time.

Taxonomy of Real-Time Applications

Now that we have a concrete idea of how real-time applications work, we can look at some different classes of applications that serve to motivate our service model. The following taxonomy owes much to the work of Clark, Braden, Shenker, and Zhang, whose papers on this subject can be

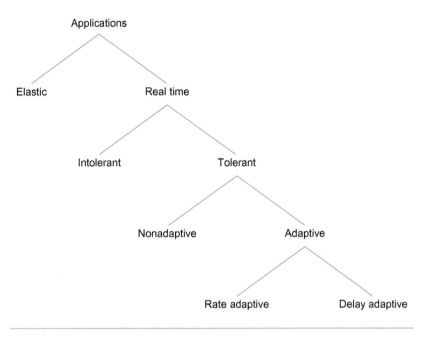

■ FIGURE 6.23 Taxonomy of applications.

found in the Further Reading section for this chapter. The taxonomy of applications is summarized in Figure 6.23.

The first characteristic by which we can categorize applications is their tolerance of loss of data, where "loss" might occur because a packet arrived too late to be played back as well as arising from the usual causes in the network. On the one hand, one lost audio sample can be interpolated from the surrounding samples with relatively little effect on the perceived audio quality. It is only as more and more samples are lost that quality declines to the point that the speech becomes incomprehensible. On the other hand, a robot control program is likely to be an example of a real-time application that cannot tolerate loss—losing the packet that contains the command instructing the robot arm to stop is unacceptable. Thus, we can categorize real-time applications as *tolerant* or *intolerant* depending on whether they can tolerate occasional loss. (As an aside, note that many real-time applications are more tolerant of occasional loss than non-real-time applications; for example, compare our audio application to FTP, where the uncorrected loss of one bit might render a file completely useless.)

A second way to characterize real-time applications is by their adaptability. For example, an audio application might be able to adapt to the amount of delay that packets experience as they traverse the network. If we notice that packets are almost always arriving within 300 ms of being sent, then we can set our playback point accordingly, buffering any packets that arrive in less than 300 ms. Suppose that we subsequently observe that all packets are arriving within 100 ms of being sent. If we moved up our playback point to 100 ms, then the users of the application would probably perceive an improvement. The process of shifting the playback point would actually require us to play out samples at an increased rate for some period of time. With a voice application, this can be done in a way that is barely perceptible, simply by shortening the silences between words. Thus, playback point adjustment is fairly easy in this case, and it has been effectively implemented for several voice applications such as the audio teleconferencing program known as vat. Note that playback point adjustment can happen in either direction, but that doing so actually involves distorting the played-back signal during the period of adjustment, and that the effects of this distortion will very much depend on how the end user uses the data.

Observe that if we set our playback point on the assumption that all packets will arrive within 100 ms and then find that some packets are arriving slightly late, we will have to drop them, whereas we would not have had to drop them if we had left the playback point at 300 ms. Thus, we should advance the playback point only when it provides a perceptible advantage and only when we have some evidence that the number of late packets will be acceptably small. We may do this because of observed recent history or because of some assurance from the network.

We call applications that can adjust their playback point *delay-adaptive* applications. Another class of adaptive applications is *rate adaptive*. For example, many video coding algorithms can trade off bit rate versus quality. Thus, if we find that the network can support a certain bandwidth, we can set our coding parameters accordingly. If more bandwidth becomes available later, we can change parameters to increase the quality.

Approaches to QoS Support

Considering this rich space of application requirements, what we need is a richer service model that meets the needs of any application. This leads us to a service model with not just one class (best effort), but with several classes, each available to meet the needs of some set of applications. Towards this end, we are now ready to look at some of the approaches that have been developed to provide a range of qualities of service. These can be divided into two broad categories:

- *Fine-grained* approaches, which provide QoS to individual applications or flows
- *Coarse-grained* approaches, which provide QoS to large classes of data or aggregated traffic

In the first category, we find *Integrated Services*, a QoS architecture developed in the IETF and often associated with the Resource Reservation Protocol (RSVP); ATM's approach to QoS was also in this category. In the second category lies *Differentiated Services*, which is probably the most widely deployed QoS mechanism at the time of writing. We discuss these in turn in the next two subsections.

Finally, as we suggested at the start of this section, adding QoS support to the network isn't necessarily the entire story about supporting real-time applications. We conclude our discussion by revisiting what the end-host might do to better support real-time streams, independent of how widely deployed QoS mechanisms like Integrated or Differentiated Services become.

6.5.2 Integrated Services (RSVP)

LAB 12:
RSVP

The term *Integrated Services* (often called IntServ for short) refers to a body of work that was produced by the IETF around 1995–97. The IntServ working group developed specifications of a number of *service classes* designed to meet the needs of some of the application types described above. It also defined how RSVP could be used to make reservations using these service classes. The following paragraphs provide an overview of these specifications and the mechanisms that are used to implement them.

Service Classes

One of the service classes is designed for intolerant applications. These applications require that a packet never arrive late. The network should guarantee that the maximum delay that any packet will experience has some specified value; the application can then set its playback point so that no packet will ever arrive after its playback time. We assume that early arrival of packets can always be handled by buffering. This service is referred to as the *guaranteed* service.

In addition to the guaranteed service, the IETF considered several other services, but eventually settled on one to meet the needs of tolerant, adaptive applications. The service is known as *controlled load* and was motivated by the observation that existing applications of this type run quite well on networks that are not heavily loaded. The audio application vat, for example, adjusts its playback point as network delay varies and produces reasonable audio quality as long as loss rates remain on the order of 10% or less.

The aim of the controlled load service is to emulate a lightly loaded network for those applications that request the service, even though the network as a whole may in fact be heavily loaded. The trick to this is to use a queuing mechanism such as WFQ (see Section 6.2) to isolate the controlled load traffic from the other traffic and some form of admission control to limit the total amount of controlled load traffic on a link such that the load is kept reasonably low. We discuss admission control in more detail below.

Clearly, these two service classes are a subset of all the classes that might be provided. In fact, other services were specified but never standardized as part of the IETF's work. So far, the two services described above (along with traditional best effort) have proven flexible enough to meet the needs of a wide range of applications.

Overview of Mechanisms

Now that we have augmented our best-effort service model with some new service classes, the next question is how we implement a network that provides these services to applications. This section outlines the key mechanisms. Keep in mind while reading this section that the mechanisms being described are still being hammered out by the Internet design community. The main thing to take away from the discussion is a general understanding of the pieces involved in supporting the service model outlined above.

First, whereas with a best-effort service we can just tell the network where we want our packets to go and leave it at that, a real-time service involves telling the network something more about the type of service we require. We may give it qualitative information such as "use a controlled load service" or quantitative information such as "I need a maximum delay of 100 ms." In addition to describing what we want, we need to tell the network something about what we are going to inject into it, since a low-bandwidth application is going to require fewer network resources than a high-bandwidth application. The set of information that we provide to the network is referred to as a *flowspec*. This name comes from the idea that a set of packets associated with a single application and that share common requirements is called a *flow*, consistent with our use of the term in Section 6.1.

Second, when we ask the network to provide us with a particular service, the network needs to decide if it can in fact provide that service. For example, if 10 users ask for a service in which each will consistently use 2 Mbps of link capacity, and they all share a link with 10-Mbps capacity, the network will have to say no to some of them. The process of deciding when to say no is called *admission control*.

Third, we need a mechanism by which the users of the network and the components of the network itself exchange information such as requests for service, flowspecs, and admission control decisions. This is sometimes called *signalling*, but since that word has several meanings, we refer to this process as *resource reservation*, and it is achieved using a resource reservation protocol.

Finally, when flows and their requirements have been described, and admission control decisions have been made, the network switches and routers need to meet the requirements of the flows. A key part of meeting these requirements is managing the way packets are queued and scheduled for transmission in the switches and routers. This last mechanism is *packet scheduling*.

Flowspecs

There are two separable parts to the flowspec: the part that describes the flow's traffic characteristics (called the *TSpec*) and the part that describes the service requested from the network (the *RSpec*). The RSpec is very service specific and relatively easy to describe. For example, with a controlled load service, the RSpec is trivial: The application just requests controlled load service with no additional parameters. With a guaranteed service, you could specify a delay target or bound. (In the IETF's guaranteed service specification, you specify not a delay but another quantity from which delay can be calculated.)

The TSpec is a little more complicated. As our example above showed, we need to give the network enough information about the bandwidth used by the flow to allow intelligent admission control decisions to be made. For most applications, however, the bandwidth is not a single number; it is something that varies constantly. A video application, for example, will generally generate more bits per second when the scene is changing rapidly than when it is still. Just knowing the long-term average bandwidth is not enough, as the following example illustrates. Suppose that we have 10 flows that arrive at a switch on separate input ports and that all leave on the same 10-Mbps link. Assume that over some suitably long interval each flow can be expected to send no more than 1 Mbps. You might think that this presents no problem. However, if these are variable bit rate applications, such as compressed video, then they will occasionally send more than their average rates. If enough sources send at above their average rates, then the total rate at which data arrives at the switch will be greater than 10 Mbps. This excess data will be queued before it can be sent on the link. The longer this condition persists, the longer the queue will get. Packets might have to be dropped and, even if it doesn't come to that, data sitting in the queue is being delayed. If packets are delayed long enough, the service that was requested will not be provided.

Exactly how we manage our queues to control delay and avoid dropping packets is something we discuss below. However, note here that we need to know something about how the bandwidth of our sources varies with time. One way to describe the bandwidth characteristics of sources is called a *token bucket* filter. Such a filter is described by two parameters: a token rate r, and a bucket depth B. It works as follows. To be able to send a byte, I must have a token. To send a packet of length n, I need n tokens. I start with no tokens and I accumulate them at a rate of r per second. I can accumulate no more than B tokens. What this means is that I can send a burst of as many as B bytes into the network as fast as I want, but over a sufficiently long interval I can't send more than r bytes per second. It turns out that this information is very helpful to the admission control algorithm when it tries to figure out whether it can accommodate a new request for service.

Figure 6.24 illustrates how a token bucket can be used to characterize a flow's bandwidth requirements. For simplicity, assume that each flow can send data as individual bytes rather than as packets. Flow A generates data at a steady rate of 1 MBps, so it can be described by a token

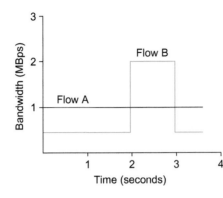

■ FIGURE 6.24 Two flows with equal average rates but different token bucket descriptions.

bucket filter with a rate $r = 1$ MBps and a bucket depth of 1 byte. This means that it receives tokens at a rate of 1 MBps but that it cannot store more than 1 token—it spends them immediately. Flow B also sends at a rate that averages out to 1 MBps over the long term, but does so by sending at 0.5 MBps for 2 seconds and then at 2 MBps for 1 second. Since the token bucket rate r is, in a sense, a long-term average rate, flow B can be described by a token bucket with a rate of 1 MBps. Unlike flow A, however, flow B needs a bucket depth B of at least 1 MB, so that it can store up tokens while it sends at less than 1 MBps to be used when it sends at 2 MBps. For the first 2 seconds in this example, it receives tokens at a rate of 1 MBps but spends them at only 0.5 MBps, so it can save up $2 \times 0.5 = 1$ MB of tokens, which it then spends in the third second (along with the new tokens that continue to accrue in that second) to send data at 2 MBps. At the end of the third second, having spent the excess tokens, it starts to save them up again by sending at 0.5 MBps again.

It is interesting to note that a single flow can be described by many different token buckets. As a trivial example, flow A could be described by the same token bucket as flow B, with a rate of 1 MBps and a bucket depth of 1 MB. The fact that it never actually needs to accumulate tokens does not make that an inaccurate description, but it does mean that we have failed to convey some useful information to the network—the fact that flow A is actually very consistent in its bandwidth needs. In general, it is good to be as explicit about the bandwidth needs of an application as possible to avoid over-allocation of resources in the network.

Admission Control

The idea behind admission control is simple: When some new flow wants to receive a particular level of service, admission control looks at the TSpec and RSpec of the flow and tries to decide if the desired service can be provided to that amount of traffic, given the currently available resources, without causing any previously admitted flow to receive worse service than it had requested. If it can provide the service, the flow is admitted; if not, then it is denied. The hard part is figuring out when to say yes and when to say no.

Admission control is very dependent on the type of requested service and on the queuing discipline employed in the routers; we discuss the latter topic later in this section. For a guaranteed service, you need to have a good algorithm to make a definitive yes/no decision. The decision is fairly straightforward if weighted fair queuing, as discussed in Section 6.2, is used at each router. For a controlled load service, the decision may be based on heuristics, such as "The last time I allowed a flow with this TSpec into this class, the delays for the class exceeded the acceptable bound, so I'd better say no" or "My current delays are so far inside the bounds that I should be able to admit another flow without difficulty."

Admission control should not be confused with *policing*. The former is a per-flow decision to admit a new flow or not. The latter is a function applied on a per-packet basis to make sure that a flow conforms to the TSpec that was used to make the reservation. If a flow does not conform to its TSpec—for example, because it is sending twice as many bytes per second as it said it would—then it is likely to interfere with the service provided to other flows, and some corrective action must be taken. There are several options, the obvious one being to drop offending packets. However, another option would be to check if the packets really are interfering with the service of other flows. If they are not interfering, the packets could be sent on after being marked with a tag that says, in effect, "This is a nonconforming packet. Drop it first if you need to drop any packets."

Admission control is closely related to the important issue of *policy*. For example, a network administrator might wish to allow reservations made by his company's CEO to be admitted while rejecting reservations made by more lowly employees. Of course, the CEO's reservation request might still fail if the requested resources aren't available, so we see that issues of policy and resource availability may both be addressed when admission control decisions are made. The application of policy to networking is an area receiving much attention at the time of writing.

Reservation Protocol

While connection-oriented networks have always needed some sort of setup protocol to establish the necessary virtual circuit state in the switches, connectionless networks like the Internet have had no such protocols. As this section has indicated, however, we need to provide a lot more information to our network when we want a real-time service from it. While there have been a number of setup protocols proposed for the Internet, the one on which most current attention is focused is the RSVP. It is particularly interesting because it differs so substantially from conventional signalling protocols for connection-oriented networks.

One of the key assumptions underlying RSVP is that it should not detract from the robustness that we find in today's connectionless networks. Because connectionless networks rely on little or no state being stored in the network itself, it is possible for routers to crash and reboot and for links to go up and down while end-to-end connectivity is still maintained. RSVP tries to maintain this robustness by using the idea of *soft state* in the routers. Soft state—in contrast to the hard state found in connection-oriented networks—does not need to be explicitly deleted when it is no longer needed. Instead, it times out after some fairly short period (say, a minute) if it is not periodically refreshed. We will see later how this helps robustness.

Another important characteristic of RSVP is that it aims to support multicast flows just as effectively as unicast flows. This is not surprising, since many of the first applications that could benefit from improved quality of service were also multicast applications—vat and vic, for example. One of the insights of RSVP's designers is that most multicast applications have many more receivers than senders, as typified by the large audience and one speaker for a lecture. Also, receivers may have different requirements. For example, one receiver might want to receive data from only one sender, while others might wish to receive data from all senders. Rather than having the senders keep track of a potentially large number of receivers, it makes more sense to let the receivers keep track of their own needs. This suggests the *receiver-oriented* approach adopted by RSVP. In contrast, connection-oriented networks usually leave resource reservation to the sender, just as it is normally the originator of a phone call who causes resources to be allocated in the phone network.

The soft state and receiver-oriented nature of RSVP give it a number of good properties. One such property is that it is very straightforward to increase or decrease the level of resource allocation provided to a receiver. Since each receiver periodically sends refresh messages to keep the soft state in place, it is easy to send a new reservation that asks for a new level of resources. Further, soft state deals gracefully with the possibility of network or node failures. In the event of a host crash, resources allocated by that host to a flow will naturally time out and be released. To see what happens in the event of a router or link failure, we need to look a little more closely at the mechanics of making a reservation.

Initially, consider the case of one sender and one receiver trying to get a reservation for traffic flowing between them. There are two things that need to happen before a receiver can make the reservation. First, the receiver needs to know what traffic the sender is likely to send so that it can make an appropriate reservation. That is, it needs to know the sender's TSpec. Second, it needs to know what path the packets will follow from sender to receiver, so that it can establish a resource reservation at each router on the path. Both of these requirements can be met by sending a message from the sender to the receiver that contains the TSpec. Obviously, this gets the TSpec to the receiver. The other thing that happens is that each router looks at this message (called a PATH message) as it goes past, and it figures out the *reverse path* that will be used to send reservations from the receiver back to the sender in an effort to get the reservation to each router on the path. Building the multicast tree in the first place is done by mechanisms such as those described in Section 4.2.

Having received a PATH message, the receiver sends a reservation back up the multicast tree in a RESV message. This message contains the sender's TSpec and an RSpec describing the requirements of this receiver. Each router on the path looks at the reservation request and tries to allocate the necessary resources to satisfy it. If the reservation can be made, the RESV request is passed on to the next router. If not, an error message is returned to the receiver who made the request. If all goes well, the correct reservation is installed at every router between the sender and the receiver. As long as the receiver wants to retain the reservation, it sends the same RESV message about once every 30 seconds.

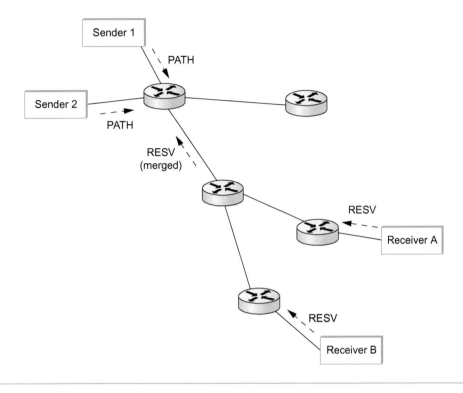

Making reservations on a multicast tree.

Now we can see what happens when a router or link fails. Routing protocols will adapt to the failure and create a new path from sender to receiver. PATH messages are sent about every 30 seconds, and may be sent sooner if a router detects a change in its forwarding table, so the first one after the new route stabilizes will reach the receiver over the new path. The receiver's next RESV message will follow the new path and, if all goes well, establish a new reservation on the new path. Meanwhile, the routers that are no longer on the path will stop getting RESV messages, and these reservations will time out and be released. Thus, RSVP deals quite well with changes in topology, as long as routing changes are not excessively frequent.

The next thing we need to consider is how to cope with multicast, where there may be multiple senders to a group and multiple receivers. This situation is illustrated in Figure 6.25. First, let's deal with multiple receivers for a single sender. As a RESV message travels up the multicast tree, it is likely to hit a piece of the tree where some other receiver's reservation has already been established. It may be the case that the resources reserved upstream of this point are adequate to serve both receivers. For example, if receiver A has already made a reservation that provides for a guaranteed delay of less than 100 ms, and the new request from receiver B is for a delay of less than 200 ms, then no new reservation is required. On the other hand, if the new request were for a delay of less than 50 ms, then the router would first need to see if it could accept the request; if so, it would send the request on upstream. The next time receiver A asked for a minimum of a 100-ms delay, the router would not need to pass this request on. In general, reservations can be merged in this way to meet the needs of all receivers downstream of the merge point.

If there are also multiple senders in the tree, receivers need to collect the TSpecs from all senders and make a reservation that is large enough to accommodate the traffic from all senders. However, this may not mean that the TSpecs need to be added up. For example, in an audioconference with 10 speakers, there is not much point in allocating enough resources to carry 10 audio streams, since the result of 10 people speaking at once would be incomprehensible. Thus, we could imagine a reservation that is large enough to accommodate two speakers and no more. Calculating the correct overall TSpec from all of the sender TSpecs is clearly application specific. Also, we may only be interested in hearing from a subset of all possible speakers; RSVP has different reservation styles to deal with such options as "Reserve resources for all speakers," "Reserve resources for any n speakers," and "Reserve resources for speakers A and B only."

Packet Classifying and Scheduling

Once we have described our traffic and our desired network service and have installed a suitable reservation at all the routers on the path, the only thing that remains is for the routers to actually deliver the requested service to the data packets. There are two things that need to be done:

- Associate each packet with the appropriate reservation so that it can be handled correctly, a process known as *classifying* packets.
- Manage the packets in the queues so that they receive the service that has been requested, a process known as packet *scheduling*.

The first part is done by examining up to five fields in the packet: the source address, destination address, protocol number, source port, and destination port. (In IPv6, it is possible that the FlowLabel field in

Where Are They Now?

RSVP AND INTEGRATED SERVICES DEPLOYMENT

RSVP and the Integrated Services architecture have, at the time of writing, not been very widely deployed, in large part because of scalability concerns described at the end of this section. In fact, it is common to assert that they are dead as technologies. However, it may be premature to write the obituaries for RSVP and Integrated Services just yet.

Separated from IntServ, RSVP has been quite widely deployed as a protocol for establishing MPLS paths for the purposes of traffic engineering, as described in Section 4.3. For this reason alone, most routers in the Internet have some sort of RSVP implementation. However, that is probably the full extent of RSVP deployment in the Internet at the time of writing. This usage of RSVP is largely independent of IntServ, but it does at least demonstrate that the protocol itself is deployable.

There is some evidence that RSVP and IntServ may get a second chance more than 10 years after they were first proposed. For example, the IETF is standardizing extensions to RSVP to support aggregate reservations—extensions that directly address the scalability concerns that have been raised about RSVP and IntServ in the past. And, there is increasing support for RSVP as a resource reservation protocol in commercial products.

Various factors can be identified that may lead to greater adoption of RSVP and IntServ in the near future. First, applications that actually require QoS, such as Voice over IP, real-time video conferencing, and entertainment video, are much more widespread than they were 10 years ago, creating a greater demand for sophisticated QoS mechanisms. Second, admission control—which enables the network to say no to an application when resources are scarce—is a good match to applications that cannot work well unless sufficient resources are available. Most users of IP telephones, for example, would prefer to get a busy signal from the network than to have a call proceed at unacceptably bad quality, and a network operator would prefer to send a busy signal to one user than to provide bad quality to a large number of users. A third factor is the large resource requirements of new applications such as high-definition video delivery: Because they need so much bandwidth to work well, it may be more cost effective to build networks that can say no occasionally than to provide enough bandwidth to meet all possible application demands. However, this is a complex tradeoff, and the debate over the value of admission control, and RSVP and IntServ as the tools to provide it, is likely to continue for some time.

the header could be used to enable the lookup to be done based on a single, shorter key.) Based on this information, the packet can be placed in the appropriate class. For example, it may be classified into the controlled load classes, or it may be part of a guaranteed flow that needs to be handled separately from all other guaranteed flows. In short, there is a mapping from the flow-specific information in the packet header to a single class identifier that determines how the packet is handled in the queue. For guaranteed flows this might be a one-to-one mapping, while for other services it might be many to one. The details of classification are closely related to the details of queue management.

It should be clear that something as simple as a FIFO queue in a router will be inadequate to provide many different services and to provide different levels of delay within each service. Several more sophisticated queue management disciplines were discussed in Section 6.2, and some combination of these is likely to be used in a router.

The details of packet scheduling ideally should not be specified in the service model. Instead, this is an area where implementors can try to do creative things to realize the service model efficiently. In the case of guaranteed service, it has been established that a weighted fair queuing discipline, in which each flow gets its own individual queue with a certain share of the link, will provide a guaranteed end-to-end delay bound that can readily be calculated. For controlled load, simpler schemes may be used. One possibility includes treating all the controlled load traffic as a single, aggregated flow (as far as the scheduling mechanism is concerned), with the weight for that flow being set based on the total amount of traffic admitted in the controlled load class. The problem is made harder when you consider that, in a single router, many different services are likely to be provided concurrently and that each of these services may require a different scheduling algorithm. Thus, some overall queue management algorithm is needed to manage the resources between the different services.

Scalability Issues

Although the Integrated Services architecture and RSVP represented a significant enhancement of the best-effort service model of IP, many Internet service providers felt that it was not the right model for them to deploy. The reason for this reticence relates to one of the fundamental design goals of IP: scalability. In the best-effort service model, routers in the

Internet store little or no state about the individual flows passing through them. Thus, as the Internet grows, the only thing routers have to do to keep up with that growth is to move more bits per second and to deal with larger routing tables, but RSVP raises the possibility that every flow passing through a router might have a corresponding reservation. To understand the severity of this problem, suppose that every flow on an OC-48 (2.5-Gbps) link represents a 64-kbps audio stream. The number of such flows is

$$2.5 \times 10^9 / 64 \times 10^3 = 39,000$$

Each of those reservations needs some amount of state that needs to be stored in memory and refreshed periodically. The router needs to classify, police, and queue each of those flows. Admission control decisions need to be made every time such a flow requests a reservation, and some mechanisms are needed to "push back" on users so that they don't make arbitrarily large reservations for long periods of time.[6]

These scalability concerns have, at the time of writing, prevented the widespread deployment of IntServ. Because of these concerns, other approaches that do not require so much "per-flow" state have been developed. The next section discusses a number of such approaches.

6.5.3 Differentiated Services (EF, AF)

Whereas the Integrated Services architecture allocates resources to individual flows, the Differentiated Services model (often called DiffServ for short) allocates resources to a small number of classes of traffic. In fact, some proposed approaches to DiffServ simply divide traffic into two classes. This is an eminently sensible approach to take: If you consider the difficulty that network operators experience just trying to keep a best-effort internet running smoothly, it makes sense to add to the service model in small increments.

LAB Appendix B: ATM

Suppose that we have decided to enhance the best-effort service model by adding just one new class, which we'll call "premium." Clearly, we will need some way to figure out which packets are premium and which are regular old best effort. Rather than using a protocol like RSVP to tell all

---

[6]Charging per reservation would be one way to push back, consistent with the telephony model of billing for each phone call. This is not the only way to push back, and per-call billing is believed to be one of the major costs of operating the phone network.

the routers that some flow is sending premium packets, it would be much easier if the packets could just identify themselves to the router when they arrive. This could obviously be done by using a bit in the packet header—if that bit is a 1, the packet is a premium packet; if it's a 0, the packet is best effort. With this in mind, there are two questions we need to address:

- Who sets the premium bit and under what circumstances?
- What does a router do differently when it sees a packet with the bit set?

There are many possible answers to the first question, but a common approach is to set the bit at an administrative boundary. For example, the router at the edge of an Internet service provider's network might set the bit for packets arriving on an interface that connects to a particular company's network. The Internet service provider might do this because that company has paid for a higher level of service than best effort. It is also possible that not all packets would be marked as premium; for example, the router might be configured to mark packets as premium up to some maximum rate and to leave all excess packets as best effort.

Assuming that packets have been marked in some way, what do the routers that encounter marked packets do with them? Here again there are many answers. In fact, the IETF standardized a set of router behaviors to be applied to marked packets. These are called *per-hop behaviors* (PHBs), a term that indicates that they define the behavior of individual routers rather than end-to-end services. Because there is more than one new behavior, there is also a need for more than 1 bit in the packet header to tell the routers which behavior to apply. The IETF decided to take the old TOS byte from the IP header, which had not been widely used, and redefine it. Six bits of this byte have been allocated for DiffServ code points (DSCPs), where each DSCP is a 6-bit value that identifies a particular PHB to be applied to a packet. (The remaining two bits are used by ECN, described in Section 6.4.2.)

The Expedited Forwarding (EF) PHB

One of the simplest PHBs to explain is known as *expedited forwarding* (EF). Packets marked for EF treatment should be forwarded by the router with minimal delay and loss. The only way that a router can guarantee this to all EF packets is if the arrival rate of EF packets at the router is strictly limited to be less than the rate at which the router can forward EF packets. For example, a router with a 100-Mbps interface needs to be sure that the arrival rate of EF packets destined for that interface never exceeds 100 Mbps. It might also want to be sure that the rate will be somewhat below 100 Mbps, so that it occasionally has time to send other packets such as routing updates.

The rate limiting of EF packets is achieved by configuring the routers at the edge of an administrative domain to allow a certain maximum rate of EF packet arrivals into the domain. A simple, albeit conservative, approach would be to ensure that the sum of the rates of all EF packets entering the domain is less than the bandwidth of the slowest link in the domain. This would ensure that, even in the worst case where all EF packets converge on the slowest link, it is not overloaded and can provide the correct behavior.

There are several possible implementation strategies for the EF behavior. One is to give EF packets strict priority over all other packets. Another is to perform weighted fair queuing between EF packets and other packets, with the weight of EF set sufficiently high that all EF packets can be delivered quickly. This has an advantage over strict priority: The non-EF packets can be assured of getting some access to the link, even if the amount of EF traffic is excessive. This might mean that the EF packets fail to get exactly the specified behavior, but it could also prevent essential routing traffic from being locked out of the network in the event of an excessive load of EF traffic.

The Assured Forwarding (AF) PHB

The *assured forwarding* (AF) PHB has its roots in an approach known as *RED* with In and Out (RIO) or Weighted RED, both of which are enhancements to the basic RED algorithm of Section 6.4.2. Figure 6.26 shows how RIO works; like Figure 6.17, we see drop probability on the y-axis increasing as average queue length increases along the x-axis. But now, for our two classes of traffic, we have two separate drop probability curves. RIO calls the two classes "in" and "out" for reasons that will become clear shortly. Because the "out" curve has a lower MinThreshold than the "in" curve, it is clear that, under low levels of congestion, only packets marked "out" will be discarded by the RED algorithm. If the congestion becomes more serious, a higher percentage of "out" packets are dropped, and then

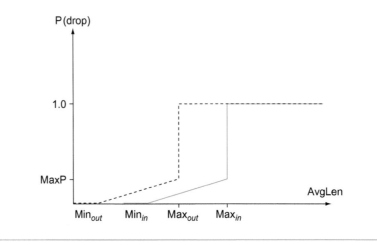

if the average queue length exceeds Min_{in}, RED starts to drop "in" packets as well.

The reason for calling the two classes of packets "in" and "out" stems from the way the packets are marked. We already noted that packet marking can be performed by a router at the edge of an administrative domain. We can think of this router as being at the boundary between a network service provider and some customer of that network. The customer might be any other network—for example, the network of a corporation or of another network service provider. The customer and the network service provider agree on some sort of profile for the assured service (and perhaps the customer pays the network service provider for this profile). The profile might be something like "Customer X is allowed to send up to y Mbps of assured traffic," or it could be significantly more complex. Whatever the profile is, the edge router can clearly mark the packets that arrive from this customer as being either in or out of profile. In the example just mentioned, as long as the customer sends less than y Mbps, all his packets will be marked "in," but once he exceeds that rate the excess packets will be marked "out."

The combination of a profile meter at the edge and RIO in all the routers of the service provider's network should provide the customer with a high assurance (but not a guarantee) that packets within his profile can be delivered. In particular, if the majority of packets, including those sent by customers who have not paid extra to establish a profile, are "out" packets, then it should usually be the case that the RIO mechanism will act to keep congestion low enough that "in" packets are rarely dropped. Clearly, there must be enough bandwidth in the network so that the "in" packets alone are rarely able to congest a link to the point where RIO starts dropping "in" packets.

Just like RED, the effectiveness of a mechanism like RIO depends to some extent on correct parameter choices, and there are considerably more parameters to set for RIO. Exactly how well the scheme will work in production networks is not known at the time of writing.

One interesting property of RIO is that it does not change the order of "in" and "out" packets. For example, if a TCP connection is sending packets through a profile meter, and some packets are being marked "in" while others are marked "out," those packets will receive different drop probabilities in the router queues, but they will be delivered to the receiver in the same order in which they were sent. This is important for most TCP implementations, which perform much better when packets arrive in order, even if they are designed to cope with misordering. Note also that mechanisms such as fast retransmit can be falsely triggered when misordering happens.

The idea of RIO can be generalized to provide more than two drop probability curves, and this is the idea behind the approach known as *weighted RED* (WRED). In this case, the value of the DSCP field is used to pick one of several drop probability curves, so that several different classes of service can be provided.

A third way to provide Differentiated Services is to use the DSCP value to determine which queue to put a packet into in a weighted fair queuing scheduler as described in Section 6.2.2. As a very simple case, we might use one code point to indicate the *best-effort* queue and a second code point to select the *premium* queue. We then need to choose a weight for the premium queue that makes the premium packets get better service than the best-effort packets. This depends on the offered load of premium packets. For example, if we give the premium queue a weight of 1 and the best-effort queue a weight of 4, that ensures that the bandwidth available to premium packets is

$$B_{premium} = W_{premium}/(W_{premium} + W_{best\_effort})$$
$$= 1/(1+4)$$
$$= 0.2$$

Where Are They Now?

THE QUIET SUCCESS OF DIFFServ

As recently as 2003, many people were ready to declare that DiffServ was dead. That year's ACM SIGCOMM conference, one of the most prestigious networking research conferences, included a workshop with the provocative title "RIPQOS"—the official name of the workshop was "Revisiting IP QoS" but the implication that QOS might be ready to rest in peace was clear in the workshop announcement. However, just as Mark Twain quipped that reports of his death were greatly exaggerated, it seems that the demise of IP QoS, and DiffServ in particular, was also overstated.

Much of the pessimism about DiffServ arose from the fact that it had not been deployed to any significant extent by Internet Service Providers. Not only that, but the fact that real-time applications such as IP telephony and video streaming appear to be working so well over the Internet without any QoS mechanisms in place makes one wonder if any QoS will ever be needed. In part, this is the result of aggressive deployment of high bandwidth links and routers by many ISPs, especially during the boom years of the late 1990s.

To see where DiffServ has succeeded, you need to look outside the ISP backbones. For example, corporations that have deployed IP telephony solutions— and there are tens of millions of enterprise-class IP phones in use at the time of writing—routinely use EF behavior for the voice media packets to ensure that they are not delayed when sharing links with other traffic. The same holds for many residential Voice over IP solutions: Just to get priority on the upstream link out of the residence (e.g., the "slow" direction of a DSL link), it is common for the voice endpoint to set the DSCP to EF, and for a consumer's router connected to the broadband link to use DiffServ to give low latency and jitter to those packets. There are even some large national telephone companies that have migrated their traditional voice services onto IP networks, with DiffServ providing the means to protect the QoS of the voice.

There are other applications beside voice that are benefiting from DiffServ, notably business data services, and no doubt the maturing of IP-based video in the coming years will provide another driver. In general, two factors make DiffServ deployment worthwhile: a high demand for QoS assurance from the application and a lack of assurance that the link bandwidth will be sufficient to deliver that QoS to *all* the traffic traversing the link. It is important to realize that DiffServ, like any other QoS mechanism, cannot create bandwidth—all it can do is ensure that what bandwidth there is gets preferentially allocated to the applications that have more demanding QoS needs.

That is, we have effectively reserved 20% of the link for premium packets, so if the offered load of premium traffic is only 10% of the link on average, then the premium traffic will behave as if it is running on a very underloaded network and the service will be very good. In particular, the delay experienced by the premium class can be kept low, since WFQ will try to transmit premium packets as soon as they arrive in this scenario. On the other hand, if the premium traffic load were 30%, it would behave like a highly loaded network, and delay could be very high for the premium packets—even worse than for the so-called best-effort packets. Thus, knowledge of the offered load and careful setting of weights is important for this type of service. However, note that the safe approach is to be very conservative in setting the weight for the premium queue. If this weight is made very high relative to the expected load, it provides a margin of error and yet does not prevent the best-effort traffic from using any bandwidth that has been reserved for premium but is not used by premium packets.

Just as in WRED, we can generalize this WFQ-based approach to allow more than two classes represented by different code points. Furthermore, we can combine the idea of a queue selector with a drop preference. For example, with 12 code points we can have four queues with different weights, each of which has three drop preferences. This is exactly what the IETF has done in the definition of "assured service."

ATM Quality of Service

ATM is a rather less important technology today than it was 10 years ago, but one of its real contributions was in the area of QoS. In some respects, the fact that ATM was designed with fairly rich QoS capabilities was one of the things that spurred interest in QoS for IP. It also helped the early adoption of ATM.

In many respects, the QoS capabilities that are provided in ATM networks are similar to those provided in an IP network using Integrated Services. However, the ATM standards bodies came up with a total of five service classes compared to the IETF's three.[7] The five ATM service classes are

- Constant bit rate (CBR)
- Variable bit rate—real-time (VBR-rt)

---

[7]We count best effort as a service class along with controlled load and guaranteed service.

- Variable bit rate—non-real-time (VBR-nrt)
- Available bit rate (ABR)
- Unspecified bit rate (UBR)

Mostly the ATM and IP service classes are quite similar, but one of them, ABR, has no real counterpart in IP. More on ABR in a moment. VBR-rt is very much like the guaranteed service class in IP Integrated Services. The exact parameters that are used to set up a VBR-rt VC are slightly different than those used to make a guaranteed service reservation, but the basic idea is the same. The traffic generated by the source is characterized by a token bucket, and the maximum total delay required through the network is specified. CBR is also similar to guaranteed service except that sources of CBR traffic are expected to send at a constant rate. Note that this is really a special case of VBR, where the source's peak rate and average rate of transmission are equal.

VBR-nrt bears some similarity to IP's controlled load service. Again, the source traffic is specified by a token bucket, but there is not the same hard delay guarantee of VBR-rt or IP's guaranteed service. UBR is ATM's best-effort service.

Finally, we come to ABR, which is more than just a service class; it also defines a set of congestion-control mechanisms. It is rather complex, so we mention only the high points.

The ABR mechanisms operate over a virtual circuit by exchanging special ATM cells called *resource management* (RM) cells between the source and destination of the VC. The goal of sending the RM cells is to get information about the state of congestion in the network back to the source so that it can send traffic at an appropriate rate. In this respect, RM cells are an explicit congestion feedback mechanism. This is similar to the DECbit (see Section 6.4.1), but contrasts with TCP's use of implicit feedback, which depends on packet losses to detect congestion. It is also similar to the new quick-start mechanism for TCP described in Section 6.3.2.

Initially, the source sends the cell to the destination and includes in it the rate at which it would like to send data cells. Switches along the path look at the requested rate and decide if sufficient resources are available to handle that rate, based on the amount of traffic being carried on other circuits. If enough resources are available, the RM cell is passed on unmodified; otherwise, the requested rate is decreased before the cell is passed along. At the destination, the RM cell is turned around and sent back to the source, which thereby learns what rate it can send at.

The intention of ABR is to allow a source to increase or decrease its allotted rate as conditions dictate. Hence, RM cells are sent periodically and may contain either higher or lower requested rates. Also, the rate at which a source is allowed to send decays with time if not used. In general, proprietary algorithms in the switches determine the rates that are placed in RM cells as they pass through the switches; the algorithms draw on a variety of information such as the current buffer occupancy and the measured arrival rates on currently active VCs. These algorithms, as is normal for congestion-control algorithms, seek to maximize throughput and to keep delay and loss low.

Given the relative decline of ATM in real networks today, the interesting point of ATM QoS is how many mechanisms are common across different technologies. Mechanisms that are found in both ATM and IP QoS include admission control, scheduling algorithms, token bucket policers, and explicit congestion feedback mechanisms.

6.5.4 Equation-Based Congestion Control

We conclude our discussion of QoS by returning full circle to TCP congestion control, but this time in the context of real-time applications. Recall that TCP adjusts the sender's congestion window (and, hence, the rate at which it can transmit) in response to ACK and timeout events. One of the strengths of this approach is that it does not require cooperation from the network's routers; it is a purely host-based strategy. Such a strategy complements the QoS mechanisms we've been considering, because (1) applications can use host-based solutions today, before QoS mechanisms are widely deployed, and (2) even with DiffServ fully deployed, it is still possible for a router queue to be oversubscribed, and we would like real-time applications to react in a reasonable way should this happen.

While we would like to take advantage of TCP's congestion control algorithm, TCP itself is not appropriate for real-time applications. One reason is that TCP is a reliable protocol, and real-time applications often cannot afford the delays introduced by retransmission. However, what if we were to decouple TCP from its congestion control mechanism, to add TCP-like congestion control to an unreliable protocol like UDP? Could real-time applications make use of such a protocol?

On the one hand, this is an appealing idea because it would cause real-time streams to compete fairly with TCP streams. The alternative (which happens today) is that video applications use UDP without any form of congestion control and, as a consequence, steal bandwidth away from TCP flows that back off in the presence of congestion. On the other hand, the sawtooth behavior of TCP's congestion-control algorithm (see Figure 6.9) is not appropriate for real-time applications; it means that the rate at which the application transmits is constantly going up and down. In contrast, real-time applications work best when they are able to sustain a smooth transmission rate over a relatively long period of time.

Is it possible to achieve the best of both worlds: compatibility with TCP congestion control for the sake of fairness, while sustaining a smooth transmission rate for the sake of the application? Recent work suggests that the answer is yes. Specifically, several so called TCP-friendly congestion-control algorithms have been proposed. These algorithms have two main goals. One is to slowly adapt the congestion window. This is done by adapting over relatively longer time periods (e.g., an RTT) rather than on a per-packet basis. This smooths out the transmission rate. The second is to be TCP friendly in the sense of being fair to competing TCP flows. This property is often enforced by ensuring that the flow's behavior adheres to an equation that models TCP's behavior. Hence, this approach is sometimes called *equation-based congestion control*.

We saw a simplified form of the TCP rate equation in Section 6.3. The interested reader is referred to the papers cited at the end of this chapter for details about the full model. For our purposes, it is sufficient to note that the equation takes this general form:

$$Rate \propto \left(\frac{1}{RTT \times \sqrt{\rho}} \right)$$

which says that to be TCP-friendly, the transmission rate must be inversely proportional to the round-trip time (RTT) and the square root of the loss rate (ρ). In other words, to build a congestion control mechanism out of this relationship, the receiver must periodically report the loss rate it is experiencing back to the sender (e.g., it might report that it failed to received 10% of the last 100 packets), and the sender then adjusts its sending rate up or down, such that this relationship continues to hold. Of course, it is still up to the application to adapt to these changes in the available rate, but as we will see in the next chapter, many real-time applications are quite adaptable.

6.6 SUMMARY

As we have just seen, the issue of resource allocation is not only central to computer networking, it is also a very hard problem. This chapter has examined two aspects of resource allocation. The first, congestion control, is concerned with preventing overall degradation of service when the demand for resources by hosts exceeds the supply available in the network. The second aspect is the provision of different qualities of service to applications that need more assurances than those provided by the best-effort model.

Most congestion-control mechanisms are targeted at the best-effort service model of today's Internet, where the primary responsibility for congestion control falls on the end nodes of the network. Typically, the source uses feedback—either implicitly learned from the network or explicitly sent by a router—to adjust the load it places on the network; this is precisely what TCP's congestion-control mechanism does.

Independent of exactly what the end nodes are doing, the routers implement a queuing discipline that governs which packets get transmitted and which packets get dropped. Sometimes this queuing algorithm is sophisticated enough to segregate traffic (e.g., WFQ); in other cases, the router attempts to monitor its queue length and then signals the source host when congestion is about to occur (e.g., RED gateways and DECbit).

Emerging quality of service approaches aim to do substantially more than just control congestion. Their goal is to enable applications with widely varying requirements for delay, loss, and throughput to have those requirements met through new mechanisms inside the network. The Integrated Services (IntServ) approach allows individual application flows to specify their needs to the routers using an explicit signalling mechanism (RSVP), while Differentiated Services (DiffServ) assigns packets into a small number of classes that receive differentiated treatment in the routers. Differentiated Services is by far the more widely deployed approach, and yet neither DiffServ nor IntServ has seen much deployment in the public Internet.

Perhaps the larger question we should be asking is how much can we expect from the network and how much responsibility will ultimately fall to the end hosts. Reservation-based strategies certainly have the advantage of providing for more varied qualities of service than today's feedback-based schemes; being able to support different qualities of service is a strong reason to put more functionality into the network's routers. Does this mean that the days of TCP-like end-to-end congestion control are numbered? Certainly not. TCP and the applications that use it are well entrenched, and in many cases have no need of much more help from the network. Furthermore, it is most unlikely that all the routers in a worldwide, heterogeneous network

WHAT'S NEXT: REFACTORING THE NETWORK

like the Internet will implement precisely the same resource reservation mechanisms. Ultimately, it seems that the endpoints are going to have to look out for themselves, at least to some extent. The end-to-end principle argues that we should be very selective about putting additional functionality inside the network. How this all plays out in the next few years, in more areas than resource allocation, will be very interesting indeed.

In some sense, the Differentiated Services approach represents the middle ground between absolutely minimal intelligence in the network and the rather significant amount of intelligence (and stored state information) that is required in an Integrated Services network. Deployments of Integrated Services and RSVP can be found today, but only in very constrained environments (mostly in corporate networks). One important question is whether the Differentiated Services approach will meet the requirements of more stringent applications. For example, if a service provider is trying to offer a large-scale video on demand service over an IP network, will Differentiated Services techniques be adequate to deliver the quality of service that traditional television viewers expect? It seems likely that yet more QoS options, with varying amounts of intelligence in the network, will need to be explored.

There are some trends that seem to point in the direction of end systems taking charge of their QoS needs, at least in the public Internet. Skype, for example, has been very successful, in part because its free service makes people more willing to tolerate a lack of QoS guarantees. From a technology point of view, the combination of rate adaptation (Skype has a variable bit-rate voice codec) and overlay routing (a technique discussed in Chapter 9) has proven fairly effective at delivering decent quality to the application in spite of a lack of help from the network. At the same time, in corporate environments where users are more demanding, network-level support of QoS continues to see increasing deployment and sophistication.

■ FURTHER READING

The recommended reading list for this chapter is long, reflecting the breadth of interesting work being done in congestion control and resource allocation. It includes the original papers introducing the various mechanisms discussed in this chapter. In addition to a more detailed description of these mechanisms, including thorough analysis of their effectiveness and fairness, these papers are must reading because of the insights they give into the interplay of the various issues related to congestion control. In addition, the first paper gives a nice overview of some of the early work on this topic, while the last is considered one of the seminal papers in the development of QoS capabilities in the Internet.

- Gerla, M., and L. Kleinrock. Flow control: A comparative survey. *IEEE Transactions on Communications* COM-28(4):553–573, April 1980.

- Demers, A., S. Keshav, and S. Shenker. Analysis and simulation of a fair queuing algorithm. *Proceedings of the SIGCOMM '89 Symposium*, pages 1–12, September 1989.

- Jacobson, V. Congestion avoidance and control. *Proceedings of the SIGCOMM '88 Symposium*, pages 314–329, August 1988.

- Floyd, S., and V. Jacobson. Random early detection gateways for congestion avoidance. *IEEE/ACM Transactions on Networking* 1(4):397–413, August 1993.

- Clark, D., S. Shenker, and L. Zhang. Supporting real-time applications in an integrated services packet network: Architecture and mechanism. *Proceedings of the SIGCOMM '92 Symposium*, pages 14–26, August 1992.

- Parekh, A. and R. Gallager. A generalized processor sharing approach to flow control in integrated services networks: The multiple node case. *IEEE/ACM Transactions on Networking* 2(2):137–150, April 1994.

Beyond these recommended papers, there is a wealth of other valuable material on resource allocation. For starters, two early papers by Kleinrock [Kle79] and Jaffe [Jaf81] set the foundation for using power as a measure of congestion-control effectiveness. Also, Jain [Jai91] gives a thorough discussion of various issues related to performance evaluation, including a description of Jain's fairness index.

More details about TCP Vegas can be found in Brakmo and Peterson [BP95], with follow-up work presented in Low et al. [LPW02b]. Improvements to TCP's congestion control algorithms continue to be explored. FAST TCP extends TCP Vegas to high delay-bandwidth scenarios [WJLH06]. CUBIC, the TCP variant now found in Linux, is described by Ha et al. [HRX08]. Floyd [Flo03] provides the specification for HighSpeed TCP, an experimental IETF standard. Congestion-avoidance techniques similar to those introduced in Section 6.4 can be found in Wang and Crowcroft [WC92] and, [WC91] and in Jain [Jai89], with the first paper giving an especially nice overview of congestion avoidance based on a common understanding of how the network changes as it approaches congestion. Some issues with and proposed modifications to the RED algorithm including Flow RED (FRED) are described by Lin et al. [LM97].

The proposed ECN standard is spelled out by Ramakrishnan, Floyd, and Black in [RFB01]. Efforts to generalize this idea in the form of active queue management are put forth by Stoica et al. [SSZ98], Low et al. [LPW$^+$02a], and Katabi et al. [KHR02]. The Katabi paper introduces XCP, one of the proposed new transport protocols that tackles the issue of improving on TCP's throughput in high bandwidth-delay product networks.

There is a considerable body of work on packet scheduling that has extended the original fair queuing and processor sharing papers cited above. Excellent examples include articles by Stoica and Zhang [SZ97], Bennett and Zhang [BZ96], and Goyal, Vin, and Chen [GVC96].

Many additional articles have been published on the Integrated Services architecture, including an overview by Braden et al. [BCS94] and a description of RSVP by Zhang et al. [ZDE$^+$93]. The first paper to address the topic of Differentiated Services is that of Clark [Cla97], which introduces the RIO mechanism as well as the overall architecture of Differentiated Services. A follow-on paper by Clark and Fang [CF98] presents some simulation results. Blake et al. [BBC$^+$98] defines the Differentiated

Services architecture, and Davie et al. [DCB+02] defines the EF per-hop behavior. To see how real-time applications fare when they try to operate reliably over the best-effort service of the Internet, we recommend the paper on Skype user satisfaction by Chen et al. [CHHL06].

Finally, in addition to the work described above on improving TCP for traditional data applications, several TCP-friendly congestion control algorithms have been proposed and tailored for use by real-time applications. These include algorithms by Floyd et al. [FHPW00], Sisalem and Schulzrinne [SS98], Rhee et al. [ROY00], and Rejaie et al. [RHE99]. These algorithms build on the earlier equation-based model of TCP throughput by Padhye et al. [PFTK98]. A TCP-friendly rate control protocol has been specified by the IETF [HFPW03], and the idea of adding congestion control to UDP has led to the Datagram Congestion Control Protocol (DCCP) [KHF06].

EXERCISES

1. It is possible to define flows on either a host-to-host basis or on a process-to-process basis.
   (a) Discuss the implications of each approach to application programs.
   (b) IPv6 includes a FlowLabel field for supplying hints to routers about individual flows. The originating host is to put here a pseudorandom hash of all the other fields serving to identify the flow; the router can thus use any subset of these bits as a hash value for fast lookup of the flow. What exactly should the FlowLabel be based on, for each of these two approaches?

2. TCP uses a host-centric, feedback-based, window-based resource allocation model. How might TCP have been designed to use instead the following models?
   (a) Host-centric, feedback-based, and rate-based.
   (b) Router-centric and feedback-based.

3. Sketch curves for throughput, delay, and power, each as a function of load, for an Ethernet as described in Exercise 51 of Chapter 2. The average packet size is 5 slot times, and when N stations are trying to transmit the average delay until one station succeeds is $N/2$ slot times. Throughput is to be measured

as a percentage of the maximum. Load is to be measured (somewhat unnaturally) as the number of stations (N) ready to send at any one time; note this implies there is always (unless $N = 0$, which you may ignore) a station ready to send. Assume each station has only one packet to send at a time.

4. Suppose two hosts A and B are connected via a router R. The A–R link has infinite bandwidth; the R–B link can send one packet per second. R's queue is infinite. Load is to be measured as the number of packets per second sent from A to B. Sketch the throughput-versus-load and delay-versus-load graphs, or if a graph cannot be drawn, explain why. Would another way to measure load be more appropriate?

5. Is it possible for TCP Reno to reach a state with the congestion window size much larger than (e.g., twice as large as) RTT× bandwidth? Is it likely?

6. Consider the arrangement of hosts H and routers R and R1 in Figure 6.27. All links are full-duplex, and all routers are faster than their links. Show that R1 cannot become congested, and for any other router R we can find a traffic pattern that congests that router alone.

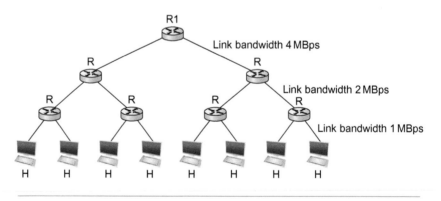

■ FIGURE 6.27 Diagram for Exercise 6.

7. Suppose a congestion-control scheme results in a collection of competing flows that achieve the following throughput rates: 200 KBps, 160 KBps, 110 KBps, 95 KBps, and 150 KBps.

(a) Calculate the fairness index for this scheme.

(b) Now add a flow with a throughput rate of 1000 KBps to the above, and recalculate the fairness index.

8. In fair queuing, the value F_i was interpreted as a timestamp: the time when the ith packet would finish transmitting. Give an interpretation of F_i for weighted fair queuing, and also give a formula for it in terms of F_{i-1}, arrival time A_i, packet size P_i, and weight w assigned to the flow.

9. Give an example of how nonpreemption in the implementation of fair queuing leads to a different packet transmission order from bit-by-bit round-robin service.

10. Suppose a router has three input flows and one output. It receives the packets listed in Table 6.1 all at about the same time, in the order listed, during a period in which the output port is busy but all queues are otherwise empty. Give the order in which the packets are transmitted, assuming

(a) Fair queuing.

(b) Weighted fair queuing, with flow 2 having weight 4, and the other two flows having weight 1.

Table 6.1 Packets for Exercise 10

Packet	Size	Flow
1	100	1
2	100	1
3	100	1
4	100	1
5	190	2
6	200	2
7	110	3
8	50	3

11. Suppose a router has three input flows and one output. It receives the packets listed in Table 6.2 all at about the same time, in the

Table 6.2 Packets for Exercise 11

Packet	Size	Flow
1	200	1
2	200	1
3	160	2
4	120	2
5	160	2
6	210	3
7	150	3
8	90	3

order listed, during a period in which the output port is busy but all queues are otherwise empty. Give the order in which the packets are transmitted, assuming

(a) Fair queuing.

(b) Weighted fair queuing with flow 2 having twice as much share as flow 1, and flow 3 having 1.5 times as much share as flow 1. Note that ties are to be resolved in the order of flow 1, flow 2, flow 3.

12. Suppose a router's drop policy is to drop the highest-cost packet whenever queues are full, where it defines the "cost" of a packet to be the product of its size by the time *remaining* that it will spend in the queue. (Note that in calculating cost it is equivalent to use the sum of the sizes of the earlier packets in lieu of remaining time.)

(a) What advantages and disadvantages might such a policy offer, compared to tail drop?

(b) Give an example of a sequence of queued packets for which dropping the highest-cost packet differs from dropping the largest packet.

(c) Give an example where two packets exchange their relative cost ranks as time progresses.

13. Two users, one using Telnet and one sending files with FTP, both send their traffic out via router R. The outbound link from R is slow enough that both users keep packets in R's queue at all

times. Discuss the relative performance seen by the Telnet user if R's queuing policy for these two flows is

(a) Round-robin service.

(b) Fair queuing.

(c) Modified fair queuing, where we count the cost only of data bytes and not IP or TCP headers.

Consider outbound traffic only. Assume Telnet packets have 1 byte of data, FTP packets have 512 bytes of data, and all packets have 40 bytes of headers.

14. Consider a router that is managing three flows, on which packets of constant size arrive at the following wall clock times:

Flow A: 1, 2, 4, 6, 7, 9, 10

Flow B: 2, 6, 8, 11, 12, 15

Flow C: 1, 2, 3, 5, 6, 7, 8

All three flows share the same outbound link, on which the router can transmit one packet per time unit. Assume that there is an infinite amount of buffer space.

(a) Suppose the router implements fair queuing. For each packet, give the wall clock time when it is transmitted by the router. Arrival time ties are to be resolved in the order of A, B, C. Note that wall clock time $T = 2$ is FQ-clock time $A_i = 1.5$.

(b) Suppose the router implements weighted fair queuing, where flows A and B are given an equal share of the capacity and flow C is given twice the capacity of flow A. For each packet, give the wall clock time when it is transmitted.

15. Consider a router that is managing three flows, on which packets of constant size arrive at the following wall clock times:

Flow A: 1, 3, 5, 6, 8, 9, 11

Flow B: 1, 4, 7, 8, 9, 13, 15

Flow C: 1, 2, 4, 6, 7, 12

All three flows share the same outbound link, on which the router can transmit one packet per time unit. Assume that there is an infinite amount of buffer space.

(a) Suppose the router implements fair queuing. For each packet, give the wall clock time when it is transmitted by the router. Arrival time ties are to be resolved in the order of A, B,

C. Note that wall clock time $T = 2$ is FQ-clock time $A_i = 1.333$.

(b) Suppose the router implements weighted fair queuing, where flows A and C are given an equal share of the capacity, and flow B is given twice the capacity of flow A. For each packet, give the wall clock time when it is transmitted.

16. Assume that TCP implements an extension that allows window sizes much larger than 64 KB. Suppose that you are using this extended TCP over a 1-Gbps link with a latency of 50 ms to transfer a 10-MB file, and the TCP receive window is 1 MB. If TCP sends 1-KB packets (assuming no congestion and no lost packets):

(a) How many RTTs does it take until slow start opens the send window to 1 MB?

(b) How many RTTs does it take to send the file?

(c) If the time to send the file is given by the number of required RTTs multiplied by the link latency, what is the effective throughput for the transfer? What percentage of the link bandwidth is utilized?

17. Consider a simple congestion-control algorithm that uses linear increase and multiplicative decrease but not slow start, that works in units of packets rather than bytes, and that starts each connection with a congestion window equal to one packet. Give a detailed sketch of this algorithm. Assume the delay is latency only and that when a group of packets is sent only a single ACK is returned. Plot the congestion window as a function of round-trip times for the situation in which the following packets are lost: 9, 25, 30, 38, and 50. For simplicity, assume a perfect timeout mechanism that detects a lost packet exactly 1 RTT after it is transmitted.

18. For the situation given in the previous problem, compute the effective throughput achieved by this connection. Assume that each packet holds 1 KB of data and that the RTT = 100 ms.

19. During linear increase, TCP computes an increment to the congestion window as:

$$\text{Increment} = \text{MSS} \times (\text{MSS/CongestionWindow})$$

Explain why computing this increment each time an ACK arrives may not result in the correct increment. Give a more precise definition for this increment. (Hint: A given ACK can acknowledge more or less than one MSS's worth of data.)

20. Under what circumstances may coarse-grained timeouts still occur in TCP even when the fast retransmit mechanism is being used?

21. Suppose that between A and B there is a router R. The A–R bandwidth is infinite (that is, packets are not delayed), but the R–B link introduces a bandwidth delay of 1 packet per second (that is, 2 packets take 2 seconds, etc.). Acknowledgments from B to R, though, are sent instantaneously. A sends data to B over a TCP connection, using slow start but with an arbitrarily large window size. R has a queue size of one, in addition to the packet it is sending. At each second, the sender first processes any arriving ACKs and then responds to any timeouts.
    (a) Assuming a fixed TimeOut period of 2 seconds, what is sent and received for $T = 0, 1, \ldots, 6$ seconds? Is the link ever idle due to timeouts?
    (b) What changes if TimeOut is 3 seconds instead?

22. Suppose A, R, and B are as in the previous exercise, except that R's queue now has a size of three packets, in addition to the one being transmitted. A starts a connection using slow start, with an infinite receive window. Fast retransmit is done on the *second* duplicate ACK (that is, the third ACK of the same packet); the TimeOut interval is infinite. Ignore fast recovery; when a packet is lost, let the window size be 1. Give a table showing, for the first 15 seconds, what A receives, what A sends, what R sends, R's queue, and what R drops.

23. Suppose the R–B link in the previous exercise changes from a bandwidth delay to a propagation delay, so that two packets now take 1 second to send. List what is sent and received during the first 8 seconds. Assume a static timeout value of 2 seconds, that slow start is used on a timeout, and that ACKs sent at about the same time are consolidated. Note that R's queue size is now irrelevant (why?).

24. Suppose host A reaches host B via routers R1 and R2: A–R1–R2–B. Fast retransmit is not used, and A calculates TimeOut as $2 \times$ EstimatedRTT. Assume that the A–R1 and R2–B links have infinite bandwidth; the R1 $\longrightarrow$ R2 link, however, introduces a 1-second-per-packet bandwidth delay for data packets (though not ACKs). Describe a scenario in which the R1–R2 link is not 100% utilized, even though A always has data ready to send. (Hint: Suppose A's CongestionWindow increases from N to $N + 1$, where N is R1's queue size.)

25. You are an Internet Service Provider; your client hosts connect directly to your routers. You know some hosts are using experimental TCPs and suspect some may be using a "greedy" TCP with no congestion control. What measurements might you make at your router to establish that a client was not using slow start at all? If a client used slow start on startup but not after a timeout, could you detect that?

26. Defeating TCP congestion-control mechanisms usually requires explicit cooperation of the sender. However, consider the receiving end of a large data transfer using a TCP modified to ACK packets that have not yet arrived. It may do this either because not all of the data is necessary or because data that is lost can be recovered in a separate transfer later. What effect does this receiver behavior have on the congestion control properties of the session? Can you devise a way to modify TCP to avoid the possibility of senders being taken advantage of in this manner?

27. Consider the TCP trace in Figure 6.28. Identify time intervals representing slow start on startup, slow start after timeout, and linear-increase congestion avoidance. Explain what is going on from $T = 0.5$ to $T = 1.9$. The TCP version that generated this trace includes a feature absent from the TCP that generated Figure 6.11. What is this feature? This trace and the one in Figure 6.13 both lack a feature. What is it?

28. Suppose you are downloading a large file over a 3-KBps phone link. Your software displays an average-bytes-per-second counter. How will TCP congestion control and occasional packet losses cause this counter to fluctuate? Assume that only a third, say, of the total RTT is spent on the phone link.

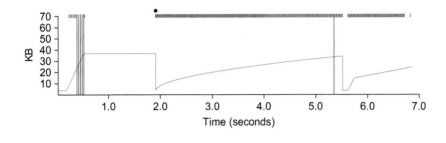

■ FIGURE 6.28 TCP trace for Exercise 27.

29. Suppose TCP is used over a lossy link that loses on average one segment in four. Assume the delay × bandwidth window size is considerably larger than four segments.

   (a) What happens when we start a connection? Do we ever get to the linear-increase phase of congestion avoidance?

   (b) Without using an explicit feedback mechanism from the routers, would TCP have any way to distinguish such link losses from congestion losses, at least over the short term?

   (c) Suppose TCP senders did reliably get explicit congestion indications from routers. Assuming links as above were common, would it be feasible to support window sizes much larger than four segments? What would TCP have to do?

30. Suppose two TCP connections share a path through a router R. The router's queue size is six segments; each connection has a stable congestion window of three segments. No congestion control is used by these connections. A third TCP connection now is attempted, also through R. The third connection does not use congestion control either. Describe a scenario in which, for at least a while, the third connection gets none of the available bandwidth, and the first two connections proceed with 50% each. Does it matter if the third connection uses slow start? How does full congestion avoidance on the part of the first two connections help solve this?

31. Suppose a TCP connection has a window size of eight segments and an RTT of 800 ms, the sender sends segments at a regular rate of one every 100 ms, and the receiver sends ACKs back at the same rate without delay. A segment is lost, and the loss is

detected by the fast retransmit algorithm on the receipt of the third duplicate ACK. At the point when the ACK of the retransmitted segment finally arrives, how much total time has the sender lost (compared to lossless transmission) if

(a) The sender waits for the ACK from the retransmitted lost packet before sliding the window forward again?

(b) The sender uses the continued arrival of each duplicate ACK as an indication it may slide the window forward one segment?

32. The text states that additive increase is a necessary condition for a congestion-control mechanism to be stable. Outline a specific instability that might arise if all increases were exponential; that is, if TCP continued to use slow start after CongestionWindow increased beyond CongestionThreshold.

33. Discuss the relative advantages and disadvantages of marking a packet (as in the DECbit mechanism) versus dropping a packet (as in RED gateways that do not implement ECN).

34. Consider a RED gateway with $\mathsf{MaxP} = 0.01$, and with an average queue length halfway between the two thresholds.

(a) Find the drop probability $\mathsf{P_{count}}$ for count $= 1$ and count $= 100$.

(b) Calculate the probability that none of the first 50 packets is dropped. Note that this is $(1 - \mathsf{P_1}) \times \cdots \times (1 - \mathsf{P_{50}})$.

✓ 35. Consider a RED gateway with $\mathsf{MaxP} = p$, and with an average queue length halfway between the two thresholds.

(a) Calculate the probability that none of the first n packets is dropped.

(b) Find p such that the probability that none of the first n packets is dropped is α.

36. Explain the intuition behind setting $\mathsf{MaxThreshold} = 2 \times \mathsf{MinThreshold}$ in RED gateways.

37. In RED gateways, explain why MaxThreshold is actually less than the actual size of the available buffer pool.

38. Explain the fundamental conflict between tolerating burstiness and controlling network congestion.

39. Why do you think that the drop probability P of a RED gateway does *not* simply increase linearly from $P = 0$ at MinThresh to $P = 1$ at MaxThresh?

40. Explicit Congestion Notification (ECN) as defined in RFC 3168 requires one bit to indicate whether the end-points are ECN capable. What would be the downside of not having this bit?

41. In TCP Vegas, the calculation of ActualRate is done by dividing the amount of data transmitted in one RTT interval by the length of the RTT.

    (a) Show that for any TCP, if the window size remains constant, then the amount of data transmitted in one RTT interval is constant once a full window-full is sent. Assume that the sender transmits each segment instantly upon receiving an ACK, packets are not lost and are delivered in order, segments are all the same size, and the first link along the path is not the slowest.

    (b) Give a timeline sketch showing that the amount of data per RTT above can be less than CongestionWindow.

42. Suppose a TCP Vegas connection measures the RTT of its first packet and sets BaseRTT to that, but then a network link failure occurs and all subsequent traffic is routed via an alternative path with twice the RTT. How will TCP Vegas respond? What will happen to the value of CongestionWindow? Assume no actual timeouts occur, and that β is much smaller than the initial ExpectedRate.

43. Consider the following two causes of a 1-second network delay (assume ACKs return instantaneously):

    - One intermediate router with a 1-second outbound per-packet bandwidth delay and no competing traffic.

    - One intermediate router with a 100-ms outbound per-packet bandwidth delay and with a steadily replenished (from another source) 10 packets in the queue.

    (a) How might a transport protocol in general distinguish between these two cases?

    (b) Suppose TCP Vegas sends over the above connections, with an initial CongestionWindow of three packets. What will happen to CongestionWindow in each case? Assume BaseRTT $= 1$ second and β is 1 packet per second.

44. Many real-time video applications run over UDP rather than TCP because they cannot tolerate retransmission delays. However, this means video applications are not constrained by TCP's congestion-control algorithm. What impact does this have on TCP traffic? Be specific about the consequences.

   Fortunately, these video applications often use RTP (Section 5.4), which results in RTCP receiver reports being sent from the sink back to the source. These reports are sent periodically (e.g., once a second) and include the percentage of packets successfully received in the last reporting period. Describe how the source might use this information to adjust its rate in a TCP-compatible way.

45. Give an argument why the congestion-control problem is better managed at the internet level than the ATM level, at least when only part of the internet is ATM. In an exclusively IP-over-ATM network, is congestion better managed at the cell level or at the TCP level? Why?

46. Consider the taxonomy of Figure 6.23.
   (a) Give an example of a real-time application that is *intolerant/rate adaptive*.
   (b) Explain why you might expect a loss-tolerant application to be at least somewhat rate adaptive.
   (c) Part (b) notwithstanding, give an example of an application that might be considered *tolerant/nonadaptive*. (Hint: Tolerating even small losses qualifies an application as loss tolerant; you will need to interpret rate adaptive as the ability to adjust to *substantial* bandwidth changes.)

47. The transmission schedule (Table 6.3) for a given flow lists for each second the number of packets sent between that time and the following second. The flow must stay within the bounds of a token bucket filter. What bucket depth does the flow need for the following token rates? Assume the bucket is initially full.
   (a) 2 packets per second
   (b) 4 packets per second

Table 6.3 Transmission Schedule for Exercise 47	
Time (seconds)	Packets Sent
0	8
1	4
2	1
3	0
4	6
5	1

48. The transmission schedule (Table 6.4) for a given flow is for each second the number of packets sent between that time and the following second. The flow must stay within the bounds of a token bucket filter. Find the necessary bucket depth D as a function of token rate r. Note that r takes only positive integer values. Assume the bucket is initially full.

Table 6.4 Transmission Schedule for Exercise 48	
Time (seconds)	Packets Sent
0	5
1	5
2	1
3	0
4	6
5	1

49. Suppose a router has accepted flows with the TSpecs shown in Table 6.5, described in terms of token bucket filters with token rate r packets per second and bucket depth B packets. All flows are in the same direction, and the router can forward one packet every 0.1 second.

Table 6.5 TSpecs for Exercise 49	
r	B
1	10
2	4
4	1

   (a) What is the maximum delay a packet might face?

   (b) What is the minimum number of packets from the third flow that the router would send over 2.0 seconds, assuming the flow sent packets at its maximum rate uniformly?

50. Suppose an RSVP router suddenly loses its reservation state, but otherwise remains running.

   (a) What will happen to the existing reserved flows if the router handles reserved and nonreserved flows via a single FIFO queue?

   (b) What might happen to the existing reserved flows if the router used weighted fair queuing to segregate reserved and nonreserved traffic?

   (c) Eventually the receivers on these flows will request that their reservations be renewed. Give a scenario in which these requests are denied.

7

A SYSTEMS APPROACH

A SYSTEMS APPROACH

A SYSTEMS APPROACH

End-to-End Data

It is a capital mistake to theorize before one has data.

–Sir Arthur Conan Doyle

From the network's perspective, application programs send messages to each other. Each of these messages is just an uninterpreted string of bytes. From the application's perspective, however, these messages contain various kinds of *data*—arrays of integers, video frames, lines of text, digital images, and so on. In other words, these bytes have meaning. We now consider the problem of how best to encode the different kinds of data that application programs want to exchange into byte strings. In many respects, this is similar to the problem of encoding byte strings into electromagnetic signals that we saw in Section 2.2.

PROBLEM: WHAT DO WE DO WITH THE DATA?

Thinking back to our discussion of encoding in Chapter 2, there were essentially two concerns. The first was that the receiver be able to extract the same message from the signal as the transmitter sent; this was the framing problem. The second was making the encoding as efficient as possible. Both of these concerns are also present when encoding application data into network messages.

In order for the receiver to extract the message sent by the transmitter, the two sides need to agree to a message format, often called the *presentation format*. If the sender wants to send the receiver an array of integers, for example, then the two sides have to agree what each integer looks like (how many bits long it is, what order the bytes are arranged in, and whether the most significant bit comes first or last, for example) and how many elements are in the array. Section 7.1 describes various encodings of traditional computer data, such as integers, floating-point numbers, character strings, arrays, and structures. Well-established formats also exist for multimedia data: Video, for example, is typically transmitted in one of the formats created by the Moving Picture Experts Group (MPEG), and still images are usually transmitted in Joint Photographic Experts Group (JPEG) format. The particular issues that arise in the encoding of multimedia data are discussed in Section 7.2.

Multimedia data types require us to think about both presentation and *compression*. The well-known formats for the transmission and storage of audio and video deal with both these issues: making sure that what was recorded, photographed, or heard at the sender can be interpreted correctly by the receiver, and doing so in a way that does not overwhelm the network with massive amounts of multimedia data.

Compression and, more generally, the efficiency of encoding have a rich history, dating back to Shannon's pioneering work on information theory in the 1940s. In effect, there are two opposing forces at work here. In one direction, you would like as much redundancy in the data as possible so that the receiver is able to extract the right data even if errors are introduced into the message. The error detection and correcting codes we saw in Section 2.4 add redundant information to messages for exactly this purpose. In the other direction, we would like to remove as much redundancy from the data as possible so that we may encode it in as few bits as possible. It turns out the multimedia data offers a wealth of opportunities for compression because of the way our senses and brains process visual and auditory signals. We don't hear high frequencies as well as lower ones, and we don't notice fine detail as much as the bigger picture in an image, especially if the image is moving.

Compression is important to the designers of networks for a wealth of reasons, not just because we rarely find ourselves with an abundance of bandwidth everywhere in the network. For example, the way we design a compression algorithm affects our sensitivity to lost or delayed data and thus may influence the design of resource allocation mechanisms and end-to-end protocols. Conversely, if the underlying network is unable to guarantee a fixed amount of bandwidth for the duration of a videoconference, we may choose to design compression algorithms that can adapt to changing network conditions.

Finally, an important aspect of both presentation formatting and data compression is that they require the sending and receiving hosts to process every byte of data in the message. It is for this reason that presentation formatting and compression are sometimes called *data manipulation* functions. This is in contrast to most of the protocols we have seen up to this point, which process a message without ever looking at its contents. Because of this need to read, compute on, and write every byte of data in a message, data manipulations affect end-to-end throughput over the network. In fact, these manipulations can be the limiting factor.

7.1 PRESENTATION FORMATTING

One of the most common transformations of network data is from the representation used by the application program into a form that is suitable for transmission over a network and *vice versa*. This transformation is typically called *presentation formatting*. As illustrated in Figure 7.1, the sending program translates the data it wants to transmit from the representation it uses internally into a message that can be transmitted over the network; that is, the data is *encoded* in a message. On the receiving side, the application translates this arriving message into a representation that it can then process; that is, the message is *decoded*. Encoding is sometimes called *argument marshalling*, and decoding is sometimes called *unmarshalling*. This terminology comes from the Remote Procedure Call (RPC) world, where the client thinks it is invoking a procedure with a set of arguments, but these arguments are then "brought together and ordered in an appropriate and effective way"[1] to form a network message.

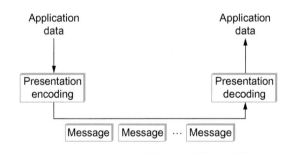

■ **FIGURE 7.1** Presentation formatting involves encoding and decoding application data.

---

[1]This is a definition of *marshalling* taken from *Webster's New Collegiate Dictionary*.

You might ask what makes this problem challenging enough to warrant a name like marshalling. One reason is that computers represent data in different ways. For example, some computers represent floating-point numbers in IEEE standard 754 format, while other machines still use their own nonstandard format. Even for something as simple as integers, different architectures use different sizes (e.g., 16-bit, 32-bit, 64-bit). To make matters worse, on some machines integers are represented in *big-endian* form (the most significant bit of a word is in the byte with the highest address), while on other machines integers are represented in *little-endian* form (the most significant bit is in the byte with the lowest address). The MIPS® and PowerPC™ processors are examples of big-endian machines, and the Intel® x86 family is an example of a little-endian architecture. The big-endian and little-endian representations of the integer 34,677,374 are given in Figure 7.2.

Another reason that marshalling is difficult is that application programs are written in different languages, and even when you are using a single language there may be more than one compiler. For example, compilers have a fair amount of latitude in how they lay out structures (records) in memory, such as how much padding they put between the fields that make up the structure. Thus, you could not simply transmit a structure from one machine to another, even if both machines were of the same architecture and the program was written in the same language, because the compiler on the destination machine might align the fields in the structure differently.

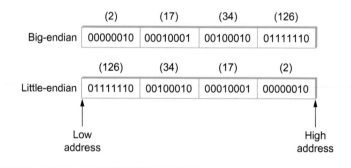

■ FIGURE 7.2 Big-endian and little-endian byte order for the integer 34,677,374.

7.1.1 Taxonomy

Although anyone who has worked on argument marshalling would tell you that no rocket science is involved—it is a small matter of bit twiddling—there are a surprising number of design choices that you must address. We begin by giving a simple taxonomy for argument marshalling systems. The following is by no means the only viable taxonomy, but it is sufficient to cover most of the interesting alternatives.

Data Types

The first question is what data types the system is going to support. In general, we can classify the types supported by an argument marshalling mechanism at three levels. Each level complicates the task faced by the marshalling system.

At the lowest level, a marshalling system operates on some set of *base types*. Typically, the base types include integers, floating-point numbers, and characters. The system might also support ordinal types and Booleans. As described above, the implication of the set of base types is that the encoding process must be able to convert each base type from one representation to another—for example, convert an integer from big-endian to little-endian.

At the next level are *flat types*—structures and arrays. While flat types might at first not appear to complicate argument marshalling, the reality is that they do. The problem is that the compilers used to compile application programs sometimes insert padding between the fields that make up the structure so as to align these fields on word boundaries. The marshalling system typically *packs* structures so that they contain no padding.

At the highest level, the marshalling system might have to deal with *complex types*—those types that are built using pointers. That is, the data structure that one program wants to send to another might not be contained in a single structure, but might instead involve pointers from one structure to another. A tree is a good example of a complex type that involves pointers. Clearly, the data encoder must prepare the data structure for transmission over the network because pointers are implemented by memory addresses, and just because a structure lives at a certain memory address on one machine does not mean it will live at the same address on another machine. In other words, the marshalling system must *serialize* (flatten) complex data structures.

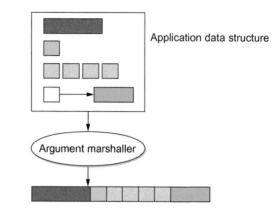

Application data structure

Argument marshaller

■ FIGURE 7.3 Argument marshalling: converting, packing, and linearizing.

In summary, depending on how complicated the type system is, the task of argument marshalling usually involves converting the base types, packing the structures, and linearizing the complex data structures, all to form a contiguous message that can be transmitted over the network. Figure 7.3 illustrates this task.

Conversion Strategy

Once the type system is established, the next issue is what conversion strategy the argument marshaller will use. There are two general options: *canonical intermediate form* and *receiver-makes-right.* We consider each, in turn.

The idea of canonical intermediate form is to settle on an external representation for each type; the sending host translates from its internal representation to this external representation before sending data, and the receiver translates from this external representation into its local representation when receiving data. To illustrate the idea, consider integer data; other types are treated in a similar manner. You might declare that the big-endian format will be used as the external representation for integers. The sending host must translate each integer it sends into big-endian form, and the receiving host must translate big-endian integers into whatever representation it uses. (This is what is done in the Internet for protocol headers.) Of course, a given host might already use big-endian form, in which case no conversion is necessary.

The alternative, receiver-makes-right, has the sender transmit data in its own internal format; the sender does not convert the base types, but usually has to pack and flatten more complex data structures. The receiver is then responsible for translating the data from the sender's format into its own local format. The problem with this strategy is that every host must be prepared to convert data from all other machine architectures. In networking, this is known as an *N-by-N solution*: Each of N machine architectures must be able to handle all N architectures. In contrast, in a system that uses a canonical intermediate form, each host needs to know only how to convert between its own representation and a single other representation—the external one.

Using a common external format is clearly the correct thing to do, right? This has certainly been the conventional wisdom in the networking community for the past 25 years. The answer is not cut and dried, however. It turns out that there are not that many different representations for the various base classes, or, said another way, N is not that large. In addition, the most common case is for two machines of the same type to be communicating with each other. In this situation, it seems silly to translate data from that architecture's representation into some foreign external representation, only to have to translate the data back into the same architecture's representation on the receiver.

A third option, although we know of no existing system that exploits it, is to use receiver-makes-right if the sender knows that the destination has the same architecture; the sender would use some canonical intermediate form if the two machines use different architectures. How would a sender learn the receiver's architecture? It could learn this information either from a name server or by first using a simple test case to see if the appropriate result occurs.

Tags

The third issue in argument marshalling is how the receiver knows what kind of data is contained in the message it receives. There are two common approaches: *tagged* and *untagged* data. The tagged approach is more intuitive, so we describe it first.

A tag is any additional information included in a message—beyond the concrete representation of the base types—that helps the receiver decode the message. There are several possible tags that might be included in a message. For example, each data item might be augmented with a

type tag. A type tag indicates that the value that follows is an integer, a floating-point number, or whatever. Another example is a *length* tag. Such a tag is used to indicate the number of elements in an array or the size of an integer. A third example is an *architecture* tag, which might be used in conjunction with the receiver-makes-right strategy to specify the architecture on which the data contained in the message was generated. Figure 7.4 depicts how a simple 32-bit integer might be encoded in a tagged message.

The alternative, of course, is not to use tags. How does the receiver know how to decode the data in this case? It knows because it was programmed to know. In other words, if you call a remote procedure that takes two integers and a floating-point number as arguments, then there is no reason for the remote procedure to inspect tags to know what it has just received. It simply assumes that the message contains two integers and a float and decodes it accordingly. Note that, while this works for most cases, the one place it breaks down is when sending variable-length arrays. In such a case, a length tag is commonly used to indicate how long the array is.

It is also worth noting that the untagged approach means that the presentation formatting is truly end to end. It is not possible for some intermediate agent to interpret the message unless the data is tagged. Why would an intermediate agent need to interpret a message, you might ask? Stranger things have happened, mostly resulting from *ad hoc* solutions to unexpected problems that the system was not engineered to handle. Poor network design is beyond the scope of this book.

Stubs

A stub is the piece of code that implements argument marshalling. Stubs are typically used to support RPC. On the client side, the stub marshals the procedure arguments into a message that can be transmitted by means of the RPC protocol. On the server side, the stub converts the message back into a set of variables that can be used as arguments to call the remote procedure. Stubs can either be interpreted or compiled.

In a compilation-based approach, each procedure has a customized client and server stub. While it is possible to write stubs by hand, they are typically generated by a stub compiler, based on a description of the procedure's interface. This situation is illustrated in Figure 7.5. Since the stub is compiled, it is usually very efficient. In an interpretation-based approach, the system provides generic client and server stubs that have their parameters set by a description of the procedure's interface. Because it is easy to change this description, interpreted stubs have the advantage of being flexible. Compiled stubs are more common in practice.

7.1.2 Examples (XDR, ASN.1, NDR)

We now briefly describe three popular network data representations in terms of this taxonomy. We use the integer base type to illustrate how each system works.

XDR

External Data Representation (XDR) is the network format used with SunRPC. In the taxonomy just introduced, XDR

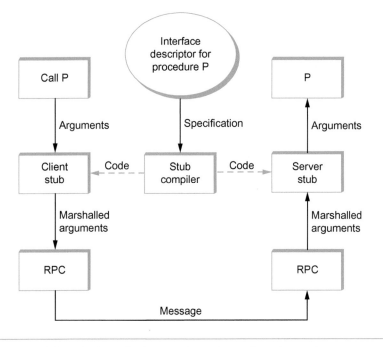

■ FIGURE 7.5 Stub compiler takes interface description as input and outputs client and server stubs.

- Supports the entire C-type system with the exception of function pointers
- Defines a canonical intermediate form
- Does not use tags (except to indicate array lengths)
- Uses compiled stubs

An XDR integer is a 32-bit data item that encodes a C integer. It is represented in twos complement notation, with the most significant byte of the C integer in the first byte of the XDR integer and the least significant byte of the C integer in the fourth byte of the XDR integer. That is, XDR uses big-endian format for integers. XDR supports both signed and unsigned integers, just as C does.

XDR represents variable-length arrays by first specifying an unsigned integer (4 bytes) that gives the number of elements in the array, followed by that many elements of the appropriate type. XDR encodes the components of a structure in the order of their declaration in the structure. For both arrays and structures, the size of each element/component is represented in a multiple of 4 bytes. Smaller data types are padded out to 4 bytes with 0s. The exception to this "pad to 4 bytes" rule is made for characters, which are encoded one per byte.

The following code fragment gives an example C structure (item) and the XDR routine that encodes/decodes this structure (xdr_item). Figure 7.6 schematically depicts XDR's on-the-wire representation of this structure when the field name is seven characters long and the array list has three values in it.

In this example, xdr_array, xdr_int, and xdr_string are three primitive functions provided by XDR to encode and decode arrays, integers, and character strings, respectively. Argument xdrs is a context variable that

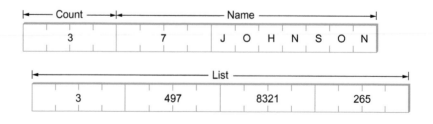

■ FIGURE 7.6 Example encoding of a structure in XDR.

XDR uses to keep track of where it is in the message being processed; it includes a flag that indicates whether this routine is being used to encode or decode the message. In other words, routines like xdr_item are used on both the client and the server. Note that the application programmer can either write the routine xdr_item by hand or use a stub compiler called rpc-gen (not shown) to generate this encoding/decoding routine. In the latter case, rpcgen takes the remote procedure that defines the data structure item as input and outputs the corresponding stub.

```
#define MAXNAME 256;
#define MAXLIST 100;

struct item {
    int     count;
    char    name[MAXNAME];
    int     list[MAXLIST];
};

bool_t
xdr_item(XDR *xdrs, struct item *ptr)
{
    return(xdr_int(xdrs, &ptr->count) &&
        xdr_string(xdrs, &ptr->name, MAXNAME) &&
        xdr_array(xdrs, &ptr->list, &ptr->count, MAXLIST,
                    sizeof(int), xdr_int));
}
```

Exactly how XDR performs depends, of course, on the complexity of the data. In a simple case of an array of integers, where each integer has to be converted from one byte order to another, an average of three instructions are required for each byte, meaning that converting the whole array is likely to be limited by the memory bandwidth of the machine. More complex conversions that require significantly more instructions per byte will be CPU limited and thus perform at a data rate less than the memory bandwidth.

ASN.1

Abstract Syntax Notation One (ASN.1) is an ISO standard that defines, among other things, a representation for data sent over a network. The representation-specific part of ASN.1 is called the *Basic Encoding Rules* (BER). ASN.1 supports the C-type system without function pointers, defines a canonical intermediate form, and uses type tags. Its stubs can be either interpreted or compiled. One of the claims to fame of ASN.1 BER is that it is used by the Internet standard Simple Network Management Protocol (SNMP).

ASN.1 represents each data item with a triple of the form

⟨ tag, length, value ⟩

The tag is typically an 8-bit field, although ASN.1 allows for the definition of multibyte tags. The length field specifies how many bytes make up the value; we discuss length more below. Compound data types, such as structures, can be constructed by nesting primitive types, as illustrated in Figure 7.7.

If the value is 127 or fewer bytes long, then the length is specified in a single byte. Thus, for example, a 32-bit integer is encoded as a 1-byte type, a 1-byte length, and the 4 bytes that encode the integer, as illustrated in Figure 7.8. The value itself, in the case of an integer, is represented in twos complement notation and big-endian form, just as in XDR. Keep in mind that, even though the value of the integer is represented in exactly the same way in both XDR and ASN.1, the XDR representation has neither the type nor the length tags associated with that integer. These two tags both take up space in the message and, more importantly, require processing during marshalling and unmarshalling. This is one reason why ASN.1 is not as efficient as XDR. Another is that the very fact that each data value is preceded by a length field means that the data value is unlikely to fall on a natural byte boundary (e.g., an integer beginning on a word boundary). This complicates the encoding/decoding process.

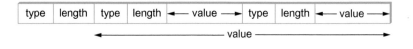

■ FIGURE 7.7 Compound types created by means of nesting in ASN.1 BER.

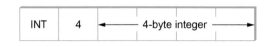

■ FIGURE 7.8 ASN.1 BER representation for a 4-byte integer.

If the value is 128 or more bytes long, then multiple bytes are used to specify its length. At this point you may be asking why a byte can specify a length of up to 127 bytes rather than 256. The reason is that 1 bit of the length field is used to denote how long the length field is. A 0 in the eighth bit indicates a 1-byte length field. To specify a longer length, the eighth bit is set to 1, and the other 7 bits indicate how many additional bytes make up the length. Figure 7.9 illustrates a simple 1-byte length and a multibyte length.

NDR

Network Data Representation (NDR) is the data-encoding standard used in the Distributed Computing Environment (DCE, which we introduced in Section 5.3). Unlike XDR and ASN.1, NDR uses receiver-makes-right. It does this by inserting an architecture tag at the front of each message; individual data items are untagged. NDR uses a compiler to generate stubs. This compiler takes a description of a program written in the Interface Definition Language (IDL) and generates the necessary stubs. IDL looks pretty much like C, and so essentially supports the C-type system.

Figure 7.10 illustrates the 4-byte architecture definition tag that is included at the front of each NDR-encoded message. The first byte contains two 4-bit fields. The first field, IntegrRep, defines the format for all integers contained in the message. A 0 in this field indicates big-endian integers, and a 1 indicates little-endian integers. The CharRep

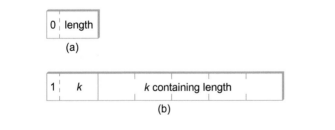

■ FIGURE 7.9 ASN.1 BER representation for length: (a) 1 byte; (b) multibyte.

0	4	8	16	24	31
IntegrRep	CharRep	FloatRep	Extension 1	Extension 2	

■ FIGURE 7.10 NDR's architecture tag.

field indicates what character format is used: 0 means ASCII (American Standard Code for Information Interchange) and 1 means EBCDIC (an older, IBM-defined alternative to ASCII). Next, the FloatRep byte defines which floating-point representation is being used: 0 means IEEE 754, 1 means VAX, 2 means Cray, and 3 means IBM. The final 2 bytes are reserved for future use. Note that, in simple cases such as arrays of integers, NDR does the same amount of work as XDR, and so it is able to achieve the same performance.

7.1.3 Markup Languages (XML)

Although we have been discussing the presentation formatting problem from the perspective of RPC—that is, how does one encode primitive data types and compound data structures so they can be sent from a client program to a server program—the same basic problem occurs in other settings. For example, how does a web server describe a Web page so that any number of different browsers know what to display on the screen? In this specific case, the answer is the HyperText Markup Language (HTML), which indicates that certain character strings should be displayed in bold or italics, what font type and size should be used, and where images should be positioned.

The enormous popularity of the Web and the availability of all sorts of applications and data on it have also created a situation in which different Web applications need to communicate with each other and understand each other's data. For example, an e-commerce website might need to talk to a shipping company's website to allow a customer to track a package without ever leaving the e-commerce website. This in fact starts to look a lot more like RPC, and the approach taken in the Web today to enable such communication among web servers is based on the *Extensible Markup Language* (XML).

Markup languages, of which HTML and XML are both examples, take the tagged data approach to the extreme. Data is represented as text, and text tags known as *markup* are intermingled with the data text to express information about the data. In the case of HTML, markup merely indicates how the text should be displayed; other markup languages like XML can express the type and structure of the data.

XML is actually a framework for defining different markup languages for different kinds of data. For example, XML has been used to define a markup language that is roughly equivalent to HTML called *Extensible HyperText Markup Language* (XHTML). XML defines a basic syntax for mixing markup with data text, but the designer of a specific markup language has to name and define its markup. It is common practice to refer to individual XML-based languages simply as XML, but we will emphasize the distinction in this introductory material.

XML syntax looks much like HTML. For example, an employee record in a hypothetical XML-based language might look like the following XML *document*, which might be stored in a file named employee.xml. The first line indicates the version of XML being used, and the remaining lines represent four fields that make up the employee record, the last of which (hiredate) contains three subfields. In other words, XML syntax provides for a nested structure of tag/value pairs, which is equivalent to a tree structure for the represented data (with employee as the root). This is similar to XDR, ASN.1, and NDR's ability to represent compound types, but in a format that can be both processed by programs and read by humans. More importantly, programs such as parsers can be used across different XML-based languages, because the definitions of those languages are themselves expressed as machine-readable data that can be input to the programs.

```
<?xml version="1.0"?>
<employee>
    <name>John Doe</name>
    <title>Head Bottle Washer</title>
    <id>123456789</id>
    <hiredate>
        <day>5</day>
        <month>June</month>
        <year>1986</year>
    </hiredate>
</employee>
```

Although the markup and the data in this document are highly suggestive to the human reader, it is the definition of the employee record language that actually determines what tags are legal, what they mean, and what data types they imply. Without some formal definition of the tags, a human reader (or a computer) can't tell whether 1986 in the year field, for example, is a string, an integer, an unsigned integer, or a floating point number.

The definition of a specific XML-based language is given by a *schema*, which is a database term for a specification of how to interpret a collection of data. Several schema languages have been defined for XML; we will focus here on the leading standard, known by the none-too-surprising name *XML Schema*. An individual schema defined using XML Schema is known as an *XML Schema Document* (XSD). The following is an XSD for the employee.xml example; in other words, it defines the language to which the example document conforms. It might be stored in a file named employee.xsd.

```
<?xml version="1.0"?>
<schema xmlns="http://www.w3.org/2001/XMLSchema">
  <element name="employee">
    <complexType>
      <sequence>
        <element name="name" type="string"/>
        <element name="title" type="string"/>
        <element name="id" type="string"/>
        <element name="hiredate">
          <complexType>
            <sequence>
              <element name="day" type="integer"/>
              <element name="month" type="string"/>
              <element name="year" type="integer"/>
            </sequence>
          </complexType>
        </element>
      </sequence>
    </complexType>
  </element>
</schema>
```

This XSD looks superficially similar to our example document employee.xml, but only because XML Schema is itself an XML-based language. There is an obvious relationship between this XSD and the document employee.xml defined above. For example,

```
<element name="title" type="string"/>
```

indicates that the value bracketed by the markup title is to be interpreted as a string. The sequence and nesting of that line in the XSD indicate that a title field must be the second item in an employee record.

Unlike some schema languages, XML Schema provides datatypes such as string, integer, decimal, and Boolean. It allows the datatypes to be combined in sequences or nested, as in employee.xsd, to create compound data types. So an XSD defines more than a syntax; it defines its own abstract data model. A document that conforms to the XSD represents a collection of data that conforms to the data model.

The significance of an XSD defining an abstract data model and not just a syntax is that there can be other ways besides XML of representing data that conforms to the model. And XML does, after all, have some shortcomings as an on-the-wire representation: it is not as compact as other data representations, and it is relatively slow to parse. A number of alternative representations described as binary are in use. The International Standards Organization (ISO) has published one called *Fast Infoset*, while the World Wide Web Consortium (W3C) has produced the *Efficient XML Interchange* (EXI) proposal. Binary representations sacrifice human readability for greater compactness and faster parsing.

XML Namespaces

XML has to solve a common problem, that of name clashes.[2] The problem arises because schema languages such as XML Schema support modularity in the sense that a schema can be reused as part of another schema. Suppose two XSDs are defined independently, and both happen to define the markup name *idNumber*. Perhaps one XSD uses that name to identify employees of a company, and the other XSD uses it to identify laptop computers owned by the company. We might like to reuse those two XSDs in a third XSD for describing which assets are associated with which employees, but to do that we need some mechanism for distinguishing employees' idNumbers from laptop idNumbers.

XML's solution to this problem is *XML namespaces*. A namespace is a collection of names. Each XML namespace is identified by a Uniform Resource Identifier (URI). URIs will be described in some detail in Section 9.1.2; for now, all you really need to know is that URIs are a form

---

[2] Naming is an important and popular problem area for computer scientists. We will talk a lot more about namespaces when we look at DNS—the naming scheme for Internet hosts—in Section 9.3.1.

of globally unique identifier.[3] A simple markup name like *idNumber* can be added to a namespace as long as it is unique within that namespace. Since the namespace is globally unique and the simple name is unique within the namespace, the combination of the two is a globally unique *qualified name* that cannot clash.

An XSD usually specifies a *target namespace* with a line like the following:

```
targetNamespace="http://www.example.com/employee"
```

http://www.example.com/employee is a Uniform Resource Identifier, identifying a made-up namespace. All the new markup defined in that XSD will belong to that namespace.

Now, if an XSD wants to reference names that have been defined in other XSDs, it can do so by qualifying those names with a namespace prefix. This prefix is a short abbreviation for the full URI that actually identifies the namespace. For example, the following line assigns emp as the namespace prefix for the employee namespace:

```
xmlns:emp="http://www.example.com/employee"
```

Any markup from that namespace would be qualified by prefixing it with emp:, as is title in the following line:

```
<emp:title>Head Bottle Washer</emp:title>
```

emp:title is a qualified name, which will not clash with the name title from some other namespace.

It is remarkable how widely XML is now used in applications that range from RPC-style communication among Web-based services to office productivity tools to instant messaging. We will see some more of its uses in Chapter 9. It is certainly one of the core protocols on which the upper layers of the Internet now depend.

7.2 MULTIMEDIA DATA

Multimedia data, comprised of audio, video, and still images, now makes up the majority of traffic on the Internet by many estimates. This is a relatively recent development—it may be hard to believe now, but there

---

[3]HTTP URLs are a particular type of URI.

was no YouTube before 2005. Part of what has made the widespread transmission of multimedia across networks possible is advances in compression technology. Because multimedia data is consumed mostly by humans using their senses—vision and hearing—and processed by the human brain, there are unique challenges to compressing it. You want to try to keep the information that is most important to a human, while getting rid of anything that doesn't improve the human's perception of the visual or auditory experience. Hence, both computer science and the study of human perception come into play. In this section, we'll look at some of the major efforts in representing and compressing multimedia data.

The uses of compression are not limited to multimedia data of course—for example, you may well have used a utility like zip or compress to compress files before sending them over a network, or to uncompress a data file after downloading. It turns out that the techniques used for compressing data—which are typically *lossless*, because most people don't like to lose data from a file—also show up as part of the solution for multimedia compression. In contrast, *lossy compression*, commonly used for multimedia data, does not promise that the data received is exactly the same as the data sent. As noted above, this is because multimedia data often contains information that is of little utility to the human who receives it. Our senses and brains can only perceive so much detail. They are also very good at filling in missing pieces and even correcting some errors in what we see or hear. And, lossy algorithms typically achieve much better compression ratios than do their lossless counterparts; they can be an order of magnitude better or more.

To get a sense of how important compression has been to the spread of networked multimedia, consider the following example. A high-definition TV screen has something like 1080×1920 pixels, each of which has 24 bits of color information, so each frame is

$$1080 \times 1920 \times 24 = 50\,\text{Mb}$$

so if you want to send 24 frames per second, that would be over 1 Gbps. That's a lot more than most Internet users can get access to, by a good margin. By contrast, modern compression techniques can get a reasonably high-quality HDTV signal down to the range of 10 Mbps, a two order of magnitude reduction and well within the reach of many broadband users. Similar compression gains apply to lower quality video such as

YouTube clips—Web video could never have reached its current popularity without compression to make all those entertaining videos fit within the bandwidth of today's networks.

Compression techniques as applied to multimedia have been an area of great innovation in recent years, particularly lossy compression. Lossless techniques also have an important role to play, however. Indeed, most of the lossy techniques include some steps that are lossless, so we begin our discussion with an overview of lossless compression.

7.2.1 Lossless Compression Techniques

In many ways, compression is inseparable from data encoding. When thinking about how to encode a piece of data in a set of bits, we might just as well think about how to encode the data in the smallest set of bits possible. For example, if you have a block of data that is made up of the 26 symbols A through Z, and if all of these symbols have an equal chance of occurring in the data block you are encoding, then encoding each symbol in 5 bits is the best you can do (since $2^5 = 32$ is the lowest power of 2 above 26). If, however, the symbol R occurs 50% of the time, then it would be a good idea to use fewer bits to encode the R than any of the other symbols. In general, if you know the relative probability that each symbol will occur in the data, then you can assign a different number of bits to each possible symbol in a way that minimizes the number of bits it takes to encode a given block of data. This is the essential idea of *Huffman codes*, one of the important early developments in data compression.

When to Compress?

It might seem that compressing your data before sending it would always be a good idea, since the network would be able to deliver compressed data in less time than uncompressed data. This is not necessarily the case, however. Compression/decompression algorithms often involve time-consuming computations. The question you have to ask is whether or not the time it takes to compress/decompress the data is worthwhile given such factors as the host's processor speed and the network bandwidth. Specifically, if B_c is the average bandwidth at which data can be pushed through the compressor and decompressor (in series), B_n is the network bandwidth (including network processing costs) for uncompressed data, and r is the average compression ratio, and if we assume that all the data is compressed before any of it is transmitted, then the time taken to send x bytes of uncompressed data is

$$x/B_n$$

whereas the time to compress it and send the compressed data is

$$x/B_c + x/(rB_n)$$

Thus, compression is beneficial if

$$x/B_c + x/(rB_n) < x/B_n$$

which is equivalent to

$$B_c > r/(r-1) \times B_n$$

For a compression ratio of 2, for example, B_c would have to be greater than $2 \times B_n$ for compression to make sense.

For many compression algorithms, we may not need to compress the *whole* data set before beginning transmission (videoconferencing would be impossible if we did), but rather we need to collect some amount of data (perhaps a few frames of video) first. The amount of data needed to "fill the pipe" in this case would be used as the value of x in the above equation.

Of course, when talking about lossy compression algorithms, processing resources are not the only factor. Depending on the exact application, users are willing to make very different tradeoffs between bandwidth (or delay) and extent of information loss due to compression. For example, a radiologist reading a mammogram is unlikely to tolerate any significant loss of image quality and might well tolerate a delay of several hours in retrieving an image over a network. By contrast, it has become quite clear that many people will tolerate questionable audio quality in exchange for free global telephone calls (not to mention the ability to talk on the phone while driving).

Run Length Encoding

Run length encoding (RLE) is a compression technique with a brute-force simplicity. The idea is to replace consecutive occurrences of a given symbol with only one copy of the symbol, plus a count of how many times that symbol occurs—hence, the name *run length*. For example, the string AAABBCDDDD would be encoded as 3A2B1C4D.

RLE turns out to be useful for compressing some classes of images. It can be used in this context by comparing adjacent pixel values and then encoding only the changes. For images that have large homogeneous regions, this technique is quite effective. For example, it is not uncommon that RLE can achieve compression ratios on the order of 8-to-1 for scanned text images. RLE works well on such files because they often contain a large amount of white space that can be removed. In fact, RLE is the key compression algorithm used to transmit faxes. However, for images with even a small degree of local variation, it is not uncommon for compression to actually increase the image byte size, since it takes 2 bytes to represent a single symbol when that symbol is not repeated.

Differential Pulse Code Modulation

Another simple lossless compression algorithm is Differential Pulse Code Modulation (DPCM). The idea here is to first output a reference symbol and then, for each symbol in the data, to output the difference between that symbol and the reference symbol. For example, using symbol A as the reference symbol, the string AAABBCDDDD would be encoded as A0001123333 because A is the same as the reference symbol, B has a difference of 1 from the reference symbol, and so on. Note that this simple example does not illustrate the real benefit of DPCM, which is that when the differences are small they can be encoded with fewer bits than the symbol itself. In this example, the range of differences, 0–3, can be represented with 2 bits each, rather than the 7 or 8 bits required by the full character. As soon as the difference becomes too large, a new reference symbol is selected.

DPCM works better than RLE for most digital imagery, since it takes advantage of the fact that adjacent pixels are usually similar. Due to this correlation, the dynamic range of the differences between the adjacent pixel values can be significantly less than the dynamic range of the original image, and this range can therefore be represented using fewer bits. Using DPCM, we have measured compression ratios of 1.5-to-1 on digital images. DPCM also works on audio, because adjacent samples of an audio waveform are likely to be close in value.

A slightly different approach, called *delta encoding*, simply encodes a symbol as the difference from the previous one. Thus, for example, AAABBCDDDD would be represented as A001011000. Note that delta encoding is likely to work well for encoding images where adjacent pixels are similar. It is also possible to perform RLE after delta encoding, since we might find long strings of 0s if there are many similar symbols next to each other.

Dictionary-Based Methods

The final lossless compression method we consider is the dictionary-based approach, of which the Lempel–Ziv (LZ) compression algorithm is the best known. The Unix compress and gzip commands use variants of the LZ algorithm.

The idea of a dictionary-based compression algorithm is to build a dictionary (table) of variable-length strings (think of them as common phrases) that you expect to find in the data and then to replace each of these strings when it appears in the data with the corresponding index to the dictionary. For example, instead of working with individual characters in text data, you could treat each word as a string and output the index in the dictionary for that word. To further elaborate on this example, the word *compression* has the index 4978 in one particular dictionary; it is the 4978th word in /usr/share/dict/words. To compress a body of text, each time the string "compression" appears, it would be replaced by 4978. Since this particular dictionary has just over 25,000 words in it, it would take 15 bits to encode the index, meaning that the string "compression" could be represented in 15 bits rather than the 77 bits required by 7-bit ASCII. This is a compression ratio of 5-to-1! At another data point, we were able to get a 2-to-1 compression ratio when we applied the compress command to the source code for the protocols described in this book.

Of course, this leaves the question of where the dictionary comes from. One option is to define a static dictionary, preferably one that is tailored for the data being compressed. A more general solution, and the one used by LZ compression, is to adaptively define the dictionary based on the contents of the data being compressed. In this case, however, the dictionary constructed during compression has to be sent along with the data so that the decompression half of the algorithm can do its job. Exactly how you build an adaptive dictionary has been a subject of extensive research; we discuss important papers on the subject at the end of this chapter.

7.2.2 Image Representation and Compression (GIF, JPEG)

Given the increase in the use of digital imagery in recent years—this use was spawned by the invention of graphical displays, not high-speed networks—the need for standard representation formats and compression algorithms for digital imagery data has grown more and more critical. In response to this need, the ISO defined a digital image format known as

JPEG, named after the Joint Photographic Experts Group that designed it. (The "Joint" in JPEG stands for a joint ISO/ITU effort.) JPEG is the most widely used format for still images in use today. At the heart of the definition of the format is a compression algorithm, which we describe below. Many techniques used in JPEG also appear in MPEG, the set of standards for video compression and transmission created by the Moving Picture Experts Group.

Before delving into the details of JPEG, we observe that there are quite a few steps to get from a digital image to a compressed representation of that image that can be transmitted, decompressed, and displayed correctly by a receiver. You probably know that digital images are made up of pixels (hence, the megapixels quoted in digital camera advertisements). Each pixel represents one location in the two-dimensional grid that makes up the image, and for color images each pixel has some numerical value representing a color. There are lots of ways to represent colors, referred to as *color spaces*; the one most people are familiar with is RGB (red, green, blue). You can think of color as being a three dimensional quantity—you can make any color out of red, green, and blue light in different amounts. In a three-dimensional space, there are lots of different, valid ways to describe a given point (consider Cartesian and polar coordinates, for example). Similarly, there are various ways to describe a color using three quantities, and the most common alternative to RGB is YUV. The Y is luminance, roughly the overall brightness of the pixel, and U and V contain chrominance, or color information. Confoundingly, there are a few different variants of the YUV color space as well. More on this in a moment.

The significance of this discussion is that the encoding and transmission of color images (either still or moving) requires agreement between the two ends on the color space. Otherwise, of course, you'd end up with different colors being displayed by the receiver than were captured by the sender. Hence, agreeing on a color space definition (and perhaps a way to communicate which particular space is in use) is part of the definition of any image or video format.

Let's look at the example of the Graphical Interchange Format (GIF). GIF uses the RGB color space and starts out with 8 bits to represent each of the three dimensions of color for a total of 24 bits. Rather than sending those 24 bits per pixel, however, GIF first reduces 24-bit color images to 8-bit color images. This is done by identifying the colors used in the picture, of which there will typically be considerably fewer than 2^{24}, and then picking the 256 colors that most closely approximate the colors used in the picture. There might be more than 256 colors, however, so the trick is to try not to distort the color too much by picking 256 colors such that no pixel has its color changed too much.

The 256 colors are stored in a table, which can be indexed with an 8-bit number, and the value for each pixel is replaced by the appropriate index. Note that this is an example of lossy compression for any picture with more than 256 colors. GIF then runs an LZ variant over the result, treating common sequences of pixels as the strings that make up the dictionary—a lossless operation. Using this approach, GIF is sometimes able to achieve compression ratios on the order of 10:1, but only when the image consists of a relatively small number of discrete colors. Graphical logos, for example, are handled well by GIF. Images of natural scenes, which often include a more continuous spectrum of colors, cannot be compressed at this ratio using GIF. It is also not too hard for a human eye to detect the distortion caused by the lossy color reduction of GIF in some cases.

The JPEG format is considerably more well suited to photographic images, as you would hope given the name of the group that created it. JPEG does not reduce the number of colors like GIF. Instead, JPEG starts off by transforming the RGB colors (which are what you usually get out of a digital camera) to the YUV space. The reason for this has to do with the way the eye perceives images. There are receptors in the eye for brightness, and separate receptors for color. Because we're very good at perceiving variations in brightness, it makes sense to spend more bits on transmitting brightness information. Since the Y component of YUV is, roughly, the brightness of the pixel, we can compress that component separately, and less aggressively, from the other two (chrominance) components.

As noted above, YUV and RGB are alternative ways to describe a point in a 3-dimensional space, and it's possible to convert from one color space to another using linear equations. For one YUV space that is commonly used to represent digital images, the equations are:

$$Y = 0.299R + 0.587G + 0.114B$$
$$U = (B - Y) \times 0.565$$
$$V = (R - Y) \times 0.713$$

The exact values of the constants here are not important, as long as the encoder and decoder agree on what they are. (The decoder will have to apply the inverse transformations to recover the RGB components needed to drive a display.) The constants are, however, carefully chosen based on the human perception of color. You can see that Y, the luminance, is a sum of the red, green, and blue components, while U and V are color difference components. U represents the difference between the luminance and blue, and V the difference between luminance and red. You may notice that setting R, G, and B to their maximum values (which would be 255 for 8-bit representations) will also produce a value of $Y = 255$ while U and V in this case would be zero. That is, a fully white pixel is (255,255,255) in RGB space and (255,0,0) in YUV space.

Once the image has been transformed into YUV space, we can now think about compressing each of the three components separately. We want to be more aggressive in compressing the U and V components, to which human eyes are less sensitive. One way to compress the U and V components is to *subsample* them. The basic idea of subsampling is to take a number of adjacent pixels, calculate the average U or V value for that group of pixels, and transmit that, rather than sending the value for every pixel. Figure 7.11 illustrates the point. The luminance (Y) component is not subsampled, so the Y value of all the pixels will be transmitted, as indicated by the 16×16 grid of pixels on the left. In the case of U and V, we treat each group of four adjacent pixels as a group, calculate the average of the U or V value for that group, and transmit that. Hence, we end up with an 8×8 grid of U and V values to transmit. Thus, in this example,

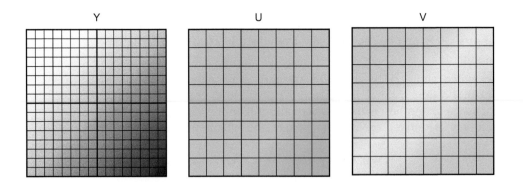

■ FIGURE 7.11 Subsampling the U and V components of an image.

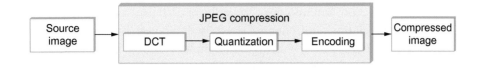

■ FIGURE 7.12 Block diagram of JPEG compression.

for every four pixels, we transmit six values (four Y and one each of U and V) rather than the original 12 values (four each for all three components), for a 50% reduction in information.

It's worth noting that you could be either more or less aggressive in the subsampling, with corresponding increases in compression and decreases in quality. The subsampling approach shown here, in which chrominance is subsampled by a factor of two in both horizontal and vertical directions (and which goes by the identification 4:2:0), happens to match the most common approach used for both JPEG and MPEG.

Once subsampling is done, we now have three grids of pixels to deal with, and each one is dealt with separately. JPEG compression of each component takes place in three phases, as illustrated in Figure 7.12. On the compression side, the image is fed through these three phases one 8×8 block at a time. The first phase applies the discrete cosine transform (DCT) to the block. If you think of the image as a signal in the spatial domain, then DCT transforms this signal into an equivalent signal in the *spatial frequency* domain. This is a lossless operation but a necessary precursor to the next, lossy step. After the DCT, the second phase applies a quantization to the resulting signal and, in so doing, loses the least significant information contained in that signal. The third phase encodes the final result, but in so doing also adds an element of lossless compression to the lossy compression achieved by the first two phases. Decompression follows these same three phases, but in reverse order.

DCT Phase

DCT is a transformation closely related to the fast Fourier transform (FFT). It takes an 8×8 matrix of pixel values as input and outputs an 8×8 matrix of frequency coefficients. You can think of the input matrix as a 64-point signal that is defined in two spatial dimensions (x and y); DCT breaks this signal into 64 spatial frequencies. To get an intuitive feel for spatial frequency, imagine yourself moving across a picture in, say, the x

direction. You would see the value of each pixel varying as some function of x. If this value changes slowly with increasing x, then it has a low spatial frequency; if it changes rapidly, it has a high spatial frequency. So the low frequencies correspond to the gross features of the picture, while the high frequencies correspond to fine detail. The idea behind the DCT is to separate the gross features, which are essential to viewing the image, from the fine detail, which is less essential and, in some cases, might be barely perceived by the eye.

DCT, along with its inverse, which is performed during decompression, is defined by the following formulas:

$$DCT(i,j) = \frac{1}{\sqrt{2N}} C(i)C(j) \sum_{x=0}^{N-1} \sum_{y=0}^{N-1} pixel(x,y)$$

$$\times \cos \left[\frac{(2x+1)i\pi}{2N} \right] \cos \left[\frac{(2y+1)j\pi}{2N} \right]$$

$$pixel(x,y) = \frac{1}{\sqrt{2N}} \sum_{i=0}^{N-1} \sum_{j=0}^{N-1} C(i)C(j)DCT(i,j)$$

$$\times \cos \left[\frac{(2x+1)i\pi}{2N} \right] \cos \left[\frac{(2y+1)j\pi}{2N} \right]$$

$$C(x) = \begin{cases} \frac{1}{\sqrt{2}} & \text{if } x = 0 \\ 1 & \text{if } x > 0 \end{cases}$$

where $pixel(x,y)$ is the grayscale value of the pixel at position (x,y) in the 8×8 block being compressed; $N = 8$ in this case.

The first frequency coefficient, at location (0,0) in the output matrix, is called the *DC coefficient*. Intuitively, we can see that the DC coefficient is a measure of the average value of the 64 input pixels. The other 63 elements of the output matrix are called the *AC coefficients*. They add the higher-spatial-frequency information to this average value. Thus, as you go from the first frequency coefficient toward the 64th frequency coefficient, you are moving from low-frequency information to high-frequency information, from the broad strokes of the image to finer and finer detail. These higher-frequency coefficients are increasingly unimportant to the perceived quality of the image. It is the second phase of JPEG that decides which portion of which coefficients to throw away.

Quantization Phase

The second phase of JPEG is where the compression becomes lossy. DCT does not itself lose information; it just transforms the image into a form that makes it easier to know what information to remove. (Although not lossy, *per se*, there is of course some loss of precision during the DCT phase because of the use of fixed-point arithmetic.) Quantization is easy to understand—it's simply a matter of dropping the insignificant bits of the frequency coefficients.

To see how the quantization phase works, imagine that you want to compress some whole numbers less than 100, such as 45, 98, 23, 66, and 7. If you decided that knowing these numbers truncated to the nearest multiple of 10 is sufficient for your purposes, then you could divide each number by the quantum 10 using integer arithmetic, yielding 4, 9, 2, 6, and 0. These numbers can each be encoded in 4 bits rather than the 7 bits needed to encode the original numbers.

Rather than using the same quantum for all 64 coefficients, JPEG uses a quantization table that gives the quantum to use for each of the coefficients, as specified in the formula given below. You can think of this table (Quantum) as a parameter that can be set to control how much information is lost and, correspondingly, how much compression is achieved. In practice, the JPEG standard specifies a set of quantization tables that have proven effective in compressing digital images; an example quantization table is given in Table 7.1. In tables like this one, the low coefficients have a quantum close to 1 (meaning that little low-frequency information

Table 7.1 Example JPEG Quantization Table

$$
\text{Quantum} =
\begin{bmatrix}
3 & 5 & 7 & 9 & 11 & 13 & 15 & 17 \\
5 & 7 & 9 & 11 & 13 & 15 & 17 & 19 \\
7 & 9 & 11 & 13 & 15 & 17 & 19 & 21 \\
9 & 11 & 13 & 15 & 17 & 19 & 21 & 23 \\
11 & 13 & 15 & 17 & 19 & 21 & 23 & 25 \\
13 & 15 & 17 & 19 & 21 & 23 & 25 & 27 \\
15 & 17 & 19 & 21 & 23 & 25 & 27 & 29 \\
17 & 19 & 21 & 23 & 25 & 27 & 29 & 31
\end{bmatrix}
$$

is lost) and the high coefficients have larger values (meaning that more high-frequency information is lost). Notice that as a result of such quantization tables many of the high-frequency coefficients end up being set to 0 after quantization, making them ripe for further compression in the third phase.

The basic quantization equation is

$$\mathsf{QuantizedValue}(i,j) = \mathsf{IntegerRound}(DCT(i,j)/\mathsf{Quantum}(i,j))$$

where

$$\mathsf{IntegerRound}(x) = \begin{cases} \lfloor x + 0.5 \rfloor & \text{if } x \geq 0 \\ \lfloor x - 0.5 \rfloor & \text{if } x < 0 \end{cases}$$

Decompression is then simply defined as

$$DCT(i,j) = \mathsf{QuantizedValue}(i,j) \times \mathsf{Quantum}(i,j)$$

For example, if the DC coefficient (i.e., DCT(0,0)) for a particular block was equal to 25, then the quantization of this value using Table 7.1 would result in

$$\lfloor 25/3 + 0.5 \rfloor = 8$$

During decompression, this coefficient would then be restored as

$$8 \times 3 = 24$$

Encoding Phase

The final phase of JPEG encodes the quantized frequency coefficients in a compact form. This results in additional compression, but this compression is lossless. Starting with the DC coefficient in position (0,0), the coefficients are processed in the zigzag sequence shown in Figure 7.13. Along this zigzag, a form of run length encoding is used—RLE is applied to only the 0 coefficients, which is significant because many of the later coefficients are 0. The individual coefficient values are then encoded using a Huffman code. (The JPEG standard allows the implementer to use an arithmetic coding instead of the Huffman code.)

In addition, because the DC coefficient contains a large percentage of the information about the 8×8 block from the source image, and

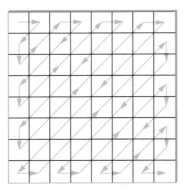

■ **FIGURE 7.13** Zigzag traversal of quantized frequency coefficients.

images typically change slowly from block to block, each DC coefficient is encoded as the difference from the previous DC coefficient. This is the delta encoding approach described in Section 7.2.1.

JPEG includes a number of variations that control how much compression you achieve versus the fidelity of the image. This can be done, for example, by using different quantization tables. These variations, plus the fact that different images have different characteristics, make it impossible to say with any precision the compression ratios that can be achieved with JPEG. Ratios of 30:1 are common, and higher ratios are certainly possible, but *artifacts* (noticeable distortion due to compression) become more severe at higher ratios.

7.2.3 Video Compression (MPEG)

We now turn our attention to the MPEG format, named after the Moving Picture Experts Group that defined it. To a first approximation, a moving picture (i.e., video) is simply a succession of still images—also called *frames* or *pictures*—displayed at some video rate. Each of these frames can be compressed using the same DCT-based technique used in JPEG. Stopping at this point would be a mistake, however, because it fails to remove the interframe redundancy present in a video sequence. For example, two successive frames of video will contain almost identical information if there is not much motion in the scene, so it would be unnecessary to send the same information twice. Even when there is motion, there may be plenty of redundancy since a moving object may not change from one frame to the next; in some cases, only its position changes. MPEG takes this interframe redundancy into consideration. MPEG also defines a mechanism for encoding an audio signal with the video, but we consider only the video aspect of MPEG in this section.

Frame Types

MPEG takes a sequence of video frames as input and compresses them into three types of frames, called *I frames* (intrapicture), *P frames* (predicted picture), and *B frames* (bidirectional predicted picture). Each frame of input is compressed into one of these three frame types. I frames can be thought of as reference frames; they are self-contained, depending on neither earlier frames nor later frames. To a first approximation, an I frame is simply the JPEG compressed version of the corresponding frame in the video source. P and B frames are not self-contained; they specify relative differences from some reference frame. More specifically, a P frame specifies the differences from the previous I frame, while a B frame gives an interpolation between the previous and subsequent I or P frames.

Figure 7.14 illustrates a sequence of seven video frames that, after being compressed by MPEG, result in a sequence of I, P, and B frames. The two I frames stand alone; each can be decompressed at the receiver independently of any other frames. The P frame depends on the preceding I frame; it can be decompressed at the receiver only if the preceding I frame also arrives. Each of the B frames depends on both the preceding I or P frame and the subsequent I or P frame. Both of these reference frames

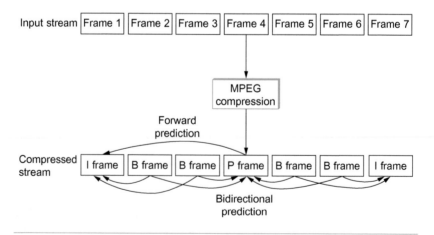

■ FIGURE 7.14 Sequence of I, P, and B frames generated by MPEG.

must arrive at the receiver before MPEG can decompress the B frame to reproduce the original video frame.

Note that, because each B frame depends on a later frame in the sequence, the compressed frames are not transmitted in sequential order. Instead, the sequence I B B P B B I shown in Figure 7.14 is transmitted as I P B B I B B. Also, MPEG does not define the ratio of I frames to P and B frames; this ratio may vary depending on the required compression and picture quality. For example, it is permissible to transmit only I frames. This would be similar to using JPEG to compress the video.

In contrast to the preceding discussion of JPEG, the following focuses on the *decoding* of an MPEG stream. It is a little easier to describe, and it is the operation that is more often implemented in networking systems today, since MPEG coding is so expensive that it is frequently done offline (i.e., not in real time). For example, in a video-on-demand system, the video would be encoded and stored on disk ahead of time. When a viewer wanted to watch the video, the MPEG stream would then be transmitted to the viewer's machine, which would decode and display the stream in real time.

Let's look more closely at the three frame types. As mentioned above, I frames are approximately equal to the JPEG compressed version of the source frame. The main difference is that MPEG works in units of 16×16 *macroblocks*. For a color video represented in YUV, the U and V components in each macroblock are subsampled into an 8×8 block, as we discussed above in the context of JPEG. Each 2×2 subblock in the macroblock is given by one U value and one V value—the average of the four pixel values. The subblock still has four Y values. The relationship between a frame and the corresponding macroblocks is given in Figure 7.15.

The P and B frames are also processed in units of macroblocks. Intuitively, we can see that the information they carry for each macroblock captures the motion in the video; that is, it shows in what direction and how far the macroblock moved relative to the reference frame(s). The following describes how a B frame is used to reconstruct a frame during decompression; P frames are handled in a similar manner, except that they depend on only one reference frame instead of two.

Before getting to the details of how a B frame is decompressed, we first note that each macroblock in a B frame is not necessarily defined relative to both an earlier and a later frame, as suggested above, but may

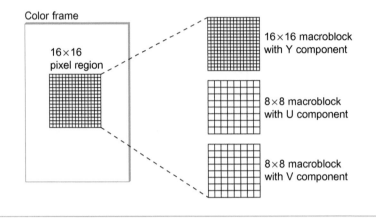

■ FIGURE 7.15 Each frame as a collection of macroblocks.

instead simply be specified relative to just one or the other. In fact, a given macroblock in a B frame can use the same intracoding as is used in an I frame. This flexibility exists because if the motion picture is changing too rapidly then it sometimes makes sense to give the intrapicture encoding rather than a forward- or backward-predicted encoding. Thus, each macroblock in a B frame includes a type field that indicates which encoding is used for that macroblock. In the following discussion, however, we consider only the general case in which the macroblock uses bidirectional predictive encoding.

In such a case, each macroblock in a B frame is represented with a 4-tuple: (1) a coordinate for the macroblock in the frame, (2) a motion vector relative to the previous reference frame, (3) a motion vector relative to the subsequent reference frame, and (4) a delta (δ) for each pixel in the macroblock (i.e., how much each pixel has changed relative to the two reference pixels). For each pixel in the macroblock, the first task is to find the corresponding reference pixel in the past and future reference frames. This is done using the two motion vectors associated with the macroblock. Then, the delta for the pixel is added to the average of these two reference pixels. Stated more precisely, if we let F_p and F_f denote the past and future reference frames, respectively, and the past/future motion vectors are given by (x_p, y_p) and (x_f, y_f), then the pixel at coordinate (x, y) in the current frame (denoted F_c) is computed as

$$F_c(x, y) = (F_p(x + x_p, y + y_p) + F_f(x + x_f, y + y_f))/2 + \delta(x, y)$$

where δ is the delta for the pixel as specified in the B frame. These deltas are encoded in the same way as pixels in I frames; that is, they are run through DCT and then quantized. Since the deltas are typically small, most of the DCT coefficients are 0 after quantization; hence, they can be effectively compressed.

It should be fairly clear from the preceding discussion how encoding would be performed, with one exception. When generating a B or P frame during compression, MPEG must decide where to place the macroblocks. Recall that each macroblock in a P frame, for example, is defined relative to a macroblock in an I frame, but that the macroblock in the P frame need not be in the same part of the frame as the corresponding macroblock in the I frame—the difference in position is given by the motion vector. You would like to pick a motion vector that makes the macroblock in the P frame as similar as possible to the corresponding macroblock in the I frame, so that the deltas for that macroblock can be as small as possible. This means that you need to figure out where objects in the picture moved from one frame to the next. This is the problem of *motion estimation*, and several techniques (heuristics) for solving this problem are known. (We discuss papers that consider this problem at the end of this chapter.) The difficulty of this problem is one of the reasons why MPEG encoding takes longer than decoding on equivalent hardware. MPEG does not specify any particular technique; it only defines the format for encoding this information in B and P frames and the algorithm for reconstructing the pixel during decompression, as given above.

Effectiveness and Performance

MPEG typically achieves a compression ratio of 90:1, although ratios as high as 150:1 are not unheard of. In terms of the individual frame types, we can expect a compression ratio of approximately 30:1 for the I frames (this is consistent with the ratios achieved using JPEG when 24-bit color is first reduced to 8-bit color), while P and B frame compression ratios are typically three to five times smaller than the rates for the I frame. Without first reducing the 24 bits of color to 8 bits, the achievable compression with MPEG is typically between 30:1 and 50:1.

MPEG involves an expensive computation. On the compression side, it is typically done offline, which is not a problem for preparing movies for a video-on-demand service. Video can be compressed in real time using hardware today, but software implementations are quickly closing the gap. On the decompression side, low-cost MPEG video boards are available, but they do little more than YUV color lookup, which fortunately is the most expensive step. Most of the actual MPEG decoding is done in software. In recent years, processors have become fast enough to keep pace with 30-frames-per-second video rates when decoding MPEG streams purely in software—modern processors can even decode MPEG streams of high definition video (HDTV).

Other Video Encoding Standards

We conclude by noting that MPEG is not by any means the only standard available for encoding video. For example, the ITU-T has also defined the *H series* for encoding real-time multimedia data. Generally, the H series includes standards for video, audio, control, and multiplexing (e.g., mixing audio, video, and data onto a single bit stream). Within the series, H.261 and H.263 are the first- and second-generation video encoding standards. Unlike early versions of MPEG, which is targeted at bit rates on the order of 1.5 Mbps, H.261 and H.263 are targeted at lower speeds. Designed for the Integrated Services Digital Network (ISDN) standards, they support video over links with bandwidth available in 64-kbps increments. In principle, both H.261 and H.263 look a lot like MPEG: They use DCT, quantization, and interframe compression. The differences between H.261/H.263 and MPEG are in the details. In fact, the newer H.264 standard is also part of the MPEG-4 standard. As video become supported on more and more devices ranging from small-screen devices connected over low-bandwidth cellular wireless links to large TVs connected to high-bandwidth fiber links, there is likely to be more demand for innovation and new standards in this space.

7.2.4 Transmitting MPEG over a Network

As we've noted, MPEG and JPEG are not just compression standards but also definitions of the format of video and images, respectively. Focusing on MPEG, the first thing to keep in mind is that it defines the format of a video *stream*; it does not specify how this stream is broken into network packets. Thus, MPEG can be used for videos stored on disk, as well as videos transmitted over a stream-oriented network connection, like that provided by TCP. More on how you might packetize an MPEG stream in a moment.

The MPEG format is one of the most complicated of any protocols discussed in this book. This complication comes from a desire to give the encoding algorithm every possible degree of freedom in how it encodes a given video stream. It also comes from the evolution of the standard over time (i.e., MPEG-1, MPEG-2, MPEG-4). What we describe below is called the *main profile* of an MPEG-2 video stream. You can think of an MPEG profile as being analogous to a "version," except the profile is not explicitly specified in an MPEG header; the receiver has to deduce the profile from the combination of header fields it sees.

A main profile MPEG-2 stream has a nested structure, as illustrated in Figure 7.16. (Keep in mind that this figure hides a *lot* of messy details.) At the outermost level, the video contains a sequence of groups of pictures (GOP) separated by a SeqHdr. The sequence is terminated by a SeqEndCode (0xb7). The SeqHdr that precedes every GOP specifies— among other things—the size of each picture (frame) in the GOP

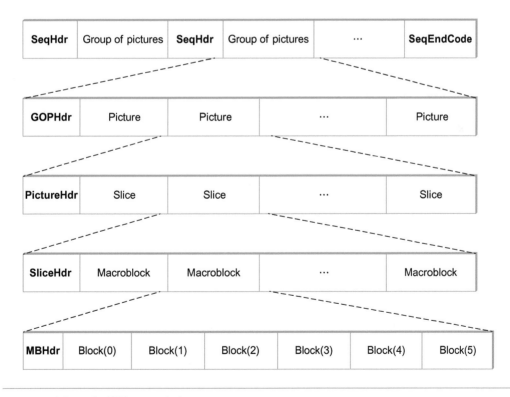

■ FIGURE 7.16 Format of an MPEG-compressed video stream.

(measured in both pixels and macroblocks), the interpicture period (measured in μs), and two quantization matrices for the macroblocks within this GOP: one for intracoded macroblocks (I blocks) and one for intercoded macroblocks (B and P blocks). Since this information is given for each GOP—rather than once for the entire video stream, as you might expect—it is possible to change the quantization table and frame rate at GOP boundaries throughout the video. This makes it possible to adapt the video stream over time, as we discuss below.

Each GOP is given by a GOPHdr, followed by the set of pictures that make up the GOP. The GOPHdr specifies the number of pictures in the GOP, as well as synchronization information for the GOP (i.e., when the GOP should play, relative to the beginning of the video). Each picture, in turn, is given by a PictureHdr and a set of *slices* that make up the picture. (A slice is a region of the picture, such as one horizontal line.) The PictureHdr identifies the type of the picture (I, B, or P) and defines a picture-specific quantization table. The SliceHdr gives the vertical position of the slice, plus another opportunity to change the quantization table—this time by a constant scaling factor rather than by giving a whole new table. Next, the SliceHdr is followed by a sequence of macroblocks. Finally, each macroblock includes a header that specifies the block address within the picture, along with data for the six blocks within the macroblock: one for the U component, one for the V component, and four for the Y component. (Recall that the Y component is 16×16, while the U and V components are 8×8.)

It should be clear that one of the powers of the MPEG format is that it gives the encoder an opportunity to change the encoding over time. It can change the frame rate, the resolution, the mix of frame types that define a GOP, the quantization table, and the encoding used for individual macroblocks. As a consequence, it is possible to adapt the rate at which a video is transmitted over a network by trading picture quality for network bandwidth. Exactly how a network protocol might exploit this adaptability is currently a subject of research (see sidebar).

Another interesting aspect of sending an MPEG stream over the network is exactly how the stream is broken into packets. If sent over a TCP connection, packetization is not an issue; TCP decides when it has enough bytes to send the next IP datagram. When using video interactively, however, it is rare to transmit it over TCP, since TCP has several features that are ill suited to highly latency-sensitive applications (such as abrupt rate changes after a packet loss and retransmission of lost packets). If we are transmitting video using UDP, say, then it makes sense to break the stream at carefully selected points, such as at macroblock boundaries. This is because we would like to confine the effects of a lost packet to a single macroblock, rather than damaging several macroblocks with a single loss. This is an example of Application Level Framing, which was discussed in Section 5.4.

Adaptive Video Coding

We have already noted that video coding using MPEG allows a tradeoff between the bandwidth consumed and the quality of the image. Conversely, it should be apparent that the output bandwidth of a video compression algorithm operating at a certain quality level will not, in general, be constant, but will vary over time depending on the amount of detail and movement in the video stream. These facts raise some interesting questions about how to design a system to transport compressed video over a packet network.

Suppose we have a video codec that outputs a compressed video stream at an average rate of R bps but occasionally bursts up to $3R$ bps. We could potentially transmit the video stream over a fixed bandwidth pipe (e.g., a leased line or CBR circuit) of capacity R, provided we passed the video stream through a smoothing buffer that smooths out the instantaneous peaks in transmission rate. Now, it could happen at some point that the smoothing buffer would fill up beyond an acceptable level, perhaps due to a long action sequence in a movie causing a long period of high output from the codec. At this point, we could increase the amount of compression for a while, thus reducing the data rate (and picture quality) and allowing the smoothing buffer to drain. When it gets close to empty, we could increase the coding quality again.

We could do pretty much the same thing over a packet-switched network, but without a smoothing buffer. Let's assume that we have some way to measure the amount of free capacity and level of congestion along a path—for example, by using an equation-based congestion control algorithm like the ones described in Section 6.5.4. As the available bandwidth fluctuates, we can feed that information back to the codec so that it adjusts its coding parameters to back off during congestion and to send more aggressively (with a higher picture quality) when the network is idle. This is analogous to the behavior of TCP, except in the video case we are actually modifying the total amount of data sent rather than how long we take to send a fixed amount of data, since we don't want to introduce delay into a video application.

> An interesting problem arises if we are *multicasting* a video stream to many receivers. How do we choose the correct rate for each receiver, since they may be experiencing wildly different levels of congestion? A cunning solution to this problem is to split the transmitted video into "layers." The first layer would have the basic level of detail needed to see some sort of useful picture, while each subsequent layer would add more detail, consisting of higher-frequency information. Each layer can then be sent to a different multicast group address, and each receiver can decide how many layers to join. If receiver A is experiencing heavy congestion, he might join only the multicast group carrying the base layer, while receiver B could join all the layers. Receiver A might periodically try to join the next layer of detail to see if more bandwidth has become available. This approach is known as *receiver-driven layered multicast* (RLM). An interesting research problem is how to create the right set of incentives to cause a receiver to join the appropriate number of groups rather than just joining all of them, since joining too many groups would cause unnecessary network congestion.

Packetizing the stream is only the first problem in sending MPEG-compressed video over a network. The next complication is dealing with packet loss. On the one hand, if a B frame is dropped by the network, then it is possible to simply replay the previous frame without seriously compromising the video; 1 frame out of 30 is no big deal. On the other hand, a lost I frame has serious consequences—none of the subsequent B and P frames can be processed without it. Thus, losing an I frame would result in losing multiple frames of the video. While you could retransmit the missing I frame, the resulting delay would probably not be acceptable in a real-time videoconference. One solution to this problem would be to use the Differentiated Services techniques described in Section 6.5.3 to mark the packets containing I frames with a lower drop probability than other packets.

One final observation is that how you choose to encode video depends on more than just the available network bandwidth. It also depends on the application's latency constraints. Once again, an interactive application like videoconferencing needs small latencies. The critical factor is the combination of I, P, and B frames in the GOP. Consider the following GOP:

I B B B B P B B B B I

The problem this GOP causes a videoconferencing application is that the sender has to delay the transmission of the four B frames until the P or I that follows them is available. This is because each B frame depends on the subsequent P or I frame. If the video is playing at 15 frames per second (i.e., one frame every 67 ms), this means the first B frame is delayed 4×67 ms, which is more than a quarter of a second. This delay is in addition to any propagation delay imposed by the network. A quarter of a second is far greater than the 100-ms threshold that humans are able to perceive. It is for this reason that many videoconference applications encode video using JPEG, which is often called motion-JPEG. (Motion-JPEG also addresses the problem of dropping a reference frame since all frames are able to stand alone.) Notice, however, that an interframe encoding that depends upon only prior frames rather than later frames is not a problem. Thus, a GOP of

$$I\ P\ P\ P\ P\ I$$

would work just fine for interactive videoconferencing.

7.2.5 Audio Compression (MP3)

Not only does MPEG define how video is compressed, but it also defines a standard for compressing audio. This standard can be used to compress the audio portion of a movie (in which case the MPEG standard defines how the compressed audio is interleaved with the compressed video in a single MPEG stream) or it can be used to compress stand-alone audio (for example, an audio CD).

To understand audio compression, we need to begin with the data. CD-quality audio, which is the *de facto* digital representation for high-quality audio, is sampled at a rate of 44.1 KHz (i.e., a sample is collected approximately once every 23 μs). Each sample is 16 bits, which means that a stereo (2-channel) audio stream results in a bit rate of

$$2 \times 44.1 \times 1000 \times 16 = 1.41\ \text{Mbps}$$

By comparison, telephone-quality voice is sampled at a rate of 8 KHz, with 8-bit samples, resulting in a bit rate of 64 kbps, which is not coincidentally the speed of an ISDN link.

Clearly, some amount of compression is going to be required to transmit CD-quality audio over, say, the 128-kbps capacity of an ISDN data/voice line pair. To make matters worse, synchronization and error correction overhead require that 49 bits be used to encode each 16-bit sample, resulting in an actual bit rate of

$$49/16 \times 1.41 \text{ Mbps} = 4.32 \text{ Mbps}$$

MPEG addresses this need by defining three levels of compression, as enumerated in Table 7.2. Of these, Layer III, which is more widely known as MP3, is the most commonly used.

To achieve these compression ratios, MP3 uses techniques that are similar to those used by MPEG to compress video. First, it splits the audio stream into some number of frequency subbands, loosely analogous to the way MPEG processes the Y, U, and V components of a video stream separately. Second, each subband is broken into a sequence of blocks, which are similar to MPEG's macroblocks except they can vary in length from 64 to 1024 samples. (The encoding algorithm can vary the block size depending on certain distortion effects that are beyond our discussion.) Finally, each block is transformed using a modified DCT algorithm, quantized, and Huffman encoded, just as for MPEG video.

The trick to MP3 is how many subbands it elects to use and how many bits it allocates to each subband, keeping in mind that it is trying to produce the highest-quality audio possible for the target bit rate. Exactly how this allocation is made is governed by psychoacoustic models that are beyond the scope of this book, but to illustrate the idea consider that it makes sense to allocate more bits to low-frequency subbands when compressing a male voice and more bits to high-frequency subbands when compressing a female voice. Operationally, MP3 dynamically changes the quantization tables used for each subband to achieve the desired effect.

Table 7.2 MP3 Compression Rates

Coding	Bit Rates	Compression Factor
Layer I	384 kbps	4
Layer II	192 kbps	8
Layer III	128 kbps	12

Once compressed, the subbands are packaged into fixed-size frames, and a header is attached. This header includes synchronization information, as well as the bit allocation information needed by the decoder to determine how many bits are used to encode each subband. As mentioned above, these audio frames can then be interleaved with video frames to form a complete MPEG stream. One interesting side note is that, while it might work to drop B frames in the network should congestion occur, experience teaches us that it is not a good idea to drop audio frames since users are better able to tolerate bad video than bad audio.

7.3 SUMMARY

This chapter has described how application data is encoded in network packets. Unlike the protocols described earlier in this book, which you can think of as processing *messages*, these transformations process *data*. Multimedia data types, such as video, still image, and audio, are increasingly driving developments in this space.

The first issue is presentation formatting, where the problem is formatting the different types of data that application programs compute on, such that they can be transmitted over a network and interpreted correctly by the receiver. Data types such as integers, floating-point numbers, character strings, arrays, and structures must be encoded in some intelligible way. This involves both translating between machine and network byte order and linearizing compound data structures. We outlined the design space for presentation formatting and discussed four specific mechanisms that fall on different points in this design space: XDR, ASN.1, NDR, and the increasingly important XML.

The second issue is compression, which is concerned with reducing the bandwidth required to transmit different types of data. Compression algorithms can be either lossless or lossy, with lossy algorithms being most appropriate for image and video data. JPEG, MPEG, and MP3 all make use of lossy compression protocols for still images, video, and audio data, respectively. Video compression and encoding formats such as the MPEG family of standards continue to evolve to meet the demand for higher quality within the limits of available bandwidth.

It hardly needs to be emphasized that video is now the major components of traffic on the Internet, with *three-screen* capability—delivered to TV sets, computers, and cell phones—an overriding goal of the computing, communication, and entertainment industries.

This raises a number of interesting issues. One is the impact that all of this video will have on the bandwidth required for the Internet. We are still a long way from having enough deployed capacity in the Internet to transmit entertainment video to everyone who watches TV or rents DVDs today. Not only is this driving demand for more network capacity, but new network architectures with names such as content-centric networking are also being proposed.

WHAT'S NEXT: VIDEO EVERYWHERE

More directly relevant to the material in this chapter is the need to converge on coding and presentation formats for video in this new video everywhere environment. As one example of the challenges in this department, consider the fact that three of the largest players in video streaming (Microsoft®, Adobe®, and Apple®) have each developed different protocols for streaming video from websites to browsers. Users can mostly get around these incompatibilities today by installing appropriate plug-ins on their browsers, but the situation gets decidedly messier on less flexible devices such as mobile phones. With the emergence of Internet-capable televisions and set-top boxes, incompatible video formats seem likely to be a continuing source of irritation for consumers.

The emerging standard for HTML5 has attempted to ensure that at least one common video codec and format is supported by all browsers as a least common denominator, but that process has so far failed to converge. Patent concerns have caused some of the participants in the standards process to be hesitant to endorse any one format for fear that a (hitherto unknown) patent holder will come out of the woodwork once their patent is infringed.

Another issue that will come to the forefront as video over IP becomes ubiquitous is the ease of configuration and management of IP devices. Although some of today's Internet users are comfortable configuring networking parameters (does my ISP use DHCP? PPoE?), it's unlikely that the average purchaser of a television wants to learn how to configure anything more complex than the channel change button. "Plug-and-play" configuration of IP devices remains an important goal, as does the ability to troubleshoot these devices without being a networking expert. This is part of the larger problem of management of devices in the home, which has now emerged as one of the hot topics in networking.

■ FURTHER READING

Our recommended reading list for this chapter includes two papers that give an overview of the JPEG and MPEG standards, respectively. Their main value is in explaining the various factors that shaped the standards. We also recommend the paper on receiver-driven layered multicast as an excellent example of a systems approach to design, embracing the issues of multicast, congestion control, and video coding.

- Wallace, G. K. The JPEG still picture compression standard. *Communications of the ACM* 34(1):30–44, April 1991.
- Le Gall, D. MPEG: A video compression standard for multimedia applications. *Communications of the ACM* 34(1):46–58, April 1991.
- McCanne, S., V. Jacobson, and M. Vetterli. Receiver-driven layered multicast. *Proceedings of the SIGCOMM '96 Symposium,* pages 117–130, September 1996.

Unfortunately, there is no single paper that gives a comprehensive treatment of presentation formatting. Aside from the XDR, ASN.1/BER, and NDR specifications (see Eisler [Eis06]; the CCITT recommendations [CCITT92a], [CCITT92b]; and the Open Software Foundation [OSF94]), three other papers cover topics related to presentation formatting are those by O'Malley et al. [OPM94], Lin [Lin93], and Chen et al. [CLNZ89]. All three discuss performance-related issues.

On the topic of compression, a good place to start is with Huffman encoding, which was originally defined in [Huf52]. The original LZ algorithm is presented in Ziv and Lempel [ZL77], and an improved version of that algorithm by the same authors can be found in [ZL78]. Both of these papers are of a theoretical nature. The work that brought the LZ approach into widespread practice can be found in Welch [Wel84]. For a more complete overview of the topic of compression, Nelson's article [Nel92] is recommended. There are many books on multimedia that cover compression. We recommend Witten et al. [WMB99], which has a relatively high science-to-hype ratio, and Buford [Buf94], which is a collection of contributed chapters that span the range of multimedia topics. Weise and

Weynand's book [WW07] covers almost every aspect of video, including compression and many other topics. For a comprehensive description of the early MPEG standards, see Mitchell et al. [MPFL96]. For a description of MP3, see Noll [Nol97].

Finally, we recommend the following live references:

- http://www.w3.org/TR/REC-xml/: The most recent XML specification
- http://mpeg.chiariglione.org/: Home page of the Motion Picture Experts Group, a source for lots of MPEG material

EXERCISES

1. Consider the following C code:

```
#define  MAXSTR 100

struct date {
    char   month[MAXSTR];
    int    day;
    int    year;
};

struct employee {
    char   name[MAXSTR];
    int    ssn;
    struct date *hireday;
    int    salary_history[5];
    int    num_raises;
};

static struct date date0 = {"DECEMBER", 2, 1998};
static struct date date1 = {"JANUARY", 7, 2002};

static struct employee employee0 = {"RICHARD", 4376,
                                   &date0,{80000, 85000,
                                   90000, 0, 0}, 2};
static struct employee employee1 = {"MARY", 4377,
                                   &date1, {90000,
                                   150000, 0, 0, 0}, 1};
```

where num_raises + 1 corresponds to the number of valid entries in array salary_history. Show the on-the-wire representation of employee0 that is generated by XDR.

2. Show the on-the-wire representation of employee1 from the previous problem that is generated by XDR.

3. For the data structures given in the previous problem, give the XDR routine that encodes/decodes these structures. If you have XDR available to you, run this routine and measure how long it takes to encode and decode an example instance of structure employee.

4. Using library functions like htonl and Unix's bcopy or Windows' CopyMemory, implement a routine that generates the same on-the-wire representation of the structures given in Exercise 1 as XDR does. If possible, compare the performance of your "by-hand" encoder/decoder with the corresponding XDR routines.

5. Use XDR and htonl to encode a 1000-element array of integers. Measure and compare the performance of each. How do these compare to a simple loop that reads and writes a 1000-element array of integers? Perform the experiment on a computer for which the native byte order is the same as the network byte order, as well as on a computer for which the native byte order and the network byte order are different.

6. Write your own implementation of htonl. Using both your own htonl and (if little-endian hardware is available) the standard library version, run appropriate experiments to determine how much longer it takes to byte-swap integers versus merely copying them.

7. Give the ASN.1 encoding for the following three integers. Note that ASN.1 integers, like those in XDR, are 32 bits in length.
   (a) 101
   (b) 10,120
   (c) 16,909,060

8. Give the ASN.1 encoding for the following three integers. Note that ASN.1 integers, like those in XDR, are 32 bits in length.
   (a) 15
   (b) 29,496,729
   (c) 58,993,458

9. Give the big-endian and little-endian representation for the integers from Exercise 7.

10. Give the big-endian and little-endian representation for the integers from Exercise 8.

11. XDR is used to encode/decode the header for the SunRPC protocol illustrated by Figure 5.18. The XDR version is determined by the RPCVersion field. What potential difficulty does this present? Would it be possible for a new version of XDR to switch to little-endian integer format?

12. The presentation-formatting process is sometimes regarded as an autonomous protocol layer, separate from the application. If this is so, why might including data compression in the presentation layer be a bad idea?

13. Suppose you have a machine with a 36-bit word size. Strings are represented as five packed 7-bit characters per word. What presentation issues on this machine have to be addressed for it to exchange integer and string data with the rest of the world?

14. Using the programming language of your choice that supports user-defined automatic type conversions, define a type netint and supply conversions that enable assignments and equality comparisons between ints and netints. Can a generalization of this approach solve the problem of network argument marshalling?

15. Different architectures have different conventions on bit order as well as byte order—whether the least significant bit of a byte, for example, is bit 0 or bit 7. RFC 791 [Pos81] defines (in its Appendix B) the standard network bit order. Why is bit order then not relevant to presentation formatting?

16. Let $p \leq 1$ be the fraction of machines in a network that are big-endian; the remaining $1 - p$ fraction are little-endian. Suppose we choose two machines at random and send an int from one to the other. Give the average number of byte-order conversions needed for both big-endian network byte order and receiver-makes-right for $p = 0.1$, $p = 0.5$, and $p = 0.9$. (Hint: The probability that both endpoints are big-endian is p^2; the

probability that the two endpoints use different byte orders is $2p(1 - p)$.)

17. Describe a representation for XML documents that would be more compact and more efficient to process than XML text.

18. Experiment with a compression utility (e.g., compress, gzip, or pkzip). What compression ratios are you able to achieve? See if you can generate data files for which you can achieve 5:1 or 10:1 compression ratios.

19. Suppose a file contains the letters a, b, c, and d. Nominally we require 2 bits per letter to store such a file.
    (a) Assume the letter a occurs 50% of the time, b occurs 30% of the time, and c and d each occurs 10% of the time. Give an encoding of each letter as a bit string that provides optimal compression. (Hint: Use a single bit for a.)
    (b) What is the percentage of compression you achieve above? (This is the average of the compression percentages achieved for each letter, weighted by the letter's frequency.)
    (c) Repeat this, assuming a and b each occurs 40% of the time, c occurs 15% of the time, and d occurs 5% of the time.

20. Suppose we have a compression function c, which takes a bit string s to a compressed string $c(s)$.
    (a) Show that for any integer N there must be a string s of length N for which $length(c(s)) \geq N$; that is, no effective compression is done.
    (b) Compress some already compressed files (try compressing with the same utility several times in sequence). What happens to the file size?
    (c) Given a compression function c as in (a), give a function c' such that for all bit strings s, $length(c'(s)) \leq \min(length(c(s)), length(s)) + 1$; that is, in the worst case, compression with c' expands the size by only 1 bit.

21. Give an algorithm for run length encoding that requires only a single byte to represent nonrepeated symbols.

22. Write a program to construct a dictionary of all "words," defined to be runs of consecutive nonwhitespace, in a given text file. We

might then compress the file (ignoring the loss of whitespace information) by representing each word as an index in the dictionary. Retrieve the file rfc791.txt containing [Pos81], and run your program on it. Give the size of the compressed file assuming first that each word is encoded with 12 bits (this should be sufficient), and then that the 128 most common words are encoded with 8 bits and the rest with 13 bits. Assume that the dictionary itself can be stored by using, for each word, $\text{length}(\text{word}) + 1$ bytes.

23. The one-dimensional discrete cosine transform is similar to the two-dimensional transform, except that we drop the second variable (j or y) and the second cosine factor. We also drop, from the inverse DCT only, the leading $1/\sqrt{2}N$ coefficient. Implement this and its inverse for $N = 8$ (a spreadsheet will do, although a language supporting matrices might be better) and answer the following:

(a) If the input data is $\langle 1, 2, 3, 5, 5, 3, 2, 1 \rangle$, which DCT coefficients are near 0?

(b) If the data is $\langle 1, 2, 3, 4, 5, 6, 7, 8 \rangle$, how many DCT coefficients must we keep so that after the inverse DCT the values are all within 1% of their original values? 10%? Assume dropped DCT coefficients are replaced with 0s.

(c) Let s_i, for $1 \leq i \leq 8$, be the input sequence consisting of a 1 in position i and 0 in position $j, j \neq i$. Suppose we apply the DCT to s_i, zero the last three coefficients, and then apply the inverse DCT. Which $i, 1 \leq i \leq 8$, results in the smallest error in the ith place in the result? The largest error?

24. Compare the size of an all-white image in JPEG format with a typical photographic image of the same dimensions. At what stage or stages of the JPEG compression process does the white image become smaller than the photographic image?

For the next three exercises, the utilities cjpeg and djpeg may be useful and can be obtained from http://www.ijg.org/. Other JPEG conversion utilities can also be used. For manual creation and examination of graphics files, the pgm portable grayscale format is recommended; see the Unix pgm(5)/ppm(5) man pages.

25. Create a grayscale image consisting of an 8×8 grid with a vertical black line in the first column. Compress into JPEG format and decompress. How far off are the resultant bytes at the default quality setting? How would you describe the inaccuracies introduced, visually? What quality setting is sufficient to recover the file exactly?

26. Create an 8×8 grayscale image consisting of a 64-character ASCII text string. Use lowercase letters only, with no whitespace or punctuation. Compress into JPEG format and decompress. How recognizable is the result, as text? Why might adding whitespace make things worse? With the quality setting at 100, would this be a plausible way of compressing text?

27. Write a program that implements forward and backward DCT, using floating-point arithmetic. Run the program on a sample grayscale image. Since DCT is lossless, the image output by the program should match the input. Now modify your program so that it zeroes some of the higher-frequency components, and see how the output image is affected. How is this different from what JPEG does?

28. Express DCT(0,0) in terms of the average of the $pixel(x,y)$s.

29. Think about what functions might reasonably be expected from a video standard: fast-forward, editing capabilities, random access, and so on. (See the paper by Le Gall, "MPEG: A video compression standard for multimedia applications," given in this chapter's Further Reading list, for more ideas.) Explain MPEG's design in terms of these features.

30. Suppose you want to implement fast-forward and reverse for MPEG streams. What problems do you run into if you limit your mechanism to displaying I frames only? If you don't, then to display a given frame in the fast-forward sequence, what is the largest number of frames in the original sequence you may have to decode?

31. Use mpeg_play to play an MPEG-encoded video. Experiment with options, particularly -nob and -nop, which are used to omit the B and P frames, respectively, from the stream. What are the visible effects of omitting these frames?

32. The mpeg_stat program can be used to display statistics for video streams. Use it to determine, for several streams:
    (a) Number and sequence of I, B, and P frames.
    (b) Average compression rate for the entire video.
    (c) Average compression rate for each type of frame.

33. Suppose we have a video of two white points moving toward each other at a uniform rate against a black background. We encode it via MPEG. In one I frame the two points are 100 pixels apart; in the next I frame they have merged. The final point of merger happens to lie at the center of a 16×16 macroblock.
    (a) Describe how you might optimally encode the Y component of the intervening B (or P) frames.
    (b) Now suppose the points are in color and that the color changes slowly as the points move. Describe what the encoding of the U and V values might look like.

Network Security

It is true greatness to have in one the frailty of a man and the security of a god.

–Seneca

omputer networks are typically a shared resource used by many applications representing different interests. The Internet is particularly widely shared, being used by competing businesses, mutually antagonistic governments, and opportunistic criminals. Unless security measures are taken, a network conversation or a distributed application may be compromised by an adversary.

Consider some threats to secure use of, for example, the World Wide Web. Suppose you are a customer using a credit card to order an item from a website. An obvious threat is that an adversary would eavesdrop on your network communica-

---

PROBLEM: SECURITY ATTACKS

tion, reading your messages to obtain your credit card information. How might that eavesdropping be accomplished? It is trivial on a broadcast network such as an Ethernet, where any node can be configured to receive all the message traffic on that network. Wireless communication can be monitored without any physical connection. More elaborate approaches include wiretapping and planting spy software on any of the chain of nodes involved. Only in the most extreme cases (e.g., national security) are serious measures taken to prevent such monitoring, and the Internet is not one of those cases. It is possible and practical, however, to encrypt messages so as to prevent an adversary from understanding the message contents. A protocol that does so is said to provide *confidentiality*. Taking the concept a step farther, concealing the quantity or destination of communication is called *traffic confidentiality*—because merely knowing how much communication is going where can be useful to an adversary in some situations.

Even with confidentiality there still remains threats for the website customer. An adversary who can't read the contents of your encrypted message might still be able to change a few bits in it, resulting in a valid order for, say, a completely different item or perhaps 1000 units of the item. There are techniques to detect, if not prevent, such tampering. A protocol that detects such message tampering provides *data integrity*. The adversary could alternatively transmit an extra copy of your message in a *replay attack*. To the website, it would appear as though you had simply ordered another of the same item you ordered the first time. A protocol that detects replays provides *originality*. Originality would not, however, preclude the adversary intercepting your order, waiting a while, then transmitting it—in effect, delaying your order. The adversary could thereby arrange for the item to arrive on your doorstep while you are away on vacation, when it can be easily snatched. A protocol that detects such delaying tactics is said to provide *timeliness*. Data integrity, originality, and timeliness are considered aspects of the more general property of *integrity*.

Another threat to the customer is unknowingly being directed to a false website. This can result from a Domain Name System (DNS) attack, in which false information is entered in a DNS server or the name service cache of the customer's computer. This leads to translating a correct URL into an incorrect IP address—the address of a false website. A protocol that ensures that you really are talking to whom you think you're talking is said to provide *authentication*. Authentication entails integrity, since it is meaningless to say that a message came from a certain participant if it is no longer the same message.

The owner of the website can be attacked as well. Some websites have been defaced; the files that make up the website content have been remotely accessed and modified without authorization. That is an issue of *access control*: enforcing the rules regarding who is allowed to do what. Websites have also been subject to denial of service (DoS) attacks, during which would-be customers are unable to access the website because it is being overwhelmed by bogus requests. Ensuring a degree of access is called *availability*.

In addition to these issues, the Internet has notably been used as a means for deploying malicious code that exploits vulnerabilities in end systems. *Worms*, pieces of self-replicating code that spread over networks, have been known for several decades and continue to cause problems, as do their relatives, *viruses*, which are spread by the transmission of infected files. Infected machines can then be arranged into *botnets*, which can be used to inflict further harm, such as launching DoS attacks.

Although the Internet was designed with the redundancy to survive problems such as the disruption of a link or router, it was not originally designed to provide the kind of security we have been discussing. Internet security mechanisms have essentially been patches. If a comprehensive redesign of the Internet were to take place, integrating security would likely be the foremost driving factor. That possibility makes this chapter all the more pertinent.

There are many tools today for securing networked systems, ranging from various forms of cryptography to specialized devices such as firewalls. This chapter will provide an introduction to these tools with a particular focus on the use of cryptographic methods to improve network security. Improving the security of networks continues to be a field of rapid change and considerable research effort.

8.1 CRYPTOGRAPHIC BUILDING BLOCKS

We introduce the concepts of cryptography-based security step by step. The first step is the cryptographic algorithms—ciphers and cryptographic hashes—that are introduced in this section. They are not a solution in themselves, but rather building blocks from which a solution can be built. Cryptographic algorithms are parameterized by *keys*, and Section 8.2 addresses the problem of distributing the keys. In the next step (Section 8.3), we describe how to incorporate the cryptographic building blocks into protocols that provide secure communication between participants who possess the correct keys. Finally, Section 8.4 examines several complete security protocols and systems in current use.

8.1.1 Principles of Ciphers

Encryption transforms a message in such a way that it becomes unintelligible to any party that does not have the secret of how to reverse the transformation. The sender applies an *encryption* function to the original *plaintext* message, resulting in a *ciphertext* message that is sent over the network, as shown in Figure 8.1. The receiver applies a secret *decryption* function—the inverse of the encryption function—to recover the original plaintext. The ciphertext transmitted across the network is unintelligible to any eavesdropper, assuming the eavesdropper doesn't know the

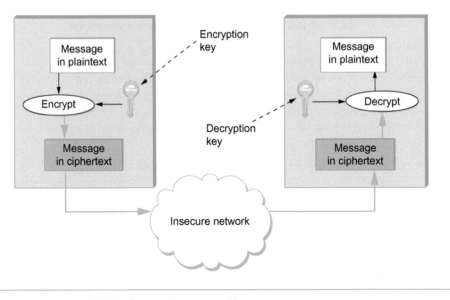

■ FIGURE 8.1 Symmetric-key encryption and decryption.

decryption function. The transformation represented by an encryption function and its corresponding decryption function is called a *cipher*.

Cryptographers have been led to the principle, first stated in 1883, that encryption and decryption functions should be parameterized by a *key*, and furthermore that the functions should be considered public knowledge—only the key need be secret. Thus, the ciphertext produced for a given plaintext message depends on both the encryption function and the key. One reason for this principle is that if you depend on the cipher being kept secret, then you have to retire the cipher (not just the keys) when you believe it is no longer secret. This means potentially frequent changes of cipher, which is problematic since it takes a lot of work to develop a new cipher. Also, one of the best ways to know that a cipher is secure is to use it for a long time—if no one breaks it, it's probably secure. (Fortunately, there are plenty of people who will try to break ciphers and who will let it be widely known when they have succeeded, so no news is generally good news.) Thus, there is considerable cost and risk in deploying a new cipher. Finally, parameterizing a cipher with keys provides us with what is in effect a very large family of ciphers; by switching keys, we essentially switch ciphers, thereby limiting the amount of data that a *cryptanalyst* (code-breaker) can use to try to break our key/cipher and the amount she can read if she succeeds.

The basic requirement for an encryption algorithm is that it turn plaintext into ciphertext in such a way that only the intended recipient—the holder of the decryption key—can recover the plaintext. What this means is that encrypted messages cannot be read by people who do not hold the key.

It is important to realize that when a potential attacker receives a piece of ciphertext, he may have more information at his disposal than just the ciphertext itself. For example, he may know that the plaintext was written in English, which means that the letter *e* occurs more often in the plaintext that any other letter; the frequency of many other letters and common letter combinations can also be predicted. This information can greatly simplify the task of finding the key. Similarly, he may know something about the likely contents of the message; for example, the word "login" is likely to occur at the start of a remote login session. This may enable a *known plaintext* attack, which has a much higher chance of success than a *ciphertext only* attack. Even better is a *chosen plaintext* attack, which may be enabled by feeding some information to the sender that you know the sender is likely to transmit—such things have happened in wartime, for example.

The best cryptographic algorithms, therefore, can prevent the attacker from deducing the key even when the individual knows both the plaintext and the ciphertext. This leaves the attacker with no choice but to try all the possible keys—exhaustive, "brute force" search. If keys have n bits, then there are 2^n possible values for a key (each of the n bits could be either a zero or a one). An attacker could be so lucky as to try the correct value immediately, or so unlucky as to try every incorrect value before finally trying the correct value of the key, having tried all 2^n possible values; the average number of guesses to discover the correct value is halfway between those extremes, $2^n/2$. This can be made computationally impractical by choosing a sufficiently large key space and by making the operation of checking a key reasonably costly. What makes this difficult is that computing speeds keep increasing, making formerly infeasible computations feasible. Furthermore, although we are concentrating on the security of data as it moves through the network—that is, the data is sometimes vulnerable for only a short period of time—in general, security people have to consider the vulnerability of data that needs to be stored in archives for tens of years. This argues for a generously large key size. On the other hand, larger keys make encryption and decryption slower.

Most ciphers are *block ciphers*; they are defined to take as input a plaintext block of a certain fixed size, typically 64 to 128 bits. Using a block cipher to encrypt each block independently—known as *electronic codebook (ECB) mode* encryption—has the weakness that a given plaintext block value will always result in the same ciphertext block. Hence, recurring block values in the plaintext are recognizable as such in the ciphertext, making it much easier for a cryptanalyst to break the cipher.

To prevent this, block ciphers are always augmented to make the ciphertext for a block vary depending on context. Ways in which a block cipher may be augmented are called *modes of operation*. A common mode of operation is *cipher block chaining* (CBC), in which each plaintext block is XORed with the previous block's ciphertext before being encrypted. The result is that each block's ciphertext depends in part on the preceding blocks (i.e., on its context). Since the first plaintext block has no preceding block, it is XORed with a random number. That random number, called an *initialization vector* (IV), is included with the series of ciphertext blocks so that the first ciphertext block can be decrypted. This mode is illustrated in Figure 8.2. Another mode of operation is *counter mode*, in which successive values of a counter (e.g., 1, 2, 3, . . .) are incorporated into the encryption of successive blocks of plaintext.

8.1.2 Symmetric-Key Ciphers

In a symmetric-key cipher, both participants[1] in a communication share the same key. In other words, if a message is encrypted using a particular key, the same key is required for decrypting the message. If the cipher illustrated in Figure 8.1 were a symmetric-key cipher, then the encryption and decryption keys would be identical. Symmetric-key ciphers are also known as secret-key ciphers since the shared key must be known only to the participants. (We'll take a look at the alternative, public-key ciphers, shortly.)

The U.S. National Institute of Standards and Technology (NIST) has issued standards for a series of symmetric-key ciphers. *Data Encryption Standard* (DES) was the first, and it has stood the test of time in that no cryptanalytic attack better than brute force search has been discovered.

---

[1]We use the term *participant* for the parties involved in a secure communication since that is the term we have been using throughout the book to identify the two endpoints of a channel. In the security world, they are typically called *principals*.

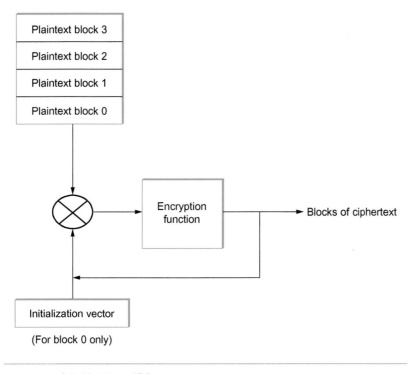

■ **FIGURE 8.2** Cipher block chaining (CBC).

Brute force search, however, has gotten faster. DES's keys (56 independent bits) are now too small given current processor speeds. DES keys have 56 independent bits (although they have 64 bits in total; the last bit of every byte is a parity bit). As noted above, you would, on average, have to search half of the space of 2^{56} possible keys to find the right one, giving $2^{55} = 3.6 \times 10^{16}$ keys. That may sound like a lot, but such a search is highly parallelizable, so it's possible to throw as many computers at the task as you can get your hands on—and these days it's easy to lay your hands on thousands of computers (Amazon.com will rent them to you for a few cents an hour, for example). By the late 1990s, it was already possible to recover a DES key after a few hours. Consequently, NIST updated the DES standard in 1999 to indicate that DES should only be used for legacy systems.

NIST also standardized the cipher *Triple DES* (3DES), which leverages the cryptanalysis resistance of DES while in effect increasing the key size. A 3DES key has 168 ($= 3 \times 56$) independent bits, and is used as three DES keys; let's call them DES-key1, DES-key2, and DES-key3. 3DES encryption of a block is performed by first DES encrypting the block using DES-key1, then DES *de*crypting the result using DES-key2, and finally DES encrypting that result using DES-key3. Decryption involves decrypting using DES-key3, then encrypting using DES-key2, then decrypting using DES-key1.[2]

Although 3DES solves DES's key-length problem, it inherits some other shortcomings. Software implementations of DES/3DES are slow because it was originally designed, by IBM, for implementation in hardware. Also, DES/3DES uses a 64-bit block size; a larger block size is more efficient and more secure.

3DES is being superseded by the *Advanced Encryption Standard* (AES) standard issued by NIST in 2001. The cipher selected to become that standard (with a few minor modifications) was originally named Rijndael (pronounced roughly like "Rhine dahl") based on the names of its inventors, Daemen and Rijmen. AES supports key lengths of 128, 192, or 256 bits, and the block length is 128 bits. AES permits fast implementations in both software and hardware. It doesn't require much memory, which makes it suitable for small mobile devices. AES has some mathematically proven security properties and, as of the time of writing, has not suffered from any significant successful attacks.[3]

8.1.3 Public-Key Ciphers

An alternative to symmetric-key ciphers is asymmetric, or public-key, ciphers. Instead of a single key shared by two participants, a public-key cipher uses a pair of related keys, one for encryption and a different one for decryption. The pair of keys is "owned" by just one participant. The owner keeps the decryption key secret so that only the owner can decrypt messages; that key is called the *private key*. The owner makes the encryption key public, so that anyone can encrypt messages for the owner; that

---

[2]The reason 3DES encryption uses DES *de*cryption with DES-key2 is to interoperate with legacy DES systems. If a legacy DES system uses a single key, then a 3DES system can perform the same encryption function by using that key for each of DES-key1, DES-key2, and DES-key3; in the first two steps, we encrypt and then decrypt with the same key, producing the original plaintext, which we then encrypt again.

[3]Since anything that can recover the plaintext with less computational effort than sheer brute force is technically classified as an attack, there are some forms of attack on AES that have been published. While they do somewhat better than brute force, they remain computationally very expensive.

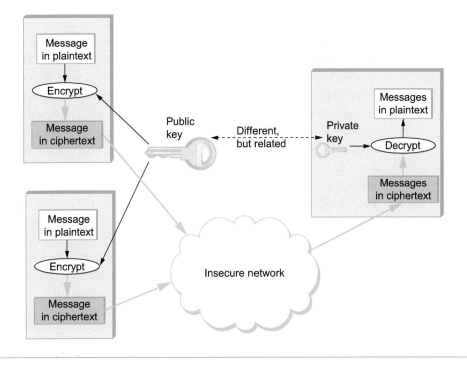

key is called the *public key*. Obviously, for such a scheme to work, it must not be possible to deduce the private key from the public key. Consequently, any participant can get the public key and send an encrypted message to the owner of the keys, and only the owner has the private key necessary to decrypt it. This scenario is depicted in Figure 8.3.

Because it is somewhat unintuitive, we emphasize that the public encryption key is useless for decrypting a message—you couldn't even decrypt a message that you yourself had just encrypted unless you had the private decryption key. If we think of keys as defining a communication channel between participants, then another difference between public-key and symmetric-key ciphers is the topology of the channels. A key for a symmetric-key cipher provides a channel that is two-way between two participants—each participant holds the same (symmetric) key that either one can use to encrypt or decrypt messages in either direction. A public/private key pair, in contrast, provides a channel that is one way and many to one from everyone who has the public key to the (unique) owner of the private key, as illustrated in Figure 8.3.

An important additional property of public-key ciphers is that the private "decryption" key can be used with the encryption algorithm to encrypt messages so that they can only be decrypted using the public "encryption" key. This property clearly wouldn't be useful for confidentiality since anyone with the public key could decrypt such a message. (Indeed, for two-way confidentiality between two participants, each participant needs its own pair of keys, and each encrypts messages using the other's public key.) This property is, however, useful for authentication since it tells the receiver of such a message that it could only have been created by the owner of the keys (subject to certain assumptions that we will get into later). This is illustrated in Figure 8.4. It should be clear from the figure that anyone with the public key can decrypt the encrypted message, and, assuming that the result of the decryption matches the expected result, it can be concluded that the private key must have been used to perform the encryption. Exactly how this operation is used to provide authentication is the topic of Section 8.3. As we will see, public-key ciphers are used primarily for authentication and to confidentially distribute symmetric keys, leaving the rest of confidentiality to symmetric-key ciphers.

A bit of interesting history: The concept of public-key ciphers was first published in 1976 by Diffie and Hellman. Subsequently, however, documents have come to light proving that Britain's Communications-Electronics Security Group had discovered public-key ciphers by 1970, and the U.S. National Security Agency (NSA) claims to have discovered them in the mid-1960s.

The best-known public-key cipher is RSA, named after its inventors: Rivest, Shamir, and Adleman. RSA relies on the high computational cost

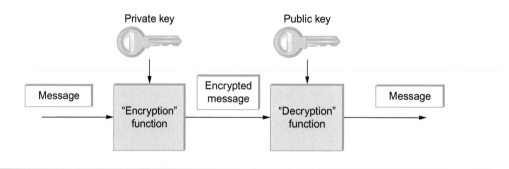

■ FIGURE 8.4 Authentication using public keys.

of factoring large numbers. The problem of finding an efficient way to factor numbers is one that mathematicians have worked on unsuccessfully since long before RSA appeared in 1978, and RSA's subsequent resistance to cryptanalysis has further bolstered confidence in its security. Unfortunately, RSA needs relatively large keys, at least 1024 bits, to be secure. This is larger than keys for symmetric-key ciphers because it is faster to break an RSA private key by factoring the large number on which the pair of keys is based than by exhaustively searching the key space.

Another public-key cipher is ElGamal. Like RSA, it relies on a mathematical problem, the discrete logarithm problem, for which no efficient solution has been found, and requires keys of at least 1024 bits. There is a variation of the discrete logarithm problem, arising when the input is an elliptic curve, that is thought to be even more difficult to compute; cryptographic schemes based on this problem are referred to as *elliptic curve cryptography*.

Public-key ciphers are, unfortunately, several orders of magnitude slower than symmetric-key ciphers. Consequently, symmetric-key ciphers are used for the vast majority of encryption, while public-key ciphers are reserved for use in authentication (Section 8.1.4) and session key establishment (Section 8.2).

8.1.4 Authenticators

Encryption alone does not provide data integrity. For example, just randomly modifying a ciphertext message could turn it into something that decrypts into valid-looking plaintext, in which case the tampering would be undetectable by the receiver. Nor does encryption alone provide authentication. It is not much use to say that a message came from a certain participant if the contents of the message have been modified after that participant created it. In a sense, integrity and authentication are fundamentally inseparable.

An *authenticator* is a value, to be included in a transmitted message, that can be used to verify simultaneously the authenticity and the data integrity of a message. We will see how authenticators can be used in protocols to Section 8.3. For now, we focus on the algorithms that produce authenticators.

You should recall that in Section 2.4.3 we looked at checksums and cyclic redundancy checks (CRCs)—added pieces of information sent with the original message—as ways of detecting when a message has been inadvertently modified by bit errors. A similar concept applies to authenticators, with the added challenge that the corruption of the message is likely to be deliberately performed by someone who wants the corruption to go undetected. To support authentication, an authenticator includes some proof that whoever created the authenticator knows a secret that is known only to the alleged sender of the message; for example, the secret could be a key, and the proof could be some value encrypted using the key. There is a mutual dependency between the form of the redundant information and the form of the proof of secret knowledge. We discuss several workable combinations.

We initially assume that the original message need not be confidential—that a transmitted message will consist of the plaintext of the original message plus an authenticator. Later we will consider the case where confidentiality is desired.

One kind of authenticator combines encryption and a *cryptographic hash function*. Cryptographic hash algorithms are treated as public knowledge, as with cipher algorithms. A cryptographic hash function (also known as a *cryptographic checksum*) is a function that outputs sufficient redundant information about a message to expose any tampering. Just as a checksum or CRC exposes bit errors introduced by noisy links, a cryptographic checksum is designed to expose deliberate corruption of messages by an adversary. The value it outputs is called a *message digest* and, like an ordinary checksum, is appended to the message. All the message digests produced by a given hash have the same number of bits regardless of the length of the original message. Since the space of possible input messages is larger than the space of possible message digests, there will be different input messages that produce the same message digest, like collisions in a hash table.

An authenticator can be created by encrypting the message digest. The receiver computes a digest of the plaintext part of the message and compares that to the decrypted message digest. If they are equal, then the receiver would conclude that the message is indeed from its alleged sender (since it would have to have been encrypted with the right key) and has not been tampered with. No adversary could get away with sending a bogus message with a matching bogus digest because she would not have the key to encrypt the bogus digest correctly. An adversary could, however, obtain the plaintext original message and its encrypted digest by eavesdropping. The adversary could then (since the hash function is public knowledge) compute the digest of the original message and generate alternative messages looking for one with the same message digest. If she finds one, she could undetectably send the new message with the old authenticator. Therefore, security requires that the hash function have the *one-way* property: It must be computationally infeasible for an adversary to find any plaintext message that has the same digest as the original.

For a hash function to meet this requirement, its outputs must be fairly randomly distributed. For example, if digests are 128 bits long and randomly distributed, then you would need to try 2^{127} messages, on average, before finding a second message whose digest matches that of a given message. If the outputs are not randomly distributed—that is, if some outputs are much more likely than others—then for some messages you could find another message with the same digest much more easily than this, which would reduce the security of the algorithm. If you were instead just trying to find any *collision*—any two messages that produce the same digest—then you would need to compute the digests of only 2^{64} messages, on average. This surprising fact is the basis of the "birthday attack"—see the exercises for more details.

There are several common cryptographic hash algorithms, including Message Digest 5 (MD5) and Secure Hash Algorithm 1 (SHA-1). MD5 outputs a 128-bit digest, and SHA-1 outputs a 160-bit digest. Weaknesses of MD5 have been known for some time, which led to recommendations to shift from MD5 to SHA-1. More recently, researchers have discovered techniques that find SHA-1 collisions somewhat more efficiently than brute force, but they are not yet computationally feasible. Although *collision attacks* (attacks based on finding any collision) are not as great a risk as *preimage attacks* (attacks based on finding a second message that collides with a given first message), these are nonetheless serious weaknesses. NIST recommended phasing out SHA-1 by 2010, in favor of four variants of SHA that are collectively known as SHA-2. There is an ongoing competition to devise a new hash known as SHA-3.

When generating an encrypted message digest, the digest encryption could use either a symmetric-key cipher or a public-key cipher. If a public-key cipher is used, the digest would be encrypted using the sender's private key (the one we normally think of as being used for decryption), and the receiver—or anyone else—could decrypt the digest using the sender's public key.

A digest encrypted with a public key algorithm but using the private key is called a *digital signature* because it provides nonrepudiation like a written signature. The receiver of a message with a digital signature can prove to any third party that the sender really sent that message, because the third party can use the sender's public key to check for herself. (Symmetric-key encryption of a digest does not have this property because only the two participants know the key; furthermore, since both participants know the key, the alleged receiver could have created the message herself.) Any public-key cipher can be used for digital signatures. *Digital Signature Standard* (DSS) is a digital signature format that has been standardized by NIST. DSS signatures may use any one of three public-key ciphers, one based on RSA, another on ElGamal, and a third called the *Elliptic Curve Digital Signature Algorithm*.

Another kind of authenticator is similar, but instead of encrypting a hash it uses a hash-like function that takes a secret value (known to only the sender and the receiver) as a parameter, as illustrated in Figure 8.5. Such a function outputs an authenticator called a *message authentication code* (MAC). The sender appends the MAC to her plaintext message. The receiver recomputes the MAC using the plaintext and the secret value and compares that recomputed MAC to the received MAC.

A common variation on MACs is to apply a cryptographic hash (such as MD5 or SHA-1) to the concatenation of the plaintext message and

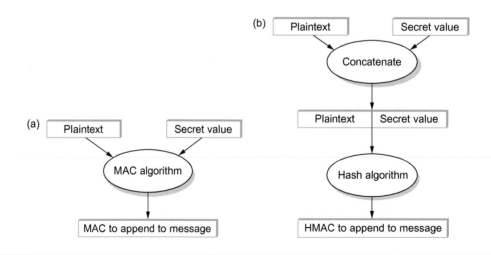

■ FIGURE 8.5 Computing a MAC (a) versus computing an HMAC (b).

the secret value, as illustrated in Figure 8.5. The resulting digest is called a *hashed message authentication code* (HMAC) since it is essentially a MAC. The HMAC, but not the secret value, is appended to the plaintext message. Only a receiver who knows the secret value can compute the correct HMAC to compare with the received HMAC. If it weren't for the one-way property of the hash, an adversary might be able to find the input that generated the HMAC and compare it to the plaintext message to determine the secret value.

Up to this point, we have been assuming that the message wasn't confidential, so the original message could be transmitted as plaintext. To add confidentiality to a message with an authenticator, it suffices to encrypt the concatenation of the entire message including its authenticator—the MAC, HMAC, or encrypted digest. Remember that, in practice, confidentiality is implemented using symmetric-key ciphers because they are so much faster than public-key ciphers. Furthermore, it costs little to include the authenticator in the encryption, and it increases security. A common simplification is to encrypt the message with its (raw) digest, such that the digest is only encrypted once; in this case, the entire ciphertext message is considered to be an authenticator.

Although authenticators may seem to solve the authentication problem, we will see in Section 8.3 that they are only the foundation of a solution. First, however, we address the issue of how participants obtain keys in the first place.

8.2 KEY PREDISTRIBUTION

To use ciphers and authenticators, the communicating participants need to know what keys to use. In the case of a symmetric-key cipher, how does a pair of participants obtain the key they share? In the case of a public-key cipher, how do participants know what public key belongs to a certain participant? The answer differs depending on whether the keys are short-lived *session keys* or longer-lived *predistributed keys*.

A session key is a key used to secure a single, relatively short episode of communication: a session. Each distinct session between a pair of participants uses a new session key, which is always a symmetric key for speed. The participants determine what session key to use by means of a protocol—a session key establishment protocol. A session key establishment protocol needs its own security (so that, for example, an adversary cannot learn the new session key); that security is based on the longer-lived predistributed keys.

There are several motivations for this division of labor between session keys and predistributed keys:

- Limiting the amount of time a key is used results in less time for computationally intensive attacks, less ciphertext for cryptanalysis, and less information exposed should the key be broken.
- Predistribution of symmetric keys is problematic.
- Public key ciphers are generally superior for authentication and session key establishment but too slow to use for encrypting entire messages for confidentiality.

This section explains how predistributed keys are distributed, and Section 8.3 will explain how session keys are then established. We henceforth use "Alice" and "Bob" to designate participants, as is common in the cryptography literature. Bear in mind that although we tend to refer to participants in anthropomorphic terms, we are more frequently concerned with the communication between software or hardware entities such as clients and servers that often have no direct relationship with any particular person.

8.2.1 Predistribution of Public Keys

The algorithms to generate a matched pair of public and private keys are publicly known, and software that does it is widely available. So, if Alice wanted to use a public-key cipher, she could generate her own pair of public and private keys, keep the private key hidden, and publicize the public key. But, how can she publicize her public key—assert that it belongs to her—in such a way that other participants can be sure it really belongs to her? Not via email or Web, because an adversary could forge an equally plausible claim that key x belongs to Alice when x really belongs to the adversary.

A complete scheme for certifying bindings between public keys and identities—what key belongs to whom—is called a *Public Key Infrastructure* (PKI). A PKI starts with the ability to verify identities and bind them to keys out of band. By "out of band," we mean something outside the network and the computers that comprise it, such as in the following scenarios. If Alice and Bob are individuals who know each other, then they could get together in the same room and Alice could give her public key to Bob directly, perhaps on a business card. If Bob is an organization, Alice the individual could present conventional identification, perhaps involving a photograph or fingerprints. If Alice and Bob are computers owned by the same company, then a system administrator could configure Bob with Alice's public key.

Establishing keys out of band doesn't sound like it would scale well, but it suffices to bootstrap a PKI. Bob's knowledge that Alice's key is x can be widely, scalably disseminated using a combination of digital signatures and a concept of trust. For example, suppose that you have received Bob's public key out of band and that you know enough about Bob to trust him on matters of keys and identities. Then Bob could send you a message asserting that Alice's key is x and—since you already know Bob's public key—you could authenticate the message as having come from Bob. (Remember that to digitally sign the statement Bob would append a cryptographic hash of it that has been encrypted using his private key.) Since you trust Bob to tell the truth, you would now know that Alice's key is x, even though you had never met her or exchanged a single message with her. Using digital signatures, Bob wouldn't even have to send you a message; he could simply create and publish a digitally signed statement that Alice's key is x. Such a digitally signed statement of a public key binding is called a *public key certificate*, or simply a certificate. Bob could send Alice a copy of the certificate, or post it on a website. If and when someone needs to verify Alice's public key, they could do so by getting a copy of the certificate, perhaps directly from Alice—as long as they trust Bob and know his public key. You can see how starting from a very small number of keys (in this case, just Bob's) you could build up a large set of trusted keys over time. Bob in this case is playing the role often referred to as a *certification authority* (CA), and much of today's Internet security depends on CAs. VeriSign® is one well-known commercial CA. We return to this topic below.

One of the major standards for certificates is known as X.509. This standard leaves a lot of details open, but specifies a basic structure. A certificate clearly must include:

- The identity of the entity being certified
- The public key of the entity being certified
- The identity of the signer

- The digital signature
- A digital signature algorithm identifier (which cryptographic hash and which cipher)

An optional component is an expiration time for the certificate. We will see a particular use of this feature below.

Since a certificate creates a binding between an identity and a public key, we should look more closely at what we mean by "identity." For example, a certificate that says, "This public key belongs to John Smith," may not be terribly useful if you can't tell which of the thousands of John Smiths is being identified. Thus, certificates must use a well-defined name space for the identities being certified; for example, certificates are often issued for email addresses and DNS domains.

There are different ways a PKI could formalize the notion of trust. We discuss the two main approaches.

Certification Authorities

In this model of trust, trust is binary; you either trust someone completely or not at all. Together with certificates, this allows the building of *chains of trust*. If X certifies that a certain public key belongs to Y, and then Y goes on to certify that another public key belongs to Z, then there exists a chain of certificates from X to Z, even though X and Z may have never met. If you know X's key—and you trust X and Y—then you can believe the certificate that gives Z's key. In other words, all you need is a chain of certificates, all signed by entities you trust, as long as it leads back to an entity whose key you already know.

A *certification authority* or *certificate authority* (CA) is an entity claimed (by someone) to be trustworthy for verifying identities and issuing public key certificates. There are commercial CAs, governmental CAs, and even free CAs. To use a CA, you must know its own key. You can learn that CA's key, however, if you can obtain a chain of CA-signed certificates that starts with a CA whose key you already know. Then you can believe any certificate signed by that new CA.

A common way to build such chains is to arrange them in a tree-structured hierarchy, as shown in Figure 8.6. If everyone has the public key of the root CA, then any participant can provide a chain of certificates to another participant and know that it will be sufficient to build a chain of trust for that participant.

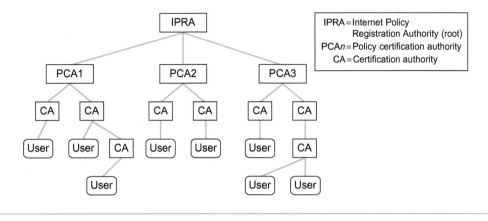

FIGURE 8.6 Tree-structured certification authority hierarchy.

There are some significant issues with building chains of trust. Most importantly, even if you are certain that you have the public key of the root CA, you need to be sure that every CA from the root on down is doing its job properly. If just one CA in the chain is willing to issue certificates to entities without verifying their identities, then what looks like a valid chain of certificates becomes meaningless. For example, a root CA might issue a certificate to a second-tier CA and thoroughly verify that the name on the certificate matches the business name of the CA, but that second-tier CA might be willing to sell certificates to anyone who asks, without verifying their identity. This problem gets worse the longer the chain of trust. X.509 certificates provide the option of restricting the set of entities that the subject of a certificate is, in turn, trusted to certify.

There can be more than one root to a certification tree, and this is common in securing Web transactions today, for example. Web browsers such as Firefox and Internet Explorer come pre-equipped with certificates for a set of CAs; in effect, the browser's producer has decided these CAs and their keys can be trusted. A user can also add CAs to those that their browser recognizes as trusted. These certificates are accepted by Secure Socket Layer (SSL)/Transport Layer Security (TLS), the protocol most often used to secure Web transactions, which we discuss below in Section 8.4.3. (If you are curious, you can poke around in the preferences settings for your browser and find the "view certificates" option to see how many CAs your browser is configured to trust.)

Web of Trust

An alternative model of trust is the *web of trust* exemplified by Pretty Good Privacy (PGP), which is further discussed in Section 8.4.3. PGP is a security system for email, so email addresses are the identities to which keys are bound and by which certificates are signed. In keeping with PGP's roots as protection against government intrusion, there are no CAs. Instead, every individual decides whom they trust and how much they trust them—in this model, trust is a matter of degree. In addition, a public key certificate can include a confidence level indicating how confident the signer is of the key binding claimed in the certificate, so a given user may have to have several certificates attesting to the same key binding before he is willing to trust it.

For example, suppose you have a certificate for Bob provided by Alice; you can assign a moderate level of trust to that certificate. However, if you have additional certificates for Bob that were provided by C and D, each of whom is also moderately trustworthy, that might considerably increase your level of confidence that the public key you have for Bob is valid. In short, PGP recognizes that the problem of establishing trust is quite a personal matter and gives users the raw material to make their own decisions, rather than assuming that they are all willing to trust in a single hierarchical structure of CAs. To quote Phil Zimmerman, the developer of PGP, "PGP is for people who prefer to pack their own parachutes."

PGP has become quite popular in the networking community, and PGP key-signing parties are a regular feature of IETF meetings. At these gatherings, an individual can

- Collect public keys from others whose identity he knows.
- Provide his public key to others.
- Get his public key signed by others, thus collecting certificates that will be persuasive to an increasingly large set of people.
- Sign the public key of other individuals, thus helping them build up their set of certificates that they can use to distribute their public keys.
- Collect certificates from other individuals whom he trusts enough to sign keys.

Thus, over time, a user will collect a set of certificates with varying degrees of trust.

Certificate Revocation

One issue that arises with certificates is how to revoke, or undo, a certificate. Why is this important? Suppose that you suspect that someone has discovered your private key. There may be any number of certificates in the universe that assert that you are the owner of the public key corresponding to that private key. The person who discovered your private key thus has everything he needs to impersonate you: valid certificates and your private key. To solve this problem, it would be nice to be able to revoke the certificates that bind your old, compromised key to your identity, so that the impersonator will no longer be able to persuade other people that he is you.

The basic solution to the problem is simple enough. Each CA can issue a *certificate revocation list* (CRL), which is a digitally signed list of certificates that have been revoked. The CRL is periodically updated and made publicly available. Because it is digitally signed, it can just be posted on a website. Now, when Alice receives a certificate for Bob that she wants to verify, she will first consult the latest CRL issued by the CA. As long as the certificate has not been revoked, it is valid. Note that, if all certificates have unlimited life spans, the CRL would always be getting longer, since you could never take a certificate off the CRL for fear that some copy of the revoked certificate might be used. For this reason, it is common to attach an expiration date to a certificate when it is issued. Thus, we can limit the length of time that a revoked certificate needs to stay on a CRL. As soon as its original expiration date is passed, it can be removed from the CRL.

8.2.2 **Predistribution of Symmetric Keys**

If Alice wants to use a secret-key cipher to communicate with Bob, she can't just pick a key and send it to to him because, without already having a key, they can't encrypt this key to keep it confidential and they can't authenticate each other. As with public keys, some predistribution scheme is needed. Predistribution is harder for symmetric keys than for public keys for two obvious reasons:

- While only one public key per entity is sufficient for authentication and confidentiality, there must be a symmetric key for each pair of entities who wish to communicate. If there are N entities, that means $N(N-1)/2$ keys.

- Unlike public keys, secret keys must be kept secret.

In summary, there are a lot more keys to distribute, and you can't use certificates that everyone can read.

The most common solution is to use a *Key Distribution Center* (KDC). A KDC is a trusted entity that shares a secret key with each other entity. This brings the number of keys down to a more manageable $N - 1$, few enough to establish out of band for some applications. When Alice wishes to communicate with Bob, that communication does not travel via the KDC. Rather, the KDC participates in a protocol that authenticates Alice and Bob—using the keys that the KDC already shares with each of them—and generates a new session key for them to use. Then Alice and Bob communicate directly using their session key. Kerberos (Section 8.3.3) is a widely used system based on this approach.

8.3 AUTHENTICATION PROTOCOLS

We described how to encrypt messages and build authenticators in Section 8.1 and how to predistribute the necessary keys in Section 8.2. It might seem as if all we have to do to make a protocol secure is append an authenticator to every message and, if we want confidentiality, encrypt the message.

There are two main reasons why it's not that simple. First, there is the problem of a *replay attack*: an adversary retransmitting a copy of a message that was previously sent. If the message was an order you had placed on a website, for example, then the replayed message would appear to the website as though you had ordered more of the same. Even though it wasn't the original incarnation of the message, its authenticator would still be valid; after all, the message was created by you, and it wasn't modified. In a variation of this attack called a *suppress-replay attack*, an adversary might merely delay your message (by intercepting and later replaying it), so that it is received at a time when it is no longer appropriate. For example, an adversary could delay your order to buy stock from an auspicious time to a time when you would not have wanted to buy. Although this message would in a sense be the original, it wouldn't be timely. Originality and timeliness may be considered aspects of integrity. Ensuring them will in most cases require a nontrivial, back-and-forth protocol.

The other problem we have not yet solved is how to establish a session key. A session key is a symmetric-key cipher key generated on the fly and used for just one session as described in Section 8.2. This too involves a nontrivial protocol.

What these two issues have in common is authentication. If a message is not original and timely, then from a practical standpoint we want to consider it as not being authentic, not being from whom it claims to be. And, obviously, when you are arranging to share a new session key with someone, you want to know you are sharing it with the right person. Usually, authentication protocols establish a session key at the same time, so that at the end of the protocol Alice and Bob have authenticated each other and they have a new symmetric key to use. Without a new session key, the protocol would just authenticate Alice and Bob at one point in time; a session key allows them to efficiently authenticate subsequent messages. Generally, session key establishment protocols perform authentication (a notable exception is Diffie–Hellman; see Section 8.3.4), so the terms *authentication protocol* and *session key establishment protocol* are almost synonymous.

There is a core set of techniques used to ensure originality and timeliness in authentication protocols. We describe those techniques before moving on to particular protocols.

8.3.1 Originality and Timeliness Techniques

We have seen that authenticators alone do not enable us to detect messages that are not original or timely. One approach is to include a timestamp in the message. Obviously the timestamp itself must be tamperproof, so it must be covered by the authenticator. The primary drawback to timestamps is that they require distributed clock synchronization. Since our system would then depend on synchronization, the clock synchronization itself would need to be defended against security threats, in addition to the usual challenges of clock synchronization. Another issue is that distributed clocks are synchronized to only a certain degree—a certain margin of error. Thus, the timing integrity provided by timestamps is only as good as the degree of synchronization.

Another approach is to include a *nonce*—a random number used only once—in the message. Participants can then detect replay attacks by checking whether a nonce has been used previously. Unfortunately, this requires keeping track of past nonces, of which a great many could accumulate. One solution is to combine the use of timestamps and nonces, so that nonces are required to be unique only within a certain span of time.

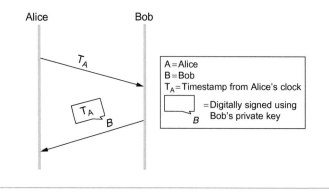

That makes ensuring uniqueness of nonces manageable while requiring only loose synchronization of clocks.

Another solution to the shortcomings of timestamps and nonces is to use one or both of them in a *challenge–response* protocol. Suppose we use a timestamp. In a challenge–response protocol, Alice sends Bob a timestamp, challenging Bob to encrypt it in a response message (if they share a symmetric key) or digitally sign it in a response message (if Bob has a public key, as in Figure 8.7). The encrypted timestamp is like an authenticator that additionally proves timeliness. Alice can easily check the timeliness of the timestamp in a response from Bob since that timestamp comes from Alice's own clock—no distributed clock synchronization needed. Suppose instead that the protocol uses nonces. Then Alice need only keep track of those nonces for which responses are currently outstanding and haven't been outstanding too long; any purported response with an unrecognized nonce must be bogus.

The beauty of challenge–response, which might otherwise seem excessively complex, is that it combines timeliness and authentication; after all, only Bob (and possibly Alice, if it's a symmetric-key cipher) knows the key necessary to encrypt the never before seen timestamp or nonce. Timestamps or nonces are used in most of the authentication protocols that follow.

8.3.2 Public-Key Authentication Protocols

In the following discussion, we assume that Alice and Bob's public keys have been predistributed to each other via some means such as a PKI

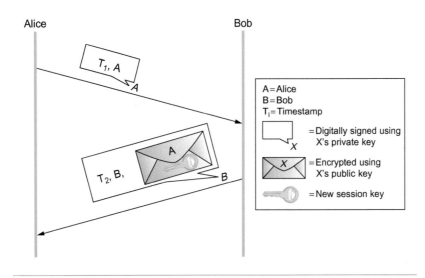

Alice   Bob

T_1, A

A

$A=$Alice
$B=$Bob
$T_i=$Timestamp

☐ $=$ Digitally signed using
  X X's private key

✉ X $=$ Encrypted using
  X's public key

🔑 $=$ New session key

$T_2, B,$ A B

■ FIGURE 8.8 A public-key authentication protocol that depends on synchronization.

(Section 8.2.1). We mean this to include the case where Alice includes her certificate in her first message to Bob, and the case where Bob searches for a certificate about Alice when he receives her first message.

This first protocol (Figure 8.8) relies on Alice and Bob's clocks being synchronized. Alice sends Bob a message with a timestamp and her identity in plaintext plus her digital signature. Bob uses the digital signature to authenticate the message and the timestamp to verify its freshness. Bob sends back a message with a timestamp and his identity in plaintext, as well as a new session key encrypted (for confidentiality) using Alice's public key, all digitally signed. Alice can verify the authenticity and freshness of the message, so she knows she can trust the new session key. To deal with imperfect clock synchronization, the timestamps could be augmented with nonces.

The second protocol (Figure 8.9) is similar but does not rely on clock synchronization. In this protocol, Alice again sends Bob a digitally signed message with a timestamp and her identity. Because their clocks aren't synchronized, Bob cannot be sure that the message is fresh. Bob sends back a digitally signed message with Alice's original timestamp, his own new timestamp, and his identity. Alice can verify the freshness of Bob's reply by comparing her current time against the timestamp that originated with her. She then sends Bob a digitally signed message with his

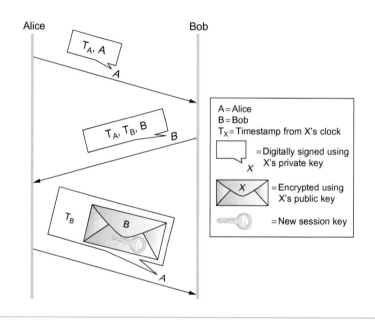

■ **FIGURE 8.9** A public-key authentication protocol that does not depend on synchronization. Alice checks her own timestamp against her own clock, and likewise for Bob.

original timestamp and a new session key encrypted using Bob's public key. Bob can verify the freshness of the message because the timestamp came from his clock, so he knows he can trust the new session key. The timestamps essentially serve as convenient nonces, and indeed this protocol could use nonces instead.

8.3.3 Symmetric-Key Authentication Protocols

As explained in Section 8.2.2, only in fairly small systems is it practical to predistribute symmetric keys to every pair of entities. We focus here on larger systems, where each entity would have its own *master key* shared only with a Key Distribution Center (KDC). In this case, symmetric-key-based authentication protocols involve three parties: Alice, Bob, and a KDC. The end product of the authentication protocol is a session key shared between Alice and Bob that they will use to communicate directly, without involving the KDC.

The Needham–Schroeder authentication protocol is illustrated in Figure 8.10. Note that the KDC doesn't actually authenticate Alice's initial message and doesn't communicate with Bob at all. Instead, the KDC

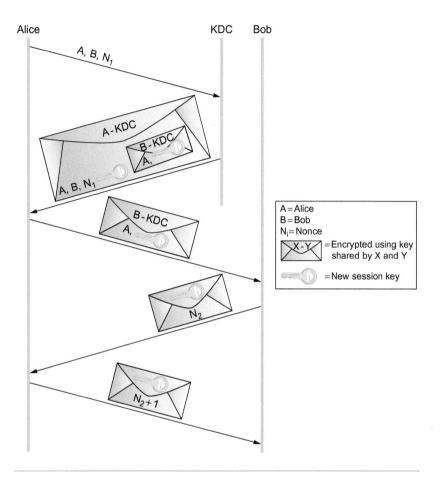

A = Alice
B = Bob
N_i = Nonce

$\boxed{X-Y}$ = Encrypted using key shared by X and Y

= New session key

■ FIGURE 8.10 The Needham–Schroeder authentication protocol.

uses its knowledge of Alice's and Bob's master keys to construct a reply that would be useless to anyone other than Alice (because only Alice can decrypt it) and contains the necessary ingredients for Alice and Bob to perform the rest of the authentication protocol themselves.

The nonce in the first two messages is to assure Alice that the KDC's reply is fresh. The second and third messages include the new session key and Alice's identifier, encrypted together using Bob's master key. It is a sort of symmetric-key version of a public-key certificate; it is in effect a signed statement by the KDC (because the KDC is the only entity besides Bob who knows Bob's master key) that the enclosed session key is owned by Alice and Bob. Although the nonce in the last two messages is intended to assure Bob that the third message was fresh, there is a flaw in this reasoning—see Exercise 4.

Kerberos

Kerberos is an authentication system based on the Needham–Schroeder protocol and specialized for client/server environments. Originally developed at MIT, it has been standardized by the IETF and is available as both open source and commercial products. We will focus here on some of Kerberos's interesting innovations.

Kerberos clients are generally human users, and users authenticate themselves using passwords. Alice's master key, shared with the KDC, is derived from her password—if you know the password, you can compute the key. Kerberos assumes anyone can physically access any client machine; therefore, it is important to minimize the exposure of Alice's password or master key not just in the network but also on any machine where she logs in. Kerberos takes advantage of Needham–Schroeder to accomplish this. In Needham-Schroeder, the only time Alice needs to use her password is when decrypting the reply from the KDC. Kerberos client-side software waits until the KDC's reply arrives, prompts Alice to enter her password, computes the master key and decrypts the KDC's reply, and then erases all information about the password and master key to minimize its exposure. Also note that the only sign a user sees of Kerberos is when the user is prompted for a password.

In Needham–Schroeder, the KDC's reply to Alice plays two roles: It gives her the means to prove her identity (only Alice can decrypt the reply), and it gives her a sort of symmetric-key certificate or "ticket" to present to Bob—the session key and Alice's identifier, encrypted with Bob's master key. In Kerberos, those two functions—and the KDC itself, in effect—are split up (Figure 8.11). A trusted server called an Authentication Server (AS) plays the first KDC role of providing Alice with something she can use to prove her identity—not to Bob this time, but to a second trusted server called a Ticket Granting Server (TGS). The TGS plays the second KDC role, replying to Alice with a ticket she can present to Bob. The attraction of this scheme is that if Alice needs to communicate with several servers, not just Bob, then she can get tickets for each of them from the TGS without going back to the AS.

In the client/server application domain for which Kerberos is intended, it is reasonable to assume a degree of clock synchronization. This

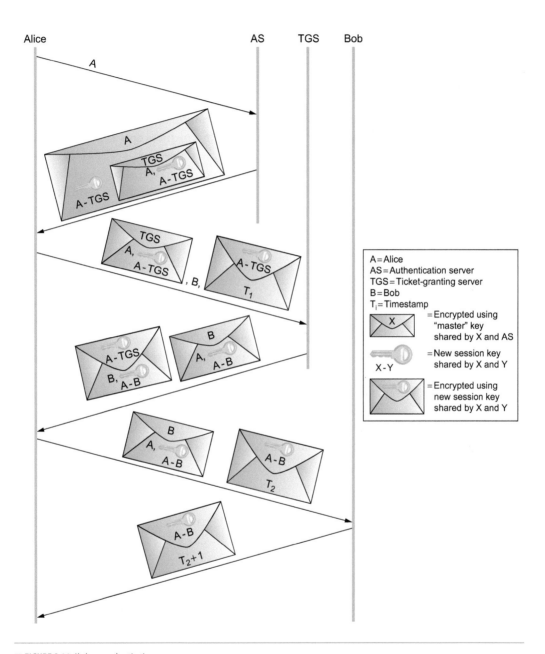

A = Alice
AS = Authentication server
TGS = Ticket-granting server
B = Bob
T_i = Timestamp

☐ = Encrypted using "master" key shared by X and AS

☐ = New session key shared by X and Y

☐ = Encrypted using new session key shared by X and Y

■ FIGURE 8.11 Kerberos authentication.

allows Kerberos to use timestamps and lifespans instead of Needham–Shroeder's nonces, and thereby eliminate the Needham-Schroeder security weakness explored in Exercise 4. Kerberos supports a choice of cryptographic algorithms including the hashes SHA-1 and MD5 and the symmetric-key ciphers AES, 3DES, and DES.

8.3.4 Diffie–Hellman Key Agreement

The Diffie–Hellman key agreement protocol establishes a session key without using any predistributed keys. The messages exchanged between Alice and Bob can be read by anyone able to eavesdrop, and yet the eavesdropper won't know the session key that Alice and Bob end up with. On the other hand, Diffie–Hellman doesn't authenticate the participants. Since it is rarely useful to communicate securely without being sure whom you're communicating with, Diffie–Hellman is usually augmented in some way to provide authentication. One of the main uses of Diffie–Hellman is in the Internet Key Exchange (IKE) protocol, a central part of the IP Security (IPsec) architecture.

The Diffie–Hellman protocol has two parameters, p and g, both of which are public and may be used by all the users in a particular system. Parameter p must be a prime number. The integers $\bmod\, p$ (short for modulo p) are 0 through $p-1$, since $x \bmod p$ is the remainder after x is divided by p, and form what mathematicians call a *group* under multiplication. Parameter g (usually called a generator) must be a *primitive root* of p: For every number n from 1 through $p-1$ there must be some value k such that $n = g^k \bmod p$. For example, if p were the prime number 5 (a real system would use a much larger number), then we might choose 2 to be the generator g since:

$$1 = 2^0 \bmod p$$

$$2 = 2^1 \bmod p$$

$$3 = 2^3 \bmod p$$

$$4 = 2^2 \bmod p$$

Suppose Alice and Bob want to agree on a shared symmetric key. Alice and Bob, and everyone else, already know the values of p and g. Alice generates a random private value a and Bob generates a random private value b. Both a and b are drawn from the set of integers $\{1, \ldots, p-1\}$. Alice and Bob derive their corresponding public values—the values they will send to each other unencrypted—as follows. Alice's public value is

$$g^a \bmod p$$

and Bob's public value is

$$g^b \bmod p$$

They then exchange their public values. Finally, Alice computes

$$g^{ab} \bmod p = (g^b \bmod p)^a \bmod p$$

and Bob computes

$$g^{ba} \bmod p = (g^a \bmod p)^b \bmod p.$$

Alice and Bob now have $g^{ab} \bmod p$ (which is equal to $g^{ba} \bmod p$) as their shared symmetric key.

Any eavesdropper would know p, g, and the two public values $g^a \bmod p$ and $g^b \bmod p$. If only the eavesdropper could determine a or b, she could easily compute the resulting key. Determining a or b from that information is, however, computationally infeasible for suitably large p, a, and b; it is known as the *discrete logarithm problem.*

On the other hand, there is the problem of Diffie–Hellman's lack of authentication. One attack that can take advantage of this is the *man-in-the-middle attack.* Suppose Mallory is an adversary with the ability to intercept messages. Mallory already knows p and g since they are public, and she generates random private values c and d to use with Alice and Bob, respectively. When Alice and Bob send their public values to each other, Mallory intercepts them and sends her own public values, as in Figure 8.12. The result is that Alice and Bob each end up unknowingly sharing a key with Mallory instead of each other.

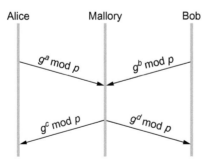

■ FIGURE 8.12 A man-in-the-middle attack.

A variant of Diffie–Hellman sometimes called *fixed Diffie–Hellman* supports authentication of one or both participants. It relies on certificates that are similar to public key certificates but instead certify the Diffie–Hellman public parameters of an entity. For example, such a certificate would state that Alice's Diffie–Hellman parameters are p, g, and $g^a \bmod p$ (note that the value of a would still be known only to Alice). Such a certificate would assure Bob that the other participant in Diffie–Hellman is Alice—or else the other participant won't be able to compute the secret key, because she won't know a. If both participants have certificates for their Diffie–Hellman parameters, they can authenticate each other. If just one has a certificate, then just that one can be authenticated. This is useful in some situations; for example, when one participant is a web server and the other is an arbitrary client, the client can authenticate the web server and establish a session key for confidentiality before sending a credit card number to the web server.

8.4 EXAMPLE SYSTEMS

At this point, we have seen many of the components that are required to provide one or two aspects of security. These components include cryptographic algorithms, key predistribution mechanisms, and authentication protocols. In this section, we examine some complete systems that use these components.

These systems can be roughly categorized by the protocol layer at which they operate. Systems that operate at the application layer include Pretty Good Privacy (PGP), which provides electronic mail security, and Secure Shell (SSH), a secure remote login facility. At the transport layer, there is the IETF's Transport Layer Security (TLS) standard and the older protocol from which it derives, Secure Socket Layer (SSL). The IPsec (IP Security) protocols, as their name implies, operate at the IP (network) layer. 802.11i provides security at the link layer of wireless networks. This section describes the salient features of each of these approaches.

You might reasonably wonder why security has to be provided at so many different layers. One reason is that different threats require different defensive measures, and this often translates into securing a different protocol layer. For example, if your main concern is with a person in the building next door snooping on your traffic as it flows between your laptop and your 802.11 access point, then you probably want security at the link layer. However, if you want to be really sure you are connected to your bank's website and preventing all the data that you send to the bank from being read by curious employees of some Internet service provider, then something that extends all the way from your machine to the bank's server—like the transport layer—may be the right place to secure the traffic. As is often the case, there is no one-size-fits-all solution.

The security systems described below have the ability to vary which cryptographic algorithms they use. The idea of making a security system algorithm independent is a very good one, because you never know when your favorite cryptographic algorithm might be proved to be insufficiently strong for your purposes. It would be nice if you could quickly change to a new algorithm without having to change the protocol specification or implementation. Note the analogy to being able to change keys without changing the algorithm; if one of your cryptographic algorithms turns out to be flawed, it would be great if your entire security architecture didn't need an immediate redesign.

8.4.1 Pretty Good Privacy (PGP)

Pretty Good Privacy (PGP) is a widely used approach to providing security for electronic mail. It provides authentication, confidentiality, data integrity, and nonrepudiation. Originally devised by Phil Zimmerman, it has evolved into an IETF standard known as OpenPGP. As we saw in Section 8.2, PGP is notable for using a "web of trust" model for distribution of keys rather than a tree-like hierarchy.

PGP's confidentiality and receiver authentication depend on the receiver of an email message having a public key that is known to the sender. To provide sender authentication and nonrepudiation, the sender must have a public key that is known by the receiver. These public keys are predistributed using certificates and a web-of-trust PKI as described in Section 8.2.1. PGP supports RSA and DSS for public key certificates. These certificates may additionally specify which cryptographic algorithms are supported or preferred by the key's owner. The certificates provide bindings between email addresses and public keys.

Consider the following example of PGP being used to provide both sender authentication and confidentiality. Suppose Alice has a message to email to Bob. Alice's PGP application goes through the steps illustrated in Figure 8.13. First, the message is digitally signed by Alice; MD5, SHA-1, and the SHA-2 family are among the hashes that may be used in

Hi... = The plaintext message

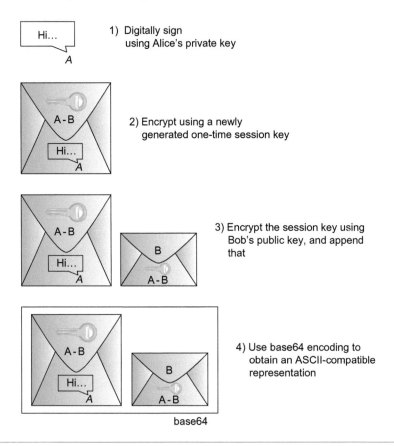

1) Digitally sign
   using Alice's private key

2) Encrypt using a newly
   generated one-time session key

3) Encrypt the session key using
   Bob's public key, and append
   that

4) Use base64 encoding to
   obtain an ASCII-compatible
   representation

base64

■ FIGURE 8.13 PGP's steps to prepare a message for emailing from Alice to Bob.

the digital signature. Her PGP application then generates a new session key for just this one message; AES and 3DES are among the supported symmetric-key ciphers. The digitally signed message is encrypted using the session key, then the session key itself is encrypted using Bob's public key and appended to the message. Alice's PGP application reminds her of the level of trust she had previously assigned to Bob's public key, based on the number of certificates she has for Bob and the trustworthiness of the individuals who signed the certificates. Finally, not for security but because email messages have to be sent in ASCII, a base64 encoding (as described in Section 9.1.1) is applied to the message to convert it to an ASCII-compatible representation. Upon receiving the PGP message in an email, Bob's PGP application reverses this process step-by-step to obtain the original plaintext message and confirm Alice's digital signature—and reminds Bob of the level of trust he has in Alice's public key.

Email has particular characteristics that allow PGP to embed an adequate authentication protocol in this one-message data transmission protocol, avoiding the need for any prior message exchange (and sidestepping some of the complexities described earlier in Section 8.3). Alice's digital signature suffices to authenticate her. Although there is no proof that the message is timely, legitimate email isn't guaranteed to be timely either. There is also no proof that the message is original, but Bob is an email user and probably a fault-tolerant human who can recover from duplicate emails (which, again, are not out of the question under normal operation anyway). Alice can be sure that only Bob could read the message because the session key was encrypted with his public key. Although this protocol doesn't prove to Alice that Bob is actually there and received the email, an authenticated email from Bob back to Alice could do this.

The preceding discussion gives a good example of why application-layer security mechanisms can be helpful. Only with a full knowledge of how the application works can you make the right choices about which attacks to defend against (like forged email) versus which to ignore (like delayed or replayed email).

8.4.2 Secure Shell (SSH)

LAB 13:
VPN

The Secure Shell (SSH) protocol is used to provide a remote login service and is intended to replace the less secure Telnet and rlogin programs used in the early days of the Internet. (SSH can also be used to remotely execute commands and transfer files, like the Unix rsh and rcp commands, respectively, but we will focus first on how SSH supports remote login.) SSH is most often used to provide strong client/server authentication/message integrity—where the SSH client runs on the user's desktop machine and the SSH server runs on some remote machine that the user wants to log into—but it also supports confidentiality. Telnet and rlogin provide none of these capabilities. Note that "SSH" is often used to refer to both the SSH protocol and applications that use it; you need to figure out which from the context.

To better appreciate the importance of SSH on today's Internet, consider a couple of the scenarios where it is used. Telecommuters, for example, often subscribe to ISPs that offer high-speed cable modem or DSL service, and they use these ISPs, and some chain of other ISPs as well, to reach machines operated by their employer. This means that when a telecommuter logs into a machine inside his employer's data center, both the passwords and all the data sent or received potentially passes through any number of untrusted networks. SSH provides a way to encrypt the data sent over these connections and to improve the strength of the authentication mechanism used to log in. A similar usage of SSH is remote login to a router, perhaps to change its configuration or read its log files; clearly, a network administrator wants to be sure that he can log into a router securely and that unauthorized parties can neither log in nor intercept the commands sent to the router or output sent back to the administrator.

The latest version of SSH, version 2, consists of three protocols:

- SSH-TRANS, a transport layer protocol
- SSH-AUTH, an authentication protocol
- SSH-CONN, a connection protocol

We focus on the first two, which are involved in remote login. We briefly discuss the purpose of SSH-CONN at the end of the section.

SSH-TRANS provides an encrypted channel between the client and server machines. It runs on top of a TCP connection. Any time a user uses an SSH application to log into a remote machine, the first step is to set up an SSH-TRANS channel between those two machines. The two machines establish this secure channel by first having the client authenticate the server using RSA. Once authenticated, the client and server establish a session key that they will use to encrypt any data sent over the channel. This high-level description skims over several details, including the fact that the SSH-TRANS protocol includes a negotiation of the encryption algorithm the two sides are going to use. For example, AES is commonly selected. Also, SSH-TRANS includes a message integrity check of all data exchanged over the channel.

The one issue we can't skim over is how the client came to possess the server's public key that it needs to authenticate the server. Strange as it may sound, the server tells the client its public key at connection time. The first time a client connects to a particular server, the SSH application warns the user that it has never talked to this machine before and asks if the user wants to continue. Although it is a risky thing to do, because

SSH is effectively not able to authenticate the server, users often say "yes" to this question. The SSH application then remembers the server's public key, and the next time the user connects to that same machine it compares this saved key with the one the server responds with. If they are the same, SSH authenticates the server. If they are different, however, the SSH application again warns the user that something is amiss, and the user is then given an opportunity to abort the connection. Alternatively, the prudent user can learn the server's public key through some out-of-band mechanism, save it on the client machine, and thus never take the "first time" risk.

Once the SSH-TRANS channel exists, the next step is for the user to actually log into the machine, or more specifically, authenticate himself or herself to the server. SSH allows three different mechanisms for doing this. First, since the two machines are communicating over a secure channel, it is OK for the user to simply send his or her password to the server. This is not a safe thing to do when using Telnet since the password would be sent in the clear, but in the case of SSH the password is encrypted in the SSH-TRANS channel. The second mechanism uses public-key encryption. This requires that the user has already placed his or her public key on the server. The third mechanism, called *host-based authentication*, basically says that any user claiming to be so-and-so from a certain set of trusted hosts is automatically believed to be that same user on the server. Host-based authentication requires that the client *host* authenticate itself to the server when they first connect; standard SSH-TRANS only authenticates the server by default.

The main thing you should take away from this discussion is that SSH is a fairly straightforward application of the protocols and algorithms we have seen throughout this chapter. However, what sometimes makes SSH a challenge to understand is all the keys a user has to create and manage, where the exact interface is operating system dependent. For example, the OpenSSH package that runs on most Unix machines supports a ssh-keygen command that can be used to create public/private key pairs. These keys are then stored in various files in directory .ssh in the user's home directory. For example, file /.ssh/known_hosts records the keys for all the hosts the user has logged into, file /.ssh/authorized_keys contains the public keys needed to authenticate the user when he or she logs into this machine (i.e., they are used on the server side), and file /.ssh/identity contains the private keys needed to authenticate the user on remote machines (i.e., they are used on the client side).

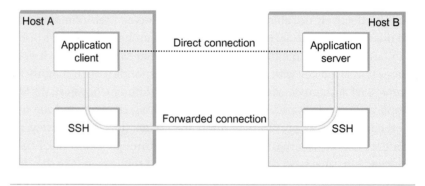

Finally, SSH has proven so useful as a system for securing remote login, it has been extended to also support other applications, such as sending and receiving email. The idea is to run these applications over a secure "SSH tunnel." This capability is called *port forwarding*, and it uses the SSH-CONN protocol. The idea is illustrated in Figure 8.14, where we see a client on host A indirectly communicating with a server on host B by forwarding its traffic through an SSH connection. The mechanism is called *port forwarding* because when messages arrive at the well-known SSH port on the server, SSH first decrypts the contents and then "forwards" the data to the actual port at which the server is listening. This is just another sort of tunnel of the sort introduced in Section 3.2.9, which in this case happens to provide confidentiality and authentication. It's possible to provide a form of virtual private network (VPN) using SSH tunnels in this way.

8.4.3 Transport Layer Security (TLS, SSL, HTTPS)

To understand the design goals and requirements for the Transport Layer Security (TLS) standard and the Secure Socket Layer (SSL) on which TLS is based, it is helpful to consider one of the main problems that they are intended to solve. As the World Wide Web became popular and commercial enterprises began to take an interest in it, it became clear that some level of security would be necessary for transactions on the Web. The canonical example of this is making purchases by credit card. There are several issues of concern when sending your credit card information to a computer on the Web. First, you might worry that the information would be intercepted in transit and subsequently used to make unauthorized purchases. You might also worry about the details of a transaction being modified, such as changing the purchase amount. And you would certainly like to know that the computer to which you are sending your credit card information is in fact one belonging to the vendor in question and not some other party. Thus, we immediately see a need for confidentiality, integrity, and authentication in Web transactions. The first widely used solution to this problem was SSL, originally developed by Netscape and subsequently the basis for the IETF's TLS standard.

The designers of SSL and TLS recognized that these problems were not specific to Web transactions (i.e., those using HTTP) and instead built a general-purpose protocol that sits between an application protocol such as HTTP and a transport protocol such as TCP. The reason for calling this "transport layer security" is that, from the application's perspective, this protocol layer looks just like a normal transport protocol except for the fact that it is secure. That is, the sender can open connections and deliver bytes for transmission, and the secure transport layer will get them to the receiver with the necessary confidentiality, integrity, and authentication. By running the secure transport layer on top of TCP, all of the normal features of TCP (reliability, flow control, congestion control, etc.) are also provided to the application. This arrangement of protocol layers is depicted in Figure 8.15.

When HTTP is used in this way, it is known as HTTPS (Secure HTTP). In fact, HTTP itself is unchanged. It simply delivers data to and accepts data from the SSL/TLS layer rather than TCP. For convenience, a default TCP port has been assigned to HTTPS (443). That is, if you try to connect to a server on TCP port 443, you will likely find yourself talking to the SSL/TLS protocol, which will pass your data through to HTTP provided all goes well with authentication and decryption. Although standalone implementations of SSL/TLS are available, it is more common for an

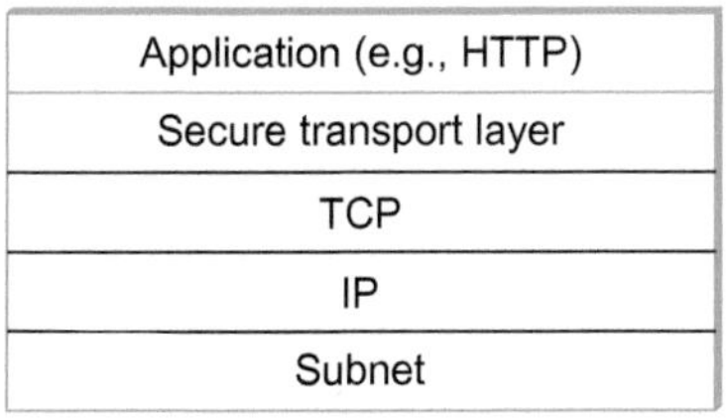

| Application (e.g., HTTP) |
| Secure transport layer |
| TCP |
| IP |
| Subnet |

■ FIGURE 8.15 Secure transport layer inserted between application and TCP layers.

implementation to be bundled with applications that need it, primarily web browsers.

In the remainder of our discussion of transport layer security, we focus on TLS. Although SSL and TLS are unfortunately not interoperable, they differ in only minor ways, so nearly all of this description of TLS applies to SSL.

The Handshake Protocol

A pair of TLS participants negotiate at runtime which cryptography to use. The participants negotiate a choice of:

- Data integrity hash (MD5, SHA-1, etc.), used to implement HMACs
- Symmetric-key cipher for confidentiality (among the possibilities are DES, 3DES, and AES)
- Session key establishment approach (among the possibilities are Diffie–Hellman, fixed Diffie–Hellman, and public-key authentication protocols using RSA or DSS)

Interestingly, the participants may also negotiate the use of a compression algorithm, not because this offers any security benefits, but because it's easy to do when you're negotiating all this other stuff and you've already decided to do some expensive per-byte operations on the data.

In TLS, the confidentiality cipher uses two keys, one for each direction, and similarly two initialization vectors. The HMACs are likewise keyed with different keys for the two participants. Thus, regardless of the choice of cipher and hash, a TLS session requires effectively six keys. TLS derives all of them from a single shared *master secret*. The master secret is a 384-bit (48-byte) value that in turn is derived in part from the "session key" that results from TLS's session key establishment protocol.

The part of TLS that negotiates the choices and establishes the shared master secret is called the *handshake protocol*. (Actual data transfer is performed by TLS's *record protocol*.) The handshake protocol is at heart a session key establishment protocol, with a master secret instead of a session key. Since TLS supports a choice of approaches to session key establishment, these call for correspondingly different protocol variants. Furthermore, the handshake protocol supports a choice between mutual authentication of both participants, authentication of just one participant (this is the most common case, such as authenticating a website but not a user), or no authentication at all (anonymous Diffie–Hellman). Thus,

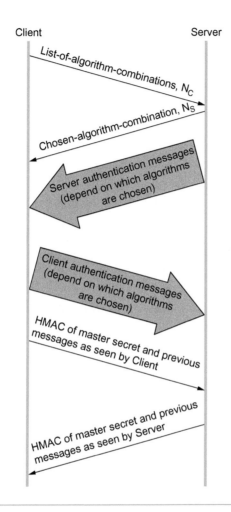

■ FIGURE 8.16 Handshake protocol to establish TLS session.

the handshake protocol knits together several session key establishment protocols into a single protocol.

Figure 8.16 shows the handshake protocol at a high level. The client initially sends a list of the combinations of cryptographic algorithms that it supports, in decreasing order of preference. The server responds, giving the single combination of cryptographic algorithms it selected from those listed by the client. These messages also contain a *client nonce* and a *server nonce*, respectively, that will be incorporated in generating the master secret later.

At this point, the negotiation phase is complete. The server now sends additional messages based on the negotiated session key establishment protocol. That could involve sending a public-key certificate or a set of Diffie–Hellman parameters. If the server requires authentication of the client, it sends a separate message indicating that. The client then responds with its part of the negotiated key exchange protocol.

Now the client and server each have the information necessary to generate the master secret. The "session key" that they exchanged is not in fact a key, but instead what TLS calls a *pre-master secret*. The master secret is computed (using a published algorithm) from this pre-master secret, the client nonce, and the server nonce. Using the keys derived from the master secret, the client then sends a message that includes a hash of all the preceding handshake messages, to which the server responds with a similar message. This enables them to detect any discrepancies between the handshake messages they sent and received, such as would result, for example, if a man in the middle modified the initial unencrypted client message to weaken its choices of cryptographic algorithms.

The Record Protocol

Within a session established by the handshake protocol, TLS's record protocol adds confidentiality and integrity to the underlying transport service. Messages handed down from the application layer are:

1. Fragmented or coalesced into blocks of a convenient size for the following steps
2. Optionally compressed
3. Integrity-protected using an HMAC
4. Encrypted using a symmetric-key cipher
5. Passed to the transport layer (normally TCP) for transmission

The record protocol uses an HMAC as an authenticator. The HMAC uses whichever hash algorithm (MD5, SHA-1, etc.) was negotiated by the participants. The client and server have different keys to use when computing HMACs, making them even harder to break. Furthermore, each record protocol message is assigned a sequence number, which is included when the HMAC is computed—even though the sequence number is never explicit in the message. This implicit sequence number prevents replays or reorderings of messages. This is needed because, although TCP can deliver sequential, unduplicated messages to the layer above it under normal assumptions, those assumptions do not include an adversary that can intercept TCP messages, modify messages, or send bogus ones. On the other hand, it is TCP's delivery guarantees that make it possible for TLS to rely on a legitimate TLS message having the next implicit sequence number in order.

Another interesting feature of the TLS protocol, which is quite a useful feature for Web transactions, is the ability to resume a session. To understand the motivation for this, it is helpful to understand how HTTP makes use of TCP connections. (The details of HTTP are presented in Section 9.1.2.) Each HTTP operation, such as getting a page of text or an image from a server, requires a new TCP connection to be opened. Retrieving a single page with a number of embedded graphical objects might take many TCP connections. Recall from Section 5.2 that opening a TCP connection requires a three-way handshake before data transmission can start. Once the TCP connection is ready to accept data, the client would then need to start the TLS handshake protocol, taking at least another two round-trip times (and consuming some amount of processing resources and network bandwidth) before actual application data could be sent. The resumption capability of TLS alleviates this problem.

Session resumption is an optimization of the handshake that can be used in those cases where the client and the server have already established some shared state in the past. The client simply includes the session ID from a previously established session in its initial handshake message. If the server finds that it still has state for that session, and the resumption option was negotiated when that session was originally created, then the server can reply to the client with an indication of success, and data transmission can begin using the algorithms and parameters previously negotiated. If the session ID does not match any session state cached at the server, or if resumption was not allowed for the session, then the server will fall back to the normal handshake process.

8.4.4 IP Security (IPsec)

Probably the most ambitious of all the efforts to integrate security into the Internet happens at the IP layer. Support for IPsec, as the architecture is called, is optional in IPv4 but mandatory in IPv6.

IPsec is really a framework (as opposed to a single protocol or system) for providing all the security services discussed throughout this chapter. IPsec provides three degrees of freedom. First, it is highly modular, allowing users (or more likely, system administrators) to select from a variety of cryptographic algorithms and specialized security protocols. Second, IPsec allows users to select from a large menu of security properties, including access control, integrity, authentication, originality, and confidentiality. Third, IPsec can be used to protect narrow streams (e.g., packets belonging to a particular TCP connection being sent between a pair of hosts) or wide streams (e.g., all packets flowing between a pair of routers).

When viewed from a high level, IPsec consists of two parts. The first part is a pair of protocols that implement the available security services. They are the Authentication Header (AH), which provides access control, connectionless message integrity, authentication, and antireplay protection, and the Encapsulating Security Payload (ESP), which supports these same services, plus confidentiality. AH is rarely used so we focus on ESP here. The second part is support for key management, which fits under an umbrella protocol known as the Internet Security Association and Key Management Protocol (ISAKMP).

The abstraction that binds these two pieces together is the *security association* (SA). An SA is a simplex (one-way) connection with one or more of the available security properties. Securing a bidirectional communication between a pair of hosts—corresponding to a TCP connection, for example—requires two SAs, one in each direction. Although IP is a connectionless protocol, security depends on connection state information such as keys and sequence numbers. When created, an SA is assigned an ID number called a *security parameters index* (SPI) by the receiving machine. A combination of this SPI and the destination IP addresses uniquely identifies an SA. An ESP header includes the SPI so the receiving host can determine which SA an incoming packet belongs to and, hence, what algorithms and keys to apply to the packet.

SAs are established, negotiated, modified, and deleted using ISAKMP. It defines packet formats for exchanging key generation and authentication data. These formats aren't terribly interesting because they provide a framework only—the exact form of the keys and authentication data depends on the key generation technique, the cipher, and the authentication mechanism that is used. Moreover, ISAKMP does not specify a particular key exchange protocol, although it does suggest the Internet Key Exchange (IKE) as one possibility, and IKE is what is used in practice.

ESP is the protocol used to securely transport data over an established SA. In IPv4, the ESP header follows the IP header; in IPv6, it is an extension

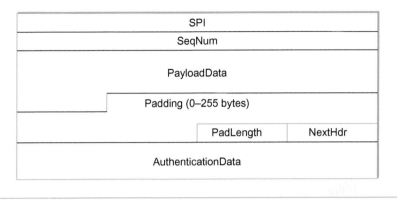

header. Its format uses both a header and a trailer, as shown in Figure 8.17. The SPI field lets the receiving host identify the security association to which the packet belongs. The SeqNum field protects against replay attacks. The packet's PayloadData contains the data described by the NextHdr field. If confidentiality is selected, then the data is encrypted using whatever cipher was associated with the SA. The PadLength field records how much padding was added to the data; padding is sometimes necessary because, for example, the cipher requires the plaintext to be a multiple of a certain number of bytes or to ensure that the resulting ciphertext terminates on a 4-byte boundary. Finally, the Authentication-Data carries the authenticator.

IPsec supports a *tunnel mode* as well as the more straightforward *transport mode*. Each SA operates in one or the other mode. In a transport mode SA, ESP's payload data is simply a message for a higher layer such as UDP or TCP. In this mode, IPsec acts as an intermediate protocol layer, much like SSL/TLS does between TCP and a higher layer. When an ESP message is received, its payload is passed to the higher level protocol.

In a tunnel mode SA, however, ESP's payload data is itself an IP packet, as in Figure 8.18. The source and destination of this inner IP packet may be different from those of the outer IP packet. When an ESP message is received, its payload is forwarded on as a normal IP packet. The most common way to use the ESP is to build an "IPsec tunnel" between two routers, typically firewalls. For example, a corporation wanting to link two sites using the Internet could open a pair of tunnel-mode SAs between a router at one site and a router at the other site, as we discussed in Section 3.2.9. An IP packet outgoing from one site would, at the outgoing

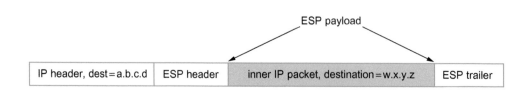

ESP payload

| IP header, dest=a.b.c.d | ESP header | inner IP packet, destination=w.x.y.z | ESP trailer |

■ **FIGURE 8.18** An IP packet with a nested IP packet encapsulated using ESP in tunnel mode. Note that the inner and outer packets have different addresses.

router, become the payload of an ESP message sent to the other site's router. The receiving router would unwrap the payload IP packet and forward it on to its true destination.

These tunnels may also be configured to use ESP with confidentiality and authentication, thus preventing unauthorized access to the data that traverses this virtual link and ensuring that no spurious data is received at the far end of the tunnel. Furthermore, tunnels can provide traffic confidentiality, since multiplexing multiple flows through a single tunnel obscures information about how much traffic is flowing between particular endpoints. A network of such tunnels can be used to implement an entire virtual private network (see Section 3.2.9). Hosts communicating over a VPN need not even be aware that it exists.

8.4.5 Wireless Security (802.11i)

Wireless links (Section 2.7) are particularly exposed to security threats due to the lack of any physical security on the medium. While the convenience of 802.11 has prompted widespread acceptance of the technology, lack of security has been a recurring problem. For example, it is all too easy for an employee of a corporation to connect an 802.11 access point to the corporate network. Since radio waves pass through most walls, if the access point lacks the correct security measures, an attacker can now gain access to the corporate network from outside the building. Similarly, a computer with a wireless network adaptor inside the building could connect to an access point outside the building, potentially exposing it to attack, not to mention the rest of the corporate network if that same computer has, say, an Ethernet connection as well.

Consequently, there has been considerable work on securing Wi-Fi links. Somewhat surprisingly, one of the early security techniques developed for 802.11, known as Wired Equivalent Privacy (WEP), turned out to be seriously flawed and quite easily breakable.

The IEEE 802.11i standard provides authentication, message integrity, and confidentiality to 802.11 (Wi-Fi) at the link layer. *WPA2* (Wi-Fi Protected Access 2) is often used as a synonym for 802.11i, although it is technically a trademark of the Wi-Fi Alliance® that certifies product compliance with 802.11i.

For backward compatibility, 802.11i includes definitions of first-generation security algorithms—including WEP—that are now known to have major security flaws. We will focus here on 802.11i's newer, stronger algorithms.

802.11i authentication supports two modes. In either mode, the end result of successful authentication is a shared Pairwise Master Key. *Personal mode*, also known as *Pre-Shared Key (PSK) mode*, provides weaker security but is more convenient and economical for situations like a home 802.11 network. The wireless device and the Access Point (AP) are preconfigured with a shared *passphrase*—essentially a very long password—from which the Pairwise Master Key is cryptographically derived.

802.11i's stronger authentication mode is based on the IEEE 802.1X framework for controlling access to a LAN, which uses an Authentication Server (AS) as in Figure 8.19. The AS and AP must be connected by a secure channel and could even be implemented as a single box, but they are logically separate. The AP forwards authentication messages between the wireless device and the AS. The protocol used for authentication is called the *Extensible Authentication Protocol* (EAP). EAP is designed to support multiple authentication methods—smart cards, Kerberos, one-time passwords, public key authentication, and so on—as well as both one-sided and mutual authentication. So EAP is better thought of as an authentication framework than a protocol. Specific EAP-compliant protocols, of which there are many, are called *EAP methods*. For example, EAP-TLS is an EAP method based on TLS authentication (see Section 8.4.3).

802.11i does not place any restrictions on what the EAP method can use as a basis for authentication. It does, however, require an EAP method that performs *mutual* authentication, because not only do we want to prevent an adversary from accessing the network via our AP, we also want to prevent an adversary from fooling our wireless devices with a bogus, malicious AP. The end result of a successful authentication is a Pairwise Master Key shared between the wireless device and the AS, which the AS then conveys to the AP.

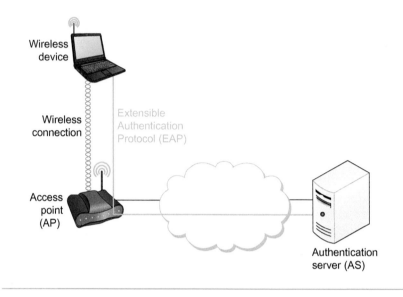

■ **FIGURE 8.19** Use of an Authentication Server in 802.11i.

One of the main differences between the stronger AS-based mode and the weaker personal mode is that the former readily supports a unique key per client. This in turn makes it easier to change the set of clients that can authenticate themselves (e.g., to revoke access to one client) without needing to change the secret stored in every client.

With a Pairwise Master Key in hand, the wireless device and the AP execute a session key establishment protocol called the 4-way handshake to establish a Pairwise Transient Key. This Pairwise Transient Key is really a collection of keys that includes a session key called a *Temporal Key*. This session key is used by the protocol, called *CCMP*, that provides 802.11i's data confidentiality and integrity.

CCMP stands for CTR (Counter Mode) with CBC-MAC (Cipher-Block Chaining with Message Authentication Code) Protocol. CCMP uses AES in counter mode to encrypt for confidentiality. Recall that in counter mode encryption successive values of a counter are incorporated into the encryption of successive blocks of plaintext (Section 8.1.1).

CCMP uses a Message Authentication Code (MAC) as an authenticator. The MAC algorithm is based on CBC (Section 8.1.1), even though CCMP doesn't use CBC in the confidentiality encryption. In effect, CBC is performed without transmitting any of the CBC-encrypted blocks, solely so that the last CBC-encrypted block can be used as a MAC (only its first

8 bytes are actually used). The role of initialization vector is played by a specially constructed first block that includes a 48-bit packet number—a sequence number. (The packet number is also incorporated in the confidentiality encryption and serves to expose replay attacks.) The MAC is subsequently encrypted along with the plaintext in order to prevent birthday attacks, which depend on finding different messages with the same authenticator (Section 8.1.4).

8.5 FIREWALLS

Whereas much of this chapter has focused on the uses of cryptography to provide such security features as authentication and confidentiality, there is a whole set of security issues that are not readily addressed by cryptographic means. For example, worms and viruses spread by exploiting bugs in operating systems and application programs (and sometimes human gullibility as well), and no amount of cryptography can help you if your machine has unpatched vulnerabilities. So other approaches are often used to keep out various forms of potentially harmful traffic. Firewalls are one of the most common ways to do this.

A firewall is a system that typically sits at some point of connectivity between a site it protects and the rest of the network, as illustrated in Figure 8.20. It is usually implemented as an "appliance" or part of a router, although a "personal firewall" may be implemented on an end-user machine. Firewall-based security depends on the firewall being the only connectivity to the site from outside; there should be no way to bypass the firewall via other gateways, wireless connections, or dial-up connections. The wall metaphor is somewhat misleading in the context of networks since a great deal of traffic passes through a firewall. One way to think of a firewall is that by default it blocks traffic unless that traffic is specifically allowed to pass through. For example, it might filter out all incoming messages except those addresses to a particular set of IP addresses or to particular TCP port numbers.

In effect, a firewall divides a network into a more-trusted zone internal to the firewall and a less-trusted zone external to the firewall.[4] This is

---

[4]The location of a firewall also often happens to be the dividing line between globally addressable regions and those that use local addresses. Hence, Network Address Translation (NAT; see Section 4.1.3) functionality and firewall functionality often are found in the same device, even though they are logically separate.

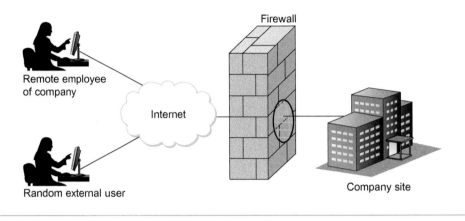

Firewall

Remote employee of company

Internet

Random external user

Company site

■ FIGURE 8.20 A firewall filters packets flowing between a site and the rest of the Internet.

useful if you do not want external users to access a particular host or service within your site. Much of the complexity comes from the fact that you want to allow different kinds of access to different external users, ranging from the general public, to business partners, to remotely located members of your organization. A firewall may also impose restrictions on outgoing traffic to prevent certain attacks and to limit losses if an adversary succeeds in getting access inside the firewall.

Firewalls may be used to create multiple *zones of trust*, such as a hierarchy of increasingly trusted zones. A common arrangement involves three zones of trust: the internal network, the *DMZ* ("demilitarized zone"); and the rest of the Internet. The DMZ is used to hold services such as DNS and email servers that need to be accessible to the outside. Both the internal network and the outside world can access the DMZ, but hosts in the DMZ cannot access the internal network; therefore, an adversary who succeeds in compromising a host in the exposed DMZ still cannot access the internal network. The DMZ can be periodically restored to a clean state.

Firewalls filter based on IP, TCP, and UDP information, among other things. They are configured with a table of addresses that characterize the packets they will, and will not, forward. By addresses, we mean more than just the destination's IP address, although that is one possibility. Generally, each entry in the table is a 4-tuple: It gives the IP address and TCP (or UDP) port number for both the source and destination.

For example, a firewall might be configured to filter out (not forward) all packets that match the following description:

⟨ 192.12.13.14, 1234, 128.7.6.5, 80 ⟩

This pattern says to discard all packets from port 1234 on host 192.12.13.14 addressed to port 80 on host 128.7.6.5. (Port 80 is the well-known TCP port for HTTP.) Of course, it's often not practical to name every source host whose packets you want to filter, so the patterns can include wildcards. For example,

⟨ *, *, 128.7.6.5, 80 ⟩

says to filter out all packets addressed to port 80 on 128.7.6.5, regardless of what source host or port sent the packet. Notice that address patterns like these require the firewall to make forwarding/filtering decisions based on level 4 port numbers, in addition to level 3 host addresses. It is for this reason that network layer firewalls are sometimes called *level 4 switches*.

In the preceding discussion, the firewall forwards everything except where specifically instructed to filter out certain kinds of packets. A firewall could also filter out everything unless explicitly instructed to forward it, or use a mix of the two strategies. For example, instead of blocking access to port 80 on host 128.7.6.5, the firewall might be instructed to only allow access to port 25 (the SMTP mail port) on a particular mail server, such as

⟨ *, *, 128.19.20.21, 25 ⟩

but to block all other traffic. Experience has shown that firewalls are very frequently configured incorrectly, allowing unsafe access. Part of the problem is that filtering rules can overlap in complex ways, making it hard for a system administrator to correctly express the intended filtering. A design principle that maximizes security is to configure a firewall to discard all packets other than those that are explicitly allowed. Of course, this means that some valid applications might be accidentally disabled; presumably users of those applications eventually notice and ask the system administrator to make the appropriate change.

Many client/server applications dynamically assign a port to the client. If a client inside a firewall initiates access to an external server, the server's response would be addressed to the dynamically assigned port. This poses a problem: How can a firewall be configured to allow an arbitrary server's response packet but disallow a similar packet for which there was no client request? This is not possible with a *stateless firewall*, which evaluates each packet in isolation. It requires a *stateful firewall*, which keeps track of the state of each connection. An incoming packet addressed to a dynamically assigned port would then be allowed only if it is a valid response in the current state of a connection on that port.

Modern firewalls also understand and filter based on many specific application-level protocols such as HTTP, Telnet, or FTP. They use information specific to that protocol, such as URLs in the case of HTTP, to decide whether to discard a message.

8.5.1 Strengths and Weaknesses of Firewalls

At best, a firewall protects a network from undesired access from the rest of the Internet; it cannot provide security to legitimate communication between the inside and the outside of the firewall. In contrast, the cryptography-based security mechanisms described in this chapter are capable of providing secure communication between any participants anywhere. This being the case, why are firewalls so common? One reason is that firewalls can be deployed unilaterally, using mature commercial products, while cryptography-based security requires support at both endpoints of the communication. A more fundamental reason for the dominance of firewalls is that they encapsulate security in a centralized place, in effect factoring security out of the rest of the network. A system administrator can manage the firewall to provide security, freeing the users and applications inside the firewall from security concerns—at least some kinds of security concerns.

Unfortunately, firewalls have serious limitations. Since a firewall does not restrict communication between hosts that are inside the firewall, the adversary who does manage to run code internal to a site can access all local hosts. How might an adversary get inside the firewall? The adversary could be a disgruntled employee with legitimate access, or the adversary's software could be hidden in some software installed from a CD or downloaded from the Web. It might be possible to bypass the firewall by using wireless communication or dial-up connections.

Another problem is that any parties granted access through your firewall, such as business partners or externally located employees, become a security vulnerability. If their security is not as good as yours, then an adversary could penetrate your security by penetrating their security.

On of the most serious problems for firewalls is their vulnerability to the exploitation of bugs in machines inside the firewall. Such bugs are discovered regularly, so a system administrator has to constantly monitor announcements of them. Administrators frequently fail to do so, since firewall security breaches routinely exploit security flaws that have been known for some time and have straightforward solutions.

Malware (for "malicious software") is the term for software that is designed to act on a computer in ways concealed from and unwanted by the computer's user. Viruses, worms, and spyware are common types of malware. (*Virus* is sometimes used synonymously with *malware*, but we will use it in the narrower sense in which it refers to only a particular kind of malware.) Malware code need not be natively executable object code; it could as well be interpreted code such as a script or an executable macro such as those used by Microsoft® Word.

Viruses and *worms* are characterized by the ability to make and spread copies of themselves; the difference between them is that a worm is a complete program that replicates itself, while a virus is a bit of code that is inserted (and inserts copies of itself) into another piece of software or a file, so that it is executed as part of the execution of that piece of software or as a result of opening the file. Viruses and worms typically cause problems such as consuming network bandwidth as mere side effects of attempting to spread copies of themselves. Even worse, they can also deliberately damage a system or undermine its security in various ways. They could, for example, install a *backdoor*—software that allows remote access to the system without the normal authentication. This could lead to a firewall exposing a service that should be providing its own authentication procedures but has been undermined by a backdoor.

Spyware is software that, without authorization, collects and transmits private information about a computer system or its users. Usually spyware is secretly embedded in an otherwise useful program and is spread by users deliberately installing copies. The problem for firewalls is that the transmission of the private information looks like legitimate communication.

A natural question to ask is whether firewalls (or cryptographic security) could keep malware out of a system in the first place. Most malware is indeed transmitted via networks, although it may also be transmitted via portable storage devices such as CDs and memory sticks. Certainly this is one argument in favor of the "block everything not explicitly allowed" approach taken by many administrators in their firewall configurations.

One approach that is used to detect malware is to search for segments of code from known malware, sometimes called a *signature*. This approach has its own challenges, as cleverly designed malware can tweak its representation in various ways. There is also a potential impact on network performance to perform such detailed inspection of data entering a network. Cryptographic security cannot eliminate the problem either, although it does provide a means to authenticate the originator of a piece of software and detect any tampering, such as when a virus inserts a copy of itself.

Related to firewalls are systems known as *intrusion detection systems* (IDS) and *intrusion prevention systems* (IPS). These systems try to look for anomalous activity, such as an unusually large amount of traffic targeting a given host or port number, for example, and generate alarms for network managers or perhaps even take direct action to limit a possible attack. While there are commercial products in this space today, it is still a developing field.

8.6 SUMMARY

Networks such as the Internet are shared by parties with conflicting interests, a situation that was not entirely foreseeable in the early days of networking. The job of network security is to keep some set of users from spying on or interfering with other users of the network. Confidentiality is achieved by encrypting messages. Data integrity can be assured using cryptographic hashing. The two techniques can be combined to guarantee authenticity of messages.

Symmetric-key ciphers such as AES and 3DES use the same secret key for both encryption and decryption, so sender and receiver must share the same key. Public-key ciphers such as RSA use a public key for encryption and a secret, private key for decryption. This means that any party can use the public key to encrypt a message such that it is readable only by the holder of the private key. The fastest technique known for breaking established ciphers such as AES and RSA is brute force search of the space of possible keys, which is made computationally infeasible by the use of large keys. Most encryption for confidentiality uses symmetric-key ciphers due to their vastly superior speed, while public-key ciphers are usually reserved for authentication and session key establishment.

An authenticator is a value attached to a message to verify the authenticity and data integrity of the message. One way to generate an authenticator is to encrypt a message digest that is output by a cryptographic hash function such as MD5 or one of the SHA family of hashes. If the message digest is encrypted using the private key of a public-key cipher, the resulting authenticator is considered a digital signature, since the public key can be used to verify that only the holder of the private key could have generated it. Another kind of authenticator is a Message Authentication Code, which is output by a hash-like function that takes a shared secret value as a parameter. A hashed MAC is a MAC computed by applying a cryptographic hash to the concatenation of the plaintext message and the secret value.

A session key is used to secure a relatively short episode of communication. The dynamic establishment of a session key depends on longer-lived predistributed keys. The ownership of a predistributed public key by a certain party can be attested to by a public key certificate that is digitally signed by a trusted party. A Public Key Infrastructure is a complete scheme for certifying such bindings and depends on a chain or web of trust. Predistribution of keys for symmetric-key ciphers is different because public certificates can't be used and because symmetric-key ciphers need a unique key for each pair of participants. A Key Distribution Center is a trusted entity that shares a predistributed secret key with each other participant, so that they can use session keys, not predistributed keys, between themselves.

Authentication and session key establishment require a protocol to assure the timeliness and originality of messages. Timestamps or nonces are used to guarantee the freshness of the messages. We saw two authentication protocols that use public-key ciphers, one that required synchronized clocks and one that did not. Needham–Schroeder is a protocol for authenticating two participants who each share a master symmetric-key cipher key with a Key Distribution Center. Kerberos is an authentication system based on the Needham–Schroeder protocol and specialized for client/server environments. The Diffie–Hellman key agreement protocol establishes a session key without predistributed keys and authentication.

We discussed several systems that provide security based on these cryptographic algorithms and protocols. At the application level, PGP can be used to protect email messages and SSH can be used to securely connect to a remote machine. At the transport level, TLS can be used to protect commercial transactions on the World Wide Web. At the network level, the IPsec architecture can be used to secure communication among any set of hosts or routers on the Internet.

A firewall filters the messages that pass between the site it protects and the rest of the network. Firewalls filter based on IP, TCP, and UDP addresses, as well as fields of some application protocols. A stateful firewall keeps track of the state of each connection so that it can allow valid responses to be delivered to dynamically assigned ports. Although firewall security has important limitations, it has the advantage of shifting some responsibility for security from users and applications to system administrators.

If you ask any Internet researcher "What would be the most important feature to include in a future Internet if we could start from scratch?" there is a pretty good chance the answer will include something about better security. One way to think about the problem is that the Internet was designed by a fairly small community who wanted access to each other's computers; today's Internet is used by a large, global community, including a reasonable number of criminals who would also like to gain access to a lot of other computers. Thus, the design of making open access the default isn't clearly a good match to today's world.

There are a lot of theories about how this situation might be improved. One problem, of course, is that the Internet

WHAT'S NEXT: COMING TO GRIPS WITH SECURITY

is such a fundamental part of everyday life now that we can't easily imagine replacing it with a new, designed-from-scratch version. There is, however, a fair amount of "clean-slate" research underway, based on the theory that working on a future Internet unhindered by questions of incremental deployment might lead to some new insights that could later be retrofitted to the current Internet. (See the Further Reading section of Chapter 3 for some references.)

The near-term outlook seems to be for a continual playing out of the cat-and-mouse game that has gone on for some time. Firewalls, intrusion detection systems, and DoS-mitigation systems get more sophisticated; attackers find new ways of working around the defenses of these systems; the systems evolve to become better at defending against the new attacks, and so on. On the positive side, many security systems work quite well; there wouldn't be nearly as much e-commerce on the Web as there is were it not for the effectiveness of Transport Layer Security and all the cryptographic methods on which it depends.

One phrase that has been used to describe a vision for a future Internet is "An Internet deserving of society's trust." It is clear that realizing that vision is a significant challenge and that securing networks will be an area of research and innovation for some time to come.

■ FURTHER READING

The first two security-related papers, taken together, give a good overview of the topic. The article by Lampson et al. contains a formal treatment of security, while the Satyanarayanan paper gives a nice description of how a secure system is designed in practice. The third paper is a thorough and somewhat alarming overview of how worms and viruses spread and how a well-planned attack could be sped up.

- Lampson, B. et al. Authentication in distributed systems: Theory and practice. *ACM Transactions on Computer Systems* 10(4):265–310, November 1992.

- Satyanarayanan, M. Integrating security in a large distributed system. *ACM Transactions on Computer Systems* 7(3):247–280, August 1989.

- Staniford, S., V. Paxson, and N. Weaver. How to Own the Internet in Your Spare Time. *USENIX Security Symposium 2002*, pp. 149–167. San Francisco, CA, August 2002.

There are several good books covering the full gamut of network security. We recommend Schneier [Sch95], Stallings [Sta03], and Kaufman et al. [KPS02]. The first two give comprehensive treatments of the topic, while the last gives a very readable overview of the subject. The full IPSec architecture is defined in a series of RFCs: [Ken05a], [Eas05], [MG98a], [MG98b], [MD98], [Ken05b], and [Kau05]. The Open PGP standard is defined in [Cal07], and the latest TLS standard is [DR08]. A book by Barrett and Silverman [Bar01] gives a thorough description of SSH. Menezes et al. [MvOV96] is a comprehensive cryptography reference (a copy can be freely downloaded from the URL listed below).

A discussion of the problem of recognizing and defending against denial-of-service attacks can be found in Moore et al. [MVS01], Spatscheck and Peterson [SP99], and Qiexh et al. [QPP02]. Recent techniques used to identify the source of attacks can be found in papers by Savage et al. [SWKA00] and Snoeren et al. [SPS+01]. The increasing threat of DDoS attacks is discussed by Garber [Gar00] and Harrison [Har00], and early approaches to defending against such attacks are reported in a paper by Park and Lee [PL01]. A novel approach to DoS prevention which falls in the "clean slate" category is the TVA approach by Yang et al. [YWA08].

Finally, we recommend the following live references:

- http://www.cert.org/: The website of CERT, an organization focused on computer security issues.
- http://www.cacr.math.uwaterloo.ca/hac/: Downloadable copy of [MvOV96] a comprehensive cryptography reference.

EXERCISES

1. Find or install an encryption utility (e.g., the Unix des command or pgp) on your system. Read its documentation and experiment with it. Measure how fast it is able to encrypt and decrypt data. Are these two rates the same? Try to compare these timing results using different key sizes; for example, compare AES with triple-DES.

2. Diagram cipher block chaining as described in Section 8.1.1.

3. Learn about a key escrow, or key surrender, scheme (for example, Clipper). What are the pros and cons of key escrow?

4. A good cryptographic hashing algorithm should produce random outputs; that is, the probability of any given hash value should be approximately the same as any other for randomly chosen input data. What would be the consequence of using a hash algorithm whose outputs were not random? Consider, for example, the case where some hash values are twice as likely to occur as others.

5. Suppose Alice uses the Needham–Schroeder authentication protocol described in Section 8.3.3 to initiate a session with Bob. Further suppose that an adversary is able to eavesdrop on the

authentication messages and, long after the session has completed, discover the (unencrypted) session key. How could the adversary deceive Bob into authenticating the adversary as Alice?

6. One mechanism for resisting replay attacks in password authentication is to use *one-time passwords*: A list of passwords is prepared, and once $password[N]$ has been accepted the server decrements N and prompts for $password[N-1]$ next time. At $N = 0$ a new list is needed. Outline a mechanism by which the user and server need only remember one master password mp and have available locally a way to compute $password[N] = f(mp, N)$. Hint: Let g be an appropriate one-way function (e.g., MD5) and let $password[N] = g^N(mp) = g$ applied N times to mp. Explain why knowing $password[N]$ doesn't help reveal $password[N-1]$.

7. Suppose a user employs one-time passwords as above (or, for that matter, reusable passwords), but that the password is transmitted sufficiently slowly.
   (a) Show that an eavesdropper can gain access to the remote server with a relatively modest number of guesses. (Hint: The eavesdropper starts guessing after the original user has typed all but one character of the password.)
   (b) To what other attacks might a user of one-time passwords be subject?

8. The Diffie–Hellman key exchange protocol is vulnerable to a "man-in-the-middle" attack as shown in Section 8.3.4 and Figure 8.12. Outline how Diffie–Hellman can be extended to protect against this possibility.

9. Suppose we have a very short secret s (e.g., a single bit or even a Social Security number), and we wish to send someone else a message m now that will not reveal s but that can be used later to verify that we did know s. Explain why $m = \mathrm{MD5}(s)$ or $m = \mathrm{E}(s)$ with RSA encryption would not be secure choices, and suggest a better choice.

10. Suppose two people want to play poker over the network. To deal the cards they need a mechanism for fairly choosing a random number x between them; each party stands to lose if the other

party can unfairly influence the choice of x. Describe such a mechanism. Hint: You may assume that if either of two bit strings x_1 and x_2 are random, then the exclusive-OR $x = x_1 \oplus x_2$ is random.

11. Estimate the probabilities of finding two messages with the same MD5 checksum, given total numbers of messages of 2^{63}, 2^{64}, and 2^{65}. Hint: This is the Birthday Problem again, as in Exercise 48 in Chapter 2, and again the probability that the $k + 1$th message has a different checksum from each of the preceding k is $1 - k/2^{128}$. However, the approximation in the hint there for simplifying the product fails rather badly now. So, instead, take the log of each side and use the approximation $\log(1 - k/2^{128}) \approx -k/2^{128}$.

12. Suppose we wanted to encrypt a Telnet session with, say, 3DES. Telnet sends lots of 1-byte messages, while 3DES encrypts in blocks of 8 bytes at a time. Explain how 3DES might be used securely in this setting.

13. Consider the following simple UDP protocol (based loosely on TFTP, *Request for Comments* 1350) for downloading files:

   ■ Client sends a file request.

   ■ Server replies with first data packet.

   ■ Client sends ACK, and the two proceed using stop-and-wait.

   Suppose client and server possess keys K_C and K_S, respectively, and that these keys are known to each other.

   (a) Extend the file downloading protocol, using these keys and MD5, to provide sender authentication and message integrity. Your protocol should also be resistant to replay attacks.

   (b) How does the extra information in your revised protocol protect against the arrival of late packets from prior connection incarnations and sequence number wraparound?

14. Using the browser of your choice, find out what certification authorities for HTTPS your browser is configured by default to trust. Do you trust these agencies? Find out what happens when you disable trust of some or all of these certification authorities.

15. Use an OpenPGP implementation such as GnuPG to do the following. Note that no email is involved—you are working exclusively with files on a single machine.

    (a) Generate a public–private key pair.

    (b) Use your public key to encrypt a file, as if for secure storage, and then use your private key to decrypt it.

    (c) Use your key pair to digitally sign an unencrypted file and then, as if you were someone else, verify your signature using your public key.

    (d) Consider the first public–private key pair as belonging to Alice, and generate a second public–private key pair, for Bob. Playing the role of Alice, encrypt and sign a file intended for Bob. (Be sure to sign as Alice, not Bob.) Then, playing the role of Bob, verify Alice's signature and decrypt the file.

16. Consider a certification hierarchy as described in Section 8.2.1. A root CA signs a certificate for a second-tier CA, and the second-tier CA signs a certificate for Alice. Bob has the public key for the root CA, so he can verify the certificate of the second-tier CA. Why might Bob still not trust that the certificate for Alice truly establishes Alice as the owner of the public key in the certificate?

17. PuTTY (pronounced "putty") is a popular free SSH client—an application that implements the client side of SSH connections—for Unix and Windows. Its documentation is accessible on the Web.

    (a) How does PuTTY handle authentication of a server that it has not previously connected to?

    (b) How are clients authenticated to servers?

    (c) PuTTY supports several ciphers. How does it determine which one to use for a particular connection?

    (d) PuTTY supports ciphers, such as DES, that might be considered too weak for some—or any—situations. Why? How does PuTTY determine which ciphers are weak, and how does it use that information?

    (e) For a given connection, PuTTY lets a user specify a maximum amount of time and/or transmitted data after which PuTTY will initiate the establishment of a new session key, which the documentation refers to as a *key exchange* or *rekeying*. What is the motivation behind this feature?

(f) Use PuTTYgen, the PuTTY key generator, to generate a public–private key pair for one of the PuTTY-supported public key ciphers.

18. Suppose you want your firewall to block all incoming Telnet connections but to allow outbound Telnet connections. One approach would be to block all inbound packets to the designated Telnet port (23).

(a) We might want to block inbound packets to other ports as well, but what inbound TCP connections *must* be permitted in order not to interfere with outbound Telnet?

(b) Now suppose your firewall is allowed to use the TCP header Flags bits in addition to the port numbers. Explain how you can achieve the desired Telnet effect here while at the same time allowing no inbound TCP connections.

19. Suppose a firewall is configured to allow outbound TCP connections but inbound connections only to specified ports. The FTP protocol now presents a problem: When an inside client contacts an outside server, the outbound TCP control connection can be opened normally but the TCP data connection traditionally is inbound.

(a) Look up the FTP protocol in, for example, *Request for Comments* 959. Find out how the **PORT** command works. Discuss how the client might be written so as to limit the number of ports to which the firewall must grant inbound access. Can the number of such ports be limited to one?

(b) Find out how the FTP **PASV** command can be used to solve this firewall problem.

20. Suppose filtering routers are arranged as in Figure 8.21; the primary firewall is R1. Explain how to configure R1 and R2 so that outsiders can Telnet to net 2 but not to hosts on net 1. To avoid "leapfrogging" break-ins to net 1, also disallow Telnet connections from net 2 to net 1.

21. Why might an Internet Service Provider want to block certain *outbound* traffic?

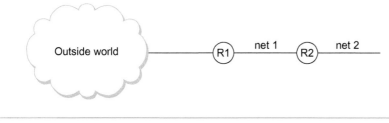

■ FIGURE 8.21 Diagram for Exercise 18.

22. It is said that IPsec may not work with Network Address
    Translation (NAT) (RFC 1631). However, whether IPsec will work
    with NAT depends on which mode of IPsec and NAT we use.
    Suppose we use true NAT, where only IP addresses are translated
    (without port translation). Will IPsec and NAT work in each of the
    following cases? Explain why or why not.
    (a) IPsec uses ESP transport mode.
    (b) IPsec uses ESP tunnel mode.
    (c) What if we use PAT (Port Address Translation), also known as
        Network Address/Port Translation (NAPT) in NAT, where in
        addition to IP addresses port numbers will be translated to
        share one IP address from outside the private network?

A SYSTEMS APPROACH

A SYSTEMS APPROACH

A SYSTEMS APPROACH

A SYSTEMS APPROACH

A SYSTEMS APPROACH

Applications

Now this is not the end. It is not even the beginning of the end. But it is, perhaps, the end of the beginning.

–Winston Churchill

We started this book by talking about application programs—everything from web browsers to videoconferencing tools—that people want to run over computer networks. In the intervening chapters, we have developed, one building block at a time, the networking infrastructure needed to make such applications possible. We have now come full circle, back to network applications. These applications are part network protocol (in the sense that they exchange messages with their peers on other machines) and part traditional application program (in the sense that they interact with the windowing system, the file

---

PROBLEM: APPLICATIONS NEED THEIR OWN PROTOCOLS

---

system, and ultimately the user). This chapter explores some of the most popular network applications available today.

Looking at applications drives home the *systems approach* that we have emphasized throughout this book. That is, the best way to build effective networked applications is to understand the building blocks that a network can provide and how those blocks can interact with each other. Thus, for example, a particular networked application might need to make use of a reliable transport protocol, authentication and privacy mechanisms, and resource allocation capabilities of the underlying network. Applications often work best when the application developer knows how to make the best use of these facilities (and there are also plenty of counter-examples of applications making poor use of available networking capabilities). Applications typically need their own protocols, too, in many cases using the same principles that we have seen in our prior examination of lower layer protocols. Thus, our focus in this chapter is on how to put together the ideas and techniques already described to build effective networked applications. Said another way, if you ever imagine yourself writing a network application, then you will by definition also become a protocol designer (and implementer).

We proceed by examining a variety of familiar, and not so familiar, network applications. These range from exchanging email and surfing the Web, to integrating applications across businesses, to multimedia applications like vic and vat, to managing a set of network elements, to emerging peer-to-peer and content distribution networks. This list is by no means exhaustive, but it does serve to illustrate many of the key principles of designing and building applications. Applications need to pick and choose the appropriate building blocks that are available at other layers either inside the network or in the host protocol stacks and then augment those underlying services to provide the precise communication service required by the application.

9.1 TRADITIONAL APPLICATIONS

We begin our discussion of applications by focusing on two of the most popular—the World Wide Web and email. Broadly speaking, both of these applications use the request/reply paradigm—users send requests to servers, which then respond accordingly. We refer to these as "traditional" applications because they typify the sort of applications that have existed since the early days of computer networks (although the Web is a lot newer than email but has its roots in file transfers that predated it). By contrast, later sections will look at a class of applications that have become feasible only relatively recently: streaming applications (e.g., multimedia applications like video and audio) and various overlay-based applications. (Note that there is a bit of a blurring between these classes, as you can of course get access to streaming multimedia data over the Web, but for now we'll focus on the general usage of the Web to request pages, images, etc.)

Before taking a close look at each of these applications, there are three general points that we need to make. The first is that it is important to distinguish between application *programs* and application *protocols*. For example, the HyperText Transport Protocol (HTTP) is an application protocol that is used to retrieve Web pages from remote servers. Many different application programs—that is, web clients like Internet Explorer, Chrome, Firefox, and Safari—provide users with a different look and feel, but all of them use the same HTTP protocol to communicate with web servers over the Internet. Indeed, it is the fact that the protocol is published and standardized that enables application programs developed by many different companies and individuals to interoperate. That is how so many browsers are able to interoperate with all the web servers (of which there are also many varieties).

This section looks at two very widely used, standardized application protocols:

- Simple Mail Transfer Protocol (SMTP) is used to exchange electronic mail.
- HyperText Transport Protocol (HTTP) is used to communicate between web browsers and web servers.

We'll also look at how custom application protocols are defined in the *Web Services* architecture.

The second point is that, since the application protocols described in this section follow the same request/reply communication pattern, you might expect that they would be built on top of a Remote Procedure Call (RPC) transport protocol. This is not the case, however, as they are instead implemented on top of TCP. In effect, each protocol reinvents a simple RPC-like mechanism on top of a reliable transport protocol (TCP). We say "simple" because each protocol is not designed to support arbitrary remote procedure calls of the sort discussed in Section 5.3, but is instead designed to send and respond to a specific set of request messages.

Finally, we observe that many application layer protocols, including HTTP and SMTP, have a companion protocol that specifies the format of the data that can be exchanged. This is one reason WHY these protocols are relatively simple: Much of the complexity is managed in this companion document. For example, SMTP is a protocol for exchanging electronic mail messages, but RFC 822 and Multipurpose Internet Mail Extensions (MIME) define the format of email messages. Similarly, HTTP is a protocol for fetching Web pages, but HyperText Markup Language (HTML) is a companion specification that defines the basic form of those pages.

9.1.1 Electronic Mail (SMTP, MIME, IMAP)

Email is one of the oldest network applications. After all, what could be more natural than wanting to send a message to the user at the other end of a cross-country link you just managed to get running? Surprisingly, the pioneers of the ARPANET had not really envisioned email as a key application when the network was created—remote access to computing resources was the main design goal—but it turned out to be a useful application that continues to be extremely popular.

As noted above, it is important (1) to distinguish the user interface (i.e., your mail reader) from the underlying message transfer protocols (such as SMTP or IMAP), and (2) to distinguish between this transfer protocol and a companion protocol (RFC 822 and MIME) that defines the format of the messages being exchanged. We start by looking at the message format.

Message Format

RFC 822 defines messages to have two parts: a *header* and a *body*. Both parts are represented in ASCII text. Originally, the body was assumed to be simple text. This is still the case, although RFC 822 has been augmented by MIME to allow the message body to carry all sorts of data. This data is still represented as ASCII text, but because it may be an encoded version of, say, a JPEG image, it's not necessarily readable by human users. More on MIME in a moment.

The message header is a series of <CRLF>-terminated lines. (<CRLF> stands for carriage return + line feed, which are a pair of ASCII control characters often used to indicate the end of a line of text.) The header is separated from the message body by a blank line. Each header line contains a type and value separated by a colon. Many of these header lines are familiar to users, since they are asked to fill them out when they compose an email message; for example, the To: header identifies the message recipient, and the Subject: header says something about the purpose of the message. Other headers are filled in by the underlying mail delivery system. Examples include Date: (when the message was transmitted), From: (what user sent the message), and Received: (each mail server that handled this message). There are, of course, many other header lines; the interested reader is referred to RFC 822.

RFC 822 was extended in 1993 (and updated quite a few times since then) to allow email messages to carry many different types of data: audio, video, images, PDF documents, and so on. MIME consists of three basic pieces. The first piece is a collection of header lines that augment the original set defined by RFC 822. These header lines describe, in various ways, the data being carried in the message body. They include MIME-Version: (the version of MIME being used), Content-Description: (a human-readable description of what's in the message, analogous to the Subject: line), Content-Type: (the type of data contained in the message), and Content-Transfer-Encoding (how the data in the message body is encoded).

The second piece is definitions for a set of content types (and subtypes). For example, MIME defines two different still image types, denoted image/gif and image/jpeg, each with the obvious meaning. As another example, text/plain refers to simple text you might find in a vanilla 822-style message, while text/richtext denotes a message that contains "marked up" text (text using special fonts, italics, etc.). As a third example, MIME defines an application type, where the subtypes correspond to the output of different application programs (e.g., application/postscript and application/msword).

MIME also defines a multipart type that says how a message carrying more than one data type is structured. This is like a programming language that defines both base types (e.g., integers and floats) and compound types (e.g., structures and arrays). One possible multipart subtype is mixed, which says that the message contains a set of independent data pieces in a specified order. Each piece then has its own header line that describes the type of that piece.

The third piece is a way to encode the various data types so they can be shipped in an ASCII email message. The problem is that, for some data types (a JPEG image, for example), any given 8-bit byte in the image might contain one of 256 different values. Only a subset of these values are valid ASCII characters. It is important that email messages contain only ASCII, because they might pass through a number of intermediate systems (gateways, as described below) that assume all email is ASCII and would corrupt the message if it contained non-ASCII characters. To address this issue, MIME uses a straightforward encoding of binary data into the ASCII character set. The encoding is called base64. The idea is to map every three bytes of the original binary data into four ASCII characters. This is done by grouping the binary data into 24-bit units and breaking each such unit into four 6-bit pieces. Each 6-bit piece maps onto one of 64 valid ASCII characters; for example, 0 maps onto A, 1 maps onto B, and so on. If you look at a message that has been encoded using the base64 encoding scheme, you'll notice only the 52 upper- and lowercase letters, the 10 digits 0 through 9, and the special characters $+$ and $/$. These are the first 64 values in the ASCII character set.

As one aside, so as to make reading mail as painless as possible for those who still insist on using text-only mail readers, a MIME message that consists of regular text only can be encoded using 7-bit ASCII. There's also a readable encoding for mostly ASCII data.

Putting this all together, a message that contains some plain text, a JPEG image, and a PostScript file would look something like this:

```
MIME-Version: 1.0
Content-Type: multipart/mixed;
boundary="-------417CA6E2DE4ABCAFBC5"
From: Alice Smith <Alice@cisco.com>
To: Bob@cs.Princeton.edu
Subject: promised material
Date: Mon, 07 Sep 1998 19:45:19 -0400


---------417CA6E2DE4ABCAFBC5
Content-Type: text/plain; charset=us-ascii
Content-Transfer-Encoding: 7bit


Bob,


Here's the jpeg image and draft report I promised.


--Alice


---------417CA6E2DE4ABCAFBC5
Content-Type: image/jpeg
Content-Transfer-Encoding: base64
... unreadable encoding of a jpeg figure
```

```
- - - - - - - - -417CA6E2DE4ABCAFBC5
Content-Type: application/postscript; name="draft.ps"
Content-Transfer-Encoding: 7bit
... readable encoding of a PostScript document
```

In this example, the Content-Type line in the message header says that this message contains various pieces, each denoted by a character string that does not appear in the data itself. Each piece then has its own Content-Type and Content-Transfer-Encoding lines.

Message Transfer

For many years, the majority of email was moved from host to host using only SMTP. While SMTP continues to play a central role, it is now just one email protocol of several, Internet Message Access Protocol (IMAP) and Post Office Protocol (POP) being two other important protocols for retrieving mail messages. We'll begin our discussion by looking at SMTP, and move on to IMAP below.

To place SMTP in the right context, we need to identify the key players. First, users interact with a *mail reader* when they compose, file, search, and read their email. Countless mail readers are available, just like there are many web browsers to choose from. In the early days of the Internet, users typically logged into the machine on which their *mailbox* resided, and the mail reader they invoked was a local application program that extracted messages from the file system. Today, of course, users remotely access their mailbox from their laptop or smartphone; they do not first log into the host that stores their mail (a mail server). A second mail transfer protocol, such as POP or IMAP, is used to remotely download email from a mail server to the user's device.

Second, there is a *mail daemon* (or process) running on each host that holds a mailbox. You can think of this process, also called a *message transfer agent* (MTA), as playing the role of a post office: Users (or their mail readers) give the daemon messages they want to send to other users, the daemon uses SMTP running over TCP to transmit the message to a daemon running on another machine, and the daemon puts incoming messages into the user's mailbox (where that user's mail reader can later find them). Since SMTP is a protocol that anyone could implement, in theory there could be many different implementations of the mail daemon. It turns out, though, that there are only a few popular implementations, with the old sendmail program from Berkeley Unix and postfix being the most widespread.

While it is certainly possible that the MTA on a sender's machine establishes an SMTP/TCP connection to the MTA on the recipient's mail server, in many cases the mail traverses one or more *mail gateways* on its route from the sender's host to the receiver's host. Like the end hosts, these gateways also run a message transfer agent process. It's not an accident that these intermediate nodes are called *gateways* since their job is to store and forward email messages, much like an "IP gateway" (which we have referred to as a *router*) stores and forwards IP datagrams. The only difference is that a mail gateway typically buffers messages on disk and is willing to try retransmitting them to the next machine for several days, while an IP router buffers datagrams in memory and is only willing to retry transmitting them for a fraction of a second. Figure 9.1 illustrates a two-hop path from the sender to the receiver.

Why, you might ask, are mail gateways necessary? Why can't the sender's host send the message to the receiver's host? One reason is that the recipient does not want to include the specific host on which he or she reads email in his or her address. Another is scale: In large organizations, it's often the case that a number of different machines hold the *mailboxes* for the organization. For example, mail delivered to Bob@cs.princeton.edu is first sent to a mail gateway in the CS Department at Princeton (that is, to the host named cs.princeton.edu), and then forwarded—involving a second connection—to the specific machine on which Bob has a mailbox. The forwarding gateway maintains a database that maps users into the machine on which their mailbox resides; the

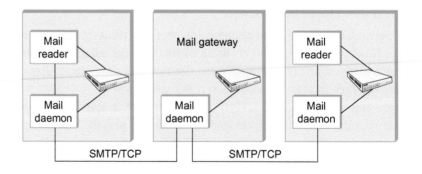

■ FIGURE 9.1 Sequence of mail gateways store and forward email messages.

sender need not be aware of this specific name. (The list of **Received:** header lines in the message will help you trace the mail gateways that a given message traversed.) Yet another reason, particularly true in the early days of email, is that the machine that hosts any given user's mailbox may not always be up or reachable, in which case the mail gateway holds the message until it can be delivered.

Independent of how many mail gateways are in the path, an independent SMTP connection is used between each host to move the message closer to the recipient. Each SMTP session involves a dialog between the two mail daemons, with one acting as the client and the other acting as the server. Multiple messages might be transferred between the two hosts during a single session. Since RFC 822 defines messages using ASCII as the base representation, it should come as no surprise to learn that SMTP is also ASCII based. This means it is possible for a human at a keyboard to pretend to be an SMTP client program.

SMTP is best understood by a simple example. The following is an exchange between sending host cs.princeton.edu and receiving host cisco.com. In this case, user Bob at Princeton is trying to send mail to users Alice and Tom at Cisco. The lines sent by cs.princeton.edu are shown in black and the lines sent by cisco.com are shown in teal. Extra blank lines have been added to make the dialog more readable.

```
HELO cs.princeton.edu
250 Hello daemon@mail.cs.princeton.edu [128.12.169.24]

MAIL FROM:<Bob@cs.princeton.edu>
250 OK

RCPT TO:<Alice@cisco.com>
250 OK

RCPT TO:<Tom@cisco.com>
550 No such user here

DATA
354 Start mail input; end with <CRLF>.<CRLF>
Blah blah blah...
...etc. etc. etc.
```

```
<CRLF>.<CRLF>
250 OK

QUIT
221 Closing connection
```

As you can see, SMTP involves a sequence of exchanges between the client and the server. In each exchange, the client posts a command (e.g., HELO, MAIL, RCPT, DATA, QUIT) and the server responds with a code (e.g., 250, 550, 354, 221). The server also returns a human-readable explanation for the code (e.g., No such user here). In this particular example, the client first identifies itself to the server with the HELO command. It gives its domain name as an argument. The server verifies that this name corresponds to the IP address being used by the TCP connection; you'll notice the server states this IP address back to the client. The client then asks the server if it is willing to accept mail for two different users; the server responds by saying "yes" to one and "no" to the other. Then the client sends the message, which is terminated by a line with a single period (".") on it. Finally, the client terminates the connection.

There are, of course, many other commands and return codes. For example, the server can respond to a client's RCPT command with a 251 code, which indicates that the user does not have a mailbox on this host, but that the server promises to forward the message onto another mail daemon. In other words, the host is functioning as a mail gateway. As another example, the client can issue a VRFY operation to verify a user's email address, but without actually sending a message to the user.

The only other point of interest is the arguments to the MAIL and RCPT operations; for example, FROM:<Bob@cs.princeton.edu> and TO:<Alice@cisco.com>, respectively. These look a lot like 822 header fields, and in some sense they are. What actually happens is that the mail daemon parses the message to extract the information it needs to run SMTP. The information it extracts is said to form an *envelope* for the message. The SMTP client uses this envelope to parameterize its exchange with the SMTP server. One historical note: The reason sendmail became so popular is that no one wanted to reimplement this message parsing function. While today's email addresses look pretty tame (e.g., Bob@cs.princeton.edu), this was not always the case. In the days before everyone was connected to the Internet, it was not uncommon to see email addresses of the form user%host@site!neighbor.

Mail Reader

The final step is for the user to actually retrieve his or her messages from the mailbox, read them, reply to them, and possibly save a copy for future reference. The user performs all these actions by interacting with a mail reader. As pointed out earlier, this reader was originally just a program running on the same machine as the user's mailbox, in which case it could simply read and write the file that implements the mailbox. This was the common case in the pre-laptop era. Today, most often the user accesses his or her mailbox from a remote machine using yet another protocol, such as POP or IMAP. It is beyond the scope of this book to discuss the user interface aspects of the mail reader, but it is definitely within our scope to talk about the access protocol. We consider IMAP, in particular.

IMAP is similar to SMTP in many ways. It is a client/server protocol running over TCP, where the client (running on the user's desktop machine) issues commands in the form of <CRLF>-terminated ASCII text lines and the mail server (running on the machine that maintains the user's mailbox) responds in kind. The exchange begins with the client authenticating him- or herself and identifying the mailbox he or she wants to access. This can be represented by the simple state transition diagram shown in Figure 9.2. In this diagram, LOGIN, AUTHENTICATE, SELECT, EXAMINE, CLOSE, and LOGOUT are example commands that the client can issue, while OK is one possible server response. Other common commands include FETCH, STORE, DELETE, and EXPUNGE, with the obvious meanings. Additional server responses include NO (client does not have permission to perform that operation) and BAD (command is ill formed).

When the user asks to FETCH a message, the server returns it in MIME format and the mail reader decodes it. In addition to the message itself, IMAP also defines a set of message *attributes* that are exchanged as part of other commands, independent of transferring the message itself. Message attributes include information like the size of the message and, more interestingly, various *flags* associated with the message (e.g., Seen, Answered, Deleted, and Recent). These flags are used to keep the client and server synchronized; that is, when the user deletes a message in the mail reader, the client needs to report this fact to the mail server. Later, should the user decide to expunge all deleted messages, the client issues an EXPUNGE command to the server, which knows to actually remove all earlier deleted messages from the mailbox.

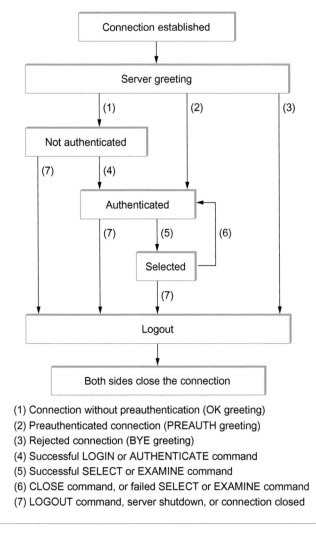

(1) Connection without preauthentication (OK greeting)
(2) Preauthenticated connection (PREAUTH greeting)
(3) Rejected connection (BYE greeting)
(4) Successful LOGIN or AUTHENTICATE command
(5) Successful SELECT or EXAMINE command
(6) CLOSE command, or failed SELECT or EXAMINE command
(7) LOGOUT command, server shutdown, or connection closed

■ FIGURE 9.2 IMAP state transition diagram.

Finally, note that when the user replies to a message, or sends a new message, the mail reader does not forward the message from the client to the mail server using IMAP, but it instead uses SMTP. This means that the user's mail server is effectively the first mail gateway traversed along the path from the desktop to the recipient's mailbox.

9.1.2 World Wide Web (HTTP)

The World Wide Web has been so successful and has made the Internet accessible to so many people that sometimes it seems to be synonymous with the Internet. In fact, the design of the system that became the Web started around 1989, long after the Internet had become a widely deployed system. The original goal of the Web was to find a way to organize and retrieve information, drawing on ideas about hypertext—interlinked documents—that had been around since at least the 1960s.[1] The core idea of hypertext is that one document can link to another document, and the protocol (HTTP) and document language (HTML) were designed to meet that goal.

One helpful way to think of the Web is as a set of cooperating clients and servers, all of whom speak the same language: HTTP. Most people are exposed to the Web through a graphical client program or web browser like Safari, Chrome, Firefox, or Internet Explorer. Figure 9.3 shows the Firefox browser in use, displaying a page of information from Princeton University.

Clearly, if you want to organize information into a system of linked documents or objects, you need to be able to retrieve one document to get started. Hence, any web browser has a function that allows the user to obtain an object by opening a URL. Uniform Resource Locators (URLs) are so familiar to most of us by now that it's easy to forget that they haven't been around forever. They provide information that allows objects on the Web to be located, and they look like the following:

http://www.cs.princeton.edu/index.html

If you opened that particular URL, your web browser would open a TCP connection to the web server at a machine called www.cs.princeton.edu and immediately retrieve and display the file called index.html. Most files on the Web contain images and text, and many have other objects such as audio and video clips, pieces of code, etc. They also frequently include URLs that point to other files that may be located on other machines, which is the core of the "hypertext" part of HTTP and HTML. A web browser has some way in which you can recognize URLs (often by highlighting or underlining some text) and then you can ask the browser to open them. These embedded URLs are called *hypertext links*. When you ask your web browser to open one of these embedded URLs (e.g., by pointing and clicking on it with a mouse), it will open a new connection and retrieve and display a new file. This is called *following a link*. It thus becomes very easy to hop from one machine to another around

---

[1]A short history of the Web provided by the World Wide Web consortium traces its roots to a 1945 article describing links between microfiche documents.

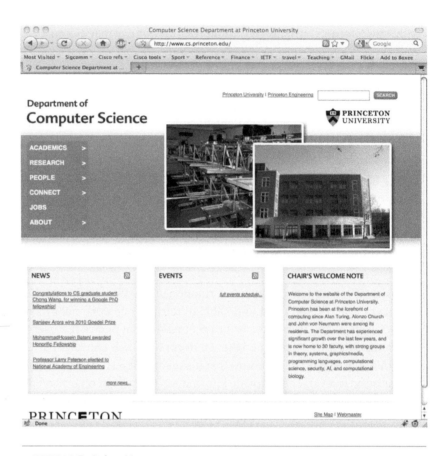

■ FIGURE 9.3 The Firefox web browser.

the network, following links to all sorts of information. Once you have a means to embed a link in a document and allow a user to follow that link to get another document, you have the basis of a hypertext system.

When you ask your browser to view a page, your browser (the client) fetches the page from the server using HTTP running over TCP. Like SMTP, HTTP is a text-oriented protocol. At its core, HTTP is a request/response protocol, where every message has the general form

```
START_LINE <CRLF>
MESSAGE_HEADER <CRLF>
<CRLF>
MESSAGE_BODY <CRLF>
```

where, as before, <CRLF> stands for carriage-return+line-feed. The first line (START_LINE) indicates whether this is a request message or a response message. In effect, it identifies the "remote procedure" to be executed (in the case of a request message), or the *status* of the request (in the case of a response message). The next set of lines specifies a collection of options and parameters that qualify the request or response. There are zero or more of these MESSAGE_HEADER lines—the set is terminated by a blank line—each of which looks like a header line in an email message. HTTP defines many possible header types, some of which pertain to request messages, some to response messages, and some to the data carried in the message body. Instead of giving the full set of possible header types, though, we just give a handful of representative examples. Finally, after the blank line comes the contents of the requested message (MESSAGE_BODY); this part of the message is where a server would place the requested page when responding to a request, and it is typically empty for request messages.

Why does HTTP run over TCP? The designers didn't have to do it that way, but TCP does provide a pretty good match to what HTTP needs, particularly by providing reliable delivery (who wants a Web page with missing data?), flow control, and congestion control. However, as we'll see below, there are a few issues that can arise from building a request/response protocol on top of TCP, especially if you ignore the subtleties of the interactions between the application and transport layer protocols.

Request Messages

The first line of an HTTP request message specifies three things: the operation to be performed, the Web page the operation should be performed on, and the version of HTTP being used. Although HTTP defines a wide assortment of possible request operations—including *write* operations that allow a Web page to be posted on a server—the two most common operations are GET (fetch the specified Web page) and HEAD (fetch status information about the specified Web page). The former is obviously used when your browser wants to retrieve and display a Web page. The latter is used to test the validity of a hypertext link or to see if a particular page has been modified since the browser last fetched it. The full set of operations is summarized in Table 9.1. As innocent as it sounds, the POST command enables much mischief (including spam) on the Internet.

Table 9.1 HTTP Request Operations

Operation	Description
OPTIONS	Request information about available options
GET	Retrieve document identified in URL
HEAD	Retrieve metainformation about document identified in URL
POST	Give information (e.g., annotation) to server
PUT	Store document under specified URL
DELETE	Delete specified URL
TRACE	Loopback request message
CONNECT	For use by proxies

For example, the START_LINE

```
GET http://www.cs.princeton.edu/index.html
HTTP/1.1
```

says that the client wants the server on host www.cs.princeton.edu to return the page named index.html. This particular example uses an *absolute* URL. It is also possible to use a *relative* identifier and specify the host name in one of the MESSAGE_HEADER lines; for example,

```
GET index.html HTTP/1.1
Host: www.cs.princeton.edu
```

Here, Host is one of the possible MESSAGE_HEADER fields. One of the more interesting of these is If-Modified-Since, which gives the client a way to conditionally request a Web page—the server returns the page only if it has been modified since the time specified in that header line.

Response Messages

Like request messages, response messages begin with a single START_LINE. In this case, the line specifies the version of HTTP being used, a three-digit code indicating whether or not the request was successful, and a text string giving the reason for the response. For example, the START_LINE

```
HTTP/1.1 202 Accepted
```

Table 9.2 Five Types of HTTP Result Codes		
Code	Type	Example Reasons
1xx	Informational	request received, continuing process
2xx	Success	action successfully received, understood, and accepted
3xx	Redirection	further action must be taken to complete the request
4xx	Client Error	request contains bad syntax or cannot be fulfilled
5xx	Server Error	server failed to fulfill an apparently valid request

indicates that the server was able to satisfy the request, while

```
HTTP/1.1 404 Not Found
```

indicates that it was not able to satisfy the request because the page was not found. There are five general types of response codes, with the first digit of the code indicating its type. Table 9.2 summarizes the five types of codes.

As with the unexpected consequences of the POST request message, it is sometimes surprising how various response messages are used in practice. For example, request redirection (specifically code 302) turns out to be a powerful mechanism that plays a big role in Content Distribution Networks (CDNs) (see Section 9.4.3) by redirecting requests to a nearby cache.

Also similar to request messages, response messages can contain one or more MESSAGE_HEADER lines. These lines relay additional information back to the client. For example, the Location header line specifies that the requested URL is available at another location. Thus, if the Princeton CS Department Web page had moved from http://www.cs.princeton.edu/index.html to http://www.princeton.edu/cs/index.html, for example, then the server at the original address might respond with

```
HTTP/1.1 301 Moved Permanently
Location: http://www.princeton.edu/cs/index.html
```

In the common case, the response message will also carry the requested page. This page is an HTML document, but since it may carry nontextual data (e.g., a GIF image), it is encoded using MIME (see

Section 9.1.1). Certain of the MESSAGE_HEADER lines give attributes of the page contents, including Content-Length (number of bytes in the contents), Expires (time at which the contents are considered stale), and Last-Modified (time at which the contents were last modified at the server).

Uniform Resource Identifiers

The URLs that HTTP uses as addresses are one type of *Uniform Resource Identifier* (URI). A URI is a character string that identifies a resource, where a resource can be anything that has identity, such as a document, an image, or a service.

The format of URIs allows various more specialized kinds of resource identifiers to be incorporated into the URI space of identifiers. The first part of a URI is a *scheme* that names a particular way of identifying a certain kind of resource, such as mailto for email addresses or file for file names. The second part of a URI, separated from the first part by a colon, is the *scheme-specific part*. It is a resource identifier consistent with the scheme in the first part, as in the URIs

```
mailto:santa@northpole.org
```

and

```
file:///C:/foo.html
```

A resource doesn't have to be retrievable or accessible. We saw an example of this earlier in Section 7.1.3—extensible markup language (XML) namespaces are identified by URIs that look an awful lot like URLs, but strictly speaking they are not *locators* because they don't tell you how to locate something; they just provide a globally unique identifier for the namespace. There is no requirement that you can retrieve anything at the URI given as the target namespace of an XML document. We'll see another example of a URI that is not a URL in Section 9.2.1.

TCP Connections

The original version of HTTP (1.0) established a separate TCP connection for each data item retrieved from the server. It's not too hard to see how this was a very inefficient mechanism: connection setup and teardown messages had to be exchanged between the client and server even if all the client wanted to do was verify that it had the most recent copy of a page.

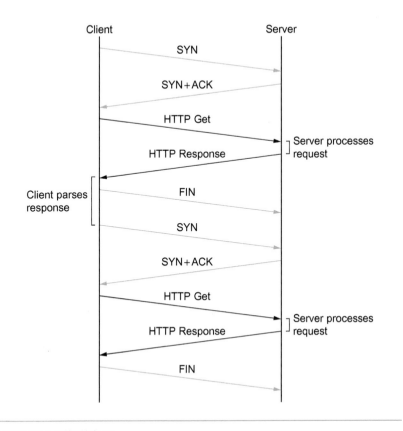

HTTP 1.0 behavior.

Thus, retrieving a page that included some text and a dozen icons or other small graphics would result in 13 separate TCP connections being established and closed. Figure 9.4 shows the sequence of events for fetching a page that has just a single embedded object. Colored lines indicate TCP messages, while black lines indicate the HTTP requests and responses. (Some of the TCP ACKs are not shown to avoid cluttering the picture.) You can see two round trip times are spent setting up TCP connections while another two (at least) are spent getting the page and image. As well as the latency impact, there is also processing cost on the server to handle the extra TCP connection establishment and termination.

To overcome this situation, HTTP version 1.1 introduced *persistent connections*—the client and server can exchange multiple request/response messages over the same TCP connection. Persistent connections have many advantages. First, they obviously eliminate the

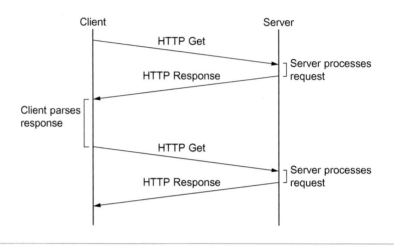

■ **FIGURE 9.5** HTTP 1.1 behavior with persistent connections.

connection setup overhead, thereby reducing the load on the server, the load on the network caused by the additional TCP packets, and the delay perceived by the user. Second, because a client can send multiple request messages down a single TCP connection, TCP's congestion window mechanism is able to operate more efficiently. This is because it's not necessary to go through the slow start phase for each page. Figure 9.5 shows the transaction from Figure 9.4 using a persistent connection in the case where the connection is already open (presumably due to some prior access of the same server).

Persistent connections do not come without a price, however. The problem is that neither the client nor server necessarily knows how long to keep a particular TCP connection open. This is especially critical on the server, which might be asked to keep connections opened on behalf of thousands of clients. The solution is that the server must time out and close a connection if it has received no requests on the connection for a period of time. Also, both the client and server must watch to see if the other side has elected to close the connection, and they must use that information as a signal that they should close their side of the connection as well. (Recall that both sides must close a TCP connection before it is fully terminated.) Concerns about this added complexity may be one reason why persistent connections were not used from the outset, but today it is widely accepted that the benefits of persistent connections more than offset the drawbacks.

Caching

One of the most active areas of research (and entrepreneurship) in the Internet today is how to effectively cache Web pages. Caching has many benefits. From the client's perspective, a page that can be retrieved from a nearby cache can be displayed much more quickly than if it has to be fetched from across the world. From the server's perspective, having a cache intercept and satisfy a request reduces the load on the server.

Caching can be implemented in many different places. For example, a user's browser can cache recently accessed pages and simply display the cached copy if the user visits the same page again. As another example, a site can support a single site-wide cache. This allows users to take advantage of pages previously downloaded by other users. Closer to the middle of the Internet, Internet Service Providers (ISPs) can cache pages. Note that, in the second case, the users within the site most likely know what machine is caching pages on behalf of the site, and they configure their browsers to connect directly to the caching host. This node is sometimes called a *proxy*. In contrast, the sites that connect to the ISP are probably not aware that the ISP is caching pages. It simply happens to be the case that HTTP requests coming out of the various sites pass through a common ISP router. This router can peek inside the request message and look at the URL for the requested page. If it has the page in its cache, it returns it. If not, it forwards the request to the server and watches for the response to fly by in the other direction. When it does, the router saves a copy in the hope that it can use it to satisfy a future request.[2]

No matter where pages are cached, the ability to cache Web pages is important enough that HTTP has been designed to make the job easier. The trick is that the cache needs to make sure it is not responding with an out-of-date version of the page. For example, the server assigns an expiration date (the **Expires** header field) to each page it sends back to the client (or to a cache between the server and client). The cache remembers this date and knows that it need not reverify the page each time it is requested until after that expiration date has passed. After that time (or if that header field is not set) the cache can use the **HEAD** or conditional **GET** operation (**GET** with **If-Modified-Since** header line) to verify that it

---

[2]There are quite a few issues with this sort of caching, ranging from the technical to the regulatory. One example of a technical challenge is the effect of *asymmetric paths*, when the request to the server and the response to the client do not follow the same sequence of router hops.

has the most recent copy of the page. More generally, there are a set of *cache directives* that must be obeyed by all caching mechanisms along the request/response chain. These directives specify whether or not a document can be cached, how long it can be cached, how fresh a document must be, and so on. We'll look at the related issue of CDNs—which are effectively distributed caches—in Section 9.4.3.

9.1.3 Web Services

So far we have focused on interactions between a human and a machine. For example, a human uses a web browser to interact with a server, and the interaction proceeds in response to input from the user (e.g., by clicking on links). However, there is increasing demand for direct computer-to-computer interaction. And, just as the applications described above need protocols, so too do the applications that communicate directly with each other. We conclude this section by looking at the challenges of building large numbers of application-to-application protocols and some of the proposed solutions.

Much of the motivation for enabling direct application-to-application communication comes from the business world. Historically, interactions between enterprises—businesses or other organizations—have involved some manual steps such as filling out an order form or making a phone call to determine whether some product is in stock. Even within a single enterprise it is common to have manual steps between software systems that cannot interact directly because they were developed independently. Increasingly, such manual interactions are being replaced with direct application-to-application interaction. An ordering application at enterprise A would send a message to an order fulfillment application at enterprise B, which would respond immediately indicating whether the order can be filled. Perhaps, if the order cannot be filled by B, the application at A would immediately order from another supplier or solicit bids from a collection of suppliers.

Here is a simple example of what we are talking about. Suppose you buy a book at an online retailer like Amazon.com. Once your book has been shipped, Amazon could send you the tracking number in an email, and then you could head over to the website for the shipping company—http://www.fedex.com, perhaps—and track the package. However, you can also track your package directly from the Amazon.com website. In order to make this happen, Amazon has to be able to send a query to FedEx, in a format that FedEx understands, interpret the result, and display it in a Web page that perhaps contains other information about your order. Underlying the user experience of getting all the information about the order served up at once on the Amazon.com Web page is the fact that Amazon and FedEx had to have a protocol for exchanging the information needed to track packages—call it the Package Tracking Protocol. It should be clear that there are so many potential protocols of this type that we'd better have some tools to simplify the task of specifying them and building them.

Network applications, even those that cross organization boundaries, are not new—email and web browsing cross such boundaries. What is new about this problem is the scale. Not scale in the size of the network, but scale in the number of different kinds of network applications. Both the protocol specifications and the implementations of those protocols for traditional applications like electronic mail and file transfer have typically been developed by a small group of networking experts. To enable the vast number of potential network applications to be developed quickly, it was necessary to come up with some technologies that simplify and automate the task of application protocol design and implementation.

Two architectures have been advocated as solutions to this problem. Both architectures are called *Web Services*, taking their name from the term for the individual applications that offer a remotely accessible service to client applications to form network applications.[3] The terms used as informal shorthand to distinguish the two Web Services architectures are *SOAP* and *REST* (as in, "the SOAP vs. REST debate"). We will discuss the technical meanings of those terms shortly.

The SOAP architecture's approach to the problem is to make it feasible, at least in theory, to generate protocols that are customized to each network application. The key elements of the approach are a framework for protocol specification, software toolkits for automatically generating protocol implementations from the specifications, and modular partial specifications that can be reused across protocols.

The REST architecture's approach to the problem is to regard individual Web Services as World Wide Web resources—identified by URIs and accessed via HTTP. Essentially, the REST architecture is just the Web

---

[3]The name *Web Services* is unfortunately so generic sounding that many mistakenly assume that it includes any sort of service associated with the Web.

architecture. The Web architecture's strengths include stability and a demonstrated scalability (in the network-size sense). It could be considered a weakness that HTTP is not well suited to the usual procedural or operation-oriented style of invoking a remote service. REST advocates argue, however, that rich services can nonetheless be exposed using a more data-oriented or document-passing style for which HTTP is well suited.

Although both architectures are being actively adopted, they are still new enough that we don't yet have much empirical data about their real-world use. One architecture may come to dominate, or they may merge in some way, or we may find that one architecture is better suited to certain kinds of applications while the other architecture is better for others.

Custom Application Protocols (WSDL, SOAP)

The architecture informally referred to as SOAP is based on *Web Services Description Language* (WSDL) and *SOAP*.[4] Both of these standards are issued by the World Wide Web Consortium (W3C). This is the architecture that people usually mean when they use the term Web Services without any preceding qualifier. As these standards are still evolving, our discussion here is effectively a snapshot.

WSDL and SOAP are frameworks for specifying and implementing application protocols and transport protocols, respectively. They are generally used together, although that is not strictly required. WSDL is used to specify application-specific details such as what operations are supported, the formats of the application data to invoke or respond to those operations, and whether an operation involves a response. SOAP's role is to make it easy to define a transport protocol with exactly the desired semantics regarding protocol features such as reliability and security.

Both WSDL and SOAP consist primarily of a protocol specification language. Both languages are based on XML (Section 7.1.3) with an eye toward making specifications accessible to software tools such as stub compilers and directory services. In a world of many custom protocols, support for automating generation of implementations is crucial to avoid the effort of manually implementing each protocol. Support software generally takes the form of toolkits and application servers developed

---

[4]Although the name *SOAP* originated as an acronym, it officially no longer stands for anything.

by third-party vendors, which allows developers of individual Web Services to focus more on the business problem they need to solve (such as tracking the package purchased by a customer).

Defining Application Protocols

WSDL has chosen a procedural *operation* model of application protocols. An abstract Web Service interface consists of a set of named operations, each representing a simple interaction between a client and the Web Service. An operation is analogous to a remotely callable procedure in an RPC system. An example from W3C's WSDL Primer is a hotel reservation Web Service with two operations, CheckAvailability and MakeReservation.

Each operation specifies a *Message Exchange Pattern* (MEP) that gives the sequence in which the messages are to be transmitted, including the fault messages to be sent when an error disrupts the message flow. Several MEPs are predefined, and new custom MEPs can be defined, but it appears that in practice only two MEPs are being used: **In-Only** (a single message from client to service) and **In-Out** (a request from client and a corresponding reply from service). These patterns should be very familiar, and suggest that the costs of supporting MEP flexibility perhaps outweigh the benefits.

MEPs are templates that have placeholders instead of specific message types or formats, so part of the definition of an operation involves specifying which message formats to map into the placeholders in the pattern. Message formats are not defined at the bit level that is typical of protocols we have discussed. They are instead defined as an abstract data model using XML Schema (Section 7.1.3). XML Schema provides a set of primitive data types and ways to define compound data types. Data that conforms to an XML Schema-defined format—its abstract data model—can be concretely represented using XML, or it can use another representation, such as the "binary" representation Fast Infoset.

WSDL nicely separates the parts of a protocol that can be specified abstractly—operations, MEPs, abstract message formats—from the parts that must be concrete. WSDL's concrete part specifies an underlying protocol, how MEPs are mapped onto it, and what bit-level representation is used for messages on the wire. This part of a specification is known as a *binding*, although it is better described as an implementation, or a mapping onto an implementation. WSDL has predefined bindings for HTTP and SOAP-based protocols, with parameters that allow the protocol designer to fine-tune the mapping onto those protocols. There is a framework for defining new bindings, but SOAP protocols dominate.

A crucial aspect of how WSDL mitigates the problem of specifying large numbers of protocols is through reuse of what are essentially specification modules. The WSDL specification of a Web Service may be composed of multiple WSDL documents, and individual WSDL documents may also be used in other Web Service specifications. This modularity makes it easier to develop a specification and easier to ensure that, if two specifications are supposed to have some elements that are identical (for example, so that they can be supported by the same tool), then those elements are indeed identical. This modularity, together with WSDL's defaulting rules, also helps keep specifications from becoming overwhelmingly verbose for human protocol designers.

WSDL modularity should be familiar to anyone who has developed moderately large pieces of software. A WSDL document need not be a complete specification; it could, for example, define a single message format. The partial specifications are uniquely identified using XML Namespaces (Section 7.1.3); each WSDL document specifies the URI of a *target namespace*, and any new definitions in the document are named in the context of that namespace. One WSDL document can incorporate components of another by *including* the second document if both share the same target namespace or *importing* it if the target namespaces differ.

Defining Transport Protocols

Although SOAP is sometimes called a protocol, it is better thought of as a framework for defining protocols. As the SOAP 1.2 specification explains, "SOAP provides a simple messaging framework whose core functionality is concerned with providing extensibility." SOAP uses many of the same strategies as WSDL, including message formats defined using XML Schema, bindings to underlying protocols, Message Exchange Patterns, and reusable specification elements identified using XML namespaces.

SOAP is used to define transport protocols with exactly the features needed to support a particular application protocol. SOAP aims to make it feasible to define many such protocols by using reusable components. Each component captures the header information and logic that go into implementing a particular feature. To define a protocol with a certain set of features, just compose the corresponding components. Let's look more closely at this aspect of SOAP.

SOAP 1.2 introduced a *feature* abstraction, which the specification describes thus: *A SOAP feature is an extension of the SOAP messaging framework. Although SOAP poses no constraints on the potential scope of such features, example features may include "reliability," "security," "correlation," "routing," and message exchange patterns (MEPs) such as request/response, one-way, and peer-to-peer conversations.* A SOAP feature specification must include:

- A URI that identifies the feature
- The state information and processing, abstractly described, that is required at each SOAP node to implement the feature
- The information to be relayed to the next node
- (If the feature is a MEP) the life cycle and temporal/causal relationships of the messages exchanged—for example, responses follow requests and are sent to the originator of the request

Note that this formalization of the concept of a protocol feature is rather low level; it is almost a design.

Given a set of features, there are two strategies for defining a SOAP protocol that will implement them. One is by layering: binding SOAP to an underlying protocol in such a way as to derive the features. For example, we could obtain a request/response protocol by binding SOAP to HTTP, with a SOAP request in an HTTP request and a SOAP reply in an HTTP response. Because this is such a common example, it happens that SOAP has a predefined binding to HTTP; new bindings may be defined using the SOAP Protocol Binding Framework.

The second and more flexible way to implement features involves *header blocks*. A SOAP message consists of an Envelope, which contains a Header that contains header blocks, and a Body, which contains the payload destined for the ultimate receiver. This message structure is illustrated in Figure 9.6.

It should be a familiar notion by now that certain header information corresponds to particular features. A digital signature is used to implement authentication, a sequence number is used for reliability, and a checksum is used to detect message corruption. A SOAP header block is intended to encapsulate the header information that corresponds to a particular feature. The correspondence is not always one-to-one since multiple header blocks could be involved in a single feature, or a single

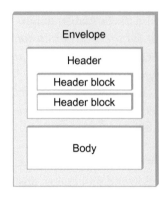

■ FIGURE 9.6 SOAP message structure.

header block could be used in multiple features. A *SOAP module* is a specification of the syntax and the semantics of one or more header blocks. Each module is intended to provide one or more features and must declare the features it implements.

The goal behind SOAP modules is to be able to compose a protocol with a set of features by simply including each of the corresponding module specifications. If your protocol is required to have at-most-once semantics and authentication, include the corresponding modules in your specification. This represents a novel approach to modularizing protocol services, an alternative to the protocol layering we have seen throughout this book. It is bit like flattening a series of protocol layers into a single protocol, but in a structured way. It remains to be seen how well SOAP features and modules, introduced in version 1.2 of SOAP, will work in practice. The main weakness of this scheme is that modules may well interfere with each other. A module specification is required to specify any *known* interactions with other SOAP modules, but clearly that doesn't do much to alleviate the problem. On the other hand, a core set of features and modules that provides the most important properties may be small enough to be well known and well understood.

Standardizing Web Services Protocols

As we've said, WSDL and SOAP aren't protocols; they are standards for *specifying* protocols. For different enterprises to implement Web Services that interoperate with each other, it is not enough to agree to use WSDL and SOAP to define their protocols; they must agree on—standardize— specific protocols. For example, you could imagine that online retailers and shipping companies might like to standardize a protocol by which they exchange information, along the lines of the simple package tracking example at the start of this section. This standardization is crucial for tool support as well as interoperability. And, yet, different network applications in this architecture must necessarily differ in at least the message formats and operations they use.

This tension between standardization and customization is tackled by establishing partial standards called *profiles*. A profile is a set of guidelines that narrow or constrain choices available in WSDL, SOAP, and other standards that may be referenced in defining a protocol. They may at the same time resolve ambiguities or gaps in those standards. In practice, a profile often formalizes an emerging *de facto* standard.

The broadest and most widely adopted profile is known as the *WS-I Basic Profile*. It was proposed by the Web Services Interoperability Organization (WS-I), an industry consortium, while WSDL and SOAP are specified by the World Wide Web Consortium (W3C). The Basic Profile resolves some of the most basic choices faced in defining a Web Service. Most notably it requires that WSDL be bound exclusively to SOAP and SOAP be bound exclusively to HTTP and use the HTTP POST method. It also specifies which versions of WSDL and SOAP must be used.

The *WS-I Basic Security Profile* adds security constraints to the Basic Profile by specifying how the SSL/TLS layer (Section 8.4.3) is to be used and requiring conformance to *WS-Security* (Web Services Security). WS-Security specifies how to use various existing techniques such as X.509 public key certificates (Section 8.2.1) and Kerberos (Section 8.3.3) to provide security features in SOAP protocols.

WS-Security is just the first of a growing suite of SOAP-level standards established by the industry consortium OASIS (Organization for the Advancement of Structured Information Standards). The standards known collectively as *WS-** include WS-Reliability, WS-Reliable-Messaging, WS-Coordination, and WS-AtomicTransaction.

A Generic Application Protocol (REST)

The WSDL/SOAP Web Services architecture is based on the assumption that the best way to integrate applications across networks is via protocols that are customized to each application. That architecture is designed to make it practical to specify and implement all those protocols. In contrast, the REST Web Services architecture is based on the assumption that the best way to integrate applications across networks is by re-applying the model underlying the World Wide Web architecture (Section 9.1.2). This model, articulated by Web architect Roy Fielding, is known as *REpresentational State Transfer* (REST). There is no need for a new REST architecture for Web Services—the existing Web architecture is sufficient, although a few extensions are probably necessary. In the Web architecture, individual Web Services are regarded as resources identified by URIs and accessed via HTTP—a single generic application protocol with a single generic addressing scheme.

Where WSDL has user-defined operations, REST uses the small set of available HTTP methods, such as **GET** and **POST** (see Table 9.1). So how can these simple methods provide an interface to a rich Web Service? By employing the REST model, in which the complexity is shifted from the protocol to the payload. The payload is a representation of the abstract state of a resource. For example, a **GET** could return a representation of the current state of the resource, and a **POST** could send a representation of a desired state of the resource.

The representation of a resource state is abstract; it need not resemble how the resource is actually implemented by a particular Web Service instance. It is not necessary to transmit a complete resource state in each message. The size of messages can be reduced by transmitting just the parts of a state that are of interest (e.g., just the parts that are being modified). And, because Web Services share a single protocol and address space with other web resources, parts of states can be passed by reference—by URI—even when they are other Web Services.

This approach is best summarized as a data-oriented or document-passing style, as opposed to a procedural style. Defining an application protocol in this architecture consists of defining the document structure (i.e., the state representation). XML and the lighter-weight JavaScript Object Notation (JSON) are the most frequently used presentation languages (Section 7.1) for this state. Interoperability depends on agreement, between a Web Service and its client, on the state representation. Of course, the same is true in the SOAP architecture; a Web Service and its client have to be in agreement on payload format. The difference is that in the SOAP architecture interoperability additionally depends on agreement on the protocol; in the REST architecture, the protocol is always HTTP, so that source of interoperability problems is eliminated.

One of the selling features of REST is that it leverages the infrastructure that has been deployed to support the Web. For example, Web proxies can enforce security or cache information. Existing content distribution networks (CDNs) can be used to support RESTful applications.

In contrast with WSDL/SOAP, the Web has had time for standards to stabilize and to demonstrate that it scales very well. It also comes with some security in the form of Secure Socket Layer (SSL)/Transport Layer Security (TLS). The Web and REST may also have an advantage in evolvability. Although the WSDL and SOAP *frameworks* are highly flexible with regard to what new features and bindings can go into the definition of a protocol, that flexibility is irrelevant once the protocol is defined. Standardized protocols such as HTTP are designed with a provision for being extended in a backward-compatible way. HTTP's own extensibility takes the form of headers, new methods, and new content types. Protocol designers using WSDL/SOAP need to design such extensibility into each of their custom protocols. Of course, the designers of state representations in a REST architecture also have to design for evolvability.

An area where WSDL/SOAP may have an advantage is in adapting or wrapping previously written, "legacy" applications to conform to Web Services. This is an important point since most Web Services will be based on legacy applications for the near future at least. These applications usually have a procedural interface that maps more easily into WSDL's operations than REST states. The REST versus WSDL/SOAP competition may very well hinge on how easy or difficult it turns out to be to devise REST-style interfaces for individual Web Services. We may find that some Web Services are better served by WSDL/SOAP and others by REST.

The online retailer Amazon.com, as it happens, was an early adopter (2002) of Web Services. Interestingly, Amazon made its systems publicly accessible via *both* of the Web Services architectures, and according to some reports a substantial majority of developers use the REST interface. Of course, this is just one data point and may well reflect factors specific to Amazon.

LAB 14:
Applications

LAB 15:
Web Caching and Data Compression

9.2 MULTIMEDIA APPLICATIONS

Just like the traditional applications described earlier in this chapter, multimedia applications such as telephony and videoconferencing need their own protocols. Much of the initial experience in designing protocols for multimedia applications came from the MBone tools—applications such as vat and vic that were developed for use on the MBone, an overlay network that supports IP multicast to enable multiparty conferencing. (More on overlay networks including the MBone in the next section.) Initially, each application implemented its own protocol (or protocols), but it became apparent that many multimedia applications have common requirements. This ultimately led to the development of a number of general-purpose protocols for use by multimedia applications.

We have already seen a number of protocols that multimedia applications use. The Real-Time Transport Protocol (RTP; described in Section 5.4) provides many of the functions that are common to multimedia applications such as conveying timing information and identifying the coding schemes and media types of an application.

The Resource Reservation Protocol (RSVP; see Section 6.5.2) can be used to request the allocation of resources in the network so that the desired quality of service (QoS) can be provided to an application. We will see how resource allocation interacts with other aspects of multimedia applications in Section 9.2.2.

In addition to these protocols for multimedia transport and resource allocation, many multimedia applications also need a signalling or *session control* protocol. For example, suppose that we wanted to be able to make telephone calls across the Internet (Voice over IP, or VoIP). We would need some mechanism to notify the intended recipient of such a call that we wanted to talk to her, such as by sending a message to some multimedia device that would cause it to make a ringing sound. We would also like to be able to support features like call forwarding, three-way calling, etc. The Session Initiation Protocol (SIP) and H.323 are examples of protocols that address the issues of session control; we begin our discussion of multimedia applications by examining these protocols.

9.2.1 Session Control and Call Control (SDP, SIP, H.323)

To understand some of the issues of session control, consider the following problem. Suppose you want to hold a videoconference at a certain time and make it available to a wide number of participants. Perhaps you have decided to encode the video stream using the MPEG-2 standard, to use the multicast IP address 224.1.1.1 for transmission of the data, and to send it using RTP over UDP port number 4000. How would you make all that information available to the intended participants? One way would be to put all that information in an email and send it out, but ideally there should be a standard format and protocol for disseminating this sort of information. The IETF has defined protocols for just this purpose. The protocols that have been defined include

- Session Description Protocol (SDP)
- Session Announcement Protocol (SAP)
- Session Initiation Protocol (SIP)
- Simple Conference Control Protocol (SCCP)

You might think that this is a lot of protocols for a seemingly simple task, but there are many aspects of the problem and several different situations in which it must be addressed. For example, there is a difference between announcing the fact that a certain conference session is going to be made available on the MBone (which would be done using SDP and SAP) and trying to make an Internet phone call to a certain user at a particular time (which could be done using SDP and SIP). In the former case, you could consider your job done once you have sent all the session information in a standard format to a well-known multicast address. In the latter, you would need to locate one or more users, get a message to them announcing your desire to talk (analogous to ringing their phone), and perhaps negotiate a suitable audio encoding among all parties. We will look first at SDP, which is common to many applications, then at SIP, which is widely used for a number of interactive applications such as Internet telephony.

Session Description Protocol (SDP)

The Session Description Protocol (SDP) is a rather general protocol that can be used in a variety of situations and is typically used in conjunction with one or more other protocols (e.g., SIP). It conveys the following information:

- The name and purpose of the session
- Start and end times for the session
- The media types (e.g., audio, video) that comprise the session
- Detailed information required to receive the session (e.g., the multicast address to which data will be sent, the transport protocol to be used, the port numbers, the encoding scheme)

SDP provides this information formatted in ASCII using a sequence of lines of text, each of the form "<type>=<value>." An example of an SDP message will illustrate the main points.

```
v=0
o=larry 2890844526 2890842807 IN IP4 128.112.136.10
s=Networking 101
i=A class on computer networking
u=http://www.cs.princeton.edu/
e=larry@cs.princeton.edu
c=IN IP4 224.2.17.12/127
t=2873397496 2873404696
m=audio 49170 RTP/AVP 0
m=video 51372 RTP/AVP 31
m=application 32416 udp wb
```

Note that SDP, like HTML, is fairly easy for a human to read but has strict formatting rules that make it possible for machines to interpret the data unambiguously. For example, the SDP specification defines all the possible information types that are allowed to appear, the order in which they must appear, and the format and reserved words for every type that is defined.

The first thing to notice is that each information type is identified by a single character. For example, the line v=0 tells us that "version" has the value zero; that is, this message is formatted according to version zero of SDP. The next line provides the "origin" of the session which contains enough information to uniquely identify the session. larry is a username of the session creator, and 128.112.136.10 is the IP address of his computer. The number following larry is a session identifier that is chosen to be unique to that machine. This is followed by a "version" number for the SDP announcement; if the session information was updated by a later message, the version number would be increased.

The next three lines (s, i, and u) provide the session name, a session description, and a session Uniform Resource Identifier (URI, as described in Section 9.1.2)—information that would be helpful to a user in deciding whether to participate in this session. Such information could be displayed in the user interface of a session directory tool that shows current and upcoming events that have been advertised using SDP. The next line (e=...) contains an email address of a person to contact regarding the

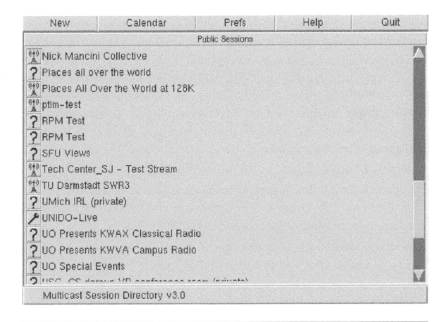

New	Calendar	Prefs	Help	Quit

Public Sessions

- Nick Mancini Collective
- Places all over the world
- Places All Over the World at 128K
- ptim-test
- RPM Test
- RPM Test
- SFU Views
- Tech Center_SJ – Test Stream
- TU Darmstadt SWR3
- UMich IRL (private)
- UNIDO–Live
- UO Presents KWAX Classical Radio
- UO Presents KWVA Campus Radio
- UO Special Events

Multicast Session Directory v3.0

■ FIGURE 9.7 A session directory tool displays information extracted from SDP messages.

session. Figure 9.7 shows a screen shot of a (somewhat archaic) session directory tool called sdr along with the descriptions of several sessions that had been announced at the time the picture was taken.

Next we get to the technical details that would enable an application program to participate in the session. The line beginning c=... provides the IP multicast address to which data for this session will be sent; a user would need to join this multicast group to receive the session. Next we see the start and end times for the session (encoded as integers according to the Network Time Protocol). Finally, we get to the information about the media for this session. This session has three media types available—audio, video, and a shared whiteboard application known as "wb." For each media type there is one line of information formatted as follows:

```
m=<media> <port> <transport> <format>
```

The media types are self-explanatory, and the port numbers in each case are UDP ports. When we look at the "transport" field, we can see that the wb application runs directly over UDP, while the audio and video are transported using "RTP/AVP." This means that they run over RTP and use the *application profile* (as defined in Section 5.4) known as *AVP*. That application profile defines a number of different encoding schemes for audio and video; we can see in this case that the audio is using encoding 0 (which is an encoding using an 8-kHz sampling rate and 8 bits per sample) and the video is using encoding 31, which represents the H.261 encoding scheme. These "magic numbers" for the encoding schemes are defined in the RFC that defines the AVP profile; it is also possible to describe nonstandard coding schemes in SDP.

Finally, we see a description of the "wb" media type. All the encoding information for this data is specific to the wb application, and so it is sufficient just to provide the name of the application in the "format" field. This is analogous to putting application/wb in a MIME message.

Now that we know how to describe sessions, we can look at how they can be initiated. One way in which SDP is used is to announce multimedia conferences, by sending SDP messages to a well-known multicast address. The session directory tool shown in Figure 9.7 would function by joining that multicast group and displaying information that it gleans from received SDP messages. SDP is also used in the delivery of entertainment video of IP (often called IPTV) to provide information about the video content on each TV channel.

SDP also plays an important role in conjunction with the Session Initiation Protocol (SIP). With the widespread adoption of Voice over IP (i.e., the support of telephony-like applications over IP networks) and IP-based video conferencing, SIP is now one of the more important members of the Internet protocol suite.

SIP

SIP is an application layer protocol that bears a certain resemblance to HTTP, being based on a similar request/response model. However, it is designed with rather different sorts of applications in mind and thus provides quite different capabilities than HTTP. The capabilities provided by SIP can be grouped into five categories:

- User location—Determining the correct device with which to communicate to reach a particular user
- User availability—Determining if the user is willing or able to take part in a particular communication session
- User capabilities—Determining such items as the choice of media and coding scheme to use

- Session setup—Establishing session parameters such as port numbers to be used by the communicating parties
- Session management—A range of functions including transferring sessions (e.g., to implement "call forwarding") and modifying session parameters

Most of these functions are easy enough to understand, but the issue of location bears some further discussion. One important difference between SIP and, say, HTTP, is that SIP is primarily used for human-to-human communication. Thus, it is important to be able to locate individual *users*, not just machines. And, unlike email, it's not good enough just to locate a server that the user will be checking on at some later date and dump the message there—we need to know where the user is right now if we want to be able to communicate with him in real time. This is further complicated by the fact that a user might choose to communicate using a range of different devices, such as using his desktop PC when he's in the office and using a handheld device when traveling. Multiple devices might be active at the same time and might have widely different capabilities (e.g., an alphanumeric pager and a PC-based video "phone"). Ideally, it should be possible for other users to be able to locate and communicate with the appropriate device at any time. Furthermore, the user must be able to have control over when, where, and from whom he receives calls.

To enable a user to exercise the appropriate level of control over his calls, SIP introduces the notion of a proxy. A SIP proxy can be thought of as a point of contact for a user to which initial requests for communication with him are sent. Proxies also perform functions on behalf of callers. We can see how proxies work best through an example.

Consider the two users in Figure 9.8. The first thing to notice is that each user has a name in the format user@domain, very much like an email

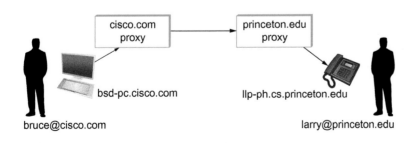

■ FIGURE 9.8 Establishing communication through SIP proxies.

address. When user Bruce wants to initiate a session with Larry, he sends his initial SIP message to the local proxy for his domain, cisco.com. Among other things, this initial message contains a *SIP URI*—these are a form of uniform resource identifier which look like this:

```
SIP:larry@princeton.edu
```

A SIP URI provides complete identification of a user, but (unlike a URL) does not provide his location, since that may change over time. We will see shortly how the location of a user can be determined.

Upon receiving the initial message from Bruce, the cisco.com proxy looks at the SIP URI and deduces that this message should be sent to the princeton.edu proxy. For now, we assume that the princeton.edu proxy has access to some database that enables it to obtain a mapping from the name larry@princeton.edu to the IP address of one or more devices at which Larry currently wishes to receive messages. The proxy can therefore forward the message on to Larry's chosen device(s). Sending the message to more than one device is called *forking* and may be done either in parallel or in series (e.g., send it to his mobile phone if he doesn't answer the phone at his desk).

The initial message from Bruce to Larry is likely to be a SIP invite message, which looks something like the following:

```
INVITE sip:larry@princeton.edu SIP/2.0
Via: SIP/2.0/UDP bsd-pc.cisco.com;branch=z9hG4bK433yte4
To: Larry <sip:larry@princeton.edu>
From: Bruce <sip:bruce@cisco.com>;tag=55123
Call-ID: xy745jj210re3@bsd-pc.cisco.com
CSeq: 271828 INVITE
Contact: <sip:bruce@bsd-pc.cisco.com>
Content-Type: application/sdp
Content-Length: 142
```

The first line identifies the type of function to be performed (invite); the resource on which to perform it, the called party (sip:larry@princeton.edu); and the protocol version (2.0). The subsequent header lines probably look somewhat familiar because of their resemblance to the header lines in an email message. SIP defines a large number of header fields, only some of which we describe here. Note that the Via: header in this example identifies the device from which this message originated. The Content-Type: and Content-Length: headers describe the contents of the message following the header, just as in a MIME-encoded email message. In this case, the content is an SDP message. That message would describe such things as the type of media (audio, video, etc.) that Bruce would like to exchange with Larry and other properties of the session such as codec types that he supports. Note that the Content-Type: field in SIP provides the capability to use any protocol for this purpose, although SDP is the most common.

Returning to the example, when the invite message arrives at the cisco.com proxy, not only does the proxy forward the message on toward princeton.edu, but it also responds to the sender of the invite. Just as in HTTP, all responses have a response code, and the organization of codes is similar to that for HTTP, as shown in Table 9.2. In Figure 9.9 we can see a sequence of SIP messages and responses.

The first response message in this figure is the provisional response 100 trying, which indicates that the message was received without error by the caller's proxy. Once the invite is delivered to Larry's phone, it alerts Larry and responds with a 180 ringing message. The arrival of this

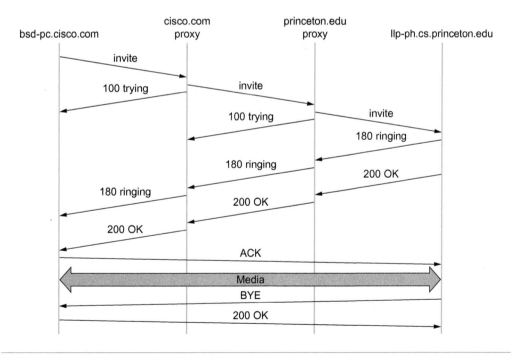

■ FIGURE 9.9 Message flow for a basic SIP session.

message at Bruce's computer is a sign that it can generate a "ringtone." Assuming Larry is willing and able to communicate with Bruce, he could pick up his phone, causing the message 200 OK to be sent. Bruce's computer responds with an ACK, and media (e.g., an RTP-encapsulated audio stream) can now begin to flow between the two parties. Note that at this point the parties know each others' addresses, so the ACK can be sent directly, bypassing the proxies. The proxies are now no longer involved in the call. Note that the media will therefore typically take a different path through the network than the original signalling messages. Furthermore, even if one or both of the proxies were to crash at this point, the call could continue on normally. Finally, when one party wishes to end the session, it sends a BYE message, which elicits a 200 OK response under normal circumstances.

There are a few details that we have glossed over. One is the negotiation of session characteristics. Perhaps Bruce would have liked to communicate using both audio and video but Larry's phone only supports audio. Thus, Larry's phone would send an SDP message in its 200 OK describing the properties of the session that will be acceptable to Larry and the device, considering the options that were proposed in Bruce's invite. In this way, mutually acceptable session parameters are agreed to before the media flow starts.

The other big issue we have glossed over is that of locating the correct device for Larry. First, Bruce's computer had to send its invite to the cisco.com proxy. This could have been a configured piece of information in the computer, or it could have been learned by DHCP. Then the cisco.com proxy had to find the princeton.edu proxy. This could be done using a special sort of DNS lookup that would return the IP address of the SIP proxy for the princeton.edu domain. (We'll discuss how DNS can do this in Section 9.3.1.) Finally, the princeton.edu proxy had to find a device on which Larry could be contacted. Typically, a proxy server has access to a location database that can be populated in several ways. Manual configuration is one option, but a more flexible option is to use the *registration* capabilities of SIP.

A user can register with a location service by sending a SIP register message to the "registrar" for his domain. This message creates a binding between an "address of record" and a "contact address." An "address of record" is likely to be a SIP URI that is the well-known address for the user (e.g., sip:larry@princeton.edu) and the "contact address" will be the address at which the user can currently be found (e.g., sip:larry@llp-ph.cs.princeton.edu). This is exactly the binding that was needed by the princeton.edu proxy in our example.

Note that a user may register at several locations and that multiple users may register at a single device. For example, one can imagine a group of people walking into a conference room that is equipped with an IP phone and all of them registering on it so that they can receive calls on that phone.

SIP is a very rich and flexible protocol that can support a wide range of complex calling scenarios as well as applications that have little or nothing to do with telephony. For example, SIP supports operations that enable a call to be routed to a "music-on-hold" server or a voice-mail server. It is also easy to see how it could be used for applications like instant messaging, and standardization of SIP extensions for such purposes is ongoing at the time of writing.

H.323

The International Telecommunication Union (ITU) has also been very active in the call control area, which is not surprising given its relevance to telephony, the traditional realm of that body. Fortunately, there has been considerable coordination between the IETF and the ITU in this instance, so that the various protocols are somewhat interoperable. The major ITU recommendation for multimedia communication over packet networks is known as *H.323*, which ties together many other recommendations, including H.225 for call control. The full set of recommendations covered by H.323 runs to many hundreds of pages, and the protocol is known for its complexity, so it is only possible to give a brief overview of it here.

H.323 is popular as a protocol for Internet telephony, including video calls, and we consider that class of application here. A device that originates or terminates calls is known as an H.323 terminal; this might be a workstation running an Internet telephony application, or it might be a specially designed "appliance"—a telephone-like device with networking software and an Ethernet port, for example. H.323 terminals can talk to each other directly, but the calls are frequently mediated by a device known as a *gatekeeper*. Gatekeepers perform a number of functions such as translating among the various address formats used for phone calls and controlling how many calls can be placed at a given time to limit the bandwidth used by the H.323 applications. H.323 also includes the

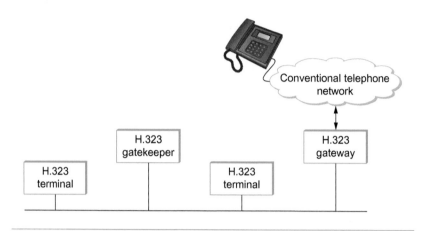

■ FIGURE 9.10 Devices in an H.323 network.

concept of a *gateway*, which connects the H.323 network to other types of networks. The most common use of a gateway is to connect an H.323 network to the public switched telephone network (PSTN) as illustrated in Figure 9.10. This enables a user running an H.323 application on a computer to talk to a person using a conventional phone on the public telephone network. One useful function performed by the gatekeeper is to help a terminal find a gateway, perhaps choosing among several options to find one that is relatively close to the ultimate destination of the call. This is clearly useful in a world where conventional phones greatly outnumber PC-based phones. When an H.323 terminal makes a call to an endpoint that is a conventional phone, the gateway becomes the effective endpoint for the H.323 call and is responsible for performing the appropriate translation of both signalling information and the media stream that need to be carried over the telephone network.

An important part of H.323 is the H.245 protocol, which is used to negotiate the properties of the call, somewhat analogously to the use of SDP described above. H.245 messages might list a number of different audio codec standards that it can support; the far endpoint of the call would reply with a list of its own supported codecs, and the two ends could pick a coding standard that they can both live with. H.245 can also be used to signal the UDP port numbers that will be used by RTP and Real-Time Control Protocol (RTCP) for the media stream (or streams—a call might include both audio and video, for example) for this call. Once this is accomplished, the call can proceed, with RTP being used to transport the media streams and RTCP carrying the relevant control information.

9.2.2 Resource Allocation for Multimedia Applications

As we have just seen, session control protocols like SIP and H.323 can be used to initiate and control communication in multimedia applications, while RTP provides transport-level functions for the data streams of the applications. A final piece of the puzzle in getting multimedia applications to work is making sure that suitable resources are allocated inside the network to ensure that the quality of service needs of the application are met. We presented a number of methods for resource allocation in Chapter 6. The motivation for developing these technologies was largely for the support of multimedia applications. So how do applications take advantage of the underlying resource allocation capabilities of the network?

It is worth noting that many multimedia applications run successfully over "best-effort" networks, such as the public Internet. The wide array of commercial VOIP services (such as Skype) are testimony to the fact that you only have to worry about resource allocation when resources are not abundant—and in many parts of today's Internet, resource abundance is the norm.

A protocol like RTCP (Section 5.4) can help applications in best-effort networks, by giving the application detailed information about the quality of service that is being delivered by the network. Recall that RTCP carries information about the loss rate and delay characteristics between participants in a multimedia application. An application can use this information to change its coding scheme—changing to a lower bitrate codec, for example, when bandwidth is scarce. Note that, while it might be tempting to change to a codec that sends additional, redundant information when loss rates are high, this is frowned upon; it is analogous to *increasing* the window size of TCP in the presence of loss, the exact opposite of what is required to avoid congestion collapse.

As discussed in Section 6.5.3, Differentiated Services (DiffServ) can be used to provide fairly basic and scalable resource allocation to applications. A multimedia application can set the differentiated services code point (DSCP) in the IP header of the packets that it generates in an effort to ensure that both the media and control packets receive appropriate quality of service. For example, it is common to mark voice media packets as "EF" (expedited forwarding) to cause them to be placed in a low-latency or priority queue in routers along the path, while the call signalling (e.g., SIP) packets are often marked with some sort of

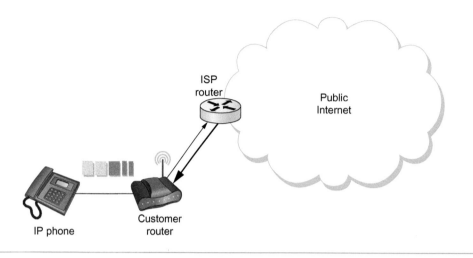

■ FIGURE 9.11 Differentiated Services applied to a VOIP application. DiffServ queueing is applied only on the upstream link from customer router to ISP.

"AF" (assured forwarding) to enable them to be queued separately from best-effort traffic and thus reduce their risk of loss.

Of course, it only makes sense to mark the packets inside the sending host or appliance if network devices such as routers pay attention to the DSCP. In general, routers in the public Internet ignore the DSCP, providing best-effort service to all packets. However, enterprise or corporate networks have the ability to use DiffServ for their internal multimedia traffic, and frequently do so. Also, even residential users of the Internet can often improve the quality of VOIP or other multimedia applications just by using DiffServ on the outbound direction of their Internet connections, as illustrated in Figure 9.11. This is effective because of the asymmetry of many broadband Internet connections: If the outbound link is substantially slower (i.e., more resource constrained) than the inbound, then resource allocation using DiffServ on that link may be enough to make all the difference in quality for latency- and loss-sensitive applications.

While DiffServ is appealing for its simplicity, it is clear that it cannot meet the needs of applications under all conditions. For example, suppose the upstream bandwidth in Figure 9.11 is only 100 kbps, and the customer attempts to place two VOIP calls, each with a 64-kbps codec. Clearly the upstream link is now more than 100% loaded, which will lead to large queueing delays and lost packets. No amount of clever queueing in the customer's router can fix that.

The characteristics of many multimedia applications are such that, rather than try to squeeze too many calls into a too-narrow pipe, it would be better to block one call while allowing another to proceed. That is, it is better to have one person carrying on a conversation successfully while another hears a busy signal than to have both callers experiencing unacceptable audio quality at the same time. We sometimes refer to such applications as having a *steep utility curve*, meaning that the utility (usefulness) of the application drops rapidly as the quality of service provided by the network degrades. Multimedia applications often have this property, whereas many traditional applications do not. Email, for example, continues to work quite well even if delays run into the hours.

Applications with steep utility curves are often well suited to some form of admission control. If you cannot be sure that sufficient resources will always be available to support the offered load of the applications, then admission control provides a way to say "no" to some applications while allowing others to get the resources they need.

We saw one way to do admission control using RSVP in Section 6.5.2, and we will return to that shortly, but multimedia applications that use session control protocols provide some other admission control options. The key point to observe here is that session control protocols like SIP or H.323 often involve some sort of message exchange between an endpoint and another entity (SIP proxy or H.323 gatekeeper) at the beginning of a call or session. This can provide a handy means to say "no" to a new call for which sufficient resources are not available.

As an example, consider the network in Figure 9.12. Suppose the wide area link from the branch office to the head office has enough bandwidth to accommodate three VOIP calls simultaneously using 64-kbps codecs. Each phone already needs to communicate with the local SIP proxy or H.323 gatekeeper when it begins to place a call, so it is easy enough for the proxy/gatekeeper to send back a message that tells the IP phone to play a busy signal if that link is already fully loaded. The proxy or gatekeeper can even deal with the possibility that a particular IP phone might be making multiple calls at the same time and that different codec speeds might be used. However, this scheme will work only if no other device can overload the link without first talking to the gatekeeper or proxy. DiffServ queueing can be used to ensure that, for example, a PC engaged in a file transfer doesn't interfere with the VOIP calls. But, suppose some VOIP application that doesn't first talk to the gatekeeper or proxy is enabled in the

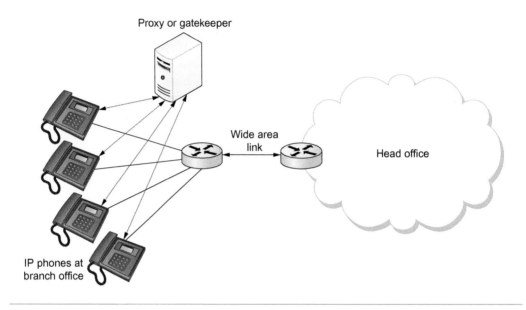

Proxy or gatekeeper

Wide area link

Head office

IP phones at branch office

■ FIGURE 9.12 Admission control using session control protocol.

remote office. Such an application, if it can get its packets marked appropriately and in the same queue as the existing VOIP traffic, can clearly drive the link to the point of overload with no feedback from the proxy or gatekeeper.

Another problem with the approach just described is that it depends on the gatekeeper or proxy having knowledge of the path that each application will use. In the simple topology of Figure 9.12 this isn't a big issue, but in more complex networks it can quickly become unmanageable. We only need to imagine the case where the remote office has two different connections to the outside world to see that we are asking the proxy or gatekeeper to understand not just SIP or H.323 but also routing, link failures, and current network conditions. This can quickly become unmanageable.

We refer to the sort of admission control just described as *off-path*, in the sense that the device making admission control decisions does not sit on the data path where resources need to be allocated. The obvious alternative is *on-path* admission control, and the standard example of a protocol that does on-path admission control in IP networks is the Resource Reservation Protocol (RSVP). We saw in Section 6.5.2 how RSVP can be used to ensure that sufficient resources are allocated along a path, and it is straightforward to use RSVP in applications like those described in this section. The one detail that still needs to be filled in is how the admission control protocol interacts with the session control protocol.

Coordinating the actions of an admission control (or resource reservation) protocol and a session control protocol is not rocket science, but it does require some attention to details. As an example, consider a simple telephone call between two parties. Before you can make a reservation, you need to know how much bandwidth the call is going to use, which means you need to know what codecs are to be used. That implies you need to do some of the session control first, to exchange information about the codecs supported by the two phones. However, you can't do *all* the session control first, because you wouldn't want the phone to ring before the admission control decision had been made, in case admission control failed. Figure 9.13 illustrates this situation where SIP is used for session control and RSVP is used to make the admission control decision (successfully in this case).

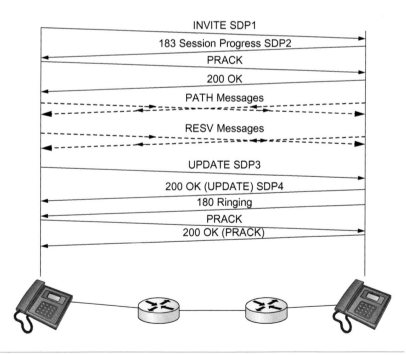

■ FIGURE 9.13 Co-ordination of SIP signalling and resource reservation.

The main thing to notice here is the interleaving of session control and resource allocation tasks. Solid lines represent SIP messages, dashed lines represent RSVP messages. Note that SIP messages are transmitted direction from phone to phone in this example (i.e., we have not shown any SIP proxies), whereas the RSVP messages are also processed by the routers in the middle as the check for sufficient resources to admit the call.

We being with an initial exchange of codec information in the first two SIP messages (recall that SDP is used to list available codecs, among other things). PRACK is a "provisional acknowledgment." Once these messages have been exchanged, RSVP PATH messages, which contain a description of the amount of resources that will be required, can be sent as the first step in reserving resources in both directions of the call. Next, RESV messages can be sent back to actually reserve the resources. Once a RESV is received by the initiating phone, it can send an updated SDP message reporting the fact that resources have been reserved in one direction. When the called phone has received both that message and the RESV from the other phone, it can start to ring and tell the other phone that resources are now reserved in both directions (with the SDP message) and also notify the calling phone that it is ringing. From here on, normal SIP signalling and media flow, similar to that shown in Figure 9.9, proceeds.

Again we see how building applications requires us to understand the interaction between different building blocks (SIP and RSVP, in this case). The designers of SIP actually made some changes to the protocol to enable this interleaving of functions between protocols with different jobs, hence our repeated emphasis in this book on focusing on complete systems rather than just looking at one layer or component in isolation from the other parts of the system.

9.3 INFRASTRUCTURE SERVICES

There are some protocols that are essential to the smooth running of the Internet but that don't fit neatly into the strictly layered model. One of these is the Domain Name System (DNS)—not an application that users normally invoke explicitly, but rather a service that almost all other applications depend upon. This is because the name service is used to translate host names into host addresses; the existence of such an application allows the users of other applications to refer to remote hosts by name rather than by address. In other words, a name service is usually used by other applications, rather than by humans.

A second critical function is network management, which although not so familiar to the average user, is the operation performed most often by system administrators. Network management is widely considered one of the hard problems of networking and continues to be the focus of much research. We'll look at some of the issues and approaches to the problem below.

9.3.1 Name Service (DNS)

In most of this book, we have been using addresses to identify hosts. While perfectly suited for processing by routers, addresses are not exactly user friendly. It is for this reason that a unique *name* is also typically assigned to each host in a network. Already in this section we have seen application protocols like HTTP using names such as www.princeton.edu. We now describe how a naming service can be developed to map user-friendly names into router-friendly addresses. Name services are sometimes called *middleware* because they fill a gap between applications and the underlying network.

Host names differ from host addresses in two important ways. First, they are usually of variable length and mnemonic, thereby making them easier for humans to remember. (In contrast, fixed-length numeric addresses are easier for routers to process.) Second, names typically contain no information that helps the network locate (route packets toward) the host. Addresses, in contrast, sometimes have routing information embedded in them; *flat* addresses (those not divisible into component parts) are the exception.

Before getting into the details of how hosts are named in a network, we first introduce some basic terminology. First, a *name space* defines the set of possible names. A name space can be either *flat* (names are not divisible into components) or *hierarchical* (Unix file names are an obvious example). Second, the naming system maintains a collection of *bindings* of names to values. The value can be anything we want the naming system to return when presented with a name; in many cases, it is an address. Finally, a *resolution mechanism* is a procedure that, when invoked with a name, returns the corresponding value. A *name server* is a specific implementation of a resolution mechanism that is available on a network and that can be queried by sending it a message.

Because of its large size, the Internet has a particularly well-developed naming system in place—the Domain Name System (DNS). We therefore use DNS as a framework for discussing the problem of naming hosts. Note that the Internet did not always use DNS. Early in its history, when there were only a few hundred hosts on the Internet, a central authority called the *Network Information Center* (NIC) maintained a flat table of name-to-address bindings; this table was called hosts.txt. Whenever a site wanted to add a new host to the Internet, the site administrator sent email to the NIC giving the new host's name/address pair. This information was manually entered into the table, the modified table was mailed out to the various sites every few days, and the system administrator at each site installed the table on every host at the site. Name resolution was then simply implemented by a procedure that looked up a host's name in the local copy of the table and returned the corresponding address.

It should come as no surprise that the hosts.txt approach to naming did not work well as the number of hosts in the Internet started to grow. Therefore, in the mid-1980s, the Domain Naming System was put into place. DNS employs a hierarchical namespace rather than a flat name space, and the "table" of bindings that implements this name space is partitioned into disjoint pieces and distributed throughout the Internet. These subtables are made available in name servers that can be queried over the network.

What happens in the Internet is that a user presents a host name to an application program (possibly embedded in a compound name such as an email address or URL), and this program engages the naming system to translate this name into a host address. The application then opens a connection to this host by presenting some transport protocol (e.g., TCP) with the host's IP address. This situation is illustrated (in the case of sending email) in Figure 9.14. While this picture makes the name resolution task look simple enough, there is a bit more to it, as we shall see.

Domain Hierarchy

DNS implements a hierarchical name space for Internet objects. Unlike Unix file names, which are processed from left to right with the naming components separated with slashes, DNS names are processed from right to left and use periods as the separator. (Although they are processed from

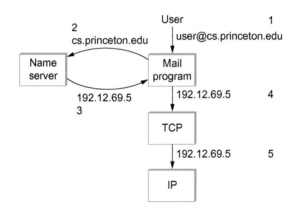

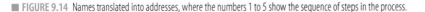

■ **FIGURE 9.14** Names translated into addresses, where the numbers 1 to 5 show the sequence of steps in the process.

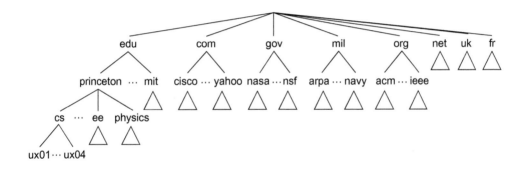

■ **FIGURE 9.15** Example of a domain hierarchy.

right to left, humans still read domain names from left to right.) An example domain name for a host is cicada.cs.princeton.edu. Notice that we said domain names are used to name Internet "objects." What we mean by this is that DNS is not strictly used to map host names into host addresses. It is more accurate to say that DNS maps domain names into values. For the time being, we assume that these values are IP addresses; we will come back to this issue later in this section.

Like the Unix file hierarchy, the DNS hierarchy can be visualized as a tree, where each node in the tree corresponds to a domain, and the leaves in the tree correspond to the hosts being named. Figure 9.15 gives an example of a domain hierarchy. Note that we should not assign any semantics to the term *domain* other than that it is simply a context in which additional names can be defined.[5]

There was actually a substantial amount of discussion that took place when the domain name hierarchy was first being developed as to what conventions would govern the names that were to be handed out near the top of the hierarchy. Without going into that discussion in any detail, notice that the hierarchy is not very wide at the first level. There are domains for each country, plus the "big six" domains: .edu, .com, .gov, .mil, .org, and .net. These six domains were all originally based in the United States (where the Internet and DNS were invented); for example, only U.S.-accredited educational institutions can register an .edu domain name. In recent years, the number of top-level domains has been expanded, partly to deal with the high demand for .com domains names. The newer top-level domains include .biz, .coop, and .info. Another recent development has been the support of domain names that are represented in character sets other than the Latin alphabet, such as Arabic and Chinese.

Name Servers

The complete domain name hierarchy exists only in the abstract. We now turn our attention to the question of how this hierarchy is actually implemented. The first step is to partition the hierarchy into subtrees called *zones*. Figure 9.16 shows how the hierarchy given in Figure 9.15 might

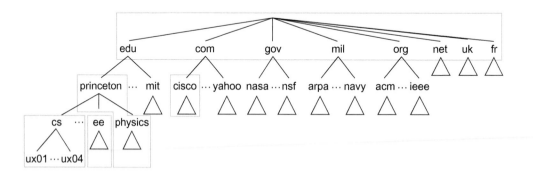

■ FIGURE 9.16 Domain hierarchy partitioned into zones.

[5]Confusingly, the word *domain* is also used in Internet routing, where it means something different than it does in DNS, being roughly equivalent to the term *autonomous system*.

be divided into zones. Each zone can be thought of as corresponding to some administrative authority that is responsible for that portion of the hierarchy. For example, the top level of the hierarchy forms a zone that is managed by the Internet Corporation for Assigned Names and Numbers (ICANN). Below this is a zone that corresponds to Princeton University. Within this zone, some departments do not want the responsibility of managing the hierarchy (and so they remain in the university-level zone), while others, like the Department of Computer Science, manage their own department-level zone.

The relevance of a zone is that it corresponds to the fundamental unit of implementation in DNS—the name server. Specifically, the information contained in each zone is implemented in two or more name servers. Each name server, in turn, is a program that can be accessed over the Internet. Clients send queries to name servers, and name servers respond with the requested information. Sometimes the response contains the final answer that the client wants, and sometimes the response contains a pointer to another server that the client should query next. Thus, from an implementation perspective, it is more accurate to think of DNS as being represented by a hierarchy of name servers rather than by a hierarchy of domains, as illustrated in Figure 9.17.

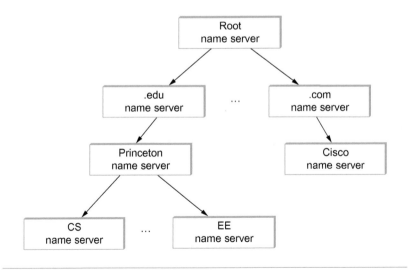

■ FIGURE 9.17 Hierarchy of name servers.

Note that each zone is implemented in two or more name servers for the sake of redundancy; that is, the information is still available even if one name server fails. On the flip side, a given name server is free to implement more than one zone.

Each name server implements the zone information as a collection of *resource records*. In essence, a resource record is a name-to-value binding or, more specifically, a 5-tuple that contains the following fields:

⟨ Name, Value, Type, Class, TTL ⟩

The Name and Value fields are exactly what you would expect, while the Type field specifies how the Value should be interpreted. For example, Type = A indicates that the Value is an IP address. Thus, A records implement the name-to-address mapping we have been assuming. Other record types include:

- NS—The Value field gives the domain name for a host that is running a name server that knows how to resolve names within the specified domain.
- CNAME—The Value field gives the canonical name for a particular host; it is used to define aliases.
- MX—The Value field gives the domain name for a host that is running a mail server that accepts messages for the specified domain.

The Class field was included to allow entities other than the NIC to define useful record types. To date, the only widely used Class is the one used by the Internet; it is denoted IN. Finally, the time-to-live (TTL) field shows how long this resource record is valid. It is used by servers that cache resource records from other servers; when the TTL expires, the server must evict the record from its cache.

To better understand how resource records represent the information in the domain hierarchy, consider the following examples drawn from the domain hierarchy given in Figure 9.15. To simplify the example, we ignore the TTL field and we give the relevant information for only one of the name servers that implement each zone.

First, a root name server contains an NS record for each top-level domain (TLD) name server. This identifies a server that can resolve queries for this part of the DNS hierarchy (.edu and .com in this example). It also has A records that translates these names into the corresponding IP addresses. Taken together, these two records effectively implement a pointer from the root name server to one of the TLD servers.

⟨edu, a3.nstld.com, NS, IN⟩

⟨a3.nstld.com, 192.5.6.32, A, IN⟩

⟨com, a.gtld-servers.net, NS, IN⟩

⟨a.gtld-servers.net, 192.5.6.30, A, IN⟩

⋮

Moving our way down the hierarchy by one level, the a3.nstld.com server has records for .edu domains like this:

⟨princeton.edu, dns.princeton.edu, NS, IN⟩

⟨dns.princeton.edu, 128.112.129.15, A, IN⟩

⋮

In this case, we get an NS record and an A record for the name server that is responsible for the princeton.edu part of the hierarchy. That server might be able to directly resolve some queries (e.g., for email.princeton.edu) while it would redirect others to a server at yet another layer in the hierarchy (e.g., for a query about penguins.cs .princeton.edu).

⟨email.princeton.edu, 128.112.198.35, A, IN⟩

⟨penguins.cs.princeton.edu, dns1.cs.princeton.edu, NS, IN⟩

⟨dns1.cs.princeton.edu, 128.112.136.10, A, IN⟩

⋮

Finally, a third-level name server, such as the one managed by domain cs.princeton.edu, contains A records for all of its hosts. It might also define a set of aliases (CNAME records) for each of those hosts. Aliases are sometimes just convenient (e.g., shorter) names for machines, but they can also be used to provide a level of indirection. For example, www.cs.princeton.edu is an alias for the host named coreweb.cs .princeton.edu. This allows the site's web server to move to another machine without affecting remote users; they simply continue to use the alias without regard for what machine currently runs the domain's web server. The mail exchange (MX) records serve the same purpose for the email application—they allow an administrator to change which host receives mail on behalf of the domain without having to change everyone's email address.

⟨penguins.cs.princeton.edu, 128.112.155.166, A, IN⟩

⟨www.cs.princeton.edu, coreweb.cs.princeton.edu, CNAME, IN⟩

⟨coreweb.cs.princeton.edu, 128.112.136.35, A, IN⟩

⟨cs.princeton.edu, mail.cs.princeton.edu, MX, IN⟩

⟨mail.cs.princeton.edu, 128.112.136.72, A, IN⟩

⋮

Note that, although resource records can be defined for virtually any type of object, DNS is typically used to name hosts (including servers) and sites. It is not used to name individual people or other objects like files or directories; other naming systems are typically used to identify such objects. For example, X.500 is an ISO naming system designed to make it easier to identify people. It allows you to name a person by giving a set of attributes: name, title, phone number, postal address, and so on. X.500 proved too cumbersome—and, in some sense, was usurped by powerful search engines now available on the Web—but it did eventually evolve into the Lightweight Directory Access Protocol (LDAP). LDAP is a subset of X.500 originally designed as a PC front end to X.500. Today, it is gaining in popularity, mostly at the enterprise level, as a system for learning information about users.

Name Resolution

Given a hierarchy of name servers, we now consider the issue of how a client engages these servers to resolve a domain name. To illustrate the basic idea, suppose the client wants to resolve the name penguins.cs.princeton.edu relative to the set of servers given in the previous subsection. The client could first send a query containing this name to one of the root servers (as we'll see below, this rarely happens in practice but will suffice to illustrate the basic operation for now). The root server, unable to match the entire name, returns the best match it

---

Naming Conventions

Our description of DNS focuses on the underlying *mechanisms*—that is, how the hierarchy is partitioned over multiple servers and how the resolution process works. There is an equally interesting, but much less technical, issue of the *conventions* that are used to decide the names to use in the mechanism. For example, it is by convention that all U.S. universities are under the .edu domain, while English universities are under the .ac (academic) subdomain of the .uk (United Kingdom) domain.

The thing to understand about conventions is that they are sometimes defined without anyone making an explicit decision. For example, by convention a site hides the exact host that serves as its mail exchange behind the MX record. An alternative would have been to adopt the convention of sending mail to user@mail.cs.princeton.edu, much as we expect to find a site's public FTP directory at ftp.cs.princeton.edu and its WWW server at www.cs.princeton.edu. This last one is so prevalent that many people do not even realize it is just a convention.

Conventions also exist at the local level, where an organization names its machines according to some consistent set of rules. Given that the host names venus, saturn, and mars are among the most popular in the Internet, it's not too hard to figure out one common naming convention. Some host naming conventions are more imaginative, however. For example, one site named its machines up, down, crashed, rebooting, and so on, resulting in confusing statements like "rebooting has crashed" and "up is down." Of course, there are also less imaginative names, such as those who name their machines after the integers.

---

has—the NS record for edu which points to the TLD server a3.nstld.com. The server also returns all records that are related to this record, in this case, the A record for a3.nstld.com. The client, having not received the answer it was after, next sends the same query to the name server at IP host 192.5.6.32. This server also cannot match the whole name and so returns the NS and corresponding A records for the princeton.edu domain. Once again, the client sends the same query as before to the server at IP host 128.112.129.15, and this time gets back the NS record and corresponding A record for the cs.princeton.edu domain. This time, the server that can fully resolve the query has been reached. A final query to the server at 128.112.136.10 yields the A record for penguins.cs.princeton.edu, and the client learns that the corresponding IP address is 128.112.155.166.

This example still leaves a couple of questions about the resolution process unanswered. The first question is how did the client locate the root server in the first place, or, put another way, how do you resolve the name of the server that knows how to resolve names? This is a fundamental problem in any naming system, and the answer is that the system has to be bootstrapped in some way. In this case, the name-to-address mapping for one or more root servers is well known; that is, it is published through some means outside the naming system itself.

In practice, however, not all clients know about the root servers. Instead, the client program running on each Internet host is initialized with the address of a *local* name server. For example, all the hosts in the Department of Computer Science at Princeton know about the server on dns1.cs.princeton.edu. This local name server, in turn, has resource records for one or more of the root servers, for example:

⟨ 'root', a.root-servers.net, NS, IN ⟩
⟨ a.root-servers.net, 198.41.0.4, A, IN ⟩

Thus, resolving a name actually involves a client querying the local server, which in turn acts as a client that queries the remote servers on the original client's behalf. This results in the client/server interactions illustrated in Figure 9.18. One advantage of this model is that all the hosts in the Internet do not have to be kept up-to-date on where the current root servers are located; only the servers have to know about the root. A second advantage is that the local server gets to see the answers that come back from queries that are posted by all the local clients. The local server *caches* these responses and is sometimes able to resolve future queries without having to go out over the network. The TTL field in the resource records returned by remote servers indicates how long each record can be safely cached. This caching mechanism can be used further up the hierarchy as well, reducing the load on the root and TLD servers.

The second question is how the system works when a user submits a partial name (e.g., penguins) rather than a complete domain name (e.g., penguins.cs.princeton.edu). The answer is that the client program is configured with the local domain in which the host resides (e.g., cs.princeton.edu), and it appends this string to any simple names before sending out a query.

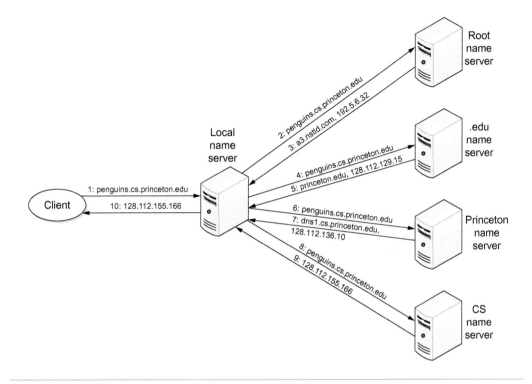

■ **FIGURE 9.18** Name resolution in practice, where the numbers 1 to 10 show the sequence of steps in the process.

Just to make sure we are clear, we have now seen three different levels of identifiers—domain names, IP addresses, and physical network addresses—and the mapping of identifiers at one level into identifiers at another level happens at different points in the network architecture. First, users specify domain names when interacting with the application. Second, the application engages DNS to translate this name into an IP address; it is the IP address that is placed in each datagram, not the domain name. (As an aside, this translation process involves IP datagrams being sent over the Internet, but these datagrams are addressed to a host that runs a name server, not to the ultimate destination.) Third, IP does forwarding at each router, which often means that it maps one IP address into another; that is, it maps the ultimate destination's address into the address for the next hop router. Finally, IP engages the Address Resolution Protocol (ARP) to translate the next hop IP address into the physical address for that machine; the next hop might be the ultimate destination or it might be an intermediate router. Frames sent over the physical network have these physical addresses in their headers.

9.3.2 Network Management (SNMP)

A network is a complex system, both in terms of the number of nodes that are involved and in terms of the suite of protocols that can be running on any one node. Even if you restrict yourself to worrying about the nodes within a single administrative domain, such as a campus, there might be dozens of routers and hundreds—or even thousands—of hosts to keep track of. If you think about all the state that is maintained and manipulated on any one of those nodes—address translation tables, routing tables, TCP connection state, and so on—then it is easy to become depressed about the prospect of having to manage all of this information.

It is easy to imagine wanting to know about the state of various protocols on different nodes. For example, you might want to monitor the number of IP datagram reassemblies that have been aborted, so as to determine if the timeout that garbage collects partially assembled datagrams needs to be adjusted. As another example, you might want to keep track of the load on various nodes (i.e., the number of packets sent or received) so as to determine if new routers or links need to be added to the network. Of course, you also have to be on the watch for evidence of faulty hardware and misbehaving software.

What we have just described is the problem of network management, an issue that pervades the entire network architecture. Since the nodes we want to keep track of are distributed, our only real option is to use the network to manage the network. This means we need a protocol that allows us to read, and possibly write, various pieces of state information on different network nodes. The most widely used protocol for this purpose is the Simple Network Management Protocol (SNMP).

SNMP is essentially a specialized request/reply protocol that supports two kinds of request messages: GET and SET. The former is used to retrieve a piece of state from some node, and the latter is used to store a new piece of state in some node. (SNMP also supports a third operation, GET-NEXT, which we explain below.) The following discussion focuses on the GET operation, since it is the one most frequently used.

SNMP is used in the obvious way. A system administrator interacts with a client program that displays information about the network. This client program usually has a graphical interface. You can think of this interface as playing the same role as a web browser. Whenever the administrator selects a certain piece of information that he or she wants to see, the client program uses SNMP to request that information from the node in question. (SNMP runs on top of UDP.) An SNMP server running on that node receives the request, locates the appropriate piece of information, and returns it to the client program, which then displays it to the user.

There is only one complication to this otherwise simple scenario: Exactly how does the client indicate which piece of information it wants to retrieve, and, likewise, how does the server know which variable in memory to read to satisfy the request? The answer is that SNMP depends on a companion specification called the *management information base* (MIB). The MIB defines the specific pieces of information—the MIB *variables*—that you can retrieve from a network node.

The current version of MIB, called MIB-II, organizes variables into 10 different *groups*. You will recognize that most of the groups correspond to one of the protocols described in this book, and nearly all of the variables defined for each group should look familiar. For example:

- System—General parameters of the system (node) as a whole, including where the node is located, how long it has been up, and the system's name

- Interfaces—Information about all the network interfaces (adaptors) attached to this node, such as the physical address of each interface and how many packets have been sent and received on each interface

- Address translation—Information about the Address Resolution Protocol, and in particular, the contents of its address translation table

- IP—Variables related to IP, including its routing table, how many datagrams it has successfully forwarded, and statistics about datagram reassembly; includes counts of how many times IP drops a datagram for one reason or another

- TCP—Information about TCP connections, such as the number of passive and active opens, the number of resets, the number of timeouts, default timeout settings, and so on; per-connection information persists only as long as the connection exists

- UDP—Information about UDP traffic, including the total number of UDP datagrams that have been sent and received.

There are also groups for Internet Control Message Protocol (ICMP), Exterior Gateway Protocol (EGP), and SNMP itself. The tenth group is used by different media.

Returning to the issue of the client stating exactly what information it wants to retrieve from a node, having a list of MIB variables is only half the battle. Two problems remain. First, we need a precise syntax for the client to use to state which of the MIB variables it wants to fetch. Second, we need a precise representation for the values returned by the server. Both problems are addressed using Abstract Syntax Notation One (ASN.1).

Consider the second problem first. As we already saw in Chapter 7, ASN.1/Basic Encoding Rules (BER) defines a representation for different data types, such as integers. The MIB defines the type of each variable, and then it uses ASN.1/BER to encode the value contained in this variable as it is transmitted over the network. As far as the first problem is concerned, ASN.1 also defines an object identification scheme; this identification system is not described in Chapter 7. The MIB uses this identification system to assign a globally unique identifier to each MIB variable. These identifiers are given in a "dot" notation, not unlike domain names. For example, 1.3.6.1.2.1.4.3 is the unique ASN.1 identifier for the IP-related MIB variable ipInReceives; this variable counts the number of IP datagrams that have been received by this node. In this example, the 1.3.6.1.2.1 prefix identifies the MIB database (remember, ASN.1 object IDs are for all possible objects in the world), the 4 corresponds to the IP group, and the final 3 denotes the third variable in this group.

Thus, network management works as follows. The SNMP client puts the ASN.1 identifier for the MIB variable it wants to get into the request message, and it sends this message to the server. The server then maps this identifier into a local variable (i.e., into a memory location where the value for this variable is stored), retrieves the current value held in this variable, and uses ASN.1/BER to encode the value it sends back to the client.

There is one final detail. Many of the MIB variables are either tables or structures. Such compound variables explain the reason for the SNMP GET-NEXT operation. This operation, when applied to a particular variable ID, returns the value of that variable plus the ID of the next variable, for example, the next item in the table or the next field in the structure. This aids the client in "walking through" the elements of a table or structure.

9.4 **OVERLAY NETWORKS**

From its inception, the Internet has adopted a clean model, in which the routers inside the network are responsible for forwarding packets from source to destination, and application programs run on the hosts connected to the edges of the network. The client/server paradigm illustrated by the applications discussed in the first two sections of this chapter certainly adhere to this model.

In the last few years, however, the distinction between *packet forwarding* and *application processing* has become less clear. New applications are being distributed across the Internet, and in many cases these applications make their own forwarding decisions. These new hybrid applications can sometimes be implemented by extending traditional routers and switches to support a modest amount of application-specific processing. For example, so-called *level-7 switches* sit in front of server clusters and forward HTTP requests to a specific server based on the requested URL. However, *overlay networks* are quickly emerging as the mechanism of choice for introducing new functionality into the Internet.

You can think of an overlay as a logical network implemented on top of some underlying network. By this definition, the Internet started out as an overlay network on top of the links provided by the old telephone network. Figure 9.19 depicts an overlay implemented on top of an underlying network. Each node in the overlay also exists in the underlying network;

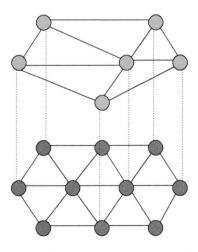

■ FIGURE 9.19 Overlay network layered on top of a physical network.

it processes and forwards packets in an application-specific way. The links that connect the overlay nodes are implemented as tunnels through the underlying network. Multiple overlay networks can exist on top of the same underlying network—each implementing its own application-specific behavior—and overlays can be nested, one on top of another. For example, all of the example overlay networks discussed in this section treat today's Internet as the underlying network.

We have already seen examples of tunneling, for example, to implement virtual private networks (VPNs). As a brief refresher, the nodes on either end of a tunnel treat the multi-hop path between them as a single logical link, the nodes that are tunneled through forward packets based on the outer header, never aware that the end nodes have attached an inner header. Figure 9.20 shows three overlay nodes (A, B, and C) connected by a pair of tunnels. In this example, overlay node B might make a forwarding decision for packets from A to C based on the inner header (IHdr), and then attach an outer header (OHdr) that identifies C as the destination in the underlying network. Nodes A, B, and C are able to interpret both the inner and outer header, whereas the intermediate routers understand only the outer header. Similarly, A, B, and C have addresses in both the overlay network and the underlying network, but they are not necessarily the same; for example, their underlying address might be a 32-bit IP address, while their overlay address might be an experimental 128-bit address. In fact, the overlay need not use conventional addresses at all but may route based on URLs, domain names, an XML query, or even the content of the packet.

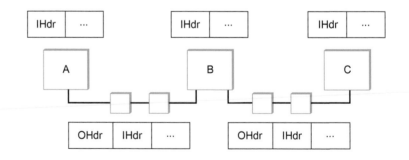

■ FIGURE 9.20 Overlay nodes tunnel through physical nodes.

Overlays and the Ossification of the Internet

Given its popularity and widespread use, it is easy to forget that at one time the Internet was a laboratory for researchers to experiment with packet-switched networking. The more the Internet has become a commercial success, however, the less useful it is as a platform for playing with new ideas. Today, commercial interests shape the Internet's continued development.

In fact, as far back as 2001, a report from the National Research Council pointed to the ossification of the Internet, both intellectually (pressure for compatibility with current standards stifles innovation) and in terms of the infrastructure itself (it is nearly impossible for researchers to affect the core infrastructure). The report went on to observe that, at the same time, a whole new set of challenges were emerging that may require a fresh approach. The dilemma, according to the report, is that

> ... successful and widely adopted technologies are subject to ossification, which makes it hard to introduce new capabilities or, if the current technology has run its course, to replace it with something better. Existing industry players are not generally motivated to develop or deploy disruptive technologies ...

Finding the right way to introduce disruptive technologies is an interesting issue. Such innovations are likely to do some things very well, but overall they lag current technology in other important areas. For example, to introduce a new routing strategy into the Internet, one would have to build a router that not only supports this new strategy but also competes with established vendors in terms of performance, reliability, management toolset, and so on. This is an extremely tall order. What the innovator needs is a way to allow users to take advantage of the new idea without having to write the hundreds of thousands of lines of code needed to support just the base system.

Overlay networks provide exactly this opportunity. Overlay nodes can be programmed to support the new capability or feature and then depend on conventional nodes to provide the underlying connectivity. Over time, if the idea deployed in the overlay proves useful, there may be economic motivation to migrate the functionality into the base system—that is, add it to the feature set of commercial routers. On the other hand, the functionality may be complex enough that an overlay layer may be exactly where it belongs.

9.4.1 Routing Overlays

The simplest kind of overlay is one that exists purely to support an alternative routing strategy; no additional application-level processing is performed at the overlay nodes. You can view a virtual private network (see Section 4.1.8) as an example of a routing overlay, but one that doesn't so much define an alternative strategy or algorithm as it does alternative routing table entries to be processed by the standard IP forwarding algorithm. In this particular case, the overlay is said to use "IP tunnels," and the ability to utilize these VPNs is supported in many commercial routers.

Suppose, however, you wanted to use a routing algorithm that commercial router vendors were not willing to include in their products. How would you go about doing it? You could simply run your algorithm on a collection of end hosts, and tunnel through the Internet routers. These hosts would behave like routers in the overlay network: As hosts they are probably connected to the Internet by only one physical link, but as a node in the overlay they would be connected to multiple neighbors via tunnels.

Since overlays, almost by definition, are a way to introduce new technologies independent of the standardization process, there are no standard overlays we can point to as examples. Instead, we illustrate the general idea of routing overlays by describing several experimental systems that have been built by network researchers.

Experimental Versions of IP

Overlays are ideal for deploying experimental versions of IP that you hope will eventually take over the world. For example, IP multicast (Section 4.2) started off as an extension to IP and even today is not enabled in many Internet routers. The MBone (multicast backbone) was an overlay network that implemented IP multicast on top of the unicast routing provided by the Internet. A number of multimedia conference tools were developed for and deployed on the Mbone. For example, IETF meetings—which are a week long and attract thousands of participants—were for many years broadcast over the MBone.

Like VPNs, the MBone used both IP tunnels and IP addresses, but unlike VPNs, the MBone implemented a different forwarding algorithm—forwarding packets to all downstream neighbors in the shortest path multicast tree. As an overlay, multicast-aware routers tunnel through legacy routers, with the hope that one day there will be no more legacy routers.

The 6-BONE was a similar overlay that was used to incrementally deploy IPv6. Like the MBone, the 6-BONE used tunnels to forward packets through IPv4 routers. Unlike the MBone, however, 6-BONE nodes did not simply provide a new interpretation of IPv4's 32-bit addresses. Instead, they forwarded packets based on IPv6's 128-bit address space. The 6-BONE also supported IPv6 multicast.

End System Multicast

Although IP multicast is popular with researchers and certain segments of the networking community, its deployment in the global Internet has been limited at best. In response, multicast-based applications like video-conferencing have recently turned to an alternative strategy, called *end system multicast*. The idea of end system multicast is to accept that IP multicast will never become ubiquitous and to instead let the end hosts that are participating in a particular multicast-based application implement their own multicast trees.

Before describing how end system multicast works, it is important to first understand that, unlike VPNs and the MBone, end system multicast assumes that only Internet hosts (as opposed to Internet routers) participate in the overlay. Moreover, these hosts typically exchange messages with each other through UDP tunnels rather than IP tunnels, making it easy to implement as regular application programs. This makes it possible to view the underlying network as a fully connected graph, since every host in the Internet is able to send a message to every other host. Abstractly, then, end system multicast solves the following problem: Starting with a fully connected graph representing the Internet, the goal is to find the embedded multicast tree that spans all the group members.

Since we take the underlying Internet to be fully connected, a naive solution would be to have each source directly connected to each member of the group. In other words, end system multicast could be implemented by having each node send unicast messages to every group member. To see the problem in doing this, especially compared to implementing IP multicast in routers, consider the example topology in Figure 9.21. Figure 9.21(a) depicts an example physical topology, where

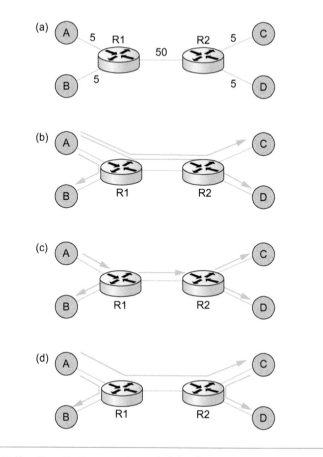

R1 and R2 are routers connected by a low-bandwidth transcontinental link; A, B, C, and D are end hosts; and link delays are given as edge weights. Assuming A wants to send a multicast message to the other three hosts, Figure 9.21(b) shows how naive unicast transmission would work. This is clearly undesirable because the same message must traverse the link A–R1 three times, and two copies of the message traverse R1–R2. Figure 9.21(c) depicts the IP multicast tree constructed by the Distance Vector Multicast Routing Protocol (DVMRP). Clearly, this approach eliminates the redundant messages. Without support from the routers, however, the best one can hope for with end system multicast is a tree similar to the one shown in Figure 9.21(d). End system multicast defines an architecture for constructing this tree.

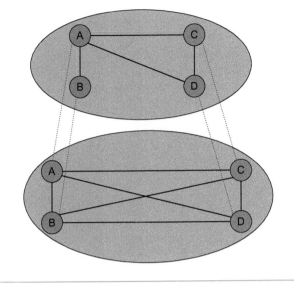

■ FIGURE 9.22 Multicast tree embedded in an overlay mesh.

The general approach is to support multiple levels of overlay networks, each of which extracts a subgraph from the overlay below it, until we have selected the subgraph that the application expects. For end system multicast, in particular, this happens in two stages: First we construct a simple *mesh* overlay on top of the fully connected Internet, and then we select a multicast tree within this mesh. The idea is illustrated in Figure 9.22, again assuming the four end hosts A, B, C, and D. The first step is the critical one: Once we have selected a suitable mesh overlay, we simply run a standard multicast routing algorithm (e.g., DVMRP) on top of it to build the multicast tree. We also have the luxury of ignoring the scalability issue that Internet-wide multicast faces since the intermediate mesh can be selected to include only those nodes that want to participate in a particular multicast group.

The key to constructing the intermediate mesh overlay is to select a topology that roughly corresponds to the physical topology of the under-lying Internet, but we have to do this without anyone telling us what the underlying Internet actually looks like since we are running only on end hosts and not routers. The general strategy is for the end hosts to measure the roundtrip latency to other nodes and decide to add links to the mesh only when they like what they see. This works as follows.

First, assuming a mesh already exists, each node exchanges the list of all other nodes it believes is part of the mesh with its directly connected neighbors. When a node receives such a membership list from a neighbor, it incorporates that information into its membership list and forwards the resulting list to its neighbors. This information eventually propagates through the mesh, much as in a distance vector routing protocol.

When a host wants to join the multicast overlay, it must know the IP address of at least one other node already in the overlay. It then sends a "join mesh" message to this node. This connects the new node to the mesh by an edge to the known node. In general, the new node might send a join message to multiple current nodes, thereby joining the mesh by multiple links. Once a node is connected to the mesh by a set of links, it periodically sends "keep alive" messages to its neighbors, letting them know that it still wants to be part of the group.

When a node leaves the group, it sends a "leave mesh" message to its directly connected neighbors, and this information is propagated to the other nodes in the mesh via the membership list described above. Alternatively, a node can fail or just silently decide to quit the group, in which case its neighbors detect that it is no longer sending "keep alive" messages. Some node departures have little effect on the mesh, but should a node detect that the mesh has become partitioned due to a departing node, it creates a new edge to a node in the other partition by sending it a "join mesh" message. Note that multiple neighbors can simultaneously decide that a partition has occurred in the mesh, leading to multiple cross-partition edges being added to the mesh.

As described so far, we will end up with a mesh that is a subgraph of the original fully connected Internet, but it may have suboptimal performance because (1) initial neighbor selection adds random links to the topology, (2) partition repair might add edges that are essential at the moment but not useful in the long run, (3) group membership may change due to dynamic joins and departures, and (4) underlying network conditions may change. What needs to happen is that the system must evaluate the value of each edge, resulting in new edges being added to the mesh and existing edges being removed over time.

To add new edges, each node i periodically probes some random member j that it is not currently connected to in the mesh, measures the round-trip latency of edge (i, j), and then evaluates the utility of adding this edge. If the utility is above a certain threshold, link (i, j) is added to the mesh. Evaluating the utility of adding edge (i, j) might look something like this:

```
EvaluateUtility(j)
    utility = 0
    for each member m not equal to i
        CL = current latency to node m along route through mesh
        NL = new latency to node m along mesh if edge (i, j) is added
        if (NL < CL) then
            utility += (CL - NL)/CL
    return utility
```

Deciding to remove an edge is similar, except each node i computes the cost of each link to current neighbor j as follows:

```
EvaluateCost(j)
    Cost_ij = number of members for which i uses j as next hop
    Cost_ji = number of members for which j uses i as next hop
    return max(Cost_ij, Cost_ji)
```

It then picks the neighbor with the lowest cost, and drops it if the cost falls below a certain threshold.

Finally, since the mesh is maintained using what is essentially a distance vector protocol, it is trivial to run DVMRP to find an appropriate multicast tree in the mesh. Note that, although it is not possible to prove that the protocol just described results in the optimum mesh network, thereby allowing DVMRP to select the best possible multicast tree, both simulation and extensive practical experience suggests that it does a good job.

Resilient Overlay Networks

Another function that can be performed by an overlay is to find alternative routes for traditional unicast applications. Such overlays exploit the observation that the triangle inequality does not hold in the Internet. Figure 9.23 illustrates what we mean by this. It is not uncommon to find three sites in the Internet—call them A, B, and C—such that the latency between A and B is greater than the sum of the latencies from A to C and from C to B. That is, sometimes you would be better off indirectly sending your packets via some intermediate node than sending them directly to the destination.

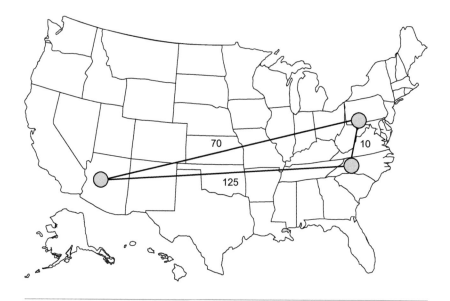

■ FIGURE 9.23 The triangle inequality does not necessarily hold in networks.

How can this be? Well, the Border Gateway Protocol (BGP) never promised that it would find the *shortest* route between any two sites; it only tries to find *some* route. To make matters more complex, BGP's routes are heavily influenced by policy issues, such as who is paying whom to carry their traffic. This often happens, for example, at peering points between major backbone ISPs. In short, that the triangle inequality does not hold in the Internet should not come as a surprise.

How do we exploit this observation? The first step is to realize that there is a fundamental tradeoff between the scalability and optimality of a routing algorithm. On the one hand, BGP scales to very large networks, but often does not select the best possible route and is slow to adapt to network outages. On the other hand, if you were only worried about finding the best route among a handful of sites, you could do a much better job of monitoring the quality of every path you might use, thereby allowing you to select the best possible route at any moment in time.

An experimental overlay, called the Resilient Overlay Network (RON), does exactly this. RON scales to only a few dozen nodes because it uses an $n \times n$ strategy of closely monitoring (via active probes) three aspects of path quality—latency, available bandwidth, and loss probability— between every pair of sites. It is then able to both select the optimal route between any pair of nodes, and rapidly change routes should network conditions change. Experience shows that RON is able to deliver modest performance improvements to applications, but more importantly, it recovers from network failures much more quickly. For example, during one 64-hour period in 2001, an instance of RON running on 12 nodes detected 32 outages lasting over 30 minutes, and it was able to recover from all of them in less than 20 seconds on average. This experiment also suggested that forwarding data through just one intermediate node is usually sufficient to recover from Internet failures.

Since RON is not designed to be a scalable approach, it is not possible to use RON to help random host A communicate with random host B; A and B have to know ahead of time that they are likely to communicate and then join the same RON. However, RON seems like a good idea in certain settings, such as when connecting a few dozen corporate sites spread across the Internet or allowing you and 50 of your friends to establish your own private overlay for the sake of running some application. The real question, though, is what happens when everyone starts to run their own RON. Does the overhead of millions of RONs aggressively probing paths swamp the network, and does anyone see improved behavior when many RONs compete for the same paths? These questions are still unanswered.

All of these overlays illustrate a concept that is central to computer networks in general: *virtualization*.[6] That is, it is possible to build a virtual network from abstract (logical) resources on top of a physical network constructed from physical resources. Moreover, it is possible to stack these virtualized networks on top of each other and for multiple virtual network to coexist at the same level. Each virtual network, in turn, provides new capabilities that are of value to some set of users, applications, or higher-level networks.

9.4.2 Peer-to-Peer Networks

Music-sharing applications like Napster® and KaZaA introduced the term "peer-to-peer" into the popular vernacular. But what exactly does it mean for a system to be "peer-to-peer"? Certainly in the context of sharing MP3 files it means not having to download music from a central site,

---

[6]The term *virtualization* is used a lot these days in the context of data center computing to refer to the virtualization of servers using hypervisors and similar technologies but it's really a much broader concept.

but instead being able to access music files directly from whoever in the Internet happens to have a copy stored on their computer. More generally then, we could say that a peer-to-peer network allows a community of users to pool their resources (content, storage, network bandwidth, disk bandwidth, CPU), thereby providing access to a larger archival store, larger video/audio conferences, more complex searches and computations, and so on than any one user could afford individually.

Quite often, attributes like *decentralized* and *self-organizing* are mentioned when discussing peer-to-peer networks, meaning that individual nodes organize themselves into a network without any centralized coordination. If you think about it, terms like these could be used to describe the Internet itself. Ironically, however, Napster was not a true peer-to-peer system by this definition since it depended on a central registry of known files, and users had to search this directory to find what machine offered a particular file. It was only the last step—actually downloading the file— that took place between machines that belong to two users, but this is little more than a traditional client/server transaction. The only difference is that the server is owned by someone just like you rather than a large corporation.

So we are back to the original question: What's interesting about peer-to-peer networks? One answer is that both the process of locating an object of interest and the process of downloading that object onto your local machine happen without your having to contact a centralized authority, and at the same time the system is able to scale to millions of nodes. A peer-to-peer system that can accomplish these two tasks in a decentralized manner turns out to be an overlay network, where the nodes are those hosts that are willing to share objects of interest (e.g., music and other assorted files), and the links (tunnels) connecting these nodes represent the sequence of machines that you have to visit to track down the object you want. This description will become clearer after we look at two examples.

Gnutella

Gnutella is an early peer-to-peer network that attempted to distinguish between exchanging music (which likely violates somebody's copyright) and the general sharing of files (which must be good since we've been taught to share since the age of two). What's interesting about Gnutella is that it was one of the first such systems to not depend on a centralized

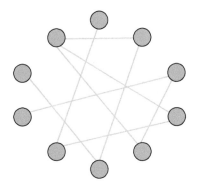

registry of objects. Instead, Gnutella participants arrange themselves into an overlay network similar to the one shown in Figure 9.24. That is, each node that runs the Gnutella software (i.e., implements the Gnutella protocol) knows about some set of other machines that also run the Gnutella software. The relationship "A and B know each other" corresponds to the edges in this graph. (We'll talk about how this graph is formed in a moment.)

Whenever the user on a given node wants to find an object, Gnutella sends a QUERY message for the object—for example, specifying the file's name—to its neighbors in the graph. If one of the neighbors has the object, it responds to the node that sent it the query with a QUERY RESPONSE message, specifying where the object can be downloaded (e.g., an IP address and TCP port number). That node can subsequently use GET or PUT messages to access the object. If the node cannot resolve the query, it forwards the QUERY message to each of its neighbors (except the one that sent it the query), and the process repeats. In other words, Gnutella floods the overlay to locate the desired object. Gnutella sets a TTL on each query so this flood does not continue indefinitely.

In addition to the TTL and query string, each QUERY message contains a unique query identifier (QID), but it does not contain the identity of the original message source. Instead, each node maintains a record of the QUERY messages it has seen recently: both the QID and the neighbor that sent it the QUERY. It uses this history in two ways. First, if it ever receives a QUERY with a QID that matches one it has seen recently, the node does not forward the QUERY message. This serves to cut off forwarding loops more quickly than the TTL might have done. Second, whenever the node receives a QUERY RESPONSE from a downstream neighbor, it knows to forward the response to the upstream neighbor that originally sent it the QUERY message. In this way, the response works its way back to the original node without any of the intermediate nodes knowing who wanted to locate this particular object in the first place.

Returning to the question of how the graph evolves, a node certainly has to know about at least one other node when it joins a Gnutella overlay. The new node is attached to the overlay by at least this one link. After that, a given node learns about other nodes as the result of QUERY RESPONSE messages, both for objects it requested and for responses that just happen to pass through it. A node is free to decide which of the nodes it discovers in this way that it wants to keep as a neighbor. The Gnutella protocol provides PING and PONG messages by which a node probes whether or not a given neighbor still exists and that neighbor's response, respectively.

It should be clear that Gnutella as described here is not a particularly clever protocol, and subsequent systems have tried to improve upon it. One dimension along which improvements are possible is in how queries are propagated. Flooding has the nice property that it is guaranteed to find the desired object in the fewest possible hops, but it does not scale well. It is possible to forward queries randomly, or according to the probability of success based on past results. A second dimension is to proactively replicate the objects, since the more copies of a given object there are, the easier it should be to find a copy. Alternatively, one could develop a completely different strategy, which is the topic we consider next.

Structured Overlays

At the same time file sharing systems have been fighting to fill the void left by Napster, the research community has been exploring an alternative design for peer-to-peer networks. We refer to these networks as *structured*, to contrast them with the essentially random (unstructured) way in which a Gnutella network evolves. Unstructured overlays like Gnutella employ trivial overlay construction and maintenance algorithms, but the best they can offer is unreliable, random search. In contrast, structured overlays are designed to conform to a particular graph structure that allows reliable and efficient (probabilistically bounded delay) object location, in return for additional complexity during overlay construction and maintenance.

If you think about what we are trying to do at a high level, there are two questions to consider: (1) How do we map objects onto nodes, and (2) How do we route a request to the node that is responsible for a given object? We start with the first question, which has a simple statement: How do we map an object with name x into the address of some node n that is able to serve that object? While traditional peer-to-peer networks have no control over which node hosts object x, if we could control how objects get distributed over the network, we might be able to do a better job of finding those objects at a later time.

A well-known technique for mapping names into an address is to use a hash table, so that

$$hash(x) \longrightarrow n$$

implies object x is first placed on node n, and at a later time a client trying to locate x would only have to perform the hash of x to determine that it is on node n. A hash-based approach has the nice property that it tends to spread the objects evenly across the set of nodes, but straightforward hashing algorithms suffer from a fatal flaw: How many possible values of n should we allow? (In hashing terminology, how many buckets should there be?) Naively, we could decide that there are, say, 101 possible hash values, and we use a modulo hash function; that is,

```
hash(x)
    return x % 101
```

Unfortunately, if there are more than 101 nodes willing to host objects, then we can't take advantage of all of them. On the other hand, if we select a number larger than the largest possible number of nodes, then there will be some values of x that will hash into an address for a node that does not exist. There is also the not-so-small issue of translating the value returned by the hash function into an actual IP address.

To address these issues, structured peer-to-peer networks use an algorithm known as *consistent hashing*, which hashes a set of objects x uniformly across a large ID space. Figure 9.25 visualizes a 128-bit ID space as a circle, where we use the algorithm to place both objects

$$hash(object\_name) \longrightarrow objid$$

and nodes

$$hash(IP\_addr) \longrightarrow nodeid$$

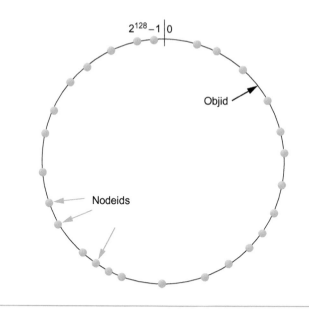

■ **FIGURE 9.25** Both nodes and objects map (hash) onto the ID space, where objects are maintained at the nearest node in this space.

onto this circle. Since a 128-bit ID space is enormous, it is unlikely that an object will hash to exactly the same ID as a machine's IP address hashes to. To account for this unlikelihood, each object is maintained on the node whose ID is *closest*, in this 128-bit space, to the object ID. In other words, the idea is to use a high-quality hash function to map both nodes and objects into the same large, sparse ID space; you then map objects to nodes by numerical proximity of their respective identifiers. Like ordinary hashing, this distributes objects fairly evenly across nodes, but, unlike ordinary hashing, only a small number of objects have to move when a node (hash bucket) joins or leaves.

We now turn to the second question—how does a user that wants to access object x know which node is closest in x's ID in this space? One possible answer is that each node keeps a complete table of node IDs and their associated IP addresses, but this would not be practical for a large network. The alternative, which is the approach used by structured peer-to-peer networks, is to *route a message to this node!* In other words, if we construct the overlay in a clever way—which is the same as saying that we need to choose entries for a node's routing table in a clever way—then we find a node simply by routing toward it. Collectively, this approach is

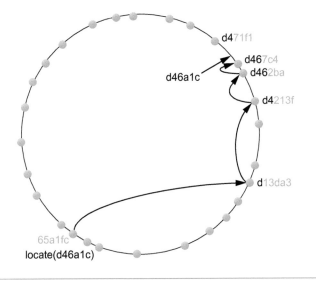

sometimes called a *distributed hash table* (DHT), since conceptually, the hash table is distributed over all the nodes in the network.

Figure 9.26 illustrates what happens for a simple 28-bit ID space. To keep the discussion as concrete as possible, we consider the approach used by a particular peer-to-peer network called *Pastry*. Other systems work in a similar manner. (See the papers cited at the end of the chapter for additional examples.)

Suppose you are at the node with id 65a1fc (hex) and you are trying to locate the object with ID d46a1c. You realize that your ID shares nothing with the object's, but you know of a node that shares at least the prefix d. That node is closer than you in the 128-bit ID space, so you forward the message to it. (We do not give the format of the message being forwarded, but you can think of it as saying "locate object d46a1c.") Assuming node d13da3 knows of another node that shares an even longer prefix with the object, it forwards the message on. This process of moving closer in ID-space continues until you reach a node that knows of no closer node. This node is, by definition, the one that hosts the object. Keep in mind that as we logically move through "ID space" the message is actually being forwarded, node to node, through the underlying Internet.

Each node maintains a both routing table (more below) and the IP addresses of a small set of numerically larger and smaller node IDs. This is called the node's *leaf set*. The relevance of the leaf set is that, once a message is routed to any node in the same leaf set as the node that hosts the object, that node can directly forward the message to the ultimate destination. Said another way, the leaf set facilitates correct and efficient delivery of a message to the numerically closest node, even though multiple nodes may exist that share a maximal length prefix with the object ID. Moreover, the leaf set makes routing more robust because any of the nodes in a leaf set can route a message just as well as any other node in the same set. Thus, if one node is unable to make progress routing a message, one of its neighbors in the leaf set may be able to. In summary, the routing procedure is defined as follows:

```
Route(D)
    if D is within range of my leaf set
        forward to numerically closest member in leaf set
    else
        let l = length of shared prefix
        let d = value of l-th digit in D's address
        if RouteTab[l, d] exists
            forward to RouteTab[l, d]
        else
            forward to known node with at least as long a shared prefix
            and numerically closer than this node
```

The routing table, denoted RouteTab, is a two-dimensional array. It has a row for every hex digit in an ID (there such 32 digits in a 128-bit ID) and a column for every hex value (there are obviously 16 such values). Every entry in row i shares a prefix of length i with this node, and within this row the entry in column j has the hex value j in the $i + 1$th position. Figure 9.27 shows the first three rows of an example routing table for node 65alfc$x$, where x denotes an unspecified suffix. This figure shows the ID prefix matched by every entry in the table. It does not show the actual value contained in this entry—the IP address of the next node to route to.

Adding a node to the overlay works much like routing a "locate object message" to an object. The new node must know of at least one current member. It asks this member to route an "add node message" to the node numerically closest to the ID of the joining node, as shown in Figure 9.28. It is through this routing process that the new node

	0	1	2	3	4	5	6	7	8	9	a	b	c	d	e	f
Row 0	0 x	1 x	2 x	3 x	4 x	5 x		7 x	8 x	9 x	a x	b x	c x	d x	e x	f x
Row 1	6 0 x	6 1 x	6 2 x	6 3 x	6 4 x		6 6 x	6 7 x	6 8 x	6 9 x	6 a x	6 b x	6 c x	6 d x	6 e x	6 f x
Row 2	6 5 0 x	6 5 1 x	6 5 2 x	6 5 3 x	6 5 4 x	6 5 5 x	6 5 6 x	6 5 7 x	6 5 8 x	6 5 9 x		6 5 b x	6 5 c x	6 5 d x	6 5 e x	6 5 f x
Row 3	6 5 a 0 x		6 5 a 2 x	6 5 a 3 x	6 5 a 4 x	6 5 a 5 x	6 5 a 6 x	6 5 a 7 x	6 5 a 8 x	6 5 a 9 x	6 5 a a x	6 5 a b x	6 5 a c x	6 5 a d x	6 5 a e x	6 5 a f x

■ **FIGURE 9.27** Example routing table at the node with ID 65a1fc𝑥.

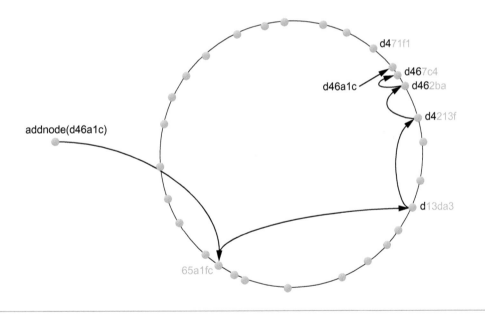

■ **FIGURE 9.28** Adding a node to the network.

learns about other nodes with a shared prefix and is able to begin filling out its routing table. Over time, as additional nodes join the overlay, existing nodes also have the option of including information about
the newly joined node in their routing tables. They do this when the

new node adds a longer prefix than they currently have in their table. Neighbors in the leaf sets also exchange routing tables with each other, which means that over time routing information propagates through the overlay.

The reader may have noticed that although structured overlays provide a probabilistic bound on the number of routing hops required to locate a given object—the number of hops in Pastry is bounded by $log_{16}N$, where N is the number of nodes in the overlay—each hop may contribute substantial delay. This is because each intermediate node may be at a random location in the Internet. (In the worst case, each node is on a different continent!) In fact, in a world-wide overlay network using the algorithm as described above, the expected delay of each hop is the average delay among all pairs of nodes in the Internet! Fortunately, one can do much better in practice. The idea is to choose each routing table entry such that it refers to a nearby node in the underlying physical network, among all nodes with an ID prefix that is appropriate for the entry. It turns out that doing so achieves end-to-end routing delays that are within a small factor of the delay between source and destination node.

Finally, the discussion up to this point has focused on the general problem of locating objects in a peer-to-peer network. Given such a routing infrastructure, it is possible to build different services. For example, a file sharing service would use file names as object names. To locate a file, you first hash its name into a corresponding object ID and then route a "locate object message" to this ID. The system might also replicate each file across multiple nodes to improve availability. Storing multiple copies on the leaf set of the node to which a given file normally routes would be one way of doing this. Keep in mind that even though these nodes are neighbors in the ID space, they are likely to be physically distributed across the Internet. Thus, while a power outage in an entire city might take down physically close replicas of a file in a traditional file system, one or more replicas would likely survive such a failure in a peer-to-peer network.

Services other than file sharing can also be built on top of distributed hash tables. Consider multicast applications, for example. Instead of constructing a multicast tree from a mesh, one could construct the tree from edges in the structured overlay, thereby amortizing the cost of overlay construction and maintenance across several applications and multicast groups.

BitTorrent

BitTorrent is a peer-to-peer file sharing protocol devised by Bram Cohen. It is based on replicating the file or, rather, replicating segments of the file, which are called *pieces*. Any particular piece can usually be downloaded from multiple peers, even if only one peer has the entire file. The primary benefit of BitTorrent's replication is avoiding the bottleneck of having only one source for a file. This is particularly useful when you consider that any given computer has a limited speed at which it can serve files over its uplink to the Internet, often quite a low limit due to the asymmetric nature of most broadband networks. The beauty of BitTorrent is that replication is a natural side effect of the downloading process: As soon as a peer downloads a particular piece, it becomes another source for that piece. The more peers downloading pieces of the file, the more piece replication occurs, distributing the load proportionately, and the more total bandwidth is available to share the file with others. Pieces are downloaded in random order to avoid a situation where peers find themselves lacking the same set of pieces.

Each file is shared via its own independent BitTorrent network, called a *swarm*. (A swarm could potentially share a set of files, but we describe the single file case for simplicity.) The lifecycle of a typical swarm is as follows. The swarm starts as a singleton peer with a complete copy of the file. A node that wants to download the file joins the swarm, becoming its second member, and begins downloading pieces of the file from the original peer. In doing so, it becomes another source for the pieces it has downloaded, even if it has not yet downloaded the entire file. (In fact, it is common for peers to leave the swarm once they have completed their downloads, although they are encouraged to stay longer.) Other nodes join the swarm and begin downloading pieces from multiple peers, not just the original peer. See Figure 9.29.

If the file remains in high demand, with a stream of new peers replacing those who leave the swarm, the swarm could remain active indefinitely; if not, it could shrink back to include only the original peer until new peers join the swarm.

Now that we have an overview of BitTorrent, we can ask how requests are routed to the peers that have a given piece. To make requests, a would-be downloader must first join the swarm. It starts by downloading a .torrent file containing meta-information about the file and swarm. The .torrent file, which may be easily replicated, is typically downloaded

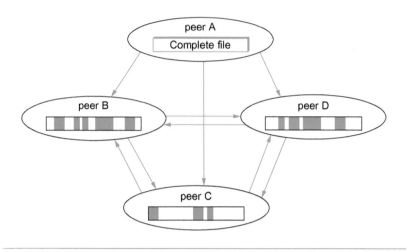

■ **FIGURE 9.29** Peers in a BitTorrent swarm download from other peers that may not yet have the complete file.

from a web server and discovered by following links from Web pages. It contains:

- The target file's size
- The piece size
- SHA-1 hash values (Section 8.1.4) precomputed from each piece
- The URL of the swarm's *tracker*

A tracker is a server that tracks a swarm's current membership. We'll see later that BitTorrent can be extended to eliminate this point of centralization, with its attendant potential for bottleneck or failure.

The would-be downloader then joins the swarm, becoming a peer, by sending a message to the tracker giving its network address and a peer ID that it has generated randomly for itself. The message also carries a SHA-1 hash of the main part of the .torrent file, which is used as a swarm ID.

Let's call the new peer P. The tracker replies to P with a partial list of peers giving their IDs and network addresses, and P establishes connections, over TCP, with some of these peers. Note that P is directly connected to just a subset of the swarm, although it may decide to contact additional peers or even request more peers from the tracker. To establish a BitTorrent connection with a particular peer after their TCP connection has been established, P sends P's own peer ID and swarm ID, and the peer replies with its peer ID and swarm ID. If the swarm IDs don't match, or the reply peer ID is not what P expects, the connection is aborted.

The resulting BitTorrent connection is symmetric: Each end can download from the other. Each end begins by sending the other a bitmap reporting which pieces it has, so each peer knows the other's initial state. Whenever a downloader (D) finishes downloading another piece, it sends a message identifying that piece to each of its directly connected peers, so those peers can update their internal representation of D's state. This, finally, is the answer to the question of how a download request for a piece is routed to a peer that has the piece, because it means that each peer knows which directly connected peers have the piece. If D needs a piece that none of its connections has, it could connect to more or different peers (it can get more from the tracker) or occupy itself with other pieces in hopes that some of its connections will obtain the piece from their connections.

How are objects—in this case, pieces—mapped onto peer nodes? Of course each peer eventually obtains all the pieces, so the question is really about which pieces a peer has at a given time before it has all the pieces or, equivalently, about the order in which a peer downloads pieces. The answer is that they download pieces in random order, to keep them from having a strict subset or superset of the pieces of any of their peers.

The BitTorrent described so far utilizes a central tracker that constitutes a single point of failure for the swarm and could potentially be a performance bottleneck. Also, providing a tracker can be a nuisance for someone who would like to make a file available via BitTorrent. Newer versions of BitTorrent additionally support "trackerless" swarms that use a DHT-based implementation. BitTorrent client software that is trackerless capable implements not just a BitTorrent peer but also what we'll call a *peer finder* (the BitTorrent terminology is simply *node*), which the peer uses to find peers.

Peer finders form their own overlay network, using their own protocol over UDP to implement a DHT. Furthermore, a peer finder network includes peer finders whose associated peers belong to different swarms. In other words, while each swarm forms a distinct network of BitTorrent peers, a peer finder network instead spans swarms.

Peer finders randomly generate their own finder IDs, which are the same size (160 bits) as swarm IDs. Each finder maintains a modest table containing primarily finders (and their associated peers) whose IDs are close to its own, plus some finders whose IDs are more distant. The following algorithm ensures that finders whose IDs are close to a given swarm

ID are likely to know of peers from that swarm; the algorithm simultaneously provides a way to look them up. When a finder F needs to find peers from a particular swarm, it sends a request to the finders in its table whose IDs are close to that swarm's ID. If a contacted finder knows of any peers for that swarm, it replies with their contact information. Otherwise, it replies with the contact information of the finders in its table that are close to the swarm, so that F can iteratively query those finders.

After the search is exhausted, because there are no finders closer to the swarm, F inserts the contact information for itself and its associated peer into the finders closest to the swarm. The net effect is that peers for a particular swarm get entered in the tables of the finders that are close to that swarm.

The above scheme assumes that F is already part of the finder network, that it already knows how to contact some other finders. This assumption is true for finder installations that have run previously, because they are supposed to save information about other finders, even across executions. If a swarm uses a tracker, its peers are able to tell their finders about other finders (in a reversal of the peer and finder roles) because the BitTorrent peer protocol has been extended to exchange finder contact information. But, how can a newly installed finder discover other finders? The .torrent files for trackerless swarms include contact information for one or a few finders, instead of a tracker URL, for just that situation.

An unusual aspect of BitTorrent is that it deals head-on with the issue of fairness, or good "network citizenship." Protocols often depend on the good behavior of individual peers without being able to enforce it. For example, an unscrupulous Ethernet peer could get better performance by using a backoff algorithm that is more aggressive than exponential backoff, or an unscrupulous TCP peer could get better performance by not cooperating in congestion control.

The good behavior that BitTorrent depends on is peers uploading pieces to other peers. Since the typical BitTorrent user just wants to download the file as quickly as possible, there is a temptation to implement a peer that tries to download all the pieces while doing as little uploading as possible—this is a bad peer. To discourage bad behavior, the BitTorrent protocol includes mechanisms that allow peers to reward or punish each other. If a peer is misbehaving by not nicely uploading to another peer, the second peer can *choke* the bad peer: It can decide to stop uploading to the bad peer, at least temporarily, and send it a message saying so.

There is also a message type for telling a peer that it has been unchoked. The choking mechanism is also used by a peer to limit the number of its active BitTorrent connections, to maintain good TCP performance. There are many possible choking algorithms, and devising a good one is an art.

9.4.3 Content Distribution Networks

We have already seen how HTTP running over TCP allows web browsers to retrieve pages from web servers. However, anyone who has waited an eternity for a Web page to return knows that the system is far from perfect. Considering that the backbone of the Internet is now constructed from OC-192 (10-Gbps) links, it's not obvious why this should happen. It is generally agreed that when it comes to downloading Web pages there are four potential bottlenecks in the system:

- *The first mile.* The Internet may have high-capacity links in it, but that doesn't help you download a Web page any faster when you're connected by a 56-Kbps modem or a poorly performing 3G wireless link.
- *The last mile.* The link that connects the server to the Internet can be overloaded by too many requests, even if the aggregate bandwidth of that link is quite high.
- *The server itself.* A server has a finite amount of resources (CPU, memory, disk bandwidth, etc.) and can be overloaded by too many concurrent requests.
- *Peering points.* The handful of ISPs that collectively implement the backbone of the Internet may internally have high-bandwidth pipes, but they have little motivation to provide high-capacity connectivity to their peers. If you are connected to ISP A and the server is connected to ISP B, then the page you request may get dropped at the point where A and B peer with each other.

There's not a lot anyone except you can do about the first problem, but it is possible to use replication to address the remaining problems. Systems that do this are often called *Content Distribution Networks* (CDNs). Akamai operates what is probably the best-known CDN.

The idea of a CDN is to geographically distribute a collection of *server surrogates* that cache pages normally maintained in some set of *backend servers*. Thus, rather than having millions of users wait forever to contact www.cnn.com when a big news story breaks—such a situation is known as a *flash crowd*—it is possible to spread this load across many servers. Moreover, rather than having to traverse multiple ISPs to reach www.cnn.com, if these surrogate servers happen to be spread across all the backbone ISPs, then it should be possible to reach one without having to cross a peering point. Clearly, maintaining thousands of surrogate servers all over the Internet is too expensive for any one site that wants to provide better access to its Web pages. Commercial CDNs provide this service for many sites, thereby amortizing the cost across many customers.

Although we call them surrogate servers, in fact, they can just as correctly be viewed as caches. If they don't have a page that has been requested by a client, they ask the backend server for it. In practice, however, the backend servers proactively replicate their data across the surrogates rather than wait for surrogates to request it on demand. It's also the case that only static pages, as opposed to dynamic content, are distributed across the surrogates. Clients have to go to the backend server for any content that either changes frequently (e.g., sports scores and stock quotes) or is produced as the result of some computation (e.g., a database query).

Having a large set of geographically distributed servers does not fully solve the problem. To complete the picture, CDNs also need to provide a set of *redirectors* that forward client requests to the most appropriate server, as shown in Figure 9.30. The primary objective of the redirectors is to select the server for each request that results in the best *response time* for the client. A secondary objective is for the system as a whole to process as many requests per second as the underlying hardware (network links and web servers) is able to support. The average number of requests that can be satisfied in a given time period—known as the *system throughput*—is primarily an issue when the system is under heavy load, such as when a flash crowd is accessing a small set of pages or a Distributed Denial of Service (DDoS) attacker is targeting a particular site, as happened to CNN, Yahoo, and several other high-profile sites in February 2000.

CDNs use several factors to decide how to distribute client requests. For example, to minimize response time, a redirector might select a server based on its *network proximity*. In contrast, to improve the overall system throughput, it is desirable to evenly *balance* the load across a set of servers. Both throughput and response time are improved if the distribution mechanism takes *locality* into consideration; that is, it selects

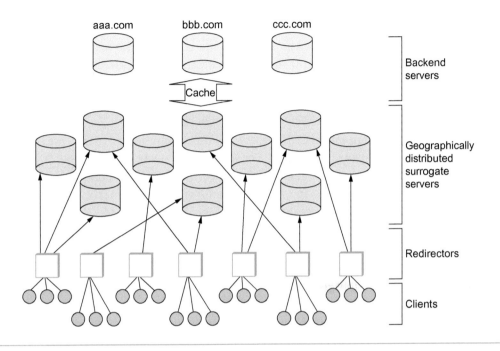

■ FIGURE 9.30 Components in a Content Distribution Network (CDN).

a server that is likely to already have the page being requested in its cache. The exact combination of factors that should be employed by a CDN is open to debate. This section considers some of the possibilities.

Mechanisms

As described so far, a redirector is just an abstract function, although it sounds like what something a router might be asked to do since it logically forwards a request message much like a router forwards packets. In fact, there are several mechanisms that can be used to implement redirection. Note that for the purpose of this discussion we assume that each redirector knows the address of every available server. (From here on, we drop the "surrogate" qualifier and talk simply in terms of a set of servers.) In practice, some form of out-of-band communication takes place to keep this information up-to-date as servers come and go.

First, redirection could be implemented by augmenting DNS to return different server addresses to clients. For example, when a client asks to resolve the name www.cnn.com, the DNS server could return the IP address of a server hosting CNN's Web pages that is known to have the lightest load. Alternatively, for a given set of servers, it might just return addresses in a round-robin fashion. Note that the granularity of DNS-based redirection is usually at the level of a site (e.g., cnn.com) rather than a specific URL (e.g., http://www.cnn.com/2002/WORLD/europe/06/21/william.birthday/index.html). However, when returning an embedded link, the server can rewrite the URL, thereby effectively pointing the client at the most appropriate server for that specific object.

Commercial CDNs essentially use a combination of URL rewriting and DNS-based redirection. For scalability reasons, the high-level DNS server first points to a regional-level DNS server, which replies with the actual server address. In order to respond to changes quickly, the DNS servers tweak the TTL of the resource records they return to a very short period, such as 20 seconds. This is necessary so clients don't cache results and thus fail to go back to the DNS server for the most recent URL-to-server mapping.

Another possibility is to use the HTTP redirect feature: The client sends a request message to a server, which responds with a new (better) server that the client should contact for the page. Unfortunately, server-based redirection incurs an additional round-trip time across the Internet, and, even worse, servers can be vulnerable to being overloaded by the redirection task itself. Instead, if there is a node close to the client (e.g., a local Web proxy) that is aware of the available servers, then it can intercept the request message and instruct the client to instead request the page from an appropriate server. In this case, either the redirector would need to be on a choke point so that all requests leaving the site pass through it, or the client would have to cooperate by explicitly addressing the proxy (as with a classical, rather than transparent, proxy).

At this point you may be wondering what CDNs have to do with overlay networks, and while viewing a CDN as an overlay is a bit of a stretch, they do share one very important trait in common. Like an overlay node, a proxy-based redirector makes an application-level routing decision. Rather than forward a packet based on an address and its knowledge of the network topology, it forwards HTTP requests based on a URL and its knowledge of the location and load of a set of servers. Today's Internet architecture does not support redirection directly—where by "directly" we mean the client sends the HTTP request to the redirector, which forwards to the destination—so instead redirection is typically implemented indirectly by having the redirector return the appropriate destination address and the client contacts the server itself.

Policies

We now consider some example policies that redirectors might use to forward requests. Actually, we have already suggested one simple policy—round-robin. A similar scheme would be to simply select one of the available servers at random. Both of these approaches do a good job of spreading the load evenly across the CDN, but they do not do a particularly good job of lowering the client-perceived response time.

It's obvious that neither of these two schemes takes network proximity into consideration, but, just as importantly, they also ignore locality. That is, requests for the same URL are forwarded to different servers, making it less likely that the page will be served from the selected server's in-memory cache. This forces the server to retrieve the page from its disk, or possibly even from the backend server. How can a distributed set of redirectors cause requests for the same page to go to the same server (or small set of servers) without global coordination? The answer is surprisingly simple: All redirectors use some form of hashing to deterministically map URLs into a small range of values. The primary benefit of this approach is that no inter-redirector communication is required to achieve coordinated operation; no matter which redirector receives a URL, the hashing process produces the same output.

So what makes for a good hashing scheme? The classic *modulo* hashing scheme—which hashes each URL modulo the number of servers—is not suitable for this environment. This is because should the number of servers change, the modulo calculation will result in a diminishing fraction of the pages keeping their same server assignments. While we do not expect frequent changes in the set of servers, the fact that the addition of new servers into the set will cause massive reassignment is undesirable.

An alternative is to use the same *consistent hashing* algorithm discussed in Section 9.4.2. Specifically, each redirector first hashes every server into the unit circle. Then, for each URL that arrives, the redirector also hashes the URL to a value on the unit circle, and the URL is assigned to the server that lies closest on the circle to its hash value. If a node fails in this scheme, its load shifts to its neighbors (on the unit circle), so the addition or removal of a server only causes local changes in request assignments. Note that unlike the peer-to-peer case, where a message is routed from one node to another in order to find the server whose ID is closest to the objects, each redirector knows how the set of servers map onto the unit circle, so they can each, independently, select the "nearest" one.

This strategy can easily be extended to take server load into account. Assume the redirector knows the current load of each of the available servers. This information may not be perfectly up-to-date, but we can imagine the redirector simply counting how many times it has forwarded a request to each server in the last few seconds and using this count as an estimate of that server's current load. Upon receiving a URL, the redirector hashes the URL plus each of the available servers and sorts the resulting values. This sorted list effectively defines the order in which the redirector will consider the available servers. The redirector then walks down this list until it finds a server whose load is below some threshold. The benefit of this approach compared to plain consistent hashing is that server order is different for each URL, so if one server fails its load is distributed evenly among the other machines. This approach is the basis for the Cache Array Routing Protocol (CARP) and is shown in pseudocode below.

```
SelectServer(URL, S)
    for = each server s_i in server set S
        weight_i = hash(URL, address(s_i))
    sort weight
    for each server s_j in decreasing order of weight_j
        if = Load(s_j) < threshold then
            return s_j
    return server with highest weight
```

As the load increases, this scheme changes from using only the first server on the sorted list to spreading requests across several servers. Some pages normally handled by busy servers will also start being handled by less busy servers. Since this process is based on aggregate server load rather than the popularity of individual pages, servers hosting some popular pages may find more servers sharing their load than servers hosting collectively unpopular pages. In the process, some unpopular pages will be replicated in the system simply because they happen to be primarily hosted on busy servers. At the same time, if some pages become extremely popular, it is conceivable that all of the servers in the system could be responsible for serving them.

Finally, it is possible to introduce network proximity into the equation in at least two different ways. The first is to blur the distinction between server load and network proximity by monitoring how long a server takes to respond to requests and using this measurement as the "server load" parameter in the preceding algorithm. This strategy tends to prefer nearby/lightly loaded servers over distant/heavily loaded servers. A second approach is to factor proximity into the decision at an earlier stage by limiting the candidate set of servers considered by the above algorithms (S) to only those that are nearby. The harder problem is deciding which of the potentially many servers are suitably close. One approach would be to select only those servers that are available on the same ISP as the client. A slightly more sophisticated approach would be to look at the map of autonomous systems produced by BGP and select only those servers within some number of hops from the client as candidate servers. Finding the right balance between network proximity and server cache locality is a subject of ongoing research.

9.5 SUMMARY

We have seen two of the most widely used client/server-based application protocols: SMTP used to exchange electronic mail and HTTP used to walk the World Wide Web. We have seen how application-to-application communication is driving the creation of new protocol development frameworks such as SOAP and REST. And we have examined session control protocols, such as SIP and H.323, which are used to control multimedia applications such as Voice over IP. In addition to these application protocols, we looked at some critical supporting protocols: the DNS protocol used by the Domain Naming System and SNMP used to query remote nodes for the sake of network management. Finally, we looked at emerging applications—including overlay, peer-to-peer, and content distribution networks—that blend application processing and packet forwarding in innovative ways.

Application protocols are a curious lot. In many ways, the traditional client/server applications are like another layer of transport protocol, except they have application-specific knowledge built into them. You could argue that they are just specialized transport protocols, and that transport protocols get layered on top of each other until producing the precise service needed by the application. Similarly, the overlay and peer-to-peer protocols can be viewed as providing an alternative routing infrastructure, but, again, one that is tailored for a particular application's needs. One sure lesson we draw from this observation is that designing application-level protocols is really no different than designing core network protocols, and that the more one understands about the latter the better they will do designing the former. We also observe that the systems approach—understanding how functions and components interact to build a complete system—applies at least as much in the design of applications as in any other aspect of networking.

It's difficult to put a finger on a specific issue in the realm of application protocols—the entire field is open as new applications are invented every day, and the networking needs of these applications are, well, application dependent. The real challenge to network designers is to recognize that what applications need from the network changes over time, and these changes drive the transport protocols we develop and the functionality we put into network routers.

Developing new transport protocols is a reasonably tractable problem. You may not be able to get the IETF to bless your transport protocol as an equal of TCP or UDP, but there's certainly nothing stopping you from designing the world's greatest multimedia application that comes bundled with a new end-to-end protocol that runs on top of UDP, much like happens with RTP.

WHAT'S NEXT: NEW NETWORK ARCHITECTURE

On the other hand, pushing application-specific knowledge into the middle of the network—into the routers—is a much more difficult problem. This is because, in order to effect a particular application, any new network service or functionality may need to be loaded into many, if not all, of the routers in the Internet. Overlay networks provide a way of introducing new functionality into the network without the cooperation of all (or even any) of the routers, but in the long run we can expect that the underlying network architecture will need to change to accommodate these overlays. We saw this issue with RON—how RON and BGP route selection interact with each other—and can expect it to be a general question as overlay networks become more prevalent.

One possibility is that an alternative *fixed* architecture does not evolve, but instead the next network architecture will be highly adaptive. In the limit, rather than defining an infrastructure for carrying data packets, the network architecture might allow packets to carry both data and code (or possibly pointers to code) that tell the router how it should process the packet. Such a network raises a host of issues, not the least of which is how to enforce security in a world where arbitrary applications can effectively program routers. Another possibility is that virtualization of networks becomes the norm, with perhaps some "slices" providing robust, well-understood, and fully debugged services while others are used for more experimental functions. This is one direction the research community is currently pursuing.

■ FURTHER READING

Our first article provides an interesting perspective on the early design and implementation of the World Wide Web, written by its inventors before it had taken the world by storm. The development of DNS is well described by Mockapetris and Dunlap. Overlays, CDNs, and peer-to-peer networks have been extensively researched in recent years, and the last six research papers provide a good place to start understanding the issues.

- Berners-Lee, T., R. Caillia, A. Luotonen, H. Nielsen, and A. Secret. The World-Wide Web. *Communications of the ACM* 37(8), pages 76–82, August 1994.

- Mockapetris, P., and K. Dunlap. Development of the Domain Name System. *Proceedings of the SIGCOMM '88 Symposium*, pages 123–133, August 1988.

- Karger, D. et al. Consistent hashing and random trees: Distributed caching protocols for relieving hot spots on the World Wide Web. *Proceedings of the ACM Symposium on Theory of Computing*, pages 654–663, May 1997.

- Chu, Y., S. Rao, and H. Zhang. A case for End System Multicast. *Proceedings of the ACM SIGMETRICS '00 Conference*, pages 1–12, June 2000.

- Andersen, D. et al. Resilient overlay networks. *Proceedings of the 18th ACM Symposium on Operating Systems Principles (SOSP)*, pages 131–145, October 2001.

- Rowstron, A., and P. Druschel. Storage management and caching in PAST, a large-scale persistent peer-to-peer storage utility. *Proceedings of the 18th ACM Symposium on Operating Systems Principles (SOSP)*, pages 188–201, October 2001.

- Stoica, I. et al. Chord: A scalable peer-to-peer lookup service for Internet applications. *Proceedings of the ACM SIGCOMM Conference*, pages 149–160, August 2001.

- Ratnasamy, S. et al. A scalable content-addressable network. *Proceedings of ACM SIGCOMM '01*, pages 161–172, August 2001.

SMTP was originally defined in RFC 821 [Pos82], and, of course, RFC 822 is RFC 822 [Cro82]. They have been, in IETF terminology, "obsoleted" by [Kle01] and [Res01], respectively. MIME is defined in a series of RFCs; the most recent version is defined in RFC 2045 [FB96], with several additional RFCs filling in details.

Version 1.0 of HTTP is specified in RFC 1945 [BLFF96], and the latest version (1.1) is defined in RFC 2616 [FGM$^+$99]. Mogul [Mog95] made the case for the persistent connections in HTTP 1.1. There is a wealth of papers written about web performance, especially web caching. A good example is a paper by Danzig on web traffic and its implications on the effectiveness of caching [Dan98]. Roy Fielding's Ph.D. thesis [Fie00] is the ultimate reference for REST.

SIP is defined in RFC 3261 [SCJ$^+$02], which contains a helpful tutorial section as well as the detailed specification of the protocol. As with MIME, there are many other RFCs that extend the protocol.

There is a wealth of papers on naming, as well as on the related issue of resource discovery (finding out what resources exist in the first place). General studies of naming can be found in Terry [Ter86], Comer and Peterson [CP89], Birrell et al. [BLNS82], Saltzer [Sal78], Shoch [Sho78], and Watson [Wat81]; attribute-based (descriptive) naming systems are described in Peterson [Pet88] and Bowman et al. [BPY90]; and resource discovery is the subject of Bowman et al. [BDMS94].

Network management is a sufficiently large and important field that the IETF devotes an entire area to it. There are well over 100 RFCs describing various aspects of SNMP and MIBs. The two key references, however, are RFC 2578 [MPS99], which defines the structure of management information for version 2 of SNMP (SNMPv2), and RFC 3416 [Pre02], which defines the protocol operations for SNMPv2. Many of the other SNMP/MIB-related RFCs define extensions to the core set of MIB variables—for example, variables that are specific to a particular network technology or to a particular vendor's product. Perkins et al. [PM97] provides a good introduction to SNMP and MIBS.

The National Research Council report on the ossification of the Internet can be found in [NRC01], and a proposal to use overlay networks to introduce disruptive technology was made by Peterson et al., Anderson, Culler, and Roscoe [PACR02]. The original case for overriding BGP routes was made by Savage et al., Collins, Hoffman, Snell, and Anderson [SCH^{+}99]. The idea of using DNS to load-balance a set of servers is described in RFC 1794 [Bri95]. A comprehensive treatment of the issue of web caching versus replicated servers can be found in Rabinovich and Spatscheck's book [RS02]. Wang, Pai, and Peterson explore the design space for redirectors [WPP02].

Finally, we recommend the following live reference to help keep tabs on the rapid evolution of the Web and for a wealth of information related to Web-related standards and history:

- http://www.w3.org/: World Wide Web Consortium.

EXERCISES

1. Discuss how you might rewrite SMTP or HTTP to make use of a hypothetical general-purpose request/reply protocol. Could an appropriate analog of persistent connections be moved from the application layer into such a transport protocol? What other application tasks might be moved into this protocol?

2. Most Telnet clients can be used to connect to port 25, the SMTP port, instead of to the Telnet port. Using such a tool, connect to an SMTP server and send yourself (or someone else, with permission) some forged email. Then examine the headers for evidence the message isn't genuine.

3. What features might be used by (or added to) SMTP and/or a mail daemon such as sendmail to provide some resistance to email forgeries as in the previous exercise?

4. Find out how SMTP hosts deal with unknown commands from the other side, and how in particular this mechanism allows for

the evolution of the protocol (e.g., to "extended SMTP"). You can either read the RFC or contact an SMTP server as in Exercise 2, above, and test its responses to nonexistent commands.

5. As presented in the text, SMTP involves the exchange of several small messages. In most cases, the server responses do not affect what the client sends subsequently. The client might thus implement *command pipelining*: sending multiple commands in a single message.
    (a) For what SMTP commands does the client need to pay attention to the server's responses?
    (b) Assume the server reads each client message with gets() or the equivalent, which reads in a string up to a <LF>. What would it have to do even to detect that a client had used command pipelining?
    (c) Pipelining is nonetheless known to break with some servers; find out how a client can negotiate its use.

6. One of the central problems faced by a protocol such as MIME is the vast number of data formats available. Consult the MIME RFC to find out how MIME deals with new or system-specific image and text formats.

7. MIME supports multiple representations of the same content using the multipart/alternative syntax; for example, text could be sent as text/plain, text/richtext, and application/postscript. Why do you think plaintext is supposed to be the *first* format, even though implementations might find it easier to place plaintext after their native format?

8. Consult the MIME RFC to find out how base64 encoding handles binary data of a length not evenly divisible by three bytes.

9. The POP3 Post Office Protocol only allows a client to retrieve email, using a password for authentication. Traditionally, to *send* email a client would simply send it to its server (using SMTP) and expect that it be relayed.
    (a) Explain why email servers often no longer permit such relaying from arbitrary clients.
    (b) Propose an SMTP option for remote client authentication.
    (c) Find out what existing methods are available for addressing this issue.

10. In HTTP version 1.0, a server marked the end of a transfer by closing the connection. Explain why, in terms of the TCP layer, this was a problem for servers. Find out how HTTP version 1.1 avoids this. How might a general-purpose request/reply protocol address this?

11. Find out how to configure an HTTP server so as to eliminate the 404 not found message and have a default (and friendlier) message returned instead. Decide if such a feature is part of the protocol or part of an implementation or is technically even permitted by the protocol. (Documentation for the apache HTTP server can be found at www.apache.org.)

12. Why does the HTTP GET command on page 712,

    ```
    GET http://www.cs.princeton.edu/index.html HTTP/1.1
    ```

    contain the name of the server being contacted? Wouldn't the server already know its name? Use Telnet, as in Exercise 2, above to connect to port 80 of an HTTP server and find out what happens if you leave the host name out.

13. When an HTTP server initiates a close() at its end of a connection, it must then wait in TCP state FIN_WAIT_2 for the client to close the other end. What mechanism within the TCP protocol could help an HTTP server deal with noncooperative or poorly implemented clients that don't close from their end? If possible, find out about the programming interface for this mechanism and indicate how an HTTP server might apply it.

14. Suppose a very large website wants a mechanism by which clients access whichever of multiple HTTP servers is "closest" by some suitable measure.
    (a) Discuss developing a mechanism within HTTP for doing this.
    (b) Discuss developing a mechanism within DNS for doing this.
    Compare the two. Can either approach be made to work without upgrading the browser?

15. Application protocols such as FTP and SMTP were designed from scratch, and they seem to work reasonably well. What is it about Business to Business and Enterprise Application Integration protocols that calls for a Web Services protocol framework?

16. Choose a Web Service with equivalent REST and SOAP interfaces, such as those offered by Amazon.com. Compare how equivalent operations are implemented in the two styles.

17. Get the WSDL for some SOAP-style Web Service and choose an operation. In the messages that implement that operation, identify the fields.

18. Suppose some receivers in a large conference can receive data at a significantly higher bandwidth than others. What sorts of things might be implemented to address this? (Hint: Consider both the Session Announcement Protocol (SAP) and the possibility of utilizing third-party "mixers.")

19. How might you encode audio (or video) data in two packets so that if one packet is lost, then the resolution is simply reduced to what would be expected with half the bandwidth? Explain why this is much more difficult if a JPEG-type encoding is used.

20. Explain the relationship between Uniform Resource Locators (URLs) and Uniform Resource Identifiers (URIs). Give an example of a URI that is *not* a URL.

21. Find out what other features DNS MX records provide in addition to supplying an alias for a mail server; the latter could, after all, be provided by a DNS CNAME record. MX records are provided to support email; would an analogous WEB record be of use in supporting HTTP?

22. ARP and DNS both depend on caches; ARP cache entry lifetimes are typically 10 minutes, while DNS cache lifetimes are on the order of days. Justify this difference. What undesirable consequences might there be in having too long a DNS cache entry lifetime?

23. IPv6 simplifies ARP out of existence by allowing hardware addresses to be part of the IPv6 address. How does this complicate the job of DNS? How does this affect the problem of finding your local DNS server?

24. DNS servers also allow reverse lookup; given an IP address 128.112.169.4, it is reversed into a text string 4.169.112.128.in-addr.arpa and looked up using DNS PTR records (which form a hierarchy of domains analogous to that for the address domain

hierarchy). Suppose you want to authenticate the sender of a packet based on its host name and are confident that the source IP *address* is genuine. Explain the insecurity in converting the source address to a name as above and then comparing this name to a given list of trusted hosts. (Hint: Whose DNS servers would you be trusting?)

25. What is the relationship between a domain name (e.g., cs.princeton.edu) and an IP subnet number (e.g., 192.12.69.0)? Do all hosts on the subnet have to be identified by the same name server? What about reverse lookup, as in the previous exercise?

26. Suppose a host elects to use a name server not within its organization for address resolution. When would this result in no more total traffic, for queries not found in any DNS cache, than with a local name server? When might this result in a better DNS cache hit rate and possibly less total traffic?

27. Figure 9.17 shows the hierarchy of name servers. How would you represent this hierarchy if one name server served multiple zones? In that setting, how does the name server hierarchy relate to the zone hierarchy? How do you deal with the fact that each zone may have multiple name servers?

28. Use the whois utility/service to find out who is in charge of your site, at least as far as the InterNIC is concerned. Look up your site both by DNS name and by IP network number; for the latter you may have to try an alternative whois server (e.g., whois-h whois.arin.net. . .). Try princeton.edu and cisco.com as well.

29. Many smaller organizations have their websites maintained by a third party. How could you use whois to find if this is the case and, if so, the identity of the third party?

30. One feature of the existing DNS .com hierarchy is that it is extremely wide.
    (a) Propose a more hierarchical reorganization of the .com hierarchy. What objections might you foresee to your proposal's adoption?
    (b) What might be some of the consequences of having most DNS domain names contain four or more levels, versus the two levels of many existing names?

31. Suppose, in the other direction, we abandon any pretense at all of DNS hierarchy and simply move all the .com entries to the root name server: www.cisco.com would become www.cisco, or perhaps just cisco. How would this affect root name server traffic in general? How would this affect such traffic for the specific case of resolving a name like cisco into a web server address?

32. What DNS cache issues are involved in changing the IP address of, say, a web server host name? How might these be minimized?

33. Take a suitable DNS-lookup utility (e.g., dig) and disable the recursive lookup feature (e.g., with +norecursive), so that when your utility sends a query to a DNS server and that server is unable to fully answer the request from its own records, the server sends back the next DNS server in the lookup sequence rather than automatically forwarding the query to that next server. Then carry out manually a name lookup such as that in Figure 9.18; try the host name www.cs.princeton.edu. List each intermediate name server contacted. You may also need to specify that queries are for NS records rather than the usual A records.

34. Find out if there is available to you an SNMP node that will answer queries you send it. If so, locate some SNMP utilities (e.g., the ucd-snmp suite) and try the following:
    (a) Fetch the entire system group, using something like

        snmpwalk *nodename* public system

        Also try the above with 1 in place of system.
    (b) Manually walk through the system group, using multiple SNMP GET-NEXT operations (e.g., using snmpgetnext or equivalent), retrieving one entry at a time.

35. Using the SNMP device and utilities of the previous exercise, fetch the tcp group (numerically group 6) or some other group. Then do something to make some of the group's counters change, and fetch the group again to show the change. Try to do this in such a way that you can be sure your actions were the cause of the change recorded.

36. What information provided by SNMP might be useful to someone planning the IP spoofing attack of Exercise 17 in Chapter 5? What other SNMP information might be considered sensitive?

37. How would one design a CDN redirection mechanism using only HTTP 302 redirects or only DNS? What are the limitations of each approach? Is a combination of the two mechanisms feasible?

38. What problem would a DNS-based redirection mechanism encounter if it wants to select an appropriate server based on current load information?

39. Imagine a situation in which multiple CDNs exist and want to peer with each other (analogous to the way autonomous systems peer with each at the IP layer) for the purpose of delivering content to a larger set of end users. For example, CDN A might serve content on behalf of one set of content providers and CDN B might serve content on behalf of another set of content providers, where both A and B have a physical footprint that allows them to deliver that content to disjoint sets of end users. Sketch how CDNs A and B can use a combination of DNS redirection and HTTP 302 redirects to deliver content from CDN A's content providers to CDN B's end users (and *vice versa*).

40. Imagine a CDN configured as a *caching hierarchy*, with end users accessing content from edge caches, which fetch the content for a parent cache upon a cache miss, and so on up to a root cache, which ultimately fetches content from an origin server. What metrics would guide provisioning decisions to (a) add more storage capacity to a given cache versus (b) adding an additional level to the caching hierarchy.

41. A multicast overlay effectively *pushes* streaming content from a single source to multiple destinations, with no caching of the stream at the intermediate nodes. A CDN effectively *pulls* content (including videos) down a caching hierarchy, caching it at the intermediate nodes. Show by example how these two can be viewed as duals of each other. Explain why a CDN can be viewed as equivalent to *asynchronous multicast*. (Hint: Think TiVo.)

42. Consider the following simplified BitTorrent scenario. There is a swarm of 2^n peers and, during the time in question, no peers join or leave the swarm. It takes a peer 1 unit of time to upload or download a piece, during which time it can only do one or the

other. Initially, one peer has the whole file and the others have nothing.

(a) If the swarm's target file consists of only 1 piece, what is the minimum time necessary for all the peers to obtain the file? Ignore all but upload/download time.

(b) Let x be your answer to the preceding question. If the swarm's target file instead consisted of 2 pieces, would it be possible for all the peers to obtain the file in less than $2x$ time units? Why or why not?

Solutions to Select
Exercises

CHAPTER 1

4. We will count the transfer as completed when the last data bit arrives at its destination

    (a) 1.5 MB = 12582912 bits. 2 initial RTTs (160 ms) + 12,582,912/10,000,000 bps (transmit) + RTT/2 (propagation) ≈ 1.458 seconds.

    (b) Number of packets required = 1.5 MB/1KB = 1536. To the above we add the time for 1535 RTTs (the number of RTTs between when packet 1 arrives and packet 1536 arrives), for a total of $1.458 + 122.8 = 124.258$ seconds.

    (c) Dividing the 1536 packets by 20 gives 76.8. This will take 76.5 RTTs (half an RTT for the first batch to arrive, plus 76 RTTs between the first batch and the 77th partial batch), plus the initial 2 RTTs, for 6.28 seconds.

    (d) Right after the handshaking is done we send one packet. One RTT after the handshaking we send two packets. At n RTTs past the initial handshaking we have sent $1 + 2 + 4 + \cdots + 2^n = 2^{n+1} - 1$ packets. At $n = 10$ we have thus been able to send all 1536 packets; the last batch arrives 0.5 RTT later. Total time is $2 + 10.5$ RTTs, or 1 second.

6. Propagation delay is 50×10^3 m$/(2 \times 10^8$ m/s$) = 250\,\mu$s. 800 bits / $250\,\mu$s is 3.2 Mbps. For 512-byte packets, this rises to 16.4 Mbps.

14. (a) Propagation delay on the link is $(55 \times 10^9)/(3 \times 10^8) = 184$ seconds. Thus, the RTT is 368 seconds.

    (b) The delay × bandwidth product for the link is $184 \times 128 \times 10^3 = 2.81$ MB.

    (c) After a picture is taken, it must be transmitted on the link and be completely propagated before Mission Control can interpret it. Transmit delay for 5 MB of data is 41,943,040 bits/$128 \times 10^3 = 328$ seconds. Thus, the total time required is transmit delay + propagation delay $= 328 + 184 = 512$ seconds.

17. (a) For each link, it takes 1 Gbps / 5 kb $= 5\,\mu$s to transmit the packet on the link, after which it takes an additional $10\,\mu$s for the last bit to propagate across the link. Thus, for a LAN with only one switch that starts forwarding only after receiving the whole packet, the total transfer delay is two transmit delays + two propagation delays $= 30\,\mu$s.

(b) For three switched and thus four links, the total delay is four transmit delays + four propagation delays $= 60\,\mu$s.

(c) For cut-through, a switch need only decode the first 128 bits before beginning to forward. This takes 128 ns. This delay replaces the switch transmit delays in the previous answer for a total delay of one transmit delay + three cut-through decoding delays + four propagation delays $= 45.384\,\mu$s.

27. (a) $1920 \times 1080 \times 24 \times 30 = 1,492,992,000 \approx 1.5$ Gbps.

(b) $8 \times 8000 = 64$ Kbps.

(c) $260 \times 50 = 13$ Kbps.

(d) $24 \times 88,200 = 216,800 \approx 2.1$ Mbps.

CHAPTER 2

3. The 4B/5B encoding of the given bit sequence is the following:

11011 11100 10110 11011 10111 11100 11100 11101

Bits 1 1 0 1 1 1 1 1 0 0 1 0 1 1 0 1 1 0 1 1 1 0 1 1 1 1 1 1 0 0 1 1 1 0 0 1 1 1 0 0 1 1 1 0 1

NRZ

7. Let $\wedge$ mark each position where a stuffed 0 bit was removed. There was one error where the sever consecutive 1s are detected (*err*) At the end of the bit sequence, the end of frame was detected (*eof*).

01101011111$\wedge$101001111111**1**$_{err}$0 110 **01111110**$_{eof}$

19. (a) We take the message 1011 0010 0100 1011, append 8 zeros and divide by 1 0000 0111 ($x^8 + x^2 + x^1 + 1$). The remainder

is 1001 0011. We transmit the original message
with this remainder appended, resulting in
1011 0010 0100 1011 1001 0011.

(b) Inverting the first bit gives 0011 0010 0100 1011 1001 0011.
Dividing by 1 0000 0111 ($x^8 + x^2 + x^1 + 1$) gives a a
remainder of 1011 0110.

25. One-way latency of the link is 100 ms. (Bandwidth)×(roundtrip
delay) is about 125 pps × 0.2 sec, or 25 packets. SWS should be
this large.

(a) If RWS = 1, the necessary sequence number space is 26.
Therefore, 5 bits are needed.

(b) If RWS = SWS, the sequence number space must cover twice
the SWS, or up to 50. Therefore, 6 bits are needed.

32. The figure that follows gives the timeline for the first case. The
second case reduces the total transaction time by roughly 1 RTT.

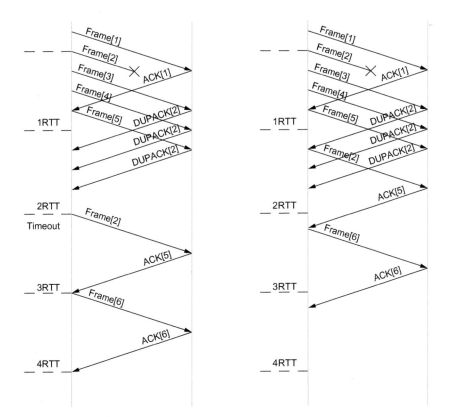

CHAPTER 3

2. The following table is cumulative; at each part the VCI tables consist of the entries at that part and also all previous entries. Note that at stage (d) we assume that VCI 0 on port 0 of switch 4 cannot be reused (it was used for a connection to H in part (a)). This would correspond to the case where VCIs are bidirectional, as they commonly are.

Exercise Part	Switch	Input Port	Input VCI	Output Port	Output VCI
(a)	1	0	0	1	0
	2	3	0	1	0
	4	3	0	0	0
(b)	2	0	0	1	1
	3	3	0	0	0
	4	3	1	1	0
(c)	1	1	1	2	0
	2	1	2	3	1
	4	2	0	3	2
(d)	1	1	2	3	0
	2	1	3	3	2
	4	0	1	3	3
(e)	2	0	1	2	0
	3	2	0	0	1
(f)	2	1	4	0	2
	3	0	2	1	0
	4	0	2	3	4

14. The following list shows the mapping between LANs and their designated bridges.

B1 dead

B2 A,B,D

B3 E,F,G,H

B4 I

B5 idle

B6 J

B7 C

16. All bridges see the packet from D to C. Only B3, B2, and B4 see the packet from C to D. Only B1, B2, and B3 see the packet from A to C.

B1	A-interface : A	B2-interface : D (not C)	
B2	B1-interface : A	B3-interface : C	B4-interface : D
B3	C-interface : C	B2-interface : A,D	
B4	D-interface : D	B2-interface : C (not A)	

27. Since the I/O bus speed is less than the memory bandwidth, it is the bottleneck. Effective bandwidth that the I/O bus can provide is 1000/2 Mbps because each packet crosses the I/O bus twice. Therefore, the number of interfaces is $(500/100) = 5$.

37. By definition, path MTU is 576 bytes. Maximum IP payload size is $576 - 20 = 556$ bytes. We need to transfer $1024 + 20 = 1044$ bytes in the IP payload. This would be fragmented into 2 fragments, the first of size 552 bytes (because the fragment needs to be a multiple of 8 bytes, so it can t be exactly 556) and the second of size $1044 - 552 = 492$ bytes. There are 2 packets in total if we use path MTU. In the previous setting we needed 3 packets.

47. (a)

Information Stored at Node	Distance to Reach Node					
	A	B	C	D	E	F
A	0	2	∞	5	∞	∞
B	2	0	2	∞	1	∞
C	∞	2	0	2	∞	3
D	5	∞	2	0	∞	∞
E	∞	1	∞	∞	0	3
F	∞	∞	3	∞	3	0

(b)

Information Stored at Node	Distance to Reach Node					
	A	B	C	D	E	F
A	0	2	4	5	3	∞
B	2	0	2	4	1	4
C	4	2	0	2	3	3
D	5	4	2	0	∞	5
E	3	1	3	∞	0	3
F	∞	4	3	5	3	0

(c)

Information Stored at Node	Distance to Reach Node					
	A	B	C	D	E	F
A	0	2	4	5	3	6
B	2	0	2	4	1	4
C	4	2	0	2	3	3
D	5	4	2	0	5	5
E	3	1	3	5	0	3
F	6	4	3	5	3	0

53. The following is an example network topology.

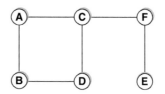

56. Apply each subnet mask and, if the corresponding subnet number matches the SubnetNumber column, then use the entry in Next-Hop.

(a) Applying the subnet mask 255.255.254.0, we get 128.96.170.0. Use interface 0 as the next hop.

(b) Applying subnet mask 255.255.254.0, we get 128.96.166.0. (Next hop is Router 2.) Applying subnet mask 255.255.252.0, we get 128.96.164.0. (Next hop is Router 3.) However, 255.255.254.0 is a longer prefix, so use Router 2 as the next hop.

(c) None of the subnet number entries match, so use default Router R4.

(d) Applying subnet mask 255.255.254.0, we get 128.96.168.0. Use interface 1 as the next hop.

(e) Applying subnet mask 255.255.252.0, we get 128.96.164.0. Use Router 3 as the next hop.

63.

Step	Confirmed	Tentative
1	(A,0,-)	
2	(A,0,-)	(B,1,B) (D,5,D)
3	(A,0,-) (B,1,B)	(D,4,B) (C,7,B)
4	(A,0,-) (B,1,B) (D,4,B)	(C,5,B) (E,7,B)
5	(A,0,-) (B,1,B) (D,4,B) (C,5,B)	(E,6,B)
6	(A,0,-) (B,1,B) (D,4,B) (C,5,B) (E,6,B)	

73. (a) F   (b) B   (c) E   (d) A   (e) D   (f) C

CHAPTER 4

15. The following figures illustrate the multicast trees for sources D and E.

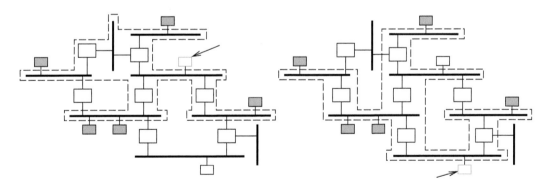

CHAPTER 5

10. The advertised window should be large enough to keep the pipe full; delay (RTT) $\times$ bandwidth here is $140\,\text{ms} \times 1\,\text{Gbps} = 10\,\text{Mb} = 17.5\,\text{MB}$ of data. This requires 25 bits ($2^{25} = 33,554,432$) for the

AdvertisedWindow field. The sequence number field must not wrap around in the maximum segment lifetime. In 60 seconds, 7.5 GB can be transmitted. 33 bits allows a sequence space of 8.6 GB, and so will not wrap in 60 seconds.

13. (a) 2^{32} B / (5 GB) = 859 ms.
    (b) 1000 ticks in 859 ms is once each 859 µs indicating wrap around in 3.7 Ms or approximately 43 days.

27. Using initial Deviation = 50 it took 20 iterations for TimeOut to fall below 300.0.

Iteration	SampleRTT	EstRTT	Dev	diff	TimeOut
0	200.0	90.0	50.0		
1	200.0	103.7	57.5	110.0	333.7
2	200.0	115.7	62.3	96.3	364.9
3	200.0	126.2	65.0	84.3	386.2
4	200.0	135.4	66.1	73.8	399.8
5	200.0	143.4	66.0	64.6	407.4
6	200.0	150.4	64.9	56.6	410.0
7	200.0	156.6	63.0	49.6	408.6
8	200.0	162.0	60.6	43.4	404.4
9	200.0	166.7	57.8	38.0	397.9
10	200.0	170.8	54.8	33.3	390.0
11	200.0	174.4	51.6	29.2	380.8
12	200.0	177.6	48.4	25.6	371.2
13	200.0	180.4	45.2	22.4	361.2
14	200.0	182.8	42.0	19.6	350.8
15	200.0	184.9	38.9	17.2	340.5
16	200.0	186.7	36.0	15.1	330.7
17	200.0	188.3	33.2	13.3	321.1
18	200.0	189.7	30.6	11.7	312.1
19	200.0	190.9	28.1	10.3	303.3
20	200.0	192.0	25.8	9.1	295.2

CHAPTER 6

11. (a) First we calculate the finishing times F_i. We don t need to
worry about clock speed here since we may take $A_i = 0$ for all
the packets. F_i thus becomes just the cumulative per- ow
size: $F_i = F_{i-1} + P_i$.

Packet	Size	Flow	F_i
1	200	1	200
2	200	1	400
3	160	2	160
4	120	2	280
5	160	2	440
6	210	3	210
7	150	3	360
8	90	3	450

We now send in increasing order of F_i: Packet 3, Packet 1,
Packet 6, Packet 4, Packet 7, Packet 2, Packet 5, Packet 8.

(b) To give ow 1 a weight of 2 we divide each of its F_i by 2:
$F_i = F_{i-1} + P_i/2$. To give ow 2 a weight of 4 we divide each
of its F_i by 4: $F_i = F_{i-1} + P_i/4$. To give ow 3 a weight of 3 we
divide each of its F_i by 3: $F_i = F_{i-1} + P_i/3$. Again, we are
using the fact that there is no waiting.

Packet	Size	Flow	Weighted F_i
1	200	1	100
2	200	1	200
3	160	2	40
4	120	2	70
5	160	2	110
6	210	3	70
7	150	3	120
8	90	3	150

Transmitting in increasing order of the weighted F_i we send as follows: Packet 3, Packet 4, Packet 6, Packet 1, Packet 5, Packet 7, Packet 8, Packet 2.

15. (a) For the ith arriving packet on a given flow we calculate its estimated finishing time F_i by the formula $F_i = \max\{A_i, F_{i-1}\} + 1$, where the clock used to measure the arrival times A_i runs slow by a factor equal to the number of active queues. The A_i clock is global; the sequence of F_i values calculated as above is local to each flow.

The following table lists all events by wall clock time. We identify packets by their flow and arrival time; thus, packet A4 is the packet that arrives on flow A at wall clock time 4 (ie., the third packet). The last three columns are the queues for each flow for the subsequent time interval, *including* the packet currently being transmitted. The number of such active queues determines the amount by which A_i is incremented on the subsequent line. Multiple packets appear on the same line if their F_i values are all the same; the F_i values are in italic when $F_i = F_{i-1} + 1$ (versus $F_i = A_i + 1$).

Wall Clock	A_i	Arrivals	F_i	Sent	A's Queue	B's Queue	C's Queue
1	1.0	A1,B1,C1	2.0	A1	A1	B1	C1
2	1.333	C2	3.0	B1		B1	C1,C2
3	1.833	A3	3.0	C1	A3		C1,C2
4	2.333	B4	3.333	A3	A3	B4	C2,C4
		C4	4.0				
5	2.666	A5	4.0	C2	A5	B4	C2,C4
6	3.0	A6	5.0	B4	A5,A6	B4	C4,C6
		C6	5.0				
7	3.333	B7	4.333	A5	A5,A6	B7	C4,C6,C7
		C7	6.0				
8	3.666	A8	6.0	C4	A6,A8	B7,B8	C4,C6,C7
		B8	5.333				
9	4	A9	7.0	B7	A6,A8,A9	B7,B8,B9	C6,C7
		B9	6.333				

(Continued)

Wall Clock	A_i	Arrivals	F_i	Sent	A's Queue	B's Queue	C's Queue
10	4.333			A6	A6,A8,A9	B8,B9	C6,C7
11	4.666	A11	8.0	C6	A8,A9,A11	B8,B9	C7
12	5	C12	7.0	B8	A8,A9,A11	B8,B9	C7,C12
13	5.333	B13	7.333	A8	A8,A9,A11	B9,B13	C7,C12
14	5.666			C7	A9,A11	B9,B13	C7,C12
15	6.0	B15	8.333	B9	A9,A11	B9,B13,B15	C12
16	6.333			A9	A9,A11	B13,B15	C12
17	6.666			C12	A11	B13,B15	C12
18	7			B13	A11	B13,B15	
19	7.5			A11	A11	B15	
20	8			B15		B15	

(b) For weighted fair queuing we have, for ow B,

$$F_i = max\{A_i, F_{i-1}\} + 0.5$$

For ows A and C, F_i is as before. Here is the table corresponding to the one above:

Wall Clock	A_i	Arrivals	F_i	Sent	A's Queue	B's Queue	C's Queue
1	1.0	A1,C1	2.0	B1	A1	B1	C1
		B1	1.5				
2	1.333	C2	3.0	A1			C1,C2
3	1.833	A3	3.0	C1	A1		C1,C2
4	2.333	B4	2.833	B4	A3	B4	C2,C4
		C4	4.0				
5	2.666	A5	4.0	A3	A3,A5		C2,C4
6	3.166	A6	5.0	C2	A5,A6		C2,C4,C6
		C6	5.0				
7	3.666	B7	4.167	A5	A5,A6	B7	C4,C6,C7
		C7	6.0				
8	4.0	A8	6.0	C4	A6,A8	B7,B8	C6,C7
		B8	4.666				

(Continued)

Wall Clock	A_i	Arrivals	F_i	Sent	A's Queue	B's Queue	C's Queue
9	4.333	A9	7.0	B7	A6,A8,A9	B7,B8,B9	C6,C7
		B9	5.166				
10	4.666			B8	A6,A8,A9	B8,B9	C6,C7
11	5.0	A11	8.0	A6	A6,A8,A9,A11	B9	C6,C7
12	5.333	C12	7.0	C6	A8,A9,A11	B9	C6,C7,C12
13	5.666	B13	6.166	B9	A8,A9,A11	B9,B13	C7,C12
14	6.0			A8	A9,A11	B13	C7,C12
15	6.333	B15	6.833	C7	A9,A11	B13,B15	C12
16	6.666			B13	A9,A11	B13,B15	C12
17	7.0			B15	A11	B15	C12
18	7.333			A9	A11		C12
19	7.833			C12	A11		C12
20	8.333			A11	A11		

35. (a) We have

$$\mathsf{TempP} = \mathsf{MaxP} \times \frac{\mathsf{AvgLen} - \mathsf{MinThreshold}}{\mathsf{MaxThreshold} - \mathsf{MinThreshold}}.$$

AvgLen is halfway between MinThreshold and MaxThreshold, which implies that the fraction here is $1/2$ and so TempP $=$ MaxP$/2 = p/2$. We now have

$$\mathsf{P}_{\mathsf{count}} = \mathsf{TempP}/(1 - \mathsf{count} \times \mathsf{TempP}) = 1/(x - \mathsf{count}),$$

where $x = 2/p$. Therefore,

$$1 - \mathsf{P}_{\mathsf{count}} = \frac{x - (\mathsf{count} + 1)}{x - \mathsf{count}}.$$

Evaluating the product

$$(1 - \mathsf{P}_1) \times \cdots \times (1 - \mathsf{P}_n)$$

gives

$$\frac{x - 2}{x - 1} \cdot \frac{x - 3}{x - 2} \cdots \cdot \frac{x - (n + 1)}{x - n} = \frac{x - (n + 1)}{x - 1},$$

where $x = 2/p$.

(b) From the result of previous question,

$$\alpha = \frac{x - (n+1)}{x - 1}.$$

Therefore,

$$x = \frac{(n+1) - \alpha}{1 - \alpha} = 2/p.$$

Accordingly,

$$p = \frac{2(1 - \alpha)}{(n+1) - \alpha}$$

48. At every second, the bucket volume must not be negative. For a given bucket depth D and token rate r, we can calculate the bucket volume $v(t)$ at time t seconds and enforce $v(t)$ being non-negative:

$$v(0) = D - 5 + r = D - (5 - r) \geq 0$$
$$v(1) = D - 5 - 5 + 2r = D - 2(5 - r) \geq 0$$
$$v(2) = D - 5 - 5 - 1 + 3r = D - (11 - 3r) \geq 0$$
$$v(3) = D - 5 - 5 - 1 + 4r = D - (11 - 4r) \geq 0$$
$$v(4) = D - 5 - 5 - 1 - 6 + 5r = D - (17 - 5r) \geq 0$$
$$v(5) = D - 5 - 5 - 1 - 6 - 1 + 6r = D - 6(3 - r) \geq 0$$

We define the functions $f_1(r), f_2(r), \ldots, f_6(r)$ as follows:

$$f_1(r) = 5 - r$$
$$f_2(r) = 2(5 - r) = 2f_1(r) \geq f_1(r) \quad (for\ 1 \leq r \leq 5)$$
$$f_3(r) = 11 - 3r \leq f_2(r) \quad (for\ r \geq 1)$$
$$f_4(r) = 11 - 4r < f_3(r) \quad (for\ r \geq 1)$$
$$f_5(r) = 17 - 5r$$
$$f_6(r) = 6(3 - r) \leq f_5(r) \quad (for\ r \geq 1)$$

First of all, for $r \geq 5$, $f_i(r) \leq 0$ for all i. This means if the token rate is faster than 5 packets per second any positive bucket depth will suffice (i.e., $D \geq 0$). For $1 \leq r \leq 5$, we only need to consider $f_2(r)$ and $f_5(r)$, since other functions are less than these functions.

One can easily find $f_2(r) - f_5(r) = 3r - 7$. Therefore, the bucket depth D is enforced by the following formula:

$$D \geq \begin{cases} f_5(r) = 17 - 5r & (r = 1, 2) \\ f_2(r) = 2(5 - r) & (r = 3, 4, 5) \\ 0 & (r \geq 5) \end{cases}$$

CHAPTER 7

2. Each string is preceded by a count of its length; the array of salaries is preceded by a count of the number of elements. That leads to the following sequence of integers and ASCII characters being sent:

   4 M A R Y 4377 7 J A N U A R Y 7 2002 2 90000 150000 1

8.

INT	4	15
INT	4	29496729
INT	4	58993458

10. 15 be 00000000 00000000 00000000 00001111
    15 le 00001111 00000000 00000000 00000000

    29496729 be 00000001 11000010 00010101 10011001
    29496729 le 10011001 00010101 11000010 00000001

    58993458 be 00000011 10000100 00101011 00110010
    58993458 le 00110010 00101011 10000100 00000011

Glossary

3DES: Triple DES, a version of DES that uses three keys, effectively increasing the key size and robustness of the encryption.

3G: Third-generation mobile wireless, a class of cellular wireless technologies based on Code Division Multiple Access (CDMA).

4B/5B: A type of bit encoding scheme used in Fiber Distributed Data Interface (FDDI), in which every 4 bits of data are transmitted as a 5-bit sequence.

4G: Fourth-generation wireless, an emerging set of standards to support higher data rates than 3G.

802.3: IEEE Ethernet standard.

802.5: IEEE token ring standard.

802.11: IEEE wireless network standard.

802.17: IEEE resilient packet ring standard.

822: Refers to RFC 822, which defines the format of Internet email messages. See *SMTP*.

AAL (ATM Adaptation Layer): A protocol layer, configured over Asynchronous Transfer Mode (ATM). Two AALs are defined for data communications, AAL3/4 and AAL5. Each protocol layer provides a mechanism to segment large packets into cells at the sender and to reassemble the cells back together at the receiver.

ABR: (1) Available bit rate. A rate-based congestion-control scheme being developed for use on Asynchronous Transfer Mode (ATM) networks. ABR is intended to allow a source to increase or decrease its allotted rate, based on feedback from switches within the network. Contrast with *CBR*, *UBR*, and *VBR*. (2) Area border router. Router at the edge of an *area* in a link-state protocol.

ACK: An abbreviation for *acknowledgment*. An acknowledgment is sent by a receiver of data to indicate to the sender that the data transmission was successful.

additive increase/multiplicative decrease: Congestion window strategy used by TCP. TCP opens the congestion window at a linear rate, but halves it when losses are experienced due to congestion. It has been shown that additive increase/multiplicative decrease is a necessary condition for a congestion-control mechanism to be stable.

AES (Advanced Encryption Standard): A cryptographic cipher that has been proposed to supersede Data Encryption Standard (DES).

AF (assured forwarding): One of the per-hop behaviors proposed for Differentiated Services.

ALF (Application Level Framing): A protocol design principle that says that application programs better understand their communication needs than do general-purpose transport protocols.

AMPS (Advance Mobile Phone System): Analog-based cell phone system. Currently being replaced by digital system, known as Personal Communication Services (PCS).

ANSI (American National Standards Institute): Private U.S. standardization body that commonly participates in the ISO standardization process. Responsible for SONET.

API (application programming interface): Interface that application programs use to access the network subsystem (usually the transport protocol). Usually OS-specific. The socket API from Berkeley Unix is a widely used example.

area: In the context of link-state routing, a collection of adjacent routers that share full routing information with each other. A routing domain is divided into areas to improve scalability.

ARP (Address Resolution Protocol): Protocol of the Internet architecture, used to translate high-level protocol addresses into physical hardware addresses. Commonly used on the Internet to map IP addresses into Ethernet addresses.

ARPA (Advanced Research Projects Agency): One of the research and development organizations within the Department of Defense. Responsible for funding the ARPANET as well as the research that led to the development of the TCP/IP Internet. Also known as DARPA, the *D* standing for Defense.

ARPANET: An experimental wide area packet-switched network funded by ARPA and begun in the late 1960s; it became the backbone of the developing Internet.

ARQ (automatic repeat request): General strategy for reliably sending packets over an unreliable link. If the sender does not receive an ACK for a packet after a certain time period, it assumes that the packet did not arrive (or was delivered with bit errors) and retransmits it. Stop-and-wait and Sliding Window are two example ARQ protocols. Contrast with *FEC*.

ASN.1 (Abstract Syntax Notation One): In conjunction with Basic Encoding Rules (BER), a presentation-formatting standard devised by the ISO as part of the OSI architecture.

ATM (Asynchronous Transfer Mode): A connection-oriented network technology that uses small, fixed-size packets (called *cells*) to carry data.

ATM Forum: A key ATM standards-setting body.

authentication: Security protocol by which two suspicious parties prove to each other that they are who they claim to be.

autonomous system (AS): A group of networks and routers, subject to a common authority and using the same intradomain routing protocol.

bandwidth: A measure of the capacity of a link or connection, usually given in units of bits per second.

Bellman–Ford: A name for the distance–vector routing algorithm, from the names of the inventors.

BER (Basic Encoding Rules): Rules for encoding data types defined by ASN.1.

best-effort delivery: The service model of the current Internet architecture. Delivery of a message is attempted but is not guaranteed.

BGP (Border Gateway Protocol): An interdomain routing protocol by which autonomous systems exchange reachability information. The most recent version is BGP-4.

BISYNC (Binary Synchronous Communication): A byte-oriented link-level protocol developed in the late 1960s by IBM.

bit stuffing: A technique used to distinguish control sequences and data on the bit level. Used by the High-Level Data Link Control (HDLC) protocol.

block: An OS term used to describe a situation in which a process suspends execution while awaiting some event, such as a change in the state of a *semaphore*.

Bluetooth®: A short-range wireless standard used to connect computers, mobile phones, and peripheral devices, among other things.

bridge: A device that forwards link-level frames from one physical network to another, sometimes called a LAN switch. Contrast with *repeater* and *router*.

broadcast: A method of delivering a packet to every host on a particular network or internet. May be implemented in hardware (e.g., Ethernet) or software (e.g., IP broadcast).

CA (certificate/certification authority): An entity that signs security certificates, thereby promising that the public key contained in the certificate belongs to the entity named in the certificate.

CBC (cipher block chaining): A cryptographic mode in which each plaintext block is XORed with the previous block of ciphertext before encryption.

CBR (constant bit rate): A class of service in ATM that guarantees transmission of data at a constant bit rate, thus emulating a dedicated transmission link. Contrast with *ABR*, *UBR*, and *VBR*.

CCITT: The now defunct *Comité Consultif International de Telegraphique et Telephonique*, a unit of the International Telecommunications Union (ITU) of the United Nations. Now replaced by ITU-T.

CDMA (Code Division Multiple Access): A form of multiplexing used in wireless networks.

CDN (content distribution network): A collection of surrogate web servers, distributed across the Internet, that respond to web HTTP requests in place of the server. The goal of widely distributing the surrogate servers is to have a surrogate close to the client, making it possible to respond to requests more quickly.

cell: A 53-byte ATM packet capable of carrying up to 48 bytes of data.

certificate: A document digitally signed by one entity that contains the name and public key of another entity. Used to distribute public keys. Also see *CA*.

channel: A generic communication term used in this book to denote a logical process-to-process connection.

checksum: Typically, a ones complement sum over some or all of the bytes of a packet, computed and appended to the packet by the sender. The receiver recomputes the checksum and compares it to the one carried in the message. Checksums are used to detect errors in a packet and may also be used to verify that the packet has been delivered to the correct host. The term *checksum* is also sometimes (imprecisely) used to refer generically to error-detecting codes.

chipping code: Random sequence of bits that is XORed with the data stream to implement the direct sequence technique of spread spectrum.

CIDR (classless interdomain routing): A method of aggregating routes that treats a block of contiguous Class C IP addresses as a single network.

circuit switching: A general strategy for switching data through a network. It involves establishing a dedicated path (circuit) between the source and destination. Contrast with *packet switching*.

client: The requester of a service in a distributed system.

CLNP (Connectionless Network Protocol): The ISO counterpart to the Internet's IP.

clock recovery: The process of deriving a valid clock from a serially transmitted digital signal.

concurrent logical channels: Multiplexing several stop-and-wait logical channels onto a single point-to-point link. No delivery order is enforced. This mechanism was used by the Interface Message Processor (IMP) IMP protocol of the ARPANET.

congestion: A state resulting from too many packets contending for limited resources (e.g., link bandwidth and buffer space on routers or switches), which may force the router (switch) to discard packets.

congestion control: Any network resource management strategy that has, as its goal, the alleviation or avoidance of congestion. A congestion-control mechanism may be implemented on the routers (switches) inside the network, by the hosts at the edges of the network, or by a combination of both.

connection: In general, a channel that must be established prior to use (e.g., by the transmission of some setup information). For example, TCP provides a connection abstraction that offers reliable, ordered delivery of a byte stream. Connection-oriented networks, such as ATM, are often said to provide a *virtual circuit* abstraction.

connectionless protocol: A protocol in which data may be sent without any advance setup. IP is an example of such a protocol.

context switch: An operation in which an operating system suspends the execution of one process and begins the execution of another. A context switch involves saving the state of the former process (e.g., the contents of all registers) and loading the state of the latter process.

controlled load: One of the service classes available in the Internet's Integrated Services architecture.

CRC (cyclic redundancy check): An error-detecting code computed over the bytes composing a packet and then appended to the packet by the network hardware (e.g., Ethernet adaptor). CRC provides stronger error detection than a simple checksum.

crossbar switch: A simple switch design in which every input is directly connected to every output and the output port is responsible for resolving contention.

CSMA/CD (Carrier Sense, Multiple Access with Collision Detect): A functionality of network hardware. "Carrier sense multiple access" means that multiple stations can listen to the link and detect when it is in use or idle; "collision detect" indicates that, if two or more stations are transmitting on the link simultaneously, they will detect the collision of their signals. Ethernet is the best-known technology that uses CSMA/CD.

cut-through: A form of switching or forwarding in which a packet starts to be transferred to an output before it has been completely received by the switching node, thus reducing latency through the node.

datagram: The basic transmission unit in the Internet architecture. A datagram contains all of the information needed to deliver it to its destination, analogous to a letter in the U.S. postal system. Datagram networks are connectionless.

DCE (Distributed Computing Environment): An RPC-based suite of protocols and standards that support distributed computing. Defined by OSF.

DDCMP (Digital Data Communication Message Protocol): A byte-oriented link-level protocol used in Digital Equipment Corporation's DECnet.

DDoS (distributed denial of service): A DoS attack in which the attack originates at a set of nodes. Each attacking node may put only a marginal load on the target machine, but the aggregate load from all the attacking nodes swamps the target machine.

DECbit: A congestion-control scheme in which routers notify the endpoints of imminent congestion by setting a bit in the header of routed packets. The endpoints decrease their sending rates when a certain percentage of received packets have the bit set.

decryption: The act of reversing an *encryption* process to recover the data from an encrypted message.

delay × bandwidth product: The product of a network's round-trip time (RTT) and bandwidth. Gives a measure of how much data can be in transit on the network.

demultiplexing: Using information contained in a packet header to direct it upward through a protocol stack. For example, IP uses the ProtNum field in the IP header to decide which higher protocol (i.e., TCP, UDP) a packet belongs to, and TCP uses the port number to demultiplex a TCP packet to the correct application process. Contrast with *multiplexing*.

demultiplexing key: A field in a packet header that enables demultiplexing to take place (e.g., ProtNum field of IP).

dense mode multicast: Protocol Independent Multicast (PIM) mode used when most routers or hosts need to receive multicast packets.

DES (Data Encryption Standard): An algorithm for data encryption based on a 64-bit secret key.

DHCP (Dynamic Host Configuration Protocol): A protocol used by a host, as it boots, to learn various network information, such as its IP address.

DHT (distributed hash table): A technique by which a message is routed toward a machine that supports a particular object, based on the object's name. The object is hashed to a unique identifier, with each intermediate node along the route forwarding the message to a node that is able to interpret a larger prefix of this ID. DHTs are often used in peer-to-peer networks.

Differentiated Services: A new architecture for providing better than best-effort service on the Internet. It has been proposed as an alternative to Integrated Services.

direct sequence: A spread spectrum technique that involves XORing the data stream with a random bit sequence known as a *chipping code*.

distance vector: A lowest-cost-path algorithm used in routing. Each node advertises reachability information and associated costs to its immediate neighbors and uses the updates it receives to construct its forwarding table. The Routing Information Protocol (RIP) uses a distance-vector algorithm. Contrast with *link state*.

DMA (direct memory access): An approach to connecting hosts to I/O devices, in which the device directly reads data from and writes data to the host's memory. Also see *PIO*.

DNA/DECnet (Digital Network Architecture): An OSI-based architecture that supports a connectionless network model and a connection-oriented transport protocol.

DNS (Domain Name System): The distributed naming system of the Internet, used to resolve host names (e.g., cicada.cs.princeton.edu) into IP addresses (e.g., 192.12.69.35). The DNS is implemented by a hierarchy of name servers.

domain: Can refer either to a context in the hierarchical DNS name space (e.g., the ".edu" domain) or to a region of the Internet that is treated as a single entity for the purpose of hierarchical routing. The latter is equivalent to *autonomous system*.

DoS (denial of service): A situation in which an attacking node floods a target node with so much work (so many packets) that it effectively keeps legitimate users from accessing the node, hence, they are denied service.

DS3: A 44.7-Mbps transmission link service offered by the phone company. Also called T3.

DSL (digital subscriber line): A family of standards for transmitting data over twisted pair telephone lines at multimegabit-per-second speeds.

duplicate ACK: A retransmission of a TCP acknowledgment. The duplicate ACK does not acknowledge any new data. The receipt of multiple duplicate ACKs triggers the TCP *fast retransmit* mechanism.

DVMRP (Distance Vector Multicast Routing Protocol): Multicast routing protocol originally used in the MBone.

DWDM (dense wavelength division multiplexing): Multiplexing multiple light waves (colors) onto a single physical fiber. The technique is "dense" in the sense that a large number of optical wavelengths can be supported.

ECN (Explicit Congestion Notification): A technique by which routers inform end hosts about congestion by setting a flag in packets they are forwarding. Used in conjunction with active queue management algorithms like random early detection (RED).

EF (expedited forwarding): One of the per-hop behaviors proposed for Differentiated Services.

EGP (Exterior Gateway Protocol): An early interdomain routing protocol of the Internet, which was used by exterior gateways (routers) of autonomous systems to exchange routing information with other autonomous systems. Replaced by BGP.

encapsulation: The operation, performed by a lower-level protocol, of attaching a protocol-specific header and/or trailer to a message passed down by a higher-level protocol. As a message travels down the protocol stack, it gathers a sequence of headers, of which the outermost corresponds to the protocol at the bottom of the stack.

encryption: The act of applying a transforming function to data, with the intention that only the receiver of the data will be able to read it (after applying the inverse function, *decryption*). Encryption generally depends on either a secret shared by the sender and receiver or a public/private key pair.

Ethernet: A popular local area network technology that uses CSMA/CD and has a bandwidth of 10 Mbps. An Ethernet itself is just a passive wire; all aspects of Ethernet transmission are completely implemented by the host adaptors.

exponential backoff: A retransmission strategy that doubles the timeout value each time a packet is retransmitted.

exposed node problem: Situation that occurs on a wireless network when two nodes receive signals from a common source but each is able to reach other nodes that do not receive this signal.

extended LAN: A collection of LANs connected by bridges.

fabric: The part of a switch that actually does the switching—that is, moves packets from input to output. Contrast with *port*.

fair queuing (FQ): A round-robin-based queuing algorithm that prevents a badly behaved process from capturing an arbitrarily large portion of the network capacity.

fast retransmit: A strategy used by TCP that attempts to avoid timeouts in the presence of lost packets. TCP retransmits a segment after receiving three consecutive duplicate ACKs, acknowledging the data up to (but not including) that segment.

FDDI (Fiber Distributed Data Interface): A high-speed token ring networking technology designed to run over optical fiber.

FEC: (1) Forward error correction. A general strategy for recovering from bit errors introduced into data packets without having to retransmit the packet. Redundant information is included with each packet that can be used by the receiver to determine which bits in a packet are incorrect. Contrast with *ARQ*.

(2) Forwarding equivalence class. A set of packets that are to receive the same forwarding treatment at a router. Multiprotocol Label Switching (MPLS) labels are normally associated with FECs.

Fibre Channel: A bidirectional link protocol commonly used to connect computers (usually supercomputers) to peripherals. Fibre Channel has a bandwidth of 100 MBps and can span up to 30 m the High-Performance Parallel Interface (HIPPI).

firewall: A router that has been configured to filter (not forward) packets from certain sources. Used to enforce a security policy.

flow control: A mechanism by which the receiver of data throttles the transmission rate of the sender so data will not arrive too quickly to be processed. Contrast with *congestion control*.

flowspec: Specification of a flow's bandwidth and delay requirements presented to the network to establish a reservation. Used with the Resource Reservation Protocol (RSVP).

forwarding: The operation performed by a router on every packet—receiving it on an input, deciding what output to send it to, and sending it there.

forwarding table: The table maintained in a router that lets it make decisions on how to forward packets. The process of building up the forwarding table is called *routing*, and thus the forwarding table is sometimes called a *routing table*. In some implementations, the routing and forwarding tables are separate data structures.

fragmentation/reassembly: A method for transmission of messages larger than the network's maximum transmission unit (MTU). Messages are fragmented into small pieces by the sender and reassembled by the receiver.

frame: Another name for a *packet*, typically used in reference to packets sent over a single link rather than a whole network. An important problem is how the receiver detects the beginning and ending of a frame, a problem known as *framing*.

Frame Relay: A connection-oriented public packet-switched service offered by the phone company.

frequency hopping: A spread spectrum technique that involves transmitting data over a random sequence of frequencies.

FTP (File Transfer Protocol): The standard protocol of the Internet architecture for transferring files between hosts. Built on top of TCP.

GMPLS (Generalized Multiprotocol Label Switching): Allows IP to run native over optically switched networks.

gopher: An early Internet information service.

GPRS (General Packet Radio Service): A packet transmission service provided by cellular wireless networks.

GSM (Global System for Mobile Communication): Widely deployed digital cellular phone system.

H.323: Session control protocol often used for Internet telephony.

handle: In programming, an identifier or pointer that is used to access an object.

hardware address: The link-level address used to identify the host adaptor on the local network.

HDLC (High-Level Data Link Control): An ISO-standard link-level protocol. It uses bit stuffing to solve the framing problem.

hidden node problem: Situation that occurs on a wireless network when two nodes are sending to a common destination but are unaware that the other exists.

hierarchical routing: A multilevel routing scheme that uses the hierarchical structure of the address space as the basis for making forwarding decisions. For example, packets might first be routed to a destination network and then to a specific host on that network.

host: A computer attached to one or more networks that supports users and runs application programs.

HTML (HyperText Markup Language): A language used to construct World Wide Web pages.

HTTP (HyperText Transport Protocol): An application-level protocol based on a request/reply paradigm and used in the World Wide Web. HTTP uses TCP connections to transfer data.

IAB (Internet Architecture Board): The main body that oversees the development and standardization of protocols of the Internet architecture. Formerly known as the Internet Activities Board.

iBGP (Interior Border Gateway Protocol): The protocol used to exchange interdomain routing information among routers in the same domain.

ICMP (Internet Control Message Protocol): This protocol is an integral part of IP. It allows a router or destination host to communicate with the source, typically to report an error in IP datagram processing.

IEEE (Institute for Electrical and Electronics Engineers): A professional society for engineers that also defines network standards, including the 802 series of LAN standards.

IETF (Internet Engineering Task Force): The main organization responsible for developing standards and best practices for the Internet.

IMAP (Internet Message Access Protocol): An application layer protocol that allows a user to retrieve his or her email from a mail server.

IMP-IMP: A byte-oriented link-level protocol used in the original ARPANET.

Integrated Services: Usually taken to mean a packet-switched network that can effectively support both conventional computer data and real-time audio and video. Also, a name given to a proposed Internet service model that was designed to supplement the current best-effort service model.

integrity: In the context of network security, a service that ensures that a received message is the same one that was sent.

interdomain routing: The process of exchanging routing among different routing domains. BGP is an example of an interdomain protocol.

internet: A collection of (possibly heterogeneous) packet-switching networks interconnected by routers. Also called an *internetwork*.

Internet: The global internet based on the Internet (TCP/IP) architecture, connecting millions of hosts worldwide.

interoperability: The ability of heterogeneous hardware and multivendor software to communicate by correctly exchanging messages.

interrupt: An event (typically generated by a hardware device) that tells the operating system to stop its current activity and take some action. For example, an interrupt is used to notify the operating system that a packet has arrived from the network.

intradomain routing: The exchange of routing information within a single domain or autonomous system. RIP and OSPF are example intradomain protocols.

IP (Internet Protocol): A protocol that provides a connectionless, best-effort delivery service of datagrams across the Internet.

IPng (Internet Protocol Next Generation; now known as IPv6): New version of IP that provides a larger, more hierarchical address space and other new features.

IPsec (IP Security): An architecture for authentication, privacy, and message integrity, among other security services to the Internet architecture.

IRTF (Internet Research Task Force): A task force responsible for charting direction in research and development for the Internet.

ISDN (Integrated Services Digital Network): A digital communication service offered by telephone carriers and standardized by ITU-T. ISDN combines voice connection and digital data services in a single physical medium.

IS-IS (Intermediate System to Intermediate System): A link-state routing protocol, similar to Open Shortest Path First (OSPF).

ISO (International Standards Organization): The international body that drafted the seven-layer OSI architecture and a suite of protocols that has not enjoyed commercial success.

ITU-T: A subcommittee of the International Telecommunications Union, a global body that drafts technical standards for all areas of international analog and digital communication. ITU-T deals with standards for telecommunications, notably ATM.

jitter: Variation in network latency. Large jitter has a negative impact on the quality of video and audio applications.

JPEG (Joint Photographic Experts Group): Typically used to refer to a widely used algorithm for compressing still images that was developed by the JPEG.

Kerberos: A TCP/IP-based authentication system developed at MIT, in which two hosts use a trusted third party to authenticate each other.

key distribution: Mechanism by which users learn each others' public keys through the exchange of digitally signed certificates.

LAN (local area network): A network based on any physical network technology that is designed to span distances of up to a few thousand meters (e.g., Ethernet or FDDI). Contrast with *SAN*, *MAN*, and *WAN*.

LAN switch: Another term for a *bridge*, usually applied to a bridge with many ports. Also called an *Ethernet switch* if the link technology it supports is Ethernet.

latency: A measure of how long it takes a single bit to propagate from one end of a link or channel to the other. Latency is measured strictly in terms of time.

LDAP (Lightweight Directory Access Protocol): A subset of the X.500 directory service that has recently become a popular directory service for information about users.

LER (label edge router): A router at the edge of a Multiprotocol Label Switching (MPLS) cloud. Performs a complete IP lookup on arriving IP packets and then applies labels to them as a result of the lookup.

link: A physical connection between two nodes of a network. It may be implemented over copper or fiber-optic cable or it may be a wireless link (e.g., a satellite).

link-level protocol: A protocol that is responsible for delivering frames over a directly connected network (e.g., an Ethernet, token ring, or point-to-point link). Also called *link-layer protocol*.

link state: A lowest-cost-path algorithm used in routing. Information on directly connected neighbors and current link costs are flooded to all routers; each router uses this information to build a view of the network on which to base forwarding decisions. The Open Shortest Path First (OSPF) routing protocol uses a link-state algorithm. Contrast with *distance vector*.

LSR (label switching router): A router that runs IP control protocols but uses the label switching forwarding algorithm of Multiprotocol Label Switching (MPLS).

MAC (media access control): Algorithms used to control access to shared-media networks like Ethernet and the Fiber Distributed Data Interface (FDDI).

MACA (Multiple Access with Collision Avoidance): Distributed algorithm used to mediate access to a shared media.

MACAW (Multiple Access with Collision Avoidance for Wireless): Enhancement of the general MACA algorithm to better support wireless networks. Used by 802.11.

MAN (metropolitan area network): A network based on any of several new network technologies that operate at high speeds (up to several Gbps) and across distances wide enough to span a metropolitan area. Contrast with *SAN, LAN,* and *WAN.*

Manchester: A bit encoding scheme that transmits the exclusive-OR of the clock and the non-return to zero (NRZ)-encoded data. Used on the Ethernet.

MBone (multicast backbone): A logical network imposed over the top of the Internet, in which multicast-enhanced routers use tunneling to forward multicast datagrams across the Internet.

MD5 (Message Digest version 5): An efficient cryptographic checksum algorithm commonly used to verify that the contents of a message are unaltered.

MIB (management information base): Defines the set of network-related variables that may be read or written on a network node. The MIB is used in conjunction with the Simple Network Management Protocol (SNMP).

MIME (Multipurpose Internet Mail Extensions): Specifications for converting binary data (such as image files) to ASCII text, which allows it to be sent via email.

Mosaic: A once-popular and free graphical World Wide Web browser developed at the National Center for Supercomputing Applications at the University of Illinois.

MP3 (MPEG Layer 3): Audio compression standard used with MPEG.

MPEG (Moving Picture Experts Group): Typically used to refer to an algorithm for compressing video streams developed by the MPEG.

MPLS (Multiprotocol Label Switching): A collection of techniques used to effectively implement IP routers on top of level 2 (e.g., ATM) switches.

MSDP (Multicast Source Discovery Protocol): A protocol used to facilitate inter-domain multicast.

MTU (maximum transmission unit): The size of the largest packet that can be sent over a physical network.

multicast: A special form of broadcast in which packets are delivered to a specified subgroup of network hosts.

multiplexing: Combining distinct channels into a single, lower-level channel. For example, separate TCP and UDP channels are multiplexed into a single host-to-host IP channel. The inverse operation, *demultiplexing*, takes place on the receiving host.

name resolution: The action of resolving host names (which are easy for humans to read) into their corresponding addresses (which machines can read). See *DNS*.

NAT (network address translation): A technique for extending the IP address space that involves translating between globally understood IP addresses and local-only addresses at the edge of a network or site.

NDR (Network Data Representation): The data-encoding standard used in the Distributed Computing Environment (DCE), as defined by the Open Software Foundation. NDR uses a receiver-makes-right strategy and inserts an architecture tag at the front of each message.

network-level protocol: A protocol that runs over switched networks, directly above the link level.

NFS (Network File System): A popular distributed file system developed by Sun Microsystems. NFS is based on SunRPC, an RPC protocol developed by Sun.

NIST (National Institute for Standards and Technology): The official U.S. standardization body.

node: A generic term used for individual computers that make up a network. Nodes include general-purpose computers, switches, and routers.

NRZ (non-return to zero): A bit encoding scheme that encodes a 1 as the high signal and a 0 as the low signal.

NRZI (non-return to zero inverted): A bit encoding scheme that makes a transition from the current signal to encode a 1 and stays at the current signal to encode a 0.

NSF (National Science Foundation): An agency of the U.S. government that funds scientific research in the United States, including research on networks and on the Internet infrastructure.

OC (Optical Carrier): The prefix for various rates of SONET optical transmission. For example, OC-1 refers to the SONET standard for 51.84-Mbps transmission over fiber. An OC-n signal differs from an STS-n signal only in that the OC-n signal is scrambled for optical transmission.

ONC (Open Network Computing): A version of SunRPC that was standardized for the Internet.

Open Software Foundation (OSF): A consortium of computer vendors that defines standards for distributed computing, including the National Data Representation (NDR) format.

optical switch: A switching device that forwards optical lightwaves from input port to output port without converting to electrical format.

OSI (Open Systems Interconnection): The seven-layer network reference model developed by the ISO that guides the design of ISO and ITU-T protocol standards.

OSPF (Open Shortest Path First): A routing protocol developed by the IETF for the Internet architecture. OSPF is based on a *link-state* algorithm, in which every node constructs a topography of the Internet and uses it to make forwarding decisions.

overlay: A virtual (logical) network running on top of an existing physical network. Overlay nodes communicate with each other through tunnels rather than over physical links. Overlays are often used to deploy new network services since they do not require the cooperation of the existing network infrastructure.

packet: A data unit sent over a packet-switched network. Also see *frame* and *segment*.

packet switching: A general strategy for switching data through a network. Packet switching uses store-and-forward switching of discrete data units called *packets* and implies *statistical multiplexing*.

participants: A generic term used to denote the processes, protocols, or hosts that are sending messages to each other.

PAWS (Protection against Wrapped Sequence Numbers): Engineering transport protocol with a large enough sequence number space to protect against the numbers wrapping around on a network where packets can be delayed for a long period of time.

PDU (protocol data unit): Another name for a packet or frame.

peer: A counterpart on another machine that a protocol module interoperates with to implement some communication service.

peer-to-peer networks: A general class of applications that integrate application logic (e.g., file storage) with routing. Popular examples include Bittorrent and Gnutella. Research prototypes often use distributed hash tables.

PEM (Privacy-Enhanced Mail): Extensions to Internet email that support privacy and integrity protection. See also *PGP*.

PGP (Pretty Good Privacy): A collection of public domain software that provides privacy and authentication capabilities using RSA and uses a mesh of trust for public key distribution.

PHB (per-hop behavior): Behavior of individual routers in the Differentiated Services architecture. AF and EF are two proposed PHBs.

physical-level protocol: The lowest layer of the OSI protocol stack. Its main function is to encode bits onto the signals that are propagated across the physical transmission media.

piconet: Wireless network spanning short distances (e.g., 10 m). Used to connect office computers (laptops, printers, PDAs, workstations, etc.) without cables.

PIM (Protocol Independent Multicast): A multicast routing protocol that can be built on top of different unicast routing protocols.

Ping: A Unix utility used to test the round-trip time (RTT) to various hosts over the Internet. Ping sends an ICMP ECHO_REQUEST message, and the remote host sends an ECHO_RESPONSE message back.

PIO (Programmed Input/Output): An approach to connecting hosts to I/O devices, in which the CPU reads data from and writes data to the I/O device. Also see *DMA*.

poison reverse: Used in conjunction with *split horizon*. A heuristic technique to avoid routing loops in distance-vector routing protocols.

port: A generic term usually used to mean the point at which a network user attaches to the network. On a switch, a port denotes the input or output on which packets are received and sent.

POTS (plain old telephone service): Used to specify the existing phone service, in contrast to ISDN, Voice over IP (VOIP), or other technologies that the telephone companies offer now or may offer in the future.

PPP (Point-to-Point Protocol): Data link protocol typically used to connect computers over a dial-up line.

process: An abstraction provided by an operating system to enable different operations to take place concurrently. For example, each user application usually runs inside its own process, while various operating system functions take place in other processes.

promiscuous mode: A mode of operation for a network adaptor in which it receives all frames transmitted on the network, not just those addressed to it.

protocol: A specification of an interface between modules running on different machines, as well as the communication service that those modules implement. The term is also used to refer to an implementation of the module that meets this specification. To distinguish between these two uses, the interface is often called a *protocol specification*.

proxy: An agent sitting between a client and server that intercepts messages and provides some service. For example, a proxy can stand in for a server by responding to client requests, perhaps using data it has cached, without contacting the server.

pseudoheader: A subset of fields from the IP header that are passed up to transport protocols TCP and UDP for use in their checksum calculation. The pseudoheader contains source and destination IP addresses and IP datagram length, thus enabling detection of corruption of these fields or delivery of a packet to an incorrect address.

public key encryption: Any of several encryption algorithms (e.g., RSA), in which each participant has a private key (shared with no one else) and a public key (available to everyone). A secure message is sent to a user by encrypting the data with that user's public key; possession of the private key is required to decrypt the message, so only the receiver can read it.

QoS (quality of service): Packet delivery guarantees provided by a network architecture. Usually related to performance guarantees, such as bandwidth and delay. The Internet offers a best-effort delivery service, meaning that every effort is made to deliver a packet but delivery is not guaranteed.

RED (random early detection): A queuing discipline for routers in which, when congestion is anticipated, packets are randomly dropped to alert the senders to slow down.

rendezvous point: A router used by PIM to allow receivers to learn about senders.

repeater: A device that propagates electrical signals from one Ethernet cable to another. There can be a maximum of two repeaters between any two hosts in an Ethernet. Repeaters forward signals, whereas *bridges* forward *frames*, and *routers* and *switches* forward *packets*.

REST (Representational State Transfer): An approach to building Web Services that uses HTTP as the generic application protocol.

RFC (Request for Comments): Internet reports that contain, among other things, specifications for protocols like TCP and IP.

RIP (Routing Information Protocol): An intradomain routing protocol supplied with Berkeley Unix. Each router running RIP dynamically builds its forwarding table based on a *distance-vector* algorithm.

router: A network node connected to two or more networks that forwards packets from one network to another. Contrast with *bridge, repeater,* and *switch.*

routing: The process by which nodes exchange topological information to build correct forwarding tables. See *forwarding, link state,* and *distance vector.*

routing table: See *forwarding table.*

RPB (Reverse Path Broadcast): A technique used to eliminate duplicate broadcast packets.

RPC (Remote Procedure Call): Synchronous request/reply transport protocol used in many client/server interactions.

RPR (Resilient Packet Ring): A type of ring network that is mostly used in metropolitan area networks. See *802.17.*

RSA: A public key encryption algorithm named after its inventors: Rivest, Shamir, and Adleman.

RSVP (Resource Reservation Protocol): A protocol for reserving resources in the network. RSVP uses the concept of *soft state* in routers and puts responsibility for making reservations on receivers instead of on senders.

RTCP (RTP Control Protocol): Control protocol associated with RTP.

RTP (Real-time Transport Protocol): An end-to-end protocol used by multimedia applications that have real-time constraints.

RTT (round-trip time): The time it takes for a bit of information to propagate from one end of a link or channel to the other and back again; in other words, double the latency of the channel.

SAN (system area network): A network that spans the components of a computer system (e.g., display, camera, disk). Sometimes stands for *storage area network* and includes interfaces the High-Performance Parallel Interface (HIPPI) such as Fibre Channel. Contrast with *LAN, MAN,* and *WAN.*

schema: A specification of how to structure and interpret a set of data. Schema are defined for XML documents.

scrambling: The process of XORing a signal with a pseudorandom bit stream before transmission to cause enough signal transitions to allow clock recovery. Scrambling is used in SONET.

SDP (Session Description Protocol): An application-layer protocol used to learn about the available audio/video channels. It reports the name and purpose of the session, start and end times for the session, the media types (e.g., audio, video) that comprise the session, and detailed information needed to receive the session (e.g., the multicast address, transport protocol, and port numbers to be used).

Secure Hash Algorithm (SHA): A family of cryptographic hash algorithms.

segment: A TCP packet. A segment contains a portion of the byte stream that is being sent by means of TCP.

SELECT: A synchronous demultiplexing protocol used to build a Remote Procedure Call (RPC) protocol.

semaphore: A variable used to support synchronization between processes. Typically, a process *blocks* on a semaphore while it waits for some other process to signal the semaphore.

server: The provider of a service in a client/server distributed system.

signalling: At the physical level, denotes the transmission of a signal over some physical medium. In ATM, signalling refers to the process of establishing a virtual circuit.

silly window syndrome: A condition occurring in TCP that may arise if each time the receiver opens its receive window a small amount the sender sends a small segment to fill the window. The result is many small segments and an inefficient use of bandwidth.

SIP (Session Initiation Protocol): An application layer protocol used in multimedia applications. It determines the correct device with which to communicate to reach a particular user, determines if the user is willing or able to take part in a particular communication, determines the choice of media and coding scheme to use, and establishes session parameters (e.g., port numbers).

sliding window: An algorithm that allows the sender to transmit multiple packets (up to the size of the window) before receiving an acknowledgment. As acknowledgments are returned for those packets in the window that were sent first, the window "slides" and more packets may be sent. The sliding window algorithm combines reliable delivery with a high throughput. See *ARQ*.

slow start: A congestion-avoidance algorithm for TCP that attempts to pace outgoing segments. For each ACK that is returned, two additional packets are sent, resulting in an exponential increase in the number of outstanding segments.

SMTP (Simple Mail Transfer Protocol): The electronic mail protocol of the Internet. See *822*.

SNA (System Network Architecture): The proprietary network architecture of IBM.

SNMP (Simple Network Management Protocol): An Internet protocol that allows the monitoring of hosts, networks, and routers.

SOAP: A component of the Web Services framework for specifying and implementing application protocols.

socket: The abstraction provided by Unix that provides the application programming interface (API) to TCP/IP.

soft state: Connection-related information contained in a router that is cached for a limited period of time rather than being explicitly established (and requiring explicit teardown) through a connection setup.

SONET (Synchronous Optical Network): A clock-based framing standard for digital transmission over optical fiber. It defines how telephone companies transmit data over optical networks.

source routing: Routing decisions performed at the source before the packet is sent. The route consists of the list of nodes that the packet should traverse on the way to the destination.

source-specific multicast: A mode of multicast in which a group may have only a single sender.

sparse mode multicast: A mode used in Protocol Independent Multicast (PIM) when relatively few hosts or routers need to receive multicast data for a certain group.

split horizon: A method of breaking routing loops in a distance-vector routing algorithm. When a node sends a routing update to its neighbors, it does not send those routes it learned from each neighbor back to that neighbor. Split horizon is used with *poison reverse*.

spread spectrum: Encoding technique that involves spreading a signal over a wider frequency than necessary to minimize the impact of interference.

SSL (Secure Socket Layer): A protocol layer that runs over TCP to provide authentication and encryption of connections. Also known as Transport Layer Security (TLS).

statistical multiplexing: Demand-based multiplexing of multiple data sources over a shared link or channel.

stop-and-wait: A reliable transmission algorithm in which the sender transmits a packet and waits for an acknowledgment before sending the next packet. Compare with *sliding window* and *concurrent logical channels*. See also *ARQ*.

STS (Synchronous Transport Signal): The prefix for various rates of SONET transmission. For example, STS-1 refers to the SONET standard for 51.84-Mbps transmission.

subnetting: The use of a single IP network address to denote multiple physical networks. Routers within the subnetwork use a subnet mask to discover the physical network to which a packet should be forwarded. Subnetting effectively introduces a third level to the two-level hierarchical IP address.

SunRPC: Remote procedure call protocol developed by Sun Microsystems. SunRPC is used to support NFS. See also *ONC*.

switch: A network node that forwards packets from inputs to outputs based on header information in each packet. Differs from a *router* mainly in that it typically does not interconnect networks of different types.

switching fabric: The component of a switch that directs packets from their inputs to the correct outputs.

T1: A standard telephone carrier service equal to 24 ISDN circuits, or 1.544 Mbps. Also called DS1.

T3: A standard telephone carrier service equal to 24 T1 circuits, or 44.736 Mbps. Also called DS3.

TCP (Transmission Control Protocol): Connection-oriented transport protocol of the Internet architecture. TCP provides a reliable, byte-stream delivery service.

TDMA (Time Division Multiple Access): A form of multiplexing used in cellular wireless networks. Also the name of a particular wireless standard.

Telnet: Remote terminal protocol of the Internet architecture. Telnet allows you to interact with a remote system as if your terminal is directly connected to that machine.

throughput: The observed rate at which data is sent through a channel. The term is often used interchangeably with *bandwidth*.

TLS (Transport Layer Security): Security services that can be layered on top of a transport protocol like TCP. It is often used by HTTP to perform secure transactions on the World Wide Web. Derived from *SSL*.

token bucket: A way to characterize or police the bandwidth used by a flow. Conceptually, processes accumulate tokens over time, and they must spend a token to transmit a byte of data and then must stop sending when they have no tokens left. Thus, overall bandwidth is limited, with the accommodation of some burstiness.

token ring: A physical network technology in which hosts are connected in a ring. A token (bit pattern) circulates around the ring. A given node must possess the token before it is allowed to transmit. 802.5 and the Fiber Distributed Data Interface (FDDI) are examples of token ring networks.

transport protocol: An end-to-end protocol that enables processes on different hosts to communicate. TCP is the canonical example.

TTL (time to live): Usually a measure of the number of hops (routers) an IP datagram can visit before it is discarded.

tunneling: Encapsulating a packet using a protocol that operates at the same layer as the packet. For example, multicast IP packets are encapsulated inside unicast IP packets to tunnel across the Internet to implement the MBone. Tunneling will also be used during the transition from IPv4 to IPv6.

two-dimensional parity: A parity scheme in which bytes are conceptually stacked as a matrix, and parity is calculated for both rows and columns.

Tymnet: An early network in which a *virtual circuit* abstraction was maintained across a set of routers.

UBR (unspecified bit rate): The "no frills" service class in ATM, offering best-effort cell delivery. Contrast with *ABR*, *CBR*, and *VBR*.

UDP (User Datagram Protocol): Transport protocol of the Internet architecture that provides a connectionless datagram service to application-level processes.

UMTS (Universal Mobile Telecommunications System): Cellular wireless standard based on wideband Code Division Multiple Access (CDMA) that offers relatively high data rates.

unicast: Sending a packet to a single destination host. Contrast with *broadcast* and *multicast*.

URI (Uniform Resource Identifier): A generalization of the URL. Used, for example, in conjunction with the Session Initiation Protocol (SIP) to set up audio/visual sessions.

URL (Uniform Resource Locator): A text string used to identify the location of Internet resources. A typical URL looks like http://www.cisco.com. In this URL, http is the protocol to use to access the resource located on host www.cisco.com.

vat: Audioconferencing tool used on the Internet that runs over RTP.

VBR (variable bit rate): One of the classes of service in ATM, intended for applications with bandwidth requirements that vary with time, such as compressed video. Contrast with *ABR*, *CBR*, and *UBR*.

VCI (virtual circuit identifier): An identifier in the header of a packet that is used for virtual circuit switching. In the case of ATM, the VPI and VCI together identify the end-to-end connection.

vic: Unix-based videoconferencing tool that uses RTP.

virtual circuit: The abstraction provided by connection-oriented networks such as ATM. Messages must usually be exchanged between participants to establish a virtual circuit (and perhaps to allocate resources to the circuit) before data can be sent. Contrast with *datagram*.

virtual clock: A service model that allows the source to reserve resources on routers using a rate-based description of its needs. Virtual clock goes beyond the best-effort delivery service of the current Internet.

VPI (virtual path identifier): An 8-bit or 12-bit field in the ATM header. VPI can be used to hide multiple virtual connections across a network inside a single virtual "path," thus decreasing the amount of connection state that the switches must maintain. See also *VCI*.

VPN (virtual private network): A logical network overlaid on top of some existing network. For example, a company with sites around the world may build a virtual network on top of the Internet rather than lease lines between each site.

WAN (wide area network): Any physical network technology that is capable of spanning long distances (e.g., cross-country). Compare with *SAN*, *LAN*, and *WAN*.

well-known port: A port number that is, by convention, dedicated for use by a particular server. For instance, the Domain Name Server receives messages at well-known UDP and TCP port 53 on every host.

WFQ (weighted fair queuing): A variation of *fair queuing* in which each flow can be given a different proportion of the network capacity.

WSDL (Web Services Description Language): A component of the Web Services framework for specifying and implementing application protocols.

WWW (World Wide Web): A hypermedia information service on the Internet.

X.25: The ITU packet-switching protocol standard.

X.400: The ITU electronic mail standard. The counterpart to the Simple Mail Transfer Protocol (SMTP) in the Internet architecture.

X.500: The ITU directory services standard, which defines an attribute-based naming service.

X.509: An ITU standard for digital certificates.

XDR (External Data Representation): Sun Microsystems' standard for machine-independent data structures. Contrast with *ASN.1* and *NDR*.

XML (Extensible Markup Language): Defines a syntax for describing data that may be passed between Internet applications.

XSD: XML Schema Definition. A schema language for defining the format and interpretation of XML objects.

zone: A partition of the domain name hierarchy, corresponding to an administrative authority that is responsible for that portion of the hierarchy. Each zone must have at least two name servers to field DNS requests for the zone.

Bibliography

[Bar01]   Barrett, D. and Silverman, R. *SSH: The Secure Shell*. O'Reilly, Sebastopol, CA, 2001.

[BCGS04]   Basagni, S., Conti, M., Giordano, S., and Stojmenovic, I., Eds. *Mobile Ad Hoc Networking*. Wiley-IEEE Press, Hoboken, NJ, 2004.

[Bat68]   Batcher, K.E. Sorting networks and their applications. *Proceedings of the AFIPS Spring Joint Computer Conference*, 32:307–314, 1968.

[BZ96]   Bennett, J. and Zhang, H. Hierarchical packet fair queueing algorithms. In *Proceedings of the SIGCOMM '96 Symposium*, pages 143–156, August 1996.

[BLFF96]   Berners-Lee, T., Fielding, R., and Frystyk, H. Hypertext Transfer Protocol — HTTP/1.0. *Request for Comments* 1945, May 1996.

[BDSZ94]   Bharghavan, V., Demers, A., Shenker, S., and Zhang, L. MACAW: a media access protocol for wireless LANs. In *Proceedings of the SIGCOMM '94 Symposium*, pages 212–225, August 1994.

[Bha03]   Bhattacharyya, S. An Overview of Source-Specific Multicast. *Request for Comments* 3569, July 2003.

[BABM05]   Bicket, J., Aguayo, D., Biswas, S., and Morris, R. Architecture and evaluation of an unplanned 802.11b mesh network. In *Proceedings of the 11th Annual International Conference on Mobile Computing and Networking*, Cologne, Germany, 2005.

[BLNS82]   Birrell, A., Levin, R., Needham, R., and Schroeder, M. Grapevine: An exercise in distributed computing. *Communications of the ACM*, 25:250–273, April 1982.

[BM05]   Biswas, S. and Morris, R. ExOR: Opportunistic multi-hop routing for wireless networks. In *Proceedings of the ACM SIGCOMM 2005 Conference*, Philadelphia, PA, August 2005.

[BG93]   Bjorkman, M. and Gunningberg, P. Locking effects in multiprocessor implementations of protocols. In *Proceedings of the SIGCOMM '93 Symposium*, pages 74–83, September 1993.

[Bla87]   Blahut, R.E. *Principles and Practice of Information Theory*. Addison-Wesley, Reading, MA, 1987.

[BBC+98]   Blake, S., Black, D., Carlson, M., Davies, E., Wang, Z., and Weiss, W. An Architecture for Differentiated Services. *Request for Comments* 2475, December 1998.

[Boo95]   Boorsook, P. How anarchy works. *Wired* 3(10):110–118, October 1995.

[BDMS94]   Bowman, C.M., Danzig, P.B., Manber, U., and Schwartz, M.F. Scalable Internet Resource Discovery: Research Problems and Approaches. *Communications of the ACM* 37(8):98–107, August 1994.

[BPY90]   Bowman, C.M., Peterson, L.L., and Yeatts, A. Univers: An attribute-based name server. *Software—Practice and Experience* 20(4):403–424, April 1990.

[BCS94]   Braden, R., Clark, D., and Shenker, S. Integrated Services in the Internet Architecture: An Overview. *Request for Comments* 1633, September 1994.

[BM95]   Bradner, S. and Mankin, A., Eds. *IPng: Internet Protocol Next Generation.* Addison-Wesley, Reading, MA, 1995.

[BP95]   Brakmo, L.S. and Peterson, L.L. TCP Vegas: End-to-end congestion avoidance on a global internet. *IEEE Journal of Selected Areas in Communication (JSAC)* 13(8):1465–1480, October 1995.

[Bri95]   Brisco, T. DNS Support for Load Balancing. *Request for Comments* 1794, April 1995.

[Buf94]   Buford, J.F. *Multimedia Systems.* ACM Press/Addison-Wesley, Reading, MA, 1994.

[Cal07]   Callas, J. et al. OpenPGP Message Format. *Request for Comments* 4880, November 2007.

[CV95]   Chandranmenon, G.P. and Varghese, G. Trading packet headers for packet processing. In *Proceedings of the SIGCOMM '95 Symposium,* pages 162–173, October 1995.

[CHHL06]   Chen, K.-T., Huang, C.-Y., Huang, P., and Lei, C.-L. Quantifying Skype user satisfaction. In *Proceedings of the ACM SIGCOMM 2006 Conference,* pp. 399–410, September 2006.

[CLNZ89]   Chen, S.K., Lazowska, D., Notkin, D., and Zahorjan, J. Performance implications of design alternatives for remote procedure call stubs. In *Proceedings of the Ninth International Conference on Distributed Computing Systems,* pages 36–41, June 1989.

[CZ85]   Cheriton, D.R. and Zwaenepoel, W. Distributed process groups in the V kernel. *ACM Transactions on Computer Systems* 3(2):77–107, May 1985.

[Cla97]   Clark, D.D. Internet Cost Allocation and Pricing. In *Internet Economics.* MIT Press, Cambridge, MA, 1997, pages 215–252.

[Cla82]   Clark, D.D. Modularity and Efficiency in Protocol Implementation. *Request for Comments* 817, July 1982.

[Cla88]   Clark, D.D. The design philosophy of the DARPA internet protocols. In *Proceedings of the SIGCOMM '88 Symposium,* pages 106–114, August 1988.

[Cla85]   Clark, D.D. The structuring of systems using upcalls. In *Proceedings of the Tenth ACM Symposium on Operating Systems Principles*, pages 171–180, December 1985.

[CF98]   Clark, D. and Fang, W. Explicit allocation of best-effort packet delivery service. *IEEE/ACM Transactions on Networking* 6(4):362–373, August 1998.

[CJRS89]   Clark, D.D., Jacobson, V., Romkey, J., and Salwen, H. An analysis of TCP processing overhead. *IEEE Communications* 27(6):23–29, June 1989.

[CPB+05]   Clark, D.D., Partridge, C., Braden, R., Davie, B.S., Floyd, S., Jacobson, V., Katabi, D., Minshall, G., Ramakrishnan, K.K., Roscoe, T., Stoica, I., Wroclawski, J., and Zhang, L. Making the world (of communications) a different place. *Computer Communication Review* 35(3):91–96, 2005.

[CHCB01]   Clausen, T., Hansen, G., Christensen, L., and Behrmann, G. The optimized link state routing protocol, evaluation through experiments and simulation. In *IEEE Symposium on Wireless Personal Mobile Communications*, September 2001.

[Com05]   Comer, D.E. *Internetworking with TCP/IP, Volume I: Principles, Protocols, and Architecture*, 5th ed. Prentice Hall, Upper Saddle River, NJ, 2005.

[CP89]   Comer, D.E. and Peterson, L.L. Understanding naming in distributed systems. *Distributed Computing* 3(2):51–60, May 1989.

[CS96]   Comer, D.E. and Stevens, D.L. *Internetworking with TCP/IP, Volume III: Client-Server Programming and Applications, BSD Socket Version*, 2nd ed. Prentice Hall, Englewood Cliffs, NJ, 1996.

[CS97]   Comer, D.E. and Stevens, D.L. *Internetworking with TCP/IP, Volume III: Client-Server Programming and Applications, Windows Sockets Version*. Prentice Hall, Englewood Cliffs, NJ, 1997.

[CS00]   Comer, D.E. and Stevens, D.L. *Internetworking with TCP/IP, Volume III: Client-Server Programming and Applications, Linux/Posix Sockets Version*. Prentice Hall, Upper Saddle River, NJ, 2000.

[CCITT92a]   Comité Consultif International de Telegraphique et Telephonique. Open systems interconnection: Specification of abstract syntax notation one (ASN.1). CCIT Recommendation X.208, 1992.

[CCITT92b]   Comité Consultif International de Telegraphique et Telephonique. Open systems interconnection: Specification of basic encoding rules for abstract syntax notation one (ASN.1). CCIT Recommendation X.209, 1992.

[Cro82]   Crocker, D. Standard for the Format of ARPA Internet Text Message. *Request for Comments* 822, August 1982.

[Dan98]   Danzig, P. NetCache architecture and deployment. *Computer Networks and ISDN Systems* 30(22–23):2081–2091, November 1998.

[DCB+02]   Davie, B., Charny, A., Bennett, J.C.R., Benson, K., Le Boudec, J.Y., Courtney, W., Davari, S., Firoiu, V., and Stiliadis, D. An Expedited Forwarding PHB (Per-Hop Behavior). *Request for Comments* 3246, March 2002.

[DR00]   Davie, B. and Rekhter, Y. *MPLS: Technology and Applications*. Morgan Kaufmann, San Francisco, CA, 2000.

[DEF+96]   Deering, S., Estrin, D., Farinacci, D., Jacobson, V., Liu, C., and Wei, L. The PIM architecture for wide-area multicast routing. *IEEE/ACM Transactions on Networking* 4(2):153–162, April 1996.

[DH98]   Deering, S. and Hinden, R. Internet Protocol, Version 6 (IPv6) Specification. *Request for Comments* 2460, December 1998.

[DBCP97]   Degermark, M., Brodnik, A., Carlsson, S., and Pink, S. Small forwarding tables for fast routing lookups. In *Proceedings of the SIGCOMM '97 Symposium*, pages 3–14, October 1997.

[DR08]   Dierks, T. and Rescorla, E. The Transport Layer Security (TLS) Protocol Version 1.2. *Request for Comments* 5246, August 2008.

[DP93]   Druschel, P. and Peterson, L.L. Fbufs: A high-bandwidth cross-domain transfer facility. In *Proceedings of the Fourteenth ACM Symposium on Operating Systems Principles*, pages 189–202, December 1993.

[DY75]   Drysdale, R.L. and Young, F.H. Improved divide/sort/merge sorting networks. *SIAM Journal on Computing* 4(3):264–270, September 1975.

[Eas05]   Eastlake 3rd, D. Cryptographic Algorithm Implementation Requirements for Encapsulating Security Payload (ESP) and Authentication Header (AH). *Request for Comments* 4305, December 2005.

[EVD04]   Eatherton, W., Varghese, G., and Dittia, Z. Tree bitmap: hardware/software IP lookups with incremental updates. *SIGCOMM Computer Communication Review* 34(2):97–122, 2004.

[Eis06]   Eisler, M. XDR: External Data Representation Standard. *Request for Comments* 4506, May 2006.

[FHHK06]   Fenner, B., Handley, M., Holbrook, H., and Kouvelas, I. Protocol Independent Multicast—Sparse Mode (PIM-SM): Protocol Specification (Revised). *Request for Comments* 4601, August 2006.

[Fie00]   Fielding, R.T. *Architectural Styles and the Design of Network-Based Software Architectures*. PhD thesis, University of California, Irvine, 2000 (http://www.ics.uci.edu/~fielding/pubs/dissertation/top.htm).

[FGM+99]   Fielding, R., Gettys, J., Mogul, J., Frystyk, H., Masinter, L., Leach, P., and Berners-Lee, T. Hypertext Transfer Protocol—HTTP/1.1. *Request for Comments* 2616, June 1999.

[Flo03]   Floyd, S. High speed TCP for Large Congestion Windows. *Request for Comments* 3649, December 2003.

[FHPW00]   Floyd, S., Handley, M., Padhye, J., and Widmer, J. Equation-based congestion control for unicast applications. In *Proceedings of the SIGCOMM 2000 Symposium*, pages 43–56, August 2000.

[FB96]   Freed, N. and Borenstein, N. Multipurpose Internet Mail Extensions (MIME) Part One: Format of Internet Message Bodies. *Request for Comments* 2045, November 1996.

[FL06]   Fuller, V. and Li, T. Classless Inter-Domain Routing (CIDR): The Internet Address Assignment and Aggregation Plan. *Request for Comments* 4632, August 2006.

[GR01]   Gao, L. and Rexford, J. Stable internet routing without global coordination. *IEEE/ACM Transactions on Networking* 9(6):681–692, December 2001.

[Gar00]   Garber, L. Technology news: Denial-of-service attacks rip the Internet. *Computer* 33(4):12–17, April 2000.

[GHMS91]   Giacopelli, J.N., Hickey, J.J., Marcus, W.S., and Sincoskie, W.D. Sunshine: A high performance self-routing broadband packet switch architecture. *IEEE Journal of Selected Areas in Communication (JSAC)* 9(8):1289–1298, October 1991.

[GG94]   Gopal, I. and Guerin, R. Network transparency: The plaNET approach. *IEEE/ACM Transactions on Networking* 2(3):226–239, June 1994.

[GVC96]   Goyal, P., Vin, H., and Chen, H. Start-time fair queueing: A scheduling algorithm for Integrated Services packet switching networks. In *Proceedings of the SIGCOMM '96 Symposium*, pages 157–168, August 1996. Also see OSDI '96.

[GK00]   Gupta, P. and Kumar, P.R. The capacity of wireless networks. *IEEE Transactions on Information Theory* 46(2):388–404, 2000.

[HRX08]   Ha, S., Rhee, I., and Xu, L. CUBIC: A new TCP-friendly high-speed TCP variant. *SIGOPS Operating Systems Review* 42(5):64–74, July 2008.

[HC99]   Handley, M. and Crowcroft, J. Internet multicast today. *The Internet Protocol Journal* 2(4), December 1999.

[HFPW03]   Handley, M., Floyd, S., Padhye, J., and Widmer, J. TCP Friendly Rate Control (TFRC): Protocol Specification. *Request for Comments* 3448, January 2003.

[Har00]   Harrison, A. Cyber assaults hit Buy.com, eBay, CNN and Amazon. In *Computerworld*, February 9, 2000.

[HP95]   Holzmann, G.J. and Pehrson, B. *The Early History of Data Networks*. IEEE Computer Society Press, Los Alamitos, CA, 1995.

[Huf52]   Huffman, D.A. A method for the construction of minimal-redundancy codes. *Proceedings of the IRE* 40(9):1098–1101, September 1952.

[HMPT89]   Hutchinson, N., Mishra, S., Peterson, L., and Thomas, V. Tools for implementing network protocols. *Software—Practice and Experience* 19(9):895–916, September 1989.

[HP91]   Hutchinson, N. and Peterson, L. The *x*-kernel: An architecture for implementing network protocols. *IEEE Transactions on Software Engineering* 17(1):64–76, January 1991.

[Jac88]   Jacobson, V. Congestion avoidance and control. In *Proceedings of the SIGCOMM '88 Symposium*, pages 314–329, August 1988.

[JBB92]   Jacobson, V., Braden, R., and Borman, D. TCP Extensions for High Performance. *Request for Comments* 1323, May 1992.

[Jaf81]   Jaffe, J.M. Flow control power is nondecentralizable. *IEEE Transactions on Communications* COM-29(9):1301–1306, September 1981.

[Jai89]   Jain, R. A delay-based approach for congestion avoidance in interconnected heterogeneous computer networks. *ACM Computer Communication Review* 19(5):56–71, October 1989.

[Jai94]   Jain, R. *FDDI Handbook: High-Speed Networking Using Fiber and Other Media*. Addison-Wesley, Reading, MA, 1994.

[Jai91]   Jain, R. *The Art of Computer Systems Performance Analysis: Techniques for Experimental Design, Measurement, Simulation, and Modeling*. John Wiley & Sons, New York, 1991.

[JB07]   Jamieson, K. and Balakrishnan, H. PPR: Partial packet recovery for wireless networks. In *Proceedings of the SIGCOMM 2007 Conference*, pages 409–420, August 2007.

[JPA04]   Johnson, D., Perkins, C., and Arkko, J. Mobility Support in IPv6. *Request for Comments* 3775, June 2004.

[KP91]   Karn, P. and Partridge, C. Improving round-trip time estimates in reliable transport protocols. *ACM Transactions on Computer Systems* 9(4):364–373, November 1991.

[KHR02]   Katabi, D., Handley, M., and Rohrs, C. Congestion control for high bandwidth-delay product networks. In *Proceedings of the ACM SIGCOMM 2002 Conference*, pages 89–102, August 2002.

[KRH+06]   Katti, S., Rahul, H., Hu, W., Katabi, D., Médard, M., and Crowcroft, J. XORs in the air: Practical wireless network coding. In *Proceedings of the SIGCOMM 2006 Conference*, pages 243–254, September 2006.

[Kau05]   Kaufman, C. Internet Key Exchange (IKEv2) Protocol. *Request for Comments* 4306, December 2005.

[KPS02]   Kaufman, C., Perlman, R., and Speciner, M. *Network Security: Private Communication in a Public World*. Prentice Hall, Englewood Cliffs, NJ, 2002.

[Ken05a]   Kent, S. IP Authentication Header. *Request for Comments* 4302, December 2005.

[Ken05b]   Kent, S. IP Encapsulating Security Payload (ESP). *Request for Comments* 4303, December 2005.

[KM87]   Kent, C. and Mogul, J. Fragmentation considered harmful. In *Proceedings of the SIGCOMM '87 Symposium*, pages 390–401, August 1987.

[Kle79]   Kleinrock, L. Power and deterministic rules of thumb for probabilistic problems in computer communications. In *Proceedings of the International Conference on Communications*, pages 43.1.1–43.1.10, June 1979.

[Kle75]   Kleinrock, L. *Queuing Systems, Volume 1: Theory.* John Wiley & Sons, New York, 1975.

[Kle01]   Klensin, J. Simple Mail Transfer Protocol. *Request for Comments* 2821, April 2001.

[KHF06]   Kohler, E., Handley, M., and Floyd, S. Datagram Congestion Control Protocol (DCCP). *Request for Comments* 4340, March 2006.

[LAAJ00]   Labovitz, C., Ahuja, A., Bose, A., and Jahanian, F. Delayed internet routing convergence. In *Proceedings of the SIGCOMM 2000 Symposium*, pages 293–306, August 2000.

[LS98]   Lakshman, T.V. and Stiliadis, D. High speed policy-based packet forwarding using efficient multi-dimensional range matching. In *Proceedings of the SIGCOMM '98 Symposium*, pages 203–214, September 1998.

[LMKQ89]   Leffler, S.J., McKusick, M.K., Karels, M.J., and Quarterman, J.S. *The Design and Implementation of the 4.3BSD UNIX Operating System.* Addison-Wesley, Reading, MA, 1989.

[LTWW94]   Leland, W., Taqqu, M., Willinger, W., and Wilson, D. On the self-similar nature of ethernet traffic. *IEEE/ACM Transactions on Networking* 2:1–15, February 1994.

[Lin93]   Lin, H.-A. Estimation of the optimal performance of ASN.1/BER transfer syntax. *Computer Communications Review* 23(3):45–58, July 1993.

[LM97]   Lin, D. and Morris, R. Dynamics of random early detection. In *Proceedings of the SIGCOMM '97 Symposium*, pages 127–136, October 1997.

[LPW+02a]   Low, S., Paganini, F., Wang, J., Adlakha, S., and Doyle, J. Dynamics of TCP/AQM and a scalable control. In *Proceedings of IEEE INFOCOM*, June 2002.

[LPW02b]   Low, S., Peterson, L., and Wang, L. Understanding TCP Vegas: A duality model. *Journal of the ACM* 49(2):207–235, March 2002.

[MD98]   Madson, C. and Doraswamy, N. The ESP DES-CBC Cipher Algorithm with Explicit IV. *Request for Comments* 2405, November 1998.

[MG98a]   Madson, C. and Glenn, R. The Use of HMAC-MD5-96 within ESP and AH. *Request for Comments* 2403, November 1998.

[MG98b]   Madson, C. and Glenn, R. The Use of HMAC-SHA-1-96 within ESP and AH. *Request for Comments* 2404, November 1998.

[Mal98]   Malkin, G. RIP Version 2. *Request for Comments* 2453, November 1998.

[Mas86]   Mashey, J. RISC, MIPS, and the motion of complexity. In *UniForum 1986 Conference Proceedings*, pages 116–124, 1986.

[MJ95]   McCanne, S. and Jacobson, V. VIC: A flexible framework for packet video. In *Proceedings of the Third ACM International Conference on Multimedia*, pages 511–522, November 1995.

[MPS99]   McCloghrie, K., Perkins, D., and Schoenwaelder, J. Structure of Management Information Version 2 (SMIv2). *Request for Comments* 2578, April 1999.

[MD93]   McKenney, P.E. and Dove, K.F. Efficient demultiplexing of incoming TCP packets. In *Proceedings of the SIGCOMM '92 Symposium*, pages 269–280, August 1993.

[MvOV96]   Menezes, A.F., van Oorschot, P.C., and Vanstone, S.A. *Handbook of Applied Cryptography*. CRC Press, Boca Raton, FL, 1996.

[Min93]   Minoli, D. *Enterprise Networking: Fractional T1 to SONET, Frame Relay to BISDN*. Artech House, Norwood, MA, 1993.

[MPFL96]   Mitchell, J.L., Pennebaker, W.B., Fogg, C.E., and LeGall, D.J. *MPEG Video: Compression Standard*. Chapman Hall, London, 1996.

[Mog95]   Mogul, J. The case for persistent-connection HTTP. In *Proceedings of the SIGCOMM '95 Symposium*, pages 299–313, August 1995.

[MD90]   Mogul, J. and Deering, S. Path MTU Discovery. *Request for Comments* 1191, November 1990.

[MP85]   Mogul, J. and Postel, J. Internet Standard Subnetting Procedure. *Request for Comments* 950, August 1985.

[MVS01]   Moore, D., Voelker, G., and Savage, S. Inferring internet denial of service activity. In *Proceedings of 2001 USENIX Security Symposium*, August 2001.

[Mor68]   Morrison, D. PATRICIA—a practical algorithm to retrieve information coded in alphanumeric. *Journal of the ACM* 15(4):514–534, October 1968.

[MPBO96]   Mosberger, D., Peterson, L., Bridges, P., and O'Malley, S. Analysis of techniques to improve protocol latency. In *Proceedings of the SIGCOMM '96 Symposium*, pages 73–84, August 1996.

[Moy98]   Moy, J. OSPF Version 2. *Request for Comments* 2328, April 1998.

[Mul90]   Mullender, S. Amoeba: A distributed operating system for the 1990s. *IEEE Computer* 23(5):44–53, May 1990.

[NYKT94]   Nahum, E.M., Yates, D.J., Kurose, J.F., and Towsley, D. Performance issues in parallelized network protocols. In *Proceedings of the First USENIX Symposium on Operating System Design and Implementation (OSDI)*, pages 125–137, November 1994.

[NRC01] National Research Council. *Looking Over the Fence at Networks.* National Academy Press, Washington, D.C., 2001.

[NRC94] National Research Council, Computer Science and Telecommunications Board. *Realizing the Information Future: The Internet and Beyond.* National Academy Press, Washington, D.C., 1994.

[Nel92] Nelson, M. *The Data Compression Book.* M&T Books, San Mateo, CA, 1992.

[Nol97] Noll, P. MPEG digital audio coding. *IEEE Signal Processing Magazine*, pages 59–81, September 1997.

[OP91] O'Malley, S. and Peterson, L. TCP Extensions Considered Harmful. *Request for Comments* 1263, October 1991.

[OPM94] O'Malley, S.W., Proebsting, T.A., and Montz, A.B. Universal stub compiler. In *Proceedings of the SIGCOMM '94 Symposium*, pages 295–306, August 1994.

[OY02] Ong, L. and Yoakum, J. An Introduction to the Stream Control Transmission Protocol (SCTP). *Request for Comments* 3286, May 2002.

[OSF94] Open Software Foundation. *OSF DCE Application Environment Specification.* Prentice Hall, Englewood Cliffs, NJ, 1994.

[OCD+88] Ousterhout, J.K., Cherenson, A.R., Douglis, F., Nelson, M.N., and Welch, B.B. The Sprite network operating system. *IEEE Computer* 21(2):23–36, February 1988.

[PFTK98] Padhye, J., Firoiu, V., Towsley, D., and Kursoe, J. Modeling TCP throughput: A simple model and its empirical validation. In *Proceedings of the ACM SIGCOMM '98 Symposium*, pages 303–314, September 1998.

[Pad85] Padlipsky, M.A. *The Elements of Networking Style and Other Essays and Animadversions on the Art of Intercomputer Networking.* Prentice Hall, Englewood Cliffs, NJ, 1985.

[PG94] Parekh, A. and Gallagher, R. A generalized processor sharing approach to flow control in integrated services networks: The multiple node case. *IEEE/ACM Transactions on Networking* 2(2):137–150, April 1994.

[PL01] Park, K. and Lee, H. On the effectiveness of route-based packet filtering for distributed DoS attack prevention in power-law internets. In *Proceedings of the ACM SIGCOMM 2001 Conference*, pages 15–26, August 2001.

[Par98] Partridge, C. et al. A 50 Gb/s IP router. *IEEE/ACM Transactions on Networking* 6(3):237–247, June 1998.

[PF94] Paxon, V. and Floyd, S. Wide-area traffic: The failure of Poisson modeling. In *Proceedings of the SIGCOMM '94 Symposium*, pages 257–268, August 1994.

[Per02] Perkins, C., Ed. IP mobility support for IPv4. *Request for Comments* 3344, August 2002.

[PM97] Perkins, D. and McGinnis, E. *Understanding SNMP MIBS*. Prentice Hall, Upper Saddle River, NJ, 1997.

[Per00] Perlman, R. *Interconnections: Bridges, Routers, Switches and Inter-networking Protocols*, 2nd ed. Addison-Wesley, Reading, MA, 2000.

[Pet88] Peterson, L.L. The Profile naming service. *ACM Transactions on Computer Systems* 6(4):341–364, November 1988.

[PACR02] Peterson, L., Anderson, T., Culler, D., and Roscoe, T. A blueprint for introducing disruptive technology into the Internet. *ACM SIG-COMM Computer Communication Review* 33(1):59–64, January 2003.

[PB61] Peterson, W.W. and Brown, D.T. Cyclic codes for error detection. *Proceedings of the IRE*, 49:228–235, January 1961.

[Pie84] Pierce, J. Telephony—a personal view. *IEEE Communications* 22(5):116–120, May 1984.

[Pos81] Postel, J. Internet Protocol. *Request for Comments* 791, September 1981.

[Pos82] Postel, J. Simple Mail Transfer Protocol. *Request for Comments* 821, August 1982.

[Pre02] Preshun, R. Version 2 of the Protocol Operations for the Simple Network Management Protocol (SNMP). *Request for Comments* 3416, December 2002.

[QPP02] Qie, X., Pang, R., and Peterson, L. In *Proceedings of 5th Symposium on Operating Systems Design and Implementation*, pages 45–60, December 2002.

[RS02] Rabinovich, M. and Spatscheck, O. *Web Caching and Replication*. Addison-Wesley, Reading, MA, 2002.

[RFB01] Ramakrishnan, K., Floyd, S., and Black, D. The Addition of Explicit Congestion Notification (ECN) to IP. *Request for Comments* 3168, September 2001.

[RS01] Ramaswami, R. and Sivarajan, K. *Optical Networks: A Practical Perspective*, 2nd ed. Morgan Kaufmann, San Francisco, CA, 2001.

[RF89] Rao, T.R.N. and Fujiwara, E. *Error-Control Coding for Computer Systems*. Prentice Hall, Englewood Cliffs, NJ, 1989.

[RHE99] Rejaie, R., Handley, M., and Estrin, D. RAP: An end-to-end rate-based congestion control mechanism for realtime streams in the internet. *INFOCOM* 3:1337–1345, March 1999.

[RDR+97] Rekhter, Y., Davie, B., Rosen, E., Swallow, G., Farinacci, D., and Katz, D. Tag switching architecture overview. *Proceeedings of the IEEE* 82(12):1973–1983, December 1997.

[Res01] Resnick, P. Internet Message Format. *Request for Comments* 2822, April 2001.

[ROY00] Rhee, I., Ozdemir, V., and Yi, Y. TEAR: TCP Emulation at Receivers—Flow Control for Multimedia Streaming, Technical

Report, Department of Computer Science, North Carolina State University, April 2000.

[Ste94] Stevens, W.R. *TCP/IP Illustrated, Volume 1: The Protocols.* Addison-Wesley, Reading, MA, 1994.

[SW95] Stevens, W.R. and Wright, G.R. *TCP/IP Illustrated, Volume 2: The Implementation.* Addison-Wesley, Reading, MA, 1995.

[Rit84] Ritchie, D. A stream input-output system. *AT&T Bell Laboratories Technical Journal* 63(8):311–324, October 1984.

[Rob93] Robertazzi, T.G., Ed. *Performance Evaluation of High Speed Switching Fabrics and Networks: ATM, Broadband ISDN, and MAN Technology.* IEEE Press, Piscataway, NJ, 1993.

[RR06] Rosen, E. and Rekhter, Y. BGP/MPLS IP Virtual Private Networks (VPNs). *Request for Comments* 4364, February 2006.

[Sal78] Saltzer, J. Naming and binding of objects. In *Operating Systems—An Advanced Course*, Bayer, R. et al., Eds., Lecture Notes on Computer Science, Vol. 60, pages 99–208. Springer-Verlag, Heidelberg, 1978.

[SK09] Saltzer, J.H. and Kaashoek, M.F. *Principles of Computer System Design: An Introduction.* Morgan Kaufmann, San Francisco, CA, 2009.

[SRC84] Saltzer, J., Reed, D., and Clark, D. End-to-end arguments in system design. *ACM Transactions on Computer Systems* 2(4):277–288, November 1984.

[SCH+99] Savage, S., Collins, A., Hoffman, E. Snell, J., and Anderson, T. The end-to-end effects of Internet path selection. In *Proceedings of the ACM SIGCOMM 1999 Conference*, pages 289–299, September 1999.

[SWKA00] Savage, S., Wetherall, D., Karlin, A., and Anderson, T. Practical network support for IP traceback. In *Proceedings of the ACM SIGCOMM 2000 Conference*, pages 295–306, August 2000.

[Sch95] Schneier, B. *Applied Cryptography: Protocols, Algorithms, and Source Code in C.* John Wiley & Sons, New York, 1995.

[SB89] Schroeder, M.D. and Burrows, M. Performance of Firefly RPC. In *Proceedings of the Twelfth ACM Symposium on Operating Systems Principles*, pages 83–90, December 1989.

[SCJ+02] Schulzrinne, H., Camarillo, G., Johnston, A., Peterson, J., Sparks, R., Handley, M., and Schooler, E. Sip: Session Initiation Protocol. *Request for Comments* 3261, June 2002.

[SC03] Schulzrinne, H. and Casner, S. RTP Profile for Audio and Video Conferences with Minimal Control. *Request for Comments* 3551, July 2003.

[SCFJ03] Schulzrinne, H., Casner, S., Frederick, R., and Jacobson, V. RTP: A Transport Protocol for Real-Time Applications. *Request for Comments* 3550, July 2003.

[Sha48]   Shannon, C. A mathematical theory of communication. *Bell Systems Technical Journal*, 27:379–423, 623–656, 1948.

[Sho78]   Schoch, J. Inter-network naming, addressing, and routing. In *Proceedings of the Seventeenth IEEE Computer Society International Conference (COMPCON)*, pages 72–79, September 1978.

[SS98]   Sisalem, D. and Schulzrinne, H. The loss-delay based adjustment algorithm: A TCP-friendly adaptation scheme. In *Proceedings of Workshop on Network and Operating System Support for Digital Audio and Video, 1998*, July 1998.

[SPS+01]   Snoeren, A.C., Partridge, C., Sanchez, L.A., Jones, C.E., Tchakountio, F., Kent, S.T., and Strayer, W.T. Hash-based IP traceback. In *Proceedings of the ACM SIGCOMM 2001 Conference*, pages 3–14, August 2001.

[SP99]   Spatscheck, O. and Peterson, L.L. Defending against denial of service attacks in Scout. In *Proceedings of the Third Symposium on Operating Systems Design and Implementation*, pages 59–72, February 1999.

[SHP91]   Spragins, J., Hammond, J., and Pawlikowski, K. *Telecommunications: Protocols and Design*. Addison-Wesley, Reading, MA, 1991.

[SVSM98]   Srinivasan, V., Vargese, G., Suri, S., and Waldvogel, M. Fast scalable level four switching. In *Proceedings of the SIGCOMM '98 Symposium*, pages 191–202, September 1998.

[Sta03]   Stallings, W. *Cryptography and Network Security*, 3rd ed. Prentice Hall, Upper Saddle River, NJ, 2003.

[Sta07]   Stallings, W. *Data and Computer Communications*, 8th ed. Prentice Hall, Upper Saddle River, NJ, 2007.

[Sta00]   Stallings, W. *Local and Metropolitan Area Networks*, 6th ed. Prentice Hall, Upper Saddle River, NJ, 2000.

[SPW02]   Staniford, S., Paxson, V., and Weaver, N. How to own the Internet in your spare time. In *Proceedings of the 11th USENIX Security Symposium*, pages 149–167, August 2002.

[Ste07]   Stewart, R., Ed. Stream Control Transmission Protocol. *Request for Comments* 4960, September 2007.

[SZ97]   Stica, I. and Zhang, H. A hierarchical fair service curve algorithm for link-sharing and priority services. In *Proceedings of the SIGCOMM '97 Symposium*, pages 29–262, October 1997.

[SSZ98]   Stoica, I., Shenker, S., and Zhang, H. Core-stateless fair queuing: A sealable architecture to approximate fair bandwidth allocation in high-speed networks. In *Proceedings of the ACM SIGCOMM '98 Symposium*, pages 33–46, August 1998.

[Tan07]   Tanenbaum, A.S. *Modern Operating Systems*, 3rd ed. Prentice Hall, Upper Saddle River, NJ, 2007.

[Ter86]   Terry, D. Structure-free name management for evolving distributed environments. In *Sixth International Conference on Distributed Computing Systems*, pages 502–508, May 1986.

[TL93]   Thekkath, C.A. and Levy, H.M. Limits to low-latency communication on high-speed networks. *ACM Transactions on Computer Systems* 11(2):179–203, May 1993.

[Tur85]   Turner, J.S. Design of an integrated services packet network. In *Proceedings of the Ninth Data Communications Symposium*, pages 124–133, September 1985.

[VL87]   Varghese, G. and Lauek, T. Hashed and hierarchical timing wheels: Data structures for the efficient implementation of a timer facility. In *Proceedings of the Eleventh ACM Symposium on Operating Systems Principles*, pages 25–38, November 1987.

[VD10]   Vasseur, J.P. and Dunkels, A. *Interconnecting Smart Objects with IP*. Morgan Kaufmann, San Francisco, CA, 2010.

[WVTP97]   Waldvogel, M., Varghese, G., Turner, J., and Plattner, B. Scalable high speed routing lookups. In *Proceedings of the SIGCOMM '97 Symposium*, pages 25–36, October 1997.

[WC91]   Wang, Z. and Crowcroft, J. A new congestion control scheme: Slow start and search (Tri-S). *ACM Computer Communication Review* 21(1):32–43, January 1991.

[WC92]   Wang, Z. and Crowcroft, J. Eliminating periodic packet losses in 4.3-Tahoe BSD TCP congestion control algorithm. *ACM Computer Communication Review* 22(2):9–16, April 1992.

[WPP02]   Wang, L., Pai, V., and Peterson, L. The effectiveness of request redirection on CDN robustness. In *Proceedings of the 5th Symposium on Operating Systems Design and Implementation*, pages 345–360, December 2002.

[Wat81]   Watson, R. Identifiers (naming) in distributed systems. In *Distributed System—Architecture and Implementation*, Lampson, B., Paul, M., and Siegert, H., Eds., pages 191–210. Springer-Verlag, New York, 1981.

[WM87]   Watson, R.W. and Mamrak, S.A. Gaining efficiency in transport services by appropriate design and implementation choices. *ACM Transactions on Computer Systems* 5(2):97–120, May 1987.

[WJLH06]   Wei, D., Jin, C., Low, S., and Hegde, S. FAST TCP: Motivation, architecture, algorithms, performance. *IEEE/ACM Transactions on Networking* 14(6):1246–1259, December 2006.

[WW07]   Weise, M. and Weynand, D. *How Video Works: From Analog to High Definition*. Focal Press, Boston, MA, 2007.

[Wel84]   Welch, T. A technique for high-performance data compression. *IEEE Computer* 17(6):8–19, June 1984.

[Wil00]   Williamson, B. *Developing IP Multicast Networks, Volume I.* Cisco Press, Indianapolis, IN, 2000.

[WMB99]   Witten, I.H., Moffat, A., and Bell, T.C. *Managing Gigabytes: Compressing and Indexing Documents and Images.* Morgan Kaufmann, San Francisco, CA, 1999.

[WYLB06]   Wong, S., Yang, H., Lu, S., and Bharghavan, V. Robust rate adaptation for 802.11 wireless networks. In *Proceedings of the 12th Annual International Conference on Mobile Computing and Networking,* pages 146–157, September 2006.

[XCL10]   Xiao, Y., Chen, H., and Li, F., Eds. *Handbook on Sensor Networks.* World Scientific, Singapore, 2010.

[YWA08]   Yang, X., Wetherall, D., and Anderson, T.E. TVA: A DoS-limiting network architecture. *IEEE/ACM Transactions on Networking,* 16(6):1267–1280, 2008.

[YHA87]   Yeh, Y.-S., Hluchyj, M.B., and Acampora, A.S. The knockout switch: A simple, modular architecture for high-performance packet switching. *IEEE Journal of Selected Areas in Communication (JSAC)* 5(8):1274–1283, October 1987.

[ZDE$^+$93]   Zhang, L., Deering, S., Estrin, D., Schenker, S., and Zappala, D. RSVP: A new resource reservation protocol. *IEEE Network* 7(9):8–18, September 1993.

[ZL77]   Ziv, J. and Lempel, A. A universal algorithm for sequential data compression. *IEEE Transactions on Information Theory* 23(3):337–343, May 1977.

[ZL78]   Ziv, J. and Lempel, A. Compression of individual sequences via variable-rate coding. *IEEE Transactions on Information Theory* 24(5):530–536, September 1978.

Index